Honda CBR600F4
Service and Repair Manual

by Matthew Coombs

Models covered
CBR600F. 599cc. 1999 to 2006
CBR600FS Sport. 599cc. 2001 to 2002

(3911-3AF1-304)

CBR600 F4

© Haynes Publishing 2006

ABCDE
FGHIJ
KLMNO
PQ

A book in the **Haynes Service and Repair Manual Series**

All rights reserved. No part of this book may be reproduced or transmitted in any form or by any means, electronic or mechanical, including photocopying, recording or by any information storage or retrieval system, without permission in writing from the copyright holder.

EAN/ISBN-13: **978 1 84425 595 5**
ISBN-10: **1 84425 595 6**

British Library Cataloguing in Publication Data
A catalogue record for this book is available from the British Library

Library of Congress Control Number 2006926140

Printed in the USA

Haynes Publishing
Sparkford, Yeovil, Somerset BA22 7JJ, England

Haynes North America, Inc
861 Lawrence Drive, Newbury Park, California 91320, USA

Editions Haynes
4, Rue de l'Abreuvoir
92415 COURBEVOIE CEDEX, France

Haynes Publishing Nordiska AB
Box 1504, 751 45 UPPSALA, Sweden

Contents

LIVING WITH YOUR HONDA CBR600F4

Introduction

The Birth of a Dream	Page	0•4
Acknowledgements	Page	0•8
About this manual	Page	0•8
Identification numbers	Page	0•9
Buying spare parts	Page	0•9
Model development	Page	0•10
Bike spec	Page	0•11
Safety first!	Page	0•12

Daily (pre-ride checks)

Engine/transmission oil level check	Page	0•13
Suspension, steering and drive chain checks	Page	0•13
Brake fluid level checks	Page	0•14
Coolant level check	Page	0•15
Tyre checks	Page	0•16
Legal and safety checks	Page	0•16

MAINTENANCE

Routine maintenance and servicing

Specifications	Page	1•1
Recommended lubricants and fluids	Page	1•2
Maintenance schedule	Page	1•2
Component locations	Page	1•4
Maintenance procedures	Page	1•5

Contents

REPAIRS AND OVERHAUL

Engine, transmission and associated systems

Engine, clutch and transmission	Page	2•1
Cooling system	Page	3•1
Fuel and exhaust systems	Page	4•1
Ignition system	Page	5•1

Chassis and bodywork components

Frame	Page	6•1
Suspension	Page	6•7
Final drive	Page	6•23
Brakes	Page	7•1
Wheels	Page	7•13
Tyres	Page	7•19
Fairing and bodywork	Page	8•1

Electrical system

Page 9•1

Wiring diagrams

Page 9•26

REFERENCE

Tools and Workshop Tips	Page	REF•2
Security	Page	REF•20
Lubricants and fluids	Page	REF•23
Conversion Factors	Page	REF•26
MOT test checks	Page	REF•27
Storage	Page	REF•32
Fault finding	Page	REF•35
Fault finding equipment	Page	REF•44
Technical terms explained	Page	REF•48

Index

Page REF•52

Introduction

The Birth of a Dream

by Julian Ryder

There is no better example of the Japanese post-war industrial miracle than Honda. Like other companies which have become household names, it started with one man's vision. In this case the man was the 40-year old Soichiro Honda who had sold his piston-ring manufacturing business to Toyota in 1945 and was happily spending the proceeds on prolonged parties for his friends. However, the difficulties of getting around in the chaos of post-war Japan irked Honda, so when he came across a job lot of generator engines he realised that here was a way of getting people mobile again at low cost.

A 12 by 18-foot shack in Hamamatsu became his first bike factory, fitting the generator motors into pushbikes. Before long he'd used up all 500 generator motors and started manufacturing his own engine, known as the 'chimney', either because of the elongated cylinder head or the smoky exhaust or perhaps both. The chimney made all of half a horsepower from its 50 cc engine but it was a major success and became the Honda A-type.

Less than two years after he'd set up in Hamamatsu, Soichiro Honda founded the Honda Motor Company in September 1948. By then, the A-type had been developed into the 90 cc B-type engine, which Mr Honda decided deserved its own chassis not a bicycle frame. Honda was about to become Japan's first post-war manufacturer of complete motorcycles. In August 1949 the first prototype was ready. With an output of three horsepower, the 98 cc D-type was still a simple two-stroke but it had a two-speed transmission and most importantly a pressed steel frame with telescopic forks and hard tail rear end. The frame was almost triangular in profile with the top rail going in a straight line from the massively braced steering head to the rear axle. Legend has it that after the D-type's first tests the entire workforce went for a drink to celebrate and try and think of a name for the bike. One man broke one of those silences you get when people are thinking, exclaiming 'This is like a dream!' 'That's it!' shouted Honda, and so the Honda Dream was christened.

> 'This is like a dream!'
> 'That's it'
> shouted Honda

Mr Honda was a brilliant, intuitive engineer and designer but he did not bother himself with the marketing side of his business. With hindsight, it is possible to see that employing Takeo Fujisawa who would both sort out the home market and plan the eventual expansion into overseas markets was a masterstroke. He arrived in October 1949 and in 1950 was made Sales Director. Another vital new name was Kiyoshi Kawashima, who along with Honda himself, designed the company's first four-stroke after Kawashima had told them that the four-stroke opposition to Honda's two-strokes sounded nicer and therefore sold better. The result of that statement was the overhead-valve 148 cc E-type which first ran in July 1951 just two months after the first drawings were made. Kawashima was made a director of the Honda Company at 34 years old.

The E-type was a massive success, over 32,000 were made in 1953 alone, a feat of mass-production that was astounding by the

Honda C70 and C90 OHV-engined models

standards of the day given the relative complexity of the machine. But Honda's lifelong pursuit of technical innovation sometimes distracted him from commercial reality. Fujisawa pointed out that they were in danger of ignoring their core business, the motorised bicycles that still formed Japan's main means of transport. In May 1952 the F-type Cub appeared, another two-stroke despite the top men's reservations. You could buy a complete machine or just the motor to attach to your own bicycle. The result was certainly distinctive, a white fuel tank with a circular profile went just below and behind the saddle on the left of the bike, and the motor with its horizontal cylinder and bright red cover just below the rear axle on the same side of the bike. This was the machine that turned Honda into the biggest bike maker in Japan with 70% of the market for bolt-on bicycle motors, the F-type was also the first Honda to be exported. Next came the machine that would turn Honda into the biggest motorcycle manufacturer in the world.

The C100 Super Cub was a typically audacious piece of Honda engineering and marketing. For the first time, but not the last, Honda invented a completely new type of motorcycle, although the term 'scooterette' was coined to describe the new bike which had many of the characteristics of a scooter but the large wheels, and therefore stability, of a motorcycle. The first one was sold in August 1958, fifteen years later over nine-million of them were on the roads of the world. If ever a machine can be said to have brought mobility to the masses it is the Super Cub. If you add in the electric starter that was added for the C102 model of 1961, the design of the Super Cub has remained substantially unchanged ever since, testament to how right Honda got it first time. The Super Cub made Honda the world's biggest manufacturer after just two years of production.

The CB250N Super Dream became a favorite with UK learner riders of the late seventies and early eighties

Honda's export drive started in earnest in 1957 when Britain and Holland got their first bikes, America got just two bikes the next year. By 1962 Honda had half the American market with 65,000 sales. But Soichiro Honda had already travelled abroad to Europe and the USA, making a special

The GL1000 introduced in 1975, was the first in Honda's line of GoldWings

Introduction

Carl Fogarty in action at the Suzuka 8 Hour on the RC45

An early CB750 Four

point of going to the Isle of Man TT, then the most important race in the GP calendar. He realised that no matter how advanced his products were, only racing success would convince overseas markets for whom 'Made in Japan' still meant cheap and nasty. It took five years from Soichiro Honda's first visit to the Island before his bikes were ready for the TT. In 1959 the factory entered five riders in the 125 class. They did not have a massive impact on the event being benevolently regarded as a curiosity, but sixth, seventh and eighth were good enough for the team prize. The bikes were off the pace but they were well engineered and very reliable.

The TT was the only time the West saw the Hondas in '59, but they came back for more the following year with the first of a generation of bikes which shaped the future of motorcycling – the double-overhead-cam four-cylinder 250. It was fast and reliable – it revved to 14,000 rpm – but didn't handle anywhere near as well as the opposition. However, Honda had now signed up non-Japanese riders to lead their challenge. The first win didn't come until 1962 (Aussie Tom Phillis in the Spanish 125 GP) and was followed up with a world-shaking performance at the TT. Twenty-one year old Mike Hailwood won both 125 and 250 cc TTs and Hondas filled the top five positions in both races. Soichiro Honda's master plan was starting to come to fruition, Hailwood and Honda won the 1961 250 cc World Championship. Next year Honda won three titles. The other Japanese factories fought back and inspired Honda to produce some of the most fascinating racers ever seen: the awesome six-cylinder 250, the five-cylinder 125, and the 500 four with which the immortal Hailwood battled Agostini and the MV Agusta.

When Honda pulled out of racing in '67 they had won sixteen rider's titles, eighteen manufacturer's titles, and 137 GPs, including 18 TTs, and introduced the concept of the modern works team to motorcycle racing. Sales success followed racing victory as Soichiro Honda had predicted, but only because the products advanced as rapidly as the racing machinery. The Hondas that came to Britain in the early '60s were incredibly sophisticated. They had overhead cams where the British bikes had pushrods, they had electric starters when the Brits relied on the kickstart, they had 12V electrics when even the biggest British bike used a 6V system. There seemed no end to the technical wizardry. It wasn't that the technology itself was so amazing but just like that first E-type, it was the fact that Honda could mass-produce it more reliably than the lower-tech competition that was so astonishing.

When in 1968 the first four-cylinder CB750 road bike arrived the world of motorcycling changed for ever, they even had to invent a new word for it, 'Superbike'. Honda raced again with the CB750 at Daytona and won the

World Endurance title with a prototype DOHC version that became the CB900 roadster. There was the six-cylinder CBX, the CX500T – the world's first turbocharged production bike, they invented the full-dress tourer with the GoldWing, and came back to GPs with the revolutionary oval-pistoned NR500 four-stroke, a much-misunderstood bike that was more a rolling experimental laboratory than a racer. Just to show their versatility Honda also came up with the weird CX500 shaft-drive V-twin, a rugged workhorse that powered a new industry, the courier companies that oiled the wheels of commerce in London and other big cities.

It was true, though, that Mr Honda was not keen on two-strokes – early motocross engines had to be explained away to him as lawnmower motors! However, in 1982 Honda raced the NS500, an agile three-cylinder lightweight against the big four-cylinder opposition in 500 GPs. The bike won in its first year and in '83 took the world title for Freddie Spencer. In four-stroke racing the V4 layout took over from the straight four, dominating TT, F1 and Endurance championships with the RVF750, the nearest thing ever built to a Formula 1 car on wheels. And when Superbike arrived Honda were ready with the RC30. On the roads the VFR V4 became an instant classic while the CBR600 invented another new class of bike on its way to becoming a best-seller. The V4 road bikes had problems to start with but the VFR750 sold world-wide over its lifetime while the VFR400 became a massive commercial success and cult bike in Japan. The original RC30 won the first two World Superbike Championships is 1988 and '89, but Honda had to wait until 1997 to win it again with the RC45, the last of the V4 roadsters. In Grands Prix, the NSR500 V4 two-stroke superseded the NS triple and became the benchmark racing machine of the '90s. Mick Doohan secured his place in history by winning five World Championships in consecutive years on it.

In yet another example of Honda inventing a new class of motorcycle, they came up with the astounding CBR900RR FireBlade, a bike with the punch of a 1000 cc motor in a package the size and weight of a 750. It became a cult bike as well as a best seller, and with judicious redesigns continues to give much more recent designs a run for their money.

When it became apparent that the high-tech V4 motor of the RC45 was too expensive to produce, Honda looked to a V-twin engine to power its flagship for the first time. Typically, the VTR1000 FireStorm was a much more rideable machine than its opposition and once accepted by the market formed the basis of the next generation of Superbike racer, the VTR-SP-1.

One of Mr Honda's mottos was that technology would solve the customers' problems, and no company has embraced cutting-edge technology more firmly than Honda. In fact Honda often developed new technology, especially in the fields of materials science and metallurgy. The embodiment of that was the NR750, a bike that was misunderstood nearly as much as the original NR500 racer. This limited-edition technological tour-de-force embodied many of Soichiro Honda's ideals. It used the latest techniques and materials in every component, from the oval piston, 32-valve V4 motor to the titanium coating on the windscreen, it was – as Mr Honda would have wanted – the best it could possibly be. A fitting memorial to the man who has shaped the motorcycle industry and motorcycles as we know them today.

The CBR600F4 models

Improving a bike that has been at the top of the class it invented 12 years ago and has dominated ever since is no mean trick. That's what Honda had to do with the fourth-generation CBR600 while maintaining its character of a user-friendly all-rounder. As the competition in the supersport 600 class is the fiercest in any market sector this is a bike that Honda had to get right in the face of race-track orientated bikes from the opposition.

The CX500 – Honda's first V-Twin and a favorite choice of dispatch riders

The VFR400R was a cult bike in Japan and a popular grey import in the UK

Introduction

The fuel injected CBR600F-1

The fuel injected CBR600FS-1 Sport

The new features of the first of the F4 generation CBRs, the 1999 F-X model, kept the Honda right up the top of the sales charts alongside the much more hard-edged sportsters from Yamaha and Suzuki. The most obvious change from previous practice was the adoption of an aluminium frame for the first time. That saved 7 kg over the old bike on its own but weight saving was a priority on all parts including the engine. The smart new frame also allowed the all-enveloping bodywork of the previous models to be tidied up.

The motor got a total redesign as well. To keep up with the Yamahas (the R6 was launched at the same time as the F4) bore was increased and stroke reduced to make the motor very over-square at 67 x 42.5 mm (from 65 x 45.2 mm). That necessitated bigger valves and carbs (flat slides) and ignition coils integral with the plug caps to burn the extra mixture efficiently. Steering head angle is two degrees steeper than on the F3 and fork stanchions up from 41 to 43 mm. Just to make sure you could differentiate the F4 from previous CBR600F3 models from a distance, three-spoke wheels were fitted for the first time. The rear is a 180, another first for the CBR.

All this sounds like pure performance enhancing modifications, and indeed the claimed 110 hp was a five per cent improvement and some testers thought they detected a concomitant dip in midrange torque. However, the F designation in CBR600F stands for the sort of all-rounder that Honda is best at, so the CBR is supposed to win the sales war against very stiff competition as well as beat them on the race track. There is no doubt that as a roadster the CBR is more usable than the harder-edged opposition as its sales figures continue to show. Well over 300,000 CR600s have been sold since '87 but it hasn't always been a winner on the race track.

The new for 2001 CBR600F-1 was designed to cure that problem. Actually, the FS-1 Sport was meant for the track but apart from a lack of centre stand and a few more revs available the two models are identical. The major mod for the latest incarnation of the 15-year old design is Honda's PGM-FI fuel injection system.

That's not the first thing you notice about the bike, though. Honda had obviously got a little fed up with suggestions that their best seller looked a little bland and given it the now obligatory aggressive twin 'fox-eye' headlights. Combined with new air-intake scoops below each headlight, the front of the bike now looks positively shark-nosed. What you can't see is the PGM-FI system. Fuel injection hasn't always been a total success on middleweight motorcycles where fine throttle control is imperative. Happily, Honda got things right with the aid of a much faster electronic engine control unit (ECU) and a bigger airbox. The only motor modifications were necessary were to the cam cover and cylinder head to cope with new sensors that supply info to the ECU. As usual, more weight was shaved off in various area – specifically inside the forks and the wheels but most of it came back again in the shape of the bigger fuel pump and generator needed to run the fuel-injection system.

There was one other big change, the digital dash – actually, the tacho stayed conventional but the speedo is digital. Riders particularly liked the four-segment reserve fuel indicator. The FS, or Sport, version is a homologation model for Supersport racing world-wide and differs in many details from the F-1. The most obvious of them are the two-piece seat and lack of a centre stand but there are extra plates in the clutch and differences in the air-intake and fuel injection systems.

The FS model was discontinued at the end of 2002, having given way to Honda's new CBR600RR. The CBR600F has, however, continued in production alongside the RR as a softer sport bike option.

Acknowledgements

Our thanks are due to Bransons Motorcycles of Yeovil who supplied the machines featured in the illustrations throughout this manual. We would also like to thank NGK Spark Plugs (UK) Ltd for supplying the colour spark plug condition photographs, the Avon Rubber Company for supplying information on tyre fitting and Draper Tools Ltd for some of the workshop tools shown.

Thanks are also due to Julian Ryder who wrote the introduction 'The Birth of a Dream' and to Honda (UK) Ltd who supplied model photographs.

About this Manual

The aim of this manual is to help you get the best value from your motorcycle. It can do so in several ways. It can help you decide what work must be done, even if you choose to have it done by a dealer; it provides information and procedures for routine maintenance and servicing; and it offers diagnostic and repair procedures to follow when trouble occurs.

We hope you use the manual to tackle the work yourself. For many simpler jobs, doing it yourself may be quicker than arranging an appointment to get the motorcycle into a dealer and making the trips to leave it and pick it up. More importantly, a lot of money can be saved by avoiding the expense the shop must pass on to you to cover its labour and overhead costs. An added benefit is the sense of satisfaction and accomplishment that you feel after doing the job yourself.

References to the left or right side of the motorcycle assume you are sitting on the seat, facing forward.

We take great pride in the accuracy of information given in this manual, but motorcycle manufacturers make alterations and design changes during the production run of a particular motorcycle of which they do not inform us. No liability can be accepted by the authors or publishers for loss, damage or injury caused by any errors in, or omissions from, the information given.

Identification numbers 0•9

Frame and engine numbers

The frame serial number is stamped into the right-hand side of the steering head. The engine number is stamped into the top of the crankcase on the left-hand side of the engine. Both of these numbers should be recorded and kept in a safe place so they can be furnished to law enforcement officials in the event of a theft. There is also a colour code label on the top of the rear mudguard (visible after removing the seat), and a VIN plate on the right-hand frame beam. The carburettors or throttle bodies also have an ID number stamped into them.

The frame serial number, engine serial number, and colour code should also be kept in a handy place (such as with your driver's licence) so they are always available when purchasing or ordering parts for your machine.

The procedures in this manual identify models by their code letter (e.g. F-X) and production year. The model code or production year is printed on the colour code label.

Buying spare parts

Once you have found all the identification numbers, record them for reference when buying parts. Since the manufacturers change specifications, parts and vendors (companies that manufacture various components on the machine), providing the ID numbers is the only way to be reasonably sure that you are buying the correct parts.

Whenever possible, take the worn part to the dealer so direct comparison with the new component can be made. Along the trail from the manufacturer to the parts shelf, there are numerous places that the part can end up with the wrong number or be listed incorrectly.

The two places to purchase new parts for your motorcycle – the franchised or main dealer and the parts/accessories store – differ in the type of parts they carry. While dealers can obtain every single genuine part for your motorcycle, the accessory store is usually limited to normal high wear items such as chains and sprockets, brake pads, spark plugs and cables, and to tune-up parts and various engine gaskets, etc. Rarely will an accessory outlet have major suspension components, camshafts, transmission gears, or engine cases.

Used parts can be obtained from breakers yards for roughly half the price of new ones, but you can't always be sure of what you're getting. Once again, take your worn part to the breaker for direct comparison, or when ordering by mail order make sure that you can return it if you are not happy.

Whether buying new, used or rebuilt parts, the best course is to deal directly with someone who specialises in your particular make.

Model – Europe	Year	Initial engine no.	Initial frame no.
CBR600F-X	1999	PC35E-2000001	JH2PC35A-XM000001
CBR600F-Y	2000	PC35E-2100001	JH2PC35A-YM100001
CBR600F-1	2001	PC35E-2200001	JH2PC35E-1M200001
CBR600FS-1	2001	PC35E-2200001	JH2PC35G-1M200001
CBR600F-2	2002	PC35E-2300001	JH2PC35E-2M300001
CBR600FS-2	2002	PC35E-2300001	JH2PC35G-2M300001
CBR600F-3	2003	PC35E-2400001	JH2PC35E-3M400001
CBR600F-4	2004	} not available	
CBR600F-5	2005		
CBR600F-6	2006		

Model – US 49-state	Year	Initial engine no.	Initial frame no.
CBR600F4	1999	PC35E-2000001	JH2PC350-XM000001
CBR600F4	2000	PC35E-2100001	JH2PC350-YM100001
CBR600F4i	2001	PC35E-2200001	JH2PC350-1M200001
CBR600F4i	2002	PC35E-2300001	JH2PC350-2M300001
CBR600F4i	2003	PC35E-2400001	JH2PC350-3M400001
CBR600F4i	2004	PC35E-2500001	JH2PC350-4M500001
CBR600F4i	2005	PC35E-2600001	JH2PC350-5M600001
CBR600F4i	2006	PC35E-2700001	JH2PC350-6M700001

Model – California	Year	Initial engine no.	Initial frame no.
CBR600F4	1999	PC35E-2000001	JH2PC351-XM000001
CBR600F4	2000	PC35E-2100001	JH2PC351-YM100001
CBR600F4i	2001	PC35E-2200001	JH2PC351-1M200001
CBR600F4i	2002	PC35E-2300001	JH2PC351-2M300001
CBR600F4i	2003	PC35E-2400001	JH2PC351-3M400001
CBR600F4i	2004	PC35E-2500001	JH2PC351-4M500001
CBR600F4i	2005	PC35E-2600001	JH2PC351-5M600001
CBR600F4i	2006	PC35E-2700001	JH2PC351-6M700001

The frame number is stamped into the right-hand side of the steering head

The engine number is stamped into the top of the crankcase on the left-hand side of the engine

The colour code label is on the topside of the mudguard

0•10 Model development

CBR600F-X (1999 model year)

The first of the F4 versions of the widely acclaimed, hugely popular, and long-running CBR600 is the F-X model introduced in 1999.

The CBR600 has an in-line four cylinder liquid-cooled engine. Drive to the double overhead camshafts which actuate the four valves per cylinder is by chain from the right-hand end of the crankshaft. The clutch is a conventional wet multi-plate unit and the gearbox is 6-speed. Drive to the rear wheel is by chain and sprockets.

The engine gets its fuel and air via four 36.5 mm CV carburettors, and this is ignited by an electronic ignition system. The exhaust system is a four-into-one design.

The engine sits in a twin-beam aluminium frame which uses the engine as a stressed member, with box-section tubing for the upper rails. Front suspension is by fully adjustable oil-damped 43 mm forks with cartridge type dampers. Rear suspension is by a fully adjustable single shock absorber via a three-way rising rate linkage.

The front brake system has two twin-opposed piston calipers acting on floating discs. The rear brake system has a single piston sliding caliper acting on a conventional disc.

Available in black, yellow/blue, red/purple.

CBR600F-Y (2000 model year)

There are no significant changes from the F-X (2000) model.

CBR600F-1 (2001 model year)

The most significant change to this model is the use of a fuel injection system to replace the carburettors, and an engine management system that controlled both the injection system and the ignition system. The injection system is Honda's PGM-FI, which is similar to that used on the FireBlade and Super Blackbird models.

There were other minor modifications to the clutch, the oil cooler, and the tail light, and the air filter housing and the air ducts to it were new. Apart from that all the changes were part of the process of replacing the carburettors with fuel injection. Minor changes were made to the suspension and braking systems, with the use of aluminium cartridge dampers in the front forks and lighter brake discs and caliper pistons. Extra bracing was added to the frame behind the steering head and the swingarm bearing arrangement was modified.

New slim-line instruments are fitted, which have an LCD display for the speedometer, fuel reserve gauge, trip meter and clock. The twin fox-eye headlights have separate lo and hi beam bulbs.

On European models Honda's HISS immobiliser system is fitted.

Available in black/silver, yellow/black, red/white/blue, and in certain markets also silver.

Note that the model available in the US for 2001 (CBR600F4i) has the same features as the Eurpean Sport model described below, the only difference being that it is not badged as such.

CBR600FS-1 Sport (2001 model year)

This is basically a more sports-focused version of the F-1, with a slightly higher tuned engine, a stronger clutch, slightly different final drive ratio. Visually the obvious changes are the black frame, single seat and modified rear bodywork with smaller tail light, plus the F Sport decals and red/black colour scheme. The centrestand is omitted on the Sport model.

CBR600F-2 and CBR600FS-2 Sport (2002 model year)

There are no significant changes from the F-1 and FS-1 (2001) models.

CBR600F-3 (2003 model year)

The CBR600F continues unchanged for the US market. The FS is discontinued in Europe and the CBR600F model is fitted with the engine from the previous year's FS, plus hard-wired lighting.

CBR600F-4 (2004 model year)

There are no significant changes from the F-3 (2003 model).

CBR600F-5 (2005 model year)

Non-adjustable front forks are fitted.

CBR600F-6 (2006 model year)

There are no significant changes from the F-5 (2005 model).

Illegal copying

It is the policy of Haynes Publishing to actively protect its Copyrights and Trade Marks. Legal action will be taken against anyone who unlawfully copies the cover or contents of this Manual. This includes all forms of unauthorised copying including digital, mechanical, and electronic in any form. Authorisation from Haynes Publishing will only be provided expressly and in writing. Illegal copying will also be reported to the appropriate statutory authorities.

Bike spec 0•11

Dimensions and weights

CBR600F-X and F-Y (1999 and 2000) models
Overall length	2060 mm
Overall width	685 mm
Overall height	1130 mm
Wheelbase	1395 mm
Seat height	810 mm
Footrest height	360 mm
Ground clearance	135 mm
Weight (dry)	169 kg
	(170 kg for California)
Engine weight (dry)	59 kg
Maximum weight capacity	
European models	189 kg
US models	175 kg
Canada models	179 kg

CBR600F-1 models onward (2001-on)
Overall length	2065 mm
Overall width	685 mm
Overall height	1135 mm
Wheelbase	1390 mm
Seat height	805 mm
Footrest height	360 mm
Ground clearance	135 mm
Weight (dry)	168 kg
	(169 kg for California)
Engine weight (dry)	59 kg
Maximum weight capacity	
European models	189 kg
US models	175 kg
Canada models	179 kg

CBR600FS models
Overall length	2100 mm
Overall width	685 mm
Overall height	1135 mm
Wheelbase	1385 mm
Seat height	805 mm
Footrest height	360 mm
Ground clearance	135 mm
Weight (dry)	169 kg
Engine weight (dry)	59 kg
Maximum weight capacity	189 kg

Engine

Type	Four-stroke in-line four cylinder 16V
Capacity	599 cc
Bore	67.0 mm
Stroke	42.5 mm
Compression ratio	12.0 to 1
Cooling system	Liquid cooled
Clutch	Wet multi-plate
Transmission	Six-speed constant mesh
Final drive	Chain and sprockets
Camshafts	DOHC, chain-driven
Fuel system	
F-X and F-Y (1999 and 2000) models	4 x 36.5 mm flat-slide Keihin CV carburettors
F-1/FS-1 models onward (2001-on)	PGM-FI fuel injection
Ignition system	Computer-controlled digital transistorised with electronic advance

Chassis

Frame type	Twin spar aluminium box section
Rake and trail	24°, 96 mm
Fuel tank capacity (including reserve)	18 litres
Front suspension	
Type	43 mm oil-damped cartridge-type telescopic forks
Travel	120 mm
Adjustment	
F-X to F-4 models and FS models	Spring pre-load, rebound and compression damping
F-5 models onward	Non-adjustable
Rear suspension	
Type	Gas-charged single shock absorber, Pro-Link rising rate linkage, box-section aluminium swingarm
Travel	120 mm
Adjustment	Spring pre-load, rebound and compression damping
Wheels	17 inch 3-spoke hollow-section alloys
Tyres	
Front	120/70-ZR17 Radial
Rear	180/55-ZR17 Radial
Front brake	Twin 296 mm floating discs with Nissin 4-piston opposed calipers
Rear brake	Single 220 mm disc with Nissin single piston sliding caliper

Safety First!

Professional mechanics are trained in safe working procedures. However enthusiastic you may be about getting on with the job at hand, take the time to ensure that your safety is not put at risk. A moment's lack of attention can result in an accident, as can failure to observe simple precautions.

There will always be new ways of having accidents, and the following is not a comprehensive list of all dangers; it is intended rather to make you aware of the risks and to encourage a safe approach to all work you carry out on your bike.

Asbestos

● Certain friction, insulating, sealing and other products - such as brake pads, clutch linings, gaskets, etc. - contain asbestos. Extreme care must be taken to avoid inhalation of dust from such products since it is hazardous to health. If in doubt, assume that they do contain asbestos.

Fire

● Remember at all times that petrol is highly flammable. Never smoke or have any kind of naked flame around, when working on the vehicle. But the risk does not end there - a spark caused by an electrical short-circuit, by two metal surfaces contacting each other, by careless use of tools, or even by static electricity built up in your body under certain conditions, can ignite petrol vapour, which in a confined space is highly explosive. Never use petrol as a cleaning solvent. Use an approved safety solvent.

● Always disconnect the battery earth terminal before working on any part of the fuel or electrical system, and never risk spilling fuel on to a hot engine or exhaust.
● It is recommended that a fire extinguisher of a type suitable for fuel and electrical fires is kept handy in the garage or workplace at all times. Never try to extinguish a fuel or electrical fire with water.

Fumes

● Certain fumes are highly toxic and can quickly cause unconsciousness and even death if inhaled to any extent. Petrol vapour comes into this category, as do the vapours from certain solvents such as trichloro-ethylene. Any draining or pouring of such volatile fluids should be done in a well ventilated area.
● When using cleaning fluids and solvents, read the instructions carefully. Never use materials from unmarked containers - they may give off poisonous vapours.
● Never run the engine of a motor vehicle in an enclosed space such as a garage. Exhaust fumes contain carbon monoxide which is extremely poisonous; if you need to run the engine, always do so in the open air or at least have the rear of the vehicle outside the workplace.

The battery

● Never cause a spark, or allow a naked light near the vehicle's battery. It will normally be giving off a certain amount of hydrogen gas, which is highly explosive.

● Always disconnect the battery ground (earth) terminal before working on the fuel or electrical systems (except where noted).
● If possible, loosen the filler plugs or cover when charging the battery from an external source. Do not charge at an excessive rate or the battery may burst.
● Take care when topping up, cleaning or carrying the battery. The acid electrolyte, evenwhen diluted, is very corrosive and should not be allowed to contact the eyes or skin. Always wear rubber gloves and goggles or a face shield. If you ever need to prepare electrolyte yourself, always add the acid slowly to the water; never add the water to the acid.

Electricity

● When using an electric power tool, inspection light etc., always ensure that the appliance is correctly connected to its plug and that, where necessary, it is properly grounded (earthed). Do not use such appliances in damp conditions and, again, beware of creating a spark or applying excessive heat in the vicinity of fuel or fuel vapour. Also ensure that the appliances meet national safety standards.
● A severe electric shock can result from touching certain parts of the electrical system, such as the spark plug wires (HT leads), when the engine is running or being cranked, particularly if components are damp or the insulation is defective. Where an electronic ignition system is used, the secondary (HT) voltage is much higher and could prove fatal.

Remember...

✗ **Don't** start the engine without first ascertaining that the transmission is in neutral.

✗ **Don't** suddenly remove the pressure cap from a hot cooling system - cover it with a cloth and release the pressure gradually first, or you may get scalded by escaping coolant.

✗ **Don't** attempt to drain oil until you are sure it has cooled sufficiently to avoid scalding you.

✗ **Don't** grasp any part of the engine or exhaust system without first ascertaining that it is cool enough not to burn you.

✗ **Don't** allow brake fluid or antifreeze to contact the machine's paintwork or plastic components.

✗ **Don't** siphon toxic liquids such as fuel, hydraulic fluid or antifreeze by mouth, or allow them to remain on your skin.

✗ **Don't** inhale dust - it may be injurious to health (see Asbestos heading).

✗ **Don't** allow any spilled oil or grease to remain on the floor - wipe it up right away, before someone slips on it.

✗ **Don't** use ill-fitting spanners or other tools which may slip and cause injury.

✗ **Don't** lift a heavy component which may be beyond your capability - get assistance.

✗ **Don't** rush to finish a job or take unverified short cuts.

✗ **Don't** allow children or animals in or around an unattended vehicle.

✗ **Don't** inflate a tyre above the recommended pressure. Apart from over-stressing the carcass, in extreme cases the tyre may blow off forcibly.

✓ **Do** ensure that the machine is supported securely at all times. This is especially important when the machine is blocked up to aid wheel or fork removal.

✓ **Do** take care when attempting to loosen a stubborn nut or bolt. It is generally better to pull on a spanner, rather than push, so that if you slip, you fall away from the machine rather than onto it.

✓ **Do** wear eye protection when using power tools such as drill, sander, bench grinder etc.

✓ **Do** use a barrier cream on your hands prior to undertaking dirty jobs - it will protect your skin from infection as well as making the dirt easier to remove afterwards; but make sure your hands aren't left slippery. Note that long-term contact with used engine oil can be a health hazard.

✓ **Do** keep loose clothing (cuffs, ties etc. and long hair) well out of the way of moving mechanical parts.

✓ **Do** remove rings, wristwatch etc., before working on the vehicle - especially the electrical system.

✓ **Do** keep your work area tidy - it is only too easy to fall over articles left lying around.

✓ **Do** exercise caution when compressing springs for removal or installation. Ensure that the tension is applied and released in a controlled manner, using suitable tools which preclude the possibility of the spring escaping violently.

✓ **Do** ensure that any lifting tackle used has a safe working load rating adequate for the job.

✓ **Do** get someone to check periodically that all is well, when working alone on the vehicle.

✓ **Do** carry out work in a logical sequence and check that everything is correctly assembled and tightened afterwards.

✓ **Do** remember that your vehicle's safety affects that of yourself and others. If in doubt on any point, get professional advice.

● If in spite of following these precautions, you are unfortunate enough to injure yourself, seek medical attention as soon as possible.

Daily (pre-ride) checks 0•13

Note: *The daily (pre-ride) checks outlined in the owner's manual covers those items which should be inspected on a daily basis.*

Engine/transmission oil level check

The correct oil
- Modern, high-revving engines place great demands on their oil. It is very important that the correct oil for your bike is used.
- Always top up with a good quality oil of the specified type and viscosity and do not overfill the engine.

Oil type	API grade SE, SF or SG
Oil viscosity	SAE 10W40

If you are using the motorcycle constantly in extreme conditions of heat or cold, other more suitable viscosity ranges may be used – refer to the viscosity table to select the oil best suited to your conditions.

Before you start:
✔ Take the motorcycle on a short run to allow it to reach normal operating temperature.
Caution: Do not run the engine in an enclosed space such as a garage or workshop.
✔ Stop the engine and support the motorcycle upright on its centre-stand if fitted, or on an auxiliary stand. Allow it to stand undisturbed for a few minutes to allow the oil level to stabilise. Make sure the motorcycle is on level ground.

Bike care:
- If you have to add oil frequently, check whether you have any oil leaks from the engine joints, seals and gaskets. If not, the engine could be burning oil, in which case there will be white smoke coming out of the exhaust – (see *Fault Finding*).

1 Wipe the oil level inspection window so that it is clean – it is located on the right-hand side of the engine and is visible via the aperture in the fairing side panel (arrow).

2 With the motorcycle vertical, the oil level should lie between the maximum and minimum level lines on the window.

3 If the level is below the minimum line, unscrew the oil filler cap from the clutch cover.

4 Top up the engine with the recommended grade and type of oil to bring the level up to the upper line on the inspection window. Do not overfill. On completion, make sure the filler cap is secure in the cover.

Suspension, steering and drive chain checks

Suspension and steering:
- Check that the front and rear suspension operates smoothly without binding (see Chapter 1).
- Check that the suspension is adjusted as required (see Chapter 6).
- Check that the steering moves smoothly from lock-to-lock.

Drive chain:
- Check that the chain isn't too loose or too tight, and adjust it if necessary (see Chapter 1).
- If the chain looks dry, lubricate it (see Chapter 1).

Daily (pre-ride) checks

Brake fluid level checks

> **Warning:** Brake hydraulic fluid can harm your eyes and damage painted surfaces, so use extreme caution when handling and pouring it and cover surrounding surfaces with rag. Do not use fluid that has been standing open for some time, as it is hygroscopic (absorbs moisture from the air) which can cause a dangerous loss of braking effectiveness.

Before you start:

✔ The front master cylinder reservoir is integral with the master cylinder on the right-hand handlebar. The rear master cylinder reservoir is located under the seat on the right-hand side.
✔ Make sure you have the correct hydraulic fluid. DOT 4 is recommended.
✔ Wrap a rag around the reservoir being worked on to ensure that any spillage does not come into contact with painted surfaces.
✔ Support the motorcycle upright on its centre-stand if fitted, or on an auxiliary stand.
Note: *When working on the front reservoir, turn the handlebars to full left lock so that the top of the reservoir is level. Access to the front reservoir cover screws is partially restricted by the windshield, so if a short or angled screwdriver is not available, slacken the screws with the handlebars on right lock* **(see illustration)**, *but do not remove them or the cover until the reservoir is level. Alternatively, remove the windshield (see Chapter 8). When working on the rear reservoir, there is very little clearance between the top of the cap and the sub-frame rail, so it may be necessary to unscrew the reservoir mounting bolt and displace the reservoir to remove the cap (though on the model we worked on this was not necessary). If you do have to displace the reservoir, make sure that you cover the area with plenty of rag and take care not to spill any fluid out of it.*

Bike care:

● The fluid in the front and rear brake master cylinder reservoirs will drop slightly as the brake pads wear down.

● If either fluid reservoir requires repeated topping-up there could be an hydraulic leak somewhere in the system, which must be investigated immediately.
● Check for signs of fluid leakage from the hydraulic hoses and components – if found, rectify immediately (see Chapter 7).
● Check the operation of both brakes before taking the machine on the road; if there is evidence of air in the system (spongy feel to lever or pedal), it must be bled (see Chapter 7).

1 The front brake fluid level is visible through the window in the reservoir body – it must be above the LOWER level line (arrowed).

2 If the level is below the LOWER level line, undo the two reservoir cover screws (see **Note** above), and remove the cover, diaphragm plate and diaphragm.

3 Top up with new clean hydraulic fluid of the recommended type, until the level is up to the UPPER level line, which is a ridge along the inside of the front wall of the reservoir. Do not overfill and take care to avoid spills (see **Warning** above).

4 Ensure that the diaphragm is correctly seated before installing the plate and cover.

5 The rear brake fluid level is visible through the reservoir body – it must be above LOWER level line.

6 If the level is below the LOWER level line, unscrew the reservoir cap (arrowed) (see **Note** above), and remove the diaphragm plate and diaphragm.

7 Top up with new clean hydraulic fluid of the recommended type, until the level is up to the UPPER level line. Do not overfill and take care to avoid spills (see **Warning** above).

8 Ensure that the diaphragm is correctly seated before installing the plate and cap.

Daily (pre-ride) checks   0•15

Coolant level check

> ⚠️ **Warning:** DO NOT remove the radiator pressure cap to add coolant. Topping up is done via the coolant reservoir tank filler. DO NOT leave open containers of coolant about, as it is poisonous.

Before you start:
✔ Make sure you have a supply of coolant available (a mixture of 50% distilled water and 50% corrosion inhibited ethylene glycol anti-freeze is needed).
✔ Always check the coolant level when the engine is at normal working temperature. Take the motorcycle on a short run to allow it to reach normal temperature.
Caution: Do not run the engine in an enclosed space such as a garage or workshop.
✔ Stop the engine and support the motorcycle upright on its centre-stand if fitted, or on an auxiliary stand. Make sure the motorcycle is on level ground.

Bike care:
● Use only the specified coolant mixture. It is important that anti-freeze is used in the system all year round, and not just in the winter. Do not top the system up using only water, as the system will become too diluted.
● Do not overfill the reservoir tank. If the coolant is significantly above the UPPER level line at any time, the surplus should be siphoned or drained off to prevent the possibility of it being expelled out of the overflow hose.
● If the coolant level falls steadily, check the system for leaks (see Chapter 1). If no leaks are found and the level continues to fall, it is recommended that the machine is taken to a Honda dealer for a pressure test.

1 On F-X and F-Y (1999 and 2000) models the coolant reservoir is located on the right-hand side of the engine, on the inside of the fairing side panel. The coolant UPPER and LOWER level lines (arrowed) are marked on the back of the reservoir and are visible via the aperture in the fairing side panel.

2 On F-1 and FS-1 models onward (2001-on) the coolant reservoir is located behind the right-hand side of the frame, below the fuel tank. The coolant UPPER and LOWER level lines (arrowed) are marked on the back of the reservoir.

3 If the coolant level is not in between the UPPER and LOWER markings, remove the reservoir filler cap – on F-X and F-Y (1999 and 2000) models, remove the right-hand fairing side panel to access the cap (see Chapter 8).

4 Top the coolant level up with the recommended coolant mixture, then fit the cap securely. On F-X and F-Y (1999 and 2000) models, install the fairing side panel (see Chapter 8).

Daily (pre-ride) checks

Tyre checks

Tyre tread depth:
- At the time of writing UK law requires that tread depth must be at least 1 mm over 3/4 of the tread breadth all the way around the tyre, with no bald patches. Many riders, however, consider 2 mm tread depth minimum to be a safer limit. Honda recommend a minimum of 1.5 mm on the front and 2 mm on the rear.
- Many tyres now incorporate wear indicators in the tread. Identify the location marking on the tyre sidewall to locate the indicator bar and replace the tyre if the tread has worn down to the bar.

The correct pressures:
- The tyres must be checked when **cold**, not immediately after riding. Note that low tyre pressures may cause the tyre to slip on the rim or come off. High tyre pressures will cause abnormal tread wear and unsafe handling.
- Use an accurate pressure gauge. Many forecourt gauges are wildly inaccurate. If you buy your own, spend as much as you can justify on a quality gauge.
- Proper air pressure will increase tyre life and provide maximum stability and ride comfort.

Tyre care:
- Check the tyres carefully for cuts, tears, embedded nails or other sharp objects and excessive wear. Operation of the motorcycle with excessively worn tyres is extremely hazardous, as traction and handling are directly affected.
- Check the condition of the tyre valve and ensure the dust cap is in place.
- Pick out any stones or nails which may have become embedded in the tyre tread. If left, they will eventually penetrate through the casing and cause a puncture.
- If tyre damage is apparent, or unexplained loss of pressure is experienced, seek the advice of a tyre fitting specialist without delay.

Loading	Front	Rear
Rider only	36 psi (2.50 Bar)	42 psi (2.90 Bar)
Rider and passenger	36 psi (2.50 Bar)	42 psi (2.90 Bar)

1 Remove the dust cap from the valve and check the tyre pressures when cold. Do not forget to fit the cap after checking the pressure.

2 Measure tread depth at the centre of the tyre using a depth gauge.

3 Tyre tread wear indicator bar and its location marking (usually either an arrow, a triangle or the letters TWI) on the sidewall.

Legal and safety checks

Lighting and signalling:
- Take a minute to check that the headlight, taillight, brake light, license plate light (where fitted), instrument lights and turn signals all work correctly.
- Check that the horn sounds when the button is pressed.
- A working speedometer, graduated in mph, is a statutory requirement in the UK.

Safety:
- Check that the throttle grip rotates smoothly when opened and snaps shut when released, in all steering positions. Also check for the correct amount of freeplay (see Chapter 1).
- Check that the engine shuts off when the kill switch is operated.
- Check that sidestand and centrestand (if fitted) return springs hold the stand(s) up securely when retracted.

Fuel:
- This may seem obvious, but check that you have enough fuel to complete your journey. If you notice signs of fuel leakage – rectify the cause immediately.
- Ensure you use the correct grade fuel – see Chapter 4 Specifications.

Chapter 1
Routine maintenance and servicing

Contents

Air filter – renewal	22
Battery – charging	see Chapter 9
Battery – check	10
Battery – removal, installation, inspection and maintenance	see Chapter 9
Brake caliper and master cylinder seal renewal	32
Brake fluid – renewal	24
Brake hoses – renewal	33
Brake pads – wear check	3
Brake system – check	14
Carburettors – synchronisation	12
Clutch – check and adjustment	4
Cooling system – check	13
Cooling system – draining, flushing and refilling	26
Cylinder compression – check	27
Drive chain and sprockets – check, adjustment, cleaning and lubrication	1
Engine oil pressure – check	28
Engine – oil change and filter change	8
Evaporative emission control (EVAP) system – check	23
Front forks – oil change	35
Fuel hoses – renewal	34
Fuel filters – cleaning and renewal	36
Fuel system – check	9
Headlight aim – check and adjustment	15
Idle speed – check and adjustment	2
Nuts and bolts – tightness check	19
Pulse secondary air injection (PAIR) system – check	21
Sidestand/centrestand – check	16
Stand(s), lever pivots and cables – lubrication	7
Spark plugs – check (F-X and F-Y models)	5
Spark plugs – check (F-1/FS-1 models onwards)	6
Steering head bearings – freeplay check and adjustment	18
Steering head bearings – re-greasing	30
Suspension – check	17
Swingarm and suspension linkage bearings – re-greasing	31
Throttle and choke cables – check	11
Valve clearances – check and adjustment	25
Wheels and tyres – general check	20
Wheel bearings – check	29

Degrees of difficulty

Easy, suitable for novice with little experience	**Fairly easy,** suitable for beginner with some experience	**Fairly difficult,** suitable for competent DIY mechanic	**Difficult,** suitable for experienced DIY mechanic	**Very difficult,** suitable for expert DIY or professional

Specifications

Engine
Cylinder numbering . . . . 1 to 4 from left to right
Spark plug type
   F-X and F-Y (1999 and 2000) models . . . . NGK CR9EH-9, or Denso U27FER-9
   F-1 to F-4, FS-1, FS-2 (2001 to 2004) models . . . . NGK IMR9A-9H, or Denso IUH27D
   F-5 models onwards (2005-on) . . . . NGK IMR9C-9H, or Denso VUH27D
Spark plug electrode gap . . . . 0.8 to 0.9 mm
Engine idle speed
   European F-X and F-Y (1999 and 2000) models . . . . 1200 ± 100 rpm
   US F-X and F-Y (1999 and 2000) models
      49-state models . . . . 1300 ± 100 rpm
      California models . . . . 1400 ± 100 rpm
   F-1/FS-1 models onwards (2001-on) . . . . 1300 ± 100 rpm
Carburettor synchronisation – max. difference between bodies . . . . . . 30 mm Hg
Valve clearances (COLD engine)
   Intake valves . . . . 0.17 to 0.23 mm
   Exhaust valves . . . . 0.25 to 0.31 mm
Cylinder compression . . . . 178 psi (12.5 Bar) @ 350 rpm
Oil pressure (at main gallery, with engine warm) . . . . 71 psi (5.0 Bar) @ 6000 rpm, oil @ 80°C

Miscellaneous
Drive chain slack . . . . 25 to 35 mm
Throttle cable freeplay . . . . 2 to 6 mm
Clutch cable freeplay . . . . 10 to 20 mm
Tyre pressures (cold) . . . . see *Daily (pre-ride) checks*

Specifications

Recommended lubricants and fluids

Engine/transmission oil type	API grade SE, SF or SG motor oil
Engine/transmission oil viscosity	SAE 10W40 (but see *Daily (pre-ride) checks*)
Engine/transmission oil capacity	
Oil change	3.0 litres
Oil and filter change	3.3 litres
Following engine overhaul – dry engine, new filter	3.7 litres
Coolant type	50% distilled water, 50% corrosion inhibited ethylene glycol anti-freeze
Coolant capacity	
Radiator and engine	2.7 litres
Reservoir	0.31 litres
Brake fluid	DOT 4
Drive chain	SAE 80 or 90 gear oil or chain lubricant suitable for O-ring chains
Steering head bearings	multi-purpose grease
Swingarm pivot bearings	multi-purpose grease
Suspension linkage bearings	multi-purpose grease
Bearing seal lips	multi-purpose grease
Gearchange lever/rear brake pedal/footrest pivots	multi-purpose grease
Clutch lever pivot	multi-purpose grease
Sidestand and centrestand pivots	multi-purpose grease
Throttle grip	multi-purpose grease or dry film lubricant
Front brake lever pivot and piston tip	silicone grease
Cables	cable lubricant

Torque settings

Rear axle nut	93 Nm
Spark plugs	12 Nm
Engine/transmission oil drain plug	29 Nm
Engine/transmission oil filter	
F-X and F-Y (1999 and 2000) models	10 Nm
F-1/FS-1 models onwards (2001-on)	26 Nm
Steering head bearing adjuster nut	25 Nm
Steering stem nut	103 Nm
Top yoke fork clamp bolts	23 Nm
Timing inspection cap	18 Nm
Main oil gallery plug	29 Nm

Maintenance schedule

Note: *The daily (pre-ride) checks outlined in the owner's manual covers those items which should be inspected on a daily basis. Always perform the pre-ride inspection at every maintenance interval (in addition to the procedures listed). The intervals listed below are the intervals recommended by the manufacturer for each particular operation during the model years covered in this manual. Your owner's manual may have different intervals for your model.*

Daily (pre-ride)
☐ See *'Daily (pre-ride) checks'* at the beginning of this manual.

After the initial 600 miles (1000 km)
Note: *This check is usually performed by a Honda dealer after the first 600 miles (1000 km) from new. Thereafter, maintenance is carried out according to the following intervals of the schedule.*

Every 500 miles (800 km) – US models
☐ Check, adjust and lubricate the drive chain (Section 1)

Every 600 miles (1000 km) – European models
☐ Check, adjust and lubricate the drive chain (Section 1)

Every 4000 miles (6000 km) or 6 months (whichever comes sooner)
☐ Check and adjust the idle speed (Section 2)
☐ Check the brake pads (Section 3)
☐ Check the clutch (Section 4)
☐ Check the spark plugs – US 1999 and 2000 models (Section 5)

Maintenance schedule

Every 8000 miles (12,000 km) or 12 months (whichever comes sooner)

Carry out all the items under the 4000 mile (6000 km) check, plus the following

☐ Check the spark plugs – European models (Section 5 or 6) and US 2001 and 2002 models (Section 6)
☐ Renew the spark plugs – US 1999 and 2000 models (Section 5)
☐ Lubricate the clutch/gearshift/brake lever/brake pedal/sidestand and centrestand pivots, and the throttle and choke cables (Section 7)
☐ Renew the engine oil and filter (Section 8)
☐ Check the fuel system and hoses (Section 9)
☐ Check the battery terminals (Section 10)
☐ Check and adjust the throttle and choke cables (Section 11)
☐ Check/adjust the carburettor synchronisation (Section 12)
☐ Check the cooling system (Section 13)
☐ Check the brake system and brake light switch operation (Section 14)
☐ Check and adjust the headlight aim (Section 15)
☐ Check the sidestand and centrestand (Section 16)
☐ Check the suspension (Section 17)
☐ Check and adjust the steering head bearings (Section 18)
☐ Check the tightness of all nuts, bolts and fasteners (Section 19)
☐ Check the condition of the wheels and tyres (Section 20)
☐ Check the pulse secondary air injection (PAIR) system (Section 21)

Every 12,000 miles (18,000 km) or 18 months (whichever comes first)

Carry out all the items under the 4000 mile (6000 km) check, plus the following

☐ Renew the air filter element (Section 22)
☐ Check the evaporative emission control (EVAP) system hoses – California models (Section 23)

Every 12,000 miles (18,000 km) or two years (whichever comes first)

Carry out all the items under the 4000 mile (6000 km) check, plus the following

☐ Renew the brake fluid (Section 24)

Every 16,000 miles (24,000 km) or two years (whichever comes sooner)

Carry out all the items under the 8000 mile (12,000 km) check, plus the following

☐ Check and adjust the valve clearances (Section 25)
☐ Renew the spark plugs – European models (Section 5 or 6) and US 2000 and 2001 models (Section 6)

Every 24,000 miles (36,000 km) or two years (whichever comes sooner)

Carry out all the items under the 12,000 mile (18,000 km) and 8000 mile (12,000 km) checks, plus the following

☐ Renew the coolant (Section 26)

Non-scheduled maintenance

☐ Check the cylinder compression (Section 27)
☐ Check the engine oil pressure (Section 28)
☐ Check the wheel bearings (Section 29)
☐ Re-grease the steering head bearings (Section 30)
☐ Re-grease the swingarm and suspension linkage bearings (Section 31)
☐ Renew the brake master cylinder and caliper seals (Section 32)
☐ Renew the brake hoses (Section 33)
☐ Renew the fuel hoses (Section 34)
☐ Renew the front fork oil (Section 35)
☐ Clean/renew the fuel filters (Section 36)

1•4 Component locations

Component locations on the right side – F-X and F-Y (1999 and 2000) models

1 Rear brake fluid reservoir
2 Idle speed adjuster
3 Clutch cable lower adjuster
4 Front brake fluid reservoir
5 Radiator pressure cap
6 Coolant reservoir
7 Engine oil level window
8 Engine oil filler cap
9 Rear brake light switch

Component locations on the right side – F-1 and FS-1 models onward (2001-on)

1 Rear brake fluid reservoir
2 Coolant reservoir
3 Clutch cable lower adjuster
4 Front brake fluid reservoir
5 Radiator pressure cap
6 Engine oil level window
7 Engine oil filler cap
8 Rear brake light switch

Component locations 1•5

Component locations on the left side – all models

1. Clutch cable upper adjuster
2. Steering head bearing adjuster
3. Air filter
4. Idle speed adjuster – F-1 and FS-1 models onward (2001-on)
5. Battery
6. Drive chain adjuster
7. Coolant drain bolt on water pump
8. Engine oil drain bolt
9. Coolant drain bolt on cylinders
10. Engine oil filter

Introduction

1 This Chapter is designed to help the home mechanic maintain his/her motorcycle for safety, economy, long life and peak performance.

2 Deciding where to start or plug into the routine maintenance schedule depends on several factors. If your motorcycle has been maintained according to the warranty standards and has just come out of warranty, start routine maintenance as it coincides with the next mileage or calendar interval. If you have owned the machine for some time but have never performed any maintenance on it, start at the nearest interval and include some additional procedures to ensure that nothing important is overlooked. If you have just had a major engine overhaul, then start the maintenance routine from the beginning. If you have a used machine and have no knowledge of its history or maintenance record, combine all the checks into one large service initially and then settle into the specified maintenance schedule.

3 Before beginning any maintenance or repair, the machine should be cleaned thoroughly, especially around the oil filter, spark plugs, valve covers, body panels, carburettors, etc. Cleaning will help ensure that dirt does not contaminate the engine and will allow you to detect wear and damage that could otherwise easily go unnoticed.

4 Certain maintenance information is sometimes printed on labels attached to the motorcycle. If the information on the labels differs from that included here, use the information on the label.

Every 500 miles (800 km) – US models
Every 600 miles (1000 km) – European models

**1 Drive chain and sprockets –
check, adjustment, cleaning
and lubrication**

Check

1 A neglected drive chain won't last long and will quickly damage the sprockets. Routine chain adjustment and lubrication isn't difficult and will ensure maximum chain and sprocket life.

2 To check the chain, place the bike on its sidestand and shift the transmission into neutral. Make sure the ignition switch is OFF.

3 Push up on the bottom run of the chain and measure the slack midway between the two sprockets, then compare your measurement to that listed in this Chapter's Specifications **(see illustration)**. As the chain stretches with wear, adjustment will periodically be necessary (see below). Since the chain will rarely wear evenly, roll the bike forward so that another section of chain can be checked (having an assistant to do this makes the task a lot easier); do this several times to check the entire length of chain, and mark the tightest spot.

4 In some cases where lubrication has been neglected, corrosion and galling may cause

1.3 Push up on the chain and measure the slack

1•6 Every 500 miles (US) or 600 miles (European models)

1.6 Check the sprockets in the areas indicated to see if they are worn excessively

1.7 Renew the chain slider if it has worn down to the line above the arrow

the links to bind and kink, which effectively shortens the chain's length. Such links should be thoroughly cleaned and worked free. If the chain is tight between the sprockets, rusty or kinked, it's time to replace it with a new one. If you find a tight area, mark it with felt pen or paint, and repeat the measurement after the bike has been ridden. If the chain's still tight in the same area, it may be damaged or worn.

Because a tight or kinked chain can damage the transmission bearings, it's a good idea to replace it with a new one.

5 Check the entire length of the chain for damaged rollers, loose links and pins, and missing O-rings and replace it with a new one if damage is found. **Note:** *Never install a new chain on old sprockets, and never use the old chain if you install new sprockets – replace the chain and sprockets as a set.*

6 Remove the front sprocket cover (see Chapter 6). Check the teeth on the front sprocket and the rear sprocket for wear **(see illustration)**.

7 Inspect the drive chain slider on the front of the swingarm for excessive wear and damage. There are wear limit lines marked by arrows on the front of the slider **(see illustration)**. Replace it with a new one if it has worn down to the lines or the tips of the arrows (see Chapter 6).

Adjustment

8 Move the bike so that the chain is positioned with the tightest point at the centre of its bottom run, then put it on the sidestand.

9 Slacken the rear axle nut **(see illustration)**.

10 Turn the adjuster bolt on each side of the swingarm evenly until the amount of freeplay specified at the beginning of the Chapter is obtained at the centre of the bottom run of the chain **(see illustration)**. Following adjustment, check that each chain adjustment marker is in the same position in relation to the mark on the swingarm **(see illustration)**. It is important the index line on the swingarm aligns with the same place on each adjuster; if not, the rear wheel will be out of alignment with the front. If the line is difficult to see, use the rear edge of the swingarm as an index instead.

11 If there is a discrepancy in the chain adjuster positions, adjust one of them so that its position is exactly the same as the other. Check the chain freeplay as described above and readjust if necessary.

12 Also check the alignment of the wear decal on the left-hand adjustment marker with the index line on the swingarm (do not use the

1.9 Slacken the axle nut (arrowed)

1.10a Turn each adjuster by an equal amount . . .

1.10b . . . then check the alignment marks as described – note the index line on the swingarm (arrowed), or use the back edge as the index

Routine maintenance and servicing 1•7

1.12 When the index line (A) meets the red zone (B), renew the chain

1.13 Tighten the axle nut to the specified torque

rear edge of the swingarm as the index) **(see illustration)**. When the index line meets the red REPLACE CHAIN zone, the drive chain has stretched excessively and must be replaced with a new one.

13 Counter-hold the axle head and tighten the axle nut to the torque setting specified at the beginning of the Chapter **(see illustration)**. Recheck the adjustment as above, then place the machine on its centrestand or an auxiliary stand and spin the wheel to make sure it runs freely.

Cleaning and lubrication

14 If required, wash the chain in paraffin (kerosene) or a suitable non-flammable or high flash-point solvent that will not damage the O-rings, using a soft brush to work any dirt out if necessary. Wipe the cleaner off the chain and allow it to dry, using compressed air if available. If the chain is excessively dirty it should be removed from the machine and allowed to soak in the paraffin or solvent (see Chapter 6).

Caution: Don't use petrol (gasoline), an unsuitable solvent or other cleaning fluids which might damage the internal sealing properties of the chain. Don't use high-pressure water to clean the chain. The entire process shouldn't take longer than ten minutes, otherwise the O-rings could be damaged.

15 For routine lubrication, the best time to lubricate the chain is after the motorcycle has been ridden. When the chain is warm, the lubricant will penetrate the joints between the sideplates better than when cold. **Note:** Honda specifies SAE 80 to SAE 90 gear oil or an aerosol chain lube that it is suitable for O-ring or X-ring (sealed) chains; do not use any other chain lubricants – the solvents could damage the chain's sealing rings. Apply the oil to the area where the sideplates overlap – not the middle of the rollers **(see illustration)**.

> **HAYNES HiNT** *Apply the lubricant to the top of the lower chain run, so centrifugal force will work the oil into the chain when the bike is moving. After applying the lubricant, let it soak in a few minutes before wiping off any excess.*

> ⚠️ **Warning: Take care not to get any lubricant on the tyres or brake system components. If any of the lubricant inadvertently contacts them, clean it off thoroughly using a suitable solvent or dedicated brake cleaner before riding the machine.**

Every 4000 miles (6000 km) or 6 months

2 Idle speed – check and adjustment

1 The idle speed should be checked and adjusted before and after the carburettors (F-X and F-Y models only) are synchronised (balanced), after checking the valve clearances, and when it is obviously too high or too low. Before adjusting the idle speed, make sure the valve clearances and spark plug gaps are correct, and the air filter is clean. Also, turn the handlebars from side-to-side and check the idle speed does not change as you do. If it does, the throttle cables may not be adjusted or routed correctly, or may be worn out. This is a dangerous condition that can cause loss of control of the bike. Be sure to correct this problem before proceeding.

2 The engine should be at normal operating temperature, which is usually reached after 10 to 15 minutes of stop-and-go riding. Place the motorcycle on its sidestand, and make sure the transmission is in neutral.

3 The idle speed adjuster is a knurled knob located on the right-hand side of the machine just ahead of the rear brake master cylinder reservoir on F-X and F-Y (1999 and 2000) models, and on the left-hand side of the machine between the frame and the fairing side panel on F-1/FS-1 models onwards (2001-on) **(see illustrations)**. With the engine

2.3a Idle speed adjuster (arrowed) – F-X and F-Y (1999 and 2000) models

2.3b Adjusting idle speed – fuel injected models

1•8 Routine maintenance and servicing

3.1a Brake pad wear indicators (arrowed) – front pads in situ

3.1b Brake pad wear indicators (arrowed) – rear pads in situ

3.1c Brake pad wear indicator (arrowed) – front pad

idling, adjust the speed by turning the adjuster until the idle speed listed in this Chapter's Specifications is obtained. Turn the screw clockwise to increase idle speed, and anti-clockwise to decrease it.

4 Snap the throttle open and shut a few times, then recheck the idle speed. If necessary, repeat the adjustment procedure.

5 If a smooth, steady idle can't be achieved on F-X and F-Y (1999 and 2000) models models, the fuel/air mixture may be incorrect (see Chapter 4) or the carburettors may need synchronising (see Section 12). Also check the intake manifold rubbers for cracks or a loose clamp which will cause an air leak, resulting in a weak mixture.

6 If a smooth, steady idle can't be achieved on F-1/FS-1 models onwards (2001-on), check the starter valve (see Chapter 4).

3 Brake pads – wear check

1 Each brake pad has wear indicators in the form of cutouts in the friction material. The wear indicators should be plainly visible by looking at the edges of the friction material from the best vantage point – on the front brake look at the bottom edge of the pad from below the caliper, and on the rear brake look at the rear edge of the pad from behind the caliper, but note that an accumulation of road dirt and brake dust could make them difficult to see **(see illustrations)**. If the indicators aren't visible, then the amount of friction material

remaining should be, and it will be obvious when the pads need replacing. Honda do not specify a minimum thickness for the friction material, but anything less than 1 mm should be considered worn. **Note:** *Some after-market pads may use different indicators to those on the original equipment.*

2 If the pads are worn to or beyond the wear indicator (i.e. the bottom of the cutout on the front pads or the beginning of the cutout on the rear pads) or there is little friction material remaining, they must be replaced with new ones, though it is advisable to replace the pads before they become this worn. If the pads are dirty or if you are in doubt as to the amount of friction material remaining, remove them for inspection (see Chapter 7). If the pads are excessively worn, check the brake discs (see Chapter 7).

3 Refer to Chapter 7 for details of pad replacement.

4 Clutch – check and adjustment

1 Check that the clutch lever operates smoothly and easily.

2 If the clutch lever operation is heavy or stiff, remove the cable (see Chapter 2) and lubricate it (see Section 7). If the cable is still stiff, replace it with a new one. Install the lubricated or new cable (see Chapter 2).

3 With the cable operating smoothly, check that the clutch lever is correctly adjusted. Periodic adjustment is necessary to

compensate for wear in the clutch plates and stretch of the cable. Check that the amount of freeplay at the clutch lever end is within the specifications listed at the beginning of the Chapter **(see illustration)**.

4 If adjustment is required, loosen the adjuster lockring at the lever end of the cable and turn the adjuster in or out until the required amount of freeplay is obtained **(see illustration)**. To increase freeplay, thread the adjuster into the lever bracket. To reduce freeplay, thread the adjuster out of the bracket. Tighten the lockring securely. When adjusting the cable make sure that the slots in the adjuster and lockring are not aligned with each other and the slot in the lever bracket – these slots are to allow removal of the cable, and if they are all aligned while the bike is in use the cable could jump out.

5 If all the adjustment has been taken up at the lever, reset the adjuster to give the maximum amount of freeplay (i.e. thread it all the way into the bracket), then set the correct amount of freeplay using the adjuster on the clutch end of cable. The adjuster is set in a bracket on the clutch cover on the right-hand side of the engine. Remove the fairing right-hand side panel for access (see Chapter 8).

6 Use the nuts on each end of the threaded section in the cable to adjust freeplay **(see illustration)**. To increase freeplay, slacken the front nut and tighten the rear nut until the freeplay is as specified, then tighten the front nut. To reduce freeplay, slacken the rear nut and tighten the front nut until the freeplay is as specified, then tighten the rear nut. Subsequent adjustments can now be made using the lever adjuster only.

4.3 Measure the amount of freeplay at the clutch lever end as shown

4.4 Slacken the lockring and turn the adjuster in or out as required

4.6 Slacken and adjust the nuts (arrowed) as described

Routine maintenance and servicing

5.4a Disconnect the coil/cap wiring connector . . .

5.4b . . . then pull the coil/cap up off the plug

5.4c If you are using the Honda tool, locate it onto the plug . . .

5 Spark plugs – check (F-X and F-Y (1999 and 2000) models)

Check and gap adjustment

Interval:
  US models: Every 4000 miles (6000 km) or 6 months
  European models: Every 8000 miles (12,000 km) or 12 months

1 Make sure your spark plug socket is the correct size before attempting to remove the plugs – a suitable one is supplied in the motorcycle's tool kit which is stored under the seat.
2 To access the plugs from the top, remove the fuel tank and the air filter housing (see Chapter 4). It is possible to access the spark plugs from the front by displacing the radiator, but access is restricted. To access from the front, displace the radiator from its mounts and move it away as much as possible (see Chapter 3) – there is no need to detach any hoses, but disconnect the wiring connector, and support or tie the radiator so that there is no danger of it scratching the front mudguard, or of the mudguard damaging the radiator fins. If access is still too restricted for you, drain the coolant (see Section 27), and remove the radiator.
3 Clean the area around the plug caps to prevent any dirt falling into the spark plug channels.
4 Check that the cylinder location is marked on each combined ignition coil/spark plug

5.4d . . . and use a ring spanner to turn it

cap, then disconnect the coil/cap wiring connectors **(see illustration)**. Pull the coil/cap off each spark plug **(see illustration)**. Using either the plug removing tool supplied in the bike's toolkit or a deep socket type wrench, unscrew and remove the plugs from the cylinder head **(see illustrations)**. Lay each plug out in relation to its cylinder; if any plug shows up a problem it will then be easy to identify the troublesome cylinder.
5 Inspect the electrodes for wear. Both the centre and side electrodes should have square edges and the side electrodes should be of uniform thickness – if not, they are worn. Look for excessive deposits and evidence of a cracked or chipped insulator around the centre electrode. Compare your spark plugs to the colour spark plug reading chart at the end of this manual. Check the threads, the washer and the ceramic insulator body for cracks and other damage.

5.4e Lift the plug out with the tool – the rubber insert should grip around the plug top

6 If the electrodes are not excessively worn, if no cracks or chips are visible in the insulator, and if the deposits can be easily removed with a wire brush, the plugs can be re-gapped and re-used. If in doubt concerning the condition of the plugs, replace them with new ones, as the expense is minimal.
7 Cleaning spark plugs by sandblasting is permitted, provided you blow out the plugs with compressed air and clean them with a high flash-point solvent afterwards.
8 Before installing the plugs, make sure they are the correct type and heat range and check the gap between the electrodes **(see illustrations)**. Compare the gap to that specified and adjust as necessary. If the gap must be adjusted, bend the side electrodes only and be very careful not to chip or crack the insulator nose **(see illustration)**. Make sure the washer is in place before installing each plug.

5.8a Using a wire type gauge to measure the spark plug electrode gap

5.8b Using a feeler gauge to measure the spark plug electrode gap

5.8c Adjust the electrode gap by bending the side electrode only

1•10 Routine maintenance and servicing

5.10 Fit the coils/caps onto the spark plugs

9 Fit the plug into the end of the tool, then use the tool to insert the plug **(see illustration 5.4e)**. Since the cylinder head is made of aluminium, which is soft and easily damaged, thread the plugs as far as possible into the head turning the tool by hand. Once the plugs are finger-tight, the job can be finished with a spanner on the tool supplied or a socket drive **(see illustration 5.4d)**. If new plugs are being used, tighten them by 1/2 a turn after the washer has seated. If the old plugs are being reused, tighten them by 1/8 to 1/4 turn after they have seated, or if a torque wrench can be applied, tighten the spark plugs to the torque setting specified at the beginning of the Chapter. Otherwise tighten them according the instructions on the box. Do not over-tighten them.

> **HAYNES HINT**: As the plugs are quite recessed, slip a short length of hose over the end of the plug to use as a tool to thread it into place. The hose will grip the plug well enough to turn it, but will start to slip if the plug begins to cross-thread in the hole – this will prevent damaged threads.

10 Install the spark plug coils/caps, making sure they locate correctly onto the plugs **(see illustration)**. Reconnect the coil/cap wiring connectors, making sure they are securely connected to the correct cylinder **(see illustration 5.4a)**. Install all other components previously removed.

> **HAYNES HINT**: Stripped plug threads in the cylinder head can be repaired with a Heli-Coil insert – see 'Tools and Workshop Tips' in the Reference section.

Renewal

Interval:
 US models: Every 8000 miles (12,000 km) or 12 months
 European models: Every 16,000 miles (24,000 km) or two years

11 Remove the existing spark plugs as described above and renew them irrespective of their apparent condition.

Every 8000 miles (12,000 km) or 12 months

Carry out all the items under the 4000 mile (6000 km) check, plus the following:

6 Spark plugs – check (F-1/FS-1 models onwards (2001-on)

Check

1 Make sure your spark plug socket is the correct size before attempting to remove the plugs – a suitable one is supplied in the motorcycle's tool kit which is stored under the seat.
2 It is possible to access the spark plugs from the front by displacing the radiator, but access is restricted. It does however mean there is no need to remove the fuel tank, which is tedious on fuel injected models. To access from the front, displace the radiator from its mounts and move it away as much as possible (see Chapter 3) – there is no need to detach any hoses, but disconnect the wiring connector, and support or tie the radiator so that there is no danger of it scratching the front mudguard, or of the mudguard damaging the radiator fins. If access is still too restricted for you, drain the coolant (see Section 27), and remove the radiator. To access the plugs from the top, remove the fuel tank and the air filter housing (see Chapter 4).
3 Clean the area around the plug caps to prevent any dirt falling into the spark plug channels.
4 Check that the cylinder location is marked on each combined ignition coil/spark plug cap, then disconnect the coil/cap wiring connectors **(see illustration 5.4a)**. Pull the coil/cap off each spark plug **(see illustration 5.4b)**. Using either the plug removing tool supplied in the bike's toolkit or a deep socket type wrench, unscrew and remove the plugs from the cylinder head **(see illustrations 5.4c, d and e)**. Lay each plug out in relation to its cylinder; if any plug shows up a problem it will then be easy to identify the troublesome cylinder.
5 At the specified interval check the condition of the electrodes, referring to the spark plug reading chart at the end of this manual if signs of contamination are evident. Contaminated plugs should be renewed and not cleaned using conventional methods.
6 Examine the pointed iridium-tipped centre electrode; if the tip has rounded off, the plug is worn **(see illustration)**. Measure the gap between the two electrodes with a wire type gauge **(see illustration)** – do not use blade type feeler gauges because the iridium tip might become damaged. The gap should be as given in the Specifications at the beginning of this chapter; if the electrodes have worn beyond this figure the plug must be renewed. Do not bend the outer electrode to adjust the gap.
7 Check the threads, the washer and the ceramic insulator body for cracks and other damage.
8 Install the plugs as described in Steps 9 and 10 above. Note that Honda advise that the specified iridium plugs must be fitted – do not substitute with conventional plugs.

Renewal

9 Renew the spark plugs at the specific interval of every 16,000 miles (24,000 km).

6.6a If the centre electrode is rounded off as shown the plug is worn – iridium plug

6.6b Measure the electrode gap with a wire type feeler gauge (arrowed) – iridium plug

Routine maintenance and servicing 1•11

7.3a Lubricating a cable with a pressure lubricator. Make sure the tool seals around the inner cable

7.3b Lubricating a cable with a makeshift funnel and motor oil

8.3 Unscrew the oil filler cap to act as a vent . . .

7 Stand(s), lever pivots and cables – lubrication

1 Since the controls, cables and various other components of a motorcycle are exposed to the elements, they should be lubricated periodically to ensure safe and trouble-free operation.

2 The footrests, clutch and brake levers, brake pedal, gearchange lever and linkage, sidestand and centrestand pivots should be lubricated frequently. In order for the lubricant to be applied where it will do the most good, the component should be disassembled. The lubricant recommended by Honda for each application is listed at the beginning of the Chapter. If chain or cable lubricant is being used, it can be applied to the pivot joint gaps and will usually work its way into the areas where friction occurs, so less disassembly of the component is needed (however it is always better to do so and clean off all dirt and old lubricant first). If motor oil or light grease is being used, apply it sparingly as it may attract dirt (which could cause the controls to bind or wear at an accelerated rate). **Note:** *One of the best lubricants for the control lever pivots is a dry-film lubricant (available from many sources by different names).*

3 To lubricate the cables, disconnect the relevant cable at its upper end, then lubricate it with a pressure adapter and aerosol lubricant, or if one is not available, using the set-up shown **(see illustrations)**. See Chapter 4 for the choke (carburettor models only) and throttle cable removal procedures.

8 Engine – oil and oil filter change

⚠️ *Warning: Be careful when draining the oil, as the exhaust pipes, the engine, and the oil itself can cause severe burns.*

1 Consistent routine oil and filter changes are the single most important maintenance procedure you can perform on a motorcycle. The oil not only lubricates the internal parts of the engine, transmission and clutch, but it also acts as a coolant, a cleaner, a sealant, and a protectant. Because of these demands, the oil takes a terrific amount of abuse and should be replaced often with new oil of the recommended grade and type. Saving a little money on the difference in cost between a good oil and a cheap oil won't pay off if the engine is damaged. The oil filter should be changed with every oil change.

2 Before changing the oil, warm up the engine so the oil will drain easily. Make sure the bike is on level ground, or if there is a slight slope make sure the front of the bike is pointing up the hill. On models equipped with a centrestand, put the motorcycle on its sidestand instead. The oil drain plug is at the back of the engine on the left-hand side so the angles created by a slope and using the sidestand will help the oil to drain. Remove the fairing side panels and centre panel (see Chapter 8).

3 Position a clean drain tray below the engine. Unscrew the oil filler cap from the clutch cover to vent the crankcase and to act as a reminder that there is no oil in the engine **(see illustration)**.

4 Unscrew the oil drain plug from the rear left-hand side of the engine and allow the oil to flow into the drain tray **(see illustration)**. Check the condition of the sealing washer on the drain plug and replace it with a new one if

8.4a . . . then unscrew the oil drain plug (arrowed) . . .

8.4b . . . and allow the oil to completely drain

1•12 Routine maintenance and servicing

8.5a Install the drain plug using a new sealing washer ...

8.5b ... and tighten it to the specified torque setting

it is damaged or worn – it is advisable to use a new one whatever the condition of the old one.

5 When the oil has completely drained, fit the plug to the sump, using a new sealing washer if necessary, and tighten it to the torque setting specified at the beginning of the Chapter **(see illustrations)**. Avoid overtightening, as it is quite easy to damage the threads in the sump.

6 Now place the drain tray below the oil filter. Unscrew the oil filter using a filter socket (one can be obtained as a kit with the new filter from Honda dealers), a filter removing strap or a chain-wrench, and tip any residual oil into the drain tray **(see illustrations)**. The filter socket is preferable because it allows a means of tightening the new filter to the correct torque.

7 Smear clean engine oil onto the rubber seal on the new filter and thread it onto the engine **(see illustrations)**. Tighten it to the specified torque setting using the filter socket if available **(see illustration)**, or tighten the filter as tight as possible by hand, or by the number of turns specified on the filter itself or its packaging. **Note:** *Do not use a strap or chain filter removing tool to tighten the filter as you will damage it.*

8 Refill the engine to the proper level using the recommended type and amount of oil (see *Daily (pre-ride) checks*). With the motorcycle vertical, the oil level should lie between the upper and lower level lines on the inspection window (see *Daily (pre-ride) checks*). Install the filler cap **(see illustration 8.3)**. Start the engine and let it run for two or three minutes (make sure that the oil pressure light extinguishes after a few seconds). Shut it off, wait a few minutes, then check the oil level. If necessary, add more oil to bring the level to the upper line. Check around the drain plug and the oil filter for leaks. A leak around the drain plug probably means a new washer is needed. A leak around the filter probably means it is not tight enough. Install the fairing centre and side panels (see Chapter 8).

> **HAYNES HiNT** *Saving a little money on the difference between good and cheap oils won't pay off if the engine is damaged as a result.*

9 The old oil drained from the engine cannot be re-used and should be disposed of properly. Check with your local refuse disposal company, disposal facility or environmental agency to see whether they will accept the used oil for recycling. Don't pour used oil into drains or onto the ground.

> **HAYNES HiNT** *Check the old oil carefully – if it is very metallic coloured, then the engine is experiencing wear from break-in (new engine) or from insufficient lubrication. If there are flakes or chips of metal in the oil, then something is drastically wrong internally and the engine will have to be disassembled for inspection and repair. If there are pieces of fibre-like material in the oil, the clutch is experiencing excessive wear and should be checked.*

9 Fuel system – check

⚠️ **Warning:** *Petrol (gasoline) is extremely flammable, so take extra precautions when you work on any part of the fuel system. Don't smoke or allow open flames or bare light bulbs near the work area, and don't work in a garage where a natural gas-type appliance is present. If you spill any fuel on your skin, rinse it off immediately with soap and water. When you perform any kind of work on the fuel system, wear safety glasses and have a fire extinguisher suitable for a Class B type fire (flammable liquids) on hand.*

8.6a Unscrew the filter using a filter removing tool ...

8.6b ... and allow the oil to drain

8.7a Smear clean oil onto the seal ...

8.7b ... then install the new filter ...

8.7c ... and tighten it as described

Routine maintenance and servicing 1•13

1 Raise the fuel tank (see Chapter 4) and check the tank, the fuel tap (carburettor models) and the fuel hoses for signs of leakage, deterioration or damage; in particular check that there is no leakage from the fuel hoses. Replace any hoses which are cracked or deteriorated with new ones.
2 On carburettor models, if the fuel tap is faulty or leaking, it must be replaced with a new one – it cannot be disassembled (see Chapter 4). If the carburettor gaskets are leaking, the carburettors should be disassembled and rebuilt using new gaskets and seals (see Chapter 4).
3 On fuel injection models, also check for signs of fuel leakage between the injectors, the fuel rail and the throttle bodies. If there are, remove the injectors and replace the O-rings and seals (see Chapter 4).
4 If there are signs of fuel starvation or the machine has covered a high mileage, the fuel filters could be in need of cleaning or renewal (see Section 36).

10 Battery – check

1 All models covered in this manual are fitted with a sealed MF (maintenance free) battery. **Note:** *Do not attempt to remove the battery caps to check the electrolyte level or battery specific gravity. Removal will damage the caps, resulting in electrolyte leakage and battery damage.* All that should be done is to check that the terminals are clean and tight and that the casing is not damaged or leaking. See Chapter 9 for further details.
2 If the machine is not in regular use, disconnect the battery and give it a refresher charge every month to six weeks (see Chapter 9).

11 Throttle and choke cables – check

Throttle cables

1 Make sure the throttle grip rotates smoothly and freely from fully closed to fully open with the front wheel turned at various angles. The grip should return automatically from fully open to fully closed when released.
2 If the throttle sticks, this is probably due to a cable fault. Remove the cables (see Chapter 4) and lubricate them (see Section 7). Check that the inner cables slide freely and easily in the outer cables. If not, replace the cables with new ones. With the cables removed, make sure the throttle twistgrip is rotates freely on the handlebar. Install the cables, making sure they are correctly routed. If this fails to improve the operation of the throttle, the cables must be replaced with new ones. Note that in very rare cases the fault

11.3 Throttle cable freeplay is measured in terms of twistgrip rotation

could lie in the carburettors or throttle bodies (according to model) rather than the cables, necessitating their removal and inspection (see Chapter 4).
3 With the throttle operating smoothly, check for a small amount of freeplay in the cables, measured in terms of the amount of twistgrip rotation before the throttle opens, and compare the amount to that listed in this Chapter's Specifications **(see illustration)**. If it's incorrect, adjust the cables to correct it as follows.
4 Freeplay adjustments can be made using the adjuster in the accelerator cable where it leaves the throttle/switch housing on the handlebar. Loosen the locknut and turn the adjuster in or out as required until the specified amount of freeplay is obtained (see this Chapter's Specifications), then retighten the locknut **(see illustration)**.
5 If the adjuster has reached its limit of adjustment, reset it so that the freeplay is at a maximum, then make adjustment at the lower end of the cable. Refer to Step 6 or 7 according to the model being worked on.
6 Remove the fuel tank (see Chapter 4) and adjust the cable at the carburettor end. The adjuster is on the upper cable in the bracket. Slacken the adjuster locknut, then screw the adjuster in or out as required, making sure the lower nut remains captive in the bracket, thereby threading itself along the adjuster as you turn it, until the specified amount of freeplay is obtained, then tighten the locknut **(see illustration)**. Further adjustments can

11.6 Throttle cable adjuster locknut (A), adjuster (B) and lower nut (C) – carburettor models

11.4 Throttle cable adjuster locknut (A) and adjuster (B) – throttle end

now be made at the throttle end. If the cable cannot be adjusted as specified, replace it with a new one (see Chapter 4). Check that the throttle twistgrip operates smoothly and snaps shut quickly when released.
7 Remove the fuel tank and the air filter housing (see Chapter 4), and adjust the cable at the throttle body end. The adjuster is on the lower cable in the bracket. Slacken the adjuster locknut, then screw the adjuster in or out as required, making sure the lower nut remains captive in the bracket, thereby threading itself along the adjuster as you turn it, until the specified amount of freeplay is obtained, then tighten the locknut **(see illustration)**. Further adjustments can now be made at the throttle end. If the cable cannot be adjusted as specified, replace it with a new one (see Chapter 4). Check that the throttle twistgrip operates smoothly and snaps shut quickly when released.

⚠️ **Warning:** *Turn the handlebars all the way through their travel with the engine idling. Idle speed should not change. If it does, the cables may be routed incorrectly. Correct this condition before riding the bike.*

Choke cable (carburettor models)

8 If the choke does not operate smoothly this is probably due to a cable fault. Remove the cable (see Chapter 4) and lubricate it (see Section 7). Check that the inner cable slides freely and easily in the outer cable. If not, replace the cable with a new one. With the

11.7 Throttle cable adjuster locknut (A), adjuster (B) and lower nut (C) – throttle body end fuel injected models

1•14 Routine maintenance and servicing

12.4 Release the clamps and detach the vacuum hoses from their stubs (arrowed)

12.5 Connect the gauge hoses to the vacuum hoses using adapters

12.7 Adjust the carburettors using the synchronisation screws (A), accessing using a screwdriver inserted from above (B)

cable removed, make sure the choke lever is able to slide freely in the switch housing. Install the cable, making sure it is correctly routed.

9 If this fails to improve the operation of the choke, the fault could lie in the carburettors rather than the cable, necessitating their removal and inspection of the choke plungers and the linkage between them (see Chapter 4).

12 Carburettors – synchronisation

⚠️ **Warning: Petrol (gasoline) is extremely flammable, so take extra precautions when you work on any part of the fuel system. Don't smoke or allow open flames or bare light bulbs near the work area, and don't work in a garage where a natural gas-type appliance is present. If you spill any fuel on your skin, rinse it off immediately with soap and water. When you perform any kind of work on the fuel system, wear safety glasses and have a fire extinguisher suitable for a Class B type fire (flammable liquids) on hand.**

Warning: Take great care not to burn your hand on the hot engine unit when accessing the gauge take-off points on the intake manifolds. Do not allow exhaust gases to build up in the work area; either perform the check outside or use an exhaust gas extraction system.

1 Carburettor synchronisation is simply the process of adjusting the carburettors so they pass the same amount of fuel/air mixture to each cylinder. This is done by measuring the vacuum produced in each intake duct. Carburettors that are out of synchronisation will result in decreased fuel mileage, increased engine temperature, less than ideal throttle response and higher vibration levels. Before synchronising the carburettors, make sure the valve clearances are properly set (see Section 25).

2 To properly synchronise the carburettors, you will need a set of vacuum gauges or calibrated tubes to indicate engine vacuum. The equipment used should be suitable for a four cylinder engine and come complete with the necessary adapters and hoses to fit the take-off points. **Note:** *Because of the nature of the synchronisation procedure and the need for special instruments, most owners leave the task to a Honda dealer.*

3 Start the engine and let it run until it reaches normal operating temperature.

⚠️ **Warning: The engine and carburettors will be hot. With the restricted access to the screws, great care must be taken not to burn yourself while synchronising the carburettors.**

4 Raise the fuel tank (see Chapter 4). Detach the vacuum hoses from the blanking stubs on the rear of the air filter housing, noting which fits where **(see illustration)**.

5 Connect the gauge hoses to the vacuum hoses using suitable adapters **(see illustration)**. Make sure they are a good fit because any air leaks will result in false readings.

6 Start the engine and adjust the idle speed (see Section 2). If using vacuum gauges fitted with damping adjustment, set this so that the needle flutter is just eliminated but so that they can still respond to small changes in pressure.

7 The vacuum readings for the Nos. 1, 2 and 3 cylinders should be the same as the No. 4 cylinder, or at least within the maximum difference specified at the beginning of the Chapter. The No.4 carburettor is the base carburettor to which all the others are matched. If the vacuum readings vary, adjust the carburettors by turning the synchronising screws situated in the throttle linkage between the carburettors until the readings are the same **(see illustration)**. **Note:** *Do not press hard on the screw whilst adjusting it, otherwise a false reading will be obtained.* First synchronise the No.3 carburettor to the No.4 using the synchronising screw situated between them. Now synchronise Nos.1 and 2 carburettors using the synchronising screw between them. Now synchronise Nos. 1 and 2 to Nos. 3 and 4 using the centre synchronising screw.

8 When the carburettors are synchronised, open and close the throttle quickly to settle the linkage, and recheck the gauge readings, readjusting if necessary.

9 When the adjustment is complete, recheck the vacuum readings, then adjust the idle speed by turning the throttle stop screw (see Section 2) until the idle speed listed in this Chapter's Specifications is obtained. Stop the engine.

10 Remove the vacuum gauges and the hose joining pieces, then fit the vacuum hoses onto their original stubs on the back of the air filter housing – the No.1 cylinder vacuum hose fits on the left-hand stub, and so on from left to right. Install the fuel tank (see Chapter 4).

13 Cooling system – check

⚠️ **Warning: The engine must be cool before beginning this procedure.**

1 Check the coolant level (see *Daily (pre-ride) checks*).

2 Remove the fairing side panels (see Chapter 8). Check the entire cooling system for evidence of leakage. Examine each rubber coolant hose along its entire length. Look for cracks, abrasions and other damage. Squeeze each hose at various points to see whether they are dried out or hard. They should feel firm, yet pliable, and return to their original shape when released. If necessary, replace them with new ones.

3 Check for evidence of leaks at each cooling system joint and around the pump on the left-hand side of the engine. Tighten the hose clips carefully to prevent future leaks. If the pump is leaking, check that the cover bolts are tight. If they are, replace the O-ring in the cover with a new one (see Chapter 3).

4 To prevent leakage of coolant from the cooling system to the lubrication system and vice versa, two seals are fitted on the pump

Routine maintenance and servicing 1•15

13.4 Check the pump drain hole (arrowed) for signs of leakage

13.7 Remove the pressure cap as described

shaft. On the bottom of the pump housing there is a drain hole **(see illustration)**. If either seal fails, the drain allows the coolant or oil to escape and prevents them mixing. The seal on the water pump side is of the mechanical type which bears on the rear face of the impeller. The second seal, which is mounted behind the mechanical seal is of the normal feathered lip type. If on inspection the drain shows signs of leakage, remove the pump and replace it with a new one – it comes as an assembly, and the seals are not available separately. Refer to Chapter 3 for details.

5 Check the radiator for leaks and other damage. Leaks in the radiator leave tell-tale scale deposits or coolant stains on the outside of the core below the leak. If leaks are noted, remove the radiator (see Chapter 3) and have it repaired or replace it with a new one – do not use a liquid leak stopping compound to try to repair leaks.

6 Check the radiator fins for mud, dirt and insects, which may impede the flow of air through the radiator. If the fins are dirty, remove the radiator (see Chapter 3) and clean it using water or low pressure compressed air directed through the fins from the inner side of the radiator. If the fins are bent or distorted, straighten them carefully with a screwdriver. If the air flow is restricted by bent or damaged fins over more than 20% of the radiator's surface area, replace the radiator with a new one.

7 Remove the pressure cap from the radiator filler neck by holding the pressure cap with a heavy cloth and turning it anti-clockwise until it reaches a stop **(see illustration)**. If you hear a hissing sound (indicating there is still pressure in the system), wait until it stops. Now press down on the cap and continue turning it until it can be removed. Check the condition of the coolant in the system. If it is rust-coloured or if accumulations of scale are visible, drain and flush the system and refill it with new coolant (See Section 26). Check the cap seal for cracks and other damage. If in doubt about the pressure cap's condition, have it tested by a Honda dealer or replace it with a new one.

8 Check the antifreeze content of the coolant with an antifreeze hydrometer. Sometimes coolant looks like it's in good condition, but might be too weak to offer adequate protection. If the hydrometer indicates a weak mixture, drain, flush and refill the system (see Section 26).

9 Install the cap by turning it clockwise until it reaches the first stop then push down on it and continue turning until it can turn no further. Start the engine and let it reach normal operating temperature, then check for leaks again. As the coolant temperature increases, the electric fan (mounted on the back of the radiator) should come on automatically and the temperature should begin to drop. If it does not, refer to Chapter 3 and check the fan and fan circuit carefully.

10 If the coolant level is consistently low, and no evidence of leaks can be found, have the entire system pressure checked by a Honda dealer.

11 Check the oil cooler on the front of the engine for any signs of oil leakage between it and the filter, and between it and the engine. Tighten the filter or the cooler bolt as required (remove the filter to access it – see Section 8), but if the leakage persists you will have to fit a new filter or a new O-ring between the cooler and the engine, as required (see Chapter 2). Check that the coolant pipes to the cooler are tight, and that there is no evidence of coolant leakage from the body of the cooler. If there is, the cooler is damaged and must be replaced with a new one.

14 Brake system – check

1 A routine general check of the brake system will ensure that any problems are discovered and remedied before the rider's safety is jeopardised.

2 Check the brake lever and pedal for loose connections, improper or rough action, excessive play, bends, and other damage. Replace any damaged parts with new ones (see Chapter 7).

3 Make sure all brake component fasteners are tight. Check the brake pads for wear (see Section 3) and make sure the fluid level in the reservoirs is correct (see *Daily (pre-ride) checks*). Look for leaks at the hose and pipe connections and check for cracks in the hoses and pipes **(see illustration)**. If the lever or pedal is spongy, bleed the brakes (see Chapter 7).

4 Make sure the brake light operates when the front brake lever is pulled in. The front brake light switch, mounted on the underside of the master cylinder, is not adjustable. If it fails to operate properly, check it (see Chapter 9).

5 Make sure the brake light is activated just before the rear brake takes effect. If adjustment is necessary, hold the switch and turn the adjuster ring on the switch body until the brake light is activated when required **(see illustration)**. The switch is mounted on the

14.3 Flex the hoses and check for cracks, bulges and leaking fluid. Also check the pipes and all connections for leaks

14.5 Hold the rear brake light switch body (A) and turn the adjuster ring (B) as required

1•16 Routine maintenance and servicing

14.6 Adjusting the front brake lever span

14.7 Slacken the locknut (A) and turn the pushrod using the hex (B) to adjust pedal height

inside of the rider's right-hand footrest bracket, just ahead of the master cylinder. If the brake light comes on too late, turn the ring clockwise. If the brake light comes on too soon or is permanently on, turn the ring anti-clockwise. If the switch doesn't operate the brake light, check it (see Chapter 9).
6 The front brake lever has a span adjuster which alters the distance of the lever from the handlebar (see illustration). Each setting is identified by a notch in the adjuster which aligns with the arrow on the lever. Turn the adjuster ring until the setting which best suits the rider is obtained.
7 The height of the rear brake pedal can be adjusted to suit the rider's preference. Slacken the clevis locknut on the master cylinder pushrod, then turn the pushrod using a spanner on the hex at the top of the rod until the pedal is at the desired height (see illustration). On completion tighten the locknut securely. Adjust the rear brake light switch after adjusting the pedal height (see Step 5). Note that Honda specify a standard pedal height of 75 mm, measured vertically from the pedal tip (brake at rest) to a line level with the top surface of the rider's footrest.

15 Headlight aim – check and adjustment

Note: *An improperly adjusted headlight may cause problems for oncoming traffic or provide poor, unsafe illumination of the road ahead. Before adjusting the headlight aim, be sure to consult with local traffic laws and regulations – for UK models refer to MOT Test Checks in the Reference section.*
1 The headlight beam can adjusted both horizontally and vertically. Before making any adjustment, check that the tyre pressures are correct and the suspension is adjusted as required. Make any adjustments to the headlight aim with the machine on level ground, with the fuel tank half full and with an assistant sitting on the seat. If the bike is usually ridden with a passenger on the back, have a second assistant to do this.
2 On F-X and F-Y (1999 and 2000) models, vertical adjustment is made by turning the adjuster screw on the top left corner of the headlight unit using a screwdriver inserted through the access hole in the cockpit trim panel (see illustration). Turn it clockwise to move the beam up, and anti-clockwise to move it down. Horizontal adjustment is made by turning the adjuster bolt on the bottom right corner of the headlight (see illustration). Turn it clockwise to move the beam to the right, and anti-clockwise to move it to the left.
3 On F-1/FS-1 models onward (2001-on), in countries that ride on the left-hand side of the road, vertical adjustment of the dipped (low) beam is made by turning the adjuster screw on the top left corner of the headlight unit using a screwdriver inserted through the access hole in the cockpit trim panel, and vertical adjustment of the main (high) beam is made by turning the adjuster screw on the top right corner of the headlight unit (see illustration).
4 On those models in countries that ride on the right-hand side of the road, vertical adjustment of the dipped (low) beam is made by turning the adjuster screw on the top right corner of the headlight unit using a screwdriver inserted through the access hole in the cockpit trim panel, and vertical adjustment of the main (high) beam is made by turning the adjuster screw on the top left corner of the headlight.
5 In all cases turn the adjuster clockwise to move the beam up, and anti-clockwise to move it down.
6 Horizontal adjustment of the beams is made by turning the adjuster screws on the bottom of the headlight unit.

15.2a Access the vertical adjustment screw as shown – carburettor models

15.2b Horizontal adjustment bolt (arrowed) – carburettor models

15.3 Vertical adjusters (A), horizontal adjusters (B) – fuel injected models

Routine maintenance and servicing 1•17

16 Sidestand and centrestand – check

1 Check the stand springs for damage and distortion. The springs must be capable of retracting the stands fully and holding them retracted when the motorcycle is in use. If a spring is sagged or broken it must be replaced with a new one.
2 Lubricate the stand pivots regularly (see Section 7).
3 Check the stands and their mounts for bends and cracks. Stands can often be repaired by welding.
4 Check the operation of the sidestand switch by shifting the transmission into neutral, retracting the stand and starting the engine. Pull in the clutch lever and select a gear. Extend the sidestand. The engine should stop as the sidestand is extended. If the sidestand switch does not operate as described, check its circuit (see Chapter 9).

17 Suspension – check

1 The suspension components must be maintained in top operating condition to ensure rider safety. Loose, worn or damaged suspension parts decrease the motorcycle's stability and control.

Front suspension

2 While standing alongside the motorcycle, apply the front brake and push on the handlebars to compress the forks several times. See if they move up-and-down smoothly without binding. If binding is felt, the forks should be disassembled and inspected (see Chapter 6).
3 Inspect the area around the dust seal for signs of oil leakage, then carefully lever up the seal using a flat-bladed screwdriver and inspect the area around the fork seal. If leakage is evident, the seals must be replaced with new ones (see Chapter 6).
4 Check the tightness of all suspension nuts and bolts to be sure none have worked loose.

Rear suspension

5 Inspect the rear shock absorber for fluid leakage and tightness of its mountings. If leakage is found, the shock must be replaced with a new one (see Chapter 6).
6 With the aid of an assistant to support the bike, compress the rear suspension several times. It should move up and down freely without binding. If any binding is felt, the worn or faulty component must be identified and checked (see Chapter 6). The problem could be due to either the shock absorber, the suspension linkage components or the swingarm components.
7 Support the motorcycle on its centrestand if fitted, or on an auxiliary stand, so that the rear wheel is off the ground. Grab the swingarm and rock it from side to side – there should be no discernible movement at the rear (see illustration). If there's a little movement or a slight clicking can be heard, inspect the tightness of all the swingarm and rear suspension mounting bolts and nuts, referring to the torque settings specified at the beginning of Chapter 6, and re-check for movement. Next, grasp the top of the rear wheel and pull it upwards – there should be no discernible freeplay before the shock absorber begins to compress (see illustration). Any freeplay felt in either check indicates worn bearings in the suspension linkage or swingarm, or worn shock absorber mountings. The worn components must be identified and replaced with new ones (see Chapter 6).
8 To make an accurate assessment of the swingarm bearings, remove the rear wheel (see Chapter 7) and the bolt securing the suspension linkage assembly to the swingarm (see Chapter 6). Grasp the rear of the swingarm with one hand and place your other hand at the junction of the swingarm and the frame. Try to move the rear of the swingarm from side-to-side. Any wear (play) in the bearings should be felt as movement between the swingarm and the frame at the front. If there is any play the swingarm will be felt to move forward and backward at the front (not from side-to-side). Next, move the swingarm up and down through its full travel. It should move freely, without any binding or rough spots. If there is any play in the swingarm or if it does not move freely, remove the bearings for inspection (see Chapter 6).

18 Steering head bearings – freeplay check and adjustment

1 This motorcycle is equipped with caged ball steering head bearings which can become dented, rough or loose during normal use of the machine. In extreme cases, worn or loose steering head bearings can cause steering wobble – a condition that is potentially dangerous.

Check

2 On F-X and F-Y (1999 and 2000) models, support the motorcycle on its centrestand, and raise the front wheel off the ground either by having an assistant push down on the rear or by placing a support under the engine (remove the fairing side panels first (see Chapter 8), and avoid placing a support on the exhaust pipes). On F-1/FS-1 models onward (2001-on), use an auxiliary stand that lifts the front wheel off the ground without loading the bearings, removing the fairing side panels and anything else that could be damaged by taking the weight of the bike first, and making sure that the bike is properly supported and secure.
3 Point the front wheel straight-ahead and slowly move the handlebars from side-to-side. Any dents or roughness in the bearing races will be felt and the bars will not move smoothly and freely. Again point the wheel straight ahead, then tap the front of the wheel to one side. The wheel should 'fall' under its own weight to the limit of its lock, indicating that the bearings are not too tight. Check for similar movement to the other side. If the steering doesn't move freely through its entire lock, and it's not due to the resistance of cables or hoses, then the bearings should be adjusted as described below.
4 Next, grasp the bottom of the forks and gently pull and push them forward and backward (see illustration). Any looseness or

17.7a Checking for play in the swingarm bearings

17.7b Checking for play in the rear shock mountings and suspension linkage bearings

18.4 Checking for play in the steering head bearings

1•18 Routine maintenance and servicing

18.7 Slacken the fork clamp bolt (arrowed) on each side

18.8 Unscrew the steering stem nut (arrowed) ...

18.9 ... and gently ease the yoke up off the forks

HAYNES HiNT *Make sure you are not mistaking any movement between the bike and stand, or between the stand and the ground, for freeplay in the bearings. Do not pull and push the forks too hard – a gentle movement is all that is needed. Freeplay in the forks themselves due to worn bushes can also be misinterpreted as steering head bearing play – do not confuse the two.*

freeplay in the steering head bearings will be felt as front-to-rear movement of the forks. If play is felt, adjust the bearings as described below.

Adjustment

5 As a precaution, remove the fuel tank (see Chapter 4) and the fairing (see Chapter 8). Though not actually necessary, this will prevent the possibility of damage should a tool slip.

6 Displace the handlebars from the top yoke (see Chapter 6). Support them so the brake master cylinder is upright to prevent the possibility of fluid leakage. There is no need to remove assemblies from the handlebars, or to disconnect any cables, hoses or wiring.

7 Slacken the fork clamp bolts in the top yoke (see illustration).

8 Remove the blanking cap from the steering stem nut. Unscrew and remove the nut **(see illustration)**.

9 Gently ease the top yoke up off the fork tubes and position it clear of the head bearings, using a rag to protect other components **(see illustration)**.

10 Bend the lockwasher tabs out of the notches in the locknut **(see illustration)**. Unscrew the locknut using either your fingers (it shouldn't be tight), a C-spanner or a suitable drift located in one of the notches **(see illustration)**. Remove the lockwasher, bending up the remaining tabs to release it from the adjuster nut if necessary **(see illustration)**. Inspect the tabs for cracks or signs of fatigue. If there is any sign of damage, discard the lockwasher and use a new one; otherwise the old one can be re-used, but note that Honda do recommend using a new one as a matter of course.

11 Using either the C-spanner or drift, slacken the adjuster nut slightly until pressure is just released, then tighten it until all freeplay is removed, yet the steering is able to move freely **(see illustration)**. The object is to set

18.10a Bend down the tabs securing the locknut ...

18.10b ... then unscrew the locknut ...

18.10c ... and remove the lockwasher

18.11 Adjust the bearings as described using either a C-spanner or a drift

Routine maintenance and servicing 1•19

18.13 Bend the tabs up into the notches in the locknut

18.14 Install the steering stem nut and tighten it to the specified torque

the adjuster nut so that the bearings are under a very light loading, just enough to remove any freeplay, but not so much that the steering does not move freely from side to side as described in the check procedure above. If the Honda service tool (part No. 07916-3710101) or a suitable peg spanner (which can be made by cutting castellations into an old socket) is available, the adjuster nut can be tightened to the torque setting specified at the beginning of the Chapter, and this should give the correct loading. Turn the steering from lock-to-lock five times after tightening and recheck the adjustment or torque setting. Do not rely on the torque setting alone and assume the loading to be correct – check the physical feel as described as well. If the bearings cannot be correctly adjusted, disassemble the steering head and check the bearings and races (see Chapter 6).

Caution: Take great care not to apply excessive pressure because this will cause premature failure of the bearings.

12 With the bearings correctly adjusted, install the lockwasher, using a new one if the tabs are weakened or cracked, onto the adjuster nut and fit two tabs into the slots in the adjuster nut **(see illustration 18.10c)**.

13 Hold the adjuster nut to prevent it from moving, then install the locknut and tighten it finger-tight **(see illustration 18.10b)**. Tighten the locknut further (but no more than 90°) until its notches align with the remaining lockwasher tabs, making sure the adjuster nut does not turn as well (though that is unlikely). Secure the locknut in position by bending up the lock washer tabs into its notches **(see illustration)**.

14 Fit the top yoke onto the steering stem **(see illustration 18.9)**. Install the steering stem nut and tighten it to the torque setting specified at the beginning of the Chapter **(see illustration)**. Now tighten both the top yoke fork clamp bolts to the specified torque **(see illustration 18.7)**.

15 Check the bearing adjustment as described above and re-adjust if necessary.

16 Install the handlebars (see Chapter 6), the fuel tank (see Chapter 4) and the fairing (see Chapter 8). Fit the blanking cap into the stem nut **(see illustration 18.8a)**.

19 Nuts and bolts – tightness check

1 Since vibration of the machine tends to loosen fasteners, all nuts, bolts, screws, etc. should be periodically checked for proper tightness.

2 Pay particular attention to the following:

Spark plugs
Engine oil drain plug and coolant drain plug
Lever and pedal bolts
Footrest and stand bolts
Engine mounting bolts
Shock absorber and suspension linkage bolts and swingarm pivot bolts
Handlebar clamp bolts
Front axle bolt and axle clamp bolts
Front fork clamp bolts (top and bottom yoke) and fork top bolts
Rear axle nut
Brake caliper and master cylinder mounting bolts
Brake hose banjo bolts and caliper bleed valves
Brake disc bolts
Exhaust system bolts/nuts

3 If a torque wrench is available, use it along with the torque specifications at the beginning of this and other Chapters.

20 Wheels and tyres – general check

Tyres

1 Check the tyre condition and tread depth thoroughly – see *Daily (pre-ride) checks*.

Wheels

2 Cast wheels are virtually maintenance free, but they should be kept clean and checked periodically for cracks and other damage. Also check the wheel runout and alignment (see Chapter 7). Never attempt to repair damaged cast wheels; they must be replaced with new ones. Check the valve rubber for signs of damage or deterioration and have it replaced if necessary. Also, make sure the valve stem cap is in place and tight.

21 Pulse secondary air injection (PAIR) system – check

1 Remove the air filter housing (see Chapter 4). Visually inspect the hoses between the reed valves on the valve cover and the PAIR control valve above it, and between the control valve and the air filter housing, for kinks and splits and any other damage or deterioration. On F-X and F-Y (1999 and 2000) models, similarly check the vacuum hose between the control valve and its take-off point on the engine near the carburettors. Make sure that all hoses are securely connected with a clamp on each end. Renew any hoses that are damaged or deteriorated.

2 See Chapter 4 for further information and tests on the system.

Routine maintenance and servicing

Every 12,000 miles (18,000 km) or 18 months

Carry out all the items under the 4000 mile (6000 km) check:

22 Air filter – renewal

Caution: *If the machine is continually ridden in wet or dusty conditions, the filter should be replaced more frequently.*

1 Raise or remove the fuel tank (see Chapter 4). On fuel injected models, disconnect the intake air temperature (IAT) sensor wiring connector **(see illustration)**. Where fitted, remove the rubber covers, noting how they locate around the collars in the air filter housing cover screw points **(see illustrations)**.

2 Undo the ten screws securing the air filter housing cover and remove it **(see illustration)**. Remove the element from the housing, noting how it fits, and discard it **(see illustration)**.

3 Fit the new filter element into the housing, making sure it is properly seated, then install the cover. On fuel injection models, connect the IAT (intake air temperature) sensor wiring connector **(see illustration 22.1)**. Where fitted, install the rubber covers, locating them onto the collars **(see illustrations 22.1b and c)**.

4 Install the fuel tank (see Chapter 4).

5 To clean the filter in between renewal intervals, tap it on a hard surface to dislodge any dirt and use compressed air to clear the element, directing the air in the opposite way to normal flow **(see illustration)**. Do not use any solvents or cleaning agents on the element as it is pre-treated with a dust adhesive. If the machine is constantly used in dirty or dusty conditions the filter should be

22.1a On fuel injection models disconnect the IAT sensor wiring connector

22.1b Where fitted, remove the rubber covers . . .

22.1c . . . noting how they locate over the collars

22.2a Undo the screws (arrowed) and remove the cover (F-X and F-Y shown) . . .

22.2b . . . and remove the element from the housing, noting how it fits

22.5 Direct the air in the opposite direction of normal flow

Routine maintenance and servicing 1•21

22.6a Remove the two screws to access each sub air filter

22.6b Lift the sub air filter out of the housing

replaced at more frequent intervals than specified.

6 On carburettor models (F-X and F-Y, 1999 and 2000), clean the direct air injection (DAI) system sub air filters whilst the main air filter is removed for cleaning or renewal. The two sub air filters are located in the base of the air filter housing – remove the two screws to release their covers and the elements **(see illustrations)**. Wash each foam filter element in soapy water then dry them thoroughly and refit them in the housing. Check that the sealing rubber in in place then refit the covers.

23 Evaporative emission control (EVAP) system – check (California models)

1 Raise the fuel tank (see Chapter 4). Visually inspect all the system hoses between the fuel tank, the purge control and solenoid valves, and the canister (mounted under the bike ahead of the rear wheel) for kinks and splits and any other damage or deterioration. Make sure that the hoses are securely connected with a clamp on each end. Replace any hoses that are damaged or deteriorated.

2 Check the EVAP canister and the two valves for cracks or other damage.

3 See Chapter 4 for further information and tests on the system. Note that there is an emission control system hose routing diagram on a label stuck to the top of the air filter housing.

Every 12,000 miles (18,000 km) or two years

24 Brake fluid – renewal

1 The brake fluid should be replaced at the prescribed interval or whenever a master cylinder or caliper overhaul is carried out. Refer to the brake bleeding section in Chapter 7, noting that all old fluid must be pumped from the fluid reservoir and hydraulic lines before filling with new fluid.

HAYNES HINT *Old brake fluid is invariably much darker in colour than new fluid, making it easy to see when all old fluid has been expelled from the system.*

Every 16,000 miles (24,000 km) or two years

Carry out all the items under the 8000 mile (12,000 km) check, plus the following:

25 Valve clearances – check and adjustment

1 The engine must be completely cool for this maintenance procedure, so let the bike stand overnight before beginning.

2 Remove the spark plugs (see Section 5). Remove the valve cover (see Chapter 2).

3 Make a chart or sketch of all valve positions so that a note of each clearance can be made against the relevant valve.

4 Referring to Chapter 2, Section 9, remove the cap bolt and sealing washer from the end of the cam chain tensioner body and retract the tensioner plunger to release all tension on the cam chain. This procedure ensures that the valve clearances are measured with the oil clearance between the camshafts and their holders taken up.

5 Unscrew the timing inspection cap from the clutch cover **(see illustration)**. To check the valve clearances the engine must be turned so that the valve being checked is closed. The engine can be turned using a suitable spanner or a socket on the timing rotor bolt and turning it in a clockwise direction only **(see illustration 26.6a)**. Alternatively, place the motorcycle on

25.5 Remove the timing inspection cap (arrowed)

1•22 Routine maintenance and servicing

25.6a Turn the engine using the timing rotor bolt (arrowed) until the line next to the T mark aligns with the notch . . .

25.6b . . . and the camshaft sprocket marks are as shown

its centrestand (where fitted) or an auxiliary stand so that the rear wheel is off the ground, select a high gear and rotate the rear wheel by hand in its normal direction of rotation.

6 Turn the engine until the line next to the 'T' mark on the timing rotor aligns with the static timing mark, which is a notch in the inspection hole rim of the clutch cover, and the IN and EX marks on the intake and exhaust camshaft sprockets respectively are facing away from each other and are flush with the cylinder head top surface **(see illustrations)**. If the sprocket marks are facing towards each other, rotate the engine clockwise one full turn (360°) until the line next to the 'T' mark again aligns with the static timing mark. The sprocket marks will now be facing away.

7 With the engine in this position, check the clearances on the Nos. 1 and 3 cylinder intake valves. Insert a feeler gauge of the same thickness as the correct valve clearance (see Specifications) between the camshaft lobe and the follower of each valve and check that it is a firm sliding fit – you should feel a slight drag when the you pull the gauge out **(see illustration)**. If not, use the feeler gauges to obtain the exact clearance. Record the measured clearance on the chart.

8 Now rotate the engine 180° clockwise until the line next to the 'T' mark on the timing rotor is diametrically opposite the static timing mark – on some models there will be a punch mark which now aligns with the notch in the rim, whereas on others there will be a scribed line on the rotor which is in the 12 o'clock position **(see illustration)**. With the engine in this position, check the clearances on the Nos. 2 and 4 cylinder exhaust valves using the method described in Step 7.

9 Now rotate the engine 180° clockwise until the line next to the 'T' mark aligns with the static timing mark again **(see illustration 26.6a)**. With the engine in this position, check the clearances on the Nos. 2 and 4 cylinder intake valves using the method described in Step 7.

10 Now rotate the engine 180° clockwise until line next to the 'T' mark on the timing rotor once again diametrically opposite the static timing mark (see Step 8). With the engine in this position, check the clearances on the Nos. 1 and 3 cylinder exhaust valves using the method described in Step 7.

11 When all clearances have been measured and charted, identify whether the clearance on any valve falls outside the specified range.

If any do, the shim must be replaced with one of a thickness which will restore the correct clearance.

12 Shim replacement requires removal of the camshafts (see Chapter 2). There is no need to remove both camshafts if shims from only one side of the cylinder need replacing. Place rags over the spark plug holes and the cam chain tunnel to prevent a shim from dropping into the engine on removal. Work on one valve at a time to prevent the possibility of mixing up the followers, which must be returned to their original location. If you want to remove more than one shim and follower at a time, store them in a marked container or bag, denoting which cylinder and which valve the shim and follower are from, so that they do not get mixed up.

13 With the camshaft removed, remove the cam follower of the valve in question, then retrieve the shim from the inside of the follower **(see illustrations)**. The follower is best removed with a magnet or using the suction created by a valve lapping tool, but long nosed pliers can be used with care. If the shim is not in the follower, pick it out of the top of the valve spring retainer using either a magnet, a screwdriver with a dab of grease on

25.7 Insert the feeler gauge between the base of the cam lobe and the top of the follower as shown

25.8 T mark positioned diametrically opposite the static timing mark

25.13a Carefully lift out the follower using grips, a lapping tool or a magnet . . .

Routine maintenance and servicing 1•23

25.13b ... and retrieve the shim from inside it ...

25.13c ... or from the top of the valve

25.14 Check the thickness of the shim using a micrometer

25.16 Fit the shim into the top of the valve ...

25.17 ... then install the follower

25.19 Fit the cap using a new O-ring and smear it and the threads with grease

it (the shim will stick to the grease), or a very small screwdriver and a pair of pliers **(see illustration)**. Do not allow the shim to fall into the engine.

14 A size mark should be stamped on one face of the shim – a shim marked 175 is 1.75 mm thick. If the mark is not visible measure the shim thickness using a micrometer **(see illustration)**. It is recommended that the shim is measured anyway to check whether it has worn.

15 Calculate the required replacement shim by using the formula $a = (b - c) + d$, where a is the required shim size, b is the measured valve clearance, c is the specified valve clearance, and d is the existing shim thickness. For example:

The measured clearance of an inlet valve is 0.24 mm, so $b = 0.24$.
The specified clearance range for an inlet valve is 0.17 to 0.23 mm, the mid-point being 0.20 mm, so $c = 0.20$.
The thickness of the existing shim is 2.200 mm, so $d = 2.2$.
Therefore, the required replacement shim $a = 0.24 - 0.20 + 2.2$ ($a = 2.24$ mm)

Note: *If the required replacement shim is greater than 2.800 mm (the largest available), the valve is probably not seating correctly due to a build-up of carbon deposits and should be checked and cleaned or resurfaced as required (see Chapter 2).*

16 Shims are available in 0.025 mm increments from 1.200 mm to 2.800 mm. Obtain the replacement shim, then lubricate it with molybdenum disulphide oil (a 50/50 mixture of molybdenum disulphide grease and engine oil) and fit it into the recess in the top of the valve spring retainer with the size mark facing up **(see illustration)**.

17 Check that the shim is correctly seated, then lubricate the follower with molybdenum disulphide oil and install it onto the valve, making sure it fits squarely in its bore **(see illustration)**. Repeat the process for any other valves until the clearances are correct, then install the camshafts (see Chapter 2).

18 Rotate the crankshaft carefully several turns to seat the new shim(s), then check the clearances again. Remove the cam chain tensioner locking key to allow the tensioner to take up cam chain slack, then install the end bolt with a new sealing washer. Check that the valve timing marks align correctly (see Step 6) before fitting the valve cover.

19 Install all disturbed components in a reverse of the removal sequence. Install the timing inspection cap using a new O-ring if required, and smear the O-ring and the cap threads with grease **(see illustration)**. Tighten the cap to the torque setting specified at the beginning of the Chapter.

20 On completion, check and adjust the idle speed (see Section 2).

Every 24,000 miles (36,000 km) or two years

Carry out all the items under the 12,000 mile (18,000 km) and 8000 mile (12,000 km) checks, plus the following

26 Cooling system – draining, flushing and refilling

⚠️ **Warning:** *Allow the engine to cool completely before performing this maintenance operation. Also, don't allow antifreeze to come into contact with your skin or the painted surfaces of the motorcycle. Rinse off spills immediately with plenty of water. Antifreeze is highly toxic if ingested. Never leave antifreeze lying around in an open container or in puddles on the floor; children and pets are attracted by its sweet smell and may drink it. Check with local authorities (councils) about disposing of antifreeze. Many communities have collection centres which will see that antifreeze is disposed of safely. Antifreeze is also combustible, so don't store it near open flames.*

Draining

1 Remove the fairing side panels (see Chapter 8). Access to the radiator cap is

1•24 Routine maintenance and servicing

26.3a Unscrew the drain plug (arrowed)...

26.3b ...and allow the coolant to drain

restricted by the air intake duct, which is secured between the fairing and the air filter housing. Removing the fairing will leave the air duct loose so that it can be lifted clear, but you may find that you can remove the cap without even disturbing the fairing. Bear in mind that the system must be filled via the radiator, so allow for that when determining you course of action. For best access and clearance, remove both the fairing and the air duct (see Chapter 8).

2 Remove the pressure cap from the top of the radiator by covering it with a heavy cloth and turning it anti-clockwise until it reaches a stop **(see illustration 13.7)**. If you hear a hissing sound (indicating there is still pressure in the system), wait until it stops. Now press down on the cap and continue turning the cap until it can be removed. Also remove the coolant reservoir cap.

3 Position a suitable container beneath the water pump on the left-hand side of the engine. Unscrew the drain plug and allow the coolant to completely drain from the system **(see illustrations)**. Retain the old sealing washer for use during flushing.

4 Now position the container beneath the front of the engine on the left-hand side.

Unscrew the cylinder drain plug and allow the coolant to completely drain from the cylinder jacket **(see illustrations)**. Retain the old sealing washer for use during flushing.

5 Place the container on the right-hand side of the engine. On F-X and F-Y (1999 and 2000) models, disconnect the radiator overflow hose from the bottom of the reservoir and allow it to drain into the container. On F-1/FS-1 models onward (2001-on), disconnect the radiator overflow hose (the top hose) from the radiator filler neck, then place it below the level of the reservoir and allow it to drain into the container. When the reservoir is empty, fit the hose back onto the reservoir or filler neck, according to model.

Flushing

6 Flush the system with clean tap water by inserting a garden hose in the radiator filler neck. Allow the water to run through the system until it is clear and flows out cleanly. If the radiator is extremely corroded, remove it (see Chapter 3) and have it cleaned by a specialist.

7 Clean the drain holes in the water pump and cylinder bock then install the drain plugs using the old sealing washers.

8 Fill the cooling system with clean water mixed with a flushing compound. Make sure the flushing compound is compatible with aluminium components, and follow the manufacturer's instructions carefully. Fit the radiator cap.

9 Start the engine and allow it to reach normal operating temperature. Let it run for about ten minutes.

10 Stop the engine. Let it cool for a while, then cover the pressure cap with a heavy rag and turn it anti-clockwise to the first stop, releasing any pressure that may be present in the system. Once the hissing stops, push down on the cap and remove it completely.

11 Drain the system once again.

12 Fill the system with clean water and repeat the procedure in Steps 6 to 10.

Refilling

13 Fit new sealing washers onto the drain plugs and tighten them securely.

14 Fill the system with the proper coolant mixture (see this Chapter's Specifications). *Note: Pour the coolant in slowly to minimise the amount of air entering the system.*

15 When the system is full (all the way up to the base of the radiator filler neck), start the engine

26.4a Unscrew the cylinder drain plug (arrowed)...

26.4b ...and drain the cylinder jacket

Routine maintenance and servicing

and allow it to idle for 2 to 3 minutes. Flick the throttle twistgrip part open 3 or 4 times, so that the engine speed rises to approximately 4000 – 5000 rpm, then stop the engine. This process will bleed any trapped air bubbles from the system.
16 If necessary, top up the coolant level to the base of the upper radiator filler neck and install the pressure cap. Also top up the coolant reservoir to the UPPER level mark (see *Daily (pre-ride) checks*).

17 Start the engine and allow it to reach normal operating temperature, then shut it off. Let the engine cool then remove the pressure cap as described in Step 2. Check that the coolant level is still up to the base of the upper radiator filler neck. If it's low, add the specified mixture until it reaches the base of the filler neck. Refit the cap.
18 Check the coolant level in the reservoir and top up if necessary.

19 Check the system for leaks. Install the fairing side panels, and the air intake duct and fairing if removed (see Chapter 8).
20 Do not dispose of the old coolant by pouring it down the drain. Instead pour it into a heavy plastic container, cap it tightly and take it into an authorised disposal site or service station – see **Warning** at the beginning of this Section.

Non-scheduled maintenance

27 Cylinder compression – check

1 Among other things, poor engine performance may be caused by leaking valves, incorrect valve clearances, a leaking head gasket, or worn pistons, rings and/or cylinder walls. A cylinder compression check will help pinpoint these conditions and can also indicate the presence of excessive carbon deposits in the cylinder heads.
2 The only tools required are a compression gauge and a spark plug wrench. A compression gauge with a threaded end for the spark plug hole is preferable to the type which requires hand pressure to maintain a tight seal. Depending on the outcome of the initial test, a squirt-type oil can may also be needed.
3 Make sure the valve clearances are correctly set (see Section 25) and that the cylinder head nuts are tightened to the correct torque setting (see Chapter 2).
4 Refer to *Fault Finding Equipment* in the Reference section for details of the compression test. Refer to the specifications at the beginning of the Chapter for compression figures.

28 Engine oil pressure – check

1 The oil pressure warning light should come on when the ignition (main) switch is turned ON and extinguish a few seconds after the engine is started – this serves as a check that the warning light bulb is sound. If the oil pressure light comes on whilst the engine is running, low oil pressure is indicated – stop the engine immediately and carry out an oil level check (see *Daily (pre-ride) checks*).
2 An oil pressure check must be carried out if the warning light comes on when the engine is running yet the oil level is good (Step 1). It can also provide useful information about the condition of the engine's lubrication system.
3 To check the oil pressure, a suitable gauge and adapter (which screws into the crankcase) will be needed. Honda provide a gauge and adapter (part Nos. 07506-3000000 and 07510 MJ10100) for this purpose, or one can be obtained commercially. You will also need some rags to catch and mop up any residual oil that gets lost in between removing the oil gallery plug and installing the gauge – on models fitted with a centrestand, place the bike on its sidestand so that the oil gathers at the other end of the gallery to reduce spillage.
4 Warm the engine up to normal operating temperature then stop it.
5 Unscrew the main oil gallery plug, which is threaded into the crankcase on the right-hand side of the engine (directly below the timing inspection cap in the front of the clutch cover), and screw the adapter in its place. Connect the oil pressure gauge to the adapter.
6 Start the engine and briefly increase the engine speed to 6000 rpm whilst watching the gauge reading. The oil pressure should be similar to that given in the Specifications at the start of this Chapter.
7 If the pressure is significantly lower than the standard, either the pressure relief valve is stuck open, the oil pump or its drive mechanism is faulty, the oil strainer or filter is blocked, or there is other engine damage. Also make sure the correct grade oil is being used. Begin diagnosis by checking the oil filter, strainer and relief valve, then the oil pump (see Chapter 2). If those items check out okay, chances are the bearing oil clearances are excessive and the engine needs to be overhauled.
8 If the pressure is too high, either an oil passage is clogged, the relief valve is stuck closed or the wrong grade of oil is being used.
9 Stop the engine and unscrew the gauge and adapter from the crankcase.
10 Install the main gallery plug, using a suitable non-permanent threadlock compound on its threads, and tighten it to the torque setting specified at the beginning of the Chapter. Check the oil level (see *Daily (pre-ride) checks*).

29 Wheel bearings – check

1 Wheel bearings will wear over a period of time and result in handling problems.
2 Support the motorcycle upright using the centrestand if fitted, or an auxiliary stand, and support it so that the wheel being checked is off the ground (remove the fairing side panels and anything else that could be damaged before placing a support under the engine). Check for any play in the bearings by pushing and pulling the wheel against the axle **(see illustration)**. Also spin the wheel and check that it rotates smoothly.
3 If any play is detected in the hub, or if the wheel does not rotate smoothly (and this is not due to brake or transmission drag), the wheel bearings must be removed and inspected for wear or damage (see Chapter 7).

30 Steering head bearings – re-greasing

1 Over a period of time the grease will harden or may be washed out of the bearings by incorrect use of jet washes.
2 Disassemble the steering head for re-greasing of the bearings. Refer to Chapter 6 for details.

31 Swingarm and suspension linkage bearings – re-greasing

1 Over a period of time the grease will harden or dirt will penetrate the bearings due to failed seals.

29.2 Checking for play in the wheel bearings

Routine maintenance and servicing

2 The suspension is not equipped with grease nipples. Remove the swingarm and suspension linkage as described in Chapter 6 for greasing of the bearings.

32 Brake caliper and master cylinder seals – renewal

1 Brake seals will deteriorate over a period of time and lose their effectiveness, leading to sticking operation or fluid loss, or allowing the ingress of air and dirt. Refer to Chapter 7 and dismantle the components for seal renewal.

33 Brake hoses – renewal

1 The hoses will in time deteriorate with age and should be renewed regardless of their apparent condition. Refer to Chapter 7 and disconnect the brake hoses from the master cylinders and calipers. Always replace the banjo union sealing washers with new ones.

34 Fuel hoses – renewal

⚠️ **Warning: Petrol (gasoline) is extremely flammable, so take extra precautions when you work on any part of the fuel system. Don't smoke or allow open flames or bare light bulbs near the work area, and don't work in a garage where a natural gas-type appliance is present. If you spill any fuel on your skin, rinse it off immediately with soap and water. When you perform any kind of work on the fuel system, wear safety glasses and have a fire extinguisher suitable for a Class B type fire (flammable liquids) on hand.**

1 The fuel system hoses should be renewed at the first signs of cracking or hardening. This includes all the vent and drain hoses, and the vacuum hoses.

2 Remove the fuel tank (see Chapter 4). Disconnect the fuel hoses from the fuel tank and the carburettors or throttle bodies, noting the routing of each hose and where it connects (see Chapter 4 if required). It is advisable to make a sketch of the various hoses before removing them to ensure they are correctly installed.

3 Secure each new hose to its unions using new clamps or sealing washers, according to model. Refer to Chapter 4 for torque settings for the fuel delivery and return hose fasteners on fuel injected models. Run the engine and check for leaks before taking the machine out on the road.

35 Front forks – oil change

1 Fork oil degrades over a period of time and loses its damping qualities. Refer to the fork oil change procedure in Chapter 6, Section 7. The forks do not need to be completely disassembled.

36 Fuel filters – cleaning and renewal

1 Cleaning or replacement of the fuel filter is advised after a particularly high mileage has been covered. It is also necessary if fuel starvation is suspected, or if the filter looks clogged or dirty. Honda do not specify a replacement interval – fuel is so clean now that this may not always be necessary. Check the condition of the inside of your tank – if it is old and there is evidence of rust, remove, drain and clean the tank and tap (see Chapter 4), and fit a new filter afterwards.

Carburettor models (F-X and F-Y, 1999 and 2000)

2 A fuel strainer is fitted in the tank and is held in place by the fuel tap. Remove the fuel tank and the fuel tap (see Chapter 4). Remove the gauze strainer and discard the O-ring. Clean off all traces of dirt and fuel sediment. Check the gauze for holes. If any are found, a new strainer must be fitted. Replace O-ring with a new one, then fit the strainer into the tank and install the tap (see Chapter 4).

3 There is also an in-line fuel filter fitted in the hose from the fuel tap to the fuel pump. To replace the filter, remove the fuel tank (see Chapter 4). Have a rag handy to soak up any residual fuel, then release the clamps and disconnect the hoses from the filter, noting which fits where **(see illustration)**. Release the filter from its holder and discard it. Install the new filter so that its arrow points in the direction of fuel flow (i.e. towards the pump).

4 Fit the hoses to the unions on the filter and secure them with the clamps. The hose from the fuel tap goes on the plain end, and the hose to the pump goes on the lipped end. Install the fuel tank (see Chapter 4). Start the engine and check that there are no leaks.

Fuel injected models (F-1/FS-1 onward, 2001-on)

5 On fuel injection models, an in-line fuel filter is fitted alongside the fuel pump inside the fuel tank. To replace the filter, remove the fuel pump assembly from the tank (see Chapter 4). Undo the clamp screw and release the filter from its holder, noting which way round it fits **(see illustration)**.

6 Have a rag handy to soak up any residual fuel, then release the clamps and disconnect the hoses from the filter, noting which fits where. Discard the filter. Install the new filter and secure it with the clamp. Fit the hoses to the unions on the filter and secure them with the clamps.

7 A fuel strainer is fitted in the base of the fuel pump assembly housing. It is basically a wad of coarse steel wool **(see illustration)**. Check that there are no large particles of dirt caught in it and clean it through using petrol if necessary. If it is clogged with debris, replace it with a new wad. Install the fuel pump assembly (see Chapter 4). Start the engine and check that there are no leaks.

36.3 In-line fuel filter (arrowed) – carburettor models

36.5 Undo the screw (A) and release the clamp, then detach the hoses (B)

36.7 The strainer (arrowed) is a wad of steel wool

Chapter 2
Engine, clutch and transmission

Contents

Alternator – removal and installation . . . . .see Chapter 9	Oil and filter – change . . . . .see Chapter 1
Camshafts – removal, inspection and installation 10	Oil cooler – removal, inspection and installation 7
Cam chain, tensioner blade and guide blades – removal, inspection and installation 11	Oil level – check . . . . .see *Daily (pre-ride) checks*
Cam chain tensioner – removal, inspection and installation 9	Oil pressure – check . . . . .see Chapter 1
Clutch – check . . . . .see Chapter 1	Oil pressure switch – check, removal and installation . . .see Chapter 9
Clutch and cable – removal, inspection and installation 16	Oil pump – removal, inspection and installation 18
Connecting rods and bearings – removal, inspection and installation 25	Oil sump, oil strainer and pressure relief valve – removal, inspection and installation 17
Crankcase halves and cylinder bores – inspection and servicing . . . 23	Operations possible with the engine in the frame 2
Crankcase halves – separation and reassembly 22	Operations requiring engine removal 3
Crankshaft and main bearings – removal, inspection and installation 28	Pistons – removal, inspection and installation 26
Cylinder head – removal and installation 12	Piston rings – inspection and installation 27
Cylinder head and valves – disassembly, inspection and reassembly 14	Pulse generator coil assembly – removal and installation . . . . .see Chapter 5
Engine – compression check .see Chapter 1	Recommended running-in procedure 32
Engine – removal and installation 5	Selector drum and forks – removal, inspection and installation 20
Engine disassembly and reassembly – general information 6	Spark plug gap – check and adjustment . . . . .see Chapter 1
Gearchange mechanism – removal, inspection and installation 19	Starter clutch – check, removal, inspection and installation 15
General information 1	Starter motor – removal and installation . . . . .see Chapter 9
Idle speed – check and adjustment . . . . .see Chapter 1	Timing rotor – removal and installation 21
Initial start-up after overhaul 31	Transmission shafts and bearings – removal and installation 29
Main and connecting rod bearings – general note 24	Transmission shafts – disassembly, inspection and reassembly . . . 30
Major engine repair – general note 4	Valve clearances – check and adjustment . . . . .see Chapter 1
Neutral switch – check, removal and installation . . . . . . .see Chapter 9	Valve cover – removal and installation 8
	Valves/valve seats/valve guides – servicing 13

Degrees of difficulty

| **Easy,** suitable for novice with little experience | **Fairly easy,** suitable for beginner with some experience | **Fairly difficult,** suitable for competent DIY mechanic | **Difficult,** suitable for experienced DIY mechanic | **Very difficult,** suitable for expert DIY or professional |

Specifications

General
Type	Four-stroke in-line four
Capacity	599 cc
Bore	67.0 mm
Stroke	42.5 mm
Compression ratio	12.0 to 1
Cylinder numbering	1 to 4 from left to right
Cooling system	Liquid cooled
Clutch	Wet multi-plate
Transmission	Six-speed constant mesh
Final drive	Chain

Camshafts and followers
Intake lobe height
  European F-X and F-Y models
    Standard .... 36.60 to 36.76 mm
    Service limit (min) .... 36.57 mm
  US 49-state 1999 and 2000 models
    Standard .... 36.60 to 36.76 mm
    Service limit (min) .... 36.57 mm
  US California 1999 and 2000 models
    Standard .... 34.64 to 34.72 mm
    Service limit (min) .... 34.61 mm
  F-1 and F-2 models (2001 and 2002)
    Standard .... 36.56 to 36.80 mm
    Service limit (min) .... 36.5 mm
  FS-1 and FS-2 models (2001 and 2002), F-3 models onward (2003-on)
    Standard .... 36.26 to 36.50 mm
    Service limit (min) .... 36.2 mm
Exhaust lobe height
  European F-X and F-Y models
    Standard .... 35.38 to 35.54 mm
    Service limit (min) .... 35.35 mm
  US 49-state 1999 and 2000 models
    Standard .... 35.38 to 35.54 mm
    Service limit (min) .... 35.35 mm
  US California 1999 and 2000 models
    Standard .... 33.92 to 34.00 mm
    Service limit (min) .... 33.89 mm
  F-1 and F-2 models (2001 and 2002)
    Standard .... 35.34 to 35.58 mm
    Service limit (min) .... 35.3 mm
  FS-1 and FS-2 models (2001 and 2002), F-3 models onward (2003-on)
    Standard .... 35.34 to 35.58 mm
    Service limit (min) .... 35.3 mm
Oil clearance
  F-X and F-Y (1999 and 2000) models
    Standard .... 0.020 to 0.062 mm
    Service limit (max) .... 0.10 mm
  F-1/FS-1 models onward (2001-on)
    Standard .... 0.030 to 0.072 mm
    Service limit (max) .... 0.10 mm
Runout (max) .... 0.05 mm
Camshaft follower diameter
  Standard .... 25.978 to 25.993 mm
  Service limit (min) .... 25.97 mm
Camshaft follower bore diameter
  Standard .... 26.010 to 26.026 mm
  Service limit (min) .... 26.04 mm

Cylinder head
Warpage (max) .... 0.10 mm

Valves, guides and springs

Valve clearances .... see Chapter 1
Stem diameter
  Intake valve
    Standard .... 3.975 to 3.990 mm
    Service limit (min) .... 3.965 mm
  Exhaust valve
    Standard .... 3.965 to 3.980 mm
    Service limit (min) .... 3.955 mm
Guide bore diameter – intake and exhaust valves
  Standard .... 4.000 to 4.012 mm
  Service limit (max) .... 4.040 mm
Stem-to-guide clearance
  Intake valve .... 0.010 to 0.037 mm
  Exhaust valve .... 0.020 to 0.047 mm
Seat width – intake and exhaust valves
  Standard .... 0.90 to 1.10 mm
  Service limit (max) .... 1.50 mm
Valve guide height above cylinder head
  Intake valve .... 16.1 to 16.4 mm
  Exhaust valve .... 14.3 to 14.6 mm
Valve spring free length
  F-X and F-Y (1999 and 2000) models
    Intake
      Standard .... 39.87 mm
      Service limit (min) .... 38.27 mm
    Exhaust
      Standard .... 36.23 mm
      Service limit (min) .... 34.73 mm
  European F-1 and F-2 models
    Intake
      Standard .... 39.5 mm
      Service limit (min) .... 38.71 mm
    Exhaust
      Standard .... 36.3 mm
      Service limit (min) .... 35.57 mm
  European FS-1 and FS-2 models, F-3 models onward
    Intake – inner spring
      Standard .... 36.4 mm
      Service limit (min) .... 35.57 mm
    Intake – outer spring
      Standard .... 42.2 mm
      Service limit (min) .... 41.36 mm
    Exhaust
      Standard .... 36.3 mm
      Service limit (min) .... 35.57 mm
  US 2001-on models
    Intake – inner spring
      Standard .... 36.4 mm
      Service limit (min) .... 35.57 mm
    Intake – outer spring
      Standard .... 42.2 mm
      Service limit (min) .... 41.36 mm
    Exhaust
      Standard .... 36.3 mm
      Service limit (min) .... 35.57 mm

Oil pump

Oil pressure .... see Chapter 1
Inner rotor tip-to-outer rotor clearance
  Standard .... 0.15 mm
  Service limit (max) .... 0.20 mm
Outer rotor-to-body clearance
  Standard .... 0.15 to 0.22 mm
  Service limit (max) .... 0.35 mm
Rotor endfloat
  Standard .... 0.02 to 0.07 mm
  Service limit (max) .... 0.10 mm

2•4 Engine, clutch and transmission

Cylinder bores
Bore
   Standard .... 67.000 to 67.015 mm
   Service limit (max) .... 67.100 mm
Warpage (max) .... 0.10 mm
Ovality (out-of-round) (max) .... 0.10 mm
Taper (max) .... 0.10 mm
Cylinder compression .... see Chapter 1

Pistons
Piston diameter (measured 15 mm up from skirt, at 90° to piston pin axis)
   Standard .... 66.965 to 66.985 mm
   Service limit (min) .... 66.90 mm
Piston-to-bore clearance
   Standard .... 0.015 to 0.050 mm
   Service limit (min) .... 0.10 mm*
Piston pin diameter
   Standard .... 16.994 to 17.000 mm
   Service limit (min) .... 16.98 mm
Piston pin bore diameter in piston
   Standard .... 17.002 to 17.008 mm
   Service limit (max) .... 17.02 mm
Piston pin-to-piston pin bore clearance
   Standard .... 0.002 to 0.014 mm
   Service limit .... 0.04 mm

If the piston-to-bore clearance exceeds the service limit, the cylinders can be rebored – Honda supply +0.25 oversize pistons. Following rebore, the piston-to-bore clearance must be as standard for normal pistons

Piston rings
Ring end gap (installed)
  Top ring
   Standard .... 0.10 to 0.20 mm
   Service limit (max) .... 0.40 mm
  Second ring
   Standard .... 0.18 to 0.30 mm
   Service limit (max) .... 0.50 mm
  Oil ring side-rail
   Standard .... 0.20 to 0.70 mm
   Service limit (max) .... 1.0 mm
Ring-to-groove clearance
  Top ring
   Standard .... 0.020 to 0.050 mm
   Service limit (max) .... 0.08 mm
  Second ring
   Standard .... 0.015 to 0.050 mm
   Service limit (max) .... 0.08 mm

Connecting rods
Small-end internal diameter
   Standard .... 17.016 to 17.034 mm
   Service limit (max) .... 17.04 mm
Small-end-to-piston pin clearance
   Standard .... 0.016 to 0.040 mm
   Service limit .... 0.06 mm
Big-end side clearance
   Standard .... 0.10 to 0.25 mm
   Service limit (max) .... 0.3 mm
Big-end oil clearance
   Standard .... 0.028 to 0.052 mm
   Service limit (max) .... 0.06 mm

Crankshaft and bearings
Main bearing oil clearance
   Standard .... 0.020 to 0.038 mm
   Service limit (max) 0.05mm
Runout (max) .... 0.05 mm

Engine, clutch and transmission 2•5

Starter clutch
Starter driven gear hub OD
   Standard .... 51.699 to 51.718 mm
   Service limit (min) .... 51.684 mm

Clutch
Friction plates
   European F models 7
   European FS models 8
   US 1999 and 2000 models 7
   US 2001-on models 8
Plain plates
   European F models 6
   European FS models 7
   US 1999 and 2000 models 6
   US 2001-on models 7
Friction plate thickness
   Standard .... 2.92 to 3.08 mm
   Service limit (min) .... 2.6 mm
Plain plate warpage (max) .... 0.3 mm
Spring free length
   European F-X, F-Y, F-1 and F-2 models
     Standard .... 46.5 mm
     Service limit (min) .... 45.2 mm
   European FS-1, FS-2, F-3 models onward
     Standard .... 44.7 mm
     Service limit (min) .... 43.4 mm
   US 1999 and 2000 models
     Standard .... 46.5 mm
     Service limit (min) .... 45.2 mm
   US 2001-on models
     Standard .... 44.7 mm
     Service limit (min) .... 43.4 mm
Clutch guide OD
   Standard .... 34.975 to 34.991 mm
   Service limit (min) 34.97mm
Clutch guide ID
   Standard .... 25.000 to 25.021 mm
   Service limit (max) .... 25.03 mm
Input shaft OD at clutch guide
   Standard .... 24.980 to 24.993 mm
   Service limit (max) .... 24.96 mm

Transmission
Gear ratios (no. of teeth)
   F-X and F-Y (1999 and 2000) models
     Primary reduction .... 1.822 to 1 (82/45T)
     Final reduction
       UK models .... 2.750 to 1 (44/16T)
       US models .... 2.812 to 1 (45/16T)
     1st gear .... 2.833 to 1 (34/12T)
     2nd gear .... 2.062 to 1 (33/16T)
     3rd gear .... 1.647 to 1 (28/17T)
     4th gear .... 1.421 to 1 (27/19T)
     5th gear .... 1.250 to 1 (25/20T)
     6th gear .... 1.130 to 1 (26/23T)
   F-1/FS-1 models onward (2001-on)
     Primary reduction .... 1.822 to 1 (82/45T)
     Final reduction
       European F models .... 2.813 to 1 (45/16T)
       European FS models and all US models .... 2.875 to 1 (46/16T)
     1st gear .... 2.833 to 1 (34/12T)
     2nd gear .... 2.062 to 1 (33/16T)
     3rd gear .... 1.647 to 1 (28/17T)
     4th gear .... 1.421 to 1 (27/19T)
     5th gear .... 1.272 to 1 (28/22T)
     6th gear .... 1.173 to 1 (27/23T)

Transmission (continued)

Input shaft 5th and 6th gears ID
- Standard ..... 28.000 to 28.021 mm
- Service limit (max) ..... 28.04 mm

Input shaft 5th and 6th gears bush OD
- Standard ..... 27.959 to 27.980 mm
- Service limit (min) ..... 27.94 mm

Input shaft 5th and 6th gears gear-to-bush clearance
- Standard ..... 0.020 to 0.062 mm
- Service limit (max) ..... 0.10 mm

Input shaft 5th gear bush ID
- Standard ..... 24.985 to 25.006 mm
- Service limit (max) ..... 25.016 mm

Input shaft OD at 5th gear bush point
- Standard ..... 24.967 to 24.980 mm
- Service limit (min) ..... 24.96 mm

Input shaft-to-bush clearance at 5th gear bush point
- Standard ..... 0.005 to 0.039 mm
- Service limit (max) ..... 0.06 mm

Output shaft 2nd, 3rd and 4th gears ID
- Standard ..... 31.000 to 31.025 mm
- Service limit (max) ..... 31.04 mm

Output shaft 2nd gear bush OD
- Standard ..... 30.955 to 30.980 mm
- Service limit (min) ..... 30.94 mm

Output shaft 3rd and 4th gears bush OD
- Standard ..... 30.950 to 30.975 mm
- Service limit (min) ..... 30.93 mm

Output shaft 2nd gear gear-to-bush clearance
- Standard ..... 0.020 to 0.070 mm
- Service limit (max) ..... 0.10 mm

Output shaft 3rd and 4th gears gear-to-bush clearance
- Standard ..... 0.025 to 0.075 mm
- Service limit (max) ..... 0.11 mm

Output shaft 2nd gear bush ID
- Standard ..... 27.985 to 28.006 mm
- Service limit (max) ..... 28.021 mm

Output shaft OD at 2nd gear bush point
- Standard ..... 27.967 to 27.980 mm
- Service limit (min) ..... 27.96 mm

Output shaft-to-bushing clearance at 2nd gear bush point
- Standard ..... 0.005 to 0.039 mm
- Service limit (max) ..... 0.06 mm

Selector drum and forks

Selector fork end thickness
- Standard ..... 5.93 to 6.00 mm
- Service limit (min) ..... 5.90 mm

Selector fork bore ID
- Standard ..... 12.000 to 12.021 mm
- Service limit (max) ..... 12.03 mm

Selector fork shaft OD
- Standard ..... 11.957 to 11.968 mm
- Service limit (min) ..... 11.95 mm

Torque settings

Cam chain front guide blade bolt	12 Nm
Cam chain tensioner blade bolt	10 Nm
Cam chain tensioner mounting bolts	10 Nm
Cam pulse generator rotor bolts – F-1/FS-1 models onward (2001-on)	12 Nm
Camshaft holder bolts	12 Nm
Camshaft sprocket bolts	20 Nm
Clutch cover bolts	12 Nm
Clutch nut	127 Nm
Clutch spring bolts	12 Nm
Connecting rod nuts	25 Nm

Torque settings (continued)

Crankcase bolts
  F-X and F-Y (1999 and 2000) models
    Lower crankcase 8 mm bolts .... 25 Nm
    Lower crankcase 10 mm bolt .... 39 Nm
    Lower crankcase 6 mm bolts .... 12 Nm
    Upper crankcase 8 mm bolts .... 25 Nm
    Upper crankcase 6 mm bolts .... 12 Nm
  F-1/FS-1 models onward (2001-on)
    Lower crankcase 8 mm bolts .... 25 Nm
    Lower crankcase 10 mm bolt .... 39 Nm
    Lower crankcase 6 mm bolts .... 12 Nm
    Lower crankcase 7 mm bolts .... 18 Nm
    Upper crankcase 8 mm bolts .... 25 Nm
    Upper crankcase 6 mm bolts .... 12 Nm
Cylinder head 6 mm bolts .... 10 Nm
Cylinder head 9 mm bolts .... 47 Nm
Engine mountings
  Left-hand centre mounting bolt .... 39 Nm
  Front mounting bolt nuts .... 39 Nm
  Adjuster bolts – see text
    F-X and F-Y (1999 and 2000) models .... 4 Nm
    F-1/FS-1 models onward (2001-on) .... 3 Nm
  Adjuster bolt locknuts *(see text)*
    Actual .... 54 Nm
    Indicated (with special tool) .... 49 Nm
  Right-hand centre mounting bolt .... 39 Nm
  Rear mounting bolt nut .... 39 Nm
Oil cooler bolt .... 64 Nm
Oil pump assembly bolt .... 8 Nm
Oil pump driven sprocket bolt .... 15 Nm
Selector drum bearing/fork shaft retainer bolts .... 12 Nm
Selector drum cam bolt .... 23 Nm
Sidestand/centrestand/suspension bracket bolt nuts ... 39 Nm
Starter clutch bolts .... 16 Nm
Stopper arm bolt .... 12 Nm
Suspension linkage arm bolt nut .... 44 Nm
Timing inspection cap .... 18 Nm
Timing rotor bolt .... 59 Nm
Transmission input shaft bearing retainer plate bolts .. 12 Nm
Valve cover bolts .... 10 Nm

1 General information

The engine/transmission unit is a liquid-cooled in-line four cylinder. The sixteen valves are operated by double overhead camshafts which are chain driven off the right-hand end of the crankshaft. The engine/transmission is a unit assembly constructed from aluminium alloy. The crankcase divides horizontally.

The crankcase incorporates a wet sump, pressure-fed lubrication system which uses a dual rotor trochoidal oil pump that is chain-driven off the back of the clutch. The system has an oil filter, an oil pressure switch, and a pressure relief valve which is in the feed from the pump to the filter.

The alternator is on the left-hand end of the crankshaft and has the starter clutch mounted behind it. The water pump is on the left-hand side of the engine, and its drive shaft is keyed to the oil pump drive shaft. The pulse generator coil and ignition timing rotor are on the right-hand end of the crankshaft.

Power from the crankshaft is routed to the transmission via the clutch. The clutch is of the wet, multi-plate type and is gear-driven off the crankshaft. The clutch is operated by cable. The transmission is a six-speed constant-mesh unit. Final drive to the rear wheel is by chain and sprockets.

2 Operations possible with the engine in the frame

The components and assemblies listed below can be removed without having to remove the engine/transmission assembly from the frame. If however, a number of areas require attention at the same time, removal of the engine is recommended.
  Valve cover
  Cam chain tensioner and blades
  Camshafts and cam chain
  Cylinder head
  Ignition timing rotor and pulse generator coil assembly
  Clutch
  Gearchange mechanism
  Alternator
  Oil filter and oil cooler
  Oil sump, oil pump, oil strainer and oil pressure relief valve
  Starter motor
  Starter clutch
  Water pump
  Selector drum and forks (though much easier with engine removed)

3 Operations requiring engine removal

It is necessary to remove the engine/transmission assembly from the frame to gain access to the following components.
  Pistons, piston rings and cylinder bores
  Transmission shafts
  Crankshaft and bearings
  Connecting rods and bearings

2•8 Engine, clutch and transmission

4 Major engine repair –
general note

1 It is not always easy to determine when or if an engine should be completely overhauled, as a number of factors must be considered.

2 High mileage is not necessarily an indication that an overhaul is needed, while low mileage, on the other hand, does not preclude the need for an overhaul. Frequency of servicing is probably the single most important consideration. An engine that has regular and frequent oil and filter changes, as well as other required maintenance, will most likely give many miles of reliable service. Conversely, a neglected engine, or one which has not been run in properly, may require an overhaul very early in its life.

3 Exhaust smoke and excessive oil consumption are both indications that piston rings and/or valve guides are in need of attention, although make sure that the fault is not due to oil leakage.

4 If the engine is making obvious knocking or rumbling noises, the connecting rods and/or main bearings are probably at fault.

5 Loss of power, rough running, excessive valve train noise and high fuel consumption may also point to the need for an overhaul, especially if they are all present at the same time. If a complete tune-up does not remedy the situation, major mechanical work is the only solution.

6 An engine overhaul generally involves restoring the internal parts to the specifications of a new engine. The piston rings and main and connecting rod bearings are usually replaced and the cylinder walls honed or, if necessary, re-bored (oversize pistons are available), during a major overhaul. Generally the valve seats are re-ground, since they are usually in less than perfect condition at this point. The end result should be a like new engine that will give as many trouble-free miles as the original.

7 Before beginning the engine overhaul, read through the related procedures to familiarise yourself with the scope and requirements of the job. Overhauling an engine is not all that difficult, but it is time consuming. Plan on the motorcycle being tied up for a minimum of two weeks. Check on the availability of parts and make sure that any necessary special tools, equipment and supplies are obtained in advance.

8 Most work can be done with typical workshop hand tools, although a number of precision measuring tools are required for inspecting parts to determine if they must be renewed. Often a dealer will handle the inspection of parts and offer advice concerning reconditioning and renewal. As a general rule, time is the primary cost of an overhaul so it does not pay to install worn or substandard parts.

9 As a final note, to ensure maximum life and minimum trouble from a rebuilt engine, everything must be assembled with care in a spotlessly clean environment.

5 Engine –
removal and installation

Caution: The engine is very heavy. Engine removal and installation should be carried out with the aid of at least one assistant; personal injury or damage could occur if the engine falls or is dropped.

Note: *As the centrestand (if fitted), the sidestand and the swingarm and suspension linkage are all attached to the engine as opposed to the frame, it is necessary to support the bike using either a hoist or some form of auxiliary stand that does not attach to either the rear wheel or swingarm. We found the best method to be two axle stands placed under the pillion footrest brackets, and as an extra precaution the bike was tied at the rear and the front wheel was secured down. It is highly advisable to tie the front brake lever to the handlebar so that the brake is applied and locking the front wheel – this will prevent the bike rolling off the axle stands should it be knocked or moved as the engine is manoeuvred out. Make sure the rear suspension is not compressed as the linkage must be separated from the engine. If the rear wheel is off the ground place a support under it so that it does not drop when the linkage is separated – ideally the rear wheel should be supported, but without any weight on it or force through it so that the shock absorber is uncompressed.*

Removal

1 Support the bike as described in the **Note** above, making sure it is on level ground. Work can be made easier by raising the machine to a suitable working height on an hydraulic ramp or a suitable platform. Make sure the motorcycle is secure and will not topple over (also see *Tools and Workshop Tips* in the Reference section).

2 Remove the seat, seat cowling, fairing and fairing side panels (see Chapter 8). If required, unscrew the bolts securing the fairing brackets to the front corners of the sump and remove the brackets, noting how they fit.

3 If the engine is dirty, particularly around its mountings, wash it thoroughly. This will make work much easier and rule out the possibility of caked on lumps of dirt falling into some vital component.

4 Drain the engine oil and the cooling system (see Chapter 1). Remove the oil filter (see Chapter 1).

5 Remove the fuel tank and the air filter housing (see Chapter 4).

6 Remove the radiator along with its hoses (see Chapter 3). On F-X and F-Y (1999 and 2000) models, also remove the coolant reservoir (see Chapter 3).

7 Remove the exhaust system (see Chapter 4). Unscrew the two bolts securing the radiator bracket to the engine and remove the bracket, noting which way up it fits **(see illustration)**.

8 If required, remove the oil cooler (see Section 7).

9 Remove the carburettors or throttle bodies (according to model) (see Chapter 4). Plug the engine inlet manifolds with clean rag.

10 Disconnect the negative (–ve) lead from the battery, and remove the battery if required (see Chapter 9).

11 Remove the thermostat housing to gain access to the starter motor (see Chapter 3). If required, remove the starter motor (see Chapter 9). If you want to leave the starter motor in situ, pull back the rubber cover on the starter motor terminal, then unscrew the nut and disconnect the lead, and unscrew the mounting bolt securing the earth lead and detach the lead **(see illustration)**.

TOOL TIP

A peg spanner is required to slacken and tighten the adjuster bolt locknuts on two of the engine mounting bolts. If the Honda service tool (Part no 07VMA-MBB0100) is not available, a suitable one will have to fabricated out of a piece of steel tubing, or an old socket

5.7 Unscrew the bolts (arrowed) and remove the bracket

5.11 Detach the starter motor lead (A) and the earth lead (B)

Engine, clutch and transmission 2•9

5.12a Unscrew the bolt (arrowed) and displace the bracket . . .

5.12b . . . then detach the end of the cable from the release arm

5.13 Disconnect the wiring connectors in the boot

12 Unscrew the bolt securing the clutch cable bracket to the clutch cover (see illustration). Displace the bracket, noting how it locates, and free the cable end from the release arm (see illustration). Position the cable clear of the engine.

13 On F-X and F-Y (1999 and 2000) models, disconnect the ignition pulse generator coil (white 2-pin), sidestand switch (green 2-pin), alternator (white 4-pin) and engine sub-harness (red 9-pin) wiring connectors – they are housed inside the rubber boot above the crankcase (see illustration). The sub-harness feeds the oil pressure switch, neutral switch, speed sensor, throttle position sensor and coolant temperature sensor. Release the wiring from any clips or ties, noting its routing, and feed it through to its source so that it does not impede engine removal. If required, disconnect the sub-leads from the neutral switch, oil pressure switch (by removing the screw) and speed sensor and remove the sub-harness.

14 On F-1/FS-1 models onward (2001-on), disconnect the sidestand switch (green 2-pin), camshaft pulse generator (plain 2-pin) and engine sub-harness (grey 12-pin) wiring connectors – they are housed inside the rubber boot above the crankcase. The sub-harness feeds the ignition pulse generator coil, oil pressure switch, neutral switch, speed sensor, rear brake light switch and coolant temperature sensor. Also disconnect the alternator (white 3-pin, three yellow wires) wiring connector, located near the top of the rear shock absorber. Release the wiring from any clips or ties, noting its routing, and feed it through to its source so that it does not impede engine removal. If required, disconnect the sub-leads from the neutral switch, oil pressure switch (by removing the screw), ignition pulse generator, speed sensor and rear brake light switch and remove the sub-harness, again releasing the leads from any clips or ties.

15 Remove the PAIR system solenoid valve and hoses (see Chapter 4).

16 Remove the spark plug caps/ignition HT coils (see Chapter 5).

17 Unscrew the gearchange linkage arm pinch bolt and slide the arm off the shaft, noting how the slot in the arm aligns with the punch mark on the shaft (see illustration).

18 Remove the front sprocket (see Chapter 6).

19 On California models, remove the EVAP system canister, on 2001 and 2002 models along with the purge control valve (see Chapter 4).

20 The cam chain tensioner can be removed to provide extra clearance when removing the engine (see Section 9). This is not essential, but with the tensioner in place it is easy to scratch the frame when manoeuvring the engine.

21 Unscrew the nuts on the right-hand side of the bracket assembly on the back of the engine and withdraw the bolt securing the suspension linkage arm, the front bracket bolt (which also secures the front of the sidestand bracket) and the top bracket bolt (see illustrations). Draw the left-hand bracket off the engine, bringing the sidestand assembly,

5.17 Note the alignment of the punch mark, then remove the bolt and slide the arm off the shaft

and where fitted the centrestand assembly, with it (the centrestand pivot is free to withdraw from the right-hand bracket) (see illustration). Draw the right-hand bracket off

5.21a Unscrew the nuts (arrowed) . . .

5.21b . . . and withdraw the linkage arm bolt . . .

5.21c . . . and the front bracket bolt and the top bracket bolt (arrowed)

5.21d Draw the left-hand bracket and stand(s) off . . .

2•10 Engine, clutch and transmission

5.21e ... then remove the right-hand bracket

5.23 Support the engine using a jack as shown

5.24a Unscrew the nuts (arrowed), then withdraw the bolts and remove the spacers

the engine and remove the dowels if they are loose **(see illustration)**.
22 Remove the swingarm pivot and displace the swingarm down from between the engine and frame, referring to Chapter 6 for details.
23 At this point, position an hydraulic or mechanical jack under the engine with a block of wood between the jack head and sump **(see illustration)**. Make sure the jack is centrally positioned so the engine will not topple in any direction when the last mounting bolt is removed. Raise the jack to take the weight of the engine, but make sure it is not lifting the bike and taking the weight of that as well. The idea is to support the engine so that there is no pressure on any of the mounting bolts once they have been slackened, so they can be easily withdrawn. Note that it may be necessary to alter the position of the jack as some of the bolts are removed to relieve the stress transferred to the other bolts.
24 On F-X and F-Y (1999 and 2000) models, unscrew the nuts, withdraw the bolts and remove the spacers from the front engine mounting bolts **(see illustration)**. Unscrew the centre mounting bolt on the left-hand side **(see illustration)**. Slacken the adjuster bolt locknuts on the right-hand centre and rear engine mounting bolts using a suitable peg spanner (see **Tool Tip** on page 2•8) **(see illustration)**. The locknuts can remain loose on the adjuster bolts, or they can be removed if required. Check that the engine is properly supported by the jack. Unscrew the centre mounting bolt on the right-hand side **(see illustration)**. Unscrew the nut on the right-hand end of the rear mounting bolt, then withdraw the bolt from the left-hand side and remove the spacers **(see illustrations)**. Partially unscrew the adjuster bolts using an Allen key, until they are flush with the inside of the frame **(see illustration 5.24c)**. The engine can now be removed (see **Caution** above). Check that all wiring, cables and hoses are well clear, then lower the jack slowly and manoeuvre the engine forward so that the cam chain tensioner (if not removed) clears the lug on the frame for the centre mounting

5.24b Remove the centre bolt on the left-hand side

5.24c Unscrew the locknuts on the right-hand centre and rear adjuster bolts

5.24d Remove the centre bolt on the right-hand side

5.24e Unscrew the nut on the right-hand end of the rear mounting bolt

5.24f Withdraw the bolt and remove the right-hand spacer ...

5.24g ... and the left-hand spacer as you do

Engine, clutch and transmission 2•11

5.24h Remove the adjuster bolts from the frame if required

5.28 Fit the spacers between the engine and frame then slide the bolts through and fit the nuts

5.30 Tighten the adjuster bolts as described using a large hex key in their centre

bolt. Fully lower the jack and manoeuvre the engine out of the frame and lift it away. If required, remove the adjuster bolts from the frame (see illustration).

25 On F-1/FS-1 models onward (2001-on), unscrew the centre mounting bolt on the right-hand side (see illustration 5.24d). Unscrew the nut on the right-hand end of the rear mounting bolt (see illustration 5.24e). Slacken the adjuster bolt locknuts on the right-hand centre and rear engine mounting bolts using a suitable peg spanner (see *Tool Tip* on page 2•8) (see illustration 5.24c). The locknuts can remain loose on the adjuster bolts, or they can be removed if required. Unscrew the centre mounting bolt on the left-hand side (see illustration 5.24b). Push the rear mounting bolt through from the right until it clears the hex in the centre of the adjuster bolt. Partially unscrew the adjuster bolts using an Allen key, until they are clear of the engine (see illustration 5.24c). Check that the engine is properly supported by the jack. Unscrew the nuts, withdraw the bolts and remove the spacers from the front engine mounting bolts (see illustration 5.24a). Withdraw the rear mounting bolt from the left-hand side and remove the spacers, noting which fits where (see illustrations 5.24f and g). The engine can now be removed from the frame (see *Caution* above). Check that all wiring, cables and hoses are well clear, then carefully lower the jack a bit and manoeuvre the engine forward so that the cam chain tensioner (if not removed) clears the lug on the frame for the centre mounting bolt. Fully lower the jack and manoeuvre the engine out of the frame and lift it away. If required, remove the adjuster bolts from the inside of the frame.

Installation

26 If removed, thread the adjuster bolts into the frame. On F-X and F-Y (1999 and 2000) models thread them in from the outside until they are flush with the inside (see illustration 5.24h). On F-1/FS-1 models onward (2001-on), thread them fully in from the inside until their flanges contact the frame.
27 Manoeuvre the engine into position under the frame and lift it onto the jack. Raise the engine to align all the mounting bolt holes, taking care not to catch the cam chain tensioner (if installed) on the frame lug. Note that it may be necessary to adjust the jack as some of the bolts are installed and tightened to realign the other bolt holes.
28 Install the centre mounting bolt on the left-hand side and tighten it finger-tight (see illustration 5.24b). Install the front mounting bolts with their spacers (see illustration), then fit the nuts and tighten them finger-tight (see illustration 5.24a). Slide the rear mounting bolt through from the left-hand side, installing the spacers as you do (see illustrations 5.24g and f) – on F-1/FS-1 models onward (2001-on) the shorter spacer fits on the left-hand side of the engine.
29 Tighten the centre mounting bolt on the left-hand side and the front mounting bolt nuts to the torque setting specified at the beginning of the Chapter (see illustrations 5.24b and a).
30 Tighten the adjuster bolts on the right-hand centre and rear engine mounts to the specified torque using an Allen key in the hex – push the rear mounting bolt in until the hex is exposed (see illustration). At this point Honda specify to then turn each adjuster bolt out by 180° (half a turn) and then to check that there is no clearance between the engine and the adjusting bolts. However, in practice, it was only found necessary to back them out by a very small amount before reaching this point.
31 If removed, thread the locknuts onto the adjuster bolts. Tighten the locknuts to the specified torque setting using the Honda special tool or the peg spanner (see *Tool Tip* on page 2•8). If you do not have the Honda special tool, which allows the adjuster bolt to be counter-held while tightening the locknut, it is advisable to make a reference mark between the adjuster bolt and the frame to make sure that it does not turn as the locknut is being tightened (see illustration). If you have the special tool, tighten the locknut to the 'indicated' specified torque setting, which allows for the extra leverage provided by the offset. If you are using a fabricated peg spanner tighten the locknut to the 'actual' specified torque setting.
32 Install the right-hand centre mounting bolt and tighten it to the specified torque setting (see illustration 5.24d). Fit the nut on to the left-hand end of the rear mounting bolt and tighten it to the specified torque setting (see illustration 5.24e).
33 The remainder of the installation procedure is the reverse of removal, noting the following points:
● Install the swingarm as described in Chapter 6, referring to the relevant Steps. Slide the centrestand off its pivot then clean it and lubricate it with multi-purpose grease. Do not forget to the fit the dowels for the right-hand bracket (see illustration). Locate the suspension linkage arm between the brackets before tightening the bracket bolts. Tighten the sidestand/centrestand/suspension bracket bolt nuts to the specified torque setting (see illustration 5.21a). Tighten the suspension

5.31 Make a reference mark between the adjuster bolt and the frame before tightening the locknut

5.33a Do not forget the dowels (arrowed) for the bracket

2•12 Engine, clutch and transmission

5.33b Align the punch mark on the shaft with the slit in the clamp

linkage arm bolt nut to the specified torque setting.
● If the cam chain tensioner was removed to improve clearance when removing and installing the engine, refit it as described in Section 9, then remove the valve cover and the inspection cap in the clutch cover and check that the valve timing marks are correctly aligned as described in Steps 2 and 3 of Section 10.
● Use new gaskets on the exhaust pipe connections.
● When fitting the gearchange linkage arm onto the gearchange shaft, align the slit in the arm with punch mark on the shaft, and tighten the pinch bolt securely **(see illustration)**.
● Make sure all wires, cables and hoses are correctly routed and connected, and secured by any clips or ties.
● Refill the engine with oil and coolant (see Chapter 1).
● Adjust the throttle and clutch cable freeplay.
● Adjust the drive chain (see Chapter 1).
● Start the engine and check that there are no oil or coolant leaks. Adjust the idle speed (see Chapter 1).

6 Engine disassembly and reassembly – general information

Disassembly

1 Before disassembling the engine, thoroughly clean and degrease its external surfaces. This will prevent contamination of the engine internals, and will also make working a lot easier and cleaner. A high flash-point solvent, such as paraffin (kerosene) can be used, or better still, a proprietary engine degreaser. Use old paintbrushes and toothbrushes to work the solvent into the various recesses of the casings. Take care to exclude solvent or water from the electrical components and intake and exhaust ports.

⚠ **Warning: The use of petrol (gasoline) as a cleaning agent should be avoided because of the risk of fire.**

2 When clean and dry, position the engine on the workbench, leaving suitable clear area for working. Gather a selection of small containers, plastic bags and some labels so that parts can be grouped together in an easily identifiable manner. Also get some paper and a pen so that notes can be taken. You will also need a supply of clean rag, which should be as absorbent as possible.
3 Before commencing work, read through the appropriate section so that some idea of the necessary procedure can be gained. When removing components note that great force is seldom required, unless specified (checking the specified torque setting of the particular bolt being removed will indicate how tight it is, and therefore how much force should be needed). In many cases, a component's reluctance to be removed is indicative of an incorrect approach or removal method – if in any doubt, re-check with the text.
4 When disassembling the engine, keep 'mated' parts together (including gears, cylinder bores, pistons, connecting rods, valves, etc. that have been in contact with each other during engine operation). These 'mated' parts must be reused or replaced as an assembly.
5 A complete engine/transmission disassembly should be done in the following general order with reference to the appropriate Sections.
 Remove the valve cover
 Remove the camshafts
 Remove the cylinder head
 Remove the clutch
 Remove the alternator/starter clutch (see Chapter 9)
 Remove the starter motor (see Chapter 9)
 Remove the gearchange mechanism
 Remove the cam chain and blades
 Remove the oil sump
 Remove the oil pump
 Remove the selector drum and forks
 Separate the crankcase halves
 Remove the connecting rods and pistons
 Remove the crankshaft
 Remove the transmission shafts

Reassembly

6 Reassembly is accomplished by reversing the general disassembly sequence.

7 Oil cooler – removal, inspection and installation

Note: *The oil cooler can be removed with the engine in the frame. If the engine has been removed, ignore the steps which do not apply.*

Removal

1 The cooler is located on the front of the engine. Remove the fairing side panels (see Chapter 8).
2 Drain the engine oil and remove the filter (see Chapter 1). Drain the coolant (see Chapter 1).
3 Slacken the clamp securing each hose to the cooler and detach the hoses **(see illustration)**.
4 Unscrew the cooler bolt using a socket and remove the washer **(see illustration)**. Remove the cooler, noting how the slotted bracket locates over the lug on the crankcase **(see illustration)**. Discard the cooler O-ring as a new one must be used.
5 Check the cooler body for cracks and dents and any evidence of coolant leakage and replace it with a new one if necessary. Also check the hoses for splits, cracks, hardening and deterioration and fit new ones if required.

Installation

6 Installation is the reverse of removal, noting the following:
● Ensure the mating surfaces of

7.3 Slacken the clamps (arrowed) and detach the hoses

7.4a Unscrew the bolt (arrowed) . . .

7.4b . . . then withdraw it with its washer and remove the cooler

Engine, clutch and transmission 2•13

7.6a Fit a new O-ring into the groove

7.6b Locate the slot in the bracket over the lug on the crankcase (arrow)

the crankcase and the cooler are clean and dry.
● Use a new O-ring on the cooler body and smear it with clean engine oil. Make sure it seats in its groove **(see illustration)**.
● Locate the slot in the bracket on the cooler over the lug on the crankcase **(see illustration)**.
● Apply clean engine oil to the cooler bolt threads and seating surface. Fit the washer with its concave side, marked with a dot, facing the cooler. Tighten the bolt to the torque setting specified at the beginning of the Chapter.
● Make sure the coolant hoses are pressed fully onto their unions and are secured by the clamps.
● Fit a new oil filter and fill the engine with oil (see Chapter 1).
● Refill the cooling system (see Chapter 1).

8.2 Release the clamps and detach the hoses (arrowed) from their unions

8 Valve cover – removal and installation

Note: *The valve cover can be removed with the engine in the frame. If the engine has been removed, ignore the steps which do not apply.*

Removal

1 On F-X and F-Y (1999 and 2000) models, remove the carburettors (see Chapter 4). On F-1/FS-1 models onward (2001-on), remove the throttle bodies (see Chapter 4).
2 Release the PAIR system solenoid valve hose clamps and detach the hoses from the reed valve housings on the valve cover **(see illustration)**.
3 If required, release the crankcase breather hose clamp and detach the hose from its union on the valve cover **(see illustration 8.5a)**.
4 Remove the spark plug caps/ignition HT coils (see Chapter 5).
5 Unscrew the valve cover bolts and lift the cover off the cylinder head **(see illustrations)**. If it is stuck, do not try to lever it off with a screwdriver. Tap it gently around the sides with a rubber hammer or block of wood to dislodge it. Note the rubber washers for the bolts fitted in the cover and remove them if they are loose **(see illustration 8.9)**. The rubber gasket is normally glued into the groove in the cover, and is best left there if it is reusable. If the gasket is in any way damaged, deformed or deteriorated, renew it.
6 Note the dowels that link the PAIR system air passages between the valve cover and cylinder head and remove them for safekeeping if they are loose (which is unlikely), taking care not to drop them if they are not in the valve cover.

8.5a Detach the breather hose (A) if required, then unscrew the bolts (B) . . .

8.5b . . . and remove the cover

2•14 Engine, clutch and transmission

8.8a Make sure the gasket locates in the groove and stays there

8.8b Apply a sealant to the cutouts in the cylinder head

Installation

7 If removed, fit the PAIR system dowels into the cylinder head, taking care not to drop them.
8 Examine the valve cover gasket for signs of damage or deterioration and replace it with new one if necessary. If a new one is used, clean all traces of the old glue from the groove in the cover and clean it and the cylinder head mating surface with solvent. Fit the new gasket into the groove, using a suitable glue, sealant or grease to hold it in place **(see illustration)**. Also apply a suitable sealant to the cutouts in the cylinder head **(see illustration)**.
9 Position the valve cover on the cylinder head, making sure the gasket stays in place **(see illustration 8.5b)**. If removed, fit the rubber washers into the cover, using new ones if required, and making sure they are installed with the 'UP' mark facing up **(see illustration)**. Install the cover bolts and tighten them to the specified torque setting **(see illustration 8.5a)**.
10 Install the remaining components in the reverse order of removal.

8.9 Install the bolts with the rubber washers, making sure their UP marks face up

9.3a Unscrew the cap bolt (arrowed) and remove the washer

9 Cam chain tensioner – removal and installation

Note: *The cam chain tensioner can be removed with the engine in the frame. If the engine has been removed, ignore the steps which do not apply.*

Removal

1 Remove the right-hand fairing side panel (see Chapter 8).
2 Remove the valve cover as described in Section 8, then set the No. 1 piston at TDC compression as described in Steps 2 and 3 of Section 10.
3 Unscrew the tensioner cap bolt and remove the sealing washer **(see illustration)**. If the Honda tensioner locking key is available, insert it in the end of the tensioner so that it engages the slotted plunger and turn it clockwise until the plunger is fully retracted, then push the key into the slots in the end of the tensioner body to lock it **(see illustration)**. Unscrew the tensioner mounting bolts and remove the sealing washers, then withdraw the tensioner from the engine. If the Honda tool is not available, a home-made equivalent can be easily made out of a piece of 1 mm steel plate cut to the dimensions shown **(see illustration)**.

9.3b Honda locking key in position with tensioner plunger retracted. Tensioner mounting bolts arrowed

9.3c A copy of Honda's locking key can be made using 1 mm thick steel cut to the dimensions shown

Engine, clutch and transmission 2•15

9.4a Slacken the mounting bolts (arrowed) slightly . . .

washers, then withdraw the tensioner from the engine and release the screwdriver – the plunger will spring back out once the screwdriver is removed, but can be easily reset on installation.

5 Discard the gasket and sealing washers as new ones must be used on installation. Do not dismantle the tensioner.

Installation

6 Check that the plunger moves smoothly when wound into the tensioner and springs back out freely when released. Ensure the tensioner and cylinder block surfaces are clean and dry.

7 If the locking key described above is being used, insert it in the end of the tensioner so that it engages the slotted plunger and turn it clockwise until the plunger is fully retracted, then push the key into the slotted end of the tensioner body to lock it in this position **(see illustrations 9.3a and b)**. Install the tensioner, using a new gasket, and its mounting bolts, using new sealing washers, and tighten them to the torque setting specified at the

4 If a locking key is not available, first slacken the tensioner mounting bolts slightly **(see illustration)**. Insert a small flat-bladed screwdriver in the end of the tensioner so that it engages the slotted plunger. Turn the screwdriver clockwise until the plunger is fully retracted and hold it in this position while unscrewing the tensioner mounting bolts **(see illustration)**. Remove the bolts and sealing

beginning of the Chapter. Remove the key, then install the tensioner cap bolt with a new sealing washer and tighten it securely **(see illustration 9.8c)**.

8 If the key is not available, insert a small flat-bladed screwdriver in the end of the tensioner so that it engages the slotted plunger **(see illustration)**. Turn the screwdriver clockwise until the plunger is fully retracted and hold it in this position whilst the tensioner is installed. Fit a new gasket onto the tensioner body, then install the tensioner and its mounting bolts, using new sealing washers, and tighten them to the torque setting specified at the beginning of the Chapter **(see illustration)**. Release and remove the screwdriver, then install the tensioner end bolt with a new sealing washer and tighten it securely **(see illustration)**.

9 With the tensioner installed, check that the valve timing marks are correctly aligned as described in Steps 2 and 3 of Section 10. Install the valve cover and all other components as described in Section 8.

10 Install the right-hand fairing side panel (see Chapter 8).

9.4b . . . then insert the screwdriver, retract the tensioner and unscrew the mounting bolts

9.8a Insert the screwdriver and retract the plunger, then install the tensioner using a new gasket . . .

9.8b . . . and fit and tighten the mounting bolts

9.8c Install the cap bolt using a new sealing washer

2•16 Engine, clutch and transmission

10.2 Remove the timing inspection cap (arrowed)

10.3a Turn the engine using the timing rotor bolt (arrowed) until the line next to the T mark aligns with the notch ...

10 Camshafts and followers – removal, inspection and installation

Note: *The camshafts can be removed with the engine in the frame. Place clean rags over the spark plug holes and the cam chain tunnel to prevent any component from dropping into the engine.*

Removal

1 Remove the valve cover (see Section 8). On F-1/FS-1 models onward (2001-on), remove the cam pulse generator (see Chapter 4).
2 Unscrew the timing inspection cap from the clutch cover **(see illustration)**. The engine must be turned so that the No. 1 piston is at TDC (top dead centre) on its compression stroke. The engine can be turned using a suitable spanner or socket on the timing rotor bolt and turning it in a clockwise direction only. Alternatively, place the motorcycle on its centrestand (or an auxiliary stand) so that the rear wheel is off the ground, select a high gear and rotate the rear wheel by hand in its normal direction of rotation (removing the spark plugs first will make this a lot easier – see Chapter 1).
3 Turn the engine until the line next to the 'T' mark on the timing rotor aligns with the static timing mark, which is a notch in the inspection hole rim, and the IN and EX marks on the intake and exhaust camshaft sprockets respectively are facing away from each other and are flush with the cylinder head top surface **(see illustrations)**. If the marks are facing towards each other, rotate the engine clockwise one full turn (360°) until the line next to the 'T' mark again aligns with the static timing mark. The sprocket marks will now be facing away.
4 Either remove the cam chain tensioner (see Section 9), or if you prefer, obtain or fabricate the tensioner locking tool, then retract and lock the tensioner plunger using the tool as described in Section 9, Steps 2 and 3. Also unscrew the bolts securing the top cam chain guide and remove it **(see illustration)**.
5 Before disturbing the camshaft holder, note the numbers marked on the holder, adjacent to each bolt. These numbers denote the **tightening** sequence for the holder bolts.
6 Unscrew the camshaft holder bolts, slackening them evenly and a very little at a time in a **reverse** of the tightening sequence marked on the holder **(see illustration)**.

Caution: *Make sure the holder lifts up squarely and is not sticking on a dowel or being distorted by some of the bolts being slackened more than the others as it could easily break.*

Remove the bolts and lift off the holder, noting how it fits **(see illustration)**. Note the sealing washers fitted with the eight bolts around the spark plug bores. Remove the sealing rings

10.3b ... and the camshaft sprocket marks are as shown

10.4 Unscrew the bolts (arrowed) and remove the guide

Engine, clutch and transmission 2•17

10.6a Unscrew and remove the holder bolts (circled)...

10.6b ...and remove the holder

from their grooves around the spark plug holes on the underside of the holder, noting how they also locate around the dowels and discard them as new ones must be used. Do not remove the dowels unless they are obviously loose and liable to drop out.

7 If both camshafts are being removed, remove the intake camshaft first. Carefully lift each camshaft off the head and disengage the sprocket from the chain **(see illustrations 10.26 and 25)**. The camshafts are marked for identification. The intake camshaft is marked IN and the exhaust camshaft is marked EX **(see illustration)**. If the marks aren't clear make your own as the camshafts must be installed in their original location. While the camshafts are out do not rotate the crankshaft – the chain may drop down and bind between the crankshaft and case, which could damage these components. Wire the chain to another component or secure it using a rod of some sort to prevent it from dropping. Place rags over the spark plug holes and the cam chain tunnel to prevent anything from dropping into the engine on removal.

8 If the followers and shims are being removed from the cylinder head, obtain a container which is divided into sixteen compartments, and label each compartment

10.6c Remove the sealing rings, noting how they fit round the dowels

with the location of a valve, i.e. intake or exhaust camshaft, left or right valve. If a container is not available, use labelled plastic bags (egg cartons also do very well!). Remove the cam follower of the valve in question, then retrieve the shim from the inside of the follower **(see illustrations)**. The follower is best removed with a magnet or using the suction created by a valve lapping tool, but long nosed pliers can be used with care. If the shim is not in the follower, pick it out of the top of the valve spring retainer using either a magnet, a screwdriver with a dab of grease on it (the shim will stick to the grease), or a very

10.7 Note the identity mark on each camshaft

small screwdriver and a pair of pliers **(see illustration)**. Do not allow the shim to fall into the engine.

9 The sprockets can be separated from the camshafts if required by removing the two bolts that hold them. Both sprockets are identical and are therefore interchangeable, but mark them according to their camshaft so they can be installed in their original position. Also make alignment marks between the sprocket and the camshaft so that the sprocket can be installed the correct way round to avoid confusion when setting up the timing. On F-1/FS-1 models onward (2001-on),

10.8a Carefully lift out the follower using a lapping tool, grips or a magnet...

10.8b ...and retrieve the shim from inside it...

10.8c ...or from the top of the valve

2•18 Engine, clutch and transmission

10.11 Measure the height of the camshaft lobes with a micrometer

10.20 Measure the diameter of each follower

also note the alignment and fitting of the cam pulse generator rotor on the left-hand end of the exhaust camshaft and remove it if required – it is secured by two bolts.

Inspection

10 Inspect the bearing surfaces of the camshaft holders and cylinder head and the corresponding journals on the camshafts. Look for score marks, deep scratches and evidence of spalling (a pitted appearance). Check the oil passages for clogging.
11 Check the camshaft lobes for heat discoloration (blue appearance), score marks, chipped areas, flat spots and spalling. Measure the height of each lobe with a micrometer **(see illustration)** and compare the results to the minimum height listed in this Chapter's Specifications. If damage is noted or wear is excessive, the camshaft must be replaced with a new one.
12 Check the amount of camshaft runout by supporting each end on V-blocks, and measuring any runout using a dial gauge. If the runout exceeds the specified limit the camshaft must be replaced with a new one.

> **HAYNES HINT**: *Refer to Tools and Workshop Tips in the Reference section for details of how to read a micrometer and dial gauge.*

13 Next, check the camshaft journal oil clearances. Clean the camshafts and the bearing surfaces in the cylinder head and camshaft holder with a clean lint-free cloth, then lay each camshaft in its correct location in the cylinder head (see Step 7) **(see illustrations 10.25 and 26)**.
14 Cut some strips of Plastigauge and lay one piece on each journal, parallel with the camshaft centreline. Make sure the camshaft holder dowels are installed **(see illustration 10.6c)**. Lay the holder in the head **(see illustration 10.6b)**. Install all the holder bolts **(see illustration**

10.6a), not forgetting the washers with the eight bolts around the spark plug bores, and tighten them as described in Step 27. While doing this, don't let the camshafts rotate, or the Plastigauge will be disturbed and you will have to start again.
15 Now unscrew the camshaft holder bolts as described in Step 6 and lift off the holder.
16 To determine the oil clearance, compare the crushed Plastigauge (at its widest point) on each journal to the scale printed on the Plastigauge container. Compare the results to this Chapter's Specifications. If the oil clearance is greater than specified, replace the camshaft with a new one and recheck the clearance. If the clearance is still too great, also replace the cylinder head and holder with new ones.

> **HAYNES HINT**: *Before replacing the camshafts, cylinder head or holders because of damage, check with local machine shops specialising in motorcycle engine work. In the case of the camshafts, it may be possible for cam lobes to be welded, reground and hardened, at a cost far lower than that of a new camshaft. If the bearing surfaces in the case or holders are damaged, it may be possible for them to be bored out to accept bearing inserts. Due to the cost of new components it is recommended that all options be explored before condemning them as trash!*

17 Except in cases of oil starvation, the cam chain should wear very little. If the chain has stretched excessively, which makes it difficult to maintain proper tension, or if it is stiff or the links are binding or kinking, replace it with a new one. Refer to Section 11 for replacement.
18 Check the sprockets for wear, cracks and other damage. If the sprockets are worn, the cam chain is also worn, and so probably is the sprocket on the crankshaft. If severe wear is apparent, the entire engine should be disassembled for inspection.

19 Inspect the cam chain guides and tensioner blade (see Section 11).
20 Inspect the outer surface of each cam follower for evidence of scoring or other damage. If a follower is in poor condition, it is probable that the bore in the cylinder head in which it works is also damaged. Check for clearance between each follower and its bore. Measure the outer diameter of each follower and the inner diameter of its bore and compare the results to the Specifications **(see illustration)**. If any follower is worn beyond its service limit replace it with a new one. If any bore is worn beyond its limit, is seriously out-of-round or tapered, replace the cylinder head with a new one.

Installation

21 If separated, fit the sprockets onto the camshafts. Make sure they are installed the correct way round and in their original location as identified by the marks made on removal (Step 9), and the accompanying illustration **(see illustration)**. Apply a suitable non-permanent

10.21 Camshaft and sprocket alignment, and timing mark alignment

10.22a Fit the shim into the top of the valve...

10.22b ...then install the follower

thread locking compound to the sprocket bolts and tighten them to the torque setting specified at the beginning of the Chapter. On F-1/FS-1 models onward (2001-on), if removed, fit the cam pulse generator rotor onto the left-hand end of the exhaust camshaft – align it so that when the No.1 cylinder (left-hand) lobe is facing up, the OUT mark on the rotor faces out, is at the top, but reads upside down. Apply a suitable non-permanent thread locking compound to the bolts and tighten them to the specified torque setting.

22 If removed, lubricate each shim and its follower with molybdenum disulphide oil (a 50/50 mixture of molybdenum disulphide grease and engine oil). Fit each shim into its recess in the top of the valve spring retainer with the size mark facing up, making sure it is correctly seated **(see illustration)**. Note: *It is most important that the shims and followers are returned to their original valves otherwise the valve clearances will be inaccurate.* Install each follower, making sure it fits squarely in its bore **(see illustration 10.9b)**.

23 Make sure the bearing surfaces on the camshafts and in the holder and cylinder head are clean, then apply molybdenum disulphide oil (a 50/50 mixture of molybdenum disulphide grease and engine oil) to each of them. Also apply it to the camshaft lobes. Make sure that none gets on the mating surfaces between the holder and the head, or in the bolt holes, as this will affect the tightness of the bolts and the seating of the holder.

24 Check that the line next to the 'T' mark on the timing rotor aligns with the notch in the inspection hole rim **(see illustration 10.3a and 10.21)**. If both camshafts have been removed, install the exhaust camshaft first, then the intake.

25 Lay the exhaust camshaft (marked EX) onto the head with the EX mark on the sprocket facing forward and level with the cylinder head, and the No.1 cylinder lobes facing diagonally forward and up **(see illustrations 10.3b and 10.21)**. Fit the cam chain around the sprocket as you install the camshaft, pulling up on the chain to remove all slack in the front run between the crankshaft and the camshaft **(see illustration)**.

26 Lay the intake camshaft (marked IN) onto the head with the IN mark on the sprocket facing back and level with the cylinder head, and the No.1 cylinder lobes facing diagonally back and up **(see illustration 10.3b and 10.21)**. Fit the cam chain around the sprocket as you install the camshaft, pulling on it to remove all slack from between the two camshaft sprockets **(see illustration)**. Any slack in the chain must lie in the rear run of the chain between the intake camshaft and the crankshaft so that it is later taken up by the tensioner.

27 Make sure the camshaft holder dowels are installed. Fit new sealing rings into the grooves around the spark plug holes on the underside of the holder, making sure they also

10.25 Install the exhaust camshaft as described...

10.26 ...then install the intake camshaft

2•20 Engine, clutch and transmission

10.27a Fit new sealing rings over the dowels and into the grooves around the plug holes

10.27b Tighten the holder bolts as described to the specified torque setting

locate around the dowels **(see illustration)**. Lay the holder in the head **(see illustration 10.6b)**. Install all the holder bolts **(see illustration 10.6a)**, not forgetting new sealing washers with the eight bolts around the spark plug bores, and tighten them evenly and a little at a time in the following numerical sequence to the torque setting specified at the beginning of the Chapter. First gradually and evenly tighten the centre bolts Nos. 6-5-8-7 in that order until the dowels in the holder enter their bores in the head. When the clearance between the holder and the head is 2 to 4 mm all round and square, tighten all the bolts evenly and a little at a time in the correct sequence (i.e. 1 to 20), again making sure the holder is being pulled down squarely **(see illustration)**.

Caution: Whilst tightening the bolts, make sure the holder is being pulled squarely down and is not binding on the dowels or tilting to one side – if it does, adjust the relevant bolts until the holder is again square to the head. The holder is likely to break if it's not tightened down evenly and squarely.

28 If the tensioner locking tool was used to retract and hold the tensioner plunger, remove it to release the plunger. If the tensioner was removed, use a piece of wooden dowel to press on the back of the cam chain tensioner blade via the tensioner bore in the cylinder block to ensure that any slack in the cam chain is taken up and transferred to the rear run of the chain (where it will later be taken up by the tensioner). At this point check that all the timing marks are still in **exact** alignment as described in Step 3 **(see illustrations 10.3a and b and 10.21)**. Note that it is easy to be slightly out (one tooth on the sprocket) without the marks appearing drastically out of alignment. If the marks are out, verify which sprocket is misaligned, then either reinstall the tensioner locking tool and retract the plunger, or remove the wooden dowel. Unscrew the sprocket's bolts and slide it off the camshaft, then disengage it from the chain. Move the camshaft round as required, then fit the sprocket back into the chain and onto the camshaft, and check the marks again. With everything correctly aligned, apply a suitable non-permanent thread locking compound to the sprocket bolts and tighten them to the torque setting specified at the beginning of the Chapter.

Caution: If the marks are not aligned exactly as described, the valve timing will be incorrect and the valves may strike the pistons, causing extensive damage to the engine.

29 Install the cam chain top guide and tighten its bolts securely **(see illustration)**. Either install the cam chain tensioner (see Section 9), or remove the tensioner locking tool, according to the method you used earlier.

30 Turn the engine clockwise through two full turns and check again that all the timing marks still align (see Step 3) **(see illustrations 10.3a and b and 10.21)**. Check the valve clearances and adjust them if necessary (see Chapter 1).

31 Install the timing inspection cap using a new O-ring if required, and smear the O-ring and the cap threads with grease **(see illustration)**. Tighten the cap to the torque setting specified at the beginning of the Chapter.

32 Install the valve cover (see Section 8). On F-1/FS-1 models onward (2001-on), install the camshaft pulse generator (see Chapter 4).

11 Cam chain, tensioner blade and guide blades – removal, inspection and installation

Note: *The cam chain and its blades can be removed with the engine in the frame. If the engine has been removed, ignore the steps which do not apply.*

Removal

Cam chain

1 Remove the camshafts (see Section 10).
2 Remove the timing rotor (see Section 21).
3 Remove the front guide blade (see below).
4 Draw the cam chain off the crankshaft sprocket and out of the engine **(see illustration)**.

10.29 Install the top cam chain guide

10.31 Fit the cap using a new O-ring and smear it and the threads with grease

11.4a Slip the cam chain off the sprocket and draw it out of the engine

Engine, clutch and transmission 2•21

If required, slide the sprocket off the end of the crankshaft, noting the wide spline that means it can only be installed in one position (see illustrations).

Tensioner blade

5 Remove the clutch cover (see Section 16). Remove the intake camshaft (see Section 10).
6 Unscrew the pivot bolt and draw the blade out of the engine, noting the washer that fits behind it (see illustrations).

Front guide blade

7 Remove the clutch cover (see Section 16). Remove the exhaust camshaft (see Section 10).
8 Remove the timing rotor (see Section 21).
9 Unscrew the pivot bolt and draw the blade out of the engine (see illustrations).

Top guide blade

10 Remove the valve cover (see Section 8). Retract the cam chain tensioner to release cam chain tension (see Section 9).
11 Unscrew the bolts securing the top cam chain guide and remove it (see illustration 10.4).

Inspection

Cam chain

12 Check the chain for binding, kinks and any obvious damage and replace it with a new one if necessary. Check the camshaft and crankshaft sprocket teeth for wear and renew the cam chain, camshaft sprockets and crankshaft as a set if necessary.

Tensioner and guide blades

13 Check the sliding surface and edges of the blades for excessive wear, deep grooves, cracking and other obvious damage, and replace them with new ones if necessary.

Installation

14 Installation of the chain and blades is the reverse of removal. Do not omit the washer that fits behind the tensioner blade. Apply a suitable non-permanent thread locking compound to the pivot bolt threads and tighten them to the torque settings specified at the beginning of the Chapter.
15 After the cam chain tensioner plunger has been released (see Section 9), check that the valve timing marks are correctly aligned as described in Steps 2 and 3 of Section 10.

11.4b Remove the sprocket if required . . .

11.4c . . . noting the wide spline

11.6a Cam chain tensioner blade bolt (A), front guide blade bolt (B)

11.6b Note the washer that fits between the blade pivot and the crankcase

12 Cylinder head – removal and installation

Caution: *The engine must be completely cool before beginning this procedure or the cylinder head may become warped.*

Removal

1 Remove the exhaust system (see Chapter 4). Remove the carburettors or throttle bodies, as applicable (see Chapter 4).
2 Remove the cam chain tensioner (see Section 9). Remove the camshafts, followers and shims (see Section 10).
3 Drain the coolant (see Chapter 1) and remove the thermostat housing (see Chapter 3).
4 The cylinder head is secured by two 6 mm

11.9a Unscrew the pivot bolt . . .

11.9b . . . and draw the blade out of the engine

2•22 Engine, clutch and transmission

12.4a Cylinder head 6 mm bolts (arrowed)

12.4b Cylinder head 9 mm bolts (arrowed)

bolts and ten 9 mm bolts **(see illustrations)**. First unscrew and remove the 6 mm bolts. Now unscrew and remove the 9 mm bolts, slackening them evenly and a little at a time in a criss-cross pattern working from the outside to the middle until they are all loose.

5 Hold the cam chain up and pull the cylinder head up off the block, then pass the cam chain down through the tunnel **(see illustration)**. Do not let the chain fall into the crankcase – secure it with a piece of wire or metal bar to prevent it from doing so. If the head is stuck, tap around the joint faces with a soft-faced mallet. Do not attempt to free the head by inserting a screwdriver between the head and block mating surfaces – you'll damage them.

6 Remove the cylinder head gasket and discard it as a new one must be used. If they are loose, remove the dowels from the crankcase or the underside of the cylinder head **(see illustration 12.10)**.

7 Check the cylinder head gasket and the mating surfaces on the cylinder head and crankcase for signs of leakage, which could indicate warpage. Refer to Section 14 and check the cylinder head gasket surface for warpage.

8 Clean all traces of old gasket material from the cylinder head and crankcase. If a scraper is used, take care not to scratch or gouge the soft aluminium. Be careful not to let any of the gasket material fall into the crankcase, the cylinder bore or the oil and coolant passages.

Installation

9 Lubricate the cylinder bores with engine oil. If removed, fit the dowels into the crankcase **(see illustration 12.10)**.

10 Ensure both cylinder head and crankcase mating surfaces are clean. Lay the new head gasket over the cam chain and blades and onto the crankcase, locating it over the dowels and making sure all the holes are correctly aligned **(see illustration)**. Never re-use the old gasket.

11 Carefully fit the cylinder head onto the block, making sure it locates correctly onto the dowels **(see illustration 12.5)**. Feed the cam chain up through the tunnel as you install the head, then secure it in place with a piece of wire to prevent it from falling back down.

12 Apply some molybdenum disulphide oil (a 50/50 mixture of molybdenum disulphide grease and engine oil) to the threads and the underside of the heads of the ten 9 mm bolts **(see illustration)**. Install the 9 mm and the 6 mm bolts and tighten them all finger-tight **(see illustration)**. Now tighten the 9 mm bolts evenly and a little at a time in a criss-cross pattern working from the middle to the outside to the torque setting specified at the beginning of the Chapter **(see illustration)**. Now tighten the 6 mm bolts to the specified torque.

13 Install the remaining components in a reverse of their removal sequence, referring to the relevant Sections or Chapters (see Steps 1 to 4).

12.5 Carefully lift the head up off the block

12.10 Install the dowels (arrowed) then lay the new gasket on the block

12.12a Lubricate the 9 mm bolts as described then fit them . . .

12.12b . . . and the 6 mm bolts . . .

12.12c . . . and tighten them as described to specified torque setting

Engine, clutch and transmission 2•23

1 Follower
2 Shim
3 Collets
4 Spring retainer
5 Inner valve spring (where fitted)
6 Outer valve spring
7 Valve stem oil seal
8 Spring seat
9 Valve guide
10 Intake valve
11 Exhaust valve

14.3 Valve components

13 Valves/valve seats/valve guides – servicing

1 Because of the complex nature of this job and the special tools and equipment required, most owners leave servicing of the valves, valve seats and valve guides to a professional. However, you can make an initial assessment of whether the valves are seating correctly, and therefore sealing, by pouring a small amount of solvent into each of the valve ports. If the solvent leaks past any valve into the combustion chamber area the valve is not seating correctly and sealing.
2 You can also remove the valves from the cylinder head, clean the components, check them for wear to assess the extent of the work needed, and, unless a valve service is required, grind in the valves (see Section 14). The head can then be reassembled.
3 A dealer service department will remove the valves and springs, replace the valves and guides, recut the valve seats, check and replace the valve springs, spring retainers and collets (as necessary), replace the valve stem seals with new ones and reassemble the valve components.
4 After the valve service has been performed, the head will be in like-new condition. When the head is returned, be sure to clean it again very thoroughly before installation on the engine to remove any metal particles or abrasive grit that may still be present from the valve service operations. Use compressed air, if available, to blow out all the holes and passages.

14 Cylinder head and valves – disassembly, inspection and reassembly

1 As mentioned in the previous section, valve overhaul should be left to a Honda dealer. However, disassembly, cleaning and inspection of the valves and related components can be done (if the necessary special tools are available) by the home mechanic. This way no expense is incurred if the inspection reveals that overhaul is not required at this time.
2 To disassemble the valve components without the risk of damaging them, a valve spring compressor is absolutely essential. Make sure it is suitable for motorcycle work.

Disassembly

3 Before proceeding, arrange to label and store the valves along with their related components in such a way that they can be returned to their original locations without getting mixed up **(see illustration)**. A good way to do this is to use the same container as the followers and shims are stored in (see Section 10), or to obtain a separate container which is divided into sixteen compartments, and label each compartment with the location of a valve, i.e. intake or exhaust camshaft, left or right valve. If a container is not available, use labelled plastic bags (egg cartons also do very well!).
4 Clean all traces of old gasket material from the cylinder head. If a scraper is used, take care not to scratch or gouge the soft aluminium; refer to Tools and Workshop Tips for details of gasket removal methods.
5 Compress the valve spring on the first valve with a spring compressor, making sure it is

TOOL TIP

The follower bore in the cylinder head can be protected from scratches by the valve spring compressor by fabricating a shield from a 35 mm film canister. Cut the canister to the dimensions shown.

2•24 Engine, clutch and transmission

14.5a Compressing the valve springs using a valve spring compressor

14.5b Make sure the compressor locates correctly both on the bottom of the valve . . .

14.5c . . . and on the top of the spring retainer

14.5d Remove the collets with needle-nose pliers, tweezers, a magnet or a screwdriver with a dab of grease on it

14.5e If the valve stem won't pull through the guide, deburr the area above the collet groove (1)

correctly located onto each end of the valve assembly **(see illustrations)**. On the underside of the head make sure the plate on the compressor only contacts the valve and not the soft aluminium of the head – if the plate is too big for the valve, use a spacer between them. Do not compress the springs any more than is absolutely necessary. Remove the collets, using either needle-nose pliers, tweezers, a magnet or a screwdriver with a dab of grease on it **(see illustration)**. Carefully release the valve spring compressor and remove it. Remove the spring retainer, noting which way up it fits **(see illustration 14.28b)**. Remove the spring(s), noting that the closer wound coils are at the bottom – European FS-1 models onward and all US 2001-on models have an inner and outer spring fitted to each intake valve, while all other models have only one spring with each **(see illustration 14.28a and 14.3)**. On all models there is one spring per exhaust valve. Press down on the top of the valve stem and draw the valve out from the underside of the head **(see illustration 14.27)**. If the valve binds in the guide (won't pull through), push it back into the head and deburr the area around the collet groove with a very fine file or whetstone **(see illustration)**.

6 Once the valve has been removed and labelled, pull the valve stem seal off the top of the valve guide with pliers and discard it (the old seals should never be reused) **(see illustration)**. Now remove the spring seat **(see illustration)**. The seat is difficult to get hold of, so either use a small magnet or turn the head upside down and tip it out, taking care not to lose it.

7 Repeat the procedure for the remaining valves. Remember to keep the parts for each valve together and in order so they can be reinstalled in the same location.

8 Next, clean the cylinder head with solvent and dry it thoroughly. Compressed air will speed the drying process and ensure that all holes and recessed areas are reached.

9 Clean all of the valve springs, collets, retainers and spring seats with solvent and dry them thoroughly. Do the parts from one valve at a time so they don't get mixed up.

10 Scrape off any deposits that may have formed on the valve, then use a motorised wire brush to remove deposits from the valve heads and stems. Again, make sure the valves do not get mixed up.

Inspection

11 Inspect the head very carefully for cracks and other damage. If cracks are found, a new head will be required. Check the camshaft bearing surfaces for wear and evidence of

14.6a Pull the seal off the valve stem . . .

14.6b . . . then remove the spring seat

Engine, clutch and transmission 2•25

14.13 Measure the valve seat width with a ruler (or for greater precision use a vernier caliper)

14.14a Measure the valve stem diameter with a micrometer

14.14b Insert a small bore gauge into the valve guide (arrowed) and expand it so there's a slight drag when it's pulled out, then measure the bore gauge with a micrometer

seizure. Check the camshafts and holders for wear as well (see Section 10).

12 Using a precision straight-edge and a feeler gauge set to the warpage limit listed in the specifications at the beginning of the Chapter, check the head gasket mating surface for warpage. Refer to *Tools and Workshop Tips* in the Reference section for details of how to use the straight-edge.

13 Examine the valve seats in the combustion chamber. If they are pitted, cracked or burned, the head will require work beyond the scope of the home mechanic. Measure the valve seat width and compare it to this Chapter's Specifications **(see illustration)**. If it exceeds the service limit, or if it varies around its circumference, overhaul is required.

14 Measure the valve stem diameter **(see illustration)**. Clean the valve guides using a guide reamer to remove any carbon build-up, then measure the inside diameters of the guides (at both ends and in the centre of the guide) with a small bore gauge, then measure the gauge with a micrometer **(see illustration)**. Measure the guides at the ends and at the centre to determine if they are worn in a bell-mouth pattern (more wear at the ends). Subtract the stem diameter from the valve guide diameter to obtain the valve stem-to-guide clearance. If the stem-to-guide clearance is greater than listed in this Chapter's Specifications, renew whichever components are worn beyond their specification limits. If the valve guide is within specifications, but is worn unevenly, it should be renewed.

15 Carefully inspect each valve face, stem and collet groove area for cracks, pits and burned spots **(see illustration)**.

16 Rotate the valve and check for any obvious indication that it is bent, in which case it must be replaced with a new one. Check the end of the stem for pitting and excessive wear. The presence of any of the above conditions indicates the need for valve servicing.

17 Check the end of each valve spring for wear and pitting. Measure the spring free lengths and compare them to the specifications **(see illustration)**. If any spring is shorter than specified it has sagged and must be replaced with a new one. Also place the spring upright on a flat surface and check it for bend by placing a ruler against it, or alternatively lay it against a set square **(see illustration)**. If the bend in any spring is excessive, it must be replaced with a new one.

18 Check the spring seats, retainers and collets for obvious wear and cracks. Any questionable parts should not be reused, as extensive damage will occur in the event of failure during engine operation.

19 If the inspection indicates that no overhaul work is required, the valve components can be reinstalled in the head.

Reassembly

20 Unless a valve service has been performed, before installing the valves in the head they should be ground in (lapped) to ensure a positive seal between the valves and seats. This procedure requires coarse and fine valve grinding compound and a valve grinding tool (either hand-held or drill driven). If a grinding tool is not available, a piece of rubber or plastic hose can be slipped over the valve stem (after the valve has been installed in the guide) and used to turn the valve.

21 Apply a small amount of coarse grinding compound to the valve face and some molybdenum disulphide oil (a 50/50 mixture of molybdenum disulphide grease and engine oil) to the valve stem, then slip the valve into the guide **(see illustration and 14.27)**.

14.15 Check the valve face (A), stem (B) and collet groove (C) for signs of wear and damage

14.17a Measure the free length of the valve springs

14.17b Check the valve springs for squareness

14.21 Apply the lapping compound very sparingly, in small dabs, to the valve face only

2•26 Engine, clutch and transmission

14.22a Rotate the valve grinding tool back and forth between the palms of your hands

14.22b The valve face and seat should show a uniform unbroken ring and the seat should be the specified width all the way round

14.25a Fit the spring seat . . .

Note: *Make sure each valve is installed in its correct guide and be careful not to get any grinding compound on the valve stem.*

22 Attach the grinding tool to the valve and rotate the tool between the palms of your hands. Use a back-and-forth motion (as though rubbing your hands together) rather than a circular motion (i.e. so that the valve rotates alternately clockwise and anti-clockwise rather than in one direction only) **(see illustration)**. If a motorised tool is being used, take note of the correct drive speed for it – if your drill runs too fast and is not variable, use a hand tool instead. Lift the valve off the seat and turn it at regular intervals to distribute the grinding compound properly. Continue the grinding procedure until the valve face and seat contact area is of uniform width, and unbroken around the entire circumference **(see illustration)**.

23 Carefully remove the valve from the guide and wipe off all traces of grinding compound, making sure none gets in the guide. Use solvent to clean the valve and wipe the seat area thoroughly with a solvent soaked cloth.

24 Repeat the procedure with fine valve grinding compound, then repeat the entire procedure for the remaining valves.

25 Working on one valve at a time, lay the spring seat in place in the cylinder head, making sure it is the correct way round **(see illustration)**. As it is easy to cock the seat on the top of the valve guide, and then tricky to get it to sit properly, install it using a rod as a guide for it to slide down as shown **(see illustration)**.

26 Fit a new valve stem seal onto the guide **(see illustration 14.6a)**, using a stem seal fitting tool or an appropriate size deep socket, to push the seal squarely onto the end of the valve guide until it is felt to clip into place **(see illustration)**.

27 Coat the valve stem with molybdenum disulphide oil (a 50/50 mixture of molybdenum disulphide grease and engine oil), then install it into its guide, rotating it slowly to avoid damaging the seal **(see illustration)**. Check that the valve moves up and down freely in the guide.

28 Next, install the spring(s), with their closer-wound coils facing down into the cylinder head **(see illustration)**. European FS models and US 2001-on models have an inner and outer spring fitted to each intake valve, while all other models have only one spring with each. On all models there is one spring per exhaust valve. Fit the spring retainer, with its shouldered side facing down so that it fits into the top of the spring(s) **(see illustration)**.

29 Compress the valve spring with a spring compressor, making sure it is correctly located onto each end of the valve assembly **(see illustrations 14.5a, b and c)**. On the underside of the head make sure the plate on the compressor only contacts the valve and not the soft aluminium of the head – if the plate is too big for the valve, use a spacer between them. Do not compress the springs any more than is necessary to slip the collets into place **(see illustration 14.5d)**. Apply a small amount of grease to the collets to help

14.25b . . . using a rod to guide it as shown if necessary

14.26 Fit a new valve stem seal using a deep socket or special tool to press it squarely into place

14.27 Lubricate the stem and slide the valve into its correct location

14.28a Fit the valve spring . . .

14.28b . . . then fit the spring retainer

Engine, clutch and transmission 2•27

hold them in place. Locate each collet in turn into the groove in the valve stem, then carefully release the compressor, making sure the collets seat and lock as you do **(see illustration)**. Check that the collets are securely locked in the retaining groove.

30 Support the cylinder head on blocks so the valves can't contact the workbench top, then very gently tap the top of the valve stem with a brass drift. This will help seat the collets in the groove. If you don't have a brass drift, fit the shim into its recess in the top of the valve spring retainer and use a soft-faced hammer and a piece of wood as an interface

HAYNES HiNT *Check for proper sealing of the valves by pouring a small amount of solvent into each of the valve ports. If the solvent leaks past any valve into the combustion chamber area the valve grinding operation on that valve should be repeated.*

31 Repeat the procedure for the remaining valves. Remember to keep the parts for each valve together, and separate from the other valves, so they can be reinstalled in the same location. After the cylinder head and camshafts have been installed, check and adjust the valve clearances as required (see Chapter 1).

15 Starter clutch – check, removal, inspection and installation

Note: *The starter clutch can be removed with the engine in the frame. If the engine has been removed, ignore the steps which do not apply.*

Check

1 The operation of the starter clutch can be checked while it is in situ. Remove the starter motor (see Chapter 9). Check that the idle/reduction gear is able to rotate freely clockwise as you look at it via the starter motor aperture, but locks when rotated anti-clockwise. If not, the starter clutch is faulty and should be removed for inspection.

14.29 Make sure both collets remain in place and lock into the groove as the compressor is released

Removal

2 Remove the alternator rotor – the starter clutch is mounted on the back of it (see Chapter 9).

Inspection

3 With the alternator rotor face down on a workbench, check that the starter driven gear rotates freely in an anti-clockwise direction and locks against the rotor in a clockwise direction. If it doesn't, the starter clutch should be dismantled for further investigation.
4 Withdraw the starter driven gear from the starter clutch **(see illustration)**. If the gear appears stuck, rotate it anti-clockwise as you withdraw it to free it from the starter clutch.
5 Check the condition of the sprags inside the clutch body and the corresponding surface on the driven gear hub **(see illustration)**. If they are damaged, marked or flattened at any point, they should be replaced with new ones. Measure the outside diameter of the hub and check that it has not worn beyond the service limit specified. To remove the sprag assembly, hold the rotor using a holding strap and unscrew the six bolts inside the rotor **(see illustration)**. Separate the sprag assembly from the rotor, noting how it fits. Install the new assembly in a reverse sequence. Apply clean engine oil to the sprags. Apply a suitable non-permanent thread locking compound to the bolts and tighten them to the torque setting specified at the beginning of the Chapter.
6 Check the needle roller bearing on the

15.4 Draw the gear out of the clutch

crankshaft and the bearing surfaces in the starter driven gear hub and on the crankshaft. If the bearing surfaces show signs of excessive wear or the bearing itself is worn or damaged, they should be replaced with new ones.
7 Check the teeth of the starter idle/reduction gear and the corresponding teeth of the starter driven gear and starter motor drive shaft. Replace the gears and/or starter motor if worn or chipped teeth are discovered on related gears. Also check the idle/reduction gear shaft for damage, and check that the gear is not a loose fit on the shaft. Replace the shaft with a new one if necessary.

Installation

8 Lubricate the needle roller bearing on the crankshaft with clean engine oil **(see illustration)**. Lubricate the outside of the starter driven gear hub with clean engine oil, then fit the gear into the clutch, rotating it anti-clockwise as you do so to spread the sprags and allow the hub to enter **(see illustration 15.4)**.
9 Install the alternator rotor (see Chapter 9).

16 Clutch and cable – removal, inspection and installation

Note 1: *The clutch can be removed with the engine in the frame. If the engine has been removed, ignore the steps which don't apply.*
Note 2: *The clutch nut must be discarded and a new one used on installation – it is best to obtain the nut in advance.*

15.5a Check the sprags (A) and the hub (B)

15.5b Unscrew the bolts (arrowed) and remove the sprag assembly

15.8 Lubricate the needle bearing with clean oil

2•28 Engine, clutch and transmission

16.2a Unscrew the bolt (arrowed) and displace the bracket . . .

16.2b . . . then detach the end of the cable from the release arm

16.3 Disconnect the ignition pulse generator wiring connector

16.4 Unscrew the bolts (arrowed) and remove the cover

Clutch removal

1 Remove the right-hand fairing side panel (see Chapter 8). Drain the engine oil (see Chapter 1). Disconnect the battery negative (-ve) lead (see Chapter 9).
2 Unscrew the bolt securing the clutch cable bracket to the clutch cover **(see illustration)**. Displace the bracket, noting how it locates, and free the cable end from the release arm **(see illustration)**. Position the cable clear of the engine.
3 Trace the ignition pulse generator coil wiring from the top of the clutch cover and disconnect it at the red 2-pin wiring connector – you should be able to access and disconnect it from the side, but if not raise the fuel tank (see Chapter 4) and do it from the top **(see illustration)**.
4 Working evenly in a criss-cross pattern, unscrew the clutch cover bolts **(see illustration)**. Remove the cover, turning the release lever arm back as you do to disengage the shaft from the pull-rod, and being prepared to catch any residual oil. Remove the four dowels from either the cover or the crankcase if they are loose.
5 Working in a criss-cross pattern, gradually slacken the clutch spring bolts until spring pressure is released **(see illustrations)**. To prevent the assembly from turning, cover it with a rag and hold it securely – the bolts are not very tight. If available, have an assistant to hold the clutch while you unscrew the bolts. Remove the bolts and springs, then remove the clutch pressure plate **(see illustrations 16.29c, b and a)**. Remove the pull-rod from either the back of the pressure plate or the end of the shaft **(see illustration 16.28)**.
6 Remove the clutch friction and plain plates, noting how they fit and keeping them in the same order as you remove them **(see illustrations 16.27d, c, b and a)**. Note how the tabs on the outer friction plate locate in the shallow slots in the housing, while the rest sit in the deep slots. On all European F models and US F models up to 2001, the outer and inner friction plates are different to the rest – they are colour-coded green, while the rest are purple, the colour being marked on the tabs. On FS models and all US F

16.5a Clutch components

1 Bolts
2 Springs
3 Pressure plate
4 Bearing
5 Pull-rod
6 Clutch nut
7 Lock washer
8 Thrust washer
9 Clutch plates
10 Anti-judder spring
11 Anti-judder spring seat
12 Clutch centre
13 Thrust washer
14 Clutch housing
15 Oil pump drive sprocket
16 Guide
17 Oil pump drive chain
18 Oil pump driven sprocket

16.5b Unscrew the pressure plate bolts (arrowed) and remove the springs

Engine, clutch and transmission 2•29

models from 2001, the outer friction plate is coded green and the inner friction plate has a larger internal diameter so that it fits over the anti-judder spring and spring seat fitted on those models. The rest of the friction plates are coded purple. If the colour codes are difficult to identify, make sure you keep the plates in the correct order. On FS models and US F models from 2001, remove the anti-judder spring and spring seat, noting which way round they fit.

7 The clutch nut is staked against the input shaft. Unstake the nut using a hammer and punch – take care not to damage the threads on the end of the shaft **(see illustration)**. To remove the clutch nut, the input shaft must be locked. This can be done in several ways. If the engine is in the frame, engage 6th gear and have an assistant hold the rear brake on hard with the rear tyre in firm contact with the ground. Alternatively, the Honda service tool (Pt. No. 07724-0050002), or a similar commercially available or home-made tool **(see Tool tip)**, can be used to stop the clutch centre from turning whilst the nut is slackened **(see illustration)**. Unscrew the nut and remove the spring washer, and on European F models and 1999/2000 US models the thrust washer, from the input shaft **(see illustrations 16.25d, c and b)**. Discard the nut as a new one must be used on installation.

8 Remove the clutch centre and the thrust washer from the shaft **(see illustrations 16.25a and 16.24)**.

9 To remove the clutch housing it is necessary to align the primary drive sub-gear teeth with the main gear. To do this, locate a suitable screwdriver or rod through the hole in the crankcase and into the holes in the gears and twist it to align the teeth **(see illustrations)**. Either remove the cam chain tensioner or retract and lock the cam chain tensioner plunger so that the tensioner blade can be lifted above the hole. If the timing rotor tangs are in the way you will have to turn the engine a little to offset them. Slide the clutch housing off the shaft, noting that you may have to prevent the guide in the centre of the housing from sliding with it by pressing on its rim using a very small screwdriver. If the guide slides with the housing, it brings the oil pump drive chain with it which could distort the chain. Note how the holes in the back of the housing engage with the pins on the oil pump drive sprocket.

10 If required, unscrew the oil pump driven sprocket bolt and remove the driven sprocket, the chain and the drive sprocket **(see illustration and 16.22d, c, b and a)**. Lock the sprocket to prevent it from turning whilst slackening the bolt by locating a rod between the one of the holes in the sprocket and the crankcase **(see illustration 16.22e)**. Also remove the clutch housing guide from the input shaft **(see illustration 16.21)**.

16.7a Unstake the nut . . .

16.7b . . . then unscrew it as described and remove the washers

A clutch centre holding tool can be made using two strips of steel with the ends bent over and filed, with a bolt in the middle to create the scissor effect

16.9a Insert a screwdriver into the hole (arrowed) . . . .

16.9b . . . and align the sub-gear (A) and main gear (B) teeth as shown and draw the housing off the shaft

16.10 Oil pump sprocket bolt (arrowed)

2•30 Engine, clutch and transmission

16.11 Measuring clutch friction plate thickness

16.12 Check the plain plates for warpage

16.15 Check the bearing in the housing and its corresponding surface on the guide

Clutch inspection

11 After an extended period of service the clutch friction plates will wear and promote clutch slip. Measure the thickness of each friction plate using a vernier caliper **(see illustration)**. If any plate has worn to or beyond the service limits given in the Specifications at the beginning of the Chapter, the friction plates must be renewed as a set. Also, if any of the plates smell burnt or are glazed, they must be renewed as a set.

12 The plain plates should not show any signs of excess heating (bluing). Check for warpage using a flat surface and feeler gauges **(see illustration)**. If any plate exceeds the maximum permissible amount of warpage, or shows signs of bluing, all plain plates must be renewed as a set.

13 Measure the free length of each clutch spring using a vernier caliper **(see illustration**

16.16 Check the pressure plate and its bearing

14.17). If any spring is below the service limit specified, renew all the springs as a set. On FS models and US 2001-on models, also check the anti-judder spring and spring seat for damage or distortion and replace them with new ones if necessary.

14 Inspect the clutch assembly for burrs and indentations on the edges of the protruding tabs of the friction plates and/or slots in the edge of the housing with which they engage. Similarly check for wear between the inner tongues of the plain plates and the slots in the clutch centre. Wear of this nature will cause clutch drag and slow disengagement during gear changes as the plates will snag when the pressure plate is lifted. With care a small amount of wear can be corrected by dressing with a fine file, but if this is excessive the worn components should be renewed.

15 Inspect the clutch housing guide bearing surface and the needle roller bearing in the clutch housing **(see illustration)**. If there are any signs of wear, pitting or other damage the affected parts must be renewed. The bearing is a press fit in the housing – refer to *Tools and Workshop Tips* in the Reference Section for details on bearing removal and installation. When removing the old bearing, note carefully at what depth it sits in the centre and install the new bearing so that it sits in exactly the same place (which should be 0.4 to 0.6 mm below the outer surface of the centre).

16 Check the pressure plate and its bearing for signs of wear or damage and roughness **(see illustration)**. Check that the bearing outer race is a good fit in the centre of the

lifter, and that the inner race rotates freely without any rough spots. Check the pull-rod end and the corresponding cutout in the release lever shaft for signs of wear or damage. Replace any parts necessary with new ones.

17 Check the release mechanism in the clutch cover for a smooth action. If the action is stiff or rough, withdraw the shaft, noting how the return spring ends locate, and remove the washer, then clean and check the oil seal and the two needle bearings in the cover **(see illustrations)**. The seal is available separately and can be renewed by levering the old one out with a screwdriver and pressing the new one in. The needle bearings for the shaft are not listed as being available separately from the cover, and so it may be necessary to fit a new cover if they are worn or damaged, though it is always worth contacting a Honda dealer and/or bearing specialist. Lubricate the bearings and shaft before installing the shaft. Make sure the return spring ends locate correctly **(see illustration)**.

18 Using a vernier caliper, measure the internal and external diameter of the clutch housing guide, and the external diameter of the input shaft where the guide sits **(see illustration 16.21)**. Compare the measurements to the specifications at the beginning of the Chapter and renew any components that are worn beyond their service limit. Also check all the above components for signs of damage or scoring, and renew if necessary.

16.17a Withdraw the shaft . . .

16.17b . . . and check the oil seal (A) and bearings (B)

16.17c Make sure the spring ends (arrowed) locate correctly

Engine, clutch and transmission 2•31

16.21 Slide the guide onto the shaft

16.22a Slide the drive sprocket onto the shaft and locate it over the guide . . .

16.22b . . . then fit the chain

19 Check the teeth of the primary driven gear on the back of the clutch housing and the corresponding teeth of the primary drive gear on the crankshaft. Renew the clutch housing and/or crankshaft if worn or chipped teeth are discovered.

Clutch installation

20 Remove all traces of old sealant from the crankcase and clutch cover surfaces.
21 If removed, smear the inside and outside of the clutch housing guide with molybdenum disulphide oil (a 50/50 mixture of molybdenum disulphide grease and engine oil), then slide the guide onto the input shaft with the flanged end inwards **(see illustration)**.

22 Slide the oil pump drive sprocket onto the shaft, making sure the pins face out, and slip the chain around the sprocket **(see illustrations)**. Engage the driven sprocket with the chain, making sure the OUT mark faces out, then locate the sprocket on the oil pump **(see illustration)**. Apply a suitable non-permanent thread locking compound to the sprocket bolt and tighten it to the torque

TOOL TIP *Insert a screwdriver or drift through one of the holes in the sprocket and lock it against the crankcase to prevent the sprocket from turning whilst tightening the bolt.*

setting specified at the beginning of the chapter (see **Tool Tip**), not forgetting its washer **(see illustrations)**.
23 To install the clutch housing it is necessary to align the primary drive sub-gear teeth with the main gear using the method employed on removal (see Step 9) **(see illustrations 16.9b and a)**. Slide the clutch housing over the housing guide on the input shaft, making sure that the pins on the oil pump drive sprocket locate in the holes in the rear of the housing – turn the sprocket with your finger while pressing on the housing until the pins are felt to locate and the housing moves in a bit further, then double-check by making sure the sprocket can't turn independently of the housing **(see illustrations)**.

16.22c Fit the driven sprocket into the chain with the OUT mark facing out and locate it onto the flats on the end of the shaft

16.22d Install the bolt with its washer . . .

16.22e . . . and tighten it to the specified torque, locking the shaft as shown

16.23a Locate the pins on the drive sprocket (B) in the holes in the back of the clutch housing (A) . . . .

16.23b . . . aligning them by turning the oil pump sprocket if necessary

2•32 Engine, clutch and transmission

16.24 Fit the thrust washer . . .

16.25a . . . and the clutch centre

16.25b Fit the thrust washer (where applicable) . . .

16.25c . . . and the spring washer, with the OUT mark facing out

16.25d Fit a new clutch nut . . .

16.25e . . . and tighten it to the specified torque

16.25f Stake the nut against the detent in the shaft end

16.26 Anti-judder spring installation details

1. Clutch centre
2. Inner friction plate with larger internal diameter
3. Spring seat
4. Anti-judder spring

24 Slide the thrust washer onto the shaft **(see illustration)**.

25 Slide the clutch centre onto the shaft splines **(see illustration)**. On European F models and 1999/2000 US models install the thrust washer **(see illustration)**. On all models install the spring washer with its OUT mark facing out **(see illustration)**. Install the new clutch nut and, using the method employed on removal to lock the input shaft (see Step 7), tighten the nut to the torque setting specified at the beginning of the Chapter **(see illustrations)**. Stake the collar of the nut into the indent on the end of the shaft **(see illustration)**.

26 On all FS models and US F models from 2001, if removed, fit the anti-judder spring seat into the clutch centre, then fit the spring so that its outer edge is raised (concave face) and facing outwards **(see illustration)**.

27 On European F models and 1999/2000 US models coat each clutch plate with engine oil prior to installation, then build up the plates as follows. Fit a green-coded friction plate, then a plain plate, then alternate purple-coded friction plates and plain plates until all except the outer green-coded friction plate are installed, then fit that with its tabs fitting into the shallow slots in the housing **(see illustrations)**.

28 On all FS models and US F models from 2001 coat each clutch plate with engine oil prior to installation, then build up the plates as follows. Fit the friction plate with the larger internal diameter over the spring and spring seat, then fit a plain plate, then alternate purple-coded friction plates and plain plates until all except the outer green-coded friction plate are installed, then fit that with its tabs fitting into the shallow slots in the housing.

16.27a Fit a green-tabbed friction plate first . . .

16.27b . . . then a plain plate . . .

Engine, clutch and transmission 2•33

16.27c ... then alternate between purple-tabbed friction plates and plain plates until they are all installed ...

16.27d ... then fit the second green-tabbed friction plate, locating its tabs into the shallow slots in the housing (arrow)

29 Lubricate the bearing in the pressure plate. Fit the pull-rod into the bearing **(see illustration)**. Fit the pressure plate onto the clutch, engaging the protrusions on its inner rim in the slots in the clutch centre **(see illustration)**. Install the springs and the bolts, not forgetting their washers, and tighten them evenly in a criss-cross sequence to the specified torque setting **(see illustrations)**. Counter-hold the clutch housing to prevent it turning when tightening the spring bolts.

30 Apply a smear of a suitable sealant (such as Three Bond 1207B) 10 to 15 mm either side of the crankcase joints on the mating surface with the clutch cover. Also apply the sealant to the entire mating surface on the clutch cover. Fit the four dowels into the crankcase if removed. Install the cover, pulling the release lever arm back as you do then moving it back round as you push the cover home on the dowels so that it engages behind the pull-rod end **(see illustration)**. Install all the bolts (except the clutch cable bracket bolt) finger tight, then tighten the numbered (1 to 4, as marked on the cover) bolts first (the ones adjacent to the dowels), evenly in 2 or 3 steps to the specified torque setting, then tighten the remaining bolts evenly in a criss-cross pattern to the specified torque setting.

31 Reconnect the pulse generator coil wiring connector **(see illustration 16.3)**. Engage the clutch cable end in the release lever arm, then locate the hole in the cable bracket onto the pin on the cover and tighten the bracket bolt to the same torque as the cover bolts **(see illustrations 16.2b and a)**.

32 Fill the engine with oil (see Chapter 1). If raised, lower the fuel tank (see Chapter 4). Install the fairing side panel (See Chapter 8). Reconnect the battery negative lead (see Chapter 9).

Clutch cable

33 Fully slacken the lockring on the adjuster at the handlebar end of the cable then screw the adjuster fully in **(see illustration)**. This provides freeplay in the cable and resets the adjuster to the beginning of its span.

16.29a Fit the pull-rod into the bearing

16.29b Fit the pressure plate ...

16.29c ... then install the springs ...

16.29d ... and tighten the bolts as described

16.30 Install the cover as described

16.33 Slacken the lockring and thread the adjuster in

2•34 Engine, clutch and transmission

16.35a Align the slots in the adjuster and lockring with that in the bracket...

16.35b ...then free the cable from the adjuster and lever

34 Remove the fairing right-hand side panel (see Chapter 8). Slacken the adjuster nuts on the section in the cable bracket on the clutch cover on the right-hand side of the engine (see illustration 16.2a). Unscrew the bolt securing the cable bracket to the cover, then free the cable end from the release lever, noting how it fits (see illustration 16.2b). Remove the bracket from the cable.

35 Align the slots in the adjuster and lockring at the handlebar end of the cable with that in the lever bracket, then pull the outer cable end from the socket in the adjuster and release the inner cable from the lever (see illustrations). Remove the cable from the machine, noting its routing through the guide on the top yoke.

> **HAYNES HiNT** *Before removing the cable from the bike, tape the lower end of the new cable to the upper end of the old cable. Slowly pull the lower end of the old cable out, guiding the new cable down into position. Using this method will ensure the cable is routed correctly.*

36 Installation is the reverse of removal. Apply grease to the cable ends. Make sure the cable is correctly routed. Adjust the amount of clutch lever freeplay (see Chapter 1).

17 Oil sump, oil strainer and pressure relief valve – removal, inspection and installation

Note: *The oil sump, strainer and pressure relief valve can be removed with the engine in the frame. If the engine has been removed, ignore the steps which don't apply.*

Removal

1 Drain the engine oil (see Chapter 1).

2 While the oil is draining, remove the exhaust system (see Chapter 4). On F-X and F-Y (1999 and 2000) models, withdraw the coolant reservoir breather hose from its guide.
3 Unscrew the sump bolts, slackening them evenly in a criss-cross sequence to prevent distortion, and remove the sump (see illustration).
4 Pull the strainer out, noting how it locates (see illustration). Remove the rubber seal and discard it as a new one must be used.
5 To remove the pressure relief valve, pull it out of its socket in the crankcase – it is a push-fit (see illustration). Discard the O-ring as a new one must be used.

Inspection

6 Remove all traces of sealant from the sump and crankcase mating surfaces, and clean the inside of the sump with solvent. Blow the sump dry with compressed air if available.
7 Clean the oil strainer in solvent and remove any debris caught in the mesh. If the strainer gauze is damaged, replace the strainer with a new one.
8 Push the relief valve plunger into the valve body and check that it moves smoothly and freely against spring pressure (see illustration). If not, remove the circlip, noting that it is under spring pressure, then remove the spring seat, spring and plunger (see

17.3 Unscrew the bolts (arrowed) and remove the sump

17.4 Remove the strainer, noting how the tab (A) locates in the groove (B)

17.5 Pull the relief valve out of its socket

17.8a Push the plunger into the body and check that it moves smoothly

Engine, clutch and transmission 2•35

17.8b Remove the circlip (arrowed) . . .

17.8c . . . and the spring seat . . .

17.8d . . . then draw out the spring . . .

17.8e . . . and the plunger

17.9 Fit a new O-ring onto the relief valve body

17.10 Lubricate the rubber seal and fit it into the crankcase

illustrations). Clean all components in solvent, then check the plunger and the valve body for evidence of scoring, wear and any other damage. If any is found, replace the relief valve with a new one – individual components are not available. Otherwise, coat the plunger with oil and fit it closed end first back into the valve and recheck the movement. If it is good, install the spring and spring seat and secure them with the circlip.

Installation

9 Fit a new O-ring onto the relief valve and smear it with clean oil, then push the valve into its socket in the sump **(see illustration and 17.5)**.
10 Fit a new rubber seal smeared with clean oil into the strainer orifice in the crankcase **(see illustration)**. Do not fit it onto the strainer as it will distort when the strainer is fitted onto the pump. Fit the strainer, locating the tab in the groove in the crankcase lug on the pump **(see illustration 17.4)**.
11 Clean the mating surfaces of the sump and crankcase with solvent. Apply a suitable sealant (such as Three Bond 1207B) to the sump mating surface **(see illustration)**. Position the sump onto the crankcase and install the bolts finger-tight **(see illustration and 17.3)**. Tighten the bolts evenly and a little at a time in a criss-cross pattern until they are secure.
12 Install the exhaust system, but do not yet fit the fairing side panels (see Chapter 4). On F-X and F-Y (1999 and 2000) models, fit the coolant reservoir breather hose into its guide.
13 Fill the engine with the correct type and quantity of oil as described in Chapter 1. Start the engine and check that there are no leaks around the sump.
14 Install the fairing side panels (see Chapter 8).

18 Oil pump – removal, inspection and installation

Note: *The oil pump can be removed with the engine in the frame. If the engine has been removed, ignore the steps which don't apply.*

Removal

1 Remove the sump and the oil strainer (see Section 17).
2 Remove the clutch, along with the oil pump drive and driven sprockets (see Section 16).
3 Unscrew the three bolts securing the pump to the crankcase, then remove the pump, noting how it fits **(see illustration)**. Remove

17.11a Apply the sealant to the sump mating surface . . .

17.11b . . . then install the sump

18.3 Unscrew the bolts (arrowed) and remove the pump

2•36 Engine, clutch and transmission

18.4a Unscrew the bolt, then remove the dowels (arrowed) . . .

18.4b . . . and remove the cover

18.5a Remove the thrust washer . . .

the dowels from either the crankcase or the pump if they are loose.

Inspection

Note: *When removing the rotors from the oil pump, note the punch mark in each outer rotor and which way it faces as the rotors must be installed the same way round so that mated surfaces continue to run together.*

4 Unscrew the single bolt securing the cover to the pump body, then remove the dowels (if in the pump and not already done) and remove the cover **(see illustrations)**.

5 Remove the thrust washer from the drive shaft **(see illustration)**. Withdraw the shaft from the pump and remove the drive pin, noting how it fits **(see illustration)**. Remove the inner and outer rotors, noting which way round they fit **(see illustrations)**.

6 Clean all the components in solvent.

7 Inspect the pump body and rotors for scoring and wear. If any damage, scoring or uneven or excessive wear is evident, replace the pump with a new one (individual components are not available).

8 Fit the inner and outer rotors into the pump body. Measure the clearance between the inner rotor tip and the outer rotor with a feeler gauge and compare it to the service limit listed in the specifications at the beginning of the Chapter **(see illustration)**. If the clearance measured is greater than the maximum listed, replace the pump with a new one.

9 Measure the clearance between the outer rotor and the pump body with a feeler gauge and compare it to the maximum clearance listed in the specifications at the beginning of the Chapter **(see illustration)**. If the clearance

measured is greater than the maximum listed, replace the pump with a new one.

10 Lay a straight-edge across the rotors and the pump body and, using a feeler gauge, measure the rotor end-float (the gap between the rotors and the straight-edge **(see illustration)**. If the clearance measured is greater than the maximum listed, replace the pump with a new one.

11 Check the pump drive chain and drive and driven sprockets for wear or damage, and renew them as a set if necessary.

12 If the pump is good, make sure all the components are clean, then lubricate them with new engine oil.

13 Fit the outer rotor into the pump body with the punch mark facing the same way as noted on removal (see **Note**) **(see illustration 18.5d)**. Fit the inner rotor into the outer

18.5b . . . then withdraw the shaft and remove the drive pin

18.5c Remove the inner rotor . . .

18.5d . . . and the outer rotor

18.8 Measure the inner rotor tip-to-outer rotor clearance as shown (cover shown removed for clarity)

18.9 Measure the outer rotor-to-body clearance as shown

18.10 Measure the rotor end-float as shown

Engine, clutch and transmission 2•37

18.13a Slide the shaft through the pump as described

18.13b Locate the drive pin ends into the cutouts in the inner rotor (arrows)

18.15 Prime the pump with some clean oil . . .

rotor with the cutouts in the inner rotor facing out **(see illustration 18.5c)**. Slide the drive shaft through the inner rotor and pump body, making sure the end with the driven sprocket bolt hole goes through to the outer side and the tabbed end remains on the inner side **(see illustration)**. Slide the drive pin into its hole in the driveshaft **(see illustration 18.5b)**, and locate it into the cutouts in the inner rotor **(see illustration)**. Slide the thrust washer onto the shaft so it covers the drive pin **(see illustration 18.58a)**. Slide the cover onto the pump, then install the single bolt and tighten it to the torque setting specified at the beginning of the Chapter **(see illustrations 18.4b and a)**. Fit the dowels into the pump **(see illustration 18.4a)**.
14 Rotate the pump shaft by hand and check it turns the rotors smoothly and freely.

Installation
15 Pour some clean engine oil into the pump and rotate the shaft to prime the pump **(see illustration)**.
16 Manoeuvre the pump into position and rotate the drive shaft to align the tab on the end with the slot in the water pump shaft. Install the pump, making sure the dowels locate correctly, and the shafts engage **(see illustration)**. Fit the mounting bolts and tighten them securely **(see illustration)**.
17 Install the pump drive and driven sprockets and chain, and the clutch (see Section 16).
18 Install the oil, strainer and sump (see Section 17).

19 Gearchange mechanism – removal, inspection and installation

Note: *The gearchange mechanism can be removed with the engine in the frame. If the engine has been removed, ignore the steps which don't apply.*

Removal
1 Make sure the transmission is in neutral. Remove the clutch (see Section 16). There is no need to remove the oil pump drive and driven sprockets and chain. Block the holes into the sump with clean rag to prevent anything falling in.
2 Unscrew the gearchange linkage arm pinch bolt and slide the arm off the shaft, noting how the slot in the arm aligns with the punch mark on the shaft **(see illustration 5.17)**.
3 Wrap a single layer of thin insulating tape around the gearchange shaft splines to protect the oil seal lips as the shaft is removed.
4 Note how the gearchange shaft centralising spring ends fit on each side of the locating pin in the casing, and how the pawls on the selector arm locate onto the pins on the end of the selector drum **(see illustration 19.10b)**. Grasp the end of the shaft and withdraw the shaft/arm assembly **(see illustration)**. Retrieve the washer from the crankcase if it didn't come with the shaft.
5 If required, note how the stopper arm

18.16a . . . then install it as described . . .

18.16b . . . and secure it with the bolts

spring ends locate and how the roller on the arm locates in the neutral detent on the selector drum cam, then unscrew the stopper arm bolt and remove the arm, the washer and the spring, noting how they fit **(see illustration)**.

Inspection
6 Check the selector arm for cracks, distortion and wear of its pawls, and check for any corresponding wear on the pins on the selector drum cam. Also check the stopper arm roller and the detents in the selector drum cam for any wear or damage, and make sure the roller turns freely. Replace any components that are worn or damaged with new ones. Remove the selector drum cam by unscrewing the bolt in its centre (see

19.4 Withdraw the shaft/arm assembly, noting how it fits

19.5 Note how the spring ends (A) locate, and how the roller sits in the neutral detent (B), then unscrew the bolt (C) and remove the arm

2•38 Engine, clutch and transmission

19.7a Check the selector arm assembly . . .

19.7b . . . and the stopper arm assembly as described

19.8a Check the oil seal (A) and renew it if required – the retainer plate is secured by the bolt (B)

illustration 20.13). Note the locating pin in the end of the drum and remove it for safekeeping if required. On installation, locate the pin in the cutout in the back of the cam. Apply a suitable non-permanent thread locking compound to the cam bolt and tighten it to the torque setting specified at the beginning of the Chapter.

7 Inspect the shaft centralising spring and the stopper arm return spring for fatigue, wear or damage **(see illustrations)**. If any is found, they must be replaced with new ones. To replace the shaft spring, remove the circlip then slide the washer and the spring off the shaft, noting how the spring ends locate. Fit the new spring, locating the ends on each side of the tab, then fit the washer and secure them with the circlip, making sure it locates in its groove. Also check that the centralising spring locating pin in the crankcase is securely tightened. If it is loose, remove it and apply a non-permanent thread locking compound to its threads, then tighten it securely.

8 Check the gearchange shaft for straightness and damage to the splines. If the shaft is bent you can attempt to straighten it, but if the splines are damaged the shaft must be replaced with a new one. Also check the condition of the shaft oil seal in the left-hand side of the crankcase **(see illustration)**. If it is damaged, deteriorated or shows signs of leakage it must be replaced with a new one. Unscrew the bolt securing the seal retainer plate and remove the plate. Lever out the old seal with a screwdriver **(see illustration)**. With the seal removed, check the condition of the needle bearing, and replace that with a new one as well if necessary **(see illustration)**. Fit the new bearing and press or drive the new seal squarely into place, with its lip facing inward, using a seal driver or suitable socket **(see illustration)**. Fit the retainer plate and tighten its bolt securely.

Installation

9 If removed, fit the bolt through the stopper arm, then fit the washer and the stopper arm return spring onto the bolt **(see illustration 19.7b)**. Apply a suitable non-permanent thread locking compound to the bolt. Install the arm, locating the roller onto the neutral detent on the selector drum and making sure the spring ends are positioned correctly **(see illustration and 19.5)**. Tighten the bolt to the torque setting specified at the beginning of the Chapter. Check that the arm and spring ends are correctly positioned.

10 Check that the shaft centralising spring is properly positioned and slide the washer onto the shaft if removed **(see illustration 19.7a)**. Apply some grease to the lips of the gearchange shaft oil seal in the left-hand side of the crankcase. Slide the shaft into place and push it all the way through the case until the splined end comes out the other side **(see illustration)**. Locate the selector arm pawls onto the pins on the selector drum and the centralising spring ends onto each side of the

19.8b Lever out the old seal with a screwdriver

19.8c Check the needle bearing (arrowed) . . .

19.8d . . . before pressing in a new seal

19.9 Locate the spring ends and stopper arm roller correctly

19.10a Slide the shaft into the engine . . .

Engine, clutch and transmission 2•39

19.10b ... and locate the selector arm as shown

20.4 Unscrew the bolts (arrowed) and remove the retainers

20.6a Withdraw the shaft and displace the forks from the selector drum ...

locating pin in the crankcase **(see illustration)**.
11 Remove the rag that was blocking the sump, then install the clutch (see Section 16).
12 Slide the gearchange linkage arm onto the shaft, aligning its slot with the punch mark on the shaft **(see illustration 5.33c)**. Install the pinch bolt and tighten it securely.

20 Selector drum and forks – removal, inspection and installation

Note: *The selector drum and forks can be removed and installed with the crankcases joined and the engine in the frame. Having said that, it is much easier if the engine is removed so that you don't have to work upside down. If the crankcases are being separated anyway, remove the selector drum and forks afterwards as it is slightly easier.*

Removal

1 The selector drum and forks are located in the lower crankcase half. If required, remove the engine (see Section 5) and, again if required, separate the crankcase halves (see Section 22). Otherwise, just remove the sump, and to improve access the oil strainer (see Section 17).
2 If not already done, remove the gearchange mechanism (see Section 19).

3 Before removing the selector forks, note that each fork carries one or more identification letters **(see illustration 20.7)**. The right-hand fork has 'RL', the centre fork 'C', and the left-hand fork 'RL'. The right-hand and left-hand forks are identical and interchangeable (but keep them in their correct order to keep mated parts together). These letters face the right-hand (clutch) side of the engine. If no letters are visible, mark them yourself using a felt pen. The right and left-hand forks fit into the output shaft and the centre fork fits into the input shaft.
4 Unscrew the bolts securing the selector drum bearing/fork shaft retainers and remove them, noting how they fit **(see illustration)**.
5 If the crankcases have been separated, support the selector forks and withdraw the shaft from the casing, then remove the forks. Withdraw the selector drum from the right-hand side of the engine.
6 If the crankcases have not been separated, withdraw the selector fork shaft from the casing, then pivot each fork out of its track in the selector drum **(see illustration)**. Withdraw the selector drum from the right-hand side of the engine **(see illustration)**. Remove the selector forks, noting how they locate in the groove in their pinion **(see illustration)**.
7 Once removed from the case, slide the forks back onto the shaft to keep them in the correct order **(see illustration)**.

Inspection

8 Inspect the selector forks for any signs of wear or damage, especially around the fork ends where they engage with the groove in the pinion. Check that each fork fits correctly in its pinion groove. Check closely to see if the forks are bent. If the forks are in any way damaged they must be replaced with new ones.
9 Measure the thickness of the fork ends and compare the readings to the specifications **(see illustration)**. Replace the forks with new ones if they are worn beyond their specifications.
10 Check that the forks fit correctly on their shaft. They should move freely with a light fit but no appreciable freeplay. Measure the

20.6b ... then remove the selector drum

20.6c ... and the selector forks, noting how and which way round they fit

20.7 Keeps the forks in the correct order and way round

20.9 Measure the fork end thickness ...

2•40 Engine, clutch and transmission

20.10 . . . the fork bore ID and the fork shaft OD

20.13 Unscrew the bolt (A) and remove the cam (B) to access the bearing (C)

20.15a Position the drum so the neutral contact is against the neutral switch contact (arrow)

internal diameter of the fork bores and the corresponding diameter of the fork shaft **(see illustration)**. Replace the forks and/or shaft with new ones if they are worn beyond their specifications. Check that the fork shaft holes in the casing are neither worn nor damaged.

11 Check the selector fork shaft for trueness by rolling it along a flat surface. A bent rod will cause difficulty in selecting gears and make the gearshift action heavy. Replace the shaft with a new one if it is bent.

12 Inspect the selector drum grooves and selector fork guide pins for signs of wear or damage. If either component shows signs of wear or damage the fork(s) and drum must be replaced with new ones.

13 Check that the selector drum bearing rotates freely and has no sign of freeplay between it and the casing. To fit a new bearing, remove the selector drum cam by unscrewing the bolt in its centre **(see illustration)**. Note the locating pin in the end of the drum and remove it for safekeeping if required. Remove the old bearing and fit a new one (see *Tools and Workshop Tips* in the Reference Section if necessary). Install the selector drum cam, locating the pin in the cutout in the back of the cam. Apply a suitable non-permanent thread locking compound to the cam bolt and tighten it to the torque setting specified at the beginning of the Chapter.

Installation

14 If the crankcases have been separated, slide the selector drum into position in the crankcase. Make sure the drum end locates into its bore in the casing, and position it so that the neutral contact is against the neutral switch **(see illustration 20.15a)**. Lubricate the selector fork shaft with clean engine oil and slide it into the crankcase, through each fork in turn (making sure they are correctly positioned – see Step3), and into its bore, locating the guide pin on the end of each fork into its groove in the drum.

15 If the crankcases have not been separated, install the selector forks, locating each in the groove of its pinion, making sure they are fitted in the correct locations (see Step 3) **(see illustration 20.6c)**. Position they forks so they will not get in the way of the selector drum when sliding it in. Slide the selector drum into position in the crankcase, making sure the drum end locates into its bore in the casing **(see illustration 20.6b)**. Position the drum so that the neutral contact is against the neutral switch **(see illustration)**. Lubricate the selector fork shaft with clean engine oil and slide it into the crankcase **(see illustration)**, through each fork in turn, and into its bore, locating the guide pin on the end of each fork into its groove in the drum **(see illustration)**.

16 Clean the threads of the selector drum retainer bolts, then apply a suitable non-permanent thread locking compound. Install the bolts and tighten them to the torque setting specified at the beginning of the Chapter **(see illustration 20.4)**.

17 Install any remaining components according to your removal procedure.

21 Timing rotor – removal and installation

Note: *The timing rotor can be removed with the engine in the frame. If the engine has been removed, ignore the steps which don't apply.*

Removal

1 Remove the clutch cover (see Section 16, Steps 1 to 4).

2 To remove the timing rotor bolt, the crankshaft must be prevented from turning. If the engine is in the frame, engage 6th gear and have an assistant hold the rear brake on hard with the rear tyre in firm contact with the ground. If the engine has been removed, remove the alternator cover (see Chapter 9) and use a rotor holding strap to counter-hold the alternator rotor while slackening the timing rotor bolt **(see illustration)**. Alternatively counter-hold the alternator rotor bolt using a spanner or socket – the alternator bolt is tighter than the timing rotor bolt so there is no danger of the wrong one coming undone.

3 Remove the bolt and its washer, then slide the timing rotor off the end of the crankshaft, noting how it locates over a wide spline so

20.15b Slide the shaft into the crankcase . . .

20.15c . . . and through each fork in turn, locating the guide pins in the drum grooves

21.2 Timing rotor bolt (arrowed)

Engine, clutch and transmission 2•41

21.3 Unscrew the bolt and remove the washer

21.4 Align the wide spline on the crankshaft with that in the rotor (arrow)

21.5 Tighten the rotor bolt to the specified torque

that it can only be fitted in one position **(see illustration)**.

Installation

4 Slide the timing rotor onto the end of the crankshaft, aligning the wide splines **(see illustration)**.
5 Apply some engine oil to the threads and the underside of the head on the bolt. Install the bolt with its washer **(see illustration 21.3)** and tighten it to the torque setting specified at the beginning of the Chapter using the same method as on removal to prevent the crankshaft turning **(see illustration)**.
6 Install the clutch cover (see Section 16, Steps 30 to 32).

22 Crankcase halves – separation and reassembly

Note: *To separate the crankcase halves, the engine must be removed from the frame.*

Separation

1 To access the pistons, connecting rods, crankshaft, bearings and transmission shafts, the crankcase must be split into two parts. The selector drum and forks can be removed and installed with the crankcases joined.
2 To enable the crankcases to be separated, the engine must be removed from the frame (see Section 5). Before the crankcases can be separated the following components must be removed:

Valve cover (Section 8).

22.3 Unscrew the bolts (arrowed) and remove the plate

Camshafts (Section 10).
Cylinder head (Section 12) – see Note.
Alternator/starter clutch (Chapter 9).
Clutch, oil pump drive chain and sprockets (Section 16).
Cam chain and blades (Section 11) – see Note.
Water pump (Chapter 3).
Gearchange mechanism (Section 19) – see Note.
Oil cooler (Section 7).
Starter motor (Chapter 9) – see Note.
Oil sump, strainer and pressure relief valve (Section 17).
Oil pump if required (Section 18).
Speed sensor (Chapter 9).

Note: *If the crankcases are being separated to inspect the crankshaft without removing it, or to remove the crankshaft without removing the connecting rods and pistons, or to inspect or remove the transmission shafts, the cylinder head can remain in situ. However, if removal of the connecting rod assemblies is intended, full disassembly of the top-end is necessary. The cam chain can remain loose on the crankshaft after the camshafts have been removed, and can be taken off after the crankshaft has been removed – this saves having to remove the timing rotor. The front guide blade must be removed, and the tensioner blade must be removed if the cylinder head is removed, but can otherwise remain in situ. The gearchange mechanism can remain in situ unless the selector drum and forks are being removed.*

3 Unscrew the bolts securing the transmission input shaft bearing retainer plate and remove the plate, noting how it fits **(see illustration)**.
4 Unscrew the seven 6 mm and five 8 mm upper crankcase bolts **(see illustration)**. Unscrew the bolts evenly, a little at a time and in a criss-cross

22.4 Upper crankcase bolts

A 6 mm bolts   B 8 mm bolts
denotes bolts with sealing washer

2•42 Engine, clutch and transmission

22.6 Lower crankcase bolts
A 6 mm bolts (F-X, F-Y models), 7 mm bolts (all later models)
B 6 mm bolts   C 10 mm bolt   D 8 mm bolts

sequence until they are finger-tight, then remove them. Note the sealing washers fitted to two of the bolts. **Note:** *As each bolt is removed, store it in its relative position in a cardboard template of the crankcase halves. This will ensure all bolts are installed in the correct location on reassembly.*

5 Turn the engine upside down.

6 On F-X and F-Y (1999 and 2000) models, unscrew the eight 6 mm and one 10 mm lower crankcase bolts **(see illustration)**. Now unscrew the ten 8 mm bolts evenly, a little at a time and in a criss-cross sequence, starting from the outside and working to the centre, until they are finger-tight, then remove them. **Note:** *As each bolt is removed, store it in its relative position in a cardboard template of the crankcase halves. This will ensure all bolts are installed in the correct location on reassembly.*

7 On F-1/FS-1 models onwards (2001-on), unscrew the two 6 mm, six 7 mm and one 10 mm lower crankcase bolts **(see illustration 22.6)**. Now unscrew the ten 8 mm bolts evenly, a little at a time and in a criss-cross sequence, starting from the outside and working to the centre, until they are finger-tight, then remove them. **Note:** *As each bolt is removed, store it in its relative position in a cardboard template of the crankcase halves. This will ensure all bolts are installed in the correct location on reassembly.*

8 Carefully lift the lower crankcase half off the upper half, using a soft-faced hammer to tap around the joint to initially separate the halves if necessary **(see illustration)**. **Note:** *If the halves do not separate easily, make sure all fasteners have been removed. Do not try and separate the halves by levering against the crankcase mating surfaces as they are easily scored and will leak oil in the future if damaged.* The lower crankcase half will come away with the gearchange mechanism and the selector drum and forks (if not already removed), leaving the crankshaft and transmission shafts in the upper crankcase half.

9 Remove the three locating dowels from the crankcase if they are loose (they could be in either crankcase half), and the two oil orifices, noting how they fit **(see illustration)**.

10 Refer to Sections 23 to 30 for the removal and installation of the components housed within the crankcases.

Reassembly

11 Remove all traces of sealant from the crankcase mating surfaces.

12 Ensure that all components and their bearings are in place in the upper and lower crankcase halves. If the transmission shafts have not been removed, check the condition of the output shaft oil seal on the left-hand end of the shaft and replace it if it is damaged or deteriorated.

13 Generously lubricate the crankshaft and transmission shafts, particularly around the bearings, with clean engine oil, then use a rag

22.8 Carefully separate the crankcase halves

22.9 Remove the dowels (A) if they are loose, and the oil orifices (B)

Engine, clutch and transmission 2•43

soaked in high flash-point solvent to wipe over the mating surfaces of both crankcase halves to remove all traces of oil.

14 If removed, install the three locating dowels and the two oil orifices in the upper crankcase half (see illustration 22.9). Make sure the orifices are installed the correct way round (see illustration).

15 Apply a small amount of suitable sealant to the outer mating surface of the lower crankcase half as shown (see illustration).

Caution: Do not apply an excessive amount of sealant as it will ooze out when the case halves are assembled and may obstruct oil passages. Do not apply the sealant on or too close to any of the bearing inserts or surfaces.

16 Check again that all components are in position, particularly that the bearing shells are still correctly located in the lower crankcase half. Carefully fit the lower crankcase half down onto the upper crankcase half, making sure the dowels all locate correctly into the lower crankcase half (see illustration 22.8). If the selector drum and forks are installed, make sure each selector fork locates correctly in the groove in its pinion.

17 Check that the lower crankcase half is correctly seated.

Caution: The crankcase halves should fit together without being forced. If the casings are not correctly seated, remove the lower crankcase half and investigate the problem. Do not attempt to pull them together using the crankcase bolts as the casing will crack and be ruined.

18 Clean the threads of the ten 8 mm lower crankcase bolts. Apply some oil to the threads and the underside of the heads of the bolts and insert them in their original locations (see illustration and 22.6). Secure all bolts finger-tight at first, then tighten them evenly and a little at a time in a criss-cross sequence starting from the centre and working outwards to the torque setting specified at the beginning of the Chapter.

19 On F-X and F-Y (1999 and 2000) models, clean the threads of the eight 6 mm and one 10 mm lower crankcase bolts and insert them in their original locations (see illustration 22.6). Secure all bolts finger-tight at first, then tighten them evenly and a little at a time in a criss-cross sequence, starting with the 10 mm bolt, to the torque settings specified at the beginning of the Chapter.

20 On F-1/FS-1 models onward (2001-on), clean the threads of the two 6 mm, six 7 mm and one 10 mm lower crankcase bolts and insert them in their original locations (see illustration 22.6). Secure all bolts finger-tight at first, then tighten them evenly and a little at a time in a criss-cross sequence, starting with the 10 mm bolt, to the torque settings specified at the beginning of the Chapter.

21 Turn the engine over. Clean the threads of the seven 6 mm and five 8 mm upper crankcase bolts and insert them in their original locations not forgetting the sealing washers fitted to the two bolts that locate in the holes marked by a triangle (see illustration 22.4). Use new washers if the old ones are damaged or deformed. Secure all bolts finger-tight at first, then tighten them evenly a little at a time in a criss-cross sequence to the torque settings specified at the beginning of the Chapter.

22 With all crankcase fasteners tightened, check that the crankshaft and transmission shafts rotate smoothly and easily. Check that the transmission shafts rotate freely and independently in neutral, then, if it is installed, rotate the selector drum by hand and select each gear in turn whilst rotating the input shaft. Check that all gears can be selected and that the shafts rotate freely in every gear. If there are any signs of undue stiffness, tight or rough spots, or of any other problem, the fault must be rectified before proceeding further.

23 Apply a suitable non-permanent thread locking compound to the transmission input shaft bearing retainer plate bolts, then install the plate with the OUTSIDE mark facing out and tighten the bolts to the specified torque setting (see illustration 22.3).

24 Install all other removed assemblies in a reverse of the sequence given in Step 2.

22.14 Install the oil orifices with the flats locating against the corresponding flats in their bores

23 Crankcase halves and cylinder bores – inspection and servicing

Crankcase halves

1 After the crankcases have been separated, remove the crankshaft, connecting rods and pistons, transmission shafts, selector drum and forks (if not already done), neutral switch and oil pressure switch, referring to the relevant Sections of this Chapter, and to Chapter 9 for the oil pressure and neutral switches. If there are any other components or assemblies that have not been removed as part of your strip-down procedure, for example the starter motor or the coolant union, remove these as well, referring to the relevant Chapter.

2 Clean the crankcases thoroughly with new solvent and dry them with compressed air. Blow out all oil passages with compressed air.

22.15 Apply sealant to the shaded areas of the lower crankcase half

22.18 Make sure the longer bolts are fitted in the correct holes

2•44 Engine, clutch and transmission

3 Remove all traces of old gasket sealant from the mating surfaces. Clean up minor damage to the surfaces with a fine sharpening stone or grindstone.
Caution: *Be very careful not to nick or gouge the crankcase mating surfaces or oil leaks will result. Check both crankcase halves very carefully for cracks and other damage.*
4 Small cracks or holes in aluminium castings can be repaired with an epoxy resin adhesive as a temporary measure. Permanent repairs can only be done by argon-arc welding, and only a specialist in this process is in a position to advise on the economy or practical aspect of such a repair. If any damage is found that can't be repaired, replace the crankcase halves as a set.
5 Damaged threads can be economically reclaimed using a diamond section wire insert, for example of the Heli-Coil type (though there are other makes), which is easily fitted after drilling and re-tapping the affected thread.
6 Sheared studs or screws can usually be removed with extractors, which consist of a tapered, left-hand thread screw of very hard steel. These are inserted into a pre-drilled hole in the stud, and usually succeed in dislodging the most stubborn stud or screw. If a stud has sheared above its bore line, it can be removed using a conventional stud extractor which avoids the need for drilling.

> **HAYNES HINT** *Refer to Tools and Workshop Tips for details of installing a thread insert and using screw extractors.*

7 Install all components and assemblies, referring to the relevant Sections of this and the other Chapters, before reassembling the crankcase halves.

Cylinder bores

Note: *Do not attempt to separate the cylinder liners from the cylinder block.*
8 Check the cylinder walls carefully for scratches and score marks.
9 Using a precision straight-edge and a feeler gauge set to the warpage limit listed in the specifications at the beginning of the Chapter, check the block gasket mating surface for warpage. Refer to *Tools and Workshop Tips* in the Reference section for details of how to use the straight-edge. If warpage is excessive the crankcases must be replaced with new ones.
10 Using telescoping gauges and a micrometer (see *Tools and Workshop Tips*), check the dimensions of each cylinder to assess the amount of wear, taper and ovality. Measure near the top (but below the level of the top piston ring at TDC), centre and bottom (but above the level of the oil ring at BDC) of the bore, both parallel to and across the crankshaft axis **(see illustration)**. Compare the results to the specifications at the beginning of the Chapter. If the cylinders are worn, oval or tapered beyond the service limit they can be rebored, an oversize (+ 0.25) set of pistons and rings and available. Note that the person carrying out the rebore must be aware of the piston-to-bore clearance for the oversize piston (see Specifications).
11 If the precision measuring tools are not available, take the crankcases to a Honda dealer or specialist motorcycle repair shop for assessment and advice.
12 If the cylinder bores are in good condition and the piston-to-bore clearance is within specifications (see Section 26), the cylinders should be honed (de-glazed). To perform this operation you will need the proper size flexible hone with fine stones, or a bottle-brush type hone, plenty of light oil or honing oil, some clean rags and an electric drill motor.
13 Hold the block sideways (so that the bores are horizontal rather than vertical) in a vice with soft jaws or cushioned with wooden blocks. Mount the hone in the drill motor, compress the stones and insert the hone into the cylinder. Thoroughly lubricate the cylinder, then turn on the drill and move the hone up and down in the cylinder at a pace which produces a fine cross-hatch pattern on the cylinder wall with the lines intersecting at an angle of approximately 60°. Be sure to use plenty of lubricant and do not take off any more material than is necessary to produce the desired effect. Do not withdraw the hone from the cylinder while it is still turning. Switch off the drill and continue to move it up and down in the cylinder until it has stopped turning, then compress the stones and withdraw the hone. Wipe the oil from the cylinder and repeat the procedure on the other cylinders. Remember, do not take too much material from the cylinder wall.
14 Wash the bores thoroughly with warm soapy water to remove all traces of the abrasive grit produced during the honing operation. Be sure to run a brush through the stud holes and flush them with running water. After rinsing, dry the cylinders thoroughly and apply a thin coat of light, rust-preventative oil to all machined surfaces.
15 If you do not have the equipment or desire to perform the honing operation, take the crankcase to a Honda dealer or specialist motorcycle repair shop.

24 Main and connecting rod bearings – general information

1 Even though main and connecting rod bearings are generally replaced with new ones during the engine overhaul, the old bearings should be retained for close examination as they may reveal valuable information about the condition of the engine.
2 Bearing failure can occur for many reasons: a of lack of lubrication, the presence of dirt or other foreign particles, overloading the engine, and corrosion. Regardless of the cause of bearing failure, it must be corrected before the engine is reassembled to prevent it from happening again.
3 When examining the main or connecting rod bearings, remove them from their journal and lay them out on a clean surface in the same general position as their location in the crankcase or on the crankshaft. This will enable you to match any noted bearing problems with the corresponding journal.
4 Dirt and other foreign particles get into the engine in a variety of ways. It may be left in the engine during assembly or it may pass through filters or breathers. It may get into the oil and from there into the bearings. Metal chips from machining operations and normal engine wear are often present. Abrasives are sometimes left in engine components after reconditioning operations, especially when parts are not thoroughly cleaned using the proper methods. Whatever the source, these foreign objects often end up imbedded in the soft bearing material and are easily recognised. Large particles will not imbed in the bearing and will score or gouge the bearing and journal. The best prevention for this is to clean all parts thoroughly and keep everything spotlessly clean during engine reassembly. Frequent and regular oil and filter changes are also recommended.
5 Lack of lubrication or lubrication breakdown has a number of interrelated causes. Excessive heat (which thins the oil), overloading (which squeezes the oil from the

23.10 Measure the cylinder bore in the directions shown with a telescoping gauge, then measure the gauge with a micrometer

Engine, clutch and transmission 2•45

25.2 Measure the connecting rod side clearance using a feeler gauge

25.5 Withdraw the piston and connecting rod assembly from the top of the cylinder

bearing face) and oil leakage or throw off (from excessive bearing clearances, worn oil pump or high engine speeds) all contribute to lubrication breakdown. Blocked oil passages will also starve a bearing and destroy it. When lack of lubrication is the cause of bearing failure, the bearing material is wiped or extruded from the steel backing of the bearing. Temperatures may increase to the point where the steel backing and the journal turn blue from overheating.
6 Riding habits can have a definite effect on bearing life. Full throttle low speed operation, or labouring the engine, puts very high loads on bearings, which tend to squeeze out the oil film. These loads cause the bearings to flex, which produces fine cracks in the bearing face (fatigue failure). Eventually the bearing material will loosen in pieces and tear away from the steel backing. Short trip riding leads to corrosion of bearings, as insufficient engine heat is produced to drive off the condensed water and corrosive gases produced. These products collect in the engine oil, forming acid and sludge. As the oil is carried to the engine bearings, the acid attacks and corrodes the bearing material.
7 Incorrect bearing installation during engine assembly will lead to bearing failure as well. Tight fitting bearings which leave insufficient bearing oil clearances result in oil starvation. Dirt or foreign particles trapped behind a bearing insert result in high spots on the bearing which lead to failure.
8 To avoid bearing problems, clean all parts thoroughly before reassembly, double check all bearing clearance measurements and lubricate the new bearings with clean engine oil during installation.

> **HAYNES HiNT** *Refer to Tools and Workshop Tips for bearing fault finding.*

25 Connecting rods and bearings – removal, inspection and installation

Note: *To remove the connecting rods the engine must be removed from the frame and the crankcases separated.*

Removal

1 Remove the engine from the frame (see Section 5) and separate the crankcase halves (see Section 22).
2 Before removing the rods from the crankshaft, measure the side clearance with a feeler gauge as shown **(see illustration)**. If the clearance is greater than the service limit listed in this Chapter's Specifications, replace the rods with new ones. If the clearance is still excessive, replace the crankshaft with a new one.
3 Using paint or a felt marker pen, mark the relevant cylinder identity on each connecting rod and cap. Mark across the cap-to-connecting rod join and note which side of the rod faces the front of the engine to ensure that the cap and rod are fitted the correct way around on reassembly. Note that the number already across the rod and cap indicates rod size grade **(see illustration 25.21b)**. The piston crown is marked IN and this mark faces the intake side of the cylinder, and the oil hole in the big-end of the connecting rod should face the same way, to the back of the engine (intake side) **(see illustration 26.2)**.
4 Remove the crankshaft (see Section 28).
5 Raise the crankcase onto wooden blocks to provide room for the connecting rod/piston assemblies to be removed from the top of the bore. Alternatively turn the crankcase on its side, but remove the transmission shafts first otherwise they will fall out (see Section 29). Push each piston/connecting rod assembly up and remove it from the top of the bore making sure the connecting rod does not mark the cylinder walls **(see illustration)**. Keep the rod, cap, nuts/bolts, and (if they are to be reused) the bearing shells together in their correct positions to ensure correct installation.

> **HAYNES HiNT** *To ease removal of the pistons, carefully remove any ridge of carbon built up on the top of each cylinder bore using a scraper. If there is a pronounced wear ridge, remove it using a ridge reamer.*

Caution: *Do not try to remove the piston/connecting rod from the bottom of the cylinder bore. The piston will not pass the crankcase main bearing webs. If the piston is pulled right to the bottom of the bore the oil control ring will expand and lock the piston in position. If this happens it is likely the ring will be broken.*
6 Immediately install the relevant bearing shells (if removed), bearing cap, and nuts on each piston/connecting rod assembly so that they are all kept together as a matched set.
7 Remove the pistons from the connecting rods if required (see Section 26).

Inspection

8 Check the connecting rods for cracks and other obvious damage.
9 Apply clean engine oil to the piston pin, insert it into the connecting rod small-end and check for any freeplay between the two **(see illustration)**. Measure the pin external

25.9a Slip the piston pin into the rod's small-end and rock it back and forth to check for looseness

2•46 Engine, clutch and transmission

25.9b Measure the external diameter of the pin . . .

25.9c . . . and the internal diameter of the connecting rod small-end

diameter and the small-end bore diameter, then calculate the difference to obtain the small-end-to-piston pin clearance **(see illustrations)**. Compare the result to the specifications at the beginning of the Chapter. If the clearance is greater than specified, renew the components that are worn beyond their specified limits.

10 Refer to Section 24 and examine the connecting rod bearing shells. If they are scored, badly scuffed, corroded, or appear to have seized, new shells must be installed. Always replace the shells in the connecting rods as a set. If they are badly damaged, check the corresponding crankpin. Evidence of extreme heat, such as discoloration, indicates that lubrication failure has occurred. Be sure to thoroughly check the oil pump and pressure regulator as well as all oil holes and passages before reassembling the engine.

11 Have the rods checked for twist and bend by a Honda dealer if you are in doubt about their straightness.

Oil clearance check

12 Whether new bearing shells are being fitted or the original ones are being re-used, the connecting rod bearing oil clearance should be checked prior to reassembly. Check the clearance on one rod at a time.

13 Clean the backs of the bearing shells and the bearing housings in both the connecting rod and cap.

14 Press the bearing shells into their housings, making sure the tab on each shell engages the notch in the connecting rod/cap **(see illustration)**. Make sure the bearings are fitted in the correct location and take care not to touch any shell's bearing surface with your fingers. Lay the crankshaft in the upper crankcase half, making sure it is the correct way round and that all the main bearing shells are installed (see Section 28).

15 Cut a length of the appropriate size Plastigauge (it should be slightly shorter than the width of the crankpin). Place a strand of Plastigauge on the (cleaned) crankpin journal, making sure it is not over the oil hole. Pull the connecting rod onto the crankpin and fit the cap onto the rod **(see illustrations 28.27 and 28.2b)**. Make sure the cap is fitted the correct way around so the previously made markings align, and that the rod is facing the right way (see Step 3). Apply some clean oil to the threads and under the heads of the connecting rod nuts. Install the nuts and tighten them evenly and alternately, in two or three stages, to the torque setting specified at the beginning of the Chapter, all the time ensuring that the connecting rod does not rotate on the crankshaft **(see illustrations 28.2b and 28.28)**. It is highly advisable to have an assistant to hold the crankshaft down in the crankcase while tightening the bolts as it could jump out.

16 Slacken the nuts and remove the connecting rod cap, again taking great care not to rotate the rod or crankshaft. Compare the width of the crushed Plastigauge on the crankpin to the scale printed on the Plastigauge envelope to obtain the connecting rod bearing oil clearance. Compare the reading to the specifications at the beginning of the Chapter.

17 On completion carefully scrape away all traces of the Plastigauge material from the crankpin and bearing shells using a fingernail or other object which is unlikely to score the shells.

18 If the clearance is within the range listed in this Chapter's Specifications and the bearings are in perfect condition, they can be reused. If the clearance is beyond the service limit, replace the bearing shells with new ones (see Steps 21 and 22). Check the oil clearance once again (the new shells may be thick enough to bring bearing clearance within the specified range). Always replace all of the shells at the same time.

19 If the clearance is still greater than the service limit listed in this Chapter's Specifications, the crankpin is worn and the crankshaft should be replaced with a new one.

20 Repeat the oil clearance check for the other connecting rods.

Bearing shell selection

21 Replacement bearing shells for the big-end bearings are supplied on a selected fit basis. Code letters and numbers stamped on the crankshaft and connecting rod are used to identify the correct replacement bearings. The crankpin journal size letters are stamped on the outside of the left-hand crankshaft web, and will be either an A or a B **(see illustration)**. The first letter, after the L, is for the No. 1 cylinder connecting rod (left-hand journal), and the letters correspond consecutively for each cylinder. The connecting rod size code number is marked across the flat face of the

25.14 Fit each shell into its housing making sure each tab locates in its notch (arrow)

25.21a Crankpin journal size letters (A), main bearing journal size numbers (B)

Engine, clutch and transmission 2•47

25.21b Connecting rod size number

25.22 The colour code is on the edge of the shell (arrow)

connecting rod and cap and will be either a 1 or a 2 **(see illustration)**.
22 A range of bearing shells is available. To select the correct bearing shell colour code for a particular big-end, use the table below and cross-refer the crankpin journal size letter (stamped on the web) with the connecting rod size number (stamped on the rod). For example, if the crankpin size is B, and the connecting rod size is 1, then the bearing required is green. The colour is marked on the side of the shell **(see illustration)**.

	Connecting rod code	
Crankpin journal code	**1 (34.000 to 34.008 mm)**	**2 (34.008 to 34.016 mm)**
A (31.492 to 31.500 mm)	C – Yellow	B – Green
B (31.484 to 31.492 mm)	B – Green	A – Brown

Installation
23 Fit the pistons onto the connecting rods (see Section 26).
24 Clean the backs of the bearing shells and the bearing housings in both cap and rod. If new shells are being fitted, ensure that all traces of the protective grease are cleaned off using paraffin (kerosene). Wipe the shells, cap and rod dry with a clean lint free cloth. Install the bearing shells in the connecting rods and caps, making sure the tab on each shell engages the notch in the connecting rod/cap **(see illustration 25.14)**. Lubricate the shells with molybdenum disulphide oil (a 50/50 mixture of molybdenum disulphide grease and clean engine oil).
25 Lubricate the pistons, rings and cylinder bore with clean engine oil **(see illustration)**. Insert the piston/connecting rod assembly into the top of its bore, taking care not to allow the connecting rod to mark the bore **(see illustration)**. Make sure the 'IN' mark on the piston crown and the connecting rod oil hole are on the intake side of the bore (see Step 3), then carefully compress and feed each piston ring into the bore until the piston crown is flush with the top of the bore **(see illustration)**. If available, a piston ring compressor makes installation a lot easier **(see illustrations)**.
26 Install the crankshaft (see Section 28).
27 Reassemble the crankcase halves (see Section 22).

26 Pistons – removal, inspection and installation

Note: *To remove the pistons the engine must be removed from the frame and the crankcase halves separated.*

Removal
1 Remove the connecting rods (see Section 25).

25.25a Lubricate the bore with clean engine oil

25.25b Lower the connecting rod and piston into the bore . . .

25.25c . . . and carefully feed each ring in

25.25d Fit the compressor over the piston and rings . . .

25.25e . . . and compress the rings by tightening the bands on the compressor using an Allen key

25.25f Position the assembly over the bore, then tap the top of the piston with a soft tool so that it enters

26.2 The IN mark (A) and the oil hole (B) must face the same way

26.3a Prise out the circlip ...

26.3b ... then push out the pin and remove the piston

2 Before removing the piston from the connecting rod, use a sharp scriber or felt marker pen to write the cylinder identity on the crown of each piston (or on the inside of the skirt if the piston is dirty and going to be cleaned). Each piston crown should already be marked IN (though the mark is likely to be invisible until the piston is cleaned) and this mark faces the intake side of the cylinder, the same way as the oil hole in the big-end of the connecting rod **(see illustration)**.

3 Carefully prise out the circlip on one side of the piston using needle-nose pliers or a small flat-bladed screwdriver inserted into the notch **(see illustration)**. Push the piston pin out from the other side to free the piston from the connecting rod **(see illustration)**. Remove the other circlip and discard them as new ones must be used. When the piston has been removed, install its pin back into its bore so that related parts do not get mixed up.

> **HAYNES HiNT**
> *If a piston pin is a tight fit in the piston bosses, soak a rag in boiling water then wring it out and wrap it around the piston – this will expand the alloy piston sufficiently to release its grip on the pin. If the piston pin is particularly stubborn, extract it using a drawbolt tool, but be careful to protect the piston's working surfaces.*

26.10 Measure the piston ring-to-groove clearance with a feeler gauge

26.11 Measure the piston diameter with a micrometer at the specified distance from the bottom of the skirt

Inspection

4 Using your thumbs or a piston ring removal and installation tool, carefully remove the rings from the pistons **(see illustrations 26.12, 11, and 9c, b and a)**. Do not nick or gouge the pistons in the process. Carefully note which way up each ring fits and in which groove as they must be installed in their original positions if being re-used. The upper surface of the top ring is marked with the letter R at one end, and the second (middle) ring is marked RN. The top and middle rings can also be identified by the fact that the top ring is narrower in width than the second (middle) ring.

5 Scrape all traces of carbon from the tops of the pistons. A hand-held wire brush or a piece of fine emery cloth can be used once most of the deposits have been scraped away. Do not, under any circumstances, use a wire brush mounted in a drill motor to remove deposits from the pistons; the piston material is soft and will be eroded away by the wire brush.

6 Use a piston ring groove cleaning tool to remove any carbon deposits from the ring grooves. If a tool is not available, a piece broken off an old ring will do the job. Be very careful to remove only the carbon deposits. Do not remove any metal and do not nick or gouge the sides of the ring grooves.

7 Once the deposits have been removed, clean the pistons with solvent and dry them thoroughly. If the identification previously marked on the piston is cleaned off, be sure to re-mark it with the correct identity. Make sure the oil return holes below the oil ring groove are clear.

8 Carefully inspect each piston for cracks around the skirt, at the pin bosses and at the ring lands. Normal piston wear appears as even, vertical wear on the thrust surfaces of the piston and slight looseness of the top ring in its groove. If the skirt is scored or scuffed, the engine may have been suffering from overheating and/or abnormal combustion, which caused excessively high operating temperatures. The oil pump should be checked thoroughly. Also check that the circlip grooves are not damaged.

9 A hole in the piston crown, an extreme to be sure, is an indication that abnormal combustion (pre-ignition) was occurring. Burned areas at the edge of the piston crown are usually evidence of spark knock (detonation). If any of the above problems exist, the causes must be corrected or the damage will occur again.

10 Measure the piston ring-to-groove clearance by laying each piston ring in its groove and slipping a feeler gauge in beside it **(see illustration)**. Make sure you have the correct ring for the groove (see Step 4). Check the clearance at three or four locations around the groove. If the clearance is greater than specified, renew both the piston and rings as a set. If new rings are being used, measure the clearance using the new rings. If the clearance is greater than that specified, the piston is worn and must be replaced with a new one.

11 Check the piston-to-bore clearance by measuring the bore (see Section 23) and the piston diameter. Make sure each piston is matched to its correct cylinder. Measure the piston 15 mm up from the bottom of the skirt and at 90° to the piston pin axis **(see illustration)**. Subtract the piston diameter from the bore diameter to obtain the clearance. If it is greater than the specified figure, the piston must be replaced with a new one (assuming the bore itself is within limits).

12 Apply clean engine oil to the piston pin, insert it into the piston and check for any

Engine, clutch and transmission 2•49

26.12a Slip the pin (A) into the piston (B) and try to rock it back and forth. If it's loose, replace the piston and pin

26.12b Measure the internal diameter of the bore in the piston

26.16a Fit a new circlip into one side . . .

26.16b . . . then fit the connecting rod and slide in the pin

freeplay between the two **(see illustration)**. Measure the pin external diameter **(see illustration 25.9b)**, and the pin bore in the piston **(see illustration)**. Calculate the difference to obtain the piston pin-to-piston pin bore clearance. Compare the result to the specifications at the beginning of the Chapter. If the clearance is greater than specified, replace the components that are worn beyond their specified limits. If not already done (see Section 25), repeat the measurements between the pin and the connecting rod small-end **(see illustration 25.9c)**.

Installation

13 Inspect and install the piston rings (see Section 27).

14 Lubricate the piston pin, the piston pin bore and the connecting rod small-end bore with molybdenum disulphide oil (a 50/50 mixture of molybdenum disulphide grease and clean engine oil).
15 When installing the pistons onto the connecting rods, make sure the IN mark on the piston crown faces the same way as the oil hole in the big-end of the connecting rod **(see illustration 26.2)**.
16 Install a *new* circlip in one side of the piston (do not re-use old circlips) **(see illustration)**. Line up the piston on its correct connecting rod, and insert the piston pin from the other side **(see illustration)**. Secure the pin with the other *new* circlip. When installing the circlips, compress them only just enough to fit them in the piston, and make sure they

are properly seated in their grooves with the open end away from the removal notch.
17 Install the connecting rods (see Section 25) and reassemble the crankcase halves (see Section 22).

27 Piston rings – inspection and installation

1 It is good practice to renew the piston rings when an engine is being overhauled. Before installing the new rings, check the end gaps with the rings installed in the bore, as follows.
2 Lay out the pistons and the new ring sets so the rings will be matched with the same piston and bore during the end gap measurement procedure and engine assembly.
3 To measure the installed ring end gap, insert the top ring into the top of the bore and square it up with the bore walls by pushing it in with the top of the piston. The ring should be about 20 mm below the top edge of the bore. Slip a feeler gauge between the ends of the ring and compare the measurement to the specifications at the beginning of the Chapter **(see illustration)**.
4 If the gap is larger than specified, double check to make sure that you have the correct rings before proceeding; excess end gap is not critical unless it exceeds the service limit. If the service limit is exceed with new rings, check the bore for wear (see Section 23).
5 Repeat the procedure for each ring that will be installed in the bore. Remember to keep the rings, pistons and bores matched up.
6 Once the ring end gaps have been checked/corrected, the rings can be installed on the pistons **(see illustration 27.11)**.
7 Install the oil control ring (lowest on the piston) first. It is composed of three separate components, namely the expander and the upper and lower side rails. Slip the expander into the groove, making sure the ends don't overlap, then install the lower side rail **(see illustrations)**. Do not use a piston ring installation tool on the side rails as they may be damaged. Instead, place one end of the side rail into the groove between the expander

27.3 Measuring piston ring installed end gap

27.7a Install the oil ring expander in its groove . . .

27.7b . . . then fit the lower side rail . . .

2•50 Engine, clutch and transmission

27.7c ... and the upper side rail on each side of it.

27.9a Note the identification letter on the top end of each ring

27.9b Install the middle ring ...

27.10 ... and the top ring as described

and the ring land. Hold it firmly in place and slide a finger around the piston while pushing the rail into the groove. Next, install the upper side rail in the same manner **(see illustration)**. Check that the ends of the expander have not overlapped.

8 After the three oil ring components have been installed, check to make sure that both the upper and lower side rails can be turned smoothly in the ring groove.

9 The upper surface of the top ring is marked with the letter R at one end, and the second (middle) ring is marked RN **(see illustration)**. The top and middle rings can also be identified by the fact that the top ring is narrower in width than the second (middle) ring. Install the second (middle) ring next. Make sure that the identification letter near the end gap is facing up. Fit the ring into the middle groove in the piston **(see illustration)**. Do not expand the ring any more than is necessary to slide it into place. To avoid breaking the ring, use a piston ring installation tool.

10 Finally, install the top ring in the same manner into the top groove in the piston **(see illustration)**. Make sure the identification letter near the end gap is facing up.

11 Once the rings are correctly installed, check they move freely without snagging and stagger their end gaps as shown **(see illustration)**.

28 Crankshaft and main bearings – removal, inspection and installation

Note: *To remove the crankshaft the engine must be removed from the frame and the crankcase halves separated.*

Removal

1 Remove the engine from the frame (see Section 5) and separate the crankcase halves (see Section 22).

2 Using paint or a felt marker pen, mark the relevant cylinder identity on each connecting rod and cap. Mark across the cap-to-connecting rod join and note which side of the cap faces the front of the engine to ensure that they are fitted the correct way around onto the correct rod on reassembly. Note that the number already across the rod and cap indicates rod size grade **(see illustration 25.21b)**. Unscrew the connecting rod cap nuts and separate the caps from the crankpin **(see illustrations)**. **Note:** *If no work is to be carried out on the piston/connecting rod assemblies there is no need to remove them from the bores, but push them up to the top of the bores so that the bottom ends are clear of the crankshaft. If you do remove them, refer to Section 25.*

27.11 Piston ring installation details – stagger the ring end gaps as shown

1 Top compression ring
2 Second compression ring
3 Oil ring expander
4 Oil ring side rails

28.2a Unscrew the nuts (arrowed) ...

Engine, clutch and transmission 2•51

28.2b ... and remove the connecting rod caps

28.3 Lift the crankshaft out of the crankcase ...

28.4 ... and remove the shells if required

3 Lift the crankshaft out of the upper crankcase half, taking care not to dislodge the main bearing shells (see illustration).
4 The main bearing shells can be removed from the crankcase halves by pushing their centres to the side, then lifting them out (see illustration). Keep the shells in order.

Inspection

5 Clean the crankshaft with solvent, squirting it under pressure through all the oil passages. If available, blow the crank dry with compressed air, and also blow through the oil passages. Check the primary drive gear and its sub-gear for wear or damage. If any of the teeth are excessively worn, chipped or broken, the crankshaft must be replaced with a new one. If wear or damage is found, also inspect the primary driven gear on the back of the clutch housing (see Section 16).
6 Check the springs between the primary drive gear and its sub-gear. To separate the sub-gear from the main gear, remove the large circlip and the sprung washer, noting which way round they fit. Discard the circlip as a new one must be used. Remove the sub-gear, noting how one of its holes aligns with the hole in the main gear – mark this alignment as an aid to installation. Remove the springs and the stopper pins, noting how they fit. When fitting the sub-gear back on, apply some molybdenum disulphide oil (a 50/50 mixture of molybdenum disulphide grease and clean engine oil) to the contact areas between the main gear, the sub gear and the sprung washer. Fit the sprung washer so that its inner rim is raised off the sub-gear and facing out, and fit the new circlip with its large tab on the right as you look at it, and aligned with the groove in the sub-gear so that the ends are at a right-angle to the cutouts in the end of the crankshaft.
7 Refer to Section 24 and examine the main bearing shells. If they are scored, badly scuffed or appear to have been seized, new bearings must be installed. Always replace the main bearings as a set. If they are badly damaged, check the corresponding crankshaft journals. Evidence of extreme heat, such as discoloration, indicates that lubrication failure has occurred. Be sure to thoroughly check the oil pump and pressure regulator as well as all oil holes and passages before reassembling the engine.
8 Give the crankshaft journals a close visual examination, paying particular attention where damaged bearings have been discovered. If the journals are scored or pitted in any way a new crankshaft will be required. Note that undersizes are not available, precluding the option of re-grinding the crankshaft.
9 Place the crankshaft on V-blocks and check the runout at the main bearing journals using a dial gauge. Compare the reading to the maximum specified at the beginning of the Chapter. If the runout exceeds the limit, the crankshaft must be replaced.

Oil clearance check

10 Whether new bearing shells are being fitted or the original ones are being re-used, the main bearing oil clearance should be checked before the engine is reassembled. Main bearing oil clearance is measured with a product known as Plastigauge.
11 Clean the backs of the bearing shells and the bearing housings in both crankcase halves.
12 Press the bearing shells into their cut-outs, ensuring that the tab on each shell engages in the notch in the crankcase (see illustration 28.24). Make sure the bearings are fitted in the correct locations and take care not to touch any shell's bearing surface with your fingers.
13 Ensure the shells and crankshaft are clean and dry. Lay the crankshaft in position in the upper crankcase (see illustration 28.3). Install the three crankcase dowels if removed (see illustration 22.9).
14 Cut five lengths of the appropriate size Plastigauge (they should be slightly shorter than the width of the crankshaft journals). Place a strand of Plastigauge on each (cleaned) journal, avoiding the oil hole. Make sure the crankshaft is not rotated.
15 Carefully fit the lower crankcase half onto the upper half (see illustration 22.8). Check that the lower half is correctly seated. Note: *Do not tighten the crankcase bolts if the casing is not correctly seated.* Clean the threads of the ten 8 mm lower crankcase bolts. Apply some oil to the threads and the underside of the heads of the bolts and insert them in their original locations. Secure all bolts finger-tight at first, then tighten them evenly and a little at a time in a criss-cross sequence starting from the centre and working outwards to the torque setting specified at the beginning of the Chapter (see illustration 22.6). Make sure that the crankshaft is not rotated as the bolts are tightened.
16 Slacken each bolt evenly a little at a time in a reverse of the tightening sequence, i.e. starting from the outside and working to the centre, until they are all finger-tight, then remove the bolts. Carefully lift off the lower crankcase half, making sure the Plastigauge is not disturbed.
17 Compare the width of the crushed Plastigauge on each crankshaft journal to the scale printed on the Plastigauge envelope to obtain the main bearing oil clearance. Compare the reading to the specifications at the beginning of the Chapter.
18 On completion carefully scrape away all traces of the Plastigauge material from the crankshaft journal and bearing shells; use a fingernail or other object which is unlikely to score them.
19 If the oil clearance falls into the specified range, no bearing shell replacement is required (provided they are in good condition). If the clearance is beyond the service limit, refer to the marks on the case and the marks on the crankshaft and select new bearing shells (see Steps 21 and 22). Install the new shells and check the oil clearance once again (the new shells may bring bearing clearance within the specified range). Always replace all of the shells at the same time.
20 If the clearance is still greater than the service limit listed in this Chapter's Specifications (even with replacement shells), the crankshaft journal is worn and the crankshaft should be replaced with a new one.

Main bearing shell selection

21 Replacement bearing shells for the main bearings are supplied on a selected fit basis. Code letters and numbers stamped on the crankshaft and crankcase are used to identify the correct replacement bearings. The crankshaft main bearing journal size numbers

2•52 Engine, clutch and transmission

28.21 Main bearing journal size letters (arrowed)

28.24a Fit the shells, locating the tabs in the notches (arrow) . . .

28.24b . . . and lubricate them with clean oil

are stamped on the outside of the left-hand crankshaft web and will be either a 1, a 2 or a 3 **(see illustration 25.21a)**. The first letter, after the L, is for the left-hand journal, and the numbers correspond consecutively for each journal. The corresponding main bearing housing size letters are stamped into the left-hand side of the upper crankcase half and will be either an A, a B or a C **(see illustration)**. The left-hand letter corresponds to the left-hand journal, and run consecutively from left to right.

22 A range of bearing shells is available. To select the correct bearing for a particular journal, use the table below and cross-refer the main bearing journal size number (stamped on the crank web) with the main bearing housing size letter (stamped on the crankcase) to determine the colour code of the bearing required. For example, if the journal code is 3, and the housing code is A, then the bearing required is Green. The colour is marked on the side of the shell **(see illustration 25.22)**.

Installation

23 Clean the backs of the bearing shells and the bearing cut-outs in both crankcase halves. If new shells are being fitted, ensure that all traces of the protective grease are cleaned off using paraffin (kerosene). Wipe the shells and crankcase halves dry with a lint-free cloth. Make sure all the oil passages and holes are clear, and blow them through with compressed air if it is available.

24 Press the bearing shells into their locations. Make sure the tab on each shell engages in the notch in the casing **(see illustration)**. Make sure the bearings are fitted in the correct locations and take care not to touch any shell's bearing surface with your fingers. Lubricate each shell with molybdenum disulphide oil (a 50/50 mixture of molybdenum disulphide grease and clean engine oil) **(see illustration)**.

25 Lower the crankshaft into position in the upper crankcase, making sure all bearings remain in place **(see illustration 28.3)**.

26 Lubricate the crankpin with molybdenum disulphide oil (a 50/50 mixture of molybdenum disulphide grease and clean engine oil). Pull the connecting rod onto the crankpin and fit the cap onto the rod **(see illustration and 28.2b)**. Make sure the cap is fitted the correct way around so the previously made markings align, and that the rod is facing the right way (see Step 2 and Section 25).

27 Apply some clean oil to the threads and under the heads of the connecting rod nuts. Install the nuts and tighten them evenly and alternately, in two or three stages, to the torque setting specified at the beginning of the Chapter **(see illustrations)**. It is highly advisable to have an assistant to hold the crankshaft down in the crankcase while tightening the bolts as it could jump out.

28 Check that the crankshaft is free to rotate easily, then install the other connecting rods in the same way. Check to make sure that all components have been returned to their original locations using the marks made on disassembly.

29 Check that the rods rotate smoothly and freely on the crankpins. If there are any signs of roughness or tightness, remove the rods and re-check the bearing clearance. Sometimes tapping the bottom of the connecting rod cap will relieve tightness, but if in doubt, recheck the clearances.

30 Reassemble the crankcase halves (see Section 22).

	Main bearing housing code		
Main bearing journal code	A (33.000 to 33.006 mm)	B (33.006 to 33.012 mm)	C (33.012 to 33.018 mm)
1 (30.000 to 30.006 mm)	E – Pink	D – Yellow	C – Green
2 (29.994 to 30.000 mm)	D – Yellow	C – Green	B – Brown
3 (29.988 to 29.994 mm)	C – Green	B – Brown	A – Black

28.26 Pull the connecting rod onto the crankpin and fit the cap

28.27a Fit the cap nuts . . .

28.27b . . . and tighten them as described to the specified torque

Engine, clutch and transmission 2•53

29.2a Remove the output shaft...

29.2b ...and the input shaft, noting how the bearings locate

29.2c Remove the bearing dowels from their holes (arrowed)...

29.2d ...and the bearing retainer from its groove

29 Transmission shafts and bearings – removal and installation

Note: *To remove the transmission shafts the engine must be removed from the frame and the crankcases separated. If the engine has already been removed, ignore the steps which do not apply.*

Removal

1 Remove the engine from the frame (see Section 5) and separate the crankcase halves (see Section 22).
2 Lift the output shaft and input shaft out of the casing, noting their relative positions, how they fit together and how the hole in each needle bearing housing locates onto the dowel **(see illustrations)**. If they are stuck, use a soft-faced hammer and gently tap on the ends of the shafts to free them. Remove the needle bearing dowels – if they are not in their holes in the crankcase, remove them from the bearings themselves on the shafts **(see illustration)**. Also remove the output shaft bearing half-ring retainer from either the crankcase or the bearing **(see illustration)**. If necessary, the input shaft and output shaft can be disassembled and inspected for wear or damage (see Section 30).
3 Referring to *Tools and Workshop Tips* (Section 5) in the Reference Section, check the bearings on the transmission shafts. Replace the bearings if necessary, noting that the output shaft left-hand bearing is not available separately from the shaft. Also check the condition of the output shaft oil seal and renew it if worn or damaged **(see illustration 29.5)**.

Installation

4 Fit the needle bearing dowels into their holes in the crankcase, and the half-ring retainer into its slot **(see illustrations 29.2c and d)**.
5 Lubricate the left-hand end of the output shaft with clean oil and slide the output shaft oil seal on, using a new one if necessary **(see illustration)**. Smear the seal lips with oil.
6 Lower the input shaft into position in the upper crankcase, making sure the hole in the

29.5 Lubricate the end of the shaft and fit the oil seal

2•54 Engine, clutch and transmission

29.7 Make sure the ring retainer (A) and the bearing pin (B) locate correctly as shown

needle bearing engages correctly with the dowel **(see illustration 29.2b)**.
7 Lower the output shaft into position in the upper crankcase **(see illustration 29.2a)**, making sure the hole in the needle bearing engages correctly with the dowel, the groove in the ball bearing engages correctly with the retainer in the bearing housing, and the locating pin sits in the cutout in the crankcase **(see illustration)**. Also ensure that the oil seal lip locates in the crankcase groove.
Caution: If the ring retainer or dowel do not locate correctly, the crankcase halves will not seat properly.

8 Make sure both transmission shafts are correctly seated and their related pinions are correctly engaged.
9 Position the gears in the neutral position and check the shafts are free to rotate easily and independently (i.e. the input shaft can turn whilst the output shaft is held stationary) before proceeding further.
10 Reassemble the crankcase halves (see Section 22).

30 Transmission shafts – disassembly, inspection and reassembly

1 Remove the transmission shafts from the crankcase (see Section 29). Always disassemble the transmission shafts separately to avoid mixing up the components.

Input shaft disassembly

HAYNES HiNT *When disassembling the transmission shafts, place the parts on a long rod or thread a wire through them to keep them in order and facing the proper direction.*

2 Slide the outer race and needle bearing off the left-hand end of the shaft, followed by the thrust washer and the 2nd gear pinion – note which way around the pinion is fitted **(see accompanying illustration and illustrations 30.20d, c, b and a)**.
3 Slide the tabbed lockwasher off the shaft, then turn the slotted splined washer to offset the splines and slide it off the shaft, noting how they fit together **(see illustrations 30.19c, b and a)**. Slide the 6th gear pinion and its bush off the shaft, followed by the splined washer **(see illustrations 30.18c, b and a)**.
4 Remove the circlip securing the combined 3rd/4th gear pinion, then slide the pinion off the shaft **(see illustrations 30.17b and a)**.
5 Remove the circlip securing the 5th gear pinion, then slide the splined washer, the pinion and its bush, and the thrust washer off the shaft **(see illustrations 30.16e, d, c, b and a)**. The 1st gear pinion is integral with the shaft **(see illustration 30.15)**.
6 If required, remove the caged ball bearing from the right-hand end of the shaft, referring to *Tools and Workshop Tips* (Section 5) in the Reference Section **(see illustration 30.15)**.

Input shaft inspection

7 Wash all of the components in clean solvent and dry them off.

30.2 Transmission input shaft components

1 Input shaft and bearing	5 2nd gear	10 Splined thrust washer	14 Splined thrust washer
2 Needle roller bearing outer race	6 Lock washer	11 Circlip	15 5th gear bushing
3 Needle roller bearing	7 Special splined washer	12 3rd/4th gear	16 5th gear
4 Thrust washer	8 6th gear splined bushing	13 Circlip	17 Thrust washer
	9 6th gear		

Engine, clutch and transmission 2•55

30.11a Measure the shaft OD . . .

30.11b . . . the bush ID . . . .

30.11c . . . the bush OD . . .

30.11d . . . and the gear ID on the relevant components as listed in the Specifications

8 Check the gear teeth for cracking, chipping, pitting and other obvious wear or damage. Any pinion that is damaged as such must be replaced.

9 Inspect the dogs and the dog holes in the gears for cracks, chips, and excessive wear especially in the form of rounded edges. Make sure mating gears engage properly. Replace the paired gears as a set if necessary.

10 Check for signs of scoring or bluing on the pinions, bushes and shaft. This could be caused by overheating due to inadequate lubrication. Check that all the oil holes and passages are clear. Replace any damaged pinions or bushes.

11 Check that each pinion moves freely on the shaft or bush but without undue freeplay. Check that each bush moves freely on the shaft but without undue freeplay. If the necessary equipment is available the individual components can be measured and the results compared with the specifications at the beginning of this Chapter **(see illustrations)**.

12 The shaft is unlikely to sustain damage unless the engine has seized, placing an unusually high loading on the transmission, or the machine has covered a very high mileage. Check the surface of the shaft, especially where a pinion turns on it, and replace the shaft if it has scored or picked up, or if there are any cracks. Damage of any kind can only be cured by replacement.

13 Check the washers and circlips and replace any that are bent or appear weakened or worn. Use new ones if in any doubt. Note that it is good practice to renew all circlips when overhauling gearshafts.

Input shaft reassembly

14 During reassembly, apply molybdenum disulphide oil (a 50/50 mixture of molybdenum disulphide grease and clean engine oil) to the mating surfaces of the shaft, pinions and bushes. When installing the circlips, do not expand their ends any further than is necessary. Install the stamped circlips and washers so that their chamfered side faces the pinion it secures **(see illustration)**.

30.14 Correct fitted orientation of input shaft thrust washers and circlips

2•56 Engine, clutch and transmission

30.15 Fit the bearing onto the shaft as shown

30.16a Slide the thrust washer . . .

30.16b . . . the 5th gear pinion bush . . .

15 If removed, fit the caged ball bearing onto the right-hand end of the shaft, referring to *Tools and Workshop Tips* (Section 5) in the Reference Section **(see illustration)**.

16 Slide the thrust washer onto the left-hand end of the shaft, followed by the 5th gear pinion bush, aligning the oil hole in the bush with the hole in the shaft **(see illustrations)**. Fit the 5th gear pinion with its dogs facing away from the integral 1st gear **(see illustration)**. Slide the splined washer onto the shaft, then fit the circlip, making sure that it locates correctly in the groove in the shaft **(see illustrations)**.

17 Slide the combined 3rd/4th gear pinion onto the shaft with the larger 4th gear pinion facing the 5th gear pinion **(see illustration)**. Fit the circlip, making sure it is locates correctly in its groove in the shaft **(see illustrations)**.

18 Slide the splined washer onto the shaft, followed by the 6th gear pinion bush, aligning the oil hole in the bush with the hole in the shaft,

30.16c . . . the 5th gear pinion . . .

30.16d . . . and the splined washer onto the shaft . . .

30.16e . . . and secure them with the circlip . . .

30.16f . . . making sure it locates properly in its groove

30.17a Slide the combined 3rd/4th gear pinion onto the shaft . . .

30.17b . . . and secure it with the circlip . . .

Engine, clutch and transmission 2•57

30.17c ... making sure it locates properly in its groove

30.18a Slide the splined washer ...

30.18b ... the 6th gear pinion bush ...

30.18c ... and the 6th gear pinion onto the shaft

30.19a Slide on the slotted splined washer ...

30.19b ... and locate it as shown ...

and the 6th gear pinion, making sure its dogs face the 3rd/4th gear pinion **(see illustrations)**.

19 Slide the slotted splined washer onto the shaft and locate it in its groove, then turn it in the groove so that the splines on the washer align with the splines on the shaft and secure the washer in the groove **(see illustrations)**. Slide the tabbed lockwasher onto the shaft, so that the tabs locate into the slots in the outer rim of the splined washer **(see illustrations)**.

20 Slide the 2nd gear pinion onto the end of the shaft so that it is the same way round as noted on removal. Fit the thrust washer, followed by the needle roller bearing and its outer race over the end of the shaft **(see illustrations)**.

30.19c ... then slide on the tabbed lockwasher ...

30.19d ... and locate it as shown

30.20a Slide the 2nd gear pinion ...

30.20b ... the thrust washer ...

30.20c ... the needle bearing ...

30.20d ... and the outer race onto the shaft

2•58 Engine, clutch and transmission

30.21 The complete assembly should be as shown

21 Check that all components have been correctly installed (see illustration).

Output shaft disassembly

22 Slide the outer race and needle bearing off the right-hand end of the shaft (see accompanying illustration and illustrations 30.37e and d).
23 Slide the thrust washer off the shaft, followed by the 1st gear pinion and its needle roller bearing, the thrust washer and the 5th gear pinion (see illustrations 30.37c, b and a, and 30.36b and a).
24 Remove the circlip securing the 4th gear pinion, then slide the splined washer, the pinion and its splined bush off the shaft (see illustrations 30.35d, c, b and a).
25 Slide the tabbed lockwasher off the shaft, then turn the slotted splined washer to offset the splines and slide it off the shaft, noting how they fit together (see illustrations 30.34c, b and a).
26 Slide the 3rd gear pinion and its splined bush, followed by the splined washer, off the shaft (see illustrations 30.33c, b and a).
27 Remove the circlip securing the 6th gear pinion, then slide the pinion off the shaft (see illustrations 30.32b and a).
28 Remove the circlip securing the 2nd gear pinion, then slide the splined washer, the pinion and its bush off the shaft (see illustrations 30.31d, c, b and a).

Output shaft inspection

29 Refer to Steps 7 to 13 above.

Output shaft reassembly

30 During reassembly, apply engine oil to the mating surfaces of the shaft, pinions and bushes. When installing the circlips, do not expand the ends any further than is necessary. Install the stamped circlips and washers so that their chamfered side faces the pinion it secures (see illustration).
31 Slide the 2nd gear pinion bush onto the shaft, aligning the oil hole in the bush with the hole in the shaft, then slide on the 2nd gear

30.22 Transmission output shaft components

1 Output shaft
2 Needle roller bearing outer race
3 Needle roller bearing
4 Thrust washer
5 1st gear
6 Needle roller bearing
7 Thrust washer
8 5th gear
9 Circlip
10 Splined thrust washer
11 4th gear
12 4th gear splined bushing
13 Lock washer
14 Special splined washer
15 3rd gear splined bushing
16 3rd gear
17 Splined thrust washer
18 Circlip
19 6th gear
20 Circlip
21 Splined thrust washer
22 2nd gear
23 2nd gear bushing

Engine, clutch and transmission 2•59

30.30 Correct fitted orientation of output shaft thrust washers and circlips

pinion with its dog holes facing away from the bearing, followed by the splined washer. Fit the circlip, making sure it is locates correctly in its groove in the shaft **(see illustrations)**.

32 Slide the 6th gear pinion with its selector fork groove facing away from the 2nd gear pinion, then fit the circlip, making sure it is locates correctly in its groove in the shaft **(see illustrations)**.

33 Slide the splined washer and the 3rd gear pinion bush onto the shaft, making sure the oil hole in the bush aligns with the hole in the shaft, then slide on the 3rd gear pinion with its dog holes facing the 6th gear pinion **(see illustrations)**.

34 Slide the slotted splined washer onto the shaft and locate it in its groove, then turn it in

30.31a Slide the 2nd gear pinion bush . . .

30.31b . . . the 2nd gear pinion . . .

30.31c . . . and the splined washer onto the shaft . . .

30.31d . . . and secure them with the circlip . . .

30.31e . . . making sure it locates in the groove

30.32a Slide the 6th gear pinion onto the shaft . . .

30.32b . . . and secure it with the circlip

30.33a Slide the splined washer . . .

2•60 Engine, clutch and transmission

30.33b ... the 3rd gear pinion bush ...

30.33c ... and the 3rd gear pinion onto the shaft

30.34a Slide the slotted splined washer onto the shaft ...

30.34b ... and locate it as shown

30.34c Slide the lockwasher onto the shaft ...

the groove so that the splines on the washer align with the splines on the shaft and secure the washer in the groove **(see illustrations)**. Slide the lockwasher onto the shaft, so that the tabs on the lockwasher locate into the slots in the outer rim of the spline washer **(see illustration)**.

35 Slide the 4th gear pinion bush onto the shaft, making sure the oil hole in the bush aligns with the hole in the shaft. Fit the 4th gear pinion so that its dog holes face away from the 3rd gear pinion. Install the splined washer, then fit the circlip, making sure it is locates correctly in its groove in the shaft **(see illustrations)**.

30.34d ... and locate it as shown

30.35a Slide the 4th gear pinion bush ...

30.35b ... the 4th gear pinion ...

30.35c ... and the splined washer onto the shaft ...

30.35d ... and secure them with the circlip ...

30.35e ... making sure it locates in the groove

Engine, clutch and transmission 2•61

30.36a Slide the 5th gear pinion . . .

30.36b . . . and the thrust washer onto the shaft

30.37a Slide the needle bearing . . .

30.37b . . . the 1st gear pinion . . .

30.37c . . . and the thrust washer onto the shaft . . .

30.37d . . . then fit the bearing onto the end of the shaft . . .

36 Slide the 5th gear pinion onto the shaft with its selector fork groove facing the 4th gear pinion, followed by the thrust washer **(see illustrations)**.
37 Slide the 1st gear pinion needle roller bearing onto the shaft, followed by the 1st gear pinion with its dog holes facing the 5th gear pinion. Fit the thrust washer then the needle roller bearing and its outer race over the end of the shaft **(see illustrations)**.
38 Check that all components have been correctly installed **(see illustration)**.

31 Initial start-up after overhaul

1 Make sure the engine oil and coolant levels are correct (see *Daily (pre-ride) checks*). Make sure there is fuel in the tank.
2 Turn the engine kill switch to the ON position and shift the gearbox into neutral. Turn the ignition ON. On F-X and F-Y (1999 and 2000) models set the choke enough to encourage the bike to start, but not so much as to allow it to race.
3 Start the engine and allow it to run at a moderately fast idle until it reaches operating temperature.

⚠ *Warning: If the oil pressure warning light doesn't go off, or it comes on while the engine is running, stop the engine immediately.*

30.37e . . . and the outer race onto the bearing

30.38 The assembled shaft should be as shown

4 Check carefully for oil and coolant leaks and make sure the transmission and controls, especially the brakes, function properly before road testing the machine. Refer to Section 32 for the recommended running-in procedure.
5 Upon completion of the road test, and after the engine has cooled down completely, recheck the valve clearances (see Chapter 1) and check the engine oil and coolant levels (see *Daily (pre-ride) checks*).

32 Recommended running-in procedure

1 Treat the machine gently for the first few miles to make sure oil has circulated throughout the engine and any new parts installed have started to seat.
2 Even greater care is necessary if new pistons/rings or a new crankcase/bores have been fitted, and the bike will have to be run in as when new. This means greater use of the transmission and a restraining hand on the throttle until at least 300 miles (500 km) have been covered. There's no point in keeping to any set speed limit – the main idea is to keep from labouring the engine and to gradually increase performance up to the 300 mile (500 km) mark. Experience is the best guide, since it's easy to tell when an engine is running freely.
3 If a lubrication failure is suspected, stop the engine immediately and try to find the cause. If an engine is run without oil, even for a short period of time, severe damage will occur.

Chapter 3
Cooling system

Contents

Coolant hoses – removal and installation 9
Coolant level check .... see Daily (pre-ride) checks
Coolant reservoir – removal and installation 8
Coolant temperature gauge and sensor – check and replacement . 4
Cooling fan and fan switch – check and replacement 3
Cooling system checks .... see Chapter 1
Cooling system draining, flushing and refilling .... see Chapter 1
General information 1
Radiator – removal and installation 6
Radiator pressure cap – check 2
Thermostat and housing – removal, check and installation 5
Water pump – check, removal and installation 7

Degrees of difficulty

| Easy, suitable for novice with little experience | Fairly easy, suitable for beginner with some experience | Fairly difficult, suitable for competent DIY mechanic | Difficult, suitable for experienced DIY mechanic | Very difficult, suitable for expert DIY or professional |

Specifications

Coolant
Mixture type and capacity .... see Chapter 1

Cooling fan switch
Switch closes (fan ON) .... 98 to 102°C
Switch opens (fan OFF) .... 93 to 97°C

Coolant temperature sensor
F-X and F-Y (1999 and 2000) models
  Resistance @ 80°C .... 47 to 57 ohms
  Resistance @ 120°C .... 14 to 18 ohms
F-1/FS-1 models onward (2001-on)
  Resistance @ 80°C .... 2.1 to 2.6 K-ohms
  Resistance @ 120°C .... 650 to 730 ohms

Thermostat
F-X and F-Y (1999 and 2000) models
  Opening temperature .... 73 to 77°C
  Fully open .... 90°C
  Valve lift .... 8 mm (min)
F-1/FS-1 models onward (2001-on)
  Opening temperature .... 80 to 84°C
  Fully open .... 90°C
  Valve lift .... 8 mm (min)

Radiator
Cap valve opening pressure .... 16 to 20 psi (1.1 to 1.4 Bar)

Torque settings
Coolant temperature sensor
  F-X and F-Y (1999 and 2000) models .... 10 Nm
  F-1/FS-1 models onward (2001-on) .... 23 Nm
Cooling fan blade nut .... 3 Nm
Cooling fan motor nuts .... 5 Nm
Fan switch .... 18 Nm
Thermostat cover bolts .... 12 Nm
Water pump bolts .... 12 Nm

3•2 Cooling system

1 General information

The cooling system uses a water/antifreeze coolant to carry away excess heat from the engine and maintain as constant a temperature as possible. The cylinders are surrounded by a water jacket from which the heated coolant is circulated by thermo-syphonic action in conjunction with a water pump, which is driven by the oil pump. The hot coolant passes upwards to the thermostat and through to the radiator. The coolant then flows across the core of the radiator, then to the water pump and back to the engine where the cycle is repeated.

A thermostat is fitted in the system to prevent the coolant flowing through the radiator when the engine is cold, therefore accelerating the speed at which the engine reaches normal operating temperature. A coolant temperature sensor (also known as a thermo sensor) mounted in the thermostat housing transmits information to the temperature gauge on the instrument panel, and on fuel-injected models to the ECM (electronic control module). A cooling fan is fitted to the back of the radiator to aid cooling in extreme conditions by drawing extra air through; a thermostatically-controlled switch fitted to the left-hand side of the radiator triggers the operation of the fan motor.

The complete cooling system is partially sealed and pressurised, the pressure being controlled by a valve contained in the spring-loaded radiator cap. By pressurising the coolant the boiling point is raised, preventing premature boiling in adverse conditions. The overflow pipe from the system is connected to a reservoir into which excess coolant is expelled under pressure. The discharged coolant automatically returns to the radiator by the vacuum created when the engine cools.

**Warning: Do not remove the pressure cap from the radiator when the engine is hot. Scalding hot coolant and steam may be blown out under pressure, which could cause serious injury. When the engine has cooled, place a thick rag, like a towel, over the pressure cap; slowly rotate the cap anti-clockwise to the first stop. This procedure allows any residual pressure to escape. When the steam has stopped escaping, press down on the cap while turning it anti-clockwise and remove it.
Caution: Do not allow antifreeze to come in contact with your skin or painted surfaces of the motorcycle. Rinse off any spills immediately with plenty of water. Antifreeze is highly toxic if ingested. Never leave antifreeze lying around in an open container or in puddles on the floor; children and pets are attracted by its sweet smell and may drink it. Check with the local authorities about disposing of used antifreeze. Many communities will have collection centres which will see that antifreeze is disposed of safely.
Caution: At all times use the specified type of antifreeze, and always mix it with distilled water in the correct proportion.**

The antifreeze contains corrosion inhibitors which are essential to avoid damage to the cooling system. A lack of these inhibitors could lead to a build-up of corrosion which would block the coolant passages, resulting in overheating and severe engine damage. Distilled water must be used as opposed to tap water to avoid a build-up of scale which would also block the passages.

2 Radiator pressure cap – check

1 If problems such as overheating or loss of coolant occur, check the entire system as described in Chapter 1. The radiator cap opening pressure should be checked by a Honda dealer with the special tester required to do the job. If the cap is defective, replace it with a new one.

3 Cooling fan and fan switch – check and replacement

Cooling fan
Check

1 If the engine is overheating and the cooling fan isn't coming on, first check the cooling fan circuit fuse (see Chapter 9). If the fuse is good, check the fan switch as described below.
2 If the fan does not come on (and the fan switch is good), the fault lies in either the cooling fan motor or the relevant wiring. Test all the wiring and connections as described in Chapter 9, following the relevant Wiring Diagram. Disconnect the fan wiring connector (see Step 3) and check that there is battery voltage at the black/blue wire terminal on the loom side of the connector with the ignition ON. If not, check the wiring.
3 To test the cooling fan motor, remove the left-hand fairing side panel (see Chapter 8). Disconnect the fan wiring connector and the fan switch wiring connector **(see illustrations)**. Using a 12 volt battery and two jumper wires with suitable connectors, connect the battery positive (+ve) lead to the black/blue wire terminal on the fan side of the wiring connector, and the battery negative (–ve) lead to the fan switch wiring connector. Once connected the fan should operate. If it does not, and the wiring is all good, then the fan motor is faulty. Individual components are available for the fan assembly.

Replacement

Warning: The engine must be completely cool before carrying out this procedure.

4 Remove the radiator (see Section 6).
5 Disconnect the wiring connector from the fan switch **(see illustration)**.
6 Undo the three screws securing the fan assembly to the radiator, noting that one screw also secures the earth (ground) wire **(see illustration)**. Free the fan wiring

3.3a Disconnect the fan wiring connector (arrowed) . . .

3.3b . . . and the fan switch wiring connector

3.5 Disconnect the switch connector (arrowed) . . .

3.6 . . . then undo the bolts (arrowed) and remove the fan assembly

Cooling system 3•3

3.14 Cooling fan switch testing set-up

connector from its lug on the radiator and all the wiring from any clamps.

7 Unscrew the fan blade nut and remove the blade. Undo the three nuts on the front of the fan motor securing it to the bracket and separate them.

8 Installation is the reverse of removal. Apply a suitable non-permanent thread locking compound the fan blade nut and tighten it to the torque setting specified at the beginning of the Chapter. Also tighten the fan motor nuts to the specified torque. Do not forget to attach the earth (ground) cable to the radiator.

9 Install the radiator (see Section 7).

Cooling fan switch

Check

10 If the engine is overheating and the cooling fan isn't coming on, first check the cooling fan circuit fuse (see Chapter 9). If the fuse is blown, check the fan circuit for a short to earth (see the wiring diagrams at the end of this book).

11 If the fuse is good, remove the left-hand fairing side panel (see Chapter 8). Disconnect the wiring connector from the fan switch on the radiator **(see illustration 3.3b)**. Using a jumper wire if necessary, connect the wire to earth (ground). Turn the ignition switch ON. The fan should come on. If it does, the fan switch is defective and must be replaced with a new one. If it does not come on, check for battery voltage at the switch wiring connector with the ignition ON. If voltage is present, test the fan motor itself (see above). If there is no voltage, check the wiring and connectors for a fault or break.

12 If the fan is on the whole time, disconnect the wiring connector. The fan should stop. If it does, the switch is defective and must be replaced with a new one. If it doesn't, check the wiring between the switch and the fan for a short to earth, and the fan itself.

13 If the fan works but is suspected of cutting in at the wrong temperature, a more comprehensive test of the switch can be made as follows.

14 Remove the switch (see Steps 16 and 17). Fill a small heatproof container with coolant and place it on a stove. Connect the positive (+ve) probe of an ohmmeter to the terminal of the switch and the negative (–ve) probe to the switch body, and using some wire or other support suspend the switch in the coolant so that just the sensing portion and the threads are submerged **(see illustration)**. Also place a thermometer capable of reading temperatures up to 110°C in the coolant so that its bulb is close to the switch. **Note:** *None of the components should be allowed to directly touch the container.*

15 Initially the ohmmeter reading should be very high indicating that the switch is open (OFF). Heat the coolant, stirring it gently.

⚠ **Warning:** *This must be done very carefully to avoid the risk of personal injury.*

When the temperature reaches around 98 to 102°C the meter reading should drop to around zero ohms, indicating that the switch has closed (ON). Now turn the heat off. As the temperature falls below 93 to 97°C the meter reading should show infinite (very high) resistance, indicating that the switch has opened (OFF). If the meter readings obtained are different, or they are obtained at different temperatures, then the switch is faulty and must be replaced with a new one. On completion, fit the switch as described in Steps 18 and 19.

Replacement

⚠ **Warning:** *The engine must be completely cool before carrying out this procedure.*

16 Drain the cooling system (see Chapter 1).

17 Disconnect the wiring connector from the fan switch on the left-hand side of the radiator **(see illustration 3.3b)**. Unscrew the switch and withdraw it from the radiator. Discard the O-ring as a new one must be used.

18 Install the switch using a new O-ring and some suitable sealant on the upper portion of the threads, and tighten it to the torque setting specified at the beginning of the Chapter. Take care not to overtighten the switch as the radiator could be damaged.

19 Reconnect the switch wiring and refill the cooling system (see Chapter 1).

4 Coolant temperature gauge and sensor – check and replacement

Coolant temperature gauge – F-X and F-Y (1999 and 2000) models

Check

1 The circuit consists of the sensor mounted in the thermostat housing and the gauge assembly mounted in the instrument cluster. If the system malfunctions check the fuse.

2 If the gauge is not working, raise or remove the fuel tank (see Chapter 4). Disconnect the wiring connector from the sensor and turn the ignition switch ON **(see illustrations)**. The temperature gauge needle should be on the 'C' on the gauge. Using a jumper wire attached to the wiring connector terminal, earth the sensor wire on the engine – the needle should swing immediately over to the 'H' on the gauge.

Caution: *Do not earth the wire for any longer than is necessary to take the reading, or the gauge may be damaged.*

If the needle moves as described above, the gauge is proven good, however the sensor is proven defective and must be replaced with a new one.

3 If the needle movement is still faulty, or if it does not move at all, the fault lies in the wiring or the gauge itself. Displace the instrument cluster and disconnect the wiring connector (see Chapter 9).

4 Check for continuity in the wire between the temperature sensor and the temperature gauge green/blue wire terminal on the wiring connector. If there is no continuity, locate the break in the wire and repair it or replace it with a new one. Also check for battery voltage at the sensor end of the wire. If voltage is present, the gauge is faulty and must be replaced with a new one (see Chapter 9).

5 If no voltage is present, check for battery voltage between the black/brown (+) and green/black (–) wire terminals on the instrument cluster wiring connector with the ignition ON. Also check for voltage between the red (+) and green/black (–) wire terminals with the ignition OFF. If there is none, check the black/brown and/or red wires and any connectors for faults. If voltage is present,

4.2a Coolant temperature sensor wiring connector (arrowed) – F-X and F-Y models

4.2b Coolant temperature sensor wiring connector (arrowed) – F-1/FS-1 models onward

3•4 Cooling system

replace the gauge with a new one (see Chapter 9). Otherwise check all the wiring, particularly check for continuity to earth in the green/black wire, referring to the *Wiring Diagrams* at the end of Chapter 9.

Replacement

6 See Chapter 9.

Coolant temperature and warning display – F-1/FS-1 models onward (2001-on)

Check

7 The circuit consists of the sensor mounted in the thermostat housing and the display which is part of the instrument cluster LCD unit. If the system malfunctions check the fuse.

8 If the display is not working at all, check the instrument cluster power input (see Chapter 9). If the power lines are good, then either the printed circuit board (PCB) or the LCD display unit could be faulty.

9 If the display as a whole works but the coolant function doesn't or is thought to be inaccurate, check the sensor (see below). If the sensor is good, remove the fairing (see Chapter 8) and check the wiring between the sensor and the instrument cluster for continuity. If the wiring is good the display is faulty.

Caution: Do not leave the ignition switched on for any longer than is necessary to take the reading, or the gauge may be damaged.

Replacement

10 The temperature display is part of the instrument cluster LCD unit in the instrument cluster (see Chapter 9).

Coolant temperature sensor

Check

11 Drain the cooling system (see Chapter 1). The sensor is mounted in the thermostat housing.

12 Remove the sensor (see Steps 15 and 16 below).

13 Fill a small heatproof container with coolant and place it on a stove. Using an ohmmeter, connect the positive (+ve) probe of the meter to the terminal on the sensor, on F-1/FS-1 models onward (2001-on) using the green/blue wire terminal, and the negative (–ve) probe to the body of the sensor. Using some wire or other support suspend the sensor in the coolant so that just the sensing head and the threads are submerged, with the head a minimum of 40 mm above the bottom of the container. Also place a thermometer capable of reading temperatures up to 130°C in the coolant so that its bulb is close to the sensor **(see illustration 3.14)**. Note: *None of the components should be allowed to directly touch the container.*

14 Begin to heat the coolant, stirring it gently.

⚠ *Warning: This must be done very carefully to avoid the risk of personal injury.*

When the temperature reaches around 80°C, turn the heat down and maintain the temperature steady for three minutes. The meter reading should be as specified at the beginning of the Chapter. Turn the heat on again. When the temperature reaches around 120°C, again turn the heat down and maintain it for three minutes. The meter reading should again be as specified at the beginning of the Chapter. If the meter readings obtained are different by a margin of 10% or more, then the sensor is faulty and must be replaced with a new one.

Replacement

⚠ *Warning: The engine must be completely cool before carrying out this procedure.*

15 Drain the cooling system (see Chapter 1). Remove the carburettors or throttle bodies, according to your model (see Chapter 4). The sensor is mounted in the thermostat housing.

16 Disconnect the sensor wiring connector **(see illustration 4.2a or b)**. Unscrew the sensor and remove it from the thermostat housing.

17 On F-X and F-Y (1999 and 2000) models, apply a smear of sealant to the threads of the new sensor, making sure none gets on the head. On F-1/FS-1 models onward (2001-on), fit a new sealing washer onto the sensor. Install the sensor and tighten it to the torque setting specified at the beginning of the Chapter. Connect the sensor wiring.

18 Install the carburettors or throttle bodies, according to your model (see Chapter 4). Refill the cooling system (see Chapter 1).

5 Thermostat and housing – removal, check and installation

Removal

Note: *The complete thermostat housing can be removed without removing the thermostat itself.*

⚠ *Warning: The engine must be completely cool before carrying out this procedure.*

1 The thermostat is automatic in operation and should give many years service without requiring attention. In the event of a failure, the valve will probably jam open, in which case the engine will take much longer than normal to warm up. Conversely, if the valve jams shut, the coolant will be unable to circulate and the engine will overheat. Neither condition is acceptable, and the fault must be investigated promptly.

2 Drain the cooling system (see Chapter 1). Remove the carburettors or throttle bodies, according to your model (see Chapter 4). The thermostat housing is on the back of the engine in the middle.

3 To remove the thermostat, unscrew the two bolts securing the cover and separate it from the housing **(see illustration)**. Withdraw the thermostat, noting how it fits **(see illustration)**. Note that the rubber seal around the thermostat should be renewed on installation.

4 To remove the thermostat housing, disconnect the coolant temperature sensor wiring connector **(see illustration 4.2a or b)**. Slacken the clamps securing all the hoses to the cover and housing and detach them, noting which fits where. Depending on your tools, you may need to remove the cover to access the right-hand bolt (see Step 3) – if you do then remove the thermostat as well to prevent the possibility of damaging it. Unscrew the bolts securing the housing to the engine and remove the housing **(see illustration)**. Discard the O-ring.

Check

5 Examine the thermostat visually before carrying out the test. If it remains in the open

5.3a Unscrew the bolts (arrowed) and detach the cover . . .

5.3b . . . then withdraw the thermostat from the housing – F-X and F-Y type shown

5.4 Detach the hoses from the housing then unscrew the mounting bolts – F-X and F-Y type shown

Cooling system 3•5

5.6 Thermostat testing set-up

5.9 Install the housing using a new O-ring

position at room temperature, it should be replaced with a new one. Check the condition of the rubber seal around the thermostat and replace it with a new one if it is damaged, deformed or deteriorated.

6 Suspend the thermostat by a piece of wire in a container of cold water. Place a thermometer capable of reading temperatures up to 110°C in the water so that the bulb is close to the thermostat **(see illustration)**. Heat the water, noting the temperature when the thermostat opens, and compare the result with the specifications given at the beginning of the Chapter. Also check the amount the valve opens after it has been heated for a few minutes and compare the measurement to the specifications. If the readings obtained differ from those given, the thermostat is faulty and must be replaced with a new one.

7 In the event of thermostat failure, as an emergency measure only, it can be removed and the machine used without it (this is better than leaving a permanently closed thermostat in, but if it is permanently open, you might as well leave it in). **Note:** *Take care when starting the engine from cold as it will take much longer than usual to warm up.* Ensure that a new unit is installed as soon as possible.

Installation

8 To install the thermostat, first make sure the seal is fitted around it and that it is in good condition, otherwise use a new one. Smear some clean coolant over the seal. Install the thermostat with the hole facing back and make sure it locates correctly **(see illustration 5.3b)**. Fit the cover onto the housing, then install the bolts and tighten them securely **(see illustration)**.

9 To install the thermostat housing, fit a new O-ring into the groove, using a dab of grease to keep it in place if required **(see illustration)**. Fit the housing and tighten the bolts securely **(see illustration 5.4)**. Fit the thermostat and cover if removed (see above). Attach the hoses to their unions on the cover and housing and tighten the clamps **(see illustration 5.3a)**. Connect the temperature sensor wiring connector **(see illustration 4.2a or b)**.

10 Install the carburettors or throttle bodies, according to your model (see Chapter 4). Refill the cooling system (see Chapter 1).

6 Radiator – removal and installation

Removal

⚠️ **Warning:** *The engine must be completely cool before carrying out this procedure.*

Note: *If the radiator is being removed as part of the engine removal procedure, detach the hoses from their unions on the engine rather than on the radiator and remove the radiator with the hoses attached to it. Note the routing of the hoses.*

1 Drain the cooling system (see Chapter 1).
2 Disconnect the fan wiring connector **(see illustration 3.3a)**.
3 To improve clearance if required, remove the horn (see Chapter 9).
4 Slacken the clamps securing the hoses to the radiator and detach them, noting which fits where **(see illustrations)**.

6.4a Detach the three hoses (arrowed) from the right-hand side of the radiator ...

6.4b ... and the two hoses (arrowed) from the left-hand side

3•6 Cooling system

6.5a Unscrew the upper and lower bolts (arrowed) . . .

6.5b . . . then draw the radiator to the right to free the grommet (A) from the lug (B)

6.5c Free the heat guard from the radiator mounts (arrows) . . .

6.5d . . . and from the engine if required (arrows)

5 Unscrew the nut on the radiator lower mounting bolt and remove the bolt **(see illustration)**. Unscrew the radiator upper mounting bolt, then draw the radiator to the right to free the top grommet from the lug **(see illustration)**. On F-X and F-Y (1999 and 2000) models, displace the rubber heat guard from the radiator mounts, noting how it fits **(see illustration)**. Release the guard from its mounts on the engine and remove it if required (for example if you are removing the engine) **(see illustration)**. Note the arrangement of the collars and rubber grommets in the radiator mounts.

6 If necessary, remove the cooling fan and its switch from the radiator (see Section 3). Check the radiator for signs of damage and clear any dirt or debris that might obstruct air flow and inhibit cooling. If the radiator fins are badly damaged or broken the radiator must be replaced with a new one. Also check the rubber mounting grommets, and renew them if necessary.

Installation

7 Installation is the reverse of removal, noting the following.

● Make sure the rubber grommet fits correctly onto the locating lug. On F-X and F-Y (1999 and 2000) models, make sure the rubber heat guard is correctly fitted on the engine and radiator, and make sure it does not get pinched between the radiator and frame on installation **(see illustrations 6.5c and d)**.
● Make sure the collars and washers are correctly installed with the mounting bolts.
● Make sure that the fan wiring is correctly connected.

7.2 Check the drain hole (arrowed) for signs of leakage

● Ensure the coolant hoses are in good condition (see Chapter 1), and are securely retained by their clamps, using new ones if necessary.
● On completion refill the cooling system as described in Chapter 1.

7 Water pump – check, removal and installation

Check

1 The water pump is located on the lower left-hand side of the engine. Visually check the area around the pump for signs of leakage.

2 To prevent leakage of water from the cooling system to the lubrication system and vice versa, two seals are fitted on the pump shaft. On the bottom of the pump housing there is also a drain hole **(see illustration)**. If either seal fails, the drain allows the coolant or oil to escape and prevents them mixing.

3 The seal on the water pump side is of the mechanical type which bears on the rear face

Cooling system 3•7

7.5a Slacken the clamps and detach the cover hoses (A) . . .

7.5b . . . then remove the cover and detach the housing hoses (B) – note that the outermost cover hose is not fitted on fuel injection models

of the impeller. The second seal, which is mounted behind the mechanical seal, is of the normal feathered lip type. If on inspection the drain shows signs of leakage, remove the pump and replace it with a new one – it comes as an assembly.

Removal

4 Drain the coolant (see Chapter 1).
5 Slacken the clamps securing the coolant hoses to the pump cover and detach the hoses, noting which fits where **(see illustrations)**. Unscrew the three remaining cover bolts and remove the pump cover (the rear bolt, marked by a triangle, will have already been removed when draining the system) **(see illustration)**. Remove the O-ring from the cover or pump and discard it as a new one must be used **(see illustration 7.9a)**.
6 Slacken the clamps securing the coolant hoses to the pump body and detach the hoses, noting which fits where **(see illustration 7.5 and b)**. Carefully draw the pump from the crankcase, noting how it fits **(see illustration)**. It may be necessary to lever it out to overcome the O-ring on the pump body. Remove the O-ring from the rear of the pump body and discard it as a new one must be used **(see illustration 7.8a)**.
7 Wiggle the water pump impeller back-and-forth and in-and-out **(see illustration)**. If there is excessive movement, replace the pump with a new one. Also check for corrosion or a build-up of scale in the pump body and clean or replace the pump as necessary.

Installation

8 Apply a smear of grease to the new pump body O-ring and fit it into the groove in the body **(see illustration)**. Slide the pump into the crankcase, aligning the slot in the impeller shaft with the tab on the oil pump shaft **(see illustration)**. If they are slightly misaligned turn the impeller as you install the pump until they are felt to locate. Fit the relevant coolant hoses onto the pump body and secure them with their clamps **(see illustrations 7.5a and b)**.
9 Smear the new cover O-ring with grease and fit it into its groove in the cover, then fit the cover onto the pump **(see**

7.5c Water pump cover and mounting bolts (arrowed)

7.6 Draw the pump out of the engine

7.7 Check the pump impeller as described

7.8a Fit a new O-ring onto the pump body . . .

7.8b . . . then install the pump, aligning the slot in the shaft (A) with the tab on the oil pump shaft (B)

3•8 Cooling system

7.9a Fit a new O-ring...

7.9b ...then install the cover...

7.9c ...fitting the long bolts in the top and bottom holes...

7.9d ...and using a new sealing washer on the rear bolt

illustrations). Install the bolts and tighten them to the torque setting specified at the beginning of the Chapter, using a new sealing washer on the rear (drain) bolt (which is marked by a triangle – the long bolts are for the top and bottom holes and the short bolts are for the left and right holes **(see illustrations)**.

10 Fit the coolant hoses onto the pump cover and secure them with their clamps **(see illustrations 7.5a and b)**.

11 Refill the cooling system (see Chapter 1).

8 Coolant reservoir – removal and installation

F-X and F-Y (1999 and 2000) models

1 The coolant reservoir is located on the right-hand side of the engine at the front. Remove the right-hand fairing side panel to access it (see Chapter 8). Note how the reservoir is located and how the various hoses and cables are routed around it before removing it.

2 Place a suitable container for catching the coolant below the reservoir. Remove the reservoir cap. Disconnect the radiator overflow hose from the bottom of the reservoir and allow it to drain into the container.

3 Release the reservoir breather hose from the bracket below the reservoir. Unscrew the reservoir mounting bolt, noting how it secures the rubber heat guard, and manoeuvre the reservoir out, noting how the lug on the bottom locates in the hole and also holds the rubber guard **(see illustrations)**.

4 Installation is the reverse of removal. On completion refill the reservoir as described in *Daily (pre-ride) checks*.

8.3a Unscrew the bolt and remove the reservoir...

8.3b ...noting how the lug on the bottom locates, and how the heat guard locates

9.4 Water inlet union bolts (arrowed)

F-1/FS-1 models onward (2001-on)

5 The coolant reservoir is located on the inside of the frame right-hand spar, near the rear shock absorber top mounting. In normal circumstances it should not require removal as it is well out of the way of all major assemblies.

6 The reservoir can be drained as described in Chapter 1. Removal of the reservoir necessitates first the removal of the rear mudguard, all electrical components which mount to the rear sub-frame, followed by removal of the sub-frame itself; the reservoir mounts to one of the sub-frame bolts and clips to the engine mounting collar via a lug moulded into its underside. Note the exact locations of the reservoir mounting collar and washer. Drain the reservoir of coolant before detaching it from the frame.

9 Coolant hoses and unions – removal and installation

Removal

1 Before removing a hose, drain the coolant (see Chapter 1).
2 Use a screwdriver to slacken the larger-bore hose clamps, then slide them back along the hose and clear of the union spigot. The smaller-bore hoses are secured by spring clamps which can be expanded by squeezing their ears together with pliers.
Caution: The radiator unions are fragile. Do not use excessive force when attempting to remove the hoses.
3 If a hose proves stubborn, release it by rotating it on its union before working it off. If all else fails, cut the hose with a sharp knife. Whilst this means replacing the hose, it is preferable to buying a new radiator.
4 The inlet union to the cylinder block can be removed by unscrewing its bolts **(see illustration)**. If the union is removed, the O-ring must be replaced with a new one. The outlet from the cylinder head goes into the thermostat housing, which is covered in Section 5.

Installation

5 Slide the clamps onto the hose and then work the hose on to its union.

> **HAYNES HiNT**
> *If the hose is difficult to push on its union, soften it by soaking it in very hot water, or alternatively a little soapy water on the union can be used as a lubricant.*

6 Rotate the hose on its unions to settle it in position before sliding the clamps into place and tightening them securely.
7 If the inlet union to the cylinder block has been removed, fit a new O-ring into the groove, using a dab of grease to hold it in place if necessary. Install the union and tighten the mounting bolts securely **(see illustration 9.4)**.

Notes

Chapter 4
Fuel and exhaust systems

Contents

Air filter renewal	see Chapter 1
Air filter housing – removal and installation	4
Carburettor overhaul – general information	6
Carburettor synchronisation	see Chapter 1
Carburettors – disassembly, cleaning and inspection	8
Carburettors – reassembly, and float height check	10
Carburettors – removal and installation	7
Carburettors – separation and joining	9
Catalytic converter (where fitted)	26
Choke cable – removal and installation	21
Direct Air Induction (DAI) system – check	23
Evaporative emission control (EVAP) system components	25
Exhaust system – removal and installation	22
Fast idle system wax unit – removal, inspection and installation	16
Fuel hoses – check and replacement	see Chapter 1
Fuel injection system – fault diagnosis and testing	12
Fuel injection system – general information	11
Fuel injection system components – check, removal and installation	13
Fuel pump – check, removal and installation	18
Fuel supply system – flow rate and pressure check	17
Fuel system – check	see Chapter 1
Fuel tank – cleaning and repair	3
Fuel tank and fuel tap – removal and installation	2
Fuel warning light/display and sensor – check and replacement	19
General information and precautions	1
Idle fuel/air mixture adjustment – general information	5
Idle speed – check and adjustment	see Chapter 1
Pulse secondary air (PAIR) system components	24
Starter valves – removal, installation and synchronisation	15
Throttle and choke cables – check and adjustment	see Chapter 1
Throttle body assembly – removal and installation	14
Throttle cables – removal and installation	20
Throttle position sensor (F-X and F-Y (1999 and 2000) models) – check, adjustment and replacement	see Chapter 5

Degrees of difficulty

Easy, suitable for novice with little experience	Fairly easy, suitable for beginner with some experience	Fairly difficult, suitable for competent DIY mechanic	Difficult, suitable for experienced DIY mechanic	Very difficult, suitable for expert DIY or professional

Specifications

Fuel

Grade	Unleaded, for the UK minimum 91 RON (Research Octane Number), for the USA minimum pump octane number 86
Fuel tank capacity (including reserve)	18.0 litres

Carburettors – F-X and F-Y (1999 and 2000) models

Type	CV
Size (throttle bore)	36.5 mm
Pilot screw setting (turns out)	see Text (and see **Note** below)
Float height	13.7 ± 0.5 mm
Idle speed	see Chapter 1
Pilot jet	40
Main jet	
European models	
Nos. 1 and 4 cylinder carburettors	130
Nos. 2 and 3 cylinder carburettors	132
US 49-state models – normal altitude (continuously below 1500 m)	
Nos. 1 and 4 cylinder carburettors	132
Nos. 2 and 3 cylinder carburettors	135
US California models – normal altitude (continuously below 1500 m)	
All carburettors	128
US 49-state models – high altitude (continuously above 2000 m)*	
Nos. 1 and 4 cylinder carburettors	130
Nos. 2 and 3 cylinder carburettors	132
US California models – high altitude (continuously above 2000 m)*	
All carburettors	125
Fuel pump minimum fuel flow rate	700 cc per minute

__Note:__ For US models that will be used continuously above an altitude of 2000m, the pilot screws should be set 1/2 turn in from their standard position

4•2 Fuel and exhaust systems

Fuel injection system – F-1/FS-1 models onward (2001-on)
Throttle bore diameter	38 mm
Idle speed	see Chapter 1
Fuel pressure at specified idle speed*	50 psi (3.5 Bar)
Minimum fuel flow rate	188 cc every 10 seconds

*Fuel pressure regulator vacuum hose disconnected and plugged

Fuel injection system test data – F-1/FS-1 models onward (2001-on)
Note: All values given are only accurate at 20°C (68°F)

Cam pulse generator minimum peak voltage output	0.7 volts
Ignition pulse generator minimum peak voltage output	0.7 volts
Engine coolant temperature (ECT) sensor resistance	2.3 to 2.6 K-ohms
Fuel injector resistance	11.1 to 12.3 ohms
Intake air temperature (IAT) sensor resistance	1 to 4 K-ohms
Oxygen sensor heater resistance	10 to 40 ohms

Emission control systems
PAIR system control valve resistance	20 to 24 ohms
EVAP system control valve resistance	30 to 34 ohms

Torque settings
Carburettor connecting bolt nuts	
6 mm nut	9 Nm
5 mm nut	5 Nm
Engine coolant temperature (ECT) sensor	23 Nm
Exhaust downpipe nuts	12 Nm
Fast idle system wax unit mounting screws	5 Nm
Fuel level sensor (F-X and F-Y (1999 and 2000) models)	23 Nm
Fuel rail bolts	10 Nm
Fuel pressure regulator bolts	10 Nm
Fuel pressure release bolt	15 Nm
Fuel pump assembly mounting plate nuts	12 Nm
Fuel supply hose banjo union nut and bolt	22 Nm
Oxygen sensor	25 Nm
Silencer clamp bolts	23 Nm

1 General information and precautions

General information

On F-X and F-Y (1999 and 2000) (carburettor) models, the fuel supply system consists of the fuel tank, strainer, fuel tap, fuel hoses, in-line filter, fuel pump, carburettors, and control cables. The fuel tap has a manually operated valve which need only be closed when the fuel tank is removed. When the manual valve is open, fuel flow is effected by a pump which is controlled by a relay that actuates the pump circuit when the engine is turned. If the manual valve is closed, fuel will not flow when the engine is turned.

On F-1/FS-1 models onward (2001-on) (fuel-injection) models, the fuel supply system consists of the fuel tank, fuel pump, filter, fuel hoses, throttle bodies, injectors, and control cables. There is no fuel tap – the fuel pump is switched on and off with the engine via a relay and supplies the fuel. The fuel flows to the fuel rail on the throttle body assembly, and this acts as a reservoir for the fuel injectors, controlled by a pressure relief valve which directs excess fuel back to the fuel tank. There is an injector for each cylinder, and these inject fuel into the throttle bodies where it mixes with the air before passing to the intake ducts. The injectors are operated by the Electronic Control Module (ECM) using the information obtained from the various sensors it monitors (refer to Section 11 for more information on the operation of the fuel injection system).

All models have a low fuel warning system in the instrument cluster which is actuated by a level sensor inside the fuel tank, and it comes on when there is approximately 3 litres (carburettor models) or 3.5 litres (fuel injection models) of fuel left. On carburettor models the system turns on a warning light in the instrument cluster. On fuel injection models the system turns on a RES indicator and segmented bar, which will thereafter flash and the segments extinguish according to how far you have travelled after initial illumination.

Many of the fuel system service procedures are considered routine maintenance items and for that reason are covered in Chapter 1.

Precautions

⚠ **Warning:** Petrol (gasoline) is extremely flammable, so take extra precautions when you work on any part of the fuel system. Always remove the battery (see Chapter 9). Don't smoke or allow open flames or bare light bulbs near the work area, and don't work in a garage where a natural gas-type appliance is present. If you spill any fuel on your skin, rinse it off immediately with soap and water. When you perform any kind of work on the fuel system, wear safety glasses and have a fire extinguisher suitable for a class B type fire (flammable liquids) on hand.

On F-1/FS-1 models onward (2001-on) (fuel-injection) models, residual pressure will remain in the fuel feed hose and fuel rail assembly long after the motorcycle was last used. Before disconnecting any fuel line, ensure the ignition is switched off then release fuel system pressure (see Section 2). It is vital that no dirt or debris is not allowed to enter the fuel tank or the fuel rail assembly whilst the fuel pipes are disconnected. Any foreign matter in the fuel system components could result in injector damage/malfunction. Ensure the ignition is switched off before disconnecting/reconnecting any fuel injection system wiring connector. If a connector is disconnected/reconnected with the ignition switched on, the engine control module (ECM) may be damaged.

Always perform service procedures in a

Fuel and exhaust systems 4•3

well-ventilated area to prevent a build-up of fumes.

Never work in a building containing a gas appliance with a pilot light, or any other form of naked flame. Ensure that there are no naked light bulbs or any sources of flame or sparks nearby.

Do not smoke (or allow anyone else to smoke) while in the vicinity of petrol (gasoline) or of components containing it. Remember the possible presence of vapour from these sources and move well clear before smoking.

Check all electrical equipment belonging to the house, garage or workshop where work is being undertaken (see the Safety first! section of this manual). Remember that certain electrical appliances such as drills, cutters etc. create sparks in the normal course of operation and must not be used near petrol (gasoline) or any component containing it. Again, remember the possible presence of fumes before using electrical equipment.

Always mop up any spilt fuel and safely dispose of the rag used.

Any stored fuel that is drained off during servicing work must be kept in sealed containers that are suitable for holding petrol (gasoline), and clearly marked as such; the containers themselves should be kept in a safe place. Note that this last point applies equally to the fuel tank if it is removed from the machine; also remember to keep its filler cap closed at all times.

Read the Safety first! section of this manual carefully before starting work.

2 Fuel tank and fuel tap – removal and installation

Warning: *Refer to the precautions given in Section 1 before starting work.*

Fuel tank – carburettor models

Removal

1 Make sure the fuel cap is secure. Remove the seat and the fuel tank trim panels (see Chapter 8).
2 To raise the tank, unscrew the front mounting bolts and remove the collars from the rubber grommets for safekeeping **(see illustrations)**. Get the rear wheel axle spanner from the toolkit. Lift the front of the tank and fit the spanner between it and the top of the shock absorber, with the handle end located in the recess in the tank **(see illustrations)**. Do not raise the tank any more than necessary to avoid damaging the rear bracket and rubbers.
3 To remove the tank, first raise it as described above. Turn the fuel tap OFF **(see illustration)**. Disconnect the fuel hose from the tap **(see illustration)**. Disconnect the fuel level sensor wiring connector **(see illustration)**. Also disconnect the overflow and breather hoses from their unions on the tank if required, again noting which fits where, or they can be left attached and drawn out with the tank, but note their routing. Remove the prop and lower the tank. Unscrew the rear mounting bolts and remove the bracket for the seat lug **(see illustration)**. Carefully lift the tank off the frame and remove it. Take care not to lose the rubbers.

2.2a Unscrew the front mounting bolts (arrowed) . . .

2.2b . . . and remove the collars

2.2c Position the tool between the tank . . .

2.2d . . . and the top of the shock as shown

2.3a Turn the fuel tap OFF

2.3b Disconnect the fuel hose . . .

2.3c . . . the wiring connectors (A) and if required the overflow hose (B) and breather hose (C)

2.3d Unscrew the rear mounting bolts (arrowed) and remove the bracket, then remove the tank

4•4 Fuel and exhaust systems

2.8 Unscrew the large nut (arrowed) and remove the tap

4 Check all the tank rubbers for signs of damage or deterioration and replace them with new ones if necessary.

Installation

5 Installation is the reverse of removal. Check that the tank mounting rubbers are fitted and in good condition. Make sure all the hoses are securely connected. Start the engine and check that there is no sign of fuel leakage. Do not forget to turn the fuel tap ON before lowering and securing the rear of the tank.

Fuel tap – carburettor models

Removal

6 If the tap is faulty, it cannot be disassembled and no individual components, so a new one will have to installed.
7 Remove the fuel tank as described above. Connect a drain hose to the fuel hose union and insert the end in a container that is suitable and large enough for storing the petrol. Turn the fuel tap to the ON position and allow the tank to drain.
8 Unscrew the large nut securing the tap and withdraw it from the tank **(see illustration)**. Withdraw the strainer as well and discard its O-ring as a new one should be used.
9 Clean the strainer to remove all traces of dirt and fuel sediment and check it for holes. If any are found, replace it with a new one.

Installation

10 Fit a new O-ring onto the strainer and insert it in the tank. Install the fuel tap, making sure it locates correctly over the strainer, and tighten the nut securely **(see illustration 2.8)**.
11 Install the fuel tank (see above).

Fuel tank – fuel injection models

Removal

Note: *Due to the arrangement of the fuel delivery and return system, which has no manual tap and no self sealing valves on the hoses, removing the tank involves a certain amount of unavoidable fuel spillage, which is obviously dangerous. Refer to the precautions given in Section 1 before starting work, and have plenty of rag on hand. Before the fuel hoses are disconnected they can be blocked using clamps, or after they have been disconnected the ends can be blocked, to prevent the tank from draining itself – a nut and bolt with sealing washers, or a suitably tight section of hose, can be used to block the supply hose banjo eye. If commercially available hose clamps are used, note that there is always a possibility of damaging a hose, especially if it is old, and that new hoses are sometimes too stiff to enable an effective seal to be made. Once the tank has been removed, store it upside down, resting it on some soft rag to prevent damaging the paintwork, and make sure the hose ends are above the level of the tank. Try to time the removal procedure with a near empty tank, which makes it much easier to lift, and means less fuel will be spilt in the event of something not going quite according to plan! To avoid unnecessary spillage, the best thing to do is to completely drain the tank before removing it. Obtain a suitable container for storing the petrol, and release the fuel pressure first, then drain the tank via the fuel return hose, disconnecting it from the fuel rail rather than the tank (see below).*

12 Make sure the fuel cap is secure. Remove the seat and the cockpit/fuel tank trim panels (see Chapter 8).

13 To raise the tank, unscrew the front mounting bolts and remove the collars from the rubber grommets for safekeeping **(see illustrations 2.2a and b)**. Obtain a suitable prop, such as a block of wood, that will fit securely between the underside of the front of the tank and the top of the frame behind the steering head. Note that a block of wood is better than something like a socket extension bar as it not only provides a wider base for extra stability, but also will not scratch or damage anything. Lift the front of the tank and fit the prop. Do not raise the tank any more than necessary to avoid damaging the rear bracket and rubbers.

14 To remove the tank, the fuel pressure must first be released and the residual fuel in the supply line drained off. Remove the battery (see Chapter 9). Raise the tank as described above. Disconnect the fuel pump and level sensor wiring connector **(see illustration)**. Place a rag and a suitable container for catching the residual fuel under the fuel supply hose union on the base of the tank, then slowly slacken the pressure release bolt in the centre of the union (not the union bolt itself) until you hear a hissing sound **(see illustration)**. At this point the fuel will spray out, so be ready with the rag to prevent it doing so. After the initial pressure has been reduced the bolt can be slackened a little further to allow the residual fuel to flow out. Once the pressure has been released, tighten the bolt.

15 As mentioned above (see **Note**), it is best to now fully drain the tank. To do this, place some fresh rag under the right-hand end of the fuel rail and position a suitable container very close by so that the supply hose end can be placed in it. Unscrew the nut securing the banjo union, counter-holding the base hex on the stud as you do, and draw the hose off the fuel rail, noting its alignment and the sealing washers, and place it immediately into the container, and allow the tank to drain **(see illustration and 2.19d, c, b and a)**. Fit the nut back onto the fuel rail stud. Now place some

2.14a Disconnect the pump wiring connector

2.14b Slacken the pressure release bolt (arrowed) and allow the pressure to escape

Fuel and exhaust systems 4•5

2.15a Counter-hold the hex (A), then unscrew the nut (B) and detach the feed hose, noting the washers

2.15b Disconnect the fuel return hose (arrowed) from the regulator

2.17a Disconnect the breather hose (A) and the overflow hose (B)

2.17b Unscrew the bolts and remove the bracket . . .

2.17c . . . and carefully remove the tank

2.19a Fit a new sealing washer . . .

fresh rag under the pressure regulator in the middle of the fuel rail, then release the clamp securing the return hose to the regulator and detach it, being prepared for some more residual fuel **(see illustration)**.

16 If you aren't draining the tank, block the banjo eye on the end of the supply hose using a nut, bolt and the sealing washers, or a short length of the correct width hose, and block the end of the return hose using a suitable bolt or plug (using a hose clamp is possible but not always that successful as the hose can be quite stiff and therefore difficult to seal, and there is always the possibility of cracking it, though a pair of long-nose mole grips with a large socket over each nose section might work – see *Tools and Workshop Tips* (Section 9) in the Reference Section.

17 Disconnect the breather and overflow hoses from their unions on the tank, again noting which fits where **(see illustration)**. Remove the prop and lower the tank. Unscrew the rear mounting bolts and remove the bracket for the seat lug **(see illustration)**. Carefully lift the tank off the frame and remove it **(see illustration)**. Take care not to lose the rubbers. If there is fuel in the tank, place it upside down on some clean soft rag.

18 Check all the tank rubbers for signs of damage or deterioration and replace them with new ones if necessary.

Installation

19 Installation is the reverse of removal. Before installing the tank, unscrew the pressure release bolt again **(see illustration 2.14b)**, then fit a new sealing washer and tighten the bolt to the torque setting specified at the beginning of the Chapter. If the supply hose was removed from the tank union, again use new sealing washers, then fit the neck of the hose between the lugs and tighten the bolt to the specified torque. Use new sealing washers on each side of the supply hose banjo union on the fuel rail and tighten the union nut to the specified torque, again counter-holding the base hex on the stud **(see illustrations)**. Make sure the return hose

4•6 Fuel and exhaust systems

2.19b ... then the feed hose ...

2.19c ... followed by another sealing washer ...

2.19d ... and the nut ...

2.19e ... then counter-hold the base hex and tighten the nut to the specified torque

4.3a Release the wiring clip ...

4.3b ... and detach the PAIR hose (A) and the vacuum hoses (B)

clamps are in good condition and use new ones if they have deformed or weakened. Check that the tank mounting rubbers are fitted and in good condition. Make sure all the hoses are securely connected. Start the engine and check that there is no sign of fuel leakage.

3 Fuel tank – cleaning and repair

1 All repairs to the fuel tank should be carried out by a professional who has experience in this critical and potentially dangerous work. Even after cleaning and flushing of the fuel system, explosive fumes can remain and ignite during repair of the tank.

2 If the fuel tank is removed from the bike, it should not be placed in an area where sparks or open flames could ignite the fumes coming out of the tank. Be especially careful inside garages where a natural gas-type appliance is located, because the pilot light could cause an explosion.

4 Air filter housing – removal and installation

Carburettor models

Removal

1 Remove the fuel tank (see Section 2).
2 On California models, displace the EVAP system purge control valve and solenoid valve from the rear of the housing.
3 Release the clip securing the wiring loom to the rear left corner of the housing **(see illustration)**. Release the clamp securing the PAIR system supply hose to the rear left of the housing and detach it from its union **(see illustration)**. Release the clamps securing the four vacuum take-off hoses to the rear of the housing and pull them off the blanking lugs.
4 Slacken the clamp screws securing the air intake ducts to the housing **(see illustration)**. Slacken the clamp screws securing the filter housing to the carburettors **(see illustration)**. Displace the housing up off the carburettors and disconnect the crankcase breather hose and the carburettor vent hoses from the unions, noting which fits

4.4a Slacken the air duct clamp screws ...

4.4b ... and the housing clamp screws (arrowed) ...

4.4c ... then displace the housing ...

Fuel and exhaust systems 4•7

4.4d ... and disconnect the breather hose (A) and vent hoses (B)

where **(see illustration)**. Remove the air filter housing.

Installation

5 Installation is the reverse of removal. Check the condition of the various hoses and their clamps and use new ones if they are in any way damaged or deteriorated.

4.7a Undo the screws (arrowed) ...

4.7b ... and remove the funnels

4.7d ... and the MAP sensor wiring connector and vacuum hose (arrowed)

4.6 Detach the PAIR hose (A) and the vacuum hoses (B)

Fuel injection models

Removal

6 Remove the fuel tank (see Section 2), and the air filter (see Chapter 1). Release the clamp securing the PAIR system supply hose to the rear right of the housing and detach it from its union **(see illustration)**. Release the clamps securing the two vacuum take-off hoses to the rear of the housing and pull them off the blanking lugs.

7 Undo the air funnel/filter housing mounting screws and remove the funnels, noting which fits where **(see illustrations)**. Displace the housing up off the throttle bodies, releasing the air ducts as you do, and disconnect the crankcase breather hose, and the MAP sensor wiring connector and vacuum hose **(see illustrations)**. Remove the air filter housing.

Installation

8 Installation is the reverse of removal. Check

4.7c Displace the housing and detach the breather hose ...

4.8 Replace the throttle body O-rings with new ones if necessary

the condition of the throttle body O-rings and use new ones if they are in any way damaged or deteriorated **(see illustration)**. Fit the shorter air intake funnels above the middle (Nos. 2 and 3) throttle bodies (each funnel pair is marked L or R to denote which side it fits on) **(see illustration 4.7b)**.

9 Check the condition of the various hoses and their clamps and use new ones if they are in any way damaged or deteriorated.

5 Idle fuel/air mixture adjustment (carburettor models) – general information

Note: *This information only applies to carburettor-equipped engines, i.e. the F-X and F-Y (1999 and 2000) models.*

Adjustment

1 If the engine runs extremely rough at idle or continually stalls, and if a carburettor overhaul does not cure the problem (and it definitely is a carburation problem – see Section 6), the pilot screws may require adjustment. It is worth noting at this point that unless you have the experience to carry this out on a multi-cylinder machine it is best to entrust the task to a motorcycle dealer, tuner or fuel systems specialist. Note that you will need a long thin flexible drive screwdriver with an angled end to access the pilot screws **(see illustration 8.11)**.

2 Before adjusting the pilot screws, warm the engine up to normal working temperature. Stop the engine and remove the tank (see Section 2). Screw in all four pilot screws until they seat lightly, then back them out to the number of turns specified below. This is the base position for adjustment.

Swiss market models . . . . $3\frac{1}{4}$ turn
Other European market models . . . . . 3 turns
California market models . . . . $2\frac{3}{8}$ turns
US 49-state and Canadian
   market models . . . . $3\frac{1}{8}$ turn

3 Arrange a temporary fuel supply using an auxiliary tank and some hosing. Start the engine and reset the idle speed to the correct level (see Chapter 1). Working on the carburettor for cylinder No. 4 first, turn the pilot screw by a small amount either side of the base position to find the point at which the highest consistent idle speed is obtained. Now do the same for the other three cylinders. Blip the throttle open a couple of times, then readjust the idle speed to the specified figure.

4 Turn the pilot screw on cylinder No. 4 carburettor in so that the idle speed drops by 50 rpm, then turn the screw out by the following amount:

Swiss market models . . . . $\frac{1}{2}$ turn
Other European market models . . . . . $\frac{3}{4}$ turn
California market models . . . . 1 turn
US 49-state and Canadian
   market models . . . . $\frac{3}{4}$ turn

4•8 Fuel and exhaust systems

5 Repeat Step 4 on cylinder Nos. 1, 2 and 3 carburettors.
Note: *For US models that will be used continuously above an altitude of 2000m, the pilot screws should be set 1/2 turn in from their standard position.*

Restrictions

6 Due to the increased emphasis on controlling exhaust emissions in certain world markets, regulations have been formulated which prevent adjustment of the air/fuel mixture. On such models the pilot screw positions are pre-set at the factory and in some cases have a limiter cap fitted to prevent tampering. Where adjustment is possible, it can only be made in conjunction with an exhaust gas analyser to ensure that the machine does not exceed the emissions regulations.

6 Carburettor overhaul – general information

Note: *This information only applies to carburettor-equipped engines, i.e. the F-X and F-Y (1999 and 2000) models.*

1 Poor engine performance, hesitation, hard starting, stalling, flooding and backfiring are all signs that major carburettor maintenance may be required.
2 Keep in mind that many so-called carburettor problems are really not carburettor problems at all, but mechanical problems within the engine or ignition system or other electrical malfunctions. Try to establish for certain that the carburettors are in need of maintenance before beginning a major overhaul.
3 Check the fuel tap and strainer, the fuel and vacuum hoses, the intake manifold joint clamps, the air filter, the ignition system, the spark plugs, valve clearance and carburettor synchronisation before assuming that a carburettor overhaul is required.
4 Most carburettor problems are caused by dirt particles, varnish and other deposits which build up in and block the fuel and air passages. Also, in time, gaskets and O-rings shrink or deteriorate and cause fuel and air leaks which lead to poor performance.

7.3a Detach the air vent hose (arrowed)...

5 When overhauling the carburettors, disassemble them completely and clean the parts thoroughly with a carburettor cleaning solvent and dry them with filtered, unlubricated compressed air. Blow through the fuel and air passages with compressed air to force out any dirt that may have been loosened but not removed by the solvent. Once the cleaning process is complete, reassemble the carburettor using new gaskets and O-rings.
6 Before disassembling the carburettors, make sure you have all necessary O-rings and other parts, some carburettor cleaner, a supply of clean rags, some means of blowing out the carburettor passages and a clean place to work. It is recommended that only one carburettor be overhauled at a time to avoid mixing up parts.

7 Carburettors – removal and installation

Note: *This information only applies to carburettor-equipped engines, i.e. the F-X and F-Y (1999 and 2000) models.*

⚠️ **Warning: Refer to the precautions given in Section 1 before starting work.**

Removal

1 Remove the fuel tank and the air filter housing (see Sections 2 and 4). Either drain the coolant (see Chapter 1), or prepare some hose clamps or blanking plugs for the

7.3b ... and the fuel supply hose

carburettor heating system hoses – there are two of them.
2 Detach the choke cable from the carburettors (see Section 21). There is no need to detach it from the handlebar end as well.
3 Detach the carburettor air vent hose (that goes to the PAIR system valve) from the T-piece union at the front of the carburettors **(see illustration)**. Detach the fuel supply hose from the T-piece union at the rear of the carburettors **(see illustration)**. On California models, disconnect the EVAP system hoses (Nos. 5 and 11) from the purge control valve.
4 Release the idle speed adjuster from its holder just ahead of the rear brake master cylinder reservoir on the right-hand side of the bike and feed it through to the base of the carburettors.
5 Fully slacken the lower clamps on the cylinder head intake manifold rubbers, accessing them using a long screwdriver via the aperture in each frame beam **(see illustration)**. Ease the carburettors up off the intakes along with the manifold rubbers, noting that they are quite a tight fit, and support them, using a rag to avoid scratching anything and to soak up any fuel that might come out.
Caution: *Tape over or stuff clean rag into each cylinder head intake after removing the throttle body assembly to prevent anything from falling in.*
6 Disconnect the throttle position sensor wiring connector **(see illustration)**.
7 Detach the throttle cables from the carburettors (see Section 20). There is no

7.5a Slacken the clamp screws, accessing them as shown ...

7.5b ... and displace the carburettors from the intakes

7.6 Disconnect the throttle position sensor wiring connector

Fuel and exhaust systems 4•9

7.8 Release the clamps and detach the hoses (arrowed) from the unions

7.9 Carburettor drain screws (arrowed)

need to detach them from the handlebar end as well.

8 Slacken the clamps securing the outer coolant hoses to the unions on the underside of the carburettors and detach the hoses, being prepared with either hose clamps or plugs to prevent the loss of coolant if it wasn't previously drained **(see illustration)**.

9 Place a suitable container below the float chambers, then slacken the drain screw on each chamber in turn and drain all the fuel from the carburettors **(see illustration)**. Discard the drain screw O-rings as new ones must be used. Once all the fuel has been drained, fit the new O-rings and tighten the drain screws securely.

10 If necessary, slacken the clamps securing the manifold rubbers to the carburettors and remove them, noting which way up and round they fit.

Installation

11 Installation is the reverse of removal, noting the following.
● Check for cracks or splits in the cylinder head intake manifold rubbers and the various hoses, and replace them with new ones if necessary.
● If removed, make sure the manifold rubbers are installed with the CARB marking facing towards the carburettor, aligning the slotted tab on the side with the projection on the carburettor, and that they are full engaged. Tighten the clamps so that the gap between the clamp ends is 11 to 13 mm.
● Make sure the manifold rubbers are fully engaged with the cylinder head when the carburettors are installed. Tighten the clamps so that the gap between the clamp ends is 3 to 5 mm.
● Make sure all hoses are correctly routed and secured and not trapped or kinked. If it was drained, do not forget to refill the cooling system (see Chapter 1). Otherwise, just check the level and top up if necessary (see Daily (pre-ride) checks).
● Check the operation of the throttle and choke cables and adjust them as necessary (see Chapter 1).
● Check idle speed and carburettor synchronisation (if overhauled) and adjust as necessary (see Chapter 1).

8 Carburettors – disassembly, cleaning and inspection

Note: *This information only applies to carburettor-equipped engines, i.e. the F-X and F-Y (1999 and 2000) models.*

⚠ **Warning: Refer to the precautions given in Section 1 before starting work.**

Disassembly

1 Remove the carburettors from the machine (see Section 7) **(see illustration)**. **Note:** *Do not separate the carburettors unless*

1 Top cover
2 Spring
3 Jet needle holder and O-ring
4 Spring
5 Jet needle
6 Washer
7 Diaphragm/piston
8 Choke plunger
9 Spring
10 Nut
11 Cap
12 Air cut-off valve
13 Pilot screw
14 Float
15 Float pin
16 Float valve
17 Float chamber
18 O-ring
19 Drain screw
20 Pilot jet
21 Main jet
22 Needle jet holder
23 Air funnel holder
24 Air funnel
25 O-ring

8.1 Carburettor components

4•10 Fuel and exhaust systems

8.2a Undo the screws (arrowed) and remove the washers . . .

8.2b . . . then release the spring end (arrowed) and remove the bar

8.2c Unscrew the nut (arrowed) and remove the spring and plunger

absolutely necessary; each carburettor can be dismantled sufficiently for all normal cleaning and adjustments while joined together. Dismantle each carburettor separately to avoid interchanging parts.

2 Remove the screws securing the choke linkage bar to the carburettors, noting the plastic washers **(see illustration)**. Release the end of the return spring from the bar, noting how it locates **(see illustration)**. Lift off the bar, noting how it fits, and remove the collars and return spring, noting how the other end locates **(see illustrations 8. 10f, e and d)**. If not already done, slacken the clamp securing the manifold rubber to the carburettor and remove it, noting which way up and round it fits. Unscrew the choke plunger nut, using a pair of thin nosed pliers if access is too restricted for a spanner, and withdraw the spring and plunger from the carburettor body **(see illustration and 10.10c, b and a)**.

3 Unscrew and remove the top cover retaining screws **(see illustration)**. Lift off the cover and remove the spring from inside the piston **(see illustration)**.

4 Carefully peel the diaphragm away from its sealing groove in the carburettor and withdraw the diaphragm and piston assembly **(see illustration)**.

Caution: Do not use a sharp instrument to displace the diaphragm as it is easily damaged.

5 Thread a 4 mm screw into the top of the needle holder (one of the top cover retaining screws is ideal), then grasp the screw head using a pair of pliers and carefully draw the holder out of the piston **(see illustrations)**. Note the spring in the base of the needle holder – it should stay in place, but take care not to lose it and remove it if it is loose **(see illustration)**. Push the needle up from the bottom of the piston and withdraw it from the top **(see illustration)**. Note the washer that fits between the needle head and the piston **(see illustration 10.7a)**. Check the condition of the O-ring on the holder and replace it with a new one if it is damaged, deformed or deteriorated **(see illustration 10.7c)**.

8.3a Undo the screws (arrowed) . . .

8.3b . . . and remove the cover and spring

8.4 Peel the diaphragm off the carburettor and withdraw the diaphragm and piston assembly

8.5a Thread the bolt into the holder . . .

8.5b . . . and draw it out of the piston

8.5c Note the spring in the holder

8.5d Push the needle up from the bottom and withdraw it from the top

Fuel and exhaust systems 4•11

8.6 Remove the screws (arrowed) and lift off the chamber

8.7 Displace the float pin and remove the float assembly (arrowed)

8.8 Remove the main jet (arrowed) . . .

6 Remove the screws securing the float chamber to the base of the carburettor and remove it **(see illustration)**. Remove the rubber gasket and discard it as a new one must be used.

7 Displace the float pin using a small screwdriver and withdraw it from the pivot **(see illustration)**. Remove the float, then slide the float needle valve off, noting how it fits **(see illustrations 10.4b and a)**.

8 Unscrew and remove the main jet from the base of the needle jet holder **(see illustration)**.

9 Unscrew and remove the needle jet holder **(see illustration)**.

10 Unscrew and remove the pilot jet **(see illustration)**.

11 The pilot screw can be removed if required, but note that its setting will be disturbed (see **Haynes Hint**). Where fitted, remove the pilot screw cap – it is probably sealed in place and will need to be prised out. Unscrew and remove the pilot screw along with its spring, washer and O-ring **(see illustration)**. Discard the O-ring as a new one must be used.

HAYNES HiNT *To record the pilot screw's current setting, turn the screw in until it seats lightly, counting the number of turns necessary to achieve this, then fully unscrew it. On installation, the screw is simply backed out the number of turns you've recorded.*

12 Do not remove the throttle position sensor unnecessarily. If you do need to remove it, undo the nut on the end of the front carburettor connecting bolt and the screw securing the throttle position sensor mounting bracket to the No. 4 carburettor and remove the bracket with the sensor attached **(see illustration)**. Do not separate the sensor from the bracket unless it is known to be faulty, and in which case refer to Chapter 5.

13 Undo the screws securing the air intake funnel assembly and remove it, noting how it fits **(see illustration)**. Separate the funnel from its holder if required by twisting it to free the tabs, noting how it fits. Discard the O-ring if it is in any way damaged, deformed or deteriorated.

Cleaning

Caution: Use only a petroleum based solvent for carburettor cleaning. Don't use caustic cleaners.

14 Submerge the metal components in the solvent, following the manufacturer's recommendations.

15 After the carburettor has soaked long enough for the cleaner to loosen and dissolve most of the varnish and other deposits, use a nylon-bristled brush to remove the stubborn deposits. Rinse it again, then dry it with compressed air.

16 Use a jet of low-pressure compressed air to blow out all of the fuel and air passages in

8.9 . . . the needle jet holder (arrowed) . . .

8.10 . . . and the pilot jet (arrowed)

8.11 If required, remove the pilot screw (arrowed) along with its O-ring, washer and spring

8.12 Unscrew the nut (A) and the screw (B) and remove the bracket with the sensor attached

8.13 Air intake funnel screws (arrowed)

4•12 Fuel and exhaust systems

8.16 Blow through the air jets as well as the fuel jets

8.17 Check the choke plunger as described

8.26 Air cut-off valve screw (arrowed)

the main and upper body, not forgetting the air jets in the carburettor intake **(see illustration)**.
Caution: Never clean the jets or passages with a piece of wire or a drill bit, as they will be enlarged, causing the fuel and air metering rates to be upset.

Inspection

17 Inspect the needle on the end of the choke plunger **(see illustration)**, the plunger shaft, the spring and the plunger linkage bar **(see illustration 8.1)**. Replace any component that is worn, damaged or bent.
18 If removed from the carburettor, check the tapered portion of the pilot screw and the spring and O-ring for wear or damage. Replace them with new ones if necessary.
19 Check the carburettor body, float chamber and top cover for cracks, distorted sealing surfaces and other damage. If any defects are found, replace the faulty component, although replacement of the entire carburettor will probably be necessary (check with a Honda dealer on the availability of separate components).
20 Check the piston diaphragm for splits, holes and general deterioration. Holding it up to a light will help to reveal problems of this nature.
21 Insert the piston in the carburettor body and check that it moves up-and-down smoothly. Check the surface of the piston for wear. If it's worn excessively or doesn't move smoothly in the guide, renew the components as necessary.
22 Check the jet needle for straightness by rolling it on a flat surface such as a piece of glass. Replace it with a new one if it's bent or if the tip is worn.
23 Check the tip of the float needle valve and the valve seat. If either has grooves or scratches in it, or is in any way worn, they should be renewed as a set. Gently push down on the rod on the top of the needle valve then release it – if it doesn't spring back, replace the valve with a new one.
24 Operate the throttle shaft to make sure the throttle butterfly valve opens and closes smoothly. If it doesn't, cleaning the throttle linkage may help. Otherwise, replace the carburettor with a new one.
25 Check the float for damage. This will usually be apparent by the presence of fuel inside the float. If the float is damaged, it must be replaced with a new one.
26 To remove the air cut-off valves for all except the No. 4 carburettor, the carburettors must be separated (see Section 9). Remove the screw securing the cut-off valve and separate it from the carburettor **(see illustration)**. Remove the air jet and O-rings **(see illustration 8.1)**. Check the condition of the O-rings and discard them if they are damaged, deformed or deteriorated. To check the valve, apply a vacuum to the hose attached to the valve cover. With the vacuum applied, air should not be able to flow between the ports in the valve. With no vacuum applied, air should be able to flow. If the valve does not behave as described, replace it with a new one.

9 Carburettors – separation and joining

Note: *This information only applies to carburettor-equipped engines, i.e. the F-X and F-Y (1999 and 2000) models.*

⚠️ **Warning: Refer to the precautions given in Section 1 before starting work.**

Separation

1 The carburettors do not need to be separated for normal overhaul. If you need to separate them (to replace a carburettor body, for example), refer to the following procedure **(see illustration)**. If required, first remove the manifold rubbers (see Section 7, Step 10), and the air intake funnels (see Section 8, Step 13).

9.1 Carburettor assembly

1 Choke linkage bar	5 Idle speed adjuster	9 Fuel tube joint
2 Choke cable bracket	6 Joining studs	10 Water tube joint
3 Throttle cable bracket	7 Air vent hose union	11 Throttle thrust spring
4 Throttle position sensor	8 Air vent hose joint	

Fuel and exhaust systems 4•13

9.5a Remove the dowel (A), the screw (B) and the bracket (C). Rear connecting bolt nut (D)

9.5b Withdraw the bolt (A) and remove the bracket (B) and the union (C)

2 Remove the carburettors from the machine (see Section 7). Mark the body of each carburettor with its cylinder number to ensure that it is positioned correctly on reassembly.

3 Remove the screws securing the choke linkage bar to the carburettors, noting the plastic washers **(see illustration 8.2a)**. Release the end of the return spring from the bar, noting how it locates **(see illustration 8.2b)**. Lift off the bar, noting how it fits, nd remove the collars and return spring, noting how the other end locates **(see illustrations 8. 10.10f, e and d)**.

4 Make a note or sketch of the arrangement of the fuel hoses, the air vent hoses and the breather hoses, and mark them according to their union. If required, release the clamps securing the hoses and carefully pull them off.

5 Undo the nut on the end of the front connecting bolt and the screw securing the throttle position sensor mounting bracket to the No. 4 carburettor and remove the bracket with the sensor attached **(see illustration 8.12)**. Do not separate the sensor from the bracket unless it is known to be faulty. Remove the locating dowel from the throttle cable bracket, then undo the screw securing the bracket and remove it and the air vent hose union, noting how they fit **(see illustration)**. Grasp the nut on the left-hand end of the connecting bolt and withdraw the bolt, then remove the bracket and the air vent hose union, noting how they fit **(see illustration)**. Withdraw the connecting bolt.

6 Make a note of how the throttle return springs, linkage assembly and carburettor synchronisation springs are arranged to ensure that they are fitted correctly on reassembly **(see illustrations)**. Also note the arrangement of the various hose unions, joint pieces and collars **(see illustration 9.1)**. Undo the synchronisation screws to relieve the pressure on the springs and remove the springs, noting how they fit.

7 Unscrew the nut from one end of the rear connecting bolt **(see illustration 9.5a)**. Withdraw the bolt from the other end of the carburettors.

8 Carefully separate carburettor Nos. 1 and 2 from Nos. 3 and 4, so they are in two pairs. Retrieve the dowels (noting which fits where) and the joint collar as they are separated.

9 Separate carburettors 1 and 2 by gently pulling them apart. Retrieve the throttle linkage spring, both dowels, joint collar, air vent joint, fuel joint and coolant joint. Carry out the same procedure to separate carburettors. 3 and 4, noting the choke cable guide.

Joining

10 Assembly is the reverse of the disassembly procedure, noting the following.
● Use new O-rings on all the air vent, fuel and coolant joint pieces **(see illustration 9.1)**.
● The carburettor joining bolts are different diameter; the front (engine side) bolt is 6 mm, whereas the rear (intake side) bolt is 5 mm diameter. Similarly, the dowels between each carburettor are sized accordingly. Tighten the nuts evenly to the specified torque setting, ensuring correct alignment of the carburettors, that there are no gaps between any of the joints between the carburettor bodies, and that no more than 3 mm of bolt thread extends from the outer face of any nut.
● Check the operation of both the choke and throttle linkages ensuring that both open smoothly and return quickly under spring pressure.
● Adjust the carburettor synchronisation settings manually at first by aligning the bottom of the No. 4 carburettor throttle butterfly with the inner edge of the outer by-pass hole using the throttle stop screw. Now set the other butterflies in the same position using the synchronisation screws. After the carburettors are installed, check carburettor synchronisation using vacuum gauges (see Chapter 1).
● If the manifold rubbers were removed, make sure they are installed with the CARB marking facing towards the carburettor, aligning the slotted tab on the side with the projection on the carburettor, and that they are full engaged. Tighten the clamps so that the gap between the clamp ends is 11 to 13 mm.

10 Carburettors – reassembly and float height check

Note: *This information only applies to carburettor-equipped engines, i.e. the F-X and F-Y (1999 and 2000) models.*

> **Warning: Refer to the precautions given in Section 1 before proceeding.**

Note: *When reassembling the carburettors, be sure to use the new O-rings, gaskets and other parts supplied in the rebuild kit. Do not overtighten the carburettor jets and screws as they are easily damaged.*

1 Install the pilot screw (if removed) along with its spring, washer and O-ring, turning it in until it seats lightly **(see illustration 8.11)**. Now, turn the screw out the number of turns previously recorded on disassembly. Where removed, fit a new cap on the screw, applying a little bonding agent to hold it in position.
2 Install the pilot jet **(see illustration)**.
3 Install the needle jet holder **(see**

9.6a Note the arrangement of the throttle linkage . . .

9.6b . . . and the synchronisation springs and screws

10.2 Install the pilot jet . . .

4•14 Fuel and exhaust systems

10.3a ... the needle jet holder ...

10.3b ... and the main jet

10.4a Fit the needle valve into the holder ...

10.4b ... then fit the float assembly, making sure the valve enters the seat (arrow) ...

10.4c ... and secure it with the pin

illustration). Screw the main jet into the end of the needle jet holder (see illustration).

4 Slide the float needle valve onto the float, then position the float assembly in the carburettor, making the needle valve locates in its seat, and install the pin, making sure it is secure (see illustrations).

5 To check the float height, hold the carburettor so the float hangs down, then tilt it back until the needle valve is just seated, but not so far that the needle's spring-loaded tip is compressed. Measure the distance between the gasket face (with the gasket removed) and the bottom of the float with an accurate ruler (see illustration). The correct setting should be as given in the Specifications at the beginning of the Chapter. If it is incorrect, replace the float and needle valve with new ones – the float height is not adjustable.

6 With the float height checked, fit a new rubber gasket onto the float chamber, making sure it is seated properly in its groove, then fit the chamber onto the carburettor and tighten the screws securely (see illustration).

7 If removed, fit the washer underneath the

10.5 Measuring the float height

10.6a Fit a new O-ring into the groove ...

10.6b ... and install the float chamber

Fuel and exhaust systems 4•15

10.7a Fit the washer onto the needle . . .

10.7b . . . then insert the needle into the piston

10.7c Fit a new O-ring . . .

10.7d . . . and the spring if removed . . .

10.7e . . . then install the holder

jet needle head **(see illustration)**. Insert the needle into the piston, making sure the washer does not fall off **(see illustration)**. Fit a new O-ring into the groove in the needle holder and smear it with oil. Check that the spring is in the base of the needle holder **(see illustration 8.5c)**, or install it if removed **(see illustration)**. Align the tabs on the holder with the slots in the piston and insert the holder, pushing it down until the O-ring is felt to locate in its groove **(see illustration)**. Remove the bolt used on removal from the holder, if not already done **(see illustration 8.5a)**.

8 Turn the diaphragm inside out so that its rim faces down **(see illustration)**. Insert the piston assembly into the carburettor, ensuring the needle is correctly aligned with the needle jet. Keep a finger on the bottom of the piston to keep it raised (inserting your finger via the air intake) so the diaphragm stays inside out – this will prevent the rim popping out of the groove. Align the loop on the diaphragm rim with its groove in the carburettor body, then press the diaphragm outer edge into its groove, making sure it is correctly seated **(see illustration)**.

9 Keeping the piston raised, fit the spring, locating it over the needle holder **(see illustration 8.3b)**. Fit the top cover onto the carburettor, locating the top of the spring inside the raised section in the cover **(see illustration)**. Align the protrusion on the cover with the loop on the diaphragm. Make sure the diaphragm rim stays seated in its groove and does not get pinched by the cover, then install the cover screws and tighten them securely. You can now let the piston drop.
10 Fit the choke plunger and spring into the carburettor body and tighten the nut to secure

10.8a Turn the diaphragm inside out and fit the assembly into the carburettor

10.8b Press the diaphragm rim into the groove, making sure the loop (arrowed) locates correctly

10.9 Fit the spring into the cover then install the cover as described

4•16 Fuel and exhaust systems

10.10a Install the choke plunger . . .

10.10b . . . and the spring . . .

10.10c . . . and secure them with the nut

it **(see illustrations)**. Check that the plunger moves smoothly out when pulled and returns quickly under spring pressure when let go. Fit the return spring over its lug, and fit the plastic collars **(see illustrations)**. Fit the choke linkage bar onto the plungers, making sure the slots locate correctly behind the nipple on the end of each choke plunger, and hook up the return spring **(see illustration)**. Fit the plastic washers and secure the linkage bar in place with the screws **(see illustration)**. Check the operation of the choke linkage bar.

11 If the air intake funnels were removed, use new O-rings if necessary and fit them into the groove in the intake side of each carburettor **(see illustration)**. Fit the air funnel into the holder and rotate it so that its tabs are locked in place **(see illustration)**. Align the cutouts in the air funnel with the corresponding raised lands on the intake bore, and fit the pins on the holder into the holes in the carburettor body **(see illustration)**. Tighten the four screws securely **(see illustration 8.13)**.

12 If removed, install the throttle position sensor (See Chapter 5).

13 Install the carburettors (see Section 7).

10.10d Fit the return spring . . .

10.10e . . . and the collars . . .

10.10f . . . then locate the bar onto the plungers and the spring end onto the bar . . .

10.10g . . . and secure the bar with the plastic washers and screws

10.11a Fit the O-ring into the groove

10.11b Fit the funnel into the holder . . .

10.11c . . . and then onto the carburettor, locating the cut-outs over the raised sections

10.11d Locate the pins on the holder into the holes in the carburettor (arrow)

Fuel and exhaust systems 4•17

11.1 Fuel injection and engine management system component location - note that on European FS-1 and FS-2 and US 2001 and 2002 models the ECM is above the battery

1 Bank angle sensor
2 Ignition (main) switch
3 PAIR solenoid valve
4 IAT sensor
5 ECT sensor
6 Throttle position sensor
7 Fuel pump
8 ECM
9 Engine stop relay
10 Fuel cut-off relay
11 Oxygen sensor (where fitted)
12 Speed sensor
13 Ignition pulse generator
14 Fuel pressure regulator
15 Injectors and rail
16 Cam pulse generator
17 MAP sensor

11 Fuel injection system – general information

Note: *This information only applies to F-1/FS-1 models onward (2001-on).*

1 F-1/FS-1 models onward (2001-on) are equipped with Honda's programmed fuel injection (PGM-FI) system. It is controlled by an engine management system which has an electronic control module (ECM) that operates both the injection and ignition systems **(see illustration)**. The fuel injection side of the system is covered in this Chapter; refer to Chapter 5 for information on the ignition system.

2 The fuel pump, contained in the fuel tank, pumps fuel to the fuel rails on the throttle body assembly, via a filter. Fuel supply pressure is controlled by the pressure regulator which keeps the pressure in the fuel rails constant, returning excess fuel to the tank via the return hose. The fuel rails act as a reservoir for the four injectors (one for each cylinder) which are operated by the Engine Control Module (ECM).

3 The engine control module (ECM) monitors signals from the following sensors.

● Throttle position sensor (TPS) – informs the ECM of the throttle position, and the rate of throttle opening or closing.
● Engine coolant temperature (ECT) sensor – informs the ECM of engine temperature. It also actuates the temperature gauge (see Chapter 3).
● Manifold absolute pressure (MAP) sensor – informs the ECM of the engine load by monitoring the pressure in the throttle body inlet tracts.
● Intake air temperature (IAT) sensor – informs the ECM of the temperature of the air entering the throttle body.
● Cam pulse generator – informs the ECM of engine speed and camshaft position.
● Ignition pulse generator – informs the ECM of engine speed and crankshaft position.
● Speed sensor – informs the ECM of the speed of the motorcycle (see Chapter 9).
● Oxygen sensor (only on models with catalytic converter – Germany and California models) – informs the ECM of the oxygen content of the exhaust gases.

4 All the information from the sensors is analysed by the ECM, and from that it determines the appropriate ignition and

4•18 Fuel and exhaust systems

1 Engine stop relay
2 Circuit fuse
3 Engine stop switch
4 Circuit fuse
5 Ignition switch
6 Main fuse
7 Bank angle sensor
8 Circuit fuse
9 Immobiliser unit
10 Battery
11 Fuel pressure regulator
12 Intake air temperature sensor
13 Combined ignition coil/spark plug caps
14 Pulse air injection solenoid valve
15 Throttle position sensor
16 Manifold absolute pressure sensor
17 Fuel injector
18 Cam pulse generator sensor
19 Pulse air injection check valve
20 Engine coolant temperature sensor
21 Crankshaft position (ignition pulse) sensor
22 Oxygen sensor
23 Coolant temperature display
24 Fuel cut-off relay
25 Fuel pump
26 Road speed sensor
27 Neutral switch
28 Clutch switch
29 Side stand switch
30 Engine management warning light
31 Immobiliser warning light
32 Diagnostic socket
33 Tachometer

11.4 PGM-FI fuel and electrical circuits

fuelling requirements of the engine **(see illustration)**. The ECM controls the fuel injector by varying its pulse width – the length of time the injector is held open – to provide more or less fuel, as appropriate. The mixture strength (fuel/air ratio) is also constantly varied by the ECM, to provide the best setting for cold starting, warm-up, idle, cruising, and acceleration. Due to the layout of the engine, the fuelling needs for each cylinder are slightly different and the ECM is programmed to compensate for this; the injection system is fully sequential, with each injector receiving its own operating signal from the ECM.

5 Cold starting and warm up idle speeds are controlled by an 'automatic fast idle system', which basically takes the place of a manual choke lever. A heat sensitive wax-filled unit that has engine coolant circulating around it actuates the starter valve arrangement in the throttle body assembly via a linkage rod. When the coolant is cold the wax unit is contracted and the starter valves are open. As the coolant heats up the wax expands, closing the starter valves. The starter valves allow additional air to bypass the throttle valves when the throttle is closed, and this increases the engine idle speed.

6 If there is an abnormality in any of the readings obtained from any sensor, the ECM enters its back-up mode. In this event, the ECM ignores the abnormal sensor signal, and assumes a pre-programmed value which will allow the engine to continue running (albeit at reduced efficiency). If the ECM enters this back-up mode, or when any faults occur, the FI warning light in the instrument cluster will come on, and the relevant fault code will be stored in the ECM memory. The fault can be identified using the fault codes which can be accessed using the self-diagnosis function (see Section 12). However if there are certain faults detected in the injectors or the cam or ignition pulse generators, the back-up mode becomes ineffective and the ECM will not allow the engine to run at all. Note that many European models have an immobiliser system (HISS – Honda Ignition Security System) which will not allow the engine to be started unless the correct key is used. A fault in this system should not be confused with a fuel injection system fault. The immobiliser system has its own fault-diagnosis function (see Chapter 5).

12 Fuel injection system – fault diagnosis and checking

Note: *This information only applies to F-1/FS-1 models onward (2001-on).*

Fault diagnosis

1 If the fuel injection system (FI) warning light on the instrument cluster illuminates when the motorcycle is running, a fault has occurred in the fuel injection/ignition system. The engine control module (ECM) will store the relevant fault code in its memory and this code can be read as follows using the self-diagnostic mode of the ECM. While the engine is running and the motorcycle is being used, the FI light will come on and stay on. When the motorcycle is on its sidestand and the engine is running below 5000 rpm, the FI light will flash, the pattern of the flashes indicating the code for the fault the ECM has identified.

2 If the engine can be started, place the motorcycle on its sidestand then start the engine and allow it to idle. Whilst the engine is idling, observe the FI warning light on the instrument cluster.

3 If the engine cannot be started, or to check for any stored fault codes even though the FI light has not illuminated, remove the seat, and on European F-1 and F-2 models the seat cowling (see Chapter 8), to gain access to the fuel injection system service check wiring connector, which is a black 3-pin (2 wire) single sided connector adjacent to the ECM on the left-hand rear sub-frame on European F-1 and F-2 models, and on the left-hand side of the battery on FS-1, FS-2 and (US 2001 and 2002) models. Ensure the ignition is switched OFF then bridge the outer terminals of the service check connector with an auxiliary wire **(see illustration)**. With the terminals connected, make sure the kill switch is in the RUN position then turn the ignition ON and observe the FI warning light. If there are no stored fault codes, the FI light will come on and stay on. If there are stored fault codes, the FI light will flash.

4 The fuel injection system warning light uses long (1.3 second) and short (0.5 second) flashes to give out the fault code. A long flash is used to indicate the first digit of a double digit fault code (i.e. 10 and above). If a single digit fault code is being displayed (i.e. 0 – 9), there will be a number of short flashes equivalent to the code being displayed. For example, two long (1.3 sec) flashes followed by five short (0.5 sec) flashes indicates the fault code number 25. If there is more than one fault code, there will be a gap before the other codes are revealed (the codes will be revealed in order, starting with the lowest and finishing with the highest). Once all codes have been revealed, the ECM will continuously run through the code(s) stored in its memory, revealing each one in turn with a short gap between them. The fault codes are as shown in the table:

12.3a Service check connector location and jumper wire (arrowed) connection - European F-1 and F-2 models

12.3b Service check connector location and jumper wire (arrowed) connection - European FS-1 and FS-2 and US 2001 and 2002 models

Fault code (No. of flashes)	Symptoms	Possible causes
0 – no code (warning light constantly on)	Engine does not start	Blown fuse (main, engine stop, PGM-FI or fuel pump) Faulty power supply to electronic control module (ECM) Faulty engine stop relay or wiring Faulty engine stop switch/open circuit on switch earth (ground) wire Faulty ignition switch Faulty bank angle sensor or wiring Faulty electronic control module (ECM)
0 – no code (warning light constantly on)	Engine runs normally	Short circuit in service check connector or wiring Faulty electronic control module (ECM)
0 – no code (warning light off)	Engine runs normally	Blown warning light bulb Open circuit in warning light wiring Faulty electronic control module (ECM)
1	Engine runs normally	Faulty manifold absolute pressure (MAP) sensor or wiring
2	Engine runs normally	Faulty manifold absolute pressure (MAP) sensor/vacuum hose
7	Engine difficult to start at low temperatures	Faulty engine coolant temperature (ECT) sensor or wiring
8	Poor throttle response	Faulty throttle position sensor or wiring
9	Engine runs normally	Faulty inlet air temperature (IAT) sensor or wiring
11	Engine operates normally	Faulty speed sensor or wiring
12	Engine does not start	Faulty No. 1 injector or wiring
13	Engine does not start	Faulty No. 2 injector or wiring
14	Engine does not start	Faulty No. 3 injector or wiring
15	Engine does not start	Faulty No. 4 injector or wiring
18	Engine does not start	Faulty cam pulse generator or wiring
19	Engine does not start	Faulty ignition pulse generator or wiring
33	Engine operates normally	Faulty EPROM in electronic control module (ECM)
The following codes are only applicable to models with catalytic converter		
21	Engine operates normally	Faulty oxygen sensor
24	Engine operates normally	Faulty oxygen sensor heating element

4•20 Fuel and exhaust systems

Once all the codes have been revealed, switch off the ignition and (where necessary) remove the auxiliary wire from the service check connector. Identify the fault using the table above, then refer below on for checking procedures.

5 Once the fault has been identified and corrected, it will be necessary to reset the system by removing the fault code from the ECM memory. To do this, ensure the ignition is switched OFF then bridge the terminals of the service check connector (see Step 3) **(see illustration 12.3a or b)**. Make sure the kill switch is in the RUN position, then turn the ignition switch ON. Disconnect the auxiliary wire from the service check connector. When the wire is disconnected the FI light should come on for about five seconds, during which time the auxiliary wire must be reconnected. The warning light should start to flash when it is reconnected, indicating that all fault codes have been erased. However if the light flashes twenty times the memory has not been erased and the procedure must be repeated. Turn off the ignition then remove the auxiliary wire. Check the operation of the warning light (in some cases it may be necessary to repeat the erasing procedure more than once) then install the seat.

Checking

6 While some of the sensors can be checked using home equipment, there are others which can only be tested using the Honda special electronic diagnostic test pin box which can be plugged into the system. If a fault appears, use the diagnostic function and fault code system described above to work out which component is faulty. First ensure that the relevant system wiring connectors are securely connected and free of corrosion – poor connections are the cause of the majority of problems. Also check the wiring itself for any obvious faults or breaks, and use a continuity tester to check the wiring between its connectors, referring to the *Wiring Diagrams* at the end of Chapter 9. Next refer to Section 13 to see if there are any other specific checks that can be made on that particular component. If this fails to reveal the cause of the problem, the motorcycle should be taken to a suitably-equipped Honda dealer for testing. They will have access to the test pin box which should locate the fault quickly and simply.

7 Also ensure that the fault is not due to poor maintenance – i.e., check that the air filter element is clean, that the spark plugs are in good condition and correctly gapped, that the valve clearances are correctly adjusted, the cylinder compression pressures are correct, and the ignition timing is correct (refer to Chapters 1, 2, 4 and 5). It is also worth removing the sensor(s) in question (see Section 13) and checking that the sensing portion is clean and not obstructed by anything. Where there is a vacuum hose to a sensor, make sure it is securely connected at both ends and has no cracks or splits.

13.3a Disconnect the wiring connector from the injector . . .

13 Fuel injection system components – check, removal and installation

Note: *This information only applies to F-1/FS-1 models onward (2001-on).*
Caution: *Ensure the ignition is switched off before disconnecting/reconnecting any fuel injection system wiring connector. If a connector is disconnected/reconnected with the ignition switched on the engine control module (ECM) could be damaged.*

Fuel rail and injectors

⚠ **Warning:** *Refer to the precautions given in Section 1 before starting work.*

Check

1 Remove the air filter housing (see Section 7).
2 If the engine runs, start it and allow it to idle. Check the operation of each injector using a stethoscope or sounding rod; an injector will emit a 'clicking' noise when functioning. If any injector is silent, either the injector or its wiring harness is faulty. **Note:** *Reconnect the wiring connector to the intake air temperature sensor (on the air filter housing cover) to prevent the ECM detecting a fault while making the check.*
3 If the engine does not run, disconnect the wiring connectors from the injectors **(see illustration)**. Connect an ohmmeter across the terminals of each injector and measure its resistance **(see illustration)**. Compare the readings obtained for each injector to that

13.6 Unscrew the bolts (arrowed) and detach the fuel rail

13.3b . . . and measure the resistance between the injector terminals (arrowed)

given in the Specifications. Also check that there is no continuity to earth on the black/white wire terminal on the injector. If the resistance of any injector differs greatly from that specified, or there is continuity to earth, the injector should be renewed. Also check for battery voltage at the black/white wire terminal in the wiring connector. If there is no voltage, check the wiring.

Removal

4 Remove the air filter housing (see Section 4). If required, remove the throttle bodies (see Section 14) – this is not essential, but will make the job less fiddly.
5 If the throttle bodies are in situ, disconnect the wiring connectors from the injectors **(see illustration 13.3a)**. Disconnect the vacuum hose from the fuel pressure regulator **(see illustration 13.14)**.
6 Unscrew the fuel rail mounting bolts **(see illustration)**. Carefully lift off the fuel rail assembly – the injectors will probably come away with the fuel rail, but could stay in the throttle body **(see illustration 13.10a)**.
7 Remove the injectors from either the fuel rail or throttle body assembly **(see illustration)**. Note the correct fitted position of the O-ring, rubber spacer and seal on each injector; the O-ring and seal must be renewed, but the spacer can be reused as long as it is not damaged, deformed or deteriorated.

Installation

8 Lubricate the new seals, spacers and O-rings with a smear of engine oil. Slide the spacer onto the top of each injector, then fit a

13.7 Pull each injector out of the fuel rail or throttle body as appropriate

Fuel and exhaust systems 4•21

13.8 Fit a new seal (A), spacer (B) and O-ring (C) onto each injector

13.10a Install the fuel rail . . .

13.10b . . . making sure the injectors seat correctly

new O-ring into the groove **(see illustration)**. Fit the seal onto the bottom of the injector.

9 Ease the injectors into position in the fuel rail, taking care not to damage the O-rings **(see illustration 13.7)**. Make sure the injector wiring connector sockets are all positioned so they will point to the rear when the fuel rail is installed.

10 Install the fuel rail assembly, making sure each injector enters its throttle body and the seals stay in place and seat correctly **(see illustrations)**. Fit the fuel rail bolts and tighten them to the torque setting specified at the beginning of the Chapter **(see illustration and 13.6)**.

11 Connect the vacuum tube to the pressure regulator **(see illustrations 13.14)**. Install the throttle bodies if removed, or reconnect the injector wiring connectors – ensure they are connected correctly **(see illustration 13.3a)**.

Fuel pressure regulator

⚠️ *Warning: Refer to the precautions given in Section 1 before starting work.*

Check

12 Check the fuel flow rate and pressure (see Section 17).

Removal

13 Remove the fuel tank (see Section 2).
14 Detach the vacuum hose from the regulator **(see illustration)**. Unscrew the regulator bolts, holding the fuel rail securely to prevent any distortion, and detach the regulator from the rail. Discard the O-ring as a new one must be used.

Installation

15 Fit a new O-ring into the groove in the regulator flange. Install the regulator, and tighten the bolts to the torque setting specified at the beginning of the Chapter, again holding the fuel rail to prevent distortion **(see illustration 13.14)**. Connect the vacuum hose to its union.
16 Install the fuel tank (see Section 2).

Throttle position sensor (TPS)

Check

17 The throttle sensor operation can only be checked using the Honda diagnostic test pin box (see Sections 11 and 12). Its power supply can be checked as follows. Raise the fuel tank (see Section 2). Disconnect the wiring connector from the sensor **(see illustration)**. Connect the positive (+) lead of a voltmeter to the yellow/red terminal of the sensor wiring connector, then connect the negative (–) lead to a good earth. Turn the ignition switch ON and check that a voltage of 4.75 to 5.25 volts is present. If it isn't, there is a fault in the yellow/red wire or the ECM. If voltage was present, now connect the negative lead to the green/orange terminal of the connector and check that the same voltage is present. If it isn't, there is a fault in the green/orange wire or the ECM. If there is voltage, check for continuity to earth in the red/yellow wire. If there is, trace the fault in the wire and repair it. If there isn't, and the sensor is proven good by the Honda tester, then the ECM is faulty.

Removal and installation

18 The throttle sensor is an integral part of the throttle body assembly and is not available separately. If the sensor is faulty, the complete throttle body assembly will have to be renewed.

Engine coolant temperature (ECT) sensor

Note: The sensor also operates the coolant temperature gauge (see Chapter 3).

Check

19 Raise or remove the fuel tank (See Section 2). The sensor is mounted in the thermostat housing on the back of the engine.
20 Disconnect the wiring connector from the sensor **(see illustration)**. With the engine cold, connect an ohmmeter across the pink and green/orange wire terminals on the sensor and measure its resistance. Compare the reading obtained to that given in the Specifications noting that the specified value is only valid at 20°C (68°F); the sensor resistance will increase at lower temperatures and decrease at higher temperatures. If the

13.14 Fuel pressure regulator vacuum hose (A) and mounting bolts (B)

13.17 Disconnect the throttle sensor wiring connector (arrowed)

13.20 Disconnect the ECT wiring connector (arrowed). The sensor screws into the thermostat housing

4•22 Fuel and exhaust systems

resistance reading differs greatly from that specified, the sensor is probably faulty.

21 If the sensor appears to be functioning correctly, check its power supply. Connect the positive (+) lead of a voltmeter to the pink terminal of the sensor wiring connector, then connect the negative (–) lead to a good earth. Turn the ignition switch ON and check that a voltage of 4.75 to 5.25 volts is present. If it isn't, there is a fault in the pink wire or the ECM. If voltage was present, now connect the negative lead to the green/orange terminal of the connector and check that the same voltage is present. If it isn't, there is a fault in the green/orange wire or the ECM. If there is voltage, the ECM is probably faulty.

Removal

⚠️ **Warning: The engine must be completely cool before carrying out this procedure.**

22 Drain the cooling system (see Chapter 1). Remove the throttle bodies (See Section 14). The sensor is mounted in the thermostat housing.
23 Disconnect the sensor wiring connector **(see illustration 13.20)**. Unscrew the sensor and remove it from the housing. Discard the sealing washer.

Installation

24 Fit a new sealing washer onto the sensor. Install the sensor in the thermostat housing and tighten it to the torque setting specified at the beginning of the Chapter. Connect the sensor wiring.
25 Install the throttle bodies (see Section 14) and refill the cooling system (see Chapter 1).

Manifold absolute pressure (MAP) sensor

Check

26 The MAP sensor can only be checked using the Honda diagnostic test pin box (see Sections 11 and 12). However you can raise the fuel tank (see Section 2) and make sure that the vacuum hose to it is securely fixed at both ends, and has no cracks or splits. The sensor is mounted on the underside of the air filter housing on the left-hand side.
27 The sensor power supply can be checked as follows. Raise the fuel tank (see Section 2). Disconnect the wiring connector from the sensor **(see illustration 4.7d)**. Connect the positive (+) lead of a voltmeter to the yellow/red terminal of the sensor wiring connector, then connect the negative (–) lead to a good earth. Turn the ignition switch ON and check that a voltage of 4.75 to 5.25 volts is present. If it isn't, there is a fault in the yellow/red wire or the ECM. If voltage was present, now connect the negative lead to the green/orange terminal of the connector and check that the same voltage is present. If it isn't, there is a fault in the green/orange wire or the ECM. If there is voltage, check that the same voltage is present between the light green/yellow terminal of the connector and the green/orange terminal. If it isn't, there is a fault in the light green/yellow wire or the ECM. If there is, and the sensor is proven good by the Honda tester, then the ECM is faulty.

Removal

28 Remove the air filter housing (see Section 4).
29 Undo the MAP sensor retaining screw and remove the sensor.

Installation

30 Installation is the reverse of removal.

Intake air temperature (IAT) sensor

Check

31 Raise or remove the fuel tank (see Section 2). The sensor is mounted in the front of the air filter housing. Disconnect its wiring connector **(see illustration)**.
32 With the sensor cold, connect an ohmmeter across the sensor terminals and measure its resistance. Compare the reading obtained to that given in the Specifications noting that the specified value is only valid at 20°C (68°F); the sensor resistance will increase at lower temperatures and decrease at higher temperatures. If the resistance reading differs greatly from that specified, the sensor is probably faulty.
33 If the sensor appears to be functioning correctly, check its power supply. Connect the positive (+) lead of a voltmeter to the grey/blue terminal of the sensor wiring connector, then connect the negative (–) lead to a good earth. Turn the ignition switch ON and check that a voltage of 4.75 to 5.25 volts is present. If it isn't, there is a fault in the grey/blue wire or the ECM. If voltage was present, now connect the negative lead to the green/orange terminal of the connector and check that the same voltage is present. If it isn't, there is a fault in the green/orange wire or the ECM. If there is voltage, the ECM is probably faulty.

Removal

34 Raise or remove the fuel tank (see Section 2). The sensor is mounted in the front of the air filter housing.
35 Disconnect the sensor wiring connector **(see illustration 13.31)**. Undo the retaining screws and remove the sensor from the housing **(see illustration)**.

Installation

36 Installation is the reverse of removal.

Cam pulse generator

Check

37 Raise or remove the fuel tank (see Section 2).
38 Trace the wiring back from the pulse generator, which is on the left-hand end of the cylinder head, to its white 2-pin wiring connector inside the rubber boot above the crankcase and disconnect it. Perform the following check(s).
39 Using an ohmmeter check for continuity between the white/yellow terminal on the sensor side of the connector and earth (ground). If there is continuity then the cam pulse generator is faulty.
40 Connect the positive (+) lead of a voltmeter and peak voltage adapter arrangement* to the grey terminal on the sensor side of the cam pulse generator connector and the negative (–) lead to the white/yellow terminal of the connector. Turn the engine over on the starter motor and note the voltage reading obtained. If this reading is below the specified minimum, the cam pulse generator is faulty. *Note: *Honda specify their own Imrie diagnostic tester (model 625), or the peak voltage adapter (Pt. No. 07HGJ-0020100) with an aftermarket digital multimeter having an impedance of 10 M-ohm/DCV minimum for this test.*
41 If the cam pulse generator functions correctly then the fault must be in the wiring harness or the ECM, and can be located by a Honda dealer with the test pin box.

Removal

42 Remove the left-hand fairing side panel (see Chapter 8). Raise or remove the fuel tank (see Section 2).
43 Trace the wiring back from the sensor, which is on the left-hand end of the cylinder head, to its white 2-pin wiring connector inside the rubber boot above the crankcase and disconnect it. Feed the wiring through to the pulse generator, noting its routing.
44 Unscrew the bolt securing the cam pulse

13.31 Disconnect the IAT sensor wiring connector

13.35 Undo the screws (arrowed) and remove the sensor

Fuel and exhaust systems 4•23

generator and draw it out of the head **(see illustration)**. Discard the O-ring.

Installation

45 Fit a new O-ring into the groove in the cam pulse generator body, then fit it into the cylinder head and secure it with the bolt.
46 Feed the wiring back to the connector and reconnect it. Install the fairing side panel and the fuel tank.

Ignition pulse generator
Check

47 Trace the wiring back from the pulse generator, which is mounted in the clutch cover on the right-hand side of the engine, to its red 2-pin wiring connector above the crankcase and disconnect it – depending on the size of your hands and general dexterity, and the tightness of the connector, you may have to either remove the right-hand fairing side panel (see Chapter 8) or raise the fuel tank (see Section 2). Perform the following checks.
48 Using an ohmmeter check for continuity between the white/yellow terminal on the sensor side of the connector and earth (ground). If there is continuity then the ignition pulse generator is faulty.
49 Connect the positive (+) lead of a voltmeter and peak voltage adapter arrangement* to the yellow terminal of the ignition pulse generator connector and the negative (–) lead to the white/yellow terminal of the connector. Turn the engine over on the starter motor and note the voltage reading obtained. If this reading is below the specified minimum, the ignition pulse generator is faulty. ***Note:*** *Honda specify their own Imrie diagnostic tester (model 625), or the peak voltage adapter (Pt. No. 07HGJ-0020100) with an aftermarket digital multimeter having an impedance of 10 M-ohm/DCV minimum for this test.*
50 If the cam pulse generator functions correctly then the fault must be in the wiring harness or the ECM, and can be located by a Honda dealer with the test pin box.

Removal

51 Remove the clutch cover (see Chapter 2, Section 16, referring to the relevant Steps). The sensor is mounted inside it.
52 Undo the sensor mounting bolts and the wire guide bolt and washer, then free the wiring grommet from the cover and remove the sensor **(see illustration)**.

Installation

53 Remove all traces of sealant from the sensor wiring grommet and clutch cover and apply a smear of fresh sealant to the grommet.
54 Locate the grommet and sensor correctly in the cover and tighten the sensor bolts securely **(see illustration 13.52)**. Route the wire and secure it the washer and bolt.
55 Install the clutch cover (see Chapter 2, Section 16, referring to the relevant Steps).

Speed sensor

56 See Chapter 9, Section 16.

13.44 Unscrew the bolt and draw the cam pulse generator (arrowed) out of the engine

Bank angle sensor
Check

57 Position the motorcycle on its centrestand if fitted or on an auxiliary stand so that the motorcycle is level. Remove the windshield (see Chapter 8). The bank angle sensor is mounted below it **(see illustration 13.62)**.
58 With the ignition switch on, connect the negative (–) lead of a voltmeter to the green terminal of the bank angle sensor connector (with the connector still connected). Connect the voltmeter positive (+) lead first to the white/black terminal and check that battery voltage (approximately 12 volts) is present, then connect it to the red/white terminal and check that between 0 to 1 volt is present.
59 Switch the ignition off then remove the retaining screws and free the bank angle sensor from its mounting (again with the connector still connected). Hold the sensor horizontal and switch the ignition on; the engine stop relay (located behind the battery) should click, indicating the power supply is closed (on). Slowly tilt the sensor to the left whilst listening to the engine stop relay; once the sensor reaches an angle of approximately 60° the relay should be heard to click, indicating the power supply is open (off). Switch the ignition off and return the sensor to the horizontal, then switch the ignition back on again (engine stop relay should click again) and tilt the sensor to the right. The engine stop relay should be heard to click again once the sensor reaches an angle of around 60°.
60 If voltage readings/relay performance are

13.62 Bank angle sensor wiring connector (A) and mounting screws (B)

13.52 Unscrew the sensor bolts (A) and the wiring guide bolt (B), and free the wiring grommet (C)

not as given, then it is likely the bank angle sensor is faulty.

Removal

61 Remove the windshield (see Chapter 8). The bank angle sensor is mounted below it.
62 Disconnect the bank angle sensor wiring connector then slacken and remove the retaining screws and remove the sensor from its mounting **(see illustration)**.

Installation

63 Installation is the reverse of removal. Make sure the sensor is fitted with its 'UP' mark facing upwards.

Engine stop relay
Check

64 Remove the relay (see below).
65 Connect an ohmmeter between the red/white and black/white terminals of the relay. Using a battery and auxiliary wires, connect the battery positive (+) terminal to the other red/white terminal of the relay and negative (–) terminal to the black terminal of the relay and note the meter reading obtained. If the relay is operating correctly there should be continuity (zero resistance) when the battery is connected and no continuity (infinite resistance) when the battery is disconnected. If this is not the case, renew the relay.

Removal

66 Remove the seat cowling (see Chapter 8). The engine stop relay is the front relay located on the right-hand side of the rear sub-frame **(see illustration)**.

13.66 Engine stop relay (A), fuel cut-off relay (B)

4•24 Fuel and exhaust systems

13.76a Release the strap and displace the ECM . . .

13.76b . . . then disconnect the wiring connectors

67 Free the relay from its mounting, then disconnect the wiring connector and remove the relay.

Installation

68 Installation is the reverse of removal.

Fuel cut-off relay

Check

69 Remove the relay (see below).
70 Connect an ohmmeter between the black/white and brown terminals of the relay. Using a battery and auxiliary wires, connect the battery positive (+) terminal to the brown/black terminal of the relay and the negative (–) terminal to the other black/white terminal of the relay and note the meter reading obtained. If the relay is operating correctly there should be continuity (zero resistance) when the battery is connected and no continuity (infinite resistance) when the battery is disconnected. If this is not the case, renew the relay.

Removal

71 Remove the seat cowling (see Chapter 8). The fuel cut-off relay is the rear relay located on the right-hand side of the rear sub-frame **(see illustration 13.66)**.
72 Free the relay from its mounting, then disconnect the wiring connector and remove the relay.

Installation

73 Installation is the reverse of removal.

Engine control module (ECM)

Check

74 The engine control module (ECM) can only be checked using the Honda diagnostic test pin box.

Removal

75 Remove the seat, and on European F models the seat cowling (see Chapter 8). Disconnect the battery negative (–) terminal.
76 On European FS models and all US models, release the ECM retaining strap and lift the ECM off the battery cover **(see illustration)**. Disconnect the wiring connectors and remove the ECM **(see illustration)**.
77 On European F models, disconnect the ECM wiring connectors, then either lift the ECM out of its holder, or draw the holder off its mounts.

Installation

78 Installation is the reverse of removal.

Oxygen sensor – models with catalytic converter

Check

79 Apart from the wiring checks that are outlined in Section 12, the operation of the oxygen sensor can only be checked using the Honda diagnostic test pin box (see Section 10)
80 To check the sensor heater, remove the seat (see Chapter 8). Trace the wiring back from the sensor to the wiring connector and disconnect it. Connect an ohmmeter between the white wire terminals on the sensor side of the connector and check that the resistance is between 10 and 40 ohms. Also check that there is no continuity to earth (ground) in either of the white wires. If the resistance is not as specified or if there is continuity to earth, replace the sensor with a new one. Otherwise check for battery voltage between the black/white (+) and black/green (-) terminals on the loom side of the connector with the ignition ON. If there is no voltage, check the wiring, using the wiring diagrams at the end of Chapter 9. Otherwise have the sensor and its circuit tested by a Honda dealer equipped with the diagnostic tester.

Removal

Note: *The oxygen sensor is delicate and will not work if it is dropped or knocked, if its power supply is disrupted, or if any cleaning materials are used on it. Ensure the exhaust system is cold before proceeding.*
81 Remove the seat (see Chapter 8).

82 Trace the wiring back from the sensor to the wiring connector and disconnect it.
83 Unscrew the oxygen sensor and remove it from the front of the exhaust silencer.

Installation

84 Installation is the reverse of removal. Tighten the sensor to the torque setting specified at the beginning of the Chapter.

14 Throttle body assembly – removal and installation

Note: *This information only applies to F-1/FS-1 models onward (2001-on).*

⚠ **Warning:** *Refer to the precautions given in Section 1 before starting work.*

Removal

1 Remove the fuel tank and the air filter housing (Sections 2 and 4). Either drain the coolant (see Chapter 1), or prepare some hose clamps or blanking plugs for the fast idle system wax unit heating system hoses – there are two of them.
2 Remove the bolts securing the throttle cable bracket to the throttle body assembly. Free both inner cables from the throttle cam. Note that if access is too restricted, this can be done after the throttle body assembly has been displaced.
Caution: *Do not snap the throttle cam/valves from fully open to fully closed once the cables have been disconnected because this can lead to engine idle speed problems.*
3 Release the idle speed adjuster from its holder and feed it through to the base of the throttle body assembly **(see illustration)**.
4 Either disconnect the wiring connector from each fuel injector and the throttle position sensor **(see illustrations 13.3a and 13.17)**, or alternatively you can disconnect the grey 10-pin sub-loom connector located on the inside of the left-hand frame beam, leaving the injector and throttle position sensor (TPS) wiring connected, noting that the inlet air temperature (IAT) sensor and manifold absolute pressure (MAP) sensor wiring will come away with the sub-loom when the throttle body assembly is removed **(see illustration)**.

14.3 Release the idle speed adjuster from its holder

14.4 Throttle body and air sensor sub-loom wiring connector

Fuel and exhaust systems 4•25

14.6a Access the clamp screws (arrowed) . . .

14.6b . . . using a long screwdriver via the aperture in the frame

14.6c Ease the throttle bodies out of the intakes . . .

5 On California models, disconnect the EVAP system solenoid valve vacuum hose from the five-way hose joint on the throttle body assembly.

6 Fully slacken the lower clamps on the cylinder head intake manifold rubbers, accessing them using a long screwdriver via the aperture in each frame beam, and noting their orientation **(see illustrations)**. Ease the throttle body assembly up off the manifold along with the intake rubbers, noting that they are quite a tight fit, and support them, using a rag to avoid scratching anything **(see illustration)**.

Caution: Tape over or stuff clean rag into each cylinder head intake after removing the throttle body assembly to prevent anything from falling in.

7 Slacken the clamps securing the coolant hoses to the fast idle system wax unit **(see illustration)**. Detach the hoses, and if the coolant wasn't drained, clamp or plug the ends.

8 If the intake rubbers shown signs of damage or deterioration they must be renewed. Note their orientation and how the clamps locate and are orientated before removing them, and on installation tighten the retaining clips so that the gap between the ends of each clip is 6 to 8 mm. Also check the throttle body vacuum hoses for signs of damage or deterioration and renew any suspect hoses **(see illustration)**.

Caution: The throttle body assembly must be treated as a sealed unit. With the exception of the fast idle system wax unit screws, NEVER loosen any of the white-painted nuts/bolts/screws on the assembly as these are pre-set at the factory to ensure correct synchronisation of the throttle valves and idle circuit. Only remove the yellow painted nuts/bolts/screws if any procedure directs it. The only components on the assembly which are serviceable are the starter valves (see Section 15) and the various vacuum hoses.

Caution: NEVER use a solvent-based carburettor cleaner to clean the throttle body assembly. The throttle bores are covered with a molybdenum coating which could be removed by the cleaner.

9 If required, disconnect the injector and throttle position sensor wiring connectors and remove the sub-harness.

Installation

10 If removed, connect the wiring sub-harness to the injectors and throttle position sensor. Remove the tape/plugs from the intakes and make sure the intake rubber retaining clip screws are correctly orientated as noted on removal.

11 Lubricate the rubbers with a light smear of engine oil to ease installation then rest the throttle body assembly in position.

12 Fit the coolant hoses onto the wax unit and tighten the clamps securely **(see illustration 14.7)**.

13 Connect the throttle inner cables to the cam, then fit the cable bracket to the throttle body and securely tighten its bolts. This can be done after the throttle bodies have been installed if required (see Section 20).

14.7 . . . and detach the coolant hoses (arrowed) from the wax unit

14.8 Vacuum hose location and routing

A All markets except California
B California market models

4•26 Fuel and exhaust systems

15.3a No. 2 cylinder starter valve nut (A), Nos. 1 and 2 starter valve arm screws (B), link arm screw (C), shaft bore collars (D)

15.3b Nos. 3 and 4 cylinder starter valve nuts (A), valve arm screws (B), shaft bore collar (C)

15.7a Unscrew the starter valves using the base nuts (arrowed) . . .

14 Ease the throttle body assembly onto the intakes **(see illustration 14.6c)**. Ensure each body is fully engaged, then tighten all the retaining clips so that the gap between the ends of each clip is 3 to 5 mm **(see illustration 14.6b)**.

15 Connect either the injector and throttle position sensor wiring connectors, or the sub-harness wiring connector, according to your removal method, making sure they are all secure **(see illustrations 13.3 and 13.17 or 14.4)**.

16 On California models, connect the EVAP system solenoid valve vacuum hose to the five-way hose joint on the throttle body assembly.

17 Fit the idle speed adjuster into its holder **(see illustration 14.3)**.

18 If the cooling system was drained, do not forget to refill it (see Chapter 1). Otherwise, just check the level and top up if necessary (see Daily (pre-ride) checks). Install the air filter housing and the fuel tank (Sections 4 and 2).

15 Starter valves – removal, installation and synchronisation

Note: *This information only applies to F-1/FS-1 models onward (2001-on).*

⚠️ **Warning: Refer to the precautions given in Section 1 before starting work.**

Removal

1 Remove the throttle body assembly (see Section 14).

2 Remove the fuel rail and injectors (see Section 13).

3 Screw the Nos. 2, 3 and 4 cylinder throttle body starter valve adjustment nuts in until they seat lightly, noting the amount of turns needed to do so on a piece of paper **(see illustrations)**. The valve for the No. 1 cylinder throttle body is the base and is pre-set and fixed.

4 To access the Nos. 1 and 2 starter valves, remove the fast idle system wax unit (see Section 16).

5 Undo the screws securing the arms for the Nos.1 and 2 starter valves and the screw securing the link arm for the wax unit and remove the arms, noting how they fit **(see illustration 15.3a)**.

6 Undo the screws securing the arm for the Nos. 3 and 4 starter valves and remove the arm, noting how it fits **(see illustration 15.3b)**.

7 Unscrew the starter valve base nuts and remove the four valves from the throttle body, keeping them in their correct fitted order **(see illustration)**.

8 If required, draw the shaft and out from the right-hand end, noting the three collars in the bores that the shaft runs in **(see illustrations 15.3a and b)**. Remove them for safekeeping if they are loose.

9 Check all components for wear and damage and renew as necessary **(see illustration)**.

Installation

10 Clean the starter valves and throttle body passages using compressed air only. Do not use a carburettor cleaner or any other solvent.

Caution: NEVER use a solvent-based carburettor cleaner to clean the throttle body components. The throttle bores are covered with a molybdenum coating which could be removed by the cleaner.

11 Install each starter valve in its original location **(see illustration 15.7b)**. Tighten the valve base nuts then check that each

15.7b . . . and remove them

valve moves smoothly and easily in its bore by pulling on the valve end, and that it closes fully under spring pressure **(see illustration 15.7a)**.

12 If removed, fit the collars into the shaft bores, noting that the bore adjacent the No.3 starter valve does not have one, and making sure they are the correct way round **(see illustrations 15.3a and b)**. Slide the shaft in from the right-hand end, making sure the collars stay in place.

13 Locate the arm for the Nos. 1 and 2 starter valves on the shaft and under the valve ends and secure it with the screws **(see illustration 15.3a)**. Make sure the arm ends engage correctly with the valves. Also fit the link arm for the wax unit and secure it with the screw.

14 Locate the arm for the Nos. 3 and 4 starter valves on the shaft and under the valve ends and secure it with the screws **(see illustration)**.

15.9 Check the action of the starter valve plunger in the body - it should move smoothly and return easily under spring pressure

15.14a Fit the arm onto the shaft . . .

Fuel and exhaust systems 4•27

15.14b . . . making sure it engages correctly behind the starter valve head

15.21a Release the clamps and detach the 1 and 2 hoses from the stubs (arrowed) . . .

15.21b . . . and pull the 3 and 4 hoses (arrowed) from the 3-way joint

Make sure the arm ends engage correctly with the valves **(see illustration)**.
15 Check the operation of the starter valve shaft before continuing; it should move smoothly and easily, drawing all the valves out as it turns, and return to the fully closed position under pressure of the return springs.
16 Install the idle system wax unit (see Section 16).
17 Turn the No. 2, 3 and 4 starter valve adjustment nuts in until they seat lightly, then back each one out by the exact amount of turns noted prior to removal **(see illustrations 15.3a and b)**.
18 Install the fuel injectors (see Section 13), then install the throttle body assembly (Section 14). On completion check the starter valve synchronisation (see below).

Synchronisation

Note: *This procedure should be carried out if the starter valves have been removed from the throttle body assembly. The procedure does not alter the setting of the throttle valves themselves (these are pre-set at the factory and fixed), but only the starter valves, which control the idle speed when the engine is cold and warming up.*

19 Starter valve synchronisation is simply the process of adjusting the valves so they pass the same amount of fuel/air mixture to each cylinder on cold start and warm-up. This is done by measuring the vacuum produced in each intake duct. Starter valves that are out of synchronisation will result in uneven idling when cold starting and warming the engine. Before synchronising the starter valves, make sure the valve clearances are properly set (see Chapter 1).
20 To properly synchronise the starter valves, you will need a set of vacuum gauges or calibrated tubes to indicate engine vacuum. The equipment used should be suitable for a four cylinder engine and come complete with the necessary adapters and hoses to fit the take-off points. **Note:** *Because of the nature of the synchronisation procedure and the need for special instruments, most owners leave the task to a Honda dealer.*
21 Raise the fuel tank (see Section 2). Detach the Nos.1 and 4 cylinder vacuum hoses from the blanking stubs on the rear of the air filter housing, noting which fits where **(see illustration)**. Detach the Nos.2 and 3 cylinder vacuum hoses from the three-way joint which directs the vacuum to the fuel pressure regulator **(see illustration)**. Also detach the air hoses from the PAIR system reed valve cover unions on the valve cover (remove the air filter housing to get at them – see Chapter 4), and fit blanking caps in their place **(see illustration)**. Install the air filter housing.
22 Connect the gauge hoses to the vacuum hoses using suitable adapters **(see illustration 12.5)**. Make sure they are a good fit because any air leaks will result in false readings.
23 Start the engine and adjust the idle speed (see Chapter 1). If using vacuum gauges fitted with damping adjustment, set this so that the needle flutter is just eliminated but so that they can still respond to small changes in pressure.
24 The vacuum readings for the Nos. 2, 3 and 4 cylinders should be the same as the No. 1 cylinder, or at least within the maximum difference specified at the beginning of the Chapter. The No. 1 cylinder starter valve is the base to which all the others are matched, and cannot itself be adjusted. If the vacuum readings vary, adjust each starter valve as required by turning the synchronising nut on the end of the valve, until the readings are the same **(see illustration)**. **Note:** *Do not press hard on the nut whilst adjusting it, otherwise a false reading will be obtained.*
25 When the adjustment is complete, recheck the vacuum readings, then adjust the idle speed by turning the throttle stop screw (see Chapter 1) until the idle speed listed in this Chapter's Specifications is obtained. Stop the engine.
26 Remove the vacuum gauges and the hose adapters. Remove the air filter housing, then fit the PAIR system hose back onto the unions on the reed valve covers and secure them with the clamps **(see illustration 12.13c)**. Install the air filter housing. Fit the Nos. 1 and 4 cylinder vacuum hoses on to their original stubs on the back of the air filter housing – the No.1 cylinder vacuum hose fits on the left-hand stub, and the No.4 on the right-hand stub **(see illustration 12.13a)**. Fit the Nos.2 and 3 cylinder vacuum hoses on to the three-way joint for the fuel pressure regulator vacuum hose **(see illustration 12.13b)**. Install the fuel tank (see Section 2).

15.21c Release the clamps and detach the hoses (arrowed), and fit blanking caps to the unions

15.24 Starter valve synchronisation nuts (arrowed) - Nos. 3 and 4 shown

16 Fast idle system wax unit – removal, inspection and installation

Note: *This information only applies to F-1/FS-1 models onward (2001-on).*

⚠ **Warning:** *Refer to the precautions given in Section 1 before starting work.*

Removal

1 Remove the throttle body assembly (see Section 14).

4•28 Fuel and exhaust systems

16.3a Undo the screws (arrowed) . . .

16.3b . . . and pivot the wax unit upwards

16.4a Open the valves by manually turning the shaft . . .

2 Remove the fuel rail and injectors (see Section 13).
3 Undo the two screws securing the wax unit and displace it upwards from its mount **(see illustration)**.
4 Turn the starter valve shaft so that the valves are open, then pivot the wax unit up further to release the pushrod pivot piece from the link arm, and remove the wax unit **(see illustration)**.

Inspection

5 Undo the three screws securing the wax unit cover and remove it **(see illustration)**. Discard the O-ring as a new one must be used. Remove the spring, spring seat and wax element from the body (or in reverse order from the cover, depending where they are). Discard the wax element O-rings.
6 Visually inspect all components for signs of wear and damage and renew them as required.
7 The wax element expands with heat. If you suspect it is not working correctly, place it first in a cold place and check that it is fully retracted. Now gently heat it using a hairdryer or equivalent and check that it expands.
8 Check that the pushrod moves smoothly in and out of the body. Check the spring for fatigue and distortion.
9 Fit new O-rings onto the wax element and the cover. Fit the wax element into the body, then fit the spring seat and the spring onto the element. Fit the cover and tighten its screws evenly and in a criss-cross pattern in three stages.

Installation

10 Turn the starter valve shaft so that the valves are open, then fit the wax unit pushrod pivot piece into the link arm **(see illustrations 16.4a and b)**.
11 Pivot the wax unit down onto its mount, then install the two screws and tighten them to the torque setting specified at the beginning of the Chapter **(see illustrations 16.3b and a)**.
12 Install the injectors and fuel rail (see Section 13).
13 Install the throttle body assembly (see Section 14).

17 Fuel supply system – flow rate and pressure check

Note: *This information only applies to F-1/FS-1 models onward (2001-on).*

⚠️ **Warning:** *Refer to the precautions given in Section 1 before starting work.*

1 If there is thought to be a problem with the fuel supply system, the fuel flow rate and fuel pressure can be checked as follows.

Fuel flow rate check

2 Remove the seat cowling (see Chapter 8). Raise and support the fuel tank (see Section 2).
3 Ensure the ignition is switched off then disconnect the wiring connector from the fuel cut-off relay, which is the rear relay located on the right-hand side of the rear sub-frame **(see illustration 13.66)**. Using an auxiliary wire, bridge between the brown and black/white wiring terminals of the connector.
4 Position a wad of rag and a graduated container suitable for holding half a litre of fuel beneath the fuel return hose union on the fuel tank and have a suitable plug ready to block the union. Working quickly to minimise fuel loss, disconnect the return hose from the tank and plug the tank union **(see illustration)**. Place the end of the return hose into the container and mop up all spilt fuel.
5 Turn on the ignition switch for exactly 10 seconds, catching all the fuel expelled from the return hose in the container, and then turn off the ignition switch. Measure the amount of fuel collected and compare this to the minimum fuel flow amount given in the Specifications.
6 If fuel flow is below the specified minimum there is a problem in the fuel supply system. Likely causes are.
● Blocked/restricted fuel feed or return hose.
● Blocked fuel filter.
● Faulty fuel pressure regulator.
● Faulty fuel pump.
7 On completion, reconnect the return hose to the fuel tank and secure it in position with the retaining clip **(see illustration 17.4)**.
8 Remove the bridging wire from the fuel cut-off relay and reconnect the wiring connector. Start the engine and check that there is no sign of fuel leakage. If all is well, lower the

16.4b . . . then release the pushrod end from the link arm

16.5 Wax unit cover screws (arrowed)

17.4 Fuel return hose union (A), fuel pump plate nuts (B)

Fuel and exhaust systems 4•29

tank back into position (see Section 2) then install the seat cowling (see Chapter 8).

Fuel pressure check

Note: *A pressure gauge will be required for this check. Honda specify the use of their gauge (Pt. No. 07406-0040002 or 3). If another gauge is used an adapter may be needed to thread into the union bolt, depending on the size of the gauge hose connector. A new sealing washer for the pressure release bolt will also be required.*

9 Remove the seat and disconnect the battery negative (–) terminal. Raise and support the fuel tank (see Section 2)

10 Disconnect the vacuum hose from the fuel pressure regulator and plug the hose end **(see illustration 13.14)**.

11 Place a rag and a suitable container for catching the residual fuel under the fuel supply hose union on the tank, then slowly slacken the pressure release bolt in the centre of the union (not the union bolt itself) until you hear a hissing sound **(see illustration 2.14b)**. At this point the fuel will spray out, so be ready with the rag to prevent it doing so. After the initial pressure has been reduced the bolt can be slackened a little further to allow the residual fuel to flow out.

12 Remove the pressure release bolt and its sealing washer and replace it with the pressure gauge, using the sealing washer if it doesn't have its own, and working quickly to minimise fuel spillage. Securely tighten the gauge to ensure there are no fuel leaks. Mop up any spilt fuel.

13 Connect the battery negative (–) lead then start the engine and allow it to idle at the specified speed. Note the pressure present in the fuel system by reading the gauge, then turn the engine off. Compare the reading obtained to that given in the Specifications.

14 If the fuel pressure is higher than specified, likely causes are.

- Blocked/restricted fuel feed or return hose.
- Faulty fuel pressure regulator.
- Faulty fuel pump (although this is unlikely).

15 If the fuel pressure is lower than specified, likely causes are.

- Leaking fuel hose union/injector.
- Blocked fuel filter.
- Faulty fuel pressure regulator.
- Faulty fuel pump.

16 On completion, disconnect the battery negative (–) lead again. Remove the fuel gauge and sealing washer, then quickly install the pressure release bolt using a new sealing washer and tighten it to the torque setting specified at the beginning of the Chapter **(see illustration 2.14b)**. Reconnect the vacuum hose to the fuel pressure regulator **(see illustration 13.14)**. Reconnect the battery then start the engine and check that there is no sign of fuel leakage. If all is well, lower the tank back into position (see Section 2).

18 Fuel pump – check, removal and installation

Warning: *Refer to the precautions given in Section 1 before starting work.*

Carburettor models

Check

1 The fuel pump is controlled through two relays, a transfer relay and a cut-off relay, so that it runs whenever the ignition is switched ON and the ignition is operative (i.e., only when the engine is turning over). As soon as the ignition is stopped, the relays cut off the fuel pump's electrical supply (so that there is no risk of fuel being sprayed out under pressure in the event of an accident).

2 The fuel pump is mounted below the rear of the fuel tank – raise or remove the fuel tank to access it **(see illustration)**. The pump transfer and cut-off relays are mounted on the right-hand side of the rear sub-frame – remove the seat cowling to access them (see Chapter 8) **(see illustrations)**.

3 It should be possible to hear or feel the fuel pump running whenever the engine is turning over – either place your ear close beside the pump or feel it with your fingertips. If you can't hear or feel anything, check the circuit fuse (see Chapter 9). If the fuse is good, check the pump and relays for loose or corroded connections or physical damage and rectify as necessary. If all is good so far, perform the following checks:

4 Place the motorcycle on its centrestand if fitted or on an auxiliary stand so that the rear wheel is off the ground. Connect the positive (+ve) probe of a voltmeter to the pink/yellow wire in the transfer relay connector (with it still connected to the relay) and the negative (-ve) probe to a good earth (ground) **(see illustration 18.2b)**. Start the engine and select a gear so that the rear wheel turns, and check the voltage reading. When the speedometer reads below 12 mph (20 km/h) there should be battery voltage, and above that speed there should be no voltage. Select neutral and stop the engine. If the readings are as stated, proceed to Step 6. If not, check the voltage at the No. 1 black/white wire in the connector with the ignition ON. If there is no voltage, there is a fault in that wire – trace and rectify the fault using the wiring diagrams at the end of Chapter 9. If there is voltage, again check for voltage at the pink/yellow wire, this time with the ignition ON but the engine stopped. If there is voltage, the transfer relay is faulty and must be replaced with a new one.

5 If there is no voltage, displace the instrument cluster, leaving the wiring connected (see Chapter 9). Perform the same dynamic voltage check as described in Step 4, but this time connect the meter probes between the pink/yellow (+ve) and green (-ve) wire terminals in the instrument wiring connector. If there is voltage below 12 mph (20 km/h), then there is a fault in the pink/yellow wire between the cluster and the relay. If there is no voltage, then the instrument cluster could be faulty.

6 If the dynamic test results from Step 4 were good, disconnect the transfer relay wiring connector. Check for continuity between the black/blue and black/yellow wire terminals on the relay – there should be continuity. Using a fully charged 12 volt battery and two insulated jumper wires, connect the positive (+) terminal of the battery to the relay's No. 1 black/white terminal, and the negative (-) terminal of the battery to the relay's pink/yellow terminal, then check again for continuity between the black/blue and black/yellow terminals – there should now be no continuity. If not, the relay is faulty. If the results are as stated, leave the battery connected and check for continuity between the black/blue and No. 2 black/white terminals – there should be continuity with the battery connected, and no continuity with the battery disconnected. If not, the relay is faulty.

18.2a Fuel pump (arrowed)

18.2b Fuel pump transfer relay (arrowed)

18.2c Fuel cut-off relay (arrowed)

4•30 Fuel and exhaust systems

If the results are as stated, check for full battery voltage at the relay connector's No. 2 black/white wire with the ignition switch ON. If there is no battery voltage, there is a fault in the black/white wire circuit – trace and rectify the fault as outlined in Chapter 9, referring to the wiring diagrams at the end of that Chapter.

7 If battery voltage was present, check for continuity between the black/blue wire terminal in the connector and earth (ground). If there is no continuity there is a fault in the black/blue or green wire, or if not then the fuel pump is faulty. If there is continuity, check for continuity in the black/yellow wire between the transfer relay and fuel cut-off relay connectors. If there is none, repair the wire. If there is continuity, check for full battery voltage at the black/white wire in the cut-off relay connector with the ignition switch ON. If there is no battery voltage, there is a fault in the black/white wire circuit. If there is voltage, now check for battery voltage at the blue/black wire in the cut-off relay connector with the ignition switch ON. If there is no voltage there is a fault in the blue/black wire. If there is voltage, the cut-off relay is faulty.

8 If the pump still does not work, trace the wiring from the pump and disconnect it at the black 2-pin wiring connector **(see illustration)**. Using a fully charged 12 volt battery and two insulated jumper wires, connect the positive (+) terminal of the battery to the pump's black/blue terminal, and the negative (-) terminal of the battery to the pump's green terminal. The pump should operate. If the pump does not operate it must be replaced with a new one. If the pump works, check for battery voltage at the black/blue terminal on the supply side of the connector. If there is no voltage, check the wiring.

9 If the pump operates but is thought to be delivering an insufficient amount of fuel, first check that all fuel hoses are in good condition and not pinched or trapped. Check that the in-line filter, the strainer in the fuel tank and the fuel delivery hoses are not blocked.

10 The fuel pump's output can be checked as follows: make sure the ignition switch is OFF. If it was removed, install the fuel tank in the raised position (see Section 2).

11 Release the clamp securing the fuel supply hose to the three-way union on the carburettors, being prepared to catch any residual fuel **(see illustration 7.3b)**. Place the end into a graduated beaker suitable for holding about 1/4 litre of petrol.

12 Disconnect the fuel transfer relay wiring connector **(see illustration 18.2b)**. Using a short length of insulated jumper wire, connect between the black/white and the black/blue wire terminals of the connector.

13 Set the kill switch to RUN, then turn the ignition switch ON and let fuel flow from the pump into the beaker for 5 seconds, then switch the ignition OFF.

14 Measure the amount of fuel that has flowed into the beaker, then multiply that amount by 12 to determine the fuel pump flow rate per minute. The minimum flow rate required is 700 cc per minute. If the flow rate recorded is below this, then the fuel pump must be replaced with a new one.

Removal

15 Make sure the ignition is switched OFF.

16 The fuel pump is mounted below the rear of the fuel tank – raise or remove the fuel tank to access it **(see illustration 18.2a)**. Trace the wiring from the pump and disconnect it at the black 2-pin wiring connector, which is to the rear of the battery **(see illustration 18.8)**. Free the wiring from any clips or ties and feed it back to the pump, noting its routing. Make a note or sketch of which fuel hose fits on which union on the pump as an aid to installation. Using a rag to mop up any spilled fuel, disconnect the two hoses from the front of the pump, then displace the pump from its mount and either disconnect the drain hose from the underside or remove the pump with it attached, noting its routing **(see illustration 18.2a)**.

17 The pump transfer and cut-off relays are mounted on the right-hand side of the rear sub-frame – remove the seat cowling to access them (see Chapter 8) **(see illustrations 18.2b and c)**. Disconnect the relay wiring connector and remove the relay from its mounting.

Installation

18 Installation is the reverse of removal. Make sure the fuel hoses are correctly and securely fitted to the pump – the hose from the in-line filter attaches to the union marked INLET; the hose to the carburettors attaches to the other union **(see illustration 18.2a)**. Start the engine and check carefully that there are no leaks at the pipe connections.

Fuel injection models

Check

19 The fuel pump is located inside the fuel tank. The fuel pump runs for a few seconds when the ignition is switched ON, to pressurise the fuel system, and then cuts out until the engine is started. Check that it does this. If the pump is thought to be faulty, first check the fuses (Chapter 9). If they are in good condition proceed as follows.

20 Raise and support the fuel tank (see Section 2).

21 Ensure the ignition is switched OFF then disconnect the fuel pump wiring connector **(see illustration 2.14a)**. Connect the positive (+) lead of a voltmeter to the brown terminal of the connector and the negative (–) lead to the green terminal of the connector. Switch the ignition ON whilst noting the reading obtained on the meter.

22 If battery voltage is present for a few seconds, the fuel pump circuit is operating correctly and the fuel pump is proven to be faulty.

23 If no reading is obtained, check the fuel pump circuit wiring for continuity and make sure all the connectors are free from corrosion and are securely connected. Repair/replace the wiring as necessary and clean the connectors using electrical contact cleaner. If this fails to reveal the fault, check the following components.

- Engine stop switch (see Chapter 9).
- Fuel cut-off relay (see Section 13).
- Engine stop relay (see Section 13).
- Bank angle sensor (see Section 13).
- Engine control module (ECM) (see Section 13).

Removal

24 Remove the fuel tank (see Section 2).

25 With the fuel tank supported upside-down, unscrew the fuel pump mounting plate nuts **(see illustration 17.4)**. Carefully remove the pump assembly from the tank along with the mounting plate seal **(see illustration)**. Discard the seal – a new one must be used on installation **(see illustration 18.32)**.

26 To remove the pump from its mounting plate, first disconnect the wiring connector from the pump **(see illustration)**.

18.8 Disconnect the fuel pump wiring connector (arrowed)

18.25 Carefully withdraw the pump assembly from the tank

18.26 Disconnect the wiring connector (arrowed)

Fuel and exhaust systems 4•31

18.27 Release the clamp (arrowed) and detach the hose

18.28a Undo the clamp screw, noting the earth wire

18.28b Check the strainer (arrowed)

27 Release the fuel hose clamp and detach the hose from the pump **(see illustration)**.
28 Undo the retaining clamp screw, noting the earth (ground) lead, and remove the clamp **(see illustration)**. Remove the pump, noting how it fits. Check the wire strainer in the base of the pump housing for signs of dirt/damage and clean/renew (as necessary) **(see illustration)**.

Installation

29 If removed, fit the pump into its housing, then secure it with the clamp and tighten the screw, not forgetting to attach the earth wire **(see illustration 18.28a)**.
30 Reconnect the fuel hose to the pump and secure it with the clamp **(see illustration 18.27)**.
31 Reconnect the pump wiring connector **(see illustration 18.26)**.
32 Ensure the mounting plate and tank surfaces are clean and dry, then fit the new seal onto the plate making sure its locating pins are all located correctly in the plate holes **(see illustration)**.
33 Manoeuvre the pump assembly into the tank, and seat it in position **(see illustration 18.25)**.
34 Fit the nuts and tighten them by hand **(see illustration 17.4)**. Now tighten them evenly and in a criss-cross pattern to the torque setting specified at the beginning of the Chapter.
35 Install the fuel tank (see Section 2).

19 Fuel warning light/display and sensor – check and replacement

Carburettor models

Check

1 The circuit consists of the sensor mounted in the fuel tank and the warning light mounted in the instrument panel. If the system malfunctions first check that the bulb and fuses are good (see Chapter 9).
2 If the warning light is permanently on, raise the fuel tank (see Section 2), then disconnect the brown/black wiring connector from the sensor **(see illustration 2.3c)**. Turn the ignition switch ON. If the warning light does not come on, replace the sensor with a new one. If it comes on, check for a short circuit to earth in the brown/black wire between the sensor and the light.
3 If the warning light does not come on at all, raise the fuel tank (see Section 2), then disconnect the wiring connectors from the sensor **(see illustration 2.3c)**. Using an insulated jumper wire, connect between the two sensor wire connectors. Turn the ignition switch ON. If the warning light comes on, replace the sensor with a new one. If it does not come on, check the wiring between the sensor and the light for continuity, referring to the *Wiring Diagrams* at the end of Chapter 9. If

the wiring is good, the instrument cluster printed circuit board could be faulty (see Chapter 9).

Replacement

4 See Chapter 9 for replacement of the warning light bulb.
5 To replace the sensor, remove the fuel tank and drain it (see Section 2).
6 Unscrew the sensor and draw it out of the tank **(see illustration)**. Discard the O-ring. Fit a new O-ring onto the sensor then install it in the tank and tighten it to the torque setting specified at the beginning of the Chapter.
7 Install the tank (see Section 2), and check carefully for leaks before using the bike.

Fuel injected models

Note: The fuel level display in the instrument LCD panel operates when the fuel quantity reaches the reserve quantity of 3.5 litres.

Check

8 The circuit consists of the sensor, which is an integral part of the fuel pump assembly mounting plate in the fuel tank, and the warning display which is incorporated in the LCD unit, which is part of the instrument cluster printed circuit board (PCB). If the system malfunctions first check that the fuses are good (see Chapter 9).
9 If the warning display does not come on, raise the fuel tank (see Section 2). Disconnect the fuel pump assembly wiring connector and bridge between the brown/black and green wire terminals on the connector using a jumper wire **(see illustration 2.14a)**. Turn the ignition switch ON – all segments of the warning display should come on. If it does, replace the pump assembly mounting plate with a new one. If it doesn't, check for continuity in the brown/black and green wires between the connector and the instrument cluster, using the *Wiring Diagrams* at the end of Chapter 9. Also check for continuity to earth (ground) in the green wire. If continuity (zero resistance) is not present, repair/replace the wiring harness. If continuity exists, then the instrument cluster could be faulty (see Chapter 9).

18.32 Fit a new seal, locating the pegs in the holes

19.6 Fuel level sensor (arrowed) - carburettor models

4•32 Fuel and exhaust systems

Replacement

10 See Chapter 9 for replacement of the instrument cluster printed circuit board.
11 The sensor is an integral part of the fuel pump assembly mounting plate in the fuel tank. Remove the fuel pump from the mounting plate and replace the plate with a new one (see Section 18).

20 Throttle cables – removal and installation

Warning: Refer to the precautions given in Section 1 before proceeding.

Removal

1 Remove the fuel tank and the air filter housing (see Sections 2 and 4). Mark each cable according to its location.
2 On carburettor models, slacken the opening (top) cable adjuster locknut and thread it fully up, then unscrew the adjuster until the captive nut is free (you may not need to do this if there is already enough clearance to release the captive nut from the bracket – it depends on the setting of the adjuster), then slip the cable out of the bracket and detach the inner cable nipple from the throttle cam on the carburettors, turning the cam by hand to make access easier if required **(see illustrations)**. Now unscrew the closing (bottom) cable hex until the captive nut is free, then slip the cable out of the bracket and detach the inner cable nipple from the cam. Withdraw the cables from the machine noting their correct routing.
3 On fuel injection models, unscrew the closing (top) cable hex until the captive nut is free, then slip the cable out of the bracket and detach the inner cable nipple from the throttle body cam. Now slacken the opening (bottom) cable adjuster locknut and thread it fully up, then unscrew the adjuster until the captive nut is free (you may not need to do this if there is already enough clearance to release the captive nut from the bracket – it depends on the setting of the adjuster), then slip the cable out of the bracket and detach the inner cable nipple from the cam. Withdraw the cables from the machine noting their correct routing.
4 Slacken the cable elbow nuts at the throttle pulley housing, then remove the housing screws and separate the halves **(see illustrations)**. Detach the cable nipples from the pulley, then fully unscrew the closing (bottom) cable elbow nut and remove the cable from the housing **(see illustration)**. Thread the opening (top) cable elbow out of the housing and withdraw the cable **(see illustration)**. Mark each cable to ensure it is connected correctly on installation.

Installation

5 Fit the opening cable elbow into the top socket of the throttle pulley housing and thread the elbow into it as far as it will go without becoming tight on the bottom of the threads – the elbow must stay loose so that it aligns itself – then thread the nut onto the elbow, again not so that it is tight **(see illustration 20.4e)**. Fit the closing cable into the bottom socket and tighten the nut finger-tight **(see illustration 20.4d)**. Lubricate the cable nipples with multi-purpose grease and fit them into the throttle pulley **(see illustration 20.4c)**. Assemble the housing onto the handlebar, making sure the pin locates in the hole in the handlebar, then install the screws and tighten them securely **(see illustration 20.4b)**. Now tighten both cable elbow nuts **(see illustration 20.4a)**.
6 Feed the cables through to the carburettors or throttle bodies, making sure they are correctly routed. The cables must not interfere with any other component and should not be kinked or bent sharply.

20.2a Opening cable locknut (A), adjuster (B) and captive nut (C). Closing cable hex (D) and captive nut (E)

20.2b Turn the throttle cam to improve access to the cable ends

20.4a Slacken the elbow nuts (arrowed) . . .

20.4b . . . then remove the housing screws and separate the halves

20.4c Detach the ends from the pulley . . .

20.4d . . . and withdraw the closing cable

20.4e Unscrew the opening cable from the housing

Fuel and exhaust systems 4•33

7 On carburettor models, lubricate the closing cable nipple with multi-purpose grease and fit it into the carburettor throttle cam **(see illustration)**. Fit the cable into the lower socket in the bracket, locating the bottom nut against the lug so that it is captive, then thread the hex into the nut until it is tight **(see illustration 20.2a)**. Lubricate the opening cable nipple with multi-purpose grease and fit it into the carburettor throttle cam **(see illustration 20.2b)**. Fit the opening cable adjuster into the upper socket in the bracket, locating the nut against the lug so that it is captive, then thread the locknut down the adjuster, but do not yet tighten it **(see illustration 20.2a)**. Thread the adjuster in or out until the specified amount of cable freeplay is obtained (see Chapter 1). Tighten the locknut against the bracket.

8 On fuel injection models, lubricate the opening cable nipple with multi-purpose grease and fit it into the throttle body cam. Fit the opening cable adjuster into the lower bracket, locating the bottom nut against the lug so that it is captive, then thread the top nut down the adjuster, but do not yet tighten it. Thread the adjuster in or out until the specified amount of cable freeplay is obtained (see Chapter 1). Tighten the locknut against the bracket. Lubricate the closing cable nipple with multi-purpose grease and fit it into the throttle body cam. Fit the cable into the upper bracket, locating the nut against the lug so that it is captive, then thread the hex into the nut until it is tight.

9 Operate the throttle to check that it opens and closes freely.

10 Check and adjust the throttle cable freeplay if required (see Chapter 1). Turn the handlebars back and forth to make sure the cable doesn't cause the steering to bind.

11 Install the air filter housing and the fuel tank (see Sections 4 and 2).

12 Start the engine and check that the idle speed does not rise as the handlebars are turned. If it does, the throttle cable is routed incorrectly. Correct the problem before riding the motorcycle.

21 Choke cable – removal and installation

Note: *This information only applies to carburettor engined models – F-X and F-Y (1999 and 2000).*

Removal

1 Remove the fuel tank and the air filter housing (see Sections 2 and 4). Unscrew the bolt securing the direct air injection (DAI) system solenoid bracket and displace it to free the choke cable **(see illustration)**.

2 Release the outer cable from its holder using a screwdriver, then free the inner cable end from its socket on the choke linkage bar **(see illustrations)**.

3 Unscrew the cable elbow locknut **(see illustration)**. Remove the left-hand switch housing screws and separate the halves from the handlebar, noting how the choke lever locates in the housing **(see illustration)**. Free the cable end from the choke lever. Withdraw the cable from the machine noting its routing.

Installation

4 Installation is the reverse of removal. Make sure the cable is correctly routed – it must not interfere with any other component and should not be kinked or bent sharply. Check the operation of the cable (see Chapter 1).

22 Exhaust system – removal and installation

⚠️ *Warning: If the engine has been running the exhaust system will be very hot. Allow the system to cool before carrying out any work.*

21.1 Unscrew the bracket bolt and free the cable

21.2a Release the outer cable end from its holder . . .

21.2b . . . and the inner cable end from its socket

21.3a Slacken the elbow nut (arrowed) . . .

21.3b . . . then undo the housing screws (arrowed)

21.3c Separate the halves . . .

21.3d . . . and free the cable end from the lever (arrow)

4•34 Fuel and exhaust systems

22.1 Slacken the clamp bolt (arrowed)

22.3 Unscrew the nut (A) and withdraw the bolt (B)

22.4 Replace the sealing ring with a new one if necessary

Removal

Silencer

1 Slacken the clamp bolt(s) securing the silencer in the downpipe assembly (see illustration).

> **HAYNES HiNT** *Exhaust system clamp bolts tend to become corroded and seized. It is advisable to spray them with WD40 or a similar product before attempting to slacken them.*

2 On California and Germany fuel injection models, remove the seat (see Chapter 8). Trace the wiring from the oxygen sensor in the front of the silencer to the wiring connector and disconnect it. Free the wiring from any clips or ties and feed it through to the sensor.
3 Unscrew the nut and remove the bolt and washer securing the rear of the silencer (see illustration). Release and withdraw the front of the silencer from the downpipe assembly and remove it.
4 Note the collar which fits into the inside of the rubber on the silencer mounting. Fit a new rubber if the old one is damaged, deformed or deteriorated. Check the condition of the sealing ring between the silencer and downpipe assembly and replace it with a new one if it is damaged or deformed (see illustration). Honda recommend always using a new one, but they can be difficult to remove, and unless they are damaged they are re-usable. It is too easy to damage a new one trying to install it to make it worthwhile destroying a good one that is already installed.

Downpipe assembly

5 Remove the fairing side panels (see Chapter 8).
6 Remove the radiator (see Chapter 3). **Note:** *Though it is possible to remove the downpipe assembly with the radiator just displaced from its mountings rather than removed altogether, there is always the possibility of damaging it when unscrewing or tightening the nuts or when manoeuvring the downpipes. As radiators are fairly fragile and easily damaged, and don't take long to remove, it is best to do so.*
7 Remove the silencer (see above).
8 Unscrew the nut and withdraw the bolt and washer securing the rear of the downpipe assembly, noting the collar that fits in the rubber dampers (see illustration).
9 Unscrew the nuts securing the header pipes to the cylinder head (see illustration). Draw the flanges off the studs and manoeuvre the downpipe assembly out of the head and remove it (see illustrations). Remove the gasket from each port in the cylinder head and discard them as new ones must be used (see illustration 22.10a).

Installation

10 Installation is the reverse of removal, noting the following:
● Use a new gasket in each cylinder head port (see illustration). Replace any damaged, deformed or deteriorated mounting rubbers with new ones.
● Use a new sealing ring between the

22.8 Downpipe assembly rear mounting bolt (arrowed)

22.9a Unscrew the nuts (arrowed) . . .

22.9b . . . and draw off the flanges . . .

22.9c . . . then manoeuvre the downpipe assembly out of the head

22.10 Use a new sealing ring in each port

Fuel and exhaust systems 4•35

downpipe assembly and the silencer if required, bearing in mind the information in Step 4 above **(see illustration 22.4)**.
● Apply a smear of copper grease to the clamp bolts to prevent them from seizing up.
● Leave all fasteners loose until the entire system has been installed, making alignment of the various sections easier. Tighten the silencer mounting last.
● Tighten the front downpipe nuts and the silencer clamp bolts to the torque settings specified at the beginning of the Chapter.
● Run the engine and check the system for leaks.

23 Direct air induction (DAI) system – check

Note: *This information only applies to carburettor engined models – F-X and F-Y (1999 and 2000).*

Check

1 The system scoops air via two main ducts and two smaller ducts in the fairing and directs it through the main air filter and a sub-air filter, and via two air vent systems controlled by a solenoid valve, as shown. On California models, the system is linked with the EVAP emission control system, and so if any of the tests below produce results which do not conform, the system should be checked in conjunction with the EVAP system. The solenoid valve is controlled via two relays (the solenoid valve relay and the fuel pump transfer relay) which are governed by the speed of the motorcycle, and switches air flow from one duct to another at a speed of 12 mph (20 kmh). A system hose routing diagram should be stuck to the air filter cover.
2 The solenoid valve is mounted behind the steering head – raise or remove the fuel tank to access it **(see illustration 7.3a)**. The solenoid valve and pump transfer relays are mounted on the right-hand side of the rear sub-frame – remove the seat cowling to access them (see Chapter 8) **(see illustration and 18.2b)**.
3 Raise or remove the fuel tank (see Chapter 4). Check that all ducts and hoses are clear, and clean any dirt or debris off the mesh in the front of the scoops in the fairing. Disconnect each tube in turn from its union and blow through it. Also check all hoses for kinks, damage or deterioration in the form of cracks, and replace them if necessary. Check that all ducts and hoses are secure on their unions.
4 Check the sub-air cleaners in the air filter housing and the air vent filter in the DAI intake for clogging and clean or replace them as required **(see illustrations)** – remove the air filter to access the sub-air cleaners (see Chapter 1).
5 It should be possible to hear the relay whenever the ignition is switched ON with the kill switch set to RUN – place your ear close beside the relay. If you can't hear anything, check the circuit fuse (see Chapter 9). If the fuse is good, check the solenoid and relays for loose or corroded connections or physical damage and rectify as necessary. Also check all the wiring and connectors between the valve and the relays. If there is still no sound, proceed to Step 9. If there is sound, perform the following checks:
6 Place the motorcycle on its centrestand if fitted or on an auxiliary stand so that the rear wheel is off the ground. Using an ohmmeter or continuity tester connect between the pink/white wire in the solenoid valve relay connector and the No. 2 black/white wire. Start the engine and select a gear so that the rear wheel turns. When the speedometer reads below 12 mph (20 kmh) there should be continuity, and above that speed there should be no continuity. Select neutral and stop the engine. If the readings are as stated, proceed to Step 10. If not, disconnect the fuel transfer relay connector and check the voltage at the No. 1 black/white wire in the connector with the ignition ON. If there is no voltage, there is a fault in that wire – trace and rectify the fault using the wiring diagrams at the end of Chapter 9. If there is voltage, check for voltage at the pink/yellow wire on the solenoid relay, this time with the ignition ON but the engine stopped. If there is no voltage, the solenoid valve relay is faulty and must be replaced with a new one.
7 If there is no voltage, connect the transfer relay wiring connector. Connect the positive (+ve) probe of a voltmeter to the pink/yellow wire in the solenoid valve relay connector and the negative (-ve) probe to a good earth (ground). Start the engine and select a gear so that the rear wheel turns, and check the voltage reading. When the speedometer reads below 12 mph (20 km/h) there should be battery voltage, and above that speed there should be no voltage. Select neutral and stop the engine. If the readings are as they should be, the solenoid valve relay is faulty.
8 If the readings are not as stated, displace the instrument cluster, leaving the wiring connected (see Chapter 9). Perform the same dynamic voltage check as described in Step 7, but this time connect the meter probes between the pink/yellow (+ve) and green (-ve) wire terminals in the instrument wiring connector. If there is voltage below 12 mph (20 km/h), then there is a fault in the pink/yellow wire between the cluster and the relay. If there is no voltage, then the instrument cluster could be faulty.
9 If there was no sound from the check in Step 5, trace the wiring from the solenoid valve and disconnect it at the 2-pin black connector and check for any loose or broken connections **(see illustration 23.11)**. With the ignition switched ON, check for battery voltage between the pink/white (positive (+ve) probe) and green (negative (-ve) probe) terminals on the wiring loom side of the connector. If there is voltage, proceed to Step 10. If no voltage is recorded, check for battery voltage at the solenoid valve relay No. 2 black/white wire with the ignition ON. If there is no voltage, there is a fault in that wire. If there is voltage, check for continuity between the pink/white and No. 2 black/white wires terminals on the solenoid with the ignition ON and the connector connected. If there is continuity, there is a fault in the pink/white or green wires. If there is no continuity, check for voltage between the No.2 black/white (+ve) and pink/yellow (-ve) terminals on the solenoid valve relay with the ignition ON. If there is no voltage, the relay is faulty. If there is voltage, disconnect the instrument cluster wiring connector and check for continuity in the pink/yellow wire to ground. If there is no continuity, the instrument cluster is faulty. If there is continuity, there is a short circuit to earth in the wire.
10 Remove the air filter housing (see Section

23.2 DAI system solenoid valve relay (arrowed)

23.4a Remove the covers . . .

23.4b . . . and check the filters

4•36 Fuel and exhaust systems

23.11 DAI system solenoid valve wiring connector (arrowed)

4). Disconnect the hose between the solenoid valve and the carburettors at the three way union **(see illustration 7.3a)**. Blow air into the hose that goes into the top left-hand side of the solenoid valve with the ignition OFF – air should flow through to the carburettor hose. Now blow air into the hose that goes into the bottom left-hand side of the valve with the ignition ON – air should flow through to the carburettor hose. If air does not flow correctly in either case, the valve is faulty and must be replaced with a new one.

Replacement

11 To replace the valve, raise the fuel tank (see Section 4). Detach the hoses, noting which fits where, and disconnect the wiring connector **(see illustration)**. then remove the screw which secures the valve bracket to the frame, noting how it holds the choke cable, and remove the valve **(see illustration 21.1)**. Install the new valve, making sure the wiring connector and all hoses are securely and correctly connected – each hose and its corresponding union on the valve should be numbered.

12 To replace the relay(s), remove the seat cowling (see Chapter 8). Disconnect the wiring connector and detach the relay from its mounting.

24 Pulse secondary air (PAIR) system

General information

1 To reduce the amount of unburned hydrocarbons released in the exhaust gases, a pulse secondary air (PAIR) system is fitted. The system consists of the control valve (mounted under the front of the air filter housing), the reed valves (fitted in the valve cover) and the hoses linking them **(see illustrations)**. The control valve is actuated by the engine vacuum on carburettor models, and electronically by the ECM on fuel injection models.

2 Under certain operating conditions, the vacuum or a signal from the ECM (according to model) opens up the PAIR control valve which then allows filtered air to be drawn through the reed valves and cylinder head passages and into the exhaust ports. The air mixes with the exhaust gases, causing any unburned particles of the fuel in the mixture to be burnt in the exhaust port/pipes. This process changes a considerable amount of hydrocarbons and carbon monoxide into relatively harmless carbon dioxide and water. The reed valves in the valve cover are fitted to prevent the flow of exhaust gases back up the cylinder head passages and into the air filter housing.

Testing

Control valve

3 Remove the valve from the motorcycle (see below).

4 Check the operation of the control valve by blowing through the air filter housing hose union; no air should flow through the reed valve hose unions. On carburettor models now apply a vacuum to the vacuum hose and repeat the check; air should now flow through the valve if it is functioning correctly. On fuel injection models, now connect battery voltage (12 volts) across the valve terminals and repeat the check; air should now flow through the valve if it is functioning correctly.

5 On fuel injection models, if an ohmmeter is available, check the resistance of the control valve windings by connecting an ohmmeter between its connector terminals and compare the reading obtained to that given in the Specifications. Renew the valve if faulty.

Reed valves

6 Disconnect the reed valve hoses from the control valve (see below).

7 Check each valve by blowing and sucking on the hose end. Air should flow through the hose only when blown down it and not when sucked back up. If this is not the case the reed valve is faulty.

24.1a PAIR system - carburettor models

1 Air filter housing
2 Reed valves
3 Control valve
4 Vacuum hose
5 Carburettor
6 Exhaust port

24.1b PAIR system - fuel injection models

1 Air filter housing
2 Reed valves
3 Control valve
4 Throttle body
5 Exhaust port

Fuel and exhaust systems 4•37

24.9 Pair control valve vacuum hose (arrowed)

24.10 Release the clamps and detach the hoses (arrowed) from the valve

24.13a Unscrew the bolts (arrowed) . . .

Component renewal

Control valve

8 Remove the air filter housing (see Section 4).

9 On carburettor models, disconnect the vacuum hose from the valve **(see illustration)**. On fuel injection models, disconnect the wiring connector.

10 Release the clamps securing the reed valve hoses and the air filter hose and disconnect them, then remove the control valve from the motorcycle **(see illustration)**.

11 Installation is the reverse of removal. Note that on California models there is an emission control system hose routing diagram on a label stuck to the top of the air filter housing.

Reed valves

12 Remove the fuel tank and the air filter housing (see Sections 2 and 4).

13 To remove either valve, first release the clamp and detach the air hose from its union **(see illustration)**. Unscrew the bolts securing the reed valve cover and remove the cover **(see illustrations)**. Remove the reed valve and the base plate, noting which way around they are fitted **(see illustrations)**.

14 Installation is the reverse of removal. Make sure the reed valve components are correctly fitted.

25 Evaporative emission control (EVAP) system

Note: *This system is fitted to California market models only.*

General information

1 The evaporative emission control system (EVAP) is fitted to minimise the escape of fuel vapour into the atmosphere. The fuel tank filler cap is sealed and a charcoal canister is mounted ahead of the rear wheel. The canister collects the fuel vapours generated when the motorcycle is parked and stores them until they can be cleared from the canister, via the control valve(s), into the throttle body inlet tracts to be burned by the engine during normal combustion. On carburettor models, the system control valves are opened and closed by the vacuum created in the inlet tracts when the engine is running. Vapour from the fuel tank is controlled by the purge control valve, while vapour from the carburettors is controlled by the carburettor air vent (CAV) valve. On fuel injection models, the purge control valve for the fuel tank vapour is opened and closed by the engine control module (ECM). There is no CAV valve.

2 The valves should be tested if there is a problem starting the engine when it is hot.

Testing

Control valves – carburettor models

3 Remove the relevant valve from the motorcycle (see below).

4 Check the operation of the purge control valve by connecting an auxiliary hose to the vacuum hose union and applying a vacuum of 250 mm Hg. Check that the valve is able to hold the vacuum once it is applied. Now blow through the inlet (canister hose) union; air should flow freely through the valve and out the outlet hose (carburettor hose) union. Disconnect the vacuum hose – no air should now flow through the valve. Now connect the auxiliary hose to the outlet hose (carburettor hose) hose union and apply a vacuum of 250 mm Hg. Check that the valve is able to hold the vacuum once it is applied. Renew the valve if it doesn't perform as described.

5 To check the operation of the CAV control valve reconnect its wiring connector. With the ignition switch OFF, blow through the inlet (carburettor hose) union; air should flow freely through the valve and out the outlet (canister hose) union. Turn the ignition ON, and again blow through the inlet (carburettor hose) union; air should now flow freely through the valve and out the open (unhosed) union, and not out of the outlet (canister hose) union. If the valve doesn't perform as described, disconnect its wiring connector and check for battery voltage using a multimeter across the

24.13b . . . and remove the cover . . .

24.13c . . . then remove the reed valve . . .

24.13d . . . and its base plate

connector terminals (positive lead to the black/brown wire terminal, negative lead to the green wire terminal) with the ignition ON. If voltage is present, the valve is faulty. If no voltage is present, check the wiring for faults and repair or renew as necessary, then check the operation of the valve again.

Control valve – fuel injection models

6 Remove the valve from the motorcycle (see below).
7 Check the operation of the control valve by blowing through the inlet (canister hose) union; air should not flow through the valve and out the outlet hose union. Connect battery voltage (12 volts) across the valve terminals and repeat the check; now air should flow through the valve if it is functioning correctly. If an ohmmeter is available, check the resistance of the control valve windings and compare the reading obtained to that given in the Specifications. Renew the valve if faulty. If it behaves as described, check for battery voltage using a multimeter across the wiring connector terminals with the ignition ON

Charcoal canister

8 No testing of the canister is possible, if it is thought to be faulty it must be renewed.

Component renewal

Control valves – carburettor models

9 To replace the purge control valve, remove the fuel tank (see Section 2). Disconnect the hoses from the valve, noting which fits where, then release the valve from its mounting.
10 To replace the CAV valve, remove the fuel tank (see Section 2). Disconnect the hoses from the valve, noting which fits where, then disconnect the wiring connector and release the valve from its mounting.
11 Installation is the reverse of removal.

Control valve – fuel injection models

12 Unscrew the bolts securing the EVAP canister bracket and displace the canister to access the valve bolts. Disconnect the wiring connector and hoses, noting which fits where, then unscrew the bolts and remove the valve.
13 Installation is the reverse of removal.

Charcoal canister

14 Unscrew the canister bracket mounting bolts and displace the canister, then disconnect the hoses, noting which fits where.
15 Installation is the reverse of removal.

26 Catalytic converter (where fitted)

General information

1 A catalytic converter is incorporated in the exhaust downpipe pipe assembly to minimise the level of exhaust pollutants released into the atmosphere.
2 The catalytic converter consists of a canister containing a fine mesh impregnated with a catalyst material, over which the hot exhaust gases pass. The catalyst speeds up the oxidation of harmful carbon monoxide, unburned hydrocarbons and soot, effectively reducing the quantity of harmful products released into the atmosphere via the exhaust gases.
3 The catalytic converter is of the closed-loop type with exhaust gas oxygen content information being fed back to the fuel injection system engine control module (ECM) by the oxygen sensor. The sensor is screwed into the front of the silencer.
4 The oxygen sensor contains a heating element which is controlled by the ECM. When the engine is cold, the ECM switches on the heating element which warms the exhaust gases as they pass over the sensor. This brings the catalytic converter quickly up to its normal operating temperature and decreases the level of exhaust pollutants emitted whilst the engine warms up. Once the engine is sufficiently warmed up, the ECM switches off the heating element.
5 Refer to Section 22 for exhaust assembly (which incorporates the catalytic converter) removal and installation, and Section 13 for oxygen sensor removal and installation information.

Precautions

6 The catalytic converter is a reliable and simple device which needs no maintenance in itself, but there are some facts of which an owner should be aware if the converter is to function properly for its full service life.
● DO NOT use leaded or lead replacement petrol (gasoline) – the additives will coat the precious metals, reducing their converting efficiency and will eventually destroy the catalytic converter.
● Always keep the ignition and fuel systems well-maintained in accordance with the manufacturer's schedule – if the fuel/air mixture is suspected of being incorrect have it checked on an exhaust gas analyser.
● If the engine develops a misfire, do not ride the bike at all (or at least as little as possible) until the fault is cured.
● DO NOT use fuel or engine oil additives – these may contain substances harmful to the catalytic converter.
● DO NOT continue to use the bike if the engine burns oil to the extent of leaving a visible trail of blue smoke.
● Remember that the catalytic converter is FRAGILE – do not strike it with tools during servicing work.

Chapter 5
Ignition system

Contents

Clutch switch – check and replacement ....see Chapter 9	Ignition system – check 2
General information 1	Ignition timing – general information and check 6
Ignition control unit – check, removal and installation 5	Immobiliser system 8
Ignition (main) switch – check, removal	Neutral switch – check and replacement ....see Chapter 9
and installation ....see Chapter 9	Sidestand switch – check and replacement ....see Chapter 9
Ignition HT coils – check, removal and installation 3	Spark plugs – gap check and renewal ....see Chapter 1
Ignition pulse generator – check, removal and installation 4	Throttle position sensor – check and replacement 7

Degrees of difficulty

Easy, suitable for novice with little experience	Fairly easy, suitable for beginner with some experience	Fairly difficult, suitable for competent DIY mechanic	Difficult, suitable for experienced DIY mechanic	Very difficult, suitable for expert DIY or professional

Specifications

General information
Cylinder numbering .... 1 to 4 from left to right
Spark plugs .... See Chapter 1

Ignition timing
F-X and F-Y (1999 and 2000) models .... 10° BTDC ('F' mark) at idle
F-1/FS-1 models onward (2001-on) .... 13° BTDC ('F' mark) at idle

Ignition HT coils
Primary winding resistance .... 1.1 to 1.5 ohms @ 20°C
Secondary winding resistance .... 11.4 to 11.8 K-ohms @ 20°C
Initial voltage (see text) .... Battery voltage (approximately 12 volts)
Minimum peak voltage (see text) .... 100 volts

Pulse generator coil – F-X and F-Y (1999 and 2000) models
Minimum peak voltage (see text) .... 0.7 volts
Note: *The ignition pulse generator for F-1/FS-1 models onward (2001-on) is covered in Chapter 4 under fuel injection system components*

Throttle position sensor – F-X and F-Y (1999 and 2000) models
Input voltage (see text) .... 4.7 to 5.3 volts
Output voltage .... see text
Resistance .... 4 to 6 K-ohms @ 20°C
Note: *The throttle position sensor for F-1/FS-1 models onward (2001-on) is covered in Chapter 4 under fuel injection system components*

Torque settings
Timing inspection cap .... 18 Nm

5•2 Ignition system

1 General information

All models are fitted with a fully transistorised electronic ignition system, which due to its lack of mechanical parts is totally maintenance free.

On F-X and F-Y (1999 and 2000) models, the system comprises the timing rotor, ignition pulse generator coil, throttle position sensor, ignition control unit, and ignition HT coils (refer to the wiring diagrams at the end of Chapter 9 for details).

On F-1/FS-1 models onward (2001-on), the system is basically the same, but control is integrated into the fuel injection system electronic control module (ECM), and the ignition pulse generator and throttle position sensor have dual roles in providing information for both the ignition and the fuelling side of the engine. All the system components for these models are therefore covered in Chapter 4.

The ignition timing rotor, which is on the right-hand end of the crankshaft, has triggers which magnetically actuate the pulse generator coil as the crankshaft rotates. The pulse generator sends a signal to the ignition control unit or ECM which then supplies the ignition HT coils with the power necessary to produce a spark at the plugs. A throttle position sensor also supplies the control unit with information that is used in determining the optimum firing point for all conditions. The system incorporates an electronic advance system controlled by the signals from the pulse generator coil and the sensors.

The system uses four HT coils, one for each cylinder. The coils are of the plug top type or 'stick coils' with the coil windings being incorporated in the spark plug cap. This eliminates the need for HT leads and saves space.

The system incorporates a safety interlock circuit which will cut the ignition if the sidestand is extended whilst the engine is running and in gear, or if a gear is selected whilst the engine is running and the sidestand is down. It also prevents the engine from being started if the sidestand is down and the engine is in gear. The engine can be started with the sidestand up when it is in gear as long as the clutch lever is pulled in.

Many models have an immobiliser system (HISS – Honda Ignition Security System) which will not allow the engine to be started unless the correct key is used. The immobiliser system has its own fault-diagnosis function.

Because of their nature, the individual ignition system components can be checked but not repaired. If ignition system troubles occur, and the faulty component can be isolated, the only cure for the problem is to replace the part with a new one. Keep in mind that most electrical parts, once purchased, cannot be returned. To avoid unnecessary expense, make very sure the faulty component has been positively identified before buying a replacement part.

Note that there is no provision for adjusting the ignition timing on these models.

2 Ignition system – check

⚠️ **Warning: The energy levels in electronic systems can be very high. On no account should the ignition be switched on whilst the plugs or plug caps are being held. Shocks from the HT circuit can be most unpleasant. Secondly, it is vital that the engine is not turned over or run with any of the plug caps removed, and that the plugs are soundly earthed (grounded) when the system is checked for sparking. The ignition system components can be seriously damaged if the HT circuit becomes isolated.**

1 As no means of adjustment is available, any failure of the system can be traced to failure of a system component or a simple wiring fault. Of the two possibilities, the latter is by far the most likely. In the event of failure, check the system in a logical fashion, as described below.

2 Working on one ignition HT coil at a time, disconnect the wiring connector – to access them refer to Section 3, Step 1 **(see illustration)**. Pull the coil off the spark plug **(see illustration)**.

Reconnect the wiring connector. Connect the HT coil to a new spark plug and lay the plug on the engine with the threads contacting it. If necessary, hold the spark plug with an insulated tool.

⚠️ **Warning: Do not remove any of the spark plugs from the engine to perform this check – atomised fuel being pumped out of the open spark plug hole could ignite, causing severe injury! Make sure the plugs are securely held against the engine – if they are not earthed when the engine is turned over, the ignition control unit/ECM could be damaged.**

3 Having observed the above precautions, check that the kill switch is in the RUN position and the transmission is in neutral, then turn the ignition switch ON and turn the engine over on the starter motor. If the system is in good condition a regular, fat blue spark should be evident at the plug electrode. If the spark appears thin or yellowish, or is non-existent, further investigation will be necessary. Turn the ignition OFF and repeat the check for each HT coil.

4 The ignition system must be able to produce a spark which is capable of jumping a particular size gap. Honda do not provide a specification, but a healthy system should produce a spark capable of jumping at least 6 mm. A simple testing tool can be made to test the minimum gap across which the spark will jump (see **Tool Tip**).

5 Connect the HT coil to the protruding electrode on the test tool, and clip the tool to a good earth (ground) on the engine or frame. Check that the kill switch is in the RUN position, turn the ignition switch ON and turn the engine over on the starter motor. If the system is in good condition a regular, fat blue spark should be seen to jump the gap between the nail ends. Repeat the test for the other HT coils. If the test results are good the entire ignition system can be considered

2.2a Disconnect the wiring connector (arrowed) . . .

2.2b . . . and pull the HT coil off the spark plug

TOOL TIP

A simple spark gap testing tool can be made from a block of wood, a large alligator clip and two nails, one of which is fashioned so that a spark plug cap or bare HT lead end can be connected to its end. Make sure the gap between the two nail ends is the same as specified

Ignition system 5•3

good. If the spark appears thin or yellowish, or is non-existent, further investigation is necessary.

6 Ignition faults can be divided into two categories, namely those where the ignition system has failed completely, and those which are due to a partial failure. The likely faults are listed below, starting with the most probable source of failure. Work through the list systematically, referring to the subsequent sections for full details of the necessary checks and tests. **Note:** *Before checking the following items ensure that the battery is fully charged and that all fuses are in good condition.*

- Loose, corroded or damaged wiring connections, broken or shorted wiring between any of the component parts of the ignition system (see Chapter 9).
- Faulty spark plug cap, faulty spark plug, dirty, worn or corroded plug electrodes, or incorrect gap between electrodes.
- Faulty ignition (main) switch or engine kill switch (see Chapter 9).
- Faulty neutral, clutch or sidestand switch (see Chapter 9).
- Faulty pulse generator coil or damaged trigger on timing rotor.
- Faulty ignition HT coil(s).
- Faulty throttle position sensor.
- Faulty ignition control unit or ECM.

7 If the above checks don't reveal the cause of the problem, have the ignition system tested by a Honda dealer.

3 Ignition HT coils – check, removal and installation

Check

1 Remove the fuel tank and air filter housing (see Chapter 4). Check the coils/caps visually for loose or damaged connectors and terminals, cracks and other damage.
2 Remove the seat (see Chapter 8). Disconnect the battery negative (–ve) lead.
3 Disconnect the wiring connector from the HT coil being tested **(see illustration 2.2a)**. Pull the coil off the spark plug **(see illustration 2.2b)**.
4 Set an ohmmeter or multimeter to the ohms x 1 scale and measure the resistance between the terminals in the coil/cap wiring connector socket **(see illustration)**. This will give a resistance reading of the primary windings of the coil and should be consistent with the value given in the Specifications at the beginning of the Chapter.
5 To check the condition of the secondary windings, set the meter to the K-ohm scale. Connect one meter probe to one of the terminals in the connector socket, and the other to the spark plug contact, using a steel rod as an extension if your probe is not long enough **(see illustration)**. If the reading obtained is not within the range shown in the Specifications, it is likely that the coil is defective. To confirm this, it must be tested as described below using the specified equipment, or by a Honda dealer.
6 Honda specify their own Imrie diagnostic tester (model 625), or the peak voltage adapter (Pt. No. 07HGJ-0020100) with an aftermarket digital multimeter having an impedance of 10 M-ohm/DCV minimum, for a complete test. If this equipment is available, reconnect the wiring connector to the coil. Connect the cap to a new spark plug and lay the plug on the engine with the threads contacting it. If necessary, hold the spark plug with an insulated tool. Connect the positive (+) lead of the voltmeter and peak voltage adapter arrangement to the blue/black (No. 1 cylinder coil), yellow/white (No. 2 coil), red/blue (No. 3 coil) or red/yellow (No. 4 coil) wire terminal on the coil, with the wiring connector still securely connected, and connect the negative (–) lead to a suitable earth (ground) point.
7 Check that the kill switch is in the RUN position and the transmission is in neutral, then turn the ignition switch ON. Note the initial voltage reading on the meter, then turn the engine over on the starter motor and note the ignition coil peak voltage reading on the meter. Once both readings have been noted, turn the ignition switch off and disconnect the meter.
8 If the initial voltage reading is not as expected or the peak voltage readings are lower than the specified minimum then a fault is present somewhere else in the ignition system circuit (see Section 2); note that the peak voltage readings for each coil can be different but each one must exceed the specified minimum.
9 If the initial and peak voltage readings are as specified and the plug does not spark, then the coil is faulty and must be replaced with a new one; the coil is a sealed unit and cannot therefore be repaired.

Removal and installation

10 Remove the fuel tank and air filter housing (see Chapter 4).
11 Disconnect the wiring connector from the coil **(see illustration 2.2a)**. Pull the coil off the spark plug **(see illustration 2.2b)**.
12 Installation is the reverse of removal.

4 Ignition pulse generator – check, removal and installation

F-X and F-Y (1999 and 2000) models

Check

1 Trace the wiring back from the pulse generator, which is mounted in the clutch cover on the right-hand side of the engine, to its red 2-pin wiring connector above the crankcase and disconnect it – depending on the size of your hands and general dexterity, and the tightness of the connector, you may have to either remove the right-hand fairing side panel (see Chapter 8) or raise the fuel tank (see Chapter 4) **(see illustration)**. Perform the following check(s).
2 Using an ohmmeter check for continuity between the white/yellow terminal on the sensor side of the connector and earth (ground). If there is continuity then the ignition pulse generator is faulty.
3 Connect the positive (+) lead of a voltmeter and peak voltage adapter arrangement* to the yellow terminal of the ignition pulse generator

3.4 To test the coil primary resistance, connect the multimeter leads between the connector socket terminals

3.5 To test the coil secondary resistance, connect the multimeter leads between one terminal and the spark plug socket

4.1 Pulse generator coil wiring connector

5•4 Ignition system

4.6 Unscrew the sensor bolts (A) and the wiring guide bolt (B), and free the wiring grommet (C)

connector and the negative (–) lead to the white/yellow terminal of the connector. Turn the engine over on the starter motor and note the voltage reading obtained. If this reading is below the specified minimum, the ignition pulse generator is faulty. *Note: Honda specify their own Imrie diagnostic tester (model 625), or the peak voltage adapter (Pt. No. 07HGJ-0020100) with an aftermarket digital multimeter having an impedance of 10 M-ohm/DCV minimum for this test.*

4 If the ignition pulse generator functions correctly then the fault must be in the wiring harness or the ignition control unit. Check the wiring between the ignition pulse generator and the ICU for continuity, referring to the wiring diagrams at the end of Chapter 9. If the wiring is good, the ICU could be faulty.

Removal and installation

5 Remove the clutch cover (see Chapter 2, Section 16, referring to the relevant Steps). The sensor is mounted inside it.
6 Undo the sensor mounting bolts and the wire guide bolt and washer, then free the wiring grommet from the cover and remove the sensor **(see illustration)**.
7 Remove all traces of sealant from the sensor wiring grommet and clutch cover and apply a smear of fresh sealant to the grommet.
8 Locate the grommet and sensor correctly in the cover and tighten the sensor bolts securely **(see illustration 4.6)**. Route the wire and secure it with the washer and bolt.
9 Install the clutch cover (see Chapter 2, Section 16, referring to the relevant Steps).

F-1/FS-1 models onward (2001-on)

10 Refer to Chapter 4, Section 13 for details of testing and removal/installation.

5 Ignition control unit – check, removal and installation

F-X and F-Y (1999 and 2000) models

Check

1 If the tests shown in the preceding Sections have failed to isolate the cause of an ignition fault, it is possible that the ignition control unit is faulty. No test details are available with which the unit can be tested on home workshop equipment. Take the machine to a Honda dealer for testing.

Removal and installation

2 Remove the seat cowling (see Chapter 8) and disconnect the battery negative (–ve) lead. The control unit is mounted on the left-hand side of the rear sub-frame **(see illustration)**.
3 Draw the ignition control unit with its rubber sleeve off the sleeve's mounting lugs, then disconnect the wiring connector and remove the unit.
4 Installation is the reverse of removal. Make sure the wiring connector is correctly and securely connected.

F-1/FS-1 models onward (2001-on)

5 The ignition system is controlled by the electronic control module (ECM). Refer to Chapter 4, Section 13 for details of testing and removal/installation.

6 Ignition timing – general information and check

General information

1 Since no provision exists for adjusting the ignition timing and since no component is subject to mechanical wear, there is no need for regular checks; only if investigating a fault such as a loss of power or a misfire, should the ignition timing be checked.
2 The ignition timing is checked dynamically (engine running) using a stroboscopic lamp. The inexpensive neon lamps should be adequate in theory, but in practice may produce a pulse of such low intensity that the timing mark remains indistinct. If possible, one of the more precise xenon tube lamps should be used, powered by an external source of the appropriate voltage. **Note:** *Do not use the machine's own battery as an incorrect reading may result from stray impulses within the machine's electrical system.*

Check

3 Warm the engine up to normal operating temperature then stop it. Remove the right-hand fairing side panel (see Chapter 8).
4 Unscrew the timing inspection cap from the clutch cover **(see illustration)**. Discard the O-ring as a new one must be used.
5 The timing mark on the rotor which indicates the firing point at idle speed for the No. 1 cylinder is a line next to an 'F' mark for UK models, the triple punch mark for US 49-state models, and the double punch mark for California models **(see illustration)**. The static timing mark with which this should align is the index line on the clutch cover.

> **HAYNES HiNT**
> *The timing marks can be highlighted with white paint to make them more visible under the stroboscope light.*

6 Connect the timing light to the No. 1 cylinder coil/cap black/white wire.
7 Start the engine and aim the light at the static timing mark.

5.2 Ignition control unit (arrowed)

6.4 Unscrew the timing inspection cap (arrowed)

6.5 'F' mark and static timing mark

Ignition system 5•5

6.10 Install the cap using a new O-ring

7.2 Disconnect the sensor wiring connector

7.8 Throttle position sensor mounting screws (arrowed)

8 With the machine idling, the appropriate timing mark next to the 'F' should align with the static timing mark (see Step 5).
9 As already stated, there is no means of adjustment of the ignition timing on these machines. If the ignition timing is incorrect, or suspected of being incorrect, one of the ignition system components is at fault, and the system must be tested as described in the preceding Sections of this Chapter.
10 When the check is complete, Install the timing inspection cap using a new O-ring, and smear it and the cap threads with grease **(see illustration)**. Tighten the cap to the torque setting specified at the beginning of the Chapter.

7 Throttle position sensor – check and replacement

F-X and F-Y (1999 and 2000) models

1 The throttle position sensor (TPS) is mounted on the right-hand side of the carburettors and is keyed to the throttle shaft. The sensor provides the ignition control unit with information on throttle position and rate of opening or closing.

Check

2 Raise or remove the fuel tank (see Chapter 4). Disconnect the sensor's wiring connector **(see illustration)**.
3 Using an ohmmeter set to the K-ohm scale, measure the resistance between the yellow/black and blue/green wire terminals on the sensor. If the reading is not as specified at the beginning of the Chapter, the sensor is faulty.
4 Now connect the meter between the yellow/blue and blue/green terminals and open and close the throttle – the resistance should increase as the throttle is opened, and decrease again as it is closed.
5 To check the input voltage to the sensor, connect the positive (+ve) lead of a voltmeter to the yellow/black wire terminal on the sensor wiring connector, and the negative (–ve) lead to the blue/green terminal. Turn the ignition switch ON and check that a voltage of 4.7 to 5.3 volts is present. If it isn't, there is a fault in the wiring or the ignition control unit. Use a multimeter set to resistance or a continuity tester, and check for continuity between the terminals on the wiring loom side of the sensor wiring connector and the corresponding terminals on the ignition control unit connector, referring to the *Wiring Diagrams* at the end of Chapter 9 (first disconnect the ICU connector). There should be continuity between each terminal. If not, this is probably due to a damaged or broken wire between the connectors; pinched or broken wires can usually be repaired. Also check the connectors for loose or corroded terminals, and check the sensor itself for cracks and other damage. If the wiring and connectors are good, check the adjustment of the sensor as described below.
6 If the readings and values were not as specified, and the wiring is good, the sensor or the ignition control unit could be faulty. Take them to a Honda dealer for further testing. If the sensor is confirmed to be faulty, it must be replaced with a new one; it is a sealed unit and cannot therefore be repaired.

Replacement

7 Remove the carburettors (see Chapter 4). The throttle sensor is mounted on the right-hand end of the carburettor assembly.
8 Undo the screws and remove the sensor, noting how it keys onto the end of the throttle shaft **(see illustration)**.
9 Install the sensor, locating the flat on the throttle shaft in the sensor so that it is keyed to it, then apply a suitable non-permanent thread locking compound to the threads of the screws and tighten them finger-tight. Now connect an ohmmeter to the top two terminals on the sensor and adjust its position on the bracket until the resistance reading is between 490 and 510 ohms, then tighten the screws securely.
10 Install the carburettors (see Chapter 4).

F-1/FS-1 models onward (2001-on)

11 Refer to Chapter 4, Section 13 for details of testing and removal/installation.

8 Immobiliser system

General information

1 An immobiliser system (known as HISS – Honda Ignition Security System) is fitted to some models as an anti-theft device. The system will only allow the machine to be started if the correct registered key is used to turn the ignition ON. The system consists of a transponder which is part of the ignition key, a receiver which is fitted around the ignition switch, and the ignition control unit (ICU) or electronic control module (ECM), depending on your model (carburettor or fuel injection).
2 When the ignition is switched ON, the ICU/ECM sends power through the receiver to the transponder. The transponder sends a coded signal back through the receiver to the ICU/ECM. If the signal sent by the transponder matches the signal stored in the ICU/ECM memory, the immobiliser indicator light in the instrument cluster (marked by a key symbol) comes on for two seconds, then goes out, and the ICU/ECM allows the engine to be started. If the key code signal is not recognised, or if there is a fault in the system, the indicator light stays on. If the light stays on, refer to the fault diagnosis and troubleshooting Sections below. Likewise if the light does not come on at all.
3 The ICU/ECM can store the codes for up to four registered keys. They keys should be kept separately (i.e. not on the same key-ring) as the proximity of another key to the one being used in the switch can lead to the signal from it being jammed, and the bike will not start. The key has a built in transponder which can be damaged if the key is dropped or knocked, gets too hot, is too close to a magnetic object, or is submerged in water for too long. If all the keys are lost, the ICU/ECM must be replaced with a new one, so always make sure you have at least one spare key. If a new key is obtained, it must be registered into the system before the bike can be started.

Key registration procedure

To register a new key

Note: *To do this you will need the Honda special tool (Part No. 07XMZ-MBW0100) which is a wiring loom adapter that plugs into the ignition pulse generator wiring connector. If this tool is not available, registration must be carried at a Honda dealer with the special tool.*

4 Obtain a new key from a Honda dealer, then have it cut to match the original key.
5 Trace the wiring back from the ignition pulse generator, which is mounted in the clutch cover on the right-hand side of the engine, to its red 2-pin wiring connector above the crankcase and disconnect it – depending on the size of your hands and general dexterity, and the tightness of the connector, you may have to either remove the right-hand fairing side panel (see Chapter 8) or raise the fuel tank (see Section 2) **(see illustration 4.1)**. Connect the special tool wiring connector to the loom side of the connector, then connect the red coloured clip of the tool to the battery positive (+ve) terminal and the green coloured clip to the battery negative (-ve) terminal.
6 Turn the ignition switch ON using your original key. The immobiliser indicator light should come on and stay on (if it starts to flash after ten seconds, then there is a fault in the system, which will have gone into fault diagnosis, and the pattern of the flashes it emits should be matched with the fault code (see below)). Now disconnect the red clip from the battery positive terminal and leave it disconnected for at least two seconds, then reconnect it. The indicator should now come on for two seconds, then begin to flash repeatedly four times. This indicates that the system is in registration mode. At this point the registrations of all keys except the one in the switch will have been cancelled, so if you have another spare apart from the new one you want to register, this will also have to registered.
7 Turn the ignition OFF and remove the original key, placing it well away from the receiver.
8 Insert the new key into the switch and turn it ON. The indicator should now come on for two seconds, then begin to flash repeatedly four times. This indicates that the system has registered the new key. Turn the ignition OFF and remove the key.
9 To register any other spare keys that will have been cancelled, repeat Steps 7 and 8. Up to four keys can be registered.
10 On completion turn the ignition OFF, then remove the special tool and reconnect the ignition pulse generator wiring connector. Now turn the ignition ON using any of the registered keys to return the system to normal mode.
11 Check that all registered keys can start the motorcycle.

To register new keys with a new ignition switch

Note: *To do this you will need the Honda special tool (Part No. 07XMZ-MBW0100) which is a wiring loom adapter that plugs into the ignition pulse generator wiring connector. If this tool is not available, registration must be carried at a Honda dealer with the special tool.*

12 Obtain a new switch and two (or more if you want) new keys (which I presume come with the switch).
13 Remove the faulty switch (see Chapter 9), but retain the receiver to fit with the new switch.
14 Trace the wiring back from the ignition pulse generator, which is mounted in the clutch cover on the right-hand side of the engine, to its red 2-pin wiring connector above the crankcase and disconnect it – depending on the size of your hands and general dexterity, and the tightness of the connector, you may have to either remove the right-hand fairing side panel (see Chapter 8) or raise the fuel tank (see Section 2) **(see illustration 4.1)**. Connect the special tool wiring connector to the loom side of the connector, then connect the red coloured clip of the tool to the battery positive (+ve) terminal and the green coloured clip to the battery negative (-ve) terminal.
15 Place one of the original registered keys for the faulty switch next to the receiver.
16 Connect the new ignition switch to its connector in the wiring loom, but keep it away from the receiver. Turn the new switch ON with one of the new keys. The immobiliser indicator light should come on and stay on, which means the ICU/ECM recognises the old key that is next to the receiver (if it starts to flash after ten seconds, then there is a fault in the system, which will have gone into fault diagnosis, and the pattern of the flashes it emits should be matched with the fault code (see below)). Now disconnect the red clip from the battery positive terminal and leave it disconnected for at least two seconds, then reconnect it. The indicator should now come on for two seconds, then begin to flash repeatedly four times. This indicates that the system is in registration mode. At this point the registrations of all keys except the one near the receiver will have been cancelled.
17 Turn the ignition OFF and remove the new key.
18 Install the new ignition switch, then fit the receiver onto it (see Chapter 9).
19 Insert the new key into the switch and turn it ON. The indicator should now come on for four seconds, then begin to flash repeatedly four times. This indicates that the system has registered the new key. Turn the ignition OFF and disconnect the red clip of the special tool from the battery positive terminal.
20 Turn the ignition ON using the newly registered key. The indicator light should come on for two seconds, then go off.
21 Turn the ignition OFF and reconnect the red clip to the battery positive terminal.
22 Turn the ignition ON using the newly registered key. The indicator light should come on and stay on. Now disconnect the red clip from the battery positive terminal and leave it disconnected for at least two seconds, then reconnect it. The indicator should now come on for two seconds, then begin to flash repeatedly four times. This indicates that the system is in registration mode. At this point the registrations of all old keys (for the faulty switch) are cancelled.
23 Turn the ignition OFF and remove the key, placing it well away from the receiver.
24 Insert the second new unregistered key and turn the ignition ON. The indicator should now come on for four seconds, then begin to flash repeatedly four times. This indicates that the system has registered the second new key. Turn the ignition OFF and remove the key.
25 To register any other new spare keys, repeat Steps 23 and 24. Up to four keys can be registered.
26 On completion turn the ignition OFF, then remove the special tool and reconnect the ignition pulse generator wiring connector. Now turn the ignition ON using any of the registered keys to return the system to normal mode.
27 Check that all newly registered keys can start the motorcycle.

To register new keys with a new ICU/ECM (electronic control module)

28 Obtain a new ICU/ECM along with two (or more if you want) new keys. Install the ICU/ECM (see Section 5 or Chapter 4). Have the keys cut to match the original key for your ignition switch.
29 Insert a new key into the switch and turn it ON. The indicator should now come on for two seconds, then begin to flash repeatedly four times. This indicates that the system has registered the new key. If the indicator stays on for ten seconds then starts to flash, then there is a fault in the system, which will have gone into fault diagnosis, and the pattern of the flashes it emits should be matched with the fault code (see below).
30 Turn the ignition OFF and remove the key.
31 Insert the second new key and turn the ignition ON. The indicator should now come on for two seconds, then begin to flash repeatedly four times. This indicates that the system has registered the second new key.
32 Turn the ignition OFF and remove the key.
33 The new ICU/ECM will only register two new keys at this stage. If you have a third key that you want to register, refer to Steps 4 to 10 to register it, noting that you will need the special tool mentioned therein.
34 Check that both newly registered keys can start the motorcycle.

Fault diagnosis

Note: *To enter the fault diagnosis mode of the system you will need the Honda special tool (Part No. 07XMZ-MBW0100) which is a wiring loom adapter that plugs into the ignition pulse generator wiring connector. If this tool is not available, fault diagnosis must be carried at a Honda dealer with the special tool.*

35 There are two fault diagnosis modes, one for if there is a fault during normal use, and one for a fault that occurs when registering a new key. Make sure you refer to the correct table below when matching the fault code pattern.

36 If the indicator light has come on and stayed on during normal use, trace the wiring back from the ignition pulse generator, which is mounted in the clutch cover on the right-hand side of the engine, to its red 2-pin wiring connector above the crankcase and disconnect it – depending on the size of your hands and general dexterity, and the tightness of the connector, you may have to either remove the right-hand fairing side panel (see Chapter 8) or raise the fuel tank (see Section 2) **(see illustration 4.1)**. Connect the special tool wiring connector to the loom side of the connector, then connect the red coloured clip of the tool to the battery positive (+ve) terminal and the green coloured clip to the battery negative (-ve) terminal.

37 Turn the ignition switch ON. The indicator light in the tachometer will come on for ten seconds, then start to flash. This means it has entered diagnostic mode, and the pattern of the flashes indicates the fault that has occurred. The pattern repeats continuously. Match the pattern with the fault codes below, making sure you refer to the relevant table. If the indicator stays on after ten seconds and does not flash, then there is no fault logged in the system.

Troubleshooting procedure

Indicator light does not come on when ignition switched ON

38 Check the fuses (see Chapter 9).
39 If the fuses are good, check whether the neutral and oil pressure warning lights have come on.
40 If the lights have not come on, remove the fairing (see Chapter 8). Disconnect the instrument cluster wiring connector. Using a voltmeter, connect the positive (+ve) probe to the black/brown wire terminal on the loom side of the indicator connector and the negative (-ve) probe to the green wire terminal on the loom side of the instrument cluster connector. With the ignition ON there should be battery voltage. If voltage is present, the instrument cluster is faulty (see Chapter 9). If there is no voltage, check for continuity in the wiring, referring to the *Wiring Diagrams* at the end of Chapter 9. The green wire goes to earth (ground).
41 If the lights have come on, remove the seat or seat cowling as required to access the ICU/ECM (see Chapter 8). Disconnect the ICU wiring connector or ECM 22-pin black wiring connector. Using a voltmeter, connect the positive (+ve) probe to the white/red wire terminal on the loom side of the indicator connector and the negative (-ve) probe to earth (ground). Turn the ignition ON – there should be battery voltage.
42 If there was no voltage, using a voltmeter, connect the positive (+ve) probe to the white/red wire terminal on the loom side of the instrument cluster connector and the negative (-ve) probe to the green wire terminal on the loom side of the instrument cluster connector. Turn the ignition ON – there should be no voltage for two seconds, then there should be battery voltage. If there is no voltage after two seconds, check for continuity in the wiring, referring to the *Wiring Diagrams* at the end of Chapter 9. The green wire goes to earth (ground). If no voltage is present, the instrument cluster is faulty (see Chapter 9). If there is voltage, check for continuity in the white/red wire between the indicator unit and the ICU/ECM.
43 If there is voltage in Step 41, disconnect the ICU wiring connector or ECM 22-pin black wiring connector. Using a voltmeter, connect the positive (+ve) probe to the black (ICU) or black/white (ECM) wire terminal on the loom side of the ICU/ECM connector and the negative (-ve) probe to earth (ground). Turn the ignition ON – there should be battery voltage. If there is no voltage, check for continuity in the black or black/white wire, referring to the *Wiring Diagrams* at the end of Chapter 9. If voltage is present, check for continuity to earth (ground) in the green wire. If the wiring is good, check the ICU/ECM connector for loose, damaged or corroded terminals. If the connector is good, then the ICU/ECM could be faulty, and should be checked by a Honda dealer.

Indicator light stays on when ignition switched ON

44 Check that none of the other registered keys are close to the receiver. If they are, remove them and try the ignition again.
45 Turn the ignition ON with a spare key and check the indicator light, which should come on for two seconds, then go out. If it does, the first key is faulty. If it doesn't, perform the fault diagnosis procedure described above. If a fault code is displayed, use the appropriate table to determine the fault and the solution.
46 If no fault code is displayed, or the system does not go into fault diagnosis mode, remove the seat or seat cowling as required to access the ICU/ECM (see Chapter 8). Disconnect the ICU wiring connector or ECM 22-pin black wiring connector. Using a voltmeter, connect the positive (+ve) probe to the white/red wire terminal on the loom side of the indicator connector and the negative (-ve) probe to earth (ground). Turn the ignition ON – there should be battery voltage. If there is no voltage, check for continuity in the white/red wire between the ICU/ECM and the indicator unit.
47 If there is voltage, check for continuity in the yellow and white/yellow wires between the ICU/ECM and the ignition pulse generator, referring to the *Wiring Diagrams* at the end of Chapter 9. If there is no continuity, trace the fault and repair or replace the wiring as necessary. If there is continuity, the ICU/ECM could be faulty and should be taken to a Honda dealer for assessment.

Fault code indicated by flash pattern

48 If the 'two short, two long' flash pattern has been indicated during the fault diagnosis procedure, remove the fairing (see Chapter 8). Trace the wiring from the receiver on the ignition switch and disconnect it at the 4-pin

Table 1: If fault is indicated during normal use

Flash pattern	Fault	Solution
Two short, one long, one short	Faulty ICU/ECM	Install new ICU/ECM
Two short, two long	Faulty receiver or wiring	Follow Troubleshooting procedure below
One long, three short	Signal jammed by other key	Place other key well away from receiver
One long, two short, one long	Signal jammed by other key	Place other key well away from receiver

Table 2: If fault is indicated during key registration

Flash pattern	Fault	Solution
One short, one long, one short, one long	Key already registered	Use a new or cancelled key
Two short, two long	Faulty receiver or wiring	Follow Troubleshooting procedure below
One short, one long, two short	Key already registered on old ECM	Use a new key

5•8 Ignition system

8.52 HISS receiver (A) and one of its screws (B)

white connector. Using a voltmeter, connect the positive (+ve) probe to the yellow/red wire terminal on the loom side of the receiver connector and the negative (-ve) probe to earth (ground). Turn the ignition ON – there should be approximately 5 volts present. If there is no voltage, check for continuity in the yellow/red wire between the ICU/ECM and the receiver, and repair or replace the wiring if there is no continuity.

49 If there is 5 volts present, check for continuity to earth (ground) in the green/orange wire, and repair or replace the wiring if there is no continuity.

50 If the wiring is good, using a voltmeter, connect the positive (+ve) probe to the pink wire terminal on the loom side of the receiver connector and the negative (-ve) probe to earth (ground). Turn the ignition ON – there should be approximately 5 volts present. If there is, the receiver is faulty.

51 If there is no voltage, check for continuity in the orange/blue and pink wires between the ICU/ECM and the receiver, and repair or replace the wiring if there is no continuity between the connectors, or if there is continuity in either to earth (ground). If the wiring is good, the receiver is faulty.

Replacement

52 To replace the receiver, remove the fairing (see Chapter 8). Trace the wiring from the receiver on the ignition switch and disconnect it at the 4-pin white connector. Undo the screws securing the receiver around the ignition switch and remove the receiver, noting how it fits **(see illustration)**. If you don't have the correct tools to easily access the screws, follow the procedure for removing the top yoke in the ignition switch replacement Section in Chapter 9.

53 To replace the ICU see Section 5, to replace the ECM see Chapter 4.

Chapter 6
Frame, suspension and final drive

Contents

Drive chain – removal, cleaning and installation	16	Sidestand and centrestand – check	see Chapter 1
Drive chain and sprockets – check, adjustment and lubrication	see Chapter 1	Sidestand and centrestand – lubrication	see Chapter 1
Footrests, brake pedal and gearchange lever – removal and installation	3	Sidestand and centrestand – removal and installation	4
Forks – disassembly, inspection and reassembly	8	Sidestand switch – check and replacement	see Chapter 9
Forks – oil change	7	Sprockets – check and replacement	17
Forks – removal and installation	6	Steering head bearings – freeplay check and adjustment	see Chapter 1
Frame – inspection and repair	2	Steering head bearings – inspection and replacement	10
General information	1	Steering head bearings – lubrication	see Chapter 1
Handlebars and levers – removal and installation	5	Steering stem – removal and installation	9
Handlebar switches – check	see Chapter 9	Suspension – adjustments	13
Handlebar switches – removal and installation	see Chapter 9	Suspension – check	see Chapter 1
Rear shock absorber– removal, inspection and installation	11	Swingarm – inspection, bearing check and replacement	15
Rear sprocket coupling/rubber damper – check and replacement	18	Swingarm – removal and installation	14
Rear suspension linkage– removal, inspection and installation	12	Swingarm and suspension linkage bearings – lubrication	see Chapter 1

Degrees of difficulty

Easy, suitable for novice with little experience	Fairly easy, suitable for beginner with some experience	Fairly difficult, suitable for competent DIY mechanic	Difficult, suitable for experienced DIY mechanic	Very difficult, suitable for expert DIY or professional

Specifications

Front forks
Fork oil type .... Pro-Honda SS8 suspension fluid or 10W fork oil
Fork oil capacity
  F-X and F-Y (1999 and 2000) models .... 475 ± 2.5 cc
  F-1 to F-4 (2001 to 2004), FS-1 and FS-2 (2001 and 2002) models . 462 ± 2.5 cc
  F-5 model onward (2005-on) .... 474 ± 2.5 cc
Fork oil level*
  F-X and F-Y (1999 and 2000) models .... 118 mm
  F-1 to F-4 (2001 to 2004), FS-1 and FS-2 (2001 and 2002) models . 116 mm
  F-5 model onward (2005-on) .... 106 mm
Fork spring free length (min)
  F-X and F-Y (1999 and 2000) models
    Standard .... 336 mm
    Service limit .... 329.9 mm
  F-1 to F-4 (2001 to 2004), FS-1 and FS-2 (2001 and 2002) models
    Standard .... 286 mm
    Service limit .... 280.3 mm
  F-5 model onward (2005-on)
    Standard .... 271.5 mm
    Service limit .... 266 mm
Fork tube runout limit .... 0.2 mm

*Oil level is measured from the top of the tube with the fork spring removed and the leg fully compressed.

Frame, suspension and final drive

Final drive

Drive chain slack and lubricant	See Chapter 1
Drive chain	
F-X and F-Y (1999 and 2000) models	
Type	DID 525HV or RK 525ROZ1
Length	110 links
F-1/FS-1 models onward (2001-on)	
Type	DID 525HV or RK GB525ROZ1
Length	108 links
Joining link pin projection from side plate (unstaked)	
DID type chain	1.15 to 1.55 mm
RK type chain	1.20 to 1.40 mm
Joining link staked ends diameter	
DID type chain	5.50 to 5.80 mm
RK type chain	5.55 to 5.85 mm
Sprocket sizes	
Front (engine) sprocket	16T
Rear (wheel) sprocket	
European F-X and F-Y models	44T
US 1999 and 2000 models	45T
European F-1 models onward	45T
European FS models, US 2001-on models	46T

Torque settings

Clutch lever bracket clamp bolts	12 Nm
Drive chain slider bolts	9 Nm
Footrest bracket mounting bolts	26 Nm
Fork damper bolt	34 Nm
Fork top bolt	23 Nm
Fork yoke clamp bolts	
Bottom yoke bolts	39 Nm
Top yoke bolts	23 Nm
Front brake master cylinder clamp bolts	12 Nm
Front sprocket bolt	54 Nm
Handlebar end-weight screws	10 Nm
Rear brake master cylinder mounting bolts	9 Nm
Rear sprocket nuts	
F-X and F-Y (1999 and 2000) models	88 Nm
F-1/FS-1 models onward (2001-on)	64 Nm
Shock absorber mounting bolt nuts	44 Nm
Sidestand bracket front bolt/nut	39 Nm
Sidestand bracket rear bolt	44 Nm
Sidestand pivot bolt	10 Nm
Sidestand pivot bolt nut	29 Nm
Sidestand/centrestand/suspension bracket bolt nuts	39 Nm
Steering head bearing adjuster nut (see text)	25 Nm
Steering stem nut	103 Nm
Suspension linkage bolt nuts	
Linkage arm to brackets	44 Nm
Linkage arm to linkage plates	44 Nm
Linkage plates to swingarm	44 Nm
Swingarm pivot adjuster bolt	
Initial torque	12 Nm
Final torque	7 Nm
Swingarm pivot adjuster bolt locknut	
Actual	64 Nm
Indicated	58 Nm
Swingarm pivot bolt nut	93 Nm

Frame, suspension and final drive 6•3

1 General information

All models have a box-section twin-spar aluminium frame which uses the engine as a stressed member.

Front suspension is by a pair of oil-damped telescopic forks. The forks have a cartridge damper and are adjustable for spring pre-load and both rebound and compression damping.

At the rear, a box-section aluminium swingarm acts on a single shock absorber via a three-way linkage. The shock absorber is adjustable for spring pre-load and both rebound and compression damping.

The drive to the rear wheel is by chain and sprockets.

2 Frame – inspection and repair

1 The frame should not require attention unless accident damage has occurred. In most cases, frame replacement is the only satisfactory remedy for such damage. A few frame specialists have the jigs and other equipment necessary for straightening the frame to the required standard of accuracy, but even then there is no simple way of assessing to what extent the frame may have been over stressed.

2 After the machine has accumulated a lot of miles, the frame should be examined closely for signs of cracking or splitting at the welded joints. Loose engine mount bolts can cause ovaling or fracturing of the mounting tabs. Minor damage can often be repaired by welding, depending on the extent and nature of the damage.

3 Remember that a frame which is out of alignment will cause handling problems. If misalignment is suspected as the result of an accident, it will be necessary to strip the machine completely so the frame can be thoroughly checked.

3.1a Remove the circlip and washer (A) and withdraw the pivot pin (B), noting the return spring ends (C) – front footrest

3 Footrests, brake pedal and gearchange lever – removal and installation

Footrests

Removal

1 Remove the split pin and washer from the bottom of the footrest pivot pin, then withdraw the pivot pin and remove the footrest (see illustrations). On the rider's footrests, note the fitting of the return spring. On the passenger's footrests, note the fitting of the detent plate, ball and spring, and take care no to let the ball and spring ping away when removing the footrest.

2 The rider's footrest rubbers can be renewed if required by removing the bolt(s) on the underside of the footrest. Note the fitting of the mounting plate for the rubber.

Installation

3 Installation is the reverse of removal.

Brake pedal

Removal

4 Slacken the master cylinder mounting bolts (see illustration). Unscrew the footrest bracket mounting bolts and displace the bracket so that you can access the back of it (see illustration). Make sure you do not strain the brake hose or the brake light switch wiring.

3.1b Remove the circlip and washer (A) and withdraw the pivot pin (B) – rear footrest

5 Unhook the brake pedal return spring and the brake light switch spring from the hook on the pedal (see illustration).
6 Remove the split pin from the clevis pin securing the brake pedal to the master cylinder pushrod (see illustration 3.5).
7 Remove the circlip, thrust washer and wave washer securing the brake pedal on its pivot (see illustration 3.5).
8 Unscrew the master cylinder mounting bolts, noting how they also secure the heel guard, then slide the pedal off the pivot. Remove the clevis pin and separate the pedal from the pushrod.

Installation

9 Installation is the reverse of removal, noting the following:
● Apply molybdenum disulphide oil to the brake pedal pivot.
● Use a new split pin on the clevis pin securing the brake pedal to the master cylinder pushrod.
● Tighten the footrest bracket mounting bolts and the master cylinder mounting bolts to the torque settings specified at the beginning of the Chapter, not forgetting to secure the heel guard with the master cylinder bolts.
● Check the operation of the rear brake light switch (see Chapter 1).

Gearchange lever and linkage

Removal

10 Slacken the gearchange lever linkage rod locknuts, then unscrew the rod and separate

3.4a Slacken the master cylinder bolts (arrowed) . . .

3.4b . . . then unscrew the bolts (B) and displace the bracket

3.5 Unhook the springs (A), remove the split pin (B), then remove the circlip and washers (C)

6•4 Frame, suspension and final drive

3.10 Slacken the locknuts (arrowed) and thread the rod out

3.11 Unscrew the bolts (arrowed) and displace the bracket . . .

3.12 . . . then remove the circlip and washers (arrowed) and remove the lever

it from the lever and the arm (the rod is reverse-threaded on one end and so will simultaneously unscrew from both lever and arm when turned in the one direction) **(see illustration)**. Note how far the rod is threaded into the lever and arm as this determines the height of the lever relative to the footrest.

11 Unscrew the footrest bracket mounting bolts and displace the bracket so that you can access the back of it **(see illustration)**

12 Remove the circlip, thrust washer and wave washer securing the gearchange lever on its pivot and slide it off **(see illustration)**.

Installation

13 Installation is the reverse of removal, noting the following:
- Apply molybdenum disulphide oil to the gear lever pivot.
- Tighten the footrest bracket mounting bolts to the torque setting specified at the beginning of the Chapter.

- Adjust the gear lever height as required by screwing the linkage rod in or out of the lever and arm. Tighten the locknuts securely.

4 Sidestand and centrestand – removal and installation

Sidestand

Removal

1 The sidestand is attached to a bracket on the frame. Springs anchored between them ensure the stand is held in the retracted or extended position. Support the bike on the centrestand; where no centrestand is fitted use an auxiliary stand.

2 To remove the sidestand without its bracket, first displace the sidestand switch (see Chapter 9). There is no need to disconnect its wiring connector or remove it completely, just let it hang from its wiring. Unhook the stand springs, then unscrew the nut from the pivot bolt **(see illustration)**. Unscrew the pivot bolt and remove the stand.

3 To remove the complete sidestand assembly, either displace the sidestand switch (see Chapter 9), or raise or remove the fuel tank (see Chapter 4), then trace the wiring from the sidestand switch and disconnect it at the green 2-pin wiring connector inside the rubber boot **(see illustration)**. Release the wiring from any clips or guides, noting its routing.

4 Unscrew the nut on the right-hand end of

the front sidestand bracket bolt, then withdraw the bolt **(see illustration)**. Unscrew the rear bracket bolt and remove the stand assembly.

Installation

5 If the stand itself has been separated from its bracket, apply grease to the pivot bolt shank and tighten the bolt and nut to the torque settings specified at the beginning of the Chapter **(see illustration 4.2)**. Reconnect the springs and check that they hold the stand securely up when not in use – an accident is almost certain to occur if the stand extends while the machine is in motion.

6 If the sidestand bracket has been removed, clean the threads of the rear bolt and apply a suitable non-permanent thread locking compound. Tighten the mounting bolt and nut to the specified torque settings **(see illustration 4.4)**.

7 If displaced, install the sidestand switch. Make sure the wiring is correctly routed and secured by any clips or guides **(see illustration 4.3)**. Check the operation of the switch (see Chapter 1).

Centrestand

Removal

8 The centrestand is attached to the brackets on the back of the engine. Springs anchored between them ensure the stand is held in the retracted or extended position. Support the bike on the sidestand.

9 Unhook the spring link plate from the lug bolt, then unscrew the lug bolt **(see illustrations)**. Support the stand, then grasp

4.2 Unhook the spring ends (A), then unscrew the nut (B)

4.3 Sidestand switch wiring connector

4.4 Sidestand bracket bolts (arrowed)

4.9a Unhook the plate . . .

Frame, suspension and final drive 6•5

4.9b . . . then unscrew the lug bolt

4.9c Withdraw the pivot and remove the stand

5.1a Disconnect the wiring connectors (arrowed)

the end of the pivot and withdraw it, and remove the stand (see illustration).

Installation

10 Apply grease to the pivot. Apply a suitable non-permanent thread locking compound to the lug bolt threads and tighten it securely. Reconnect the spring link plate and check that the springs hold the stand securely up when not in use – an accident could occur if the stand extends while the machine is in motion.

5 Handlebars and levers – removal and installation

Right handlebar removal

Note: *To merely displace the handlebar from the top yoke without having to remove the individual assemblies follow Step 4.*

1 Disconnect the wires from the brake light switch **(see illustration)**. Unscrew the two master cylinder assembly clamp bolts and position the assembly clear of the handlebar, making sure no strain is placed on the hydraulic hose **(see illustration)**. Keep the master cylinder reservoir upright to prevent possible fluid leakage.

2 Unscrew the two handlebar switch housing screws and separate the halves. If required, free the throttle cable ends from the throttle pulley, creating slack in the cable as necessary using the adjusters (see Chapter 1). To avoid having to do this, note that the throttle pulley can be slid off the end of the handlebar with the cables still attached after the handlebar has been displaced from the fork.

3 Unscrew the handlebar end-weight retaining screw, then remove the weight from the end of the handlebar. If the throttle cables have been detached, slide the twistgrip off the handlebar.

4 Prise the snap-ring from the top of the fork using a small screwdriver inserted in the slit in the handlebar clamp **(see illustration)**. Slacken the handlebar clamp bolt, then ease the handlebar up and off the fork **(see illustrations)**.

5 If required, slide the throttle twistgrip and switch housing assembly off the handlebar.

Left handlebar removal

Note: *To merely displace the handlebar from the top yoke without having to remove the individual assemblies follow Step 9.*

6 Disconnect the wires from the clutch switch **(see illustration)**. Unscrew the two clutch lever bracket bolts and position the assembly clear of the handlebar **(see illustration)**.

5.1b Unscrew the master cylinder clamp bolts (arrowed) and displace the assembly

5.4a Remove the snap-ring . . .

5.4b . . . then slacken the clamp bolt (arrowed) . . .

5.4c . . . and slide the handlebar up and off the fork

5.6a Disconnect the wiring connectors (arrowed)

5.6b Unscrew the clamp bolts (arrowed) and displace the lever bracket

6•6 Frame, suspension and final drive

5.7a Undo the screws (arrowed) and displace the switch housing

5.7b Free the choke cable end from the lever slot (arrowed)

5.9a Remove the snap-ring . . .

7 Unscrew the two handlebar switch housing screws and separate the halves, noting how the choke lever or blanking plug (according to model) locates in the housing **(see illustration)**. On carburettor models, free the choke cable end from the lever.

8 If required, unscrew the handlebar end-weight retaining screw, then remove the weight from the end of the handlebar and slide off the grip. If the grip has been glued on, you will probably have to slit it with a knife to remove it. Also slide the choke lever or blanking plug (according to models) off the handlebar.

9 Prise the snap-ring from the top of the fork using a small screwdriver inserted in the slit in the handlebar clamp **(see illustration)**. Slacken the handlebar clamp bolt, then ease the handlebar up and off the fork **(see illustrations)**.

Handlebar installation

10 Installation is the reverse of removal, noting the following.

● When installing the right handlebar, apply some grease to it. If the throttle cables were not detached, slide the throttle twistgrip and cable housing assembly onto the handlebar before fitting the handlebar onto the fork.
● When installing the left handlebar, if removed do not forget to slide the choke lever or blanking plug (according to model) onto the handlebar before fitting the grip or the switch housing.
● When fitting the handlebars onto the forks,

5.9b . . . then slacken the clamp bolt (arrowed) . . .

locate the lug on the bottom of each handlebar clamp in the slot in the yoke, so that the handlebars are set in the correct position **(see illustration)**.
● Tighten the handlebar clamp bolts securely. Fit the snap-ring into its groove **(see illustration 5.9a)**.
● Make sure the front brake master cylinder and clutch lever assembly clamps are installed with the UP mark facing up, and with the clamp mating surfaces aligned with the punch mark on the top of the handlebar. Tighten the master cylinder clamp bolts to the specified torque setting, tightening the top bolt first **(see illustration 5.1b)**.
● Make sure the pin in each switch housing locates in its hole in the handlebar. Tighten the front housing screw first, then the rear **(see illustration 5.7a)**.
● When installing the handlebar end-weights,

5.9c . . . and slide the handlebar up and off the fork

align the boss with the groove on the inner weight inside the handlebar. Use new end-weight retaining screws and tighten them to the specified torque setting. If new grips are being fitted, secure them using a suitable adhesive.
● Do not forget to reconnect the front brake light switch and clutch switch wiring connectors **(see illustrations 5.1a and 5.6a)**.

Handlebar lever removal

11 To remove the front brake lever, undo the lever pivot screw locknut, then undo the pivot screw and remove the lever **(see illustration)**.
12 To remove the clutch lever, slacken the clutch cable adjuster lockring and thread the adjuster fully into the bracket to provide maximum freeplay in the cable **(see illustration)**.
13 Undo the lever pivot screw locknut, then

5.10 Locate the lug (A) in the slot (B)

5.11 Undo the nut (A), then undo the pivot screw (B) and remove the lever

5.12 Slacken the lockring and thread the adjuster in

Frame, suspension and final drive 6•7

5.13 Undo the nut (A), then undo the pivot screw (B) and remove the lever

6.5a Slacken the fork clamp bolt (arrowed) in the top yoke . . .

6.5b . . . and if required the fork top bolt

undo the pivot screw and remove the lever, detaching the cable nipple as you do **(see illustration)**.

Handlebar lever installation

14 Installation is the reverse of removal. Apply silicone grease to the contact area between the front brake master cylinder pushrod tip and the brake lever. Apply lithium or molybdenum grease to the pivot screw shafts and the contact areas between the lever and its bracket. Apply a spray lubricant such as WD40, or a dry-film Teflon lubricant to the brake lever span adjuster mechanism.

6 Forks – removal and installation

Removal

Caution: Although not strictly necessary, before removing the forks it is recommended that the fairing and fairing panels are removed (see Chapter 8). This will prevent accidental damage to the paintwork.

1 Displace the handlebars and tie them up using cable ties, making sure no strain is placed on the master cylinder hoses (see Section 5). There is no need to detach or disconnect anything from the handlebars.
2 Remove the front mudguard (see Chapter 8).
3 Remove the front wheel (see Chapter 7). Tie

the front brake calipers and hoses back so that they are out of the way.
4 Slacken the cable tie(s) around the fork tube, noting which side of the tube the wiring routes. Also note the routing of any cables and hoses.
5 Working on one fork at a time, slacken the fork clamp bolt in the top yoke **(see illustration)**. If the fork is to be disassembled, or if the fork oil is being changed, it is advisable to slacken the fork top bolt at this stage **(see illustration)**. Note the amount of protrusion of the fork above the top yoke.
6 Slacken the fork clamp bolt in the bottom yoke, and remove the fork by twisting it and pulling it downwards **(see illustrations)**.

> **HAYNES HiNT** *If the fork legs are seized in the yokes, spray the area with penetrating oil and allow time for it to soak in before trying again.*

Installation

7 Remove all traces of corrosion from the fork tube and the yokes. Slide the fork up through the bottom yoke and into the top yoke, making sure it passes through the cable tie(s) and all cables, hoses and wiring are routed on the correct side of the fork **(see illustration 6.6b)**.
8 Set the amount of protrusion of the fork tube above the top yoke at 33 mm, noting that the measurement is from the top surface of

the top yoke to the top edge of the fork tube, and not the top of the fork top bolt **(see illustration)**. Make sure it is the same on both sides.
9 Tighten the fork clamp bolt in the bottom yoke to the torque setting specified at the beginning of the Chapter **(see illustration)**. If the fork has been dismantled or if the fork oil was changed, tighten the fork top bolt to the specified torque setting **(see illustration 6.5b)**. Now tighten the fork clamp bolt in the top yoke **(see illustration 6.5a)**.
10 Install the front wheel (see Chapter 7), the front mudguard (see Chapter 8), and the handlebars (see Section 5). Pull the cable tie(s) around the fork tubes so they are not loose, but not too tight.
11 Check the operation of the front forks and brakes before taking the machine out on the road.

6.6a Bottom yoke fork clamp bolts (arrowed)

6.6b Draw the fork down and out of the yokes

6.8 Set the fork height as shown, making sure it is the same on both sides

6.9 Tighten the bottom yoke clamp bolt to the specified torque setting

6•8 Frame, suspension and final drive

7.3 Thread the top bolt out of the tube...

7.4 ...then counter-hold the hex and thread the top bolt off the rod

7.5a Remove the slotted collar...

7 Forks – oil change

CBR600F-X, F-Y, F-1 to F-4 models (1999 to 2004) and all FS models (2001 and 2002)

1 Remove the forks (see Section 6). Always work on the fork legs separately to avoid interchanging parts and thus causing an accelerated rate of wear.
2 If the fork top bolt was not slackened with the fork in situ, carefully clamp the fork tube in a vice equipped with soft jaws, taking care not to overtighten or score its surface, and slacken the top bolt (see illustration 6.5b).
3 Note the number of lines on the pre-load adjuster that are visible above the top bolt. Unscrew the fork top bolt from the top of the fork tube (see illustration). The bolt will remain threaded on the damper rod.
4 Carefully clamp the fork slider in a vice and slide the fork tube down into the slider a little way (wrap a rag around the top of the tube to minimise oil spillage) while, with the aid of an assistant if necessary, keeping the damper rod fully extended. Note the number of lines on the pre-load adjuster that are visible above the top bolt. Counter-hold the hex on the base of the adjuster and thread the top bolt off (see illustration).
5 Slide the slotted collar from between the pre-load adjuster and the spacer, then remove the spacer, the spring seat and the spring (see illustrations).
6 Invert the fork leg over a suitable container and pump the fork and damper rod vigorously to expel as much fork oil as possible (see illustrations). Support the fork upside down in the container for a while to allow as much oil as possible to drain, and pump the fork and rod again.
7 Slowly pour in the specified quantity of the specified grade of fork oil and pump the fork and damper rod at least ten times each to distribute it evenly, and until oil appears from the hole in the top (see illustrations). Fully compress the fork tube and damper rod into the slider and measure the oil level, and make any adjustment by adding more or tipping some out until it is at the level specified at the beginning of the Chapter.
8 Fit a new O-ring smeared with fork oil onto the pre-load adjuster. Clamp the slider in a vice via the brake caliper mounting lugs, taking care not to overtighten and damage them. Pull the fork tube and damper rod out of the slider as far as possible, then install the spring with its closer-wound coils at the

7.5b ...the spacer...

7.5c ...spring seat and the spring

7.6a Invert the fork over a container and pump the tube...

7.6b ...and the rod to expel the oil

7.7a Pour the oil into the top of the tube...

7.7b ...and pump the damper rod until oil appears from the hole (arrowed)

Frame, suspension and final drive 6•9

7.13 Unscrew the top bolt...

7.14 ...then counter-hold the nut and thread the top bolt off the rod

7.15a Remove the spacer...

bottom **(see illustration 7.5d)**. Install the spring seat **(see illustration 7.5c)**. Install the spacer **(see illustration 7.5b)**. Slide the slotted collar between the top of the spacer and the bottom of the pre-load adjuster, locating the hex into the bowl in the collar **(see illustration 7.5a)**.

9 Fit a new O-ring smeared with fork oil onto the fork top bolt. Counter-hold the hex on the bottom of the adjuster and thread the top bolt onto it, setting it in the position noted on removal **(see illustration 7.4)**.

10 Withdraw the tube fully from the slider and carefully screw the top bolt into it, making sure it does not cross-thread **(see illustration 7.3)**. Note: *The top bolt can be tightened to the specified torque setting at this stage if the tube is held between the padded jaws of a vice, but do not risk distorting the tube by doing so. A better method is to tighten the top bolt when the fork leg is being installed and is securely held in the bottom yoke.*

11 Install the forks (see Section 6).

CBR600F-5 models onward (2005-on)

12 Remove the forks (see Section 6). Always work on the fork legs separately to avoid interchanging parts and thus causing an accelerated rate of wear.

13 If the fork top bolt was not slackened with the fork in situ, carefully clamp the fork tube in a vice equipped with soft jaws, taking care not to overtighten or score its surface, and slacken the top bolt **(see illustration)**.

7.15b ...the spring seat...

Unscrew the fork top bolt from the top of the fork tube; the bolt will remain threaded on the damper rod.

14 Carefully clamp the fork slider in a vice and slide the fork tube down into the slider a little way (wrap a rag around the top of the tube to minimise oil spillage) while, with the aid of an assistant if necessary, keeping the damper rod fully extended. Counter-hold the nut on the damper rod and thread the top bolt off **(see illustration)**. Thread the nut fully down the rod.

15 Remove the spacer, the spring upper seat and the spring **(see illustrations)**. Also remove the spring lower seat, which may be stuck in the base of the spring.

16 Invert the fork leg over a suitable container and pump the fork and damper rod vigorously to expel as much fork oil as possible. Support the fork upside down in the container for a

7.15c ...and the spring

while to allow as much oil as possible to drain, and pump the fork and rod again.

17 Slowly pour in the specified quantity of the specified grade of fork oil and pump the fork and damper rod at least ten times each to distribute it evenly **(see illustration)**. Fully compress the fork tube and damper rod into the slider and measure the oil level, and make any adjustment by adding more or tipping some out until it is at the level specified at the beginning of the Chapter **(see illustration)**.

18 Clamp the slider in a vice via the brake caliper mounting lugs, taking care not to overtighten and damage them. Pull the fork tube and damper rod out of the slider as far as possible, then install the spring with its closer-wound coils at the bottom and with its spring seat located in its lower end. Install the spring upper seat **(see illustration)**. Install the spacer **(see illustration 7.15a)**.

7.17a Pour the oil slowly into the top of the fork tube while pumping the damper rod

7.17b Measure the oil level with the fork held vertical

7.18 Install the spring upper seat

6•10 Frame, suspension and final drive

7.19 Thread the top bolt onto the rod

7.20 Thread the top bolt into the slider

19 Fit a new O-ring smeared with fork oil onto the fork top bolt. Make sure the damper rod nut is at the base of the threads on the rod, then thread the top bolt onto the rod until it seats **(see illustration)**. Counterhold the top bolt and use an open-ended spanner to tighten the nut up against it **(see illustration 7.14)**.

20 Withdraw the tube fully from the slider and carefully screw the top bolt into it, making sure it does not cross-thread **(see illustration)**. **Note:** *The top bolt can be tightened to the specified torque setting at this stage if the tube is held between the padded jaws of a vice, but do not risk distorting the tube by doing so. A better method is to tighten the top bolt when the fork leg is being installed and is securely held in the bottom yoke.*

21 Install the forks (see Section 6).

8 Forks – disassembly, inspection and reassembly

Disassembly

1 Remove the forks (see Section 6). Always dismantle the fork legs separately to avoid interchanging parts and thus causing an accelerated rate of wear. Store all components in separate, clearly marked containers **(see illustrations)**.

2 Prise the stone guard off the top of the fork slider, taking care not to scratch the fork **(see illustration)**.

3 Before dismantling the fork, it is advisable to slacken the damper cartridge bolt now so that there is less chance of the damper rotating with it (due to the pressure of the spring). Compress the fork tube in the slider so that the spring exerts maximum pressure on the damper head, then have an assistant slacken the bolt in the base of the fork slider **(see illustration)**.

4 If the fork top bolt was not slackened with the fork in situ, carefully clamp the fork tube in a vice equipped with soft jaws, taking care not to overtighten or score its surface, and slacken the top bolt.

5 On CBR600F-X, F-Y, F-1 to F-4 models (1999 to 2004) and all FS models (2001 and 2002) note the number of lines on the pre-load adjuster that are visible above the top bolt, then unscrew the fork top bolt from the top of the fork tube **(see illustration 7.3)**; the bolt will remain threaded on the damper rod. Carefully clamp the fork slider in a vice and slide the fork tube down into the slider a little way (wrap a rag around the top of the tube to minimise oil spillage) while, with the aid of an assistant if necessary, keeping the damper rod fully extended. Counter-hold the hex on the base of the adjuster and thread the top bolt off **(see illustration 7.4)**. Slide the slotted collar from between the pre-load adjuster and the spacer, then remove the spacer, the spring seat and the spring **(see illustrations 7.5a, b, c and d)**.

6 On CBR600F-5 (2005-on) models, unscrew the fork top bolt from the top of the fork tube; the bolt will remain threaded on the damper rod. Carefully clamp the fork slider in a vice and slide the fork tube down into the slider a little way (wrap a rag around the top of the tube to minimise oil spillage) while, with the aid of an assistant if necessary, keeping the damper rod fully extended. Counter-hold the nut on the damper rod and thread the top bolt off **(see illustration 7.14)**. Thread the nut fully down the rod. Remove the spacer, the spring upper seat and the spring **(see illustrations 7.15a, b and c)**. Also remove the spring lower seat, which may be stuck in the base of the spring.

7 Invert the fork leg over a suitable container and pump the fork and damper rod vigorously to expel as much fork oil as possible **(see illustrations 7.6a and b)**.

8 Remove the previously slackened damper bolt and its copper sealing washer from the bottom of the slider **(see illustration)**. Discard the sealing washer as a new one must be used on reassembly.

9 Withdraw the damper cartridge from inside the fork tube **(see illustration)**.

8.1a Front fork components – CBR600F-X, F-Y, F-1 to F-4 models (1999 to 2004) and all FS models (2001 and 2002)

1 Top bolt	8 Damper cartridge	15 Oil seal
2 O-ring	9 Fork tube	16 Washer
3 Slotted collar	10 Bottom bush	17 Top bush
4 Spacer	11 Damper cartridge seat	18 Stone guard
5 Spring seat	12 O-ring	19 Fork slider
6 Spring	13 Dust seal	20 Damper cartridge bolt
7 O-ring	14 Retaining clip	21 Sealing washer

Frame, suspension and final drive 6•11

8.1b Front fork components – CBR600F-5 onwards (2005-on)

1 Top bolt
2 O-ring
3 Nut
4 Spacer
5 Spring seats
6 Spring
7 Dust seal
8 Retaining clip
9 Oil seal
10 Washer
11 Top bush
12 Fork tube
13 Lower bush
14 Damper cartridge
15 Seat
16 Stone guard
17 Slider
18 Damper cartridge bolt

8.2 Remove the stone guard as described

8.3 Slacken the damper rod bolt

10 Carefully prise out the dust seal from the top of the slider to gain access to the oil seal retaining clip **(see illustration)**. Discard the dust seal as a new one must be used.

11 Carefully remove the retaining clip, taking care not to scratch the surface of the tube; compress the fork to avoid damaging its working surface **(see illustration)**.

12 To separate the tube from the slider it is necessary to displace the oil seal and top bush. The bottom bush does not pass through the top bush, and this can be used to good effect. Push the tube gently inwards until it stops against the damper seat. Take care not to do this forcibly or the seat may be damaged. Now pull the tube sharply outwards until the bottom bush strikes the top bush **(see illustration)**. Repeat this operation until the top bush and seal are tapped out of the slider **(see illustration)**.

8.8 Unscrew and remove the damper rod bolt

8.9 Withdraw the damper from the tube

8.10 Prise out the dust seal using a flat-bladed screwdriver

8.11 Prise out the retaining clip using a flat-bladed screwdriver

8.12a To separate the fork tube from the slider, pull them apart firmly several times . . .

8.12b . . . the slide-hammer effect will displace the oil seal and bush

6•12 Frame, suspension and final drive

8.14a Push the damper rod seat up the slider . . .

8.14b . . . and withdraw it from the top

8.17 Check the compression and rebound springs

13 With the tube removed, slide off the oil seal, washer and top bush, noting which way up they fit **(see illustration 8.13b)**. Discard the oil seal as a new one must be used.
Caution: *Do not remove the bottom bush from the tube unless it is to be replaced.*
14 Draw the damper seat out of the slider – you will probably have to push it from the bottom via the damper bolt hole, and then grasp it with a long pair of thin-nosed pliers **(see illustrations)**. Discard the O-ring as a new one must be used.

Inspection

15 Clean all parts in solvent and blow them dry with compressed air, if available. Check the fork tube for score marks, scratches, flaking of the chrome finish and excessive or abnormal wear. Look for dents in the tube and replace the tube in both forks if any are found. Check the fork seal seat for nicks, gouges and scratches. If damage is evident, leaks will occur. Also check the oil seal washer for damage or distortion and replace it if necessary.
16 Check the fork tube for runout using V-blocks and a dial gauge. If the amount of runout exceeds the service limit specified, the tube should be replaced.

⚠ **Warning: *If the tube is bent or exceeds the runout limit, it should not be straightened; replace it with a new one.***

17 Check the spring (both the main spring and the rebound spring on the damper cartridge) for cracks and other damage **(see illustration)**. Measure the main spring free length and compare the measurement to the specifications at the beginning of the Chapter. If it is defective or sagged below the service limit, replace the main springs in both forks with new ones. Never replace only one spring. The rebound spring is not available separate from the damper cartridge, so if it is damaged (unlikely) the whole damper has to be renewed.
18 Examine the working surfaces of the two bushes; if worn or scuffed they must be replaced **(see illustration)**. To remove the bottom bush from the fork tube, prise it apart at the slit using a flat-bladed screwdriver and slide it off. Make sure the new one seats properly.
19 Check the damper cartridge assembly for damage and wear, and replace it if necessary. Holding the outside of the damper, pump the rod in and out. If it does not move smoothly the damper must be replaced with a new one.

Reassembly

20 Fit the damper seat squarely into the top of the slider – on CBR600F-X, F-Y, F-1 to F-4 models (1999 to 2004) and all FS models (2001 and 2002) check the condition of the O-ring around the damper seat before installing it **(see illustrations)**.
21 Oil the fork tube and bottom bush with the specified fork oil. Insert the tube into the slider, locating it over the damper seat, and push it fully down until the seat contacts the bottom of the slider **(see illustration)**.
22 Slide the damper cartridge fully into the fork tube and into its seat **(see illustration)**. Fit a new copper sealing washer onto the damper bolt and apply a few drops of a suitable non-permanent thread locking compound **(see illustration)**. Fit the bolt into the bottom of the slider and tighten it to the specified torque setting **(see illustrations)**. If the damper cartridge rotates inside the tube as you tighten the bolt, wait until the fork is fully reassembled and tighten it then (the

8.18 Check the top bush (A) and bottom bush (B) for wear and damage

8.20a Fit a new O-ring onto the damper seat . . .

8.20b . . . then fit the seat into the slider

8.21 Slide the tube into the slider

8.22a Slide the damper cartridge into the tube . . .

Frame, suspension and final drive 6•13

8.22b ... then fit the bolt using a new sealing washer ...

8.22c ... and tighten it to the specified torque

8.23a Install the top bush ...

8.23b ... followed by the washer

8.23c A drift can be used to tap the bush into place

8.25a Smear the oil seal with clean fork oil ...

8.25b ... then slide it down the tube

pressure of the spring on the cartridge will prevent it from turning).

23 Push the fork tube fully into the slider, then oil the top bush and slide it down over the tube **(see illustration)**. Press the bush squarely into its recess in the slider as far as possible, then install the oil seal washer with its flat side facing up **(see illustration)**. Use either the Honda service tool (Pt. Nos. 07947-KA50100 and 07947-KA40200) or a suitable piece of tubing to tap the bush fully into place; the tubing must be slightly larger in diameter than the fork tube and slightly smaller in diameter than the bush recess in the slider. Take care not to scratch the fork tube during this operation; wind insulating tape around the exposed length of tube, and push the tube fully into the slider so that any accidental scratching is confined to the area above the oil seal. A drift or punch can be used, but this does not help the bush enter squarely, and the angle narrows as the bush gets deeper and makes it more difficult to make a good contact with a hammer **(see illustration)**.

24 Remove the washer to check the bush is seated fully and squarely in its recess in the slider, then wipe the recess clean.

25 Smear the lips of the new fork seal with fork oil and slide it over the tube so that its markings face upwards **(see illustrations)**. Press the seal into the slider, then drive it fully into place as

---

TOOL TiP

A clutch holding tool or similar can be placed around the tube and onto the piece of tubing as shown to make it easier to drive in and make sure the bush enters squarely. An axle stand can also be used as shown if it is of the correct dimensions (as this Draper one is), but make sure you deburr or tape up any rough edges first as they will scratch the tube, and apply tape to the fork tube to protect it further.

HAYNES HiNT

Wrap some insulating tape around the retaining ring groove in the top of the fork tube – this will prevent the possibility of damage to the oil seal lips as it is slid down the tube.

6•14 Frame, suspension and final drive

8.25c Press it into the top of the slider with your fingers, then drive it in as described

described in Step 23 until the retaining clip groove is visible above it **(see illustration)**.

> **HAYNES HiNT**: Place the old oil seal on top of the new one to protect it when driving the seal into place.

26 Once the seal is correctly seated, fit the retaining clip, making sure it is correctly located in its groove **(see illustration)**.
27 Lubricate the lips of the new dust seal then slide it down the fork tube and press it into position **(see illustration)**.
28 Refill the fork with oil, check the level and install the spring and top bolt components. On CBR600F-X, F-Y, F-1 to F-4 models (1999 to 2004) and all FS models (2001 and 2002) refer to Section 7 Steps 7 to 10. On CBR600F-5 models (2005-on) refer to Section 7, Steps 17 to 20.
29 If the damper rod bolt requires tightening (see Step 22), clamp the fork slider between the padded jaws of a vice and have an

8.26 Install the retaining clip . . .

assistant compress the tube into the slider so that maximum spring pressure is placed on the damper rod head – tighten the damper rod bolt to the specified torque setting.
30 Remove the insulating tape from around the circlip groove in the fork tube. Fit the fork protector onto the top of the slider **(see illustration 8.2)**.
31 Install the forks (see Section 6).

9 Steering stem – removal and installation

Removal
1 Remove the fuel tank (see Chapter 4) and the fairing (see Chapter 8). This will prevent the possibility of damage should a tool slip. Also remove the front forks (see Section 6).
2 Disconnect the horn wiring connectors, and if required unscrew the mounting bolt and remove the horn **(see illustration)**. Unscrew the bolt securing the front brake hose guide

8.27 . . . followed by the dust seal

bracket to the bottom yoke and displace it. Take care not to strain or knock the brake hoses when removing the steering stem.
3 If the top yoke is being removed from the bike rather than just being displaced, trace the wiring from the ignition switch, and where fitted the HISS receiver, and disconnect it/them at the white connector(s) inside the rubber boot in front of the instrument cluster. Release the wiring from any clips or ties and feed it through to the yoke.
4 Pull the cap out of the steering stem nut, then unscrew the nut **(see illustration)**. Lift the top yoke up off the steering stem and position it clear, using a rag to protect the tank or other components if it is only being displaced **(see illustration)**.
5 Bend down the tabs on the steering stem lockwasher to release it from the locknut, then unscrew and remove the locknut using either your fingers (it shouldn't be tight) or a suitable C-spanner or a drift located in one of the notches **(see illustrations)**. Remove the lockwasher, bending up the remaining tabs to release it from the adjuster nut if necessary **(see illustration)**.

9.2 Horn wiring connectors (A) and mounting bolt (B), brake hose guide bolt (C)

9.4a Unscrew the nut . . .

9.4b . . . and lift off the top yoke

9.5a Bend down the lockwasher tabs . . .

9.5b . . . then unscrew the locknut . . .

9.5c . . . and remove the lockwasher

Frame, suspension and final drive 6•15

9.6a Unscrew and remove the adjuster nut . . .

9.6b . . . and the grease seal

9.7 Draw the bottom yoke/steering stem out of the steering head

Inspect the tabs for cracks or signs of fatigue. If there are any, discard the lockwasher and use a new one; otherwise the old one can be reused.

6 Supporting the bottom yoke, unscrew the adjuster nut using either a C-spanner, a peg-spanner or socket, or a drift located in one of the notches **(see illustration)**. Remove the adjuster nut and the grease seal from the steering stem **(see illustration)**. Check the condition of the grease seal and discard it if it is damaged.

7 Gently lower the bottom yoke and steering stem out of the frame **(see illustration)**.

8 Remove the inner race and bearing from the top of the steering head **(see illustrations 9.10b and a)**. Remove the bearing from the base of the steering stem **(see illustration 8.9)**. Remove all traces of old grease from the bearings and races and check them for wear or damage as described in Section 9. **Note:** *Do not attempt to remove the races from the steering head or the steering stem unless they are to be replaced with new ones.*

Installation

9 Smear a liberal quantity of multi-purpose grease onto the bearing races, and work some grease well into both the upper and lower bearings. Also smear the grease seal lip, using a new seal if necessary. Fit the lower bearing onto the steering stem **(see illustration)**.

10 Carefully lift the steering stem/bottom yoke up through the steering head **(see illustration 9.7)**. Fit the upper bearing and its inner race into the top of the steering head, then install the grease seal **(see illustrations 9.6b)**. Apply some clean engine oil to the adjuster nut and thread the nut on the steering stem **(see illustration 9.6a)**.

11 If the correct tools are available, tighten the adjuster nut to the torque setting specified at the beginning of the Chapter, then turn the steering stem through its full lock at least five times and re-tighten the adjuster nut to the specified setting. Ensure that the steering stem is able to move freely from lock to lock following adjustment – if necessary reset the bearing adjustment as described in Chapter 1.

9.9 Fit the lower bearing onto the steering stem

9.10a Fit the upper bearing . . .

9.10b . . . and its inner race . . .

9.12 Tighten the adjuster nut as described

9.13 Bend the lockwasher tabs up into the notches in the lockwasher

9.14a Fit the steering stem nut . . .

9.14b . . . and tighten it to the specified torque

6•16 Frame, suspension and final drive

10.4a Drive the bearing races out with a brass drift . . .

10.4b . . . locating it as shown

10.6 Drawbolt arrangement for fitting steering stem bearing races

1 Long bolt or threaded bar
2 Thick washer
3 Guide for lower race

10.7 Remove the lower bearing race using a puller if necessary

10.9 Drive the new bearing race on using a suitable bearing driver or a length of pipe that bears only against its top edge and not against its working surface

12 If the correct tools are not available, tighten the nut using a C-spanner or drift so that bearing play is eliminated, but the steering stem is able to move freely from lock to lock – refer to the procedure in Chapter 1 for details, but note that setting the bearings is a lot easier and more accurate after the forks and wheel are installed as their leverage and inertia need to be taken into account **(see illustration)**. To do it that way, make sure the nut is tight enough to hold the steering stem in the head without any play, then install the forks and wheel, then refer to the procedure in Chapter 1.
Caution: Take great care not to apply excessive pressure because this will cause premature failure of the bearings.
13 When the bearings are correctly adjusted, install the lockwasher, using a new one if the tabs are weakened or cracked, onto the adjuster nut and fit the two bent tabs into the slots in the adjuster nut **(see illustration 9.5c)**. Install the locknut and tighten it finger-tight, then tighten it further (to a maximum of 90°) until the remaining tabs on the lockwasher align with the slots in the locknut **(see illustration 9.5b)**. Hold the adjuster nut to prevent it from moving if necessary. Secure the locknut in position by bending up the other lockwasher tabs into its notches **(see illustration)**.
14 Fit the top yoke onto the steering stem **(see illustration 9.4b)**, then install steering stem nut and tighten it finger-tight **(see illustration)**. Temporarily install one of the forks to align the top and bottom yokes, and secure it by tightening the bottom yoke clamp bolt only. Now tighten the steering stem nut to the torque setting specified at the beginning of the Chapter **(see illustration)**. Fit the rubber cap into the nut.
15 Install the remaining components in a reverse of the removal procedure, referring to the relevant Sections or Chapters, and to the torque settings specified at the beginning of the Chapter.
16 Carry out a check of the steering head bearing freeplay as described in Chapter 1, and if necessary re-adjust.

10 Steering head bearings – inspection and replacement

Inspection

1 Remove the steering stem (see Section 9).
2 Remove all traces of old grease from the bearings and races and check them for wear or damage.
3 The outer races should be polished and free from indentations. Inspect the bearing rollers for signs of wear, damage or discoloration, and examine the roller retainer cage for signs of cracks or splits. If there are any signs of wear on any of the above components both upper and lower bearing assemblies must be renewed as a set. Only remove the outer races in the steering head and the lower bearing inner race on the steering stem if they need to be replaced – do not re-use them once they have been removed.

Replacement

4 The outer races are an interference fit in the steering head and can be tapped from position with a suitable drift **(see illustrations)**. Tap firmly and evenly around each race to ensure that it is driven out squarely. It may prove advantageous to curve the end of the drift slightly to improve access.
5 Alternatively, the races can be removed using a slide-hammer type bearing extractor; these can often be hired from tool shops.
6 The new outer races can be pressed into the head using a drawbolt arrangement **(see illustration)**, or by using a large diameter tubular drift. Ensure that the drawbolt washer or drift (as applicable) bears only on the outer edge of the race and does not contact the working surface. Alternatively, have the races installed by a Honda dealer equipped with the bearing race installation tools.

HAYNES HiNT *Installation of new bearing outer races is made much easier if the races are left overnight in the freezer. This causes them to contract slightly making them a looser fit. Alternatively, use a freeze spray.*

7 The lower bearing inner race should only be removed from the steering stem if a new one is being fitted. To remove the race, use two screwdrivers placed on opposite sides to work it free, using blocks of wood to improve leverage and protect the yoke, or tap under it using a cold chisel. If the race is firmly in place it will be necessary to use a puller **(see illustration)**.
8 Remove the dust seal from the bottom of the stem and replace it with a new one. Smear the new one with grease.
9 Fit the new lower race onto the steering stem. A length of tubing with an internal diameter slightly larger than the steering stem will be needed to tap the new race into position **(see illustration)**.
10 Install the steering stem (see Section 9).

Frame, suspension and final drive 6•17

11.3a Slacken the clamp screw (arrowed) . . .

11.3b . . . and draw the reservoir out

11.4 Unscrew the nut and withdraw the lower mounting bolt

11 Rear shock absorber – removal, inspection and installation

Warning: Do not attempt to disassemble this shock absorber. It is nitrogen-charged under high pressure. Improper disassembly could result in serious injury. Instead, take the shock to a dealer service department with the proper equipment to do the job.

Removal

1 Support the motorcycle on its centrestand if fitted, or on an auxiliary stand that does not take the weight through any part of the rear suspension, or by using a hoist. Position a support under the rear wheel or swingarm so that it does not drop when the shock absorber is removed, but also making sure that the weight of the machine is off the rear suspension so that the shock is not compressed.
2 Remove the fuel tank (see Chapter 4).

3 Slacken the reservoir clamp screw and draw the reservoir out of the clamp **(see illustrations)**.
4 Unscrew the nut and withdraw the bolt securing the bottom of the shock absorber to the linkage plates **(see illustration)**.
5 Unscrew the nut on the shock absorber upper mounting bolt **(see illustration)**. Withdraw the bolt and manoeuvre the shock out of the top of the frame **(see illustrations)**.

Inspection

6 Inspect the shock absorber for obvious physical damage and oil leakage, and the coil spring for looseness, cracks or signs of fatigue.
7 Withdraw the spacer from the lower mounting. Inspect the pivot hardware at the top and bottom of the shock for wear or damage.
8 Check the condition of the grease seals in the bottom mount and replace them with new ones if they are damaged, deformed or deteriorated. Lever out the old ones using a flat bladed screwdriver and press the new ones squarely into place.
9 With the dust seals removed, check the condition of the bearing and replace it with a new one if necessary. Refer to *Tools and Workshop Tips* in the Reference Section for more information on bearing checks and replacement methods.
10 With the exception of the bottom pivot hardware, individual components are not available for the shock absorber. If it is worn or damaged, it must be replaced with a new one.

Installation

11 Installation is the reverse of removal. Apply multi-purpose grease to the shock absorber

and linkage plate pivot points. Do not forget to fit the spacer into the bottom mounting. Install the shock absorber with the rebound damping adjuster (on the bottom of the shock) facing the right-hand side. Install the bolts from the right-hand side and do not tighten the nuts until both bolts (or all components if the suspension linkage has been removed as well) are in position, then tighten them to the torque setting specified at the beginning of the Chapter.

12 Rear suspension linkage – removal, inspection and installation

Removal

1 Support the motorcycle on its centrestand if fitted, or on an auxiliary stand that does not take the weight through any part of the rear suspension, or by using a hoist. Position a support under the rear wheel or swingarm so that it does not drop when the shock absorber is detached, but also making sure that the weight of the machine is off the rear suspension so that the shock is not compressed.
2 For best access to the suspension linkage arm lower bolt and to avoid the possibility of damage, remove the fairing side panels (see Chapter 8).
3 Unscrew the nut and withdraw the bolt securing the linkage plates to the shock absorber **(see illustration 11.4)**. Unscrew the nut and withdraw the bolt securing the linkage plates to the linkage arm **(see illustration)**.

11.5a Unscrew the nut (arrowed) . . .

11.5b . . . then withdraw the upper mounting bolt . . .

11.5c . . . and remove the shock absorber from the top

12.3 Unscrew the nut and withdraw the linkage plates-to-arm bolt

6•18 Frame, suspension and final drive

12.4 Unscrew the nut and withdraw the bolt securing the plates to the swingarm and remove the plates

12.5a Unscrew the linkage arm-to-bracket nut (A) . . .

12.5b . . . and withdraw the bolt. If the arm is tight in the brackets, slacken the bracket nuts (B on 12.5a)

12.6a Withdraw the spacers . . .

12.6b . . . and lever out the grease seals

12.8 Check the needle bearings for wear and damage

4 Unscrew the nut and withdraw the bolt securing the linkage plates to the swingarm and remove the plates, noting which way round they fit **(see illustration)**.
5 Unscrew the nut and withdraw bolt securing the linkage arm to the sidestand/centrestand/suspension brackets on the engine and remove the arm, noting which way round it fits **(see illustrations)**. If the arm is tight in the brackets, slacken the nuts on the bracket bolts to give some clearance, but before doing so, if you are using either the centrestand if fitted or the sidestand to take any of the weight, make sure you transfer the weight to an auxiliary stand as the installed stands are mounted through these brackets.

Inspection

6 Withdraw the spacers from the linkage arm and swingarm, noting any difference in sizes, then lever out the grease seals **(see illustrations)**. Thoroughly clean all components, removing all traces of dirt, corrosion and grease.
7 Inspect all components closely, looking for obvious signs of wear such as heavy scoring, or for damage such as cracks or distortion. Slip each spacer back into its bearing and check that there is not an excessive amount of freeplay between the two components. Renew any components as required.
8 Check the condition of the needle roller bearings **(see illustration)**. Refer to *Tools and Workshop Tips* (Section 5) in the Reference section for more information on bearings. If the linkage plate bearings in the swingarm need to be renewed, remove the swingarm (see Section 14).
9 Worn bearings can be drifted out of their bores, but note that removal will destroy them; new bearings should be obtained before work commences. The new bearings should be pressed or drawn into their bores rather than driven into position. In the absence of a press, a suitable drawbolt tool can be made up as described in *Tools and Workshop Tips* in the Reference section. Set the bearings centrally in their bores.
10 Check the condition of the grease seals and renew them if they are damaged, deformed or deteriorated. Lubricate the needle bearings, spacers and seals with multi-purpose grease **(see illustration)**.
11 Press the seals squarely into place **(see illustration)**. Install the spacers **(see illustration 12.6a)**.

Installation

12 Installation is the reverse of removal. Apply multi-purpose grease to the pivot points. Install the linkage plates with the arrow before the FR mark pointing to the front **(see illustration 12.3)**. Insert the linkage plate bolts from the right-hand side, and the linkage arm lower bolt from the left-hand side. Install the bolts and nuts finger-tight only until all components are in position, then tighten the nuts to the torque settings specified at the beginning of the Chapter. Do not forget to tighten the sidestand/centrestand/suspension bracket nuts, also to the specified torque, if they were loosened.

13 Suspension – adjustments

Front forks
F-X and F-Y (1999 and 2000) models

1 The front forks are adjustable for spring pre-load and both rebound and compression damping.

12.10 Smear the bearings with grease . . .

12.11 . . . and press the grease seals in

Frame, suspension and final drive 6•19

13.2 Spring pre-load adjuster (arrowed)

13.3 Rebound damping adjuster (arrowed)

13.4 Compression damping adjuster (arrowed)

2 Spring pre-load is adjusted using a suitable spanner on the adjuster flats **(see illustration)**. Turn it clockwise to increase pre-load and anti-clockwise to decrease it. The amount of pre-load is indicated by grooves on the adjuster. The standard position is with the 3rd groove aligned with the top of the hex on the fork bolt. Always make sure both adjusters are set equally.

3 Rebound damping is adjusted using a screwdriver in the slot in the top of the damper rod protruding from the pre-load adjuster **(see illustration)**. Turn it clockwise to increase damping and anti-clockwise to decrease it. To set the standard position, turn the adjuster fully clockwise until it stops, then turn it anti-clockwise approximately 1 full turn until the punch mark on the adjuster aligns with the reference mark on the directional arrow.

4 Compression damping is adjusted using a screwdriver in the slot in the adjuster which is on the bottom of the fork **(see illustration)**. Turn it clockwise to increase damping and anti-clockwise to decrease it. To set the standard position, turn the adjuster fully clockwise until it stops, then turn it anti-clockwise approximately 1½ turns until the punch mark on the adjuster aligns with the reference mark on the directional arrow.

F-1 to F-4 (2001 to 2004) models, all FS models

5 The front forks are adjustable for spring pre-load and both rebound and compression damping.

6 Spring pre-load is adjusted using a suitable spanner on the adjuster flats **(see illustration 13.2)**. Turn it clockwise to increase pre-load and anti-clockwise to decrease it. The amount of pre-load is indicated by grooves on the adjuster. The standard position is with the 4th groove aligned with the top of the hex on the fork bolt. Always make sure both adjusters are set equally.

7 Rebound damping is adjusted using a screwdriver in the slot in the top of the damper rod protruding from the pre-load adjuster **(see illustration 13.3)**. Turn it clockwise to increase damping and anti-clockwise to decrease it. To set the standard position, turn the adjuster fully clockwise until it stops, then turn it anti-clockwise approximately 1¾ turns until the punch mark on the adjuster aligns with the reference mark on the directional arrow.

8 Compression damping is adjusted using a screwdriver in the slot in the adjuster which is on the bottom of the fork **(see illustration 13.4)**. Turn it clockwise to increase damping and anti-clockwise to decrease it. To set the standard position, turn the adjuster fully clockwise until it stops, then turn it anti-clockwise approximately 1¼ turns until the punch mark on the adjuster aligns with the reference mark on the directional arrow.

F-5 models onward (2005-on)

9 The forks are not adjustable.

Rear shock absorber

F-X and F-Y (1999 and 2000) models

10 The shock absorber is adjustable for spring pre-load and both rebound and compression damping.

11 Spring pre-load is adjusted using a suitable C-spanner (one is provided in the toolkit) to turn the spring seat on the bottom of the shock absorber **(see illustration)**. There are seven positions. Position 1 is the softest setting, position 2 the standard, and position 7 the hardest. Align the setting required with the adjustment stopper.

12 Rebound damping adjustment is made by turning the adjuster on the bottom of the shock absorber on the right-hand side using a flat-bladed screwdriver **(see illustration)**. To increase the damping, turn the adjuster clockwise. To decrease the damping, turn the adjuster anti-clockwise. To set the standard position, turn the adjuster clockwise until it stops, then turn it anti clockwise 1 turn until the punch mark on the adjuster aligns with the index mark on the shock absorber.

13 Compression damping adjustment is made by turning the adjuster on the shock absorber reservoir mounted on the left-hand side of the rear sub-frame using a flat-bladed screwdriver **(see illustration)**. To increase the damping, turn the adjuster clockwise. To decrease the damping, turn the adjuster anti-clockwise. To set the standard position, turn the adjuster clockwise until it stops, then turn it anti clockwise 1 turn until the punch mark on the adjuster aligns with the index mark on the shock absorber.

F-1/FS-1 models onward (2001-on)

14 The shock absorber is adjustable for spring pre-load on all models. Rebound and compression damping are adjustable on F-1 to F-4 models (2001 to 2004) and all FS models.

13.10 Spring pre-load adjuster (arrowed)

13.11 Rebound damping adjuster (arrowed)

13.12 Compression damping adjuster (arrowed)

6•20 Frame, suspension and final drive

14.2a Unscrew the brake hose guide bolts (arrowed)

14.2b Detach the caliper assembly from the swingarm and tie it to the frame, noting how the slot in the bracket locates onto the lug on the swingarm (arrow)

14.3 Unscrew the bolts (arrowed) and remove the chain guard

14.4 Unscrew the nut (arrowed) and withdraw the linkage plate-to-swingarm bolt

14.5a Unscrew the nut and remove the washer

14.5b Withdraw the pivot bolt from the right-hand side

14.6a Slacken the locknut (and remove it if required) . . .

14.6b . . . using the special tool if available

15 Spring pre-load is adjusted using a suitable C-spanner (one is provided in the toolkit) to turn the spring seat on the bottom of the shock absorber **(see illustration 13.10)**. There are seven positions. Position 1 is the softest setting and position 7 the hardest – the standard setting is 3 on F-5 models onward (2005-on) and 2 on all earlier models. Align the setting required with the adjustment stopper.

16 Rebound damping adjustment is made by turning the adjuster on the bottom of the shock absorber on the right-hand side using a flat-bladed screwdriver **(see illustration 13.11)**. To increase the damping, turn the adjuster clockwise. To decrease the damping, turn the adjuster anti-clockwise. To set the standard position, turn the adjuster clockwise until it stops, then turn it anti clockwise 1½ turns until the punch mark on the adjuster aligns with the index mark on the shock absorber.

17 Compression damping adjustment is made by turning the adjuster on the shock absorber reservoir mounted on the left-hand side of the rear sub-frame using a flat-bladed screwdriver **(see illustration 13.12)**. To increase the damping, turn the adjuster clockwise. To decrease the damping, turn the adjuster anti-clockwise. To set the standard position, turn the adjuster clockwise until it stops, then turn it anti clockwise 1½ turns until the punch mark on the adjuster aligns with the index mark on the shock absorber.

14 Swingarm – removal and installation

Removal

1 For best access, remove the silencer (see Chapter 4). Remove the rear wheel (see Chapter 7).

2 Unscrew the bolt securing each rear brake hose guide to the swingarm **(see illustration)**. Displace the rear brake caliper and bracket assembly from the swingarm (there is no need to disconnect the brake hose), noting how it locates, and tie it to the frame, making sure no strain is placed on the hose **(see illustration)**.

3 Unscrew the bolts securing the chain guard to the swingarm and remove the guard, noting how it locates **(see illustration)**.

4 Support the swingarm, then unscrew the nut and withdraw the bolt securing the suspension linkage plates to the swingarm **(see illustration)**.

5 Unscrew the nut on the left-hand end of the swingarm pivot bolt and remove the washer **(see illustration)**. Withdraw the pivot bolt from the right-hand side **(see illustration)**.

6 Slacken the locknut on each adjuster bolt – you do not have to thread it fully off the adjuster unless you want to **(see illustration)**. The locknut requires a Honda service tool, Pt. No. 07908-4690003, which is a special wrench **(see illustration)**. Alternatively the locknut can be unscrewed using a suitable peg spanner, which can be fabricated by cutting castellations into an old socket.

7 Support the swingarm then slacken and partially unscrew each adjuster bolt so that its

Frame, suspension and final drive 6•21

14.7 Unscrew the adjuster bolts and remove the swingarm

14.8a Remove the right-hand adjuster bolt . . .

14.8b . . . and the left-hand adjuster bolt, noting which fits where

inner end is clear of the swingarm, i.e. flush with or just inset from the inside of the frame **(see illustration 14.13b)**. Manoeuvre the swingarm clear of the shock absorber and out of the frame **(see illustration)**.

8 Remove the adjuster bolts (with the locknuts if not already removed) if required, noting which fits where **(see illustrations)**.

9 Remove the chain slider from the swingarm if necessary, noting the collars that fit with the bolts **(see illustration)**. If it is badly worn or damaged, it should be replaced with a new one – there are some wear limit arrows on the front **(see illustration)**. Inspect all pivot components for wear or damage as described in Section 15.

Installation

10 Remove the collar from each swingarm pivot, noting which fits where **(see illustrations)**. Also withdraw the spacer from the suspension linkage plate pivot **(see illustration 12.6a)**. Clean off all old grease, then lubricate the grease seals, bearings, collars, spacer and the pivot bolt with multi-purpose grease. Insert the collars and spacer. Similarly clean and lubricate the suspension linkage plate to swingarm pivot components.

11 If removed, install the chain slider, making sure it locates correctly at the front **(see illustration 14.9a)**. Apply a suitable non-permanent thread locking compound to the slider mounting bolts, then fit them with their collars and tighten them to the torque setting specified at the beginning of the Chapter.

12 If removed, thread each adjuster bolt a little way into the frame, making sure it does not protrude from the inside **(see illustrations 14.8a and b)**.

13 Offer up the swingarm and have an assistant hold it in place **(see illustration 14.7)**. Make sure the drive chain is looped over the front of the swingarm. Slide the pivot bolt through the left-hand adjuster bolt and swingarm and into the inner end of the right-hand adjuster so that it supports the swingarm, but leave it clear of the hex in the right-hand adjuster so that it can be tightened **(see illustration)**. Tighten the right-hand adjuster bolt to the initial torque setting specified at the beginning of the Chapter, then back it off and tighten it to the final torque setting specified **(see illustration)**.

14 Install the right-hand adjuster bolt locknut (if removed) and tighten it as much as

14.9a The chain slider is secured by two bolts, one on the top and one underneath

14.9b Renew the chain slider if it has worn to the tips of the arrows

14.10a Remove the collars . . .

14.10b . . . noting which fits where

14.13a Temporarily fit the pivot in from the left-hand side as described . . .

14.13b . . . then tighten the right-hand adjuster bolt as described

6•22 Frame, suspension and final drive

14.14a Fit the locknut . . .

14.14b . . . and tighten it to the specified torque as described

14.15a Tighten the adjuster bolt . . .

14.15b . . . and the locknut as described

14.16 Tighten the pivot bolt nut to the specified torque

possible by hand **(see illustration)**. Tighten the locknut further using the service tool as described in Step 6 or a suitable alternative **(see illustration)**. If you have the service tool, counter-hold the adjuster bolt using an Allen key applied through the middle of the tool to prevent it from turning, and tighten it to the indicated torque setting specified at the beginning of the Chapter (which takes into account the extra leverage provided by the offset in the tool for the torque wrench). Otherwise make a reference mark between the bolt and the frame so you can check that the adjuster hasn't moved while tightening the locknut, and tighten it to the actual torque setting specified using a peg spanner.

15 Support the swingarm on the left-hand side and withdraw the pivot bolt **(see illustration 14.13a)**, then re-insert it from the right-hand side, leaving the hex in the left-hand adjuster bolt clear **(see illustration 14.5b)**. Tighten the left-hand adjuster bolt to the specified torque setting **(see illustration)**, then fit the locknut if removed **(see illustration 14.6a)** and tighten to the specified torque setting **(see illustration)**.

16 Push the pivot bolt all the way through, then fit the washer and nut **(see illustration 14.5a)**. Counter-hold the head of the pivot bolt and tighten the nut to the specified torque setting **(see illustration)**.

17 Align the rear suspension linkage plates with the swingarm, then install the bolt and tighten the nut to the specified torque setting **(see illustration 14.4)**.

18 Install the chain guard, making sure it locates correctly, and tighten the bolts securely **(see illustration 14.3)**.

19 Fit the rear brake caliper and bracket assembly onto the swingarm, locating the slot in the bracket onto the lug on the swingarm **(see illustration 14.2b)**. Fit the brake hose guides and tighten their bolts securely **(see illustration 14.2a)**.

20 Install the rear wheel (see Chapter 7). If removed, install the silencer (see Chapter 4).

21 Check and adjust the drive chain slack (see Chapter 1). Check the operation of the rear suspension and brake before taking the machine on the road.

15 Swingarm – inspection, bearing check and replacement

Inspection

1 Remove the swingarm (see Section 14).
2 Thoroughly clean the swingarm, removing all traces of dirt, corrosion and grease.
3 Inspect the swingarm closely, looking for obvious signs of wear such as heavy scoring, and cracks or distortion due to accident damage. Any damaged or worn component must be replaced.
4 Check the swingarm pivot bolt for straightness by rolling it on a flat surface such as a piece of plate glass (first wipe off all old grease and remove any corrosion using fine emery cloth). Renew the pivot bolt if it is bent.

Bearing check and replacement

5 Remove the collar from each swingarm pivot, noting which fits where **(see illustrations 14.10a and b)**. Lever out the grease seal from each side of the pivot **(see illustrations)**.
6 Refer to *Tools and Workshop Tips* (Section 5) in the Reference section and check the bearings – on F-X and F-Y (1999 and 2000) models there are two caged ball bearings separated by a spacer in the right-hand pivot, and a needle bearing in the left-hand pivot. On F-1/FS-1 models onward (2001-on), there is a caged ball bearing and a needle bearing in the right-hand pivot, and a needle bearing in the left-hand pivot. Clean them and inspect them for wear or damage. If the bearings do not run smoothly and freely or if there is excessive freeplay, they must be replaced with new ones – refer to the Reference Section for removal and installation methods. The caged ball bearing(s) in the right-hand pivot are held

15.5a Lever out the grease seals (arrow) . . .

15.5b . . . and check the bearings as described

Frame, suspension and final drive 6•23

by a circlip. The needle bearing(s) must be renewed if removed – they cannot be reused **(see illustration 15.5b)**.
7 Check the condition of the grease seals and replace them if they are damaged, deformed or deteriorated.
8 Lubricate the bearings and grease seal lips with multi-purpose grease.

16 Drive chain – removal, cleaning and installation

Removal

Note: *The original equipment drive chain fitted to these models has a staked-type master (joining) link which can be disassembled using either Honda service tool, Pt. No. 07HMH-MR10103 for UK models, or 07HMH-MR1010B for US models, or one of several commercially-available drive chain cutting/staking tools. Such chains can be recognised by the master link side plate's identification marks (and usually its different colour), as well as by the staked ends of the link's two pins which look as if they have been deeply centre-punched, instead of peened over as with all the other pins.*

⚠ **Warning: NEVER install a drive chain which uses a clip-type master (split) link. Use ONLY the correct service tools to secure the staked-type of master link – if you do not have access to such tools, have the chain replaced by a dealer service department or bike repair shop to be sure of having it securely installed.**

1 Support the motorcycle on its centrestand (where fitted) or an auxiliary stand so that the rear wheel is off the ground. Locate the joining link in a suitable position to work on by rotating the back wheel. Slacken the drive chain as described in Chapter 1.
2 Unscrew the bolts securing the chainguard to the swingarm and remove the guard, noting how it locates **(see illustration 14.3)**.
3 Remove the front sprocket cover (see Section 17).
4 Split the chain at the joining link using the chain cutter, following carefully the manufacturer's operating instructions (see also Section 8 in *Tools and Workshop Tips* in the Reference Section). Remove the chain from the bike, noting its routing around the swingarm.

Cleaning

5 Refer to Chapter 1, Section 1 for details of routine cleaning with the chain installed on the sprockets.
6 If the chain is extremely dirty remove it from the motorcycle and soak it in paraffin (kerosene) for approximately five or six minutes, then clean it using a soft brush. **Caution: Don't use gasoline (petrol), solvent or other cleaning fluids which might damage its internal sealing properties. Don't use high-pressure water. Remove the chain, wipe it off, then blow dry it with compressed air immediately. The entire process shouldn't take longer than ten minutes – if it does, the O-rings in the chain rollers could be damaged.**

Installation

⚠ **Warning: NEVER install a drive chain which uses a clip-type master (split) link. If you do not have access to a chain riveting tool, have the chain fitted by a dealer service department.**

7 Fit the drive chain around the swingarm and sprockets, leaving the two ends in a convenient position to work on.
8 Refer to Section 8 in *Tools and Workshop Tips* in the Reference Section. Install the new joining link from the inside with the four O-rings correctly located between the link plate and side plate. Install the new side plate with its identification marks facing out. Measure the amount that the joining link pins project from the side plate and check they are within the measurements specified at the beginning of the Chapter. Stake the new link using the drive chain cutting/staking tool, following carefully the instructions of both the chain manufacturer and the tool manufacturer. DO NOT re-use old joining link components.
9 After staking, check the joining link and staking for any signs of cracking. If there is any evidence of cracking, the joining link, O-rings and side plate must be replaced. Measure the diameter of the staked ends in two directions and check that it is evenly staked and within the measurements specified at the beginning of the Chapter. Check that the link pivots freely.
10 Install the sprocket cover (see Section 17).
11 Install the chainguard, making sure it locates correctly, and tighten the bolts securely **(see illustration 14.3)**.
12 On completion, adjust and lubricate the chain following the procedures described in Chapter 1.

17 Sprockets – check and replacement

Check

1 Unscrew the bolts securing the front sprocket cover and remove the cover and the guide plate **(see illustration)**.
2 Check the wear pattern on both sprockets (see Chapter 1, Section 1). If the sprocket teeth are worn excessively, replace the chain and both sprockets as a set. Whenever the sprockets are inspected, the drive chain should be inspected also (see Chapter 1). Always renew the chain and sprockets as a set – worn sprockets can ruin a new drive chain and vice versa.
3 Adjust and lubricate the chain following the procedures described in Chapter 1.

Replacement

Front sprocket

4 Unscrew the bolts securing the front sprocket cover and remove the cover and the guide plate **(see illustration 17.1)**.
5 Have an assistant apply the rear brake, then unscrew the sprocket bolt and remove the washer **(see illustration)**.
6 Slacken the drive chain as described in Chapter 1.
7 Slide the sprocket and chain off the shaft and slip the sprocket out of the chain **(see illustration)**.
8 Engage the new sprocket with the chain, making sure the marked side is facing out,

17.1 Unscrew the bolts (arrowed) and remove the cover

17.5 Unscrew the bolt (arrowed) and remove the washer

17.7 Draw the sprocket off the shaft and disengage the chain

6•24 Frame, suspension and final drive

17.9 Install the bolt with its washer and tighten it to the specified torque

17.10 Fit the guide plate and cover

17.12 Rear sprocket nuts (arrowed)

and slide it on the shaft **(see illustration 17.7)**. Take up the slack in the chain.

9 Install the sprocket bolt with its washer and tighten it to the torque setting specified at the beginning of the Chapter, using the rear brake to prevent the sprocket turning **(see illustration)**.

10 Fit the guide plate and sprocket cover and tighten its bolts **(see illustration)**. Adjust and lubricate the chain following the procedures described in Chapter 1.

Rear sprocket

11 Remove the rear wheel (see Chapter 7).
12 Unscrew the nuts securing the sprocket to the hub assembly, and if fitted remove the washers **(see illustration)**. Remove the sprocket, noting which way round it fits.
13 Install the sprocket onto the hub with the stamped mark facing out. Install the nuts, with their washers if fitted, and tighten them evenly and in a criss-cross sequence to the torque setting specified at the beginning of the Chapter.
14 Install the rear wheel (see Chapter 7).

18 Rear sprocket coupling/rubber dampers – check and replacement

1 Remove the rear wheel (see Chapter 7). *Caution: Do not lay the wheel down on the disc as it could become warped. Lay the wheel on wooden blocks so that the disc is off the ground.*
2 Lift the sprocket coupling away from the wheel leaving the rubber dampers in position **(see illustration)**. Note the spacer inside the coupling – it should be a tight fit but remove it if it is likely to drop out. Check the coupling for cracks or any obvious signs of damage. Also check the sprocket studs for wear or damage.
3 Lift the rubber damper segments from the wheel and check them for cracks, hardening and general deterioration **(see illustration)**. Renew them as a set if necessary.
4 Check the condition of the hub O-ring and replace it with a new one if it is damaged, deformed or deteriorated **(see illustration)**.
5 Checking and replacement procedures for the sprocket coupling bearing are described in Chapter 7.
6 Installation is the reverse of removal. Make sure the spacer is still correctly installed in the coupling, or install it if it was removed.
7 Install the rear wheel (see Chapter 7).

18.2 Lift the sprocket coupling out of the wheel

18.3 Check the rubber dampers . . .

18.4 . . . and the O-ring

Chapter 7
Brakes, wheels and tyres

Contents

Brake discs – inspection, removal and installation	3
Brake fluid level check	see Daily (pre-ride) checks
Brake light switches – check and replacement	see Chapter 9
Brake pads – renewal	2
Brake pad wear check	see Chapter 1
Brake hoses – inspection and replacement	8
Brake system – bleeding and fluid renewal	9
Brake system check	see Chapter 1
Front brake calipers – removal, overhaul and installation	4
Front brake master cylinder – removal, overhaul and installation	6
Front wheel – removal and installation	12
General information	1
Rear brake caliper – removal, overhaul and installation	5
Rear brake master cylinder – removal, overhaul and installation	7
Rear wheel – removal and installation	13
Tyres – general information and fitting	15
Tyres – pressure, tread depth and condition	see Daily (pre-ride) checks
Wheels – general check	see Chapter 1
Wheel bearings – check	see Chapter 1
Wheel bearings – renewal	14
Wheels – alignment check	11
Wheels – inspection and repair	10

Degrees of difficulty

Easy, suitable for novice with little experience	**Fairly easy,** suitable for beginner with some experience	**Fairly difficult,** suitable for competent DIY mechanic	**Difficult,** suitable for experienced DIY mechanic	**Very difficult,** suitable for expert DIY or professional

Specifications

Front brakes

Brake fluid type	DOT 4
Caliper bore ID	
Upper bore	
Standard	33.96 to 34.01 mm
Service limit	34.02 mm
Lower bore	
Standard	32.030 to 32.080 mm
Service limit	32.09 mm
Caliper piston OD	
F-X and F-Y (1999 and 2000) models	
Upper bore	
Standard	33.895 to 33.928 mm
Service limit	33.87 mm
Lower bore	
Standard	31.965 to 31.998 mm
Service limit	31.94 mm
F-1/FS-1 models onward (2001-on)	
Upper bore	
Standard	33.802 to 33.835 mm
Service limit	33.794 mm
Lower bore	
Standard	31.877 to 31.910 mm
Service limit	31.869 mm
Master cylinder bore ID	
Standard	15.870 to 15.913 mm
Service limit	15.925 mm
Master cylinder piston OD	
Standard	15.827 to 15.854 mm
Service limit	15.815 mm
Disc thickness	
Standard	4.4 to 4.6 mm
Service limit	3.5 mm
Disc maximum runout	
F-X and F-Y (1999 and 2000) models	0.3 mm
F-1/FS-1 models onward (2001-on)	0.2 mm

7•2 Brakes, wheels and tyres

Rear brake

Brake fluid type	DOT 4
Caliper bore ID	
Standard	38.180 to 38.230 mm
Service limit	38.240 mm
Caliper piston OD	
Standard	38.098 to 38.148 mm
Service limit	38.09 mm
Master cylinder bore ID	
Standard	14.000 to 14.043 mm
Service limit	14.055 mm
Master cylinder piston OD	
Standard	13.957 to 13.984 mm
Service limit	13.945 mm
Disc thickness	
Standard	4.8 to 5.2 mm
Service limit	4.0 mm
Disc maximum runout	0.3 mm

Wheels

Maximum wheel runout (front and rear)	
Axial (side-to-side)	2.0 mm
Radial (out-of-round)	2.0 mm
Maximum axle runout (front and rear)	0.20 mm

Tyres

Tyre pressures	see *Daily (pre-ride)* checks
Tyre sizes*	
Front	120/70-ZR17 58W
Rear	180/55-ZR17 73W

Refer to the owners handbook or the tyre information label on the swingarm for approved tyre brands.

Torque settings

Front brake caliper mounting bolts	30 Nm
Brake caliper bleed valves	6 Nm
Brake caliper body joining bolts (front calipers)	23 Nm
Brake caliper rear mounting bolt/slider pin (rear caliper)	23 Nm
Brake caliper front slider pin (rear caliper)	27 Nm
Brake disc bolts	
Front	20 Nm
Rear	42 Nm
Brake hose banjo bolts	34 Nm
Brake master cylinder	
Clamp bolts (front brake)	12 Nm
Mounting bolts (rear brake)	9 Nm
Brake pad retaining pins	18 Nm
Footrest bracket mounting bolts	26 Nm
Front axle bolt	59 Nm
Front axle clamp bolts	22 Nm
Rear axle nut	93 Nm

1 General information

All models covered in this manual are fitted with cast alloy wheels designed for tubeless tyres only. Both front and rear brakes are hydraulically operated disc brakes.

On all models the front brakes have twin opposed piston calipers and the rear brake has a single piston sliding caliper.

Caution: *If an hydraulic brake line is loosened, the entire system must be disassembled, drained, cleaned and then properly filled and bled upon reassembly.*

Do not use solvents on internal brake components. Solvents will cause the seals to swell and distort. Use only clean brake fluid or denatured alcohol for cleaning. Use care when working with brake fluid as it can injure your eyes and it will damage painted surfaces and plastic parts.

2 Brake pads – renewal

Warning: *The dust created by the brake system may contain asbestos, which is harmful to your health. Never blow it out with compressed air and don't inhale any of it. An approved filtering mask should be worn when working on the brakes.*

Front brake pads

Note 1: *Honda recommend using new caliper bolts when the old ones are removed. This is because the bolts are pre-treated with a locking compound. It is possible, however, to clean up the old bolts and reinstall them using a suitable non-permanent thread locking compound that is commercially available.*

Note 2: *If the pads are being removed for cleaning and inspection purposes only and are not going to renewed, the calipers do not*

Brakes, wheels and tyres 7•3

2.1a Slacken the brake pad retaining pins (arrowed) . . .

2.1b . . . then unscrew the mounting bolts (arrowed) . . .

2.1c . . . and slide the caliper off the disc

2.2 Press the pistons in as described to make clearance for new pads

2.3a Unscrew the pins and remove the spring . . .

2.3b . . . and the pads

need to be displaced – ignore Steps 1 and 2 and start at Step 3 and remove the pads with the calipers in situ. The calipers only need to be displaced for the purpose of pushing the pistons back in to create the clearance for new pads to be installed (which are obviously that much thicker than worn ones).

1 Slacken the pad retaining pins **(see illustration)**. Unscrew the caliper mounting bolts and slide the caliper off the disc **(see illustrations)**.

2 To allow for the increased friction material thickness of new pads, push the pistons as far back into the caliper as possible using a piece of wood, a metal bar or a screwdriver inserted between the old pads, using a rag to protect the caliper body (if there is not enough room you can do this after the pads have been removed, but then should only use wood or you fingers) **(see illustration)**. It may be necessary to remove the master cylinder reservoir cover and diaphragm and siphon out some fluid (see *Daily (pre-ride) checks*). If the pistons are difficult to push back, attach a length of clear hose to the bleed valve and place the open end in a suitable container, then open the valve and try again. Take great care not to draw any air into the system. If in doubt, bleed the brakes afterwards (see Section 9).

3 Unscrew and remove the pad retaining pins (pressing down on the pad spring makes the pins easier to withdraw), then lift off the pad spring, noting how it fits, and remove the pads **(see illustrations)**.

4 Inspect the surface of each pad for contamination and check whether the friction material has worn beyond its service limit (see Chapter 1, Section 3). If either pad is worn to or beyond the service limit, is fouled with oil or grease, or is heavily scored or damaged by dirt and debris, both sets of pads must be renewed as a set.

5 If the pads are in good condition clean them carefully, using a fine wire brush which is completely free of oil and grease to remove all traces of road dirt and corrosion. Using a pointed instrument, clean out the grooves in the friction material and dig out any embedded particles of foreign matter. Any areas of glazing may be removed using emery cloth. Spray with a dedicated brake cleaner to remove any dust. It is also worth spraying the inside of the caliper to remove any dust there, and also to spray the discs.

6 Check the condition of the brake disc (see Section 3).

7 Remove all traces of corrosion from the pad pin and check that it is not bent or damaged. Smear the pin, the back of the pads and the leading and trailing edges of the backing material with copper-based grease, making sure that none gets on the friction material.

8 Insert the pads into the caliper so that the friction material of each pad faces the disc **(see illustration 2.3b)**. Fit the pad spring onto the pads, making sure the arrow points to the top of the caliper **(see illustration)**. Insert one pad retaining pin through the hole in the outer pad, then press down on the pad spring and push the pin through the spring and the hole in the inner pad **(see illustration)**. Tighten the pin finger-tight. Install the second pin in the same way **(see illustration 2.3a)**.

9 Slide the caliper onto the disc, making sure

2.8a Locate the pad spring onto the caliper with the arrow pointing up . . .

2.8b . . . then install the pin

7•4 Brakes, wheels and tyres

2.9 Apply a thread-locking compound if using the old bolts

2.12 Push the caliper against the disc to force the piston in

2.13a Unscrew the pin plug . . .

2.13b . . . then slacken the pin and unscrew the rear bolt/slider pin (arrowed)

2.14 Pivot the caliper up then remove the pin and the pads

2.16a Install the pads . . .

the pads sit squarely on either side **(see illustration 2.1c)**. Install the caliper mounting bolts, either using new ones or cleaning and applying a suitable non-permanent thread locking compound to the threads of the old ones (see **Note** above), and tighten them to the torque setting specified at the beginning of the Chapter **(see illustration)**. Now tighten the pad retaining pins to the specified torque **(see illustration 2.1a)**.

10 Top up the master cylinder reservoir if necessary (see *Daily (pre-ride) checks*).

11 Operate the brake lever several times to bring the pads into contact with the disc. Repeat the procedure on the other front brake caliper. Check the operation of the brake before riding the motorcycle.

Rear brake pads

12 To allow for the increased friction material thickness of new pads, push the brake caliper against the disc so that the piston is forced back into the caliper **(see illustration)**. It may be necessary to remove the master cylinder reservoir cover and diaphragm and siphon out some fluid. If the pistons are difficult to push back, attach a length of clear hose to the bleed valve and place the open end in a suitable container, then open the valve and try again. Take great care not to draw any air into the system. If in doubt, bleed the brake afterwards (see Section 9).

13 Unscrew the pad retaining pin plug, then slacken the pad retaining pin and unscrew the caliper rear mounting bolt/slider pin **(see illustrations)**.

14 Pivot the back of the caliper up off the disc then unscrew the pad retaining pin and remove the pads, noting how they fit **(see illustration)**. Note the pad spring in the top of caliper and the pad guide on the caliper bracket and remove them if required for cleaning or replacement, noting how they fit.

15 Inspect the pads as described in Steps 4 to 7 above.

16 Fit the pads into the caliper so that the friction material of each pad faces the disc, making sure the leading edges locate correctly against the guide **(see illustrations)**. Pivot the caliper down onto the disc while keeping the pads held in position. Apply a suitable non-permanent thread locking compound to the rear mounting bolt/slider pin and tighten it to the torque setting specified at the beginning of the Chapter **(see illustrations)**. Press the pads up against the pad spring to align the holes and insert the pad pin, then tighten it to the specified torque

2.16b . . . making sure they locate correctly

2.16c Apply a thread-locking compound to the bolt . . .

2.16d . . . and tighten it to the specified torque

Brakes, wheels and tyres 7•5

2.16e Press the pads up against the spring and install the pin

3.2a Checking front disc runout

3.2b Checking rear disc runout

setting (see illustration). Install the pad pin plug (see illustration 2.13a).
17 Top up the master cylinder reservoir if necessary (see *Daily (pre-ride) checks*).
18 Operate the brake lever several times to bring the pads into contact with the disc. Check the operation of the brake before riding the motorcycle.

3 Brake discs – inspection, removal and installation

Note: *Honda recommend using new disc mounting bolts when the old ones are removed. This is because the bolts are pre-treated with a locking compound. It is possible, however, to clean up the old bolts and reinstall them using a suitable non-permanent thread locking compound that is commercially available.*

Inspection

1 Visually inspect the surface of the disc for score marks and other damage. Light scratches are normal after use and won't affect brake operation, but deep grooves and heavy score marks will reduce braking efficiency and accelerate pad wear. If a disc is badly grooved it must be machined or replaced with a new one.
2 To check disc runout, position the bike on its centrestand if fitted or on an auxiliary stand so that the wheel being checked is off the ground. Mount a dial gauge to a fork leg or on the swingarm, according to wheel, with the plunger on the gauge touching the surface of the disc about 10 mm (1/2 in) from the outer edge (see illustrations). Rotate the wheel and watch the indicator needle, comparing the reading with the limit listed in the Specifications at the beginning of the Chapter. If the runout is greater than the service limit, check the wheel bearings for play (see Chapter 1). If the bearings are worn, replace them with new ones (see Section 14) and repeat this check. It is also worth removing the disc (see below) and checking for built-up corrosion (see Step 6) as this will cause runout. If the runout is still excessive, it will have to be replaced with a new one, although machining by an engineer may be possible.
3 The disc must not be machined or allowed to wear down to a thickness less than the service limit as listed in this Chapter's Specifications and as marked on the disc itself (see illustration). Check the thickness of the disc using a micrometer (see illustration). If the thickness of the disc is less than the service limit, it must be replaced with a new one.

Removal

4 Remove the wheel (see Section 12 or 13). **Caution:** *Do not lay the wheel down and allow it to rest on the disc – the disc could become warped. Set the wheel on wood blocks so the disc doesn't support the weight of the wheel.*
5 Mark the relationship of the disc to the wheel, so it can be installed in the same position. Unscrew the disc retaining bolts, loosening them a little at a time in a criss-cross pattern to avoid distorting the disc, then remove the disc from the wheel (see illustrations).

3.3a The minimum thickness is marked on each disc

3.3b Checking front disc thickness

3.3c Checking rear disc thickness

3.5a Front disc mounting bolts (arrowed)

3.5b Rear disc mounting bolts (arrowed)

7•6 Brakes, wheels and tyres

4.1a Unscrew the bolt and displace the guide from the fork

4.1b Brake hose banjo bolt (arrowed)

4.2 Brake caliper body joining bolts (arrowed)

Installation

6 Before installing the disc, make sure there is no dirt or corrosion where the disc seats on the hub, particularly right in the angle of the seat, as this will not allow the disc to sit flat when it is bolted down and it will appear to be warped when checked or when using the brake.

7 Install the disc on the wheel, making sure the directional arrow is on the outside and pointing in the direction of normal (i.e. forward) rotation. Align the previously applied matchmarks (if you're reinstalling the original disc).

8 Install the disc mounting bolts, either using new ones or cleaning and applying a suitable non-permanent thread locking compound to the threads of the old ones (see **Note** above), and tighten them evenly in a criss-cross pattern to the torque setting specified at the beginning of the Chapter **(see illustration 3.5a or b)**. Clean off all grease from the brake disc(s) using acetone or brake system cleaner. If a new brake disc has been installed, remove any protective coating from its working surfaces.

9 Install the wheel (see Section 13 or 14). When installing a new disc always fit new brake pads (see Section 2).

10 Operate the brake lever and pedal several times to bring the pads into contact with the disc. Check the operation of the brakes carefully before riding the bike.

4 Front brake calipers – removal, overhaul and installation

⚠️ **Warning:** *If a caliper indicates the need for an overhaul (usually due to leaking fluid or sticky operation), all old brake fluid should be flushed from the system. Also, the dust created by the brake system may contain asbestos, which is harmful to your health. Never blow it out with compressed air and don't inhale any of it. An approved filtering mask should be worn when working on the brakes. Do not, under any circumstances, use petroleum-based solvents to clean brake parts. Use clean brake fluid, brake cleaner or denatured alcohol only. Use care when working with brake fluid as it can injure your eyes and it will damage painted surfaces and plastic parts.*

Note: *Honda recommend using new mounting bolts and caliper body joining bolts when the old ones are removed. This is because the bolts are pre-treated with a locking compound. It is possible, however, to clean up the old bolts and reinstall them using a suitable non-permanent thread locking compound that is commercially available.*

Removal

1 If the calipers are just being displaced and not completely removed or overhauled, do not disconnect the brake hoses, but unscrew the bolt securing each hose guide to the front fork **(see illustration)**. If the calipers are being completely removed or overhauled, remove the brake hose banjo bolt and detach the hose, noting the alignment with the caliper **(see illustration)**. Plug the hose end or wrap a plastic bag tightly around to minimise fluid loss and prevent dirt entering the system. Discard the sealing washers as new ones must be used on installation. **Note:** *If you are planning to overhaul the caliper and don't have a source of compressed air to blow out the pistons, just loosen the banjo bolt at this stage and retighten it lightly. The bike's hydraulic system can then be used to force the pistons out of the body once the pads have been removed. Disconnect the hose once the pistons have been sufficiently displaced.*

2 If the calipers are being overhauled, slacken the caliper body joining bolts slightly, then nip them up again so they are secure but not tight **(see illustration)**. Remove the brake pads (see Section 2) – this procedure incorporates removing the caliper.

3 If the calipers are just being displaced, unscrew the mounting bolts and slide the caliper off the disc **(see illustrations 2.1b and c)**.

Overhaul

4 Clean the exterior of the caliper with denatured alcohol or brake system cleaner **(see illustration)**.

4.4 Front brake caliper components

1 Joining bolts
2 Caliper body halves
3 Piston seals
4 Dust seals
5 Upper pistons (34 mm)
6 Lower pistons (32 mm)
7 O-ring
8 Bleed valve

Brakes, wheels and tyres 7•7

4.18 The captive nut (arrowed) is easily dislodged

5 Displace the pistons as far as possible from the caliper body, either by pumping them out by operating the front brake lever, or by forcing them out using compressed air, until they meet in the middle. If the compressed air method is used, place a piece of cardboard between the pistons to act as a cushion, then use compressed air directed into the fluid inlet to force the pistons out of the body. Use only low pressure to ease the pistons out and make sure all pistons are displaced at the same time. If the air pressure is too high and the pistons are forced out, the caliper and/or pistons may be damaged.

⚠ **Warning: Never place your fingers in front of the pistons in an attempt to catch or protect them when applying compressed air, as serious injury could result.**

6 Unscrew the caliper body joining bolts and separate the caliper halves. Mark each piston head and caliper body with a felt marker to ensure that the pistons can be matched to their original bores on reassembly, then remove the pistons. Remove the caliper seal from either half of the caliper body and discard it as a new one must be used.

Caution: Do not try to remove the pistons by levering them out, or by using pliers or any other grips.

7 Using a wooden or plastic tool, remove the dust seals from the caliper bores. Discard them as new ones must be used on installation. If a metal tool is being used, take great care not to damage the caliper bores.

8 Remove and discard the piston seals in the same way.

9 Clean the pistons and bores with clean brake fluid of the specified type. If compressed air is available, use it to dry the parts thoroughly (make sure it's filtered and unlubricated).

Caution: Do not, under any circumstances, use a petroleum-based solvent to clean brake parts.

10 Inspect the caliper bores and pistons for signs of corrosion, nicks and burrs and loss of plating. If surface defects are present, the caliper assembly must be renewed. If the necessary measuring equipment is available, compare the dimensions of the caliper bores and piston diameters to those specified at the beginning of the Chapter, and install a new caliper or pistons if necessary. If the caliper is in bad shape the master cylinder should also be checked.

11 Lubricate the new piston seals with clean brake fluid and fit them into their grooves in the caliper bores. Note that different sizes of bore and piston are used (see Specifications), and care must therefore be taken to ensure that the correct size seals are fitted to the correct bores. The same applies when fitting the new dust seals and pistons.

12 Lubricate the new dust seals with silicone grease and fit them into their grooves in the caliper bores.

13 Lubricate the pistons with clean brake fluid and fit them closed-end first into the caliper bores. Using your thumbs, push the pistons all the way in, making sure they enter the bore squarely.

14 Lubricate the new caliper seal with clean brake fluid and install it in the fluid passage orifice in the caliper body, then join the body halves together. Apply a suitable non-permanent thread locking compound to the caliper body joining bolts, and tighten them to the torque setting specified at the beginning of the Chapter (note that they can be fully tightened after the calipers have been installed if required, to prevent having to hold the calipers by hand – just tighten them as much as possible before installing them).

Installation

15 If the calipers have been overhauled, install the brake pads (see Section 2). If not, slide the caliper onto the disc, making sure the pads sit squarely on either side **(see illustration 2.1c)**. Install the caliper mounting bolts, either using new ones or cleaning and applying a suitable non-permanent thread locking compound to the threads of the old ones (see **Note** above), and tighten them to the torque setting specified at the beginning of the Chapter **(see illustration 2.9)**.

16 If the calipers have been overhauled, and if not already done, tighten the body joining bolts to the specified torque **(see illustration 4.2)**.

17 If detached, connect the brake hose to the caliper, using new sealing washers on each side of the fitting. Align the hose as noted on removal **(see illustration 4.1b)**. Tighten the banjo bolt to the torque setting specified at the beginning of the Chapter.

18 If removed, when installing the brake hose guide bolts **(see illustration 4.1a)**, note that they thread into a captive nut on the inside of the mudguard **(see illustration)**. Take care not to dislodge the nuts when installing the bolts.

19 Fill the master cylinder reservoir with DOT 4 brake fluid (see *Daily (pre-ride) checks*) and bleed the hydraulic system as described in Section 9.

20 Check for leaks and thoroughly test the operation of the brakes before riding the motorcycle on the road.

5 Rear brake caliper – removal, overhaul and installation

⚠ **Warning: If a caliper indicates the need for an overhaul (usually due to leaking fluid or sticky operation), all old brake fluid should be flushed from the system. Also, the dust created by the brake system may contain asbestos, which is harmful to your health. Never blow it out with compressed air and don't inhale any of it. An approved filtering mask should be worn when working on the brakes. Do not, under any circumstances, use petroleum-based solvents to clean brake parts. Use clean brake fluid, brake cleaner or denatured alcohol only. Use care when working with brake fluid as it can injure your eyes and it will damage painted surfaces and plastic parts.**

Removal

1 If the caliper is just being displaced and not completely removed or overhauled, do not disconnect the brake hose. If the caliper is being completely removed or overhauled, remove the brake hose banjo bolt and detach the hose, noting the alignment with the caliper **(see illustration)**. Plug the hose end or wrap a plastic bag tightly around to minimise fluid loss and prevent dirt entering the system. Discard the sealing washers as new ones must be used on installation. **Note:** *If you are planning to overhaul the caliper and don't have a source of compressed air to blow out the piston, just loosen the banjo bolt at this stage and retighten it lightly. The bike's hydraulic system can then be used to force the piston out of the body once the pads have been removed. Disconnect the hose once the piston have been sufficiently displaced.*

2 If the caliper is being overhauled, remove the brake pads (see Section 2), then slide the caliper off the bracket and remove it.

3 If the caliper is just being displaced, remove the brake pads (see Section 2), then unscrew the caliper front slide pin and remove the caliper (this must be done as the brake hose will not allow the caliper to be pivoted up enough to

5.1 Brake hose banjo bolt (arrowed)

7•8 Brakes, wheels and tyres

5.3a Unscrew the front slide pin and remove the caliper

5.3b Remove the pad spring (arrowed) from the caliper . . .

5.3c . . . and the guide (arrowed) from the bracket, noting how they fit

clear the disc when sliding it off the front pin) **(see illustration)**. If required, remove the pad spring from the caliper and the guide from the bracket, noting how they fit **(see illustrations)**.

Overhaul

4 Clean the exterior of the caliper with denatured alcohol or brake system cleaner **(see illustration)**.
5 Remove the piston from the caliper body, either by pumping it out by operating the brake pedal, or by using compressed air. If the compressed air method is used, place a wad of rag over the piston to act as a cushion, then use compressed air directed into the fluid inlet to force the pistons out of the body. Use only low pressure to ease the piston out and make sure. If the air pressure is too high and the piston is forced out, the caliper and/or piston may be damaged.

⚠ **Warning:** *Never place your fingers in front of the piston in an attempt to catch or protect it when applying compressed air, as serious injury could result. Place the caliper piston side down on a bench, with the rag between them, and let the air lift the caliper off the piston.*

6 Using a wooden or plastic tool, remove the dust seal from the caliper bore. Discard it as a new one must be used on installation. If a metal tool is being used, take great care not to damage the caliper bore.
7 Remove and discard the piston seal in the same way.
8 Clean the piston and bore with denatured alcohol, clean brake fluid or brake system cleaner. If compressed air is available, use it to dry the parts thoroughly (make sure it's filtered and unlubricated).

Caution: Do not, under any circumstances, use a petroleum-based solvent to clean brake parts.

9 Inspect the caliper bores and pistons for signs of corrosion, nicks and burrs and loss of plating. If surface defects are present, the caliper assembly must be replaced. If the necessary measuring equipment is available, compare the dimensions of the pistons and bores to those given in the Specifications Section of this Chapter, replacing any component that is worn beyond the service limit. If the caliper is in bad shape the master cylinder should also be checked.
10 Remove the collar from the rear slide pin rubber boot and remove the boots from the caliper and the bracket **(see illustrations)**. Clean

5.4 Rear brake caliper components

1 Caliper front slide pin
2 Bleed valve
3 Rear slide pin collar
4 Rubber dust boot
5 Pad spring
6 Fluid seal
7 Dust seal
8 Piston

5.10a Remove the collar from the caliper boot . . .

5.10b . . . then remove the boot . . .

5.10c . . . and the bracket boot

Brakes, wheels and tyres 7•9

6.3 Slacken the reservoir cover screws (arrowed)

6.4 Disconnect the brake light switch wiring connectors (arrowed)

off all traces of corrosion and hardened grease from the collar, boots and pins. Renew the rubber boots if they are damaged, deformed or deteriorated. Apply a smear of silicone based grease to the collar, boots and slider pins. Fit the boots into their bores, then fit the collar into the rear boot **(see illustrations 5.10c, b and a)**.

11 Lubricate the new piston seal with clean brake fluid and install it in its groove in the caliper bore.

12 Lubricate the new dust seal with clean brake fluid and install it in its groove in the caliper bore.

13 Lubricate the piston with clean brake fluid and install it closed-end first into the caliper bore. Using your thumbs, push the piston all the way in, making sure it enters the bore squarely.

Installation

14 If the caliper has not been overhauled, remove the collar from the rear slider pin rubber boot and remove the boots from the caliper and the bracket **(see illustrations 5.10a, b and c)**. Clean off all traces of corrosion and hardened grease from the collar, boots and pins. Renew the rubber boots if they are damaged, deformed or deteriorated. Apply a smear of silicone based grease to the collar, boots and slider pins. Fit the boots into their bores, then fit the collar into the rear boot **(see illustrations 5.10c, b and a)**.

15 Make sure that the pad spring and pad guide are correctly fitted **(see illustrations 5.3b and c)**. If the front slider pin was removed, locate the caliper onto the bracket then apply a suitable non-permanent thread locking compound to the pin threads and tighten it to the torque setting specified at the beginning of the Chapter (it can be fully tightened after the rear mounting bolt/slider pin has been installed if necessary) **(see illustration 5.3a)**. If the pin was not removed, slide the caliper into the bracket.

16 Install the brake pads (see Section 2). If it was removed and has not yet been tightened, now tighten the front slider pin to the specified torque.

17 If detached, connect the brake hose to the caliper, using new sealing washers on each side of the fitting. Align the hose as noted on removal **(see illustration 5.1)**. Tighten the banjo bolt to the torque setting specified at the beginning of the Chapter.

18 Fill the master cylinder reservoir with DOT 4 brake fluid (see *Daily (pre-ride) checks*) and bleed the hydraulic system as described in Section 9.

19 Check for leaks and thoroughly test the operation of the brake before riding the motorcycle.

6 Front brake master cylinder – removal, overhaul and installation

1 If the master cylinder is leaking fluid, or if the lever does not produce a firm feel when the brake is applied, and bleeding the brakes does not help (see Section 9), and the hydraulic hoses and unions are all in good condition, then master cylinder overhaul is recommended.

2 Before disassembling the master cylinder, read through the entire procedure and make sure that you have the correct rebuild kit. Also, you will need some new DOT 4 brake fluid, some clean rags and internal circlip pliers. **Note:** *To prevent damage to the paint from spilled brake fluid, always cover the fuel tank when working on the master cylinder.*

Caution: *Disassembly, overhaul and reassembly of the brake master cylinder must be done in a spotlessly clean work area to avoid contamination and possible failure of the brake hydraulic system components. Use care when working with brake fluid as it can injure your eyes and it will damage painted surfaces and plastic parts.*

Removal

Note: *If the master cylinder is being displaced from the handlebar and not being removed completely or overhauled, follow Steps 4 and 7 only.*

3 Loosen, but do not remove, the screws holding the reservoir cover in place **(see illustration)**.

4 Disconnect the electrical connectors from the brake light switch **(see illustration)**.

5 Remove the front brake lever (see Chapter 6, Section 5).

6 Unscrew the brake hose banjo bolt and separate the hose from the master cylinder, noting its alignment **(see illustration)**. Discard the two sealing washers as they must be replaced with new ones. Wrap the end of the hose in a clean rag and suspend it in an upright position or bend it down and place the open end in a clean container. The objective is to prevent excessive loss of brake fluid, fluid spills and system contamination.

7 Unscrew the master cylinder clamp bolts, then lift the master cylinder and reservoir away from the handlebar, noting how the top mating surfaces of the clamp align with the punch mark on the top of the handlebar **(see illustration)**.

6.6 Brake hose banjo bolt (arrowed)

6.7 Front master cylinder clamp bolts (arrowed)

7•10 Brakes, wheels and tyres

Caution: Do not tip the master cylinder upside down or brake fluid will run out.

8 Remove the reservoir cover, diaphragm plate and rubber diaphragm. Drain the brake fluid from the reservoir into a suitable container. Wipe any remaining fluid out of the reservoir with a clean rag.
9 If required undo the brake light switch screw and remove the switch, noting how it fits.

Overhaul

10 Carefully remove the dust boot from the end of the master cylinder and from around the piston, noting how it locates **(see illustration)**.
11 Push the piston in and, using circlip pliers, remove the circlip from its groove in the master cylinder and slide out the piston assembly and the spring, noting how they fit. If they are difficult to remove, apply low pressure compressed air to the fluid outlet. Lay the parts out in order as you remove them to prevent confusion during reassembly.
12 Clean all parts with clean brake fluid or denatured alcohol. If compressed air is available, use it to dry the parts thoroughly (make sure it's filtered and unlubricated).
Caution: Do not, under any circumstances, use a petroleum-based solvent to clean brake parts.
13 Check the master cylinder bore for corrosion, scratches, nicks and score marks. If the necessary measuring equipment is available, compare the dimensions of the piston and bore to those given in the Specifications Section of this Chapter. If damage or wear is evident, the master cylinder must be replaced with a new one. If the master cylinder is in poor condition, then the calipers should be checked as well. Check that the fluid inlet and outlet ports in the master cylinder are clear.
14 The dust boot, circlip, piston, seal, cup and spring are included in the rebuild kit. Use all of the new parts, regardless of the apparent condition of the old ones. If the seal is not already on the piston, fit it according to the layout of the old one.
15 Fit the cup over the end of the spring so that its inner raised section fits into the outer coil on the spring. Lubricate the cup, seal and piston with clean brake fluid.
16 Install the spring in the master cylinder with the cup facing out, then fit the piston into the master cylinder, making sure it is the correct way round. Make sure the lips on the cup and seal do not turn inside out when they enter the bore. Depress the piston and install the new circlip, making sure that it locates in the groove in the master cylinder.
17 Install the rubber dust boot, making sure it is seated properly in the groove in the master cylinder and around the piston.
18 Inspect the reservoir rubber diaphragm and renew it if it is damaged or deteriorated.

Installation

19 Locate the brake light switch on the underside of the master cylinder and secure it with the screw.
20 Attach the master cylinder to the handlebar and fit the clamp with its UP mark facing up **(see illustration 6.7)**. Align the top mating surfaces of the clamp with the punch mark on the top of the handlebar, then tighten the top bolt first, then the bottom bolt to the torque setting specified at the beginning of the Chapter.
21 Connect the brake hose to the master cylinder, using new sealing washers on each side of the union, and aligning the hose as noted on removal **(see illustration 6.6)**. Tighten the banjo bolt to the torque setting specified at the beginning of the Chapter.
22 Install the brake lever (see Chapter 6, Section 5).
23 Connect the brake light switch wiring **(see illustration 6.4)**.
24 Fill the fluid reservoir with new DOT 4 brake fluid as described in *Daily (pre-ride) checks*. Refer to Section 9 of this Chapter and bleed the air from the system.
25 Fit the rubber diaphragm, making sure it is correctly seated, the diaphragm plate and the cover or cap onto the reservoir.
26 Check the operation of the front brake and brake light before riding the motorcycle.

7 Rear brake master cylinder – removal, overhaul and installation

1 If the master cylinder is leaking fluid, or if the lever does not produce a firm feel when the brake is applied, and bleeding the brakes does not help (see Section 9), and the hydraulic hoses and unions are all in good condition, then master cylinder overhaul is recommended.
2 Before disassembling the master cylinder, read through the entire procedure and make sure that you have the correct rebuild kit. Also, you will need some new DOT 4 brake fluid, some clean rags and internal circlip pliers. **Note:** *To prevent damage to the paint from spilled brake fluid, always cover the surrounding components when working on the master cylinder.*
Caution: Disassembly, overhaul and reassembly of the brake master cylinder must be done in a spotlessly clean work area to avoid contamination and possible failure of the brake hydraulic system components. Use care when working with brake fluid as it can injure your eyes and it will damage painted surfaces and plastic parts.

Removal

3 Unscrew the bolt securing the master

6.10 Front master cylinder components

1 Dust boot
2 Circlip
3 Seals
4 Piston and cup assembly
5 Spring
6 Pivot screw
7 Cover screws
8 Cover
9 Diaphragm plate
10 Rubber diaphragm
11 Body
12 Brake light switch
13 Brake light switch screw
14 Pivot screw locknut
15 Brake lever

Brakes, wheels and tyres 7•11

7.3a Unscrew the bolt (arrowed) and drain the reservoir ...

7.3b ... then release the clamp and detach the hose from its union on the master cylinder (arrowed)

7.4 Brake hose banjo bolt (arrowed)

cylinder reservoir **(see illustration)**. Undo the reservoir cap and remove the diaphragm plate and diaphragm, then pour the fluid into a container. Separate the fluid reservoir hose from the elbow on the master cylinder by releasing the hose clamp **(see illustration)**.

4 Unscrew the brake hose banjo bolt and separate the hose from the master cylinder, noting its alignment **(see illustration)**. Discard the sealing washers as they must be replaced with new ones. Wrap the end of the hose in a clean rag and suspend it in an upright position, or bend it down carefully and place the open end in a clean container. The objective is to prevent excessive loss of brake fluid, fluid spills and system contamination.

5 Remove the rear brake pedal (see Chapter 6) – this procedure involves separating the master cylinder from its bracket.

Overhaul

6 If necessary, slacken the clevis locknut and remove the clevis from the pushrod, noting how far up it is threaded **(see illustration)**.

7 Dislodge the rubber dust boot from the base of the master cylinder and from around the pushrod, noting how it locates.

8 Push the pushrod in and, using circlip pliers, remove the circlip from its groove in the master cylinder and slide out the piston assembly and the spring, noting how they fit. If they are difficult to remove, apply low pressure compressed air to the fluid outlet. Lay the parts out in the proper order to prevent confusion during reassembly.

9 If required, remove the screw securing the fluid reservoir hose union and detach it from the master cylinder. Discard the O-ring as a new one must be used. Inspect the reservoir hose for cracks or splits and replace with a new one if necessary.

10 Clean all of the parts with clean brake fluid or denatured alcohol.

Caution: Do not, under any circumstances, use a petroleum-based solvent to clean brake parts. If compressed air is available, use it to dry the parts thoroughly (make sure it's filtered and unlubricated).

11 Check the master cylinder bore for corrosion, scratches, nicks and score marks. If the necessary measuring equipment is available, compare the dimensions of the piston and bore to those given in the Specifications Section of this Chapter. If damage is evident, the master cylinder must be replaced with a new one. If the master cylinder is in poor condition, then the caliper should be checked as well.

12 The dust boot, circlip, piston, seal, cup and spring are included in the rebuild kit. Use all of the new parts, regardless of the apparent condition of the old ones. If the seal is not already on the piston, fit it according to the layout of the old one.

13 Fit the cup over the end of the spring so that its inner raised section fits into the outer coil on the spring. Lubricate the cup, seal and piston with clean brake fluid.

14 Install the spring in the master cylinder with the cup facing out, then fit the piston into the master cylinder, making sure it is the correct way round. Make sure the lips on the cup and seal do not turn inside out when they enter the bore.

15 Apply some silicone grease to the end of the pushrod and fit it into the master cylinder. Depress the pushrod, then install the new circlip, making sure it is properly seated in the groove.

16 Install the rubber dust boot, making sure it is seated properly in the groove in the master cylinder and around the pushrod.

17 If removed, fit a new O-ring to the fluid reservoir hose union, then install the union

7.6 Rear master cylinder components

1 Reservoir cap	6 Elbow	11 Dust boot
2 Diaphragm plate	7 O-ring	12 Circlip
3 Diaphragm	8 Split pin	13 Pushrod
4 Reservoir	9 Clevis pin	14 Piston assembly
5 Connecting hose	10 Clevis	15 Spring

7•12 Brakes, wheels and tyres

onto the master cylinder and secure it with its screw.

18 If removed, thread the clevis locknut and the clevis onto the master cylinder pushrod end. Set the clevis position as noted on removal. Honda specify the distance between the eye in the clevis and the lower mounting bolt hole should be 100 mm. Tighten the clevis locknut securely against the clevis.

Installation

19 Install the rear brake pedal (see Chapter 6) – this procedure involves mounting the master cylinder on its bracket.
20 Connect the brake hose to the master cylinder, using new sealing washers on each side of the union. Align the hose as noted on removal and tighten the banjo bolt to the specified torque setting **(see illustration 7.4)**.
21 Fit the fluid reservoir on its mount and secure it with its bolt **(see illustration 7.3a)**. Ensure that the hose is correctly routed then connect it to the union on the master cylinder and secure it with the clamp **(see illustration 7.3b)**. Check that the hose is secure and clamped at the reservoir end as well. If the clamps have weakened, use new ones.
22 Fill the fluid reservoir with new DOT 4 brake fluid (see *Daily (pre-ride) checks*) and bleed the system following the procedure in Section 9.
23 Check the operation of the brake and brake light carefully before riding the motorcycle.

8 Brake hoses – inspection and replacement

Inspection

1 Brake hose condition should be checked regularly and the hoses replaced at the specified interval (see Chapter 1).
2 Twist and flex the rubber hoses while looking for cracks, bulges and seeping fluid **(see illustration)**. Check extra carefully around the areas where the hoses connect with the banjo fittings, as these are common areas for hose failure.
3 Inspect the metal joints and the banjo union fittings connected to the brake hoses. If the fittings are rusted, scratched or cracked, replace them.

Replacement

⚠️ **Warning: Use care when working with brake fluid as it can injure your eyes and it will damage painted surfaces and plastic parts.**

4 The brake hoses have banjo union fittings on each end **(see illustrations 7.4, 6.6, 5.1, and 4.1)**. Cover the surrounding area with plenty of rags and unscrew the banjo bolt at each end of the hose, noting its alignment. Free the hose from any clips or guides and remove it. Discard the sealing washers on the hose banjo unions.

8.2 Flex the brake hoses and check for cracks, bulges and leaking fluid

5 Position the new hose, making sure it isn't twisted or otherwise strained, and abut the tab on the hose union with the lug on the component casting, where present. Otherwise align the hose as noted on removal **(see illustrations 7.4, 6.6, 5.1, and 4.1)**. Install the hose banjo bolts using new sealing washers on both sides of the unions. Tighten the banjo bolts to the torque setting specified at the beginning of this Chapter. Make sure the hoses are correctly aligned and routed clear of all moving components.
6 Flush the old brake fluid from the system, refill with new DOT 4 brake fluid (see *Daily (pre-ride) checks*) and bleed the air from the system (see Section 9). Check the operation of the brakes carefully before riding the motorcycle.

9 Brake system – bleeding and fluid renewal

Note: *Honda recommend using a commercially available vacuum-type brake bleeding tool* **(see illustration)**. *If bleeding the system using the conventional method does not work sufficiently well, it is advisable to obtain a bleeder and repeat the procedure detailed below, following the manufacturers instructions for using the tool. If the tool is not available, take the machine to a Honda dealer.*

⚠️ **Warning: Use care when working with brake fluid as it can injure your eyes and it will damage painted surfaces and plastic parts.**

9.5a Brake caliper bleed valve (arrowed)

9. NOTE Bleeding the brakes using a commercial vacuum-operated bleeding tool

Bleeding

1 Bleeding the brakes is simply the process of removing all the air bubbles from the brake fluid reservoirs, the hoses and the brake calipers. Bleeding is necessary whenever a brake system hydraulic connection is loosened, when a component or hose is replaced, or when the master cylinder or caliper is overhauled. Leaks in the system may also allow air to enter, but leaking brake fluid will reveal their presence and warn you of the need for repair.
2 To bleed the brakes, you will need some new DOT 4 brake fluid, a length of clear vinyl or plastic tubing, a small container partially filled with clean brake fluid, some rags and a ring spanner to fit the brake caliper bleed valves.
3 Cover the fuel tank, fairing panels, front mudguard and other painted components to prevent damage in the event that brake fluid is spilled.
4 Remove the reservoir cover or cap, diaphragm plate and diaphragm (see *Daily (pre-ride) checks*) and slowly pump the brake lever or pedal a few times, until no air bubbles can be seen floating up from the holes in the bottom of the reservoir. Doing this bleeds the air from the master cylinder end of the line. Loosely refit the reservoir cover.
5 Pull the dust cap off the bleed valve **(see illustration)**. Attach one end of the clear vinyl or plastic tubing to the bleed valve and submerge the other end in the brake fluid in the container **(see illustration)**.

9.5b To bleed the brakes, you need a spanner, a short section of clear tubing, and a clear container half-filled with brake fluid

Brakes, wheels and tyres 7•13

6 Remove the reservoir cap or cover and check the fluid level. Do not allow the fluid level to drop below the lower mark during the bleeding process.

7 Carefully pump the brake lever or pedal three or four times and hold it in (front) or down (rear) while opening the caliper bleed valve. When the valve is opened, brake fluid will flow out of the caliper into the clear tubing and the lever will move toward the handlebar or the pedal will move down.

8 Retighten the bleed valve, then release the brake lever or pedal gradually. Repeat the process until no air bubbles are visible in the brake fluid leaving the caliper and the lever or pedal is firm when applied. On completion, disconnect the bleeding equipment, then tighten the bleed valve to the torque setting specified at the beginning of the chapter and install the dust cap.

9 Install the diaphragm, plate and cover or cap assembly, wipe up any spilled brake fluid and check the entire system for leaks.

HAYNES HiNT *If it's not possible to produce a firm feel to the lever or pedal the fluid my be aerated. Let the brake fluid in the system stabilise for a few hours and then repeat the procedure when the tiny bubbles in the system have settled out. Also check to make sure that there are no 'high-spots' in the brake hose in which an air bubble can become trapped – this will occur most often in an incorrectly mounted hose union, but can also arise through bleeding the brakes while some of the brake system components are at such an angle to encourage this. Reversing the angle or displacing and moving the offending component around will normally dislodge any trapped air.*

Renewing the fluid

10 Changing the brake fluid is a similar process to bleeding the brakes and requires the same materials plus a suitable tool for siphoning the fluid out of the hydraulic reservoir. Also ensure that the container is large enough to take all the old fluid when it is flushed out of the system.

11 Follow Steps 3 and 5, then remove the reservoir cap, diaphragm plate and diaphragm and siphon the old fluid out of the reservoir. Fill the reservoir with new brake fluid, then follow Step 7.

12 Retighten the bleed valve, then release the brake lever or pedal gradually. Keep the reservoir topped-up with new fluid to above the LOWER level at all times or air may enter the system and greatly increase the length of the task. Repeat the process until new fluid can be seen emerging from the bleed valve.

10.2 Check the wheel for radial (out-of-round) runout (A) and axial (side-to-side) runout (B)

HAYNES HiNT *Old brake fluid is invariably much darker in colour than new fluid, making it easy to see when all old fluid has been expelled from the system.*

13 Disconnect the hose, then tighten the bleed valve to the specified torque setting and install the dust cap.

14 Top-up the reservoir, install the diaphragm, plate and cover or cap, and wipe up any spilled brake fluid. Check the entire system for fluid leaks.

15 Check the operation of the brakes before riding the motorcycle.

10 Wheels – inspection and repair

1 Position the motorcycle on its centrestand if fitted or on an auxiliary stand. When checking the front wheel, support the bike so that it is raised off the ground. Clean the wheels thoroughly to remove mud and dirt that may interfere with the inspection procedure or mask defects. Make a general check of the wheels (see Chapter 1) and tyres (see *Daily (pre-ride) checks*).

2 To check axial (side-to-side) runout, attach a dial gauge to the fork slider or the swingarm and position its stem against the side of the rim **(see illustration)**. Spin the wheel slowly and check the amount of runout at the rim. To accurately check radial (out of round) runout with the dial gauge, remove the wheel from the machine, and the tyre from the wheel.

With the axle clamped in a vice and the dial gauge positioned on the top of the rim, rotate the wheel and check the runout.

3 An easier, though slightly less accurate, method is to attach a stiff wire pointer to the fork slider or the swingarm and position the end a fraction of an inch from the wheel (where the wheel and tyre join). If the wheel is true, the distance from the pointer to the rim will be constant as the wheel is rotated. **Note:** *If wheel runout is excessive, check the wheel bearings and axle very carefully before replacing.*

4 Visually inspect the wheels for cracks, flat spots on the rim, and other damage. Look very closely for dents in the area where the tyre bead contacts the rim. Dents in this area may prevent complete sealing of the tyre against the rim, which leads to deflation of the tyre over a period of time. If damage is evident, or if runout in either direction is excessive, the wheel will have to be replaced with a new one. Never attempt to repair a damaged cast alloy wheel.

11 Wheels – alignment check

1 Misalignment of the wheels, which may be due to a cocked rear wheel or a bent frame or fork yokes, can cause strange and possibly serious handling problems. If the frame or yokes are at fault, repair by a frame specialist or replacement with new parts are the only alternatives.

2 To check the alignment you will need an assistant, a length of string or a perfectly straight piece of wood and a ruler. A plumb bob or other suitable weight will also be required.

3 Place the bike on the centrestand if fitted, or an auxiliary stand. Measure the width of both tyres at their widest points. Subtract the smaller measurement from the larger measurement, then divide the difference by two. The result is the amount of offset that should exist between the front and rear tyres on both sides.

4 If a string is used, have your assistant hold one end of it about halfway between the floor and the rear axle, touching the rear sidewall of the tyre.

5 Run the other end of the string forward and pull it tight so that it is roughly parallel to the floor **(see illustration)**. Slowly bring the string

11.5 Wheel alignment check using string

7•14 Brakes, wheels and tyres

11.7 Wheel alignment check using a straight-edge

into contact with the front sidewall of the rear tyre, then turn the front wheel until it is parallel with the string. Measure the distance from the front tyre sidewall to the string.
6 Repeat the procedure on the other side of the motorcycle. The distance from the front tyre sidewall to the string should be equal on both sides.
7 As previously mentioned, a perfectly straight length of wood or metal bar may be substituted for the string (see illustration). The procedure is the same.
8 If the distance between the string and tyre is greater on one side, or if the rear wheel appears to be cocked, refer to Chapter 1 and check that the chain adjuster markings are in the same position on each side of the swingarm.
9 If the front-to-back alignment is correct, the wheels still may be out of alignment vertically.
10 Using a plumb bob, or other suitable weight, and a length of string, check the rear wheel to make sure it is vertical. To do this, hold the string against the tyre upper sidewall and allow the weight to settle just off the floor. When the string touches both the upper and lower tyre sidewalls and is perfectly straight, the wheel is vertical. If it is not, place thin spacers under one leg of the stand until it is.
11 Once the rear wheel is vertical, check the front wheel in the same manner. If both wheels are not perfectly vertical, the frame and/or major suspension components are bent.

12 Front wheel – removal and installation

Removal

1 Position the motorcycle on its centrestand if fitted or on an auxiliary stand and support it so that the front wheel is off the ground. Always make sure the motorcycle is properly supported, and remove the fairing side panels to prevent the possibility of damaging them if necessary (see Chapter 8).
2 Unbolt the front brake calipers and slide them off the disc. Unbolt the hose guide from the fork legs. Support the calipers with a cable tie or a bungee cord so that no strain is placed on the hydraulic hoses. There is no need to disconnect the hoses from the calipers. **Note:** *Do not operate the front brake lever with the calipers removed.*
3 If required, remove the front mudguard (see Chapter 8). Whether you need to or not depends on how high the front wheel is off the ground. As the mudguard extends round the wheel, the wheel has to be lowered rather than drawn forward, so if the wheel is only just off the ground, you will need to remove it.
4 Slacken the axle clamp bolts on the bottom of the right-hand fork, then unscrew the axle bolt from the right-hand end of the axle **(see illustration)**.
5 Slacken the axle clamp bolts on the bottom of the left-hand fork. Support the wheel, then withdraw the axle from the left-hand side, using a screwdriver inserted through the holes in the end of the axle as a handle, and carefully lower the wheel **(see illustrations)**.
6 Remove the long wheel spacer from the right-hand side of the wheel and the short spacer from the left-hand side **(see illustrations)**.

Caution: *Don't lay the wheel down and allow it to rest on a disc – the disc could become warped. Set the wheel on wood blocks so the disc doesn't support the weight of the wheel.*

7 Check the axle for straightness by rolling it on a flat surface such as a piece of plate glass (first wipe off all old grease and remove any

12.4 Slacken the axle clamp bolts (A), then unscrew the axle bolt (B)

12.5a Insert a screwdriver or rod into the end of the axle . . .

12.5b . . . and use it to pull the axle out

12.6a Remove the long right-hand spacer . . .

12.6b . . . and the short left-hand spacer

Brakes, wheels and tyres 7•15

12.12a Install the axle bolt ...

12.12b ... and tighten it to the specified torque

corrosion using fine emery cloth). If the equipment is available, place the axle in V-blocks and measure the runout using a dial gauge. If the axle is bent or the runout exceeds the limit specified, replace it with a new one.

8 Check the condition of the grease seals and wheel bearings (see Section 14).

Installation

9 Apply a smear of grease to the inside of the wheel spacers, and also to the outside where they fit into the wheel. Fit the long spacer into the right-hand side of the wheel and the short spacer into the left-hand side (see illustration 12.6a and b). Each side of the wheel can be identified using the directional arrow cast into one of the spokes near the rim. The arrow denotes the normal direction of wheel rotation.

10 Manoeuvre the wheel into position between the fork sliders, making sure the directional arrow is pointing in the normal direction of rotation. Apply a thin coat of grease to the axle.

11 Lift the wheel into place, making sure the spacers remain in position. Slide the axle in from the left-hand side (see illustration 12.5b).

12 Install the axle bolt and tighten it to the torque setting specified at the beginning of the Chapter (see illustrations). Use a screwdriver inserted through the hole in the left-hand end of the axle to counter-hold it (see illustration 12.5a).

13 Tighten the axle clamp bolts on the bottom of the right-hand fork to the specified torque setting (see illustration 12.4).

14 Lower the front wheel to the ground, then install the brake calipers as described in Section 4 (note that comments relating to the caliper mounting bolts). If removed, install the front mudguard (see Chapter 8).

15 Apply the front brake a few times to bring the pads back into contact with the discs. Move the motorcycle off its stand, apply the front brake and pump the front forks a few times to settle all components in position. Now tighten the axle clamp bolts on the bottom of the left-hand fork to the specified torque.

16 Check for correct operation of the brakes before riding the motorcycle. Check that there is at least 0.7 mm clearance between each front brake disc and the caliper bracket – make the check using a feeler gauge.

13 Rear wheel – removal and installation

Removal

1 Position the motorcycle on its centrestand if fitted or on an auxiliary stand and support it so that the rear wheel is off the ground. Always make sure the motorcycle is properly supported.

2 Unscrew the axle nut and remove the washer (see illustration).

3 Support the wheel, then withdraw the axle from the left-hand side and lower the wheel to the ground (see illustration). Disengage the chain from the sprocket and remove the wheel from the swingarm (see illustration). If the axle is difficult to withdraw, either drift it through, making sure you don't damage the threads, or preferably create some slack in the chain (see Chapter 1).

4 Note how the rear brake caliper bracket locates against the swingarm, and support it so that it will not fall off. If required, displace it from the swingarm, noting how it fits, and tie it to the pillion footrest bracket, making sure no strain is placed on the hose (see illustration).

13.2 Unscrew the axle nut and remove the washer

13.3a Withdraw the axle ...

13.3b ... then lower the wheel to the ground and disengage the chain

13.4 Note how the caliper bracket locates onto the swingarm (arrow)

7•16 Brakes, wheels and tyres

13.5a Remove the spacer from the right-hand side . . .

13.5b . . . and from the left-hand side, noting which fits where

Caution: *Do not lay the wheel down and allow it to rest on the disc or the sprocket – they could become warped. Set the wheel on wood blocks so the disc or the sprocket doesn't support the weight of the wheel. Do not operate the brake pedal with the wheel removed.*

5 Remove the spacer from each side of the wheel for safekeeping, noting which fits where **(see illustrations)**.

13.10 Make sure the disc slides between the pads without dislodging them

6 Check the axle for straightness by rolling it on a flat surface such as a piece of plate glass (if the axle is corroded, first remove the corrosion with fine emery cloth). If the equipment is available, place the axle in V-blocks and check the runout using a dial indicator. If the axle is bent or the runout exceeds the limit specified at the beginning of the Chapter, replace it with a new one.

7 Check the condition of the grease seals and wheel bearings (see Section 14).

Installation

8 Apply a smear of grease to the inside of the wheel spacers, and also to the outside where they fit into the wheel. Fit the plain spacer into the right-hand side of the wheel and the collared spacer into the left-hand side **(see illustration 13.5a and b)**. If displaced, locate the brake caliper bracket onto the swingarm **(see illustration 13.4)**.

9 Manoeuvre the wheel so that it is in between the ends of the swingarm. Apply a thin coat of grease to the axle. Make sure the brake caliper bracket is still correctly positioned against the swingarm.

10 Engage the drive chain with the sprocket and lift the wheel into position **(see illustration 13.3b)**. Make sure the spacers and caliper bracket remain correctly in place, and that the brake disc fits squarely into the caliper, and with the pads positioned correctly either side of the disc **(see illustration)**. If there is not enough slack in the chain to align the wheel with the swingarm and chain adjusters, slacken the adjuster bolts and tap the ends to move them up in the swingarm.

11 Install the axle from the left, making sure it passes through the chain adjusters, spacers and the caliper bracket **(see illustration)**. Check that everything is correctly aligned. Fit the washer and nut **(see illustration 13.2)**, then check and adjust the drive chain slack (see Chapter 1). On completion tighten the nut to the torque setting specified at the beginning of the Chapter, counter-holding the axle head on the other side of the wheel to prevent it turning if necessary **(see illustration)**.

12 Operate the brake pedal several times to bring the pads into contact with the disc. Check the operation of the rear brake carefully before riding the bike.

13.11a Slide the axle through . . .

13.11b . . . then fit the washer and tighten the nut to the specified torque

Brakes, wheels and tyres 7•17

14.3 Lever out the grease seal on each side

14.4a Knock out the bearings using a drift...

14.4b ...locating it as shown

14 Wheel bearings – renewal

HAYNES HiNT *Refer to Tools and Workshop Tips (Section 5) for more information about bearings.*

Front wheel bearings

Note: *Always renew the wheel bearings in pairs. Never renew the bearings individually. Avoid using a high pressure cleaner on the wheel bearing area.*

1 Remove the wheel, and if not already done remove the spacers from it (see Section 12).
2 Rotate the inner race of each bearing to check their operation. If the inner race of either bearing doesn't turn smoothly, has rough spots or is noisy, renew the two bearings.
3 Set the wheel on blocks so as not to allow the weight to rest on the brake disc. Prise out the seal on each side of the wheel using a flat-bladed screwdriver, taking care not to damage the rim of the hub (see illustration). Discard the seals as new ones should be used.
4 Using a metal rod (preferably a brass drift punch) inserted through the centre of the upper bearing, tap evenly around the inner race of the lower bearing to drive it from the hub (see illustrations). The bearing spacer will also come out.
5 Lay the wheel on its other side so that the remaining bearing faces down. Remove the seal and drive the bearing out of the wheel using the same technique as above.
6 Thoroughly clean the hub area of the wheel. Install one new bearing into the recess in the hub, with the marked or sealed side facing outwards. Using the old bearing, a bearing driver or a socket large enough to contact the outer race of the bearing, drive it in until it's completely seated (see illustration).
7 Turn the wheel over and install the bearing spacer. Drive the other new bearing into place as described above.
8 Apply a smear of grease to the lips of the new seals, then press them into the wheel (see illustration). Gently drive them into place if necessary using a seal or bearing driver, a suitable socket or a flat piece of wood (see illustration). As the seals sit flush with the top surface of their housing, using a piece of wood as shown will automatically set them flush without the risk of setting them too deep and having to lever them out again.
9 Clean off all grease from the brake discs using acetone or brake system cleaner then install the wheel (see Section 12).

Rear wheel bearings

Note: *Always renew the wheel bearings in pairs. Never renew the bearings individually. Avoid using a high pressure cleaner on the wheel bearing area.*

10 Remove the rear wheel, and if not already done remove the spacers from it (see Section 13). Lift the sprocket coupling out of the wheel, taking care not to lose the spacer if it is loose (see illustration).
11 Rotate the inner race of each bearing to check their operation. If the inner race of either bearing doesn't turn smoothly, has rough spots or is noisy, renew the two bearings.
12 Set the wheel on blocks so as not to allow the weight of the wheel to rest on the brake disc.
13 Lever out the grease seal on the right-hand side of the wheel using a flat-bladed screwdriver, taking care not to damage the

14.6 A socket can be used to drive in the bearing

14.8a Fit the grease seal and press or tap it into place...

14.8b ...using a piece of wood ensures the seal sits flush with the rim

14.10 Lift the sprocket coupling out of the wheel

7•18 Brakes, wheels and tyres

14.13 Lever out the grease seal

14.15 Drive the bearings out as described

14.17 A socket can be used to drive in the bearing

rim of the hub **(see illustration)**. Discard the seal as a new one should be used.

14 Using a metal rod (preferably a brass drift punch) inserted through the centre of the right-hand bearing, tap evenly around the inner race of the left-hand bearing to drive it from the hub **(see illustrations 14.4a and b)**. The bearing spacer will also come out.

15 Lay the wheel on its other side so that the remaining bearing faces down. Drive the bearing out of the wheel using the same technique as above **(see illustration)**.

16 Thoroughly clean the hub area of the wheel. First install the new right-hand bearing into its recess in the hub, with the marked or sealed side facing outwards. Using the old bearing (if new ones are being fitted), a bearing driver or a socket large enough to contact the outer race of the bearing, drive it in squarely until it's completely seated.

17 Turn the wheel over and install the bearing spacer. Drive the new left-hand side bearing into place as described above **(see illustration)**.

18 Check the condition of the hub O-ring and renew it if it is damaged, deformed or deteriorated **(see illustration)**.

19 Apply a smear of grease to the lips of the new grease seal, and press it into the right-hand side of the wheel, using a seal or bearing driver, a suitable socket or a flat piece of wood to drive it into place if necessary **(see illustrations)**. As the seal sits flush with the top surface of its housing, using a piece of wood as shown will automatically set it flush without the risk of setting it too deep and having to lever it out again.

20 Clean off all grease from the brake disc using acetone or brake system cleaner. Fit the sprocket coupling assembly onto the wheel, ensuring that its spacer is in place **(see illustration 14.10)**. Install the wheel (see Section 13).

Sprocket coupling bearing

21 Remove the rear wheel, and if not already done remove the spacers from it (see Section 13). Lift the sprocket coupling out of the wheel, noting how it fits **(see illustration 14.10)**.

22 Rotate the inner race of the bearing to check its operation. If the inner race doesn't turn smoothly, has rough spots or is noisy, the bearing must be renewed.

23 Using a flat-bladed screwdriver, lever out the grease seal from the outside of the coupling **(see illustration)**.

24 Remove the spacer from the inside of the coupling bearing, noting which way round it fits. The spacer could be a tight fit and may have to be driven out using a suitable socket or piece of tubing **(see illustration)**. Support the coupling on blocks of wood to do this.

25 Support the coupling on blocks of wood and drive the bearing out from the inside

14.18 Check the O-ring and fit a new one if necessary

14.19a Fit the grease seal and press or tap it into place . . .

14.19b . . . using a piece of wood ensures the seal sits flush with the rim

14.23 Lever out the grease seal

14.24 Drive out the spacer . . .

Brakes, wheels and tyres 7•19

14.25 ... then drive out the bearing

14.26 Drive in the new bearing

using a bearing driver or socket **(see illustration)**.
26 Thoroughly clean the bearing recess then install the new bearing into the coupling, with the marked or sealed side facing out. Using the old bearing, a bearing driver or a socket large enough to contact the outer race of the bearing, drive it in until it is completely seated **(see illustration)**.
27 Fit the spacer into the inside of the coupling, making sure it is the correct way round and fits squarely into the bearing. Drive it into place if it is tight, supporting the bearing on a suitable socket as you do to prevent it from being driven out at the same time **(see illustration)**.
28 Check the condition of the hub O-ring and replace it with a new one if it is damaged, deformed or deteriorated **(see illustration 14.18)**.
29 Apply a smear of grease to the lips of the new seal, and press it into the coupling, using a seal or bearing driver, a suitable socket or a flat piece of wood to drive it into place if necessary **(see illustration)**. As the seal sits flush with the top surface of their housing, using a piece of wood as shown will automatically set it flush without the risk of setting it too deep and having to lever it out again **(see illustration 14.19)**.
30 Check the sprocket coupling/rubber dampers (see Chapter 6).
31 Clean off all grease from the brake disc using acetone or brake system cleaner. Fit the sprocket coupling into the wheel **(see illustration 14.10)**, then install the wheel (see Section 13).

15 Tyres – general information and fitting

General information

1 The wheels fitted to all models are designed to take tubeless tyres only. Tyre sizes are given in the Specifications at the beginning of this chapter.
2 Refer to the *Daily (pre-ride) checks* listed at the beginning of this manual for tyre maintenance.

Fitting new tyres

3 When selecting new tyres, refer to the tyre information label on the swingarm and the tyre options listed in the owners handbook. Ensure that front and rear tyre types are compatible, the correct size and correct speed rating; if necessary seek advice from a Honda dealer or tyre fitting specialist **(see illustration overleaf)**.
4 It is recommended that tyres are fitted by a motorcycle tyre specialist rather than attempted in the home workshop. This is particularly relevant in the case of tubeless tyres because the force required to break the seal between the wheel rim and tyre bead is substantial, and is usually beyond the capabilities of an individual working with normal tyre levers. Additionally, the specialist will be able to balance the wheels after tyre fitting.
5 Refer to the advice in the owner's manual supplied with the motorcycle concerning the repair of punctured tyres and for details of safe reduced speeds when riding on repaired tyres. Also seek advice from a Honda dealer or motorcycle tyre fitting specialist on the tyre's suitability for repair.

14.27 Support the bearing on a socket when driving in the spacer

14.29 Press or drive the seal into the coupling

7•20 Brakes, wheels and tyres

15.3 Common tyre sidewall markings

Chapter 8
Bodywork

Contents

Fairing and bodypanels – removal and installation 4
Front mudguard – removal and installation 5
General information 1
Seat – removal and installation 2
Rear view mirrors – removal and installation 3

Degrees of difficulty

| Easy, suitable for novice with little experience | Fairly easy, suitable for beginner with some experience | Fairly difficult, suitable for competent DIY mechanic | Difficult, suitable for experienced DIY mechanic | Very difficult, suitable for expert DIY or professional |

1 General information

This Chapter covers the procedures necessary to remove and install the body parts. Since many service and repair operations on these motorcycles require the removal of body parts, the procedures are grouped here and referred to from other Chapters.

In the case of damage to the body parts, it is usually necessary to remove the broken component and replace it with a new (or used) one. The material that the body panels are composed of doesn't lend itself to conventional repair techniques. There are however some shops that specialise in 'plastic welding', so it may be worthwhile seeking the advice of one of these specialists before consigning an expensive component to the bin.

When attempting to remove any body panel, first study it closely, noting any fasteners and associated fittings, to be sure of returning everything to its correct place on installation. In some cases the aid of an assistant will be required when removing panels, to help avoid the risk of damage to paintwork. Once the evident fasteners have been removed, try to withdraw the panel as described but DO NOT FORCE IT – if it will not release, check that all fasteners have been removed and try again. Where a panel engages another by means of tabs, be careful not to break the tab or its mating slot or to damage the paintwork. Remember that a few moments of patience at this stage will save you a lot of money in replacing broken fairing panels!

When installing a body panel, first study it closely, noting any fasteners and associated fittings removed with it, to be sure of returning everything to its correct place. Check that all fasteners are in good condition, including all trim nuts or clips and damping/rubber mounts; any of these must be replaced if faulty before the panel is reassembled. Check also that all mounting brackets are straight and repair or replace them if necessary before attempting to install the panel. Where assistance was required to remove a panel, make sure your assistant is on hand to install it. Tighten the fasteners securely, but be careful not to overtighten any of them or the panel may break (not always immediately) due to the uneven stress.

Where trim clips are used, to release them unscrew the centre of the clip, then pull the body of the clip out of the panel **(see illustration)**. When installing them, fit the body of the clip onto the panel then push the centre fully into the body. As they are made of plastic, the threads easily become worn and the centres may not unscrew, in which case lever the centre out of the body using a small screwdriver.

HAYNES HINT *Note that a small amount of lubricant (liquid soap or similar) applied to the mounting rubber grommets of the seat cowling will assist the lugs to engage without the need for undue pressure.*

8•2 Bodywork

2.1a Unlock the seat . . .

2.1b . . . then lift it up at the rear and draw it back

2.2 Pull up the rear corners to access the bolts

2.3 Unlock the seat and remove it, noting how it fits

2 Seat –
removal and installation

Removal

European F models, US 1999 and 2000 models

1 Insert the ignition key into the seat lock located at the back on the left-hand side and turn it clockwise to unlock the seat **(see illustration)**. Remove the seat by drawing it back and up, noting how it locates **(see illustration)**.

European FS models, US 2001-on models

2 To remove the rider's seat, pull back each rear corner to access the bolts and unscrew them **(see illustration)**. Draw the seat back and up to remove it, noting how it locates.

3 To remove the pillion seat, insert the ignition key into the seat lock located at the back on the left-hand side and turn it clockwise to unlock the seat **(see illustration)**. Remove the seat by lifting it up at the back and then drawing it back, noting how it locates.

Installation

4 Installation is the reverse of removal. Make sure the hooks and tabs locate correctly. Push down on the rear to engage the latch.

3 Rear view mirrors –
removal and installation

1 Unscrew the two mounting bolts and remove the mirror **(see illustration)**.
2 Installation is the reverse of removal.

3.1 Unscrew the bolts and remove the mirror

Bodywork 8•3

4.1 The panel is secured by a trim clip (A), nut and bolt (B) and two screws (C)

4.4 Remove the panel, noting how it fits

4 Fairing and body panels – removal and installation

Cockpit trim panels – F-X and F-Y (1999 and 2000) models

1 Remove the trim clip from below the instrument cluster (see illustration).
2 Remove the rearmost windscreen nut and bolt (see illustration 4.1).
3 Undo the two screws (see illustration 4.1).
4 Remove the panel, noting how it fits (see illustration).
5 Installation is the reverse of removal.

Fuel tank trim panels – F-X and F-Y (1999 and 2000) models

6 Remove the fairing side panel (see below).
7 Undo the two screws and remove the panel, noting how it fits (see illustrations).
8 Installation is the reverse of removal.

Cockpit/fuel tank trim panels – F-1/FS-1 models onward (2001-on)

9 Remove the fairing side panel (see below).
10 Undo the two screws securing the front and back of the panel. Draw it away from the fuel tank to release the peg from the grommet and remove the panel, noting how it fits.
11 Installation is the reverse of removal.

Windshield

12 On F-X and F-Y (1999 and 2000) models, remove the rearmost nuts and bolts securing the windshield to the cockpit trim panel (see illustration 4.1).
13 Undo the remaining screws securing the windshield, noting the washers, and manoeuvre it carefully out of the fairing, noting how it fits.
14 Remove the threaded rubber collars from the fairing for safekeeping if they are loose.
15 Installation is the reverse of removal.

Fairing – F-X and F-Y (1999 and 2000) models

16 Remove the cockpit trim panels (see above).
17 Detach the direct air injection (DAI) system hose at the three-way union (see illustration).
18 Remove the rear view mirrors (see Section 3).
19 Remove the trim clips from the inside of the fairing where it joins to the centre panel (see illustration). Undo the six screws (three on each side) securing the fairing to the fairing side panels (see illustration 4.32).
20 Carefully draw the fairing forward to

4.7a Undo the screws (arrowed) . . .

4.7b . . . and remove the panel

4.17 Detach the DAI hose at the union (arrowed)

4.19 Remove the trim clip (arrowed) on each side

8•4 Bodywork

4.20a Draw the fairing forward, noting the peg (arrowed), . . .

4.20b . . . and disconnect the headlight wiring connector . . .

4.20c . . . and the sidelight and turn signal wiring connectors

4.25 Disconnect the wiring connector

4.27 Note how the pegs (A) locate in the grommets (B)

4.28 Unhook and remove the air ducts if required

release the pegs from the grommets on the fairing/instrument bracket **(see illustration)**. Note how the front sections of the air ducts locate into the rear sections. Disconnect the headlight, sidelight and turn signal wiring connectors when accessible, then draw the fairing off the bike **(see illustrations)**.

21 If required, slacken the clamps securing the air duct rear sections in the air filter housing, then release the DAI system hose from the right-hand duct and the wiring loom from the left-hand duct and remove them, noting how they fit. Remove the headlight from the fairing if required (see Chapter 9).

22 Installation is the reverse of removal. Make sure the wiring connector is correctly and securely connected.

Fairing – F-1/FS-1 models onward (2001-on)

23 Remove the cockpit/fuel tank trim panels (see above). Remove the windshield (see above).
24 Remove the rear view mirrors (see Section 3).
25 Disconnect the front sub-loom wiring connector **(see illustration)**.
26 Remove the trim clips from the inside of the fairing where it joins to the centre panel **(see illustration 4.19)**. Undo the six screws (three on each side) securing the fairing to the fairing side panels **(see illustration 4.32b)**.
27 Carefully draw the fairing forward to release the pegs from the grommets on the fairing/instrument bracket, then draw the fairing off the bike **(see illustration)**. Note how the front sections of the air ducts locate into the mid sections.
28 If required, unhook the mid air duct sections and remove them, noting how they fit **(see illustration)**. Remove the headlight from the fairing if required (see Chapter 9).
29 Installation is the reverse of removal. Make sure the wiring connector is correctly and securely connected.

Fairing side panels and centre panel

30 Remove the trim clips securing the side panel to the centre panel **(see illustration)**.
31 Remove the trim clips securing the side panels to each other on the underside **(see illustration)**.
32 Unscrew the bolts securing the side panel to the fairing, the frame and centre panel **(see illustrations)**. Carefully remove the panel,

4.30 Remove the trim clip (arrowed) on each side

4.31 Remove the trim clips (arrowed)

4.32a Remove the two screws (arrowed) . . .

Bodywork 8•5

4.32b ... the side panel-to-fairing bolts (A) and side panel-to-frame bolts (B)

4.32c Remove the panel, noting how it fits ...

4.32d ... pulling it away to release the peg from the grommet ...

4.32e ... and how the hoses are routed on the left-hand panel

4.36 Release the bulbholders from the tail light

pulling it away at the top to release the peg from the grommet, and noting how it fits **(see illustrations)**. When removing the left-hand panel, note how the fuel tank drain and breather hoses route through the cut-out **(see illustration)**.

33 If required, release the trim clips securing the centre panel and remove it, noting how it locates.

34 Installation is the reverse of removal. When installing the left-hand panel, route the fuel tank drain and breather hoses through the cut-out **(see illustration 8.32d)**.

Seat cowling

European F models and US 1999 and 2000 models

35 Remove the seat (see Section 2).
36 Release the bulbholders from the tail light by twisting them anti-clockwise and drawing them out **(see illustration)**.
37 Remove the caps from the grab-rail bolts **(see illustration)**. Unscrew the four bolts and remove the grab-rail **(see illustration)**.
38 Remove the two screws, two trim clips and two bolts, then carefully draw the cowling back and off the bike **(see illustrations)**.
39 Installation is the reverse of removal.

European FS models and US 2001-on models

40 Remove the seats (see Section 2). Remove the four trim clips, two screws, and two bungee-hook bolts, then carefully draw the cowling back

4.37a Remove the caps, then unscrew the bolts ...

4.37b ... and remove the grab-rail. Then undo the two screws (arrowed) ...

4.38a ... and the trim clip (A) and bolt (B) on each side ...

8•6 Bodywork

4.38b ... and remove the cowling

4.40a Remove the two trim clips (arrowed) on each side ...

4.40b ... and the screw (A) and bolt (B) on each side

and off the bike, pulling the sides out as you do to create clearance **(see illustrations)**.
41 Installation is the reverse of removal.

5 Front mudguard – removal and installation

1 Unscrew the four bolts securing the mudguard to the fork sliders and remove the mudguard forwards, noting how it fits and how the rear bolts secure the brake hose guides **(see illustration)**.
2 Installation is the reverse of removal. When installing the brake hose guide bolts, note that they thread into a captive nut on the inside of the mudguard **(see illustration)**. Take care not to dislodge the nuts when installing the bolts.

5.1 Unscrew the bolts (arrowed) on each side

5.2 The captive nut (arrowed) is easily dislodged

Chapter 9
Electrical system

Contents

Alternator – removal, inspection and installation 32
Battery – charging 4
Battery – removal, installation, inspection and maintenance 3
Brake light switches – check and replacement 14
Brake/tail light bulb and license plate bulb – replacement 9
Charging system – leakage and output test 31
Charging system testing – general information and precautions . . . 30
Clutch switch – check and replacement 24
Diode – check and replacement 25
Electrical system – fault finding 2
Fuses – check and replacement 5
General information 1
Handlebar switches – check 20
Handlebar switches – removal and installation 21
Headlight aim – check and adjustment . . . . .see Chapter 1
Headlight bulb and sidelight bulb – replacement 7
Headlight assembly – removal and installation 8
Horn – check and replacement 26
Ignition (main) switch – check, removal and installation 19
Ignition system components . . . . .see Chapter 5
Instrument and warning light bulbs – replacement 17
Instrument cluster – removal and installation 15
Instruments and speed sensor – check and replacement 16
Lighting system – check 6
Neutral switch – check, removal and installation 22
Oil pressure switch – check, removal and installation 18
Regulator/rectifier – check and replacement 33
Sidestand switch – check and replacement 23
Speed sensor – check and replacement 16
Starter motor – disassembly, inspection and reassembly 29
Starter motor – removal and installation 28
Starter relay – check and replacement 27
Tail light assembly – removal and installation 10
Turn signal bulbs – replacement 12
Turn signal assemblies – removal and installation 13
Turn signal circuit – check 11

Degrees of difficulty

Easy, suitable for novice with little experience	Fairly easy, suitable for beginner with some experience	Fairly difficult, suitable for competent DIY mechanic	Difficult, suitable for experienced DIY mechanic	Very difficult, suitable for expert DIY or professional

Specifications

Battery
Capacity
  F-X and F-Y (1999 and 2000) models . . . . 12 V, 8 Ah
  F-1/FS-1 models onward (2001-on) . . . . 12 V, 8.6 Ah
Voltage
  Fully charged . . . . 13.0 to 13.2 V
  Uncharged . . . . below 12.3 V
Charging rate
  Normal . . . . 0.9 A for 5 to 10 hrs
  Quick
    F-X and F-Y (1999 and 2000) models . . . . 4.0 A for 1.0 hr
    F-1/FS-1 models onward (2001-on) . . . . 4.5 A for 0.5 hr
Current leakage
  F-X and F-Y (1999 and 2000) models . . . . 0.1 mA (max)
  F-1/FS-1 models onward (2001-on) . . . . 2.0 mA (max)

Alternator
Stator coil resistance .... 0.1 to 1.0 ohms
Output
    F-X and F-Y (1999 and 2000) models .... 343 W @ 5000 rpm
    F-1/FS-1 models onward (2001-on) .... 433 W @ 5000 rpm

Regulator/rectifier
Regulated voltage output .... 14.7 to 15.5 V @ 5000 rpm

Starter motor
Brush length
    Standard .... 12.0 to 13.0 mm
    Service limit (min) .... 6.5 mm

Instruments
Tachometer peak voltage (fuel injection models) (see Text) .... 10.5 V min.

Fuses
F-X and F-Y (1999 and 2000) models
    Main .... 30 A
    Others .... 10 A x 4
F-1/FS-1 models onward (2001-on)
    Main .... 30 A
    PGM-FI (fuel injection system) .... 20 A
    Fusebox fuses – F-1/FS-1 (2001) models .... 10 A x 6
    Fusebox fuses – F-2/FS-2 models onward (2002-on) ...... 10 A x 5, 20 A x 1

Bulbs
Headlight
    F-X and F-Y (1999 and 2000) models .... 60/55 W halogen
    F-1/FS-1 models onward (2001-on) .... 55 W halogen x 2
Sidelight (where fitted) .... 5.0 W
License plate light (where fitted) .... 5.0 W (4 CP)
Brake/tail light .... 21/5 W x 2
Turn signal lights
    European spec .... 21 W x 4
    US spec
        Front .... 32/3 CP (23/8 W) x 2
        Rear .... 32 CP (23 W) x 2
Instrument lights
    F-X and F-Y (1999 and 2000) models .... 1.1 W x 3
    F-1/FS-1 models onward (2001-on) .... LED
Turn signal indicator light
    F-X and F-Y (1999 and 2000) models .... 1.1 W x 2
    F-1/FS-1 models onward (2001-on) .... LED
High beam indicator light
    F-X and F-Y (1999 and 2000) models .... 1.1 W
    F-1/FS-1 models onward (2001-on) .... LED
Neutral indicator light
    F-X and F-Y (1999 and 2000) models .... 1.1 W
    F-1/FS-1 models onward (2001-on) .... LED
Oil pressure indicator light
    F-X and F-Y (1999 and 2000) models .... 1.1 W
    F-1/FS-1 models onward (2001-on) .... LED
PGM-FI indicator light (fuel injection models) .... LED
Immobiliser indicator light .... LED

Torque settings
Alternator rotor bolt .... 103 Nm
Alternator stator bolts .... 12 Nm
Footrest bracket mounting bolts .... 26 Nm
Ignition switch bolts (US models) .... 25 Nm
Neutral switch .... 12 Nm
Oil pressure switch .... 12 Nm
Sidestand switch bolt .... 10 Nm

Electrical system 9•3

1 General information

All models have a 12-volt electrical system charged by a three-phase alternator with a separate regulator/rectifier.

The regulator maintains the charging system output within the specified range to prevent overcharging, and the rectifier converts the ac (alternating current) output of the alternator to dc (direct current) to power the lights and other components and to charge the battery. The alternator rotor is mounted on the left-hand end of the crankshaft.

The starter motor is mounted on the top of the crankcase behind the cylinders on the left-hand side. The starting system includes the motor, the battery, the relay and the various wires and switches. If the engine kill switch is in the RUN position and the ignition (main) switch is ON, a starter interlock system prevents the engine from being started if the sidestand is down and the engine is in gear. The engine can be started with the sidestand up when it is in gear as long as the clutch lever is pulled in.

Note: *Keep in mind that electrical parts, once purchased, often cannot be returned. To avoid unnecessary expense, make very sure the faulty component has been positively identified before buying a replacement part.*

2 Electrical system – fault finding

Warning: *To prevent the risk of short circuits, the ignition (main) switch must always be OFF and the battery negative (–ve) terminal should be disconnected before any of the bike's other electrical components are disturbed. Don't forget to reconnect the terminal securely once work is finished or if battery power is needed for circuit testing.*

1 A typical electrical circuit consists of an electrical component, the switches, relays, etc. related to that component and the wiring and connectors that link the component to the battery and the frame. To aid in locating a problem in any electrical circuit, refer to the wiring diagrams at the end of this Chapter.

2 Before tackling any troublesome electrical circuit, first study the wiring diagram (see end of Chapter) thoroughly to get a complete picture of what makes up that individual circuit. Trouble spots, for instance, can often be narrowed down by noting if other components related to that circuit are operating properly or not. If several components or circuits fail at one time, chances are the fault lies in the fuse or earth (ground) connection, as several circuits often are routed through the same fuse and earth (ground) connections.

3 Electrical problems often stem from simple causes, such as loose or corroded connections or a blown fuse. Prior to any electrical fault finding, always visually check the condition of the fuse, wires and connections in the problem circuit. Intermittent failures can be especially frustrating, since you can't always duplicate the failure when it's convenient to test. In such situations, a good practice is to clean all connections in the affected circuit, whether or not they appear to be good. All of the connections and wires should also be wiggled to check for looseness which can cause intermittent failure.

4 If testing instruments are going to be utilised, use the wiring diagram to plan where you will make the necessary connections in order to accurately pinpoint the trouble spot.

5 The basic tools needed for electrical fault finding include a battery and bulb test circuit or a continuity tester, a test light, and a jumper wire. A multimeter capable of reading volts, ohms and amps is a very useful alternative and performs the functions of all of the above, and is necessary for performing more extensive tests and checks where specific voltage, current or resistance values are needed.

HAYNES HiNT *Refer to Fault Finding Equipment in the Reference section for details of how to use electrical test equipment.*

3 Battery – removal, installation, inspection and maintenance

Caution: *Be extremely careful when handling or working around the battery. The electrolyte is very caustic and an explosive gas (hydrogen) is given off when the battery is charging.*

Removal and installation

1 Make sure the ignition is switched OFF. Remove the seat (see Chapter 8). On European FS models and US 2001-on models, remove the electronic control module (ECM) as described in Chapter 4.

2 Release the battery cover clips by pulling out their centres and open the cover **(see illustration)**.

3 Unscrew the negative (–ve) terminal bolt first and disconnect the lead from the battery **(see illustration)**. Lift up the red insulating cover to access the positive (+ve) terminal, then unscrew the bolt and disconnect the lead **(see illustrations)**. Lift the battery from the bike **(see illustration)**.

4 On installation, clean the battery terminals and lead ends with a wire brush or knife and emery paper. Reconnect the leads, connecting the positive (+ve) terminal first.

3.2 Release the clips and open the cover

3.3a Disconnect the negative lead first . . .

3.3b . . . then lift the terminal cover . . .

3.3c . . . disconnect the positive lead . . .

3.3d . . . and remove the battery

9•4 Electrical system

> **HAYNES HINT**: *Battery corrosion can be kept to a minimum by applying a layer of petroleum jelly to the terminals after the cables have been connected. There are also dedicated sprays commercially available.*

5 Fit the battery cover and secure it by pressing in the centres of the clips. On European FS models and US 2001-on models, install the ECM (See Chapter 4). Install the seat (see Chapter 8).

Inspection and maintenance

6 The battery fitted to all models covered in this manual is of the maintenance free (sealed) type, therefore requiring no scheduled maintenance. However, the following checks should still be regularly performed.

7 Check the battery terminals and leads for tightness and corrosion. If corrosion is evident, unscrew the terminal screws and disconnect the leads from the battery, disconnecting the negative (–ve) terminal first, and clean the terminals and lead ends with a wire brush or knife and emery paper. Reconnect the leads, connecting the negative (–ve) terminal last, and apply a thin coat of petroleum jelly to the connections to slow further corrosion.

8 Keep the battery case clean to prevent current leakage, which can discharge the battery over a period of time (especially when it sits unused). Wash the outside of the case with a solution of baking soda and water. Rinse the battery thoroughly, then dry it.

9 Look for cracks in the case and replace the battery with a new one if any are found. If acid has been spilled on the frame or battery box, neutralise it with a baking soda and water solution, dry it thoroughly, then touch up any damaged paint.

10 If the motorcycle sits unused for long periods of time, disconnect the cables from the battery terminals, negative (–ve) terminal first. Refer to Section 4 and charge the battery

4.2 If the charger doesn't have ammeter built in, connect one in series as shown. DO NOT connect the ammeter between the battery terminals or it will be ruined

once every month to six weeks.

11 Check the condition of the battery by measuring the voltage present at the battery terminals. Connect the voltmeter positive (+ve) probe to the battery positive (+ve) terminal, and the negative (–ve) probe to the battery negative (–ve) terminal. When fully charged there should be 13.0 to 13.2 volts present. If the voltage falls below 12.3 volts the battery must be removed, disconnecting the negative (–ve) terminal first, and recharged as described below in Section 4.

4 Battery – charging

Caution: Be extremely careful when handling or working around the battery. The electrolyte is very caustic and an explosive gas (hydrogen) is given off when the battery is charging.

1 Remove the battery (see Section 3). Connect the charger to the battery, making sure that the positive (+ve) lead on the charger is connected to the positive (+ve) terminal on the battery, and the negative (–ve) lead is connected to the negative (–ve) terminal.

2 Honda recommend that the battery is charged at the normal rate specified at the beginning of the Chapter. Exceeding this figure can cause the battery to overheat, buckling the plates and rendering it useless. Few owners will have access to an expensive current controlled charger, so if a normal domestic charger is used check that after a possible initial peak, the charge rate falls to a safe level **(see illustration)**. If the battery becomes hot during charging **stop**. Further charging will cause damage. **Note:** *In emergencies the battery can be charged at the quick rate specified. However, this is not recommended and the normal charging rate is by far the safer method of charging the battery.*

3 If the recharged battery discharges rapidly if left disconnected it is likely that an internal short caused by physical damage or sulphation has occurred. A new battery will be required. A sound item will tend to lose its charge at about 1% per day.

4 Install the battery (see Section 3).

5 If the motorcycle sits unused for long periods of time, charge the battery once every month to six weeks and leave it disconnected.

5 Fuses – check and replacement

1 The electrical system is protected by fuses of different ratings. All except the main fuse, and on F-1/FS-1 models onward (2001-on) the PGM-FI (fuel injection system) fuse are housed in the fusebox, which is located under the seat behind the battery on the left-hand side **(see illustration)**. The main fuse is integral with the starter relay, which is on the left-hand end of the battery. The PGM-FI fuel injection system fuse is located in its own housing mounted on the front of the fusebox.

2 To access all fuses, remove the seat (see Chapter 8). To access the fusebox fuses unclip the fusebox lid **(see illustration)**. To access the main fuse, disconnect the starter

5.1 The fusebox is behind the battery

5.2a Unclip the lid to access the fuses. Spare main fuse (arrowed) – European F models

Electrical system 9•5

5.2b Remove the starter relay wiring connector to access the main fuse (arrowed)

5.2c PGM-FI fuse (A) – fuel injection models. Spare main fuse (B) – European FS models

relay wiring connector **(see illustration)**. To access the PGM-FI fuse unclip the fuseholder cap **(see illustration)**.

3 The fuses can be removed and checked visually. If you can't pull the fuse out with your fingertips, use a pair of suitable pliers. A blown fuse is easily identified by a break in the element **(see illustration)**. Each fuse is clearly marked with its rating and must only be replaced by a fuse of the correct rating. A spare fuse of each rating except the main fuse is housed in the fusebox, and a spare main fuse is housed behind the fusebox on European F models and US 1999 and 2000 models **(see illustration 5.2a)**, and behind the starter relay on European FS models and US 2001-on models **(see illustration 5.2c)**. If a spare fuse is used, always replace it so that a spare of each rating is carried on the bike at all times.

⚠ **Warning: Never put in a fuse of a higher rating or bridge the terminals with any other substitute, however temporary it may be. Serious damage may be done to the circuit, or a fire may start.**

4 If the new fuse blows immediately check the wiring circuit very carefully for evidence of a short-circuit. Look for bare wires and chafed, melted or burned insulation.

5 Occasionally a fuse will blow or cause an open-circuit for no obvious reason. Corrosion of the fuse ends and fusebox terminals may occur and cause poor fuse contact. If this happens, remove the corrosion with a wire brush or emery paper, then spray the fuse end and terminals with electrical contact cleaner.

6 Lighting system – check

1 The battery provides power for operation of the headlight, tail light, brake light and instrument cluster lights. If none of the lights operate, always check battery voltage before proceeding. Low battery voltage indicates either a faulty battery or a defective charging system. Refer to Section 3 for battery checks and Sections 30 and 31 for charging system tests. Also, check the condition of the fuses. Note that if there is more than one problem at the same time, it is likely to be a fault relating to a multi-function component, such as one of the fuses governing more than one circuit, or the ignition switch.

Headlight

2 F-X and F-Y (1999 and 2000) models have one dual-filament headlight bulb. F-1/FS-1 models onward (2001-on) have two single filament bulbs. If either or both headlight beams fail to work, first check the fuse (see Section 5), and then the bulb(s) (see Section 7). If they are good, use jumper wires to connect the bulb in question directly to the battery terminals. If the light comes on, the problem lies in the wiring or connectors, the HI beam relay (F-1/FS-1 models onward (2001-on)) or the switches in the circuit. Refer to Section 20 for the switch testing procedures, and also to the wiring diagrams at the end of this Chapter.

3 On F-1/FS-1 models onward (2001-on), if the high beam does not work and the relay is suspected of being faulty, the easiest way to tell is to substitute it with another one, if available. Remove the fairing to access the relay – it is mounted on the back of the headlight unit in the centre **(see illustration)**. If the beam then works, the faulty relay must be replaced with a new one. If a substitute is not available, remove the suspect one and test it as follows: set a multimeter to the ohms x 1 scale and connect it across the relay's blue and black/red wire terminals. There should be no continuity (infinite resistance). Using a fully-charged 12 volt battery and two insulated jumper wires, connect the positive (+ve) terminal of the battery to the white wire terminal of the relay, and the negative (–ve) terminal to the green wire terminal. At this point the relay should be heard to click and the meter read 0 ohms (continuity). If this is the case the relay is good. If the relay does not click when battery voltage is applied and indicates no continuity (infinite resistance) across its terminals, it is faulty and must be replaced with a new one.

4 If the relay is good, check for battery voltage at the black/red wire terminal on the relay wiring connector with the ignition ON. If there is no voltage, check the wiring between the relay wiring connector and the ignition switch, via the fusebox, then check the switch itself (see Section 19). If voltage is present,

5.3 A blown fuse can be identified by a break in its element

6.3 Headlight relay (A), turn signal relay (B) – F-1/FS-1 models on

9•6 Electrical system

check that there is continuity to the headlight wiring connector in the blue wire, and continuity to earth (ground) in the green wire from the headlight connector. Also check for battery voltage at the white wire terminal on the relay wiring connector with the ignition ON, the light switch ON and the dimmer switch set to HI. If voltage is present, check for continuity to earth (ground) in the green wire from the relay wiring connector. Repair or renew the wiring or connectors as necessary.

5 If the low beam does not work, check for battery voltage at the blue/white terminal on the headlight wiring connector with the ignition ON, the light switch ON and the dimmer switch set to LO. If voltage is present, check for continuity to earth (ground) in the green wire from the relay wiring connector. Repair or renew the wiring or connectors as necessary.

Tail light

6 If either or both tail lights fail to work, first check the fuse (see Section 5), and then the bulbs (see Section 9). If they are good, use jumper wires to connect the bulb in question directly to the battery terminals. If the light comes on, the problem lies in the wiring or connectors, or the switches in the circuit. Refer to Section 20 for the switch testing procedures, and also to the wiring diagrams at the end of this Chapter.

7 Check for battery voltage at the brown or brown/white (according to model) wire terminal on the tail light wiring connectors. If voltage is present, check for continuity to earth (ground) in the green wire from the wiring connector. If no voltage is indicated, check the wiring and connectors between the tail light and the ignition switch, via the fusebox and the handlebar switch, then check the ignition switch itself (see Section 19).

Brake light

8 If either or both brake lights fail to work, first check the fuse (see Section 5), and then the bulbs (see Section 9). If they are good, use jumper wires to connect the bulb in question directly to the battery terminals. If the light comes on, the problem lies in the wiring or connectors, or the switches in the circuit.

9 Check for battery voltage at the green/yellow wire terminal on the tail light wiring connectors, first with the front brake lever on, then with the rear brake pedal on. If voltage is present with one brake on but not the other, then the switch or its wiring is faulty. If voltage is present in both cases, check for continuity to earth (ground) in the green wire from the wiring connectors. If no voltage is indicated, check the wiring and connectors between the brake light and the brake switches, the fusebox, and the ignition switch, then check the switches themselves (see Section 14 for the brake light switches and Section 19 for the ignition switch).

Instrument and warning lights

10 See Section 17 for instrument and warning light bulb replacement.

Turn signals

11 See Section 11 for turn signal circuit check.

7 Headlight bulb and sidelight bulb – replacement

Note: *The headlight bulbs are of the quartz-halogen type. Do not touch the bulb glass as skin acids will shorten the bulb's service life. If the bulb is accidentally touched, it should be wiped carefully when cold with a rag soaked in methylated spirit and dried before fitting.*

⚠️ **Warning:** *Allow the bulb time to cool before removing it if the headlight has just been on.*

7.2a Disconnect the wiring connector . . .

7.2b . . . and remove the dust cover

Headlight

1 On F-1/FS-1 models onward (2001-on), remove the cockpit/fuel tank trim panel for the side being changed, then unhook the air duct from its hanger (see Chapter 8).

2 Disconnect the wiring connector from the back of the headlight and remove the rubber dust cover, noting how it fits **(see illustrations)**.

3 Release the bulb retaining clip, noting how it fits, then remove the bulb **(see illustrations)**.

4 Fit the new bulb, bearing in mind the information in the **Note** above. Make sure the tabs on the bulb fit correctly in the slots in the bulb housing, and secure it in position with the retaining clip.

5 Install the dust cover, making sure it is correctly seated and with the 'TOP' mark at the top, and connect the wiring connector.

6 Check the operation of the headlight. On F-1/FS-1 models onward (2001-on), hook up the air duct and install the trim panel (see Chapter 8).

HAYNES HINT *Always use a paper towel or dry cloth when handling new bulbs to prevent injury if the bulb should break and to increase bulb life.*

Sidelight

7 On F-X and F-Y (1999 and 2000) models, draw the bulbholder out of its socket in the base of the headlight, accessing it via the cut-out in the underside of the fairing **(see illustration)**.

7.3a Release the clip . . .

7.3b . . . and remove the bulb

7.7a Draw out the bulbholder . . .

Electrical system 9•7

Carefully pull the bulb out of the holder **(see illustration)**. Fit the new bulb in the bulbholder, then install the holder. Make sure it is correctly seated.

8 On F-1/FS-1 models onward (2001-on), twist the bulbholder anti-clockwise and draw it out of its socket in the centre of the headlight **(see illustration)**. Carefully pull the bulb out of the holder. Fit the new bulb in the bulbholder, then install the holder and turn it clockwise to secure it. Make sure it is correctly seated.

9 Check the operation of the sidelight.

8 Headlight assembly – removal and installation

Removal

1 Remove the fairing (see Chapter 8). On F-X and F-Y (1999 and 2000) models free the direct air induction (DAI) hose and the wiring from the clips **(see illustration)**.

7.7b ... and remove the bulb

2 Undo the four bolts securing the headlight assembly to the fairing and remove the headlight, noting how it fits **(see illustrations)**. On F-X and F-Y (1999 and 2000) models note the wiring clips secured by the bottom bolts.

3 On F-1/FS-1 models onward (2001-on), if required release the sub-loom wiring from its clips, then disconnect the wiring connectors and remove the sub-loom **(see illustration)**.

7.8 Turn the bulbholder anti-clockwise to release it from the headlight

Also remove the relays and the bank angle sensor if required.

Installation

4 Installation is the reverse of removal. Make sure all the wiring is correctly connected and secured. Check the operation of the headlight and sidelight. Check the headlight aim (see Chapter 1).

8.1 Release the hose and wiring from the clips (arrowed)

8.2a Headlight screws (arrowed) – F-X and F-Y models

8.2b Headlight screws (arrowed) – F-1/FS-1 models on

8.3 Disconnect the relevant connectors and free the wiring from the clips to remove the sub-loom

9•8 Electrical system

9.2 Remove the bulbholder from the tail light . . .

9.3 . . . and the bulb from the holder

9.6 Undo the bolts (arrowed) and detach the light . . .

9 Brake/tail light bulb and license plate bulb – replacement

Note: *It is a good idea to use a paper towel or dry cloth when handling the new bulb to prevent injury if it breaks, and to increase bulb life.*

Brake/tail light bulb

1 Remove the seat (pillion seat only on European FS models and US 2001-on models) (see Chapter 8).
2 Turn the bulbholder anti-clockwise and withdraw it from the tail light **(see illustration)**.
3 Carefully pull the bulb out of the socket **(see illustration)**. Check the socket terminals for corrosion and clean them if necessary. Install the new bulb by pushing it into the socket – it can be installed either way round.
4 Fit the bulbholder into the tail light and turn it clockwise to secure it.
5 Install the seat.

License plate light bulb (where fitted)

6 Unscrew the bolts securing the license plate bracket and light and detach them from the rear mudguard **(see illustration)**.
7 Undo the screws on the back of the light and detach the lens cover and lens **(see illustration)**.
8 Push the bulb into the holder and twist it anti-clockwise to remove it. Check the socket terminals for corrosion and clean them if necessary. Line up the pins of the new bulb with the slots in the socket, then push the bulb in and turn it clockwise until it locks into place. *It is a good idea to use a paper towel or dry cloth when handling the new bulb to prevent injury if the bulb should break and to increase bulb life.*
9 Fit the lens and its cover back onto the light. Secure the light to the bracket, then fit the assembly back on the mudguard.

10 Tail light assembly – removal and installation

Removal

Tail light

1 Remove the seat cowling (see Chapter 8).
2 On European F models and US 1999 and 2000 models undo the screws securing the tail light in the seat cowling and remove it, noting how it fits **(see illustration)**. Remove the mounting brackets if required by undoing their screws, noting how they locate on the pegs.
3 On European FS models and US 2001-on models turn the bulbholders anti-clockwise and withdraw them from the tail light **(see illustration)**.
4 Unscrew the nuts securing the tail light assembly and carefully withdraw it from the back of the bike, noting the washers and the wiring clip **(see illustration 10.3)**. Check the

9.7 . . . then undo the screws and detach the lens

10.2 Undo the screws (arrowed) and remove the light

10.3 Release the bulbholders (A) then undo the nuts (B)

Electrical system 9•9

10.6 License plate light wiring connector (A), rear turn signal wiring connectors (B)

11.2 Turn signal relay (arrowed) – F-X and F-Y models

condition of the rubber mounts and replace them with new ones if they are damaged, deformed or deteriorated.

License plate light (where fitted)

5 Remove the seat (see Chapter 8).
6 Trace the wiring and disconnect it at the connector **(see illustration)**. Feed the wiring through to the light.
7 Unscrew the bolts securing the license plate bracket and light and detach them from the rear mudguard **(see illustration 9.6)**. If required, undo the screws and separate the light from the bracket **(see illustration 9.7)**.

Installation

8 Installation is the reverse of removal. Check the operation of the tail and brake lights.

11 Turn signal circuit – check

Note: *On US models the front turn signals also function as running lights and have dual filament bulbs. When checking for faults, refer to the wiring diagram at the end of this Chapter.*
1 Most turn signal problems are the result of a burned out bulb or corroded socket. This is especially true when the turn signals function properly in one direction, but fail to flash in the other direction. If this is the case, first check the bulbs, the sockets and the wiring connectors. If all the turn signals fail to work, first check the fuse (see Section 5), and then the relay (see below). If they are good, the problem lies in the wiring or connectors, or the switch. Refer to Section 20 for the switch testing procedures, and also to the wiring diagrams at the end of this Chapter.
2 To check the relay, on F-X and F-Y (1999 and 2000) models remove the seat cowling (see Chapter 8) – the relay is mounted on the right-hand side of the rear sub-frame **(see illustration)**. On F-1/FS-1 models onward (2001-on) remove the fairing (see Chapter 8) – the relay is mounted on the back of the headlight unit in the centre **(see illustration 6.3)**. The easiest way to tell if the relay is faulty is to substitute it with another one, if available. If the turn signals then work, replace the faulty relay with a new one.
3 If a substitute is not available, or if it does not solve the problem, displace the relay and disconnect the wiring connector. Check for battery voltage at the black/brown (F-X and F-Y) or white/green (F-1/FS-1 onward) wire terminal on the loom side of the connector with the ignition ON. Turn the ignition OFF when the check is complete. If no voltage was present, check the wiring from the relay to the ignition (main) switch (via the fusebox) for continuity. Where the relay has a green wire, check the green wire from the connector for continuity to earth (ground). Repair or renew the wiring or connectors as necessary.
4 Using a jumper wire, connect between the black/brown and grey wire terminals on the connector. Turn the ignition ON and operate the turn signal switch. If the turn signals now work, replace the relay with a new one.
5 If the turn signals still don't work, use the appropriate wiring diagram at the end of this Chapter and check the wiring and connectors between the relay, turn signal switch and turn signal lights for continuity. Repair or renew the wiring, connectors or switch as necessary.

12 Turn signal bulbs – replacement

1 Remove the screw securing the lens and detach the lens from the housing, noting how it fits **(see illustrations)**. Remove the rubber gasket if it is free, and discard it if it is damaged, deformed or deteriorated.
2 Push the bulb into the holder and twist it anti-clockwise to remove it **(see illustration)**.

12.1a Remove the screw . . .

12.1b . . . and detach the lens . . .

12.2 . . . then remove the bulb from the holder – European FS models shown

9•10 Electrical system

13.2 Disconnect the wiring connector (left-hand connector shown)

13.3 Undo the screw (arrowed), noting the plate

13.5 Rear turn signal wiring connectors

13.6 Rear turn signal nut (arrowed)

Check the socket terminals for corrosion and clean them if necessary. Line up the pins of the new bulb with the slots in the socket, then push the bulb in and turn it clockwise until it locks into place. **Note:** *It is a good idea to use a paper towel or dry cloth when handling the new bulb to prevent injury if the bulb should break and to increase bulb life.*

3 Fit a new rubber gasket onto the housing if required, and make sure it is properly seated and does not get pinched by the lens. On European F models and US 1999 and 2000 models, fit the lens onto the housing, locating the cutout on the outer end of the lens over the tab on the housing, and install the screw. On European FS models and US 2001-on models, fit the lens onto the housing, locating the tab on the inner end of the lens into the cutout on the housing, and install the screw. Do not overtighten the screw as it is easy to strip the threads or crack the lens.

13 Turn signal assemblies – removal and installation

Removal

Front turn signals

1 Remove the fairing side panel (see Chapter 8).
2 On F-1/FS-1 models onward (2001-on) disconnect the turn signal wiring connector **(see illustration)**. Carefully draw the wiring through to the stem.
3 Unscrew the nut securing the stem to the inside of the fairing and remove the mounting plate **(see illustration)**. Remove the turn signal, taking care as you draw the wiring through.

Rear turn signals

4 Remove the seat (see Chapter 8).

5 Disconnect the turn signal wiring connector(s) **(see illustration or 10.6)**. Carefully draw the wiring through to the stem under the mudguard, taking care not to snag it.
6 Unscrew the nut securing the stem to the inside of the rear mudguard and remove the mounting plate **(see illustration)**. Remove the turn signal, again taking care as you draw the wiring through.

Installation

7 Installation is the reverse of removal. Check the operation of the turn signals.

14 Brake light switches – check and replacement

Circuit check

1 Before checking the switches, and if not already done, check the brake light circuit (see Section 6, Steps 8 and 9).
2 The front brake light switch is mounted on the underside of the brake master cylinder. Disconnect the wiring connectors from the switch **(see illustration)**. Using a continuity tester, connect the probes to the terminals of the switch. With the brake lever at rest, there should be no continuity. With the brake lever applied, there should be continuity. If the switch does not behave as described, replace it with a new one.
3 The rear brake light switch is mounted on the inside of the right-hand riders footrest bracket, above the brake pedal **(see illustration)**. Remove the seat to access the wiring connector (see Chapter 8). Trace the wiring from the switch and disconnect it at the connector **(see illustration)**. Using a continuity tester, connect the probes to the terminals on the switch side of the wiring connector. With the brake pedal at rest, there should be no continuity. With the brake pedal applied, there should be continuity. If the switch does not behave as described, replace it with a new one, although check first that switch is adjusted correctly (see Step 10).
4 If the switches are good, check for voltage at the black/brown wire terminal on the connector with the ignition switch ON – there

14.2 Front brake switch wiring connectors (arrowed)

14.3a Rear brake light switch (arrowed)

14.3b Rear brake light switch wiring connector

Electrical system 9•11

14.6 Front brake switch screw (arrowed)

15.2 Remove the blanking plug to access the bolt (arrowed)

15.3 Note how the pegs locate in the grommets (arrow)

should be battery voltage. If there's no voltage present, check the wiring between the switch and the ignition switch via the fusebox (see the *wiring diagrams* at the end of this Chapter). If voltage is present, check the green/yellow wire for continuity to the brake light bulb wiring connector, referring to the relevant Wiring Diagram. Repair or renew the wiring as necessary.

Switch replacement

Front brake lever switch

5 The switch is mounted on the underside of the brake master cylinder. Disconnect the wiring connectors from the switch **(see illustration 14.2)**.
6 Remove the single screw securing the switch to the master cylinder and remove the switch **(see illustration)**.
7 Installation is the reverse of removal. The switch isn't adjustable.

Rear brake pedal switch

8 The rear brake light switch is mounted on the inside of the right-hand riders footrest bracket, above the brake pedal **(see illustration 14.3a)**. Remove the seat to access the wiring connector (see Chapter 8). Trace the wiring from the switch and disconnect it at the connector **(see illustration 14.3b)**.
9 Detach the lower end of the switch spring from the brake pedal, then either release the switch with its adjustment nut from the mounting by squeezing the tabs on the underside of the nut, or thread the switch itself out of the nut, leaving the nut in the mounting. Displace the footrest bracket by unscrewing its bolts for better access if required.
10 Installation is the reverse of removal. Make sure the brake light is activated just before the rear brake pedal takes effect. If adjustment is necessary, hold the switch body and turn the adjustment nut as required (either raising or lowering the switch) until the brake light is activated correctly. If the footrest bracket was displaced, tighten the bolts to the torque setting specified at the beginning of the Chapter.

15 Instrument cluster – removal and installation

Removal

F-X and F-Y (1999 and 2000) models

1 Remove the cockpit trim panels (see Chapter 8).
2 Remove the blanking plug from the bottom of the instrument cluster to access the mounting bolt **(see illustration)**.
3 Unscrew the bolt, then draw the instrument cluster down to free the top corner mounting lugs from the grommets **(see illustration)**.
4 Disconnect the wiring connector when it is accessible and manoeuvre the cluster out of the fairing **(see illustration)**. Note the collar for the bolt fitted in the mounting grommet.

F-1/FS-1 models onward (2001-on)

5 Remove the fairing (see Chapter 8).
6 Trace the wiring from the instrument cluster and disconnect it at the connectors **(see illustration)**.
7 Undo three screws and remove the washers securing the instrument cluster, then displace it from the bracket **(see illustration)**. Note the rubber grommets fitted in the mounts.

Installation

8 Installation is the reverse of removal. Check the rubber grommets for damage, deformation and deterioration and replace them with new ones if necessary. Make sure that the wiring connectors are correctly routed and secured.

16 Instruments and speed sensor – check and replacement

Instrument cluster – power check

1 If none of the instruments or displays are working, first check the fuse (see Section 5).
2 If the fuse is good, on F-X and F-Y (1999 and 2000) models displace the instrument cluster (see Section 15) and disconnect the wiring connector **(see illustration 15.4)**. On F-1/FS-1 models onward (2001-on) remove the fairing (see Chapter 8), then trace the wiring from the instrument cluster and

15.4 Disconnect the wiring connector

15.6 Disconnect the wiring connectors . . .

15.7 . . . then undo the screws (arrowed) and remove the instruments

9•12 Electrical system

disconnect it at the connectors **(see illustration 15.6)**. Check the connectors for loose or broken connections.

3 To check the power input line, check for battery voltage between the black/brown wire terminal on the wiring loom side of the connector and a good earth (ground) with the ignition switch ON. There should be battery voltage. If there is no voltage, refer to the wiring diagrams and check the black/brown circuit for loose or broken connections or a damaged wire.

4 To check the back-up power line, check for battery voltage between the red or red/green (according to model) wire terminal on the wiring loom side of the connector and a good earth (ground) with the ignition switch OFF. There should be battery voltage. If there is no voltage, refer to the wiring diagrams and check the red or red/green circuit for loose or broken connections or a damaged wire.

5 If there is voltage, and to check the earth(ground) line, check for continuity between the green/black wire terminal on the loom side of the instrument cluster wiring connector and earth (ground). If there is no continuity, check the circuit for loose or broken connections or a damaged wire.

6 On F-1/FS-1 models onward (2001-on), if no faults can be found, also check the wiring between the cluster connectors and the cluster itself for continuity – there is a panel on the back of the cluster that can be removed to access the internal connectors.

Speedometer and speed sensor

Check

7 First check the fuse (see Section 5).
8 Raise or remove the fuel tank (see Chapter 4). Trace the wiring from the speed sensor, which is mounted on the crankcase behind the cylinders, and disconnect it at the 3-pin connector **(see illustration)**. With the ignition switch ON, check for battery voltage between the black and green wire terminals on the wiring loom side of the connector. If no voltage, refer to the wiring diagrams and check the circuit for loose or broken connections or a damaged wire.

16.8 Trace the wiring from the speed sensor (arrowed) and disconnect the wiring connector

9 If there is voltage, reconnect the wiring connector, then connect a voltmeter between the pink and green wire terminals on the connector. With the machine on its centrestand or an auxiliary stand, transmission in neutral and the ignition switch ON, turn the rear wheel by hand and check that a fluctuating voltage reading between 0 – 5 volts is obtained. If no reading is obtained, and the wiring is good, then the speed sensor is faulty.

10 If a reading is obtained, on F-X and F-Y (1999 and 2000) models displace the instrument cluster (see Section 15) and disconnect the wiring connector **(see illustration 15.4)**. On F-1/FS-1 models onward (2001-on) remove the fairing (see Chapter 8), then trace the wiring from the instrument cluster and disconnect it at the connectors **(see illustration 15.6)**. Check the connectors for loose or broken connections, then repeat the check in Step 8, but connect the meter between the pink/green and green/black wire terminals on the loom side of the cluster wiring connector. If no fluctuating voltage is obtained, check for continuity in the wiring between the speed sensor wiring connector and the instrument cluster wiring connector(s), referring to the Wiring Diagrams and noting that the wires change colour at the sub-loom wiring connector after the speed sensor. On F-1/FS-1 models onward (2001-on) also check the wiring between the connectors on the cluster side and the cluster itself for continuity – there is a panel on the back of the cluster that can be removed to access the internal connectors.

11 If the wiring is all good, either the speedometer (F-X and F-Y, 1999 and 2000) models or the LCD display (F-1/FS-1 models onward, 2001-on) is faulty. On F-X and F-Y (1999 and 2000) models, special instruments are required to properly check the operation of the speedometer. Take the machine to a Honda dealer service department or other qualified repair shop for diagnosis. If the meter is good, replace the PCB with a new one. On F-1/FS-1 models onward (2001-on), no replacement parts are available for the instrument cluster.

Replacement

Speedometer

12 Remove the instrument cluster (see Section 15).
13 On F-X and F-Y (1999 and 2000) models, remove the cover screws from the back of the housing and lift off the rear cover **(see illustrations)**.
14 Carefully remove the printed circuit board (PCB) from the housing, noting how it fits – the instruments will come with it **(see illustration)**. Separate the instrument(s) from the PCB (each is secured by two small screws) and replace the faulty component with a new one.
15 On F-1/FS-1 models onward (2001-on), no replacement parts are available for the instrument cluster.
16 Installation is the reverse of removal.

Speed Sensor

17 The speed sensor is mounted on the crankcase behind the cylinders on the left-hand side. Depending on the tools you have available, the size of your hands and your general dexterity, you might be able to access the sensor from the left-hand side of the engine after removing the fairing side panel (see Chapter 8). Otherwise you will have to remove either the carburettors or the throttle bodies (according to model – see Chapter 4) and access the sensor from the top.
18 Trace the wiring from the sensor and disconnect it at the 3-pin connector **(see illustration 16.8)**.
19 Unscrew the sensor mounting bolts and

16.13a Undo the screws (arrowed) . . .

16.13b . . . and remove the rear cover . . .

16.14 . . . then carefully lift out the PCB

Electrical system 9•13

16.19a Undo the bolts and remove the sensor

16.19b Replace the O-ring with a new one

remove the sensor **(see illustration)**. Remove and discard its O-ring as a new one must be used **(see illustration)**. Plug the sensor orifice with clean rag to prevent anything falling into the engine.

20 Installation is the reverse of removal, using a new O-ring.

Tachometer

Check

21 First check the fuse (see Section 5).
22 If the fuse is good, on F-X and F-Y (1999 and 2000) models displace the instrument cluster (see Section 15) and disconnect the wiring connector **(see illustration 15.4)**. On F-1/FS-1 models onward (2001-on) remove the fairing (see Chapter 8), then trace the wiring from the instrument cluster and disconnect it at the connectors **(see illustration 15.6)**. Check the connectors for loose or broken connections.
23 On F-X and F-Y (1999 and 2000) models, check for battery voltage between the yellow/green and green/black wire terminals on the loom side of the connector with the ignition ON. If no voltage is present, refer to the wiring diagrams and check the circuit for loose or broken connections or a damaged wire. If voltage is present, replace the instrument cluster printed circuit board (PCB) with a new one.
24 On F-1/FS-1 models onward (2001-on), switch the ignition ON – the tachometer needle should swing right round to the end of its scale then swing back to zero. If not, check the power input line (see above).
25 If the power line to the cluster is good, check the tachometer input peak voltage. Honda specify their own Imrie diagnostic tester (model 625), or the peak voltage adapter (Pt. No. 07HGJ-0020100) with an aftermarket digital multimeter having an impedance of 10 M-ohm/DCV minimum, for this test. Connect the positive (+) lead of the voltmeter and peak voltage adapter arrangement to the yellow/green wire terminal on the loom side of the connector and the negative (–) lead to the green wire terminal. Start the engine and measure the tachometer input peak voltage, which should be at least 10.5 volts. If the peak voltage is normal then the instrument cluster printed circuit board could be faulty, though it is worth checking

the wiring between the connectors and the cluster itself for continuity – there is a panel on the back of the cluster that can be removed to access the internal connectors.
26 If there is no reading, remove the seat (see Chapter 8), and disconnect the ECM wiring connector (see Chapter 4). Check for continuity in the yellow/green wire between the ECM wiring connector and the instrument cluster wiring connector. If there is no continuity there is a break in the wire or faulty connector. Refer to the wiring diagrams and trace and rectify the fault.

Replacement

27 Remove the instrument cluster (see Section 15).
28 On F-X and F-Y (1999 and 2000) models, remove the cover screws from the back of the housing and lift off the rear cover **(see illustrations 16.13a and b)**.
29 Carefully remove the printed circuit board (PCB) from the housing, noting how it fits – the instruments will come with it **(see illustration 16.14)**. Separate the instrument(s) from the PCB (each is secured by two small screws) and replace the faulty component with a new one.
30 On F-1/FS-1 models onward (2001-on), no replacement parts are available for the instrument cluster.
31 Installation is the reverse of removal.

Coolant temperature gauge – F-X and F-Y (1999 and 2000) models

Check

32 See Chapter 3.

Replacement

33 Remove the instrument cluster (see Section 15).
34 Remove the cover screws from the back of the housing and lift off the rear cover **(see illustrations 16.13a and b)**.
35 Carefully remove the printed circuit board (PCB) from the housing, noting how it fits – the instruments will come with it **(see illustration 16.14)**. Separate the instrument(s) from the PCB (each is secured by two small screws) and replace the faulty component with a new one.
36 Installation is the reverse of removal.

Fuel warning light

37 Refer to Chapter 4, Section 19 for checking details.
38 To renew the bulb on F-X and F-Y models (1999 and 2000) refer to Section 17. The LCD fitted to F-1/FS-1 models onward (2001-on) is not available separately from the instrument cluster.

LCD display – F-1/FS-1 models onward (2001-on)

Check

39 If the display is not working at all, check the instrument cluster power input (see above). If the power lines are good, then either the printed circuit board (PCB) or the LCD display unit is faulty.

Replacement

40 The instrument cluster is only available as a unit with no individual components available separately.

17 Instrument and warning light bulbs – replacement

F-X and F-Y (1999 and 2000) models

1 Remove the instrument cluster (see Section 16).
2 Remove the blanking cap from the relevant bulb location **(see illustration)**. Using a screwdriver turn the bulb 1/8 of a turn (45°) and pull it out of the instrument housing. Install a new bulb and turn it 1/8 of a turn (45°) to lock it, then fit the cap.
3 Install the instrument cluster (see Section 16).

F-1/FS-1 models onward (2001-on)

4 All instrument and warning lights are LED's, which are part of the printed circuit board and are not available individually. If one of the LED's fails the entire instrument cluster must be renewed as no individual components are listed as being available.

17.2 Remove the relevant blanking plug to access the bulb

9•14 Electrical system

18.3a Pull back the rubber . . .

18.3b . . . then remove the terminal screw and detach the wiring

18.8 Unscrew and remove the switch

18 Oil pressure switch – check, removal and installation

Check

1 The oil pressure warning light should come on when the ignition (main) switch is turned ON and extinguish a few seconds after the engine is started. If the oil pressure warning light comes on whilst the engine is running, stop the engine immediately and carry out an oil level check, and if the level is correct, an oil pressure check (see Chapter 1).
2 If the oil pressure warning light does not come on when the ignition is turned on, check the bulb (see Section 17) and fuse (see Section 5).
3 The oil pressure switch is screwed into the crankcase on the right-hand side. Remove the right-hand fairing side panel for access (see Chapter 8). Pull the rubber cover off the switch and remove the screw securing the wiring connector **(see illustrations)**. With the ignition switched ON, earth (ground) the wire on the crankcase and check that the warning light comes on. If the light comes on, the switch is defective and must be replaced with a new one.
4 If the light still does not come on, check for voltage at the wire terminal. If there is no voltage present, check the wire between the switch, the instrument cluster and fusebox for continuity (see the *wiring diagrams* at the end of this Chapter).
5 If the warning light comes on whilst the engine is running, yet the oil pressure is satisfactory, remove the wire from the oil pressure switch. With the wire detached and the ignition switched ON the light should be out. If it is illuminated, the wire between the switch and instrument cluster must be earthed (grounded) at some point. If the wiring is good, the switch must be assumed faulty and replaced.

Removal

6 The oil pressure switch is screwed into the crankcase on the right-hand side. Depending on the tools you have available, the size of your hands and your general dexterity, you might be able to access the sensor from the right-hand side of the engine after removing the fairing side panel (see Chapter 8). Otherwise you will have to raise or remove the fuel tank and possibly remove either the carburettors or the throttle bodies (according to model – see Chapter 4) and access the sensor from the top.
7 Pull the rubber cover off the switch, then remove the screw securing the wiring connector **(see illustrations 18.3a and b)**.
8 Unscrew the oil pressure switch and withdraw it from the crankcase **(see illustration)**.

Installation

9 Apply a suitable sealant to the upper portion of the switch threads near the switch body, leaving the bottom 3 to 4 mm of thread clean. Install the switch in the crankcase and tighten it to the torque setting specified at the beginning of the Chapter **(see illustration 18.8)**. Attach the wiring connector and secure it with the screw, then fit the rubber cover **(see illustrations 18.3a and b)**.
10 Run the engine and check that the switch operates correctly without leakage.
11 Install the carburettors or throttle bodies, fuel tank or fairing side panel according to your removal method.

19 Ignition (main) switch – check, removal and installation

⚠ **Warning: To prevent the risk of short circuits, disconnect the battery negative (–ve) lead before making any ignition (main) switch checks.**

Check

1 On F-X and F-Y (1999 and 2000) models, remove the left-hand cockpit trim panel (see Chapter 8). Trace the wiring from the ignition switch and disconnect it at the 4-pin white connector inside the black rubber boot on the left-hand end of the instrument cluster, but note that if the connector is tight or you have large hands it may be wiser to remove the fairing for better access – if you are applying a lot of 'pull' to the connector with the fairing in place there is the possibility of damaging it or yourself.
2 On F-1/FS-1 models onward (2001-on), remove the fairing (see Chapter 8). Trace the wiring from the ignition switch and disconnect it at the 4-pin white connector inside the black rubber boot below the instrument cluster **(see illustration)**.
3 Using an ohmmeter or a continuity tester, check the continuity of the connector terminal pairs (see the *Wiring Diagrams* at the end of this Chapter). Continuity should exist between the terminals connected by a solid line on the diagram when the switch is in the indicated position.
4 If the switch fails any of the tests, replace it with a new one.

Removal

Note: *On European models, two shear-head bolts mount the ignition switch to the underside of the top yoke – these bolts can only be used once. Obtain new bolts before starting. US models use standard bolts.*

5 On F-X and F-Y (1999 and 2000) models, remove the left-hand cockpit trim panel (see Chapter 8). Trace the wiring from the ignition switch and disconnect it at the 4-pin white connector inside the black rubber boot on the left-hand end of the instrument cluster, but note that if the connector is tight or you have large hands it may be wiser to remove the fairing for better access – if you are applying a lot of 'pull' to the connector with the fairing in place there is the possibility of damaging it or

19.2 Ignition switch wiring connector

Electrical system 9•15

yourself. Work back along the harness, freeing it from any clips and ties, noting its correct routing.

6 On F-1/FS-1 models onward (2001-on), remove the fairing (see Chapter 8). Trace the wiring from the ignition switch and disconnect it at the 4-pin white connector inside the black rubber boot below the instrument cluster **(see illustration 19.2)**. Work back along the harness, freeing it from any clips and ties, noting its correct routing.

7 On European models heads of the bolts must be drifted round using a suitable punch or drift, or drilled or ground off, before the switch can be removed, and so the top yoke must be removed as described below. On US models with standard bolts, you should be able to get at them with the switch in situ. If not you will have to remove the top yoke as described below.

8 Remove the fuel tank (see Chapter 4) and the fairing (see Chapter 8). This will prevent the possibility of damage should a tool slip.

9 Displace the handlebars from the top yoke (see Chapter 6). There is no need to remove assemblies from the handlebars.

10 Displace the top yoke from the forks and steering stem as described in Chapter 1, Section 18, following the relevant Steps.

11 On models fitted with the HISS immobiliser system, undo the screws securing the receiver around the ignition switch and remove it, noting how it fits **(see illustration)**.

12 Remove the bolts (see Step 7) and withdraw the switch from the top yoke.

Installation

13 Installation is the reverse of removal. On European models tighten the new bolts until the heads shear off. On US models tighten the bolts to the torque setting specified at the beginning of the Chapter. Make sure wiring connectors are securely connected and correctly routed.

14 Fit the top yoke onto the steering stem and forks as described in Chapter 1, Section 18, following the relevant Steps.

15 Install the handlebars (see Chapter 6), the fuel tank (see Chapter 4), and the fairing (see Chapter 8) as required.

20 Handlebar switches – check

1 Generally speaking, the switches are reliable and trouble-free. Most troubles, when they do occur, are caused by dirty or corroded contacts, but wear and breakage of internal parts is a possibility that should not be overlooked. If breakage does occur, the entire switch and related wiring harness will have to be replaced with a new one, as individual parts are not available.

2 The switches can be checked for continuity using an ohmmeter or a continuity test light. Always disconnect the battery negative (–ve) cable, which will prevent the possibility of a short circuit, before making the checks.

19.11 Immobiliser receiver screw (A), ignition switch bolt (B)

3 On F-X and F-Y (1999 and 2000) models, remove the left-hand cockpit trim panel (see Chapter 8). Trace the wiring from the relevant switch and disconnect it at the connector inside the black rubber boot on the left-hand end of the instrument cluster, but note that if the connector is tight or you have large hands it may be wiser to remove the fairing for better access – if you are applying a lot of 'pull' to the connector with the fairing in place there is the possibility of damaging it or yourself.

4 On F-1/FS-1 models onward (2001-on), remove the fairing (see Chapter 8). Trace the wiring from the relevant switch and disconnect it at the connector inside the black rubber boot below the instrument cluster.

5 Check for continuity between the terminals of the switch connector with the switch in the various positions (i.e. switch off – no continuity, switch on – continuity) – see the *wiring diagrams* at the end of this Chapter. Continuity should exist between the terminals connected by a solid line on the diagram when the switch is in the indicated position.

6 If the continuity check indicates a problem exists, refer to Section 21, displace the switch housing and spray the switch contacts with electrical contact cleaner (there is no need to remove the switch completely). If they are accessible, the contacts can be scraped clean with a knife or polished with crocus cloth. If switch components are damaged or broken, it will be obvious when the switch is disassembled.

21 Handlebar switches – removal and installation

Removal

1 On F-X and F-Y (1999 and 2000) models, if the switch is to be removed from the bike, rather than just displaced from the handlebar, remove the left-hand cockpit trim panel (see Chapter 8). Trace the wiring from the relevant switch and disconnect it at the connector inside the black rubber boot on the left-hand end of the instrument cluster, but note that if the connector is tight or you have large hands it may be wiser to remove the fairing for better access – if you are applying a lot of 'pull' to the connector with the fairing in place there is the possibility of damaging it or yourself. Work back along the harness, freeing it from any clips and ties, noting its correct routing.

2 On F-1/FS-1 models onward (2001-on), if the switch is to be removed from the bike, rather than just displaced from the handlebar, remove the fairing (see Chapter 8). Trace the wiring from the relevant switch and disconnect it at the connector inside the black rubber boot below the instrument cluster. Work back along the harness, freeing it from any clips and ties, noting its correct routing.

3 Disconnect the two wires from the brake light switch (if removing the right-hand switch) or the clutch switch and the horn (if removing the left-hand switch – the horn is on the underside of the bottom yoke) **(see illustration 14.2 or 24.2)**.

4 When working on the right-hand switch, refer to Chapter 4 for removal of the throttle cables, which involves separating the switch from the handlebars. Free the throttle cables from the twistgrip and remove them from the housing.

5 When working on the left-hand switch, unscrew the two handlebar switch screws and free the switch from the handlebar by separating the halves **(see illustrations)**. On

21.5a Undo the screws (arrowed) . . .

21.5b . . . then separate the halves . . .

9•16 Electrical system

21.5c ... and detach the choke cable (arrowed)

22.2a Neutral switch (arrowed)

22.2b Disconnect the wiring connector

F-X and F-Y (1999 and 2000) models, free the choke cable and lever from the housing **(see illustration)**. On F-1/FS-1 models onward (2001-on), note the blanking cap that fits in the housing.

Installation

6 Installation is the reverse of removal. Make sure the locating pin in the switch housing locates in the hole in the handlebar. Refer to Chapter 4 for installation of the throttle and choke cables.

22 Neutral switch – check, removal and installation

Check

1 Before checking the electrical circuit, check the bulb (see Section 17) and fuse (see Section 5).
2 The switch is located in the left-hand side of the transmission casing below the front sprocket cover **(see illustration)**. Detach the wiring connector from the switch **(see illustration)**. Make sure the transmission is in neutral.
3 With the connector disconnected and the ignition switch ON, the neutral light should be out. If not, the wire between the connector and instrument cluster must be earthed (grounded) at some point.
4 Check for continuity between the switch terminal and the crankcase. With the transmission in neutral, there should be continuity. With the transmission in gear, there should be no continuity. If the tests prove otherwise, then the switch is faulty.
5 If the continuity tests prove the switch is good, check for voltage at the wire terminal using. If there's no voltage present, check the wire between the switch, the instrument cluster and fusebox (see the *wiring diagrams* at the end of this Chapter).

Removal

6 The switch is located in the left-hand side of the transmission casing below the front sprocket cover **(see illustration 22.2a)**.

7 Detach the wiring connector from the switch **(see illustration 22.2b)**.
8 Clean the area around the switch, then unscrew it from the crankcase. Discard the sealing washer as a new one should be used.

Installation

9 Install the switch using a new washer and tighten it to the torque setting specified at the beginning of the Chapter.
10 Connect the wiring connector and check the operation of the neutral light **(see illustration 22.2b)**.
11 Install the fairing side panel (see Chapter 6).

23 Sidestand switch – check and replacement

Check

1 The sidestand switch is mounted on the back of the sidestand. The switch is part of the safety circuit which prevents or stops the engine running if the transmission is in gear whilst the sidestand is down, and prevents the engine from starting if the transmission is in gear unless the sidestand is up, and unless the clutch is pulled in. Before checking the electrical circuit, check the fuse (see Section 5).
2 Raise or remove the fuel tank (see Chapter 4) to access the wiring connector. Trace the wiring back from the switch and disconnect at

23.2 Sidestand switch wiring connector

the 2-pin green wiring connector inside the rubber boot **(see illustration)**.
3 Check the operation of the switch using an ohmmeter or continuity test light. Connect the meter between the terminals on the switch side of the connector. With the sidestand up there should be continuity (zero resistance) between the terminals, and with the stand down there should be no continuity (infinite resistance).
4 If the switch does not perform as expected, it is faulty and must be replaced with a new one.
5 If the switch is good, check the wiring and connectors between the various components in the starter safety circuit using a continuity tester (see the *wiring diagrams* at the end of this book). Also check for voltage at the green/white wire terminal on the loom side of the connector with the ignition ON – there should be battery voltage. Repair or renew the wiring as required.

Replacement

6 The sidestand switch is mounted on the back of the sidestand. Raise or remove the fuel tank (see Chapter 4) to access the wiring connector. Trace the wiring back from the switch and disconnect at the 2-pin green wiring connector inside the rubber boot **(see illustration 23.2)**. Work back along the switch wiring, freeing it from any clips and ties, noting its correct routing.
7 Unscrew the switch bolt and remove the switch from the stand, noting how it fits **(see illustration)**. Note that Honda specify that the

23.7 Sidestand switch mounting bolt (arrowed)

Electrical system 9•17

24.2 Clutch switch wiring connectors (arrowed)

24.5 Release the catch via the hole in the underside of the bracket and withdraw the switch

switch bolt be renewed every time it is disturbed – the new bolt has a locking compound already applied to its threads.

8 Fit the new switch onto the sidestand, making sure the pin locates in the hole in the sidestand, and the lug on the stand bracket locates into the cutout in the switch body. Secure the switch with a new bolt and tighten it to the torque setting specified at the beginning of the Chapter **(see illustration 23.7)**.

9 Make sure the wiring is correctly routed up to the connector and retained by any clips and ties.

10 Reconnect the wiring connector and check the operation of the sidestand switch **(see illustration 23.2)**.

11 Install the fuel tank (see Chapter 4).

24 Clutch switch –
check and replacement

Check

1 The clutch switch is mounted in the clutch lever bracket. The switch is part of the safety circuit which prevents or stops the engine running if the transmission is in gear whilst the sidestand is down, and prevents the engine from starting if the transmission is in gear unless the sidestand is up and the clutch lever is pulled in. The switch isn't adjustable.

2 To check the switch, disconnect the wiring connectors from it **(see illustration)**. Connect the probes of an ohmmeter or a continuity tester to the two switch terminals. With the clutch lever pulled in, continuity should be indicated. With the clutch lever out, no continuity (infinite resistance) should be indicated.

3 If the switch is good, check the other components in the starter circuit as described in the relevant sections of this Chapter. If all components are good, check the wiring between the various components (see the *wiring diagrams* at the end of this book).

Replacement

4 The clutch switch is mounted in the clutch lever bracket.

5 Disconnect the wiring connectors from the switch **(see illustration 24.2)**. Release the switch from the bracket by pressing up on the small catch via the opening in the underside of the lever bracket and draw it out **(see illustration)**.

6 Installation is the reverse of removal. Install the switch with the small catch at the bottom and press it in until the catch is felt to locate.

25 Diode –
check and replacement

Check

1 The diode is a small block that plugs into a connector in the fusebox, which is located under the seat. The diode is part of the safety circuit which prevents or stops the engine running if the transmission is in gear whilst the sidestand is down, and prevents the engine from starting if the transmission is in gear unless the sidestand is up and the clutch lever is pulled in.

2 Remove the seat (see Chapter 8), open the fusebox lid and pull the diode out of its socket **(see illustration)**.

3 Using an ohmmeter or continuity tester, connect the positive (+ve) probe to one of the outer terminals of the diode and the negative (–ve) probe to the middle terminal of the diode. The diode should show continuity. Now reverse the probes. The diode should show no continuity. Repeat the tests between the other outer terminal and the middle terminal. The same results should be achieved. If it doesn't behave as stated, replace the diode with a new one.

4 If the diode is good, check the other components in the starter circuit as described in the relevant sections of this Chapter. If all components are good, check the wiring between the various components (see the *wiring diagrams* at the end of this book).

Replacement

5 The diode is a small block that plugs into a connector in the fusebox, which is located under the seat.

6 Remove the seat (see Chapter 8), open the fusebox lid and pull the diode out of its socket **(see illustration 25.2)**.

7 Push the diode back into position to install it.

26 Horn –
check and replacement

Check

1 The horn is mounted on the bottom yoke – remove the fairing for access if required, though you should be able to get at it quite easily (see Chapter 8).

2 Unplug the wiring connectors from the horn **(see illustration)**. Using two jumper wires, apply battery voltage directly to the terminals on the horn. If the horn sounds, check the switch (see Section 21). Also check for voltage at the light green wire connector with the ignition ON and the horn button pressed. If voltage is present, check the green wire for continuity to earth. If no voltage was present, check the light green wire for continuity between the horn and the switch, and in the black/brown or white/green (according to model) wire from the switch to the fusebox, and then to the ignition switch (see the *wiring diagrams* at the end of this Chapter). With the

25.2 The diode (arrowed) is in the fusebox

26.2 Horn wiring connectors (A), horn mounting bolt (B)

9•18 Electrica system

27.2 Starter relay battery and starter motor leads (A) and wiring connector (B)

ignition switch ON, there should be voltage at the black/brown or white/green wire to the horn button in the left-hand switch gear.

3 If the horn doesn't sound, replace it with a new one.

Replacement

4 The horn is mounted on the bottom yoke – remove the fairing for access if required, though you should be able to get at it quite easily (see Chapter 8).

5 Unplug the wiring connectors from the horn **(see illustration 26.2)**. Unscrew the bolt securing the horn and remove it from the bike.

6 Install the horn and securely tighten the bolt. Connect the wiring to the horn. Check that it works, then install the fairing (see Chapter 8).

27 Starter relay – check and replacement

Check

1 If the starter circuit is faulty, first check the fuse (see Section 5).

2 The starter relay is located on the left-hand end of the battery **(see illustration)** – remove the seat for access (see Chapter 8).

3 Lift the rubber terminal cover and unscrew the bolt securing the starter motor lead; position the lead away from the relay terminal. With the ignition switch ON, the engine kill switch in the RUN position, and the transmission in neutral, press the starter switch. The relay should be heard to click.

4 If the relay doesn't click, switch off the ignition and remove the relay as described below; test it as follows.

5 Set a multimeter to the ohms x 1 scale and connect it across the relay's starter motor and battery lead terminals **(see illustration 27.2)**. There should be no continuity. Using a fully-charged 12 volt battery and two insulated jumper wires, connect the positive (+ve) terminal of the battery to the yellow/red wire terminal of the relay, and the negative (–ve) terminal to the green/red wire terminal of the relay. At this point the relay should be heard to click and the multimeter read 0 ohms (continuity). If this is the case the relay is proved good. If the relay does not click when battery voltage is applied and indicates no continuity (infinite resistance) across its terminals, it is faulty and must be replaced with a new one.

6 If the relay is good, check for continuity in the main lead from the battery to the relay. Also check that the terminals and connectors at each end of the lead are tight and corrosion-free. Next check for battery voltage at the yellow/red wire when the starter button is pressed. If there is no voltage, check the wiring between the relay wiring connector and the starter button. If voltage is present, check that there is continuity to earth in the green/red wire with the transmission in neutral, the clutch lever pulled in and the sidestand up (note that there will be a very slight resistance due to the diode). If there is no continuity, check the other components in the starter circuit as described in the relevant sections of this Chapter. If all components are good, check the wiring between the various components (see the *wiring diagrams* at the end of this book).

Replacement

7 The starter relay is located on the left-hand end of the battery **(see illustration 27.2)** – remove the seat for access (see Chapter 8).

8 Disconnect the battery terminals, remembering to disconnect the negative (–ve) terminal first.

9 Disconnect the relay wiring connector, then lift the insulating cover and unscrew the bolts securing the starter motor and battery leads to the relay and detach the leads **(see illustration 27.2)**. Remove the relay with its rubber sleeve from its mounting lug on the frame. If the relay is being replaced with a new one, remove the main fuse from the relay, and remove the relay from its sleeve.

10 Installation is the reverse of removal. Make sure the terminal bolts are securely tightened. Do not forget to fit the main fuse into the relay, if removed. Connect the negative (–ve) lead last when reconnecting the battery.

28 Starter motor – removal and installation

Removal

1 Remove the seat (see Chapter 8). Disconnect the battery negative (–ve) lead. The starter motor is mounted on the crankcase behind the cylinders on the left-hand side.

2 Drain the cooling system (see Chapter 1). Remove the thermostat housing (see Chapter 3).

3 Peel back the rubber terminal cover on the starter motor **(see illustration)**. Unscrew the nut securing the starter lead to the motor and detach the lead **(see illustration)**.

4 Unscrew the two bolts securing the starter motor to the crankcase, noting the earth lead secured by one of the bolts **(see illustration)**. Slide the starter motor out and remove it.

5 Remove the O-ring on the end of the starter motor and discard it as a new one must be used.

Installation

6 Fit a new O-ring onto the end of the starter motor, making sure it is seated in its groove **(see illustration)**. Apply a smear of engine oil to the O-ring to aid installation.

7 Manoeuvre the motor into position and slide

28.3a Pull back the terminal cover . . .

28.3b . . . then unscrew the nut and detach the lead

28.4 Unscrew the two bolts (arrowed), noting the earth lead, and remove the starter motor

Electrical system 9•19

28.6 Fit a new O-ring and lubricate it . . .

28.7 . . . then install the starter motor and secure it with the bolts

it into the crankcase (see illustration). Ensure that the starter motor teeth mesh correctly with those of the starter idle/reduction gear. Install the mounting bolts, not forgetting to secure the earth lead, and tighten them securely.

8 Connect the starter lead to the motor and secure it with the nut (see illustration 28.3b). Fit the rubber cover over the terminal (see illustration 28.3a).

9 Install the thermostat housing (see Chapter 3). Fill the cooling system (see Chapter 1).

10 Install the fuel tank (see Chapter 4). Connect the battery negative (–ve) lead and install the seat (see Chapter 8).

29 Starter motor – disassembly, inspection and reassembly

Disassembly

1 Remove the starter motor (see Section 28) (see illustration).

2 Note the alignment marks between the main housing and the front and rear covers, or make your own if they aren't clear (see illustration).

3 Unscrew the two long bolts, noting the O-rings, then remove the front cover from the motor along with its sealing ring (see illustration). Discard the sealing ring as a new

29.1 Starter motor assembly

1 Long bolts and O-rings
2 Front cover
3 Tabbed washer
4 Insulating washer
5 Shims
6 Sealing rings
7 Housing
8 Armature
9 Shims
10 Brushplate
11 Brush springs
12 Terminal bolt
13 Insulator
14 O-ring
15 Insulating washers
16 Plain washer
17 Nut
18 Rear cover

29.2 Note the alignment marks between the housing and the covers

29.3a Unscrew and remove the two bolts (arrowed) . . .

9•20 Electrical system

29.3b ... then remove the front cover and sealing ring (arrowed)

29.3c Remove the tabbed washer ...

29.3d ... and the shims

29.4 Remove the rear cover and its sealing ring (arrowed)

29.6a Check for continuity between the terminal and the brush ...

29.6b ... between the terminal and the cover ...

29.6c ... and between the brush and the brushplate

29.7a Unscrew the nut (A) and remove the large (B) and small (C) insulating washers and the O-ring (D)

29.7b Remove the brushplate assembly ...

29.7c ... and the insulator (arrowed)

one must be used. Remove the tabbed washer from the cover and slide the insulating washer and shim(s) from the front end of the armature, noting the number of shims and their correct fitted order (see illustrations).

4 Remove the rear cover from the motor along with its sealing ring (see illustration). Discard the sealing ring as a new one must be used. Remove the shim(s) from the rear end of the armature noting how many and their correct fitted positions (see illustration 29.17a).

5 Withdraw the armature from the main housing.

6 At this stage check for continuity between the terminal bolt and the brush with insulation (see illustration). There should be continuity (zero resistance). Check for continuity between the terminal bolt and the cover (see illustration). There should be no continuity (infinite resistance). Also check for continuity between the brush with uninsulated wire and the brushplate (see illustration). There should be continuity (zero resistance). If there is no continuity when there should be or vice versa, identify the faulty component and replace it with a new one.

7 Noting the correct fitted location of each component, unscrew the nut from the terminal bolt and remove the plain washer, the one large and two small insulating washers and the rubber O-ring (see illustration). Remove the brushplate assembly and terminal bolt from the rear cover, noting how it locates, and recover the insulator (see illustrations).

Electrical system 9•21

29.8 Place the brush spring ends onto the top of the brush housings and slide the brushes out

29.9 Measure the length of each brush

29.11a Continuity should exist between the commutator bars

8 Lift each brush spring end onto the top of each brush housing and slide the brushes out **(see illustration)**.

Inspection

9 The parts of the starter motor that are most likely to require attention are the brushes. Measure the length of each brush and compare the results to the Specifications at the beginning of the Chapter **(see illustration)**. If the brushes are worn beyond the service limit, replace the brushplate assembly with a new one. If the brushes are not worn excessively, nor cracked, chipped, or otherwise damaged, they may be re-used.

10 Inspect the commutator bars on the armature for scoring, scratches and discoloration. The commutator can be cleaned and polished with crocus cloth, but do not use sandpaper or emery paper. After cleaning, wipe away any residue with a cloth soaked in electrical system cleaner or denatured alcohol.

11 Using an ohmmeter or a continuity tester, check for continuity between the commutator bars **(see illustration)**. Continuity should exist between each bar and all of the others. Also, check for continuity between the commutator bars and the armature shaft **(see illustration)**. There should be no continuity (infinite resistance) between the commutator and the shaft. If the checks indicate otherwise, the armature is defective.

12 Check the starter pinion gear for worn, cracked, chipped and broken teeth. If the gear is damaged or worn, replace the starter motor.

13 Inspect the end covers for signs of cracks or wear. Check the needle bearing in the front cover and the bush in the rear cover for wear and damage **(see illustrations)**. Inspect the magnets in the main housing and the housing itself for cracks.

14 Inspect the insulating washers, O-ring, sealing rings and front cover oil seal for signs of damage deformation and deterioration and renew if necessary.

Reassembly

15 Slide the brushes back into position in their housings and locate the brush spring ends onto the outer ends of the brushes **(see illustration 29.8)**.

16 Fit the insulator into the rear cover **(see illustration 29.7c)**, then insert the terminal

29.11b There should be no continuity between the commutator bars and the armature shaft

bolt through it and the cover and fit the brushplate into the rear cover, making sure its tab is correctly located in the groove **(see illustration 29.7b and 29.13b)**. Slide the rubber O-ring and small insulating washers onto the terminal bolt, followed by the large insulating washer and the plain washer **(see illustration 29.7a)**. Fit the nut onto the terminal bolt and tighten it securely.

17 Fit the shims onto the rear of the armature

29.13a Check the needle bearing (arrowed) in the front cover ...

29.13b ... and the bush (arrowed) in the rear cover

9•22 Electrical system

29.17a Fit the shims onto the shaft . . .

29.17b . . . then fit the armature into the rear cover . . .

29.17c . . . making sure the brushes locate correctly onto the commutator

shaft **(see illustration)**. Apply a smear of grease to the end of the shaft. Insert the armature into the brushplate at an angle so that the brushes locate against the commutator, then straighten the armature, pushing the brushes back into their housings against the springs, and insert it into the rear cover so that the shaft end locates in its bore **(see illustrations)**.
18 Fit the sealing ring onto the rear of the housing **(see illustration)**. Slide the housing onto the armature, making sure the end with the cut-out faces the rear cover and aligns with the brushplate outer tab (aligning the marks between the cover and housing (Step 2) will help) **(see illustration)**, and noting that the magnets in the housing will forcibly draw it onto the armature.
19 Apply a smear of grease to the front cover oil seal lip. Fit the toothed washer into the cover so that its teeth are correctly located with the cover ribs **(see illustration 29.3c)**.
20 Slide the shim(s) onto the front end of the armature shaft then fit the insulating washer **(see illustration 29.3d)**. Fit the sealing ring onto the front of the housing **(see illustration)**. Slide the front cover into position, aligning the marks made on removal **(see illustration 29.3b)**.
21 Check the marks made on removal are correctly aligned then fit the long bolts, not forgetting the O-rings (and using new ones if necessary) and tighten them securely **(see illustration)**.
22 Install the starter motor (see Section 29).

30 Charging system testing – general information and precautions

1 If the performance of the charging system is suspect, the system as a whole should be checked first, followed by testing of the individual components. **Note:** *Before beginning the checks, make sure the battery is fully charged and that all system connections are clean and tight.*
2 Checking the output of the charging system and the performance of the various components within the charging system requires the use of a multimeter (with voltage, current and resistance checking facilities).
3 When making the checks, follow the procedures carefully to prevent incorrect connections or short circuits, as irreparable damage to electrical system components may result if short circuits occur.
4 If a multimeter is not available, the job of checking the charging system should be left to a Honda dealer.

31 Charging system – leakage and output test

1 If the charging system of the machine is thought to be faulty, remove the seat (see Chapter 8) and perform the following checks.

Leakage test

Caution: Always connect an ammeter in series, never in parallel with the battery, otherwise it will be damaged. Do not turn the ignition ON or operate the starter motor when the ammeter is connected – a sudden surge in current will blow the meter's fuse.
2 Turn the ignition switch OFF and disconnect the lead from the battery negative (–ve) terminal.
3 Set the multimeter to the Amps function and connect its negative (–ve) probe to the battery negative (–ve) terminal, and positive (+ve) probe to the disconnected negative (–ve)

29.18a Fit a new sealing ring onto the rear of the housing . . .

29.18b . . . then fit the housing onto the armature

29.20 Fit a new sealing ring onto the front of the housing

29.21 Fit the long bolts with their O-rings and tighten them securely

Electrical system 9•23

31.3 Checking the charging system leakage rate – connect the meter as shown

lead (see illustration). Always set the meter to a high amps range initially and then bring it down to the mA (milli Amps) range; if there is a high current flow in the circuit it may blow the meter's fuse.

4 If the current leakage indicated exceeds the amount specified at the beginning of the Chapter, there is probably a short circuit in the wiring. Use the wiring diagrams at the end of this book and systematically disconnect individual electrical components until the source is identified.

5 Disconnect the meter and connect the negative (–ve) lead to the battery, tightening it securely.

Output test

6 Start the engine and warm it up to normal operating temperature.
7 To check the voltage output, allow the engine to idle and connect a multimeter set to the 0-20 volts DC scale (voltmeter) across the terminals of the battery (positive (+ve) lead to battery positive (+ve) terminal, negative (–ve) lead to battery negative (–ve) terminal). Slowly increase the engine speed to 5000 rpm and note the reading obtained. The regulated voltage should be as specified at the beginning of the Chapter. If the voltage is outside these limits, check the alternator and the regulator (see Sections 32 and 33).

HAYNES HiNT *Clues to a faulty regulator are constantly blowing bulbs, with brightness varying considerably with engine speed, and battery overheating.*

32 Alternator – check, removal and installation

Check

1 Trace the wiring back from the alternator cover on the left-hand side of the engine and

32.1 Disconnect the alternator wiring connector

disconnect it the white wiring connector containing the three yellow wires in the rubber boot above the crankcase on the left-hand side – you may be able to access the connector after removing the left-hand fairing side panel if your hands aren't too big (see Chapter 8), otherwise raise the fuel tank (see Chapter 4) (see illustration). Check the connector terminals for corrosion and security.

2 Using a multimeter set to the ohms x 1 (ohmmeter) scale measure the resistance between each of the yellow wires on the alternator side of the connector, taking a total of three readings, then check for continuity between each terminal and ground (earth). If the stator coil windings are in good condition the three readings should be within the range shown in the Specifications at the start of this Chapter, and there should be no continuity (infinite resistance) between any of the terminals and ground (earth). If not, the alternator stator coil assembly is at fault and should be replaced with a new one. **Note:** *Before condemning the stator coils, check the fault is not due to damaged wiring between the connector and the coils.*

Removal

3 Remove the left-hand fairing side panel (see Chapter 8). Either drain the engine oil (see Chapter 1), or place a container under the engine to catch the oil that will come out when the alternator cover is removed. If your model has a centrestand place the bike on it so that

32.5 Alternator cover bolts (arrowed)

it is level – this minimises oil loss. If your model does not have a centrestand and you do not have an auxiliary stand it is best to drain the oil.

4 Trace the wiring back from the alternator cover on the left-hand side of the engine and disconnect it the white wiring connector containing the three yellow wires in the rubber boot above the crankcase on the left-hand side – you may be able to access the connector with the left-hand fairing side panel removed if your hands aren't too big, otherwise raise the fuel tank (see Chapter 4) (see illustration 32.1). Release the wiring from any clips or ties.

5 Working in a criss-cross pattern, evenly slacken the alternator cover bolts (see illustration). Lift the cover away from the engine, noting that it will be restrained by the force of the rotor magnets, and be prepared to catch any residual oil. Remove the gasket and discard it. Remove the dowel from either the cover or the crankcase if it is loose.

6 Withdraw the idle/reduction gear shaft from the crankcase and remove the gear, noting which way round it fits (see illustration).

7 To remove the rotor bolt it is necessary to stop the rotor from turning. The best way is to use a commercially available rotor strap (see illustration). If one is not available, try placing the transmission in gear and having an

32.6 Withdraw the shaft and remove the gear

32.7 Using a rotor strap to hold the rotor while unscrewing the bolt

9•24 Electrical system

32.8a Using a puller to remove the rotor

32.8b Remove the Woodruff key if it is loose

32.9 Unscrew the stator bolts (A) and the wiring clamp bolt (B) and free the grommet (C)

assistant apply the rear brake hard. Unscrew the bolt. Note the washer fitted with the bolt.

8 To remove the rotor, complete with starter gear, from the shaft it is necessary to use a rotor puller. Thread the rotor puller into the centre of the rotor and turn it until the rotor is displaced from the shaft, holding the rotor to prevent the engine turning **(see illustration)**. Remove the Woodruff key from its slot in the crankcase if it is loose **(see illustration)**. Separate the starter clutch from the rotor if required (see Chapter 2).

9 To remove the stator from the cover, unscrew the bolts securing the stator, and the bolt securing the wiring clamp, then remove the assembly, noting how the rubber wiring grommet fits **(see illustration)**.

Installation

10 Fit the stator into the cover, aligning the rubber wiring grommet with the groove **(see illustration 32.9)**. Install the bolts and tighten them to the torque setting specified at the beginning of the Chapter. Apply a suitable sealant to the wiring grommet, then press it into the cut-out in the cover. Secure the wiring with its clamp and tighten the bolt securely.

11 If separated, fit the starter clutch onto the back of the rotor (see Chapter 2). Apply some oil to the needle bearing on the end of the crankshaft.

12 Clean the tapered end of the crankshaft and the corresponding mating surface on the inside of the rotor with a suitable solvent. Fit the Woodruff key into its slot in the crankshaft if removed **(see illustration)**. Make sure that no metal objects have attached themselves to the magnet on the inside of the rotor. Slide the rotor onto the shaft, making sure the groove on the inside of the rotor is aligned with and fits over the Woodruff key **(see illustration)**. Make sure the Woodruff key does not become dislodged when installing the rotor.

13 Apply some clean oil to the rotor bolt threads and the underside of the head. Install the rotor bolt with its washer and tighten it to the torque setting specified at the beginning of the Chapter, using the method employed on removal to prevent the rotor from turning **(see illustrations)**.

14 Lubricate the idle/reduction gear shaft with clean engine oil. Position the gear in the crankcase, making sure the smaller pinion faces outwards and its teeth mesh correctly with the teeth of the starter driven gear, and the teeth of the larger pinion mesh correctly with the teeth on the starter motor, then slide the shaft into the gear **(see illustration 32.6)**.

15 Apply a smear of suitable sealant to the area around the crankcase joints **(see illustration)**. Fit the dowel into the crankcase if removed. Install the alternator cover using a new gasket, making sure they locate onto the

32.12a Fit the Woodruff key into its slot . . .

32.12b . . . then slide the rotor onto the shaft, aligning the cut-out with the Woodruff key

32.13a Install the bolt with its washer . . .

32.13b . . . and tighten it to the specified torque

32.15a Apply the sealant over the crankcase joints

Electrical system 9•25

32.15b Locate the new gasket onto the dowel (arrowed) . . .

32.15c . . . then install the cover

dowel **(see illustrations)**. Tighten the cover bolts evenly in a criss-cross sequence.

16 Reconnect the wiring at the connector and secure it with any clips or ties previously released **(see illustration 32.1)**.

17 Fill the engine with oil, or top it up to the correct level, according to you removal method (see Chapter 1). Install the fairing side panel and fuel tank if raised (see Chapters 8 and 4).

33 Regulator/rectifier – check and replacement

Check

1 Remove the seat cowling (see Chapter 8). The regulator/rectifier is mounted on the right-hand side of the rear sub-frame on European F models and US 1999 and 2000 models **(see illustration)**, and on the right-hand side of the sub-frame on European FS models and US 2001-on models **(see illustration)**. On F-X and F-Y (1999 and 2000) models, disconnect the wiring connector from the regulator/rectifier. On all other models, trace the wiring from the regulator/rectifier and disconnect it at the wiring connectors – raise the fuel tank to access them (see Chapter 4) **(see illustration and 32.1)**. Check the connectors for loose, damaged or corroded terminals.

2 Set the multimeter to the 0 to 20 dc volts setting. Connect the meter positive (+ve) probe to the red/white wire terminal on the loom side of the connector and the negative (–ve) probe to a suitable ground (earth) and check for voltage. Full battery voltage should be present at all times.

3 Switch the multimeter to the resistance (ohms) scale. Check for continuity between the green wire terminal on the loom side of the connector and ground (earth). There should be continuity.

4 Set the multimeter to the ohms x 1 (ohmmeter) scale and measure the resistance between each of the yellow wires on the alternator (loom) side of the connector, taking a total of three readings, then check for continuity between each terminal and ground (earth). The three readings should be within the range shown in the Specifications for the alternator stator coil at the start of this Chapter, and there should be no continuity (infinite resistance) between any of the terminals and ground (earth).

5 If the above checks do not provide the expected results check the wiring and connectors between the battery, regulator/rectifier and alternator for shorts, breaks, and loose or corroded terminals (see the *wiring diagrams* at the end of this book).

6 If the wiring checks out, the regulator/rectifier unit is probably faulty. Honda provide no test data for the unit itself. Take it to a Honda dealer for confirmation of its condition before replacing it with a new one.

Replacement

7 Remove the seat cowling (see Chapter 8). The regulator/rectifier is mounted on the right-hand side of the rear sub-frame on European F models and US 1999 and 2000 models **(see illustration 33.1a)**, and on the right-hand side of the sub-frame on European FS models and US 2001-on models **(see illustration 33.1b)**. On F-X and F-Y (1999 and 2000) models, disconnect the wiring connector from the regulator/rectifier. On all other models, trace the wiring from the regulator/rectifier and disconnect it at the wiring connectors – raise the fuel tank to access them (see Chapter 4) **(see illustrations 33.1c and 32.1)**. Free the wiring from any clips or ties and feed it back to the regulator/rectifier.

8 Unscrew the two bolts securing the regulator/rectifier and remove it.

9 Install the new unit and tighten its bolts securely. Connect the wiring connector(s).

10 Install the fuel tank if necessary and the seat cowling (see Chapters 4 and 8).

33.1a Regulator/rectifier (arrowed) – F-X and F-Y models

33.1b Regulator/rectifier – FS models

33.1c One of the two regulator/rectifier wiring connectors on F-1/FS-1 (2001-on) models

9•26 Wiring diagrams

CBR600 F-X and F-Y European models

Wiring diagrams 9•27

CBR600 F-X and F-Y European models

9•28 Wiring diagrams

CBR600 F-1, F-2, FS-1 and FS-2 European models

Wiring diagrams 9•29

CBR600 F-1, F-2, FS-1 and FS-2 European models

9•30 Wiring diagrams

CBR600 F-3 onward European models

Wiring diagrams 9•31

CBR600 F-3 onward European models

9•32 Wiring diagrams

CBR600 F-X and F-Y US 49-state and Canada models

Wiring diagrams 9•33

CBR600 F-X and F-Y 49-State and Canada models

9•34 Wiring diagrams

CBR600 F-X and F-Y US California models

Wiring diagrams 9•35

CBR600 F-X and F-Y US California models

9•36 Wiring diagrams

CBR600 F-1 onward US and Canada models

Wiring diagrams 9•37

CBR600 F-1 onward US and Canada models

Notes

Reference

Tools and Workshop Tips — REF•2
- Building up a tool kit and equipping your workshop ● Using tools ● Understanding bearing, seal, fastener and chain sizes and markings ● Repair techniques

Security — REF•20
- Locks and chains ● U-locks ● Disc locks ● Alarms and immobilisers ● Security marking systems ● Tips on how to prevent bike theft

Lubricants and fluids — REF•23
- Engine oils ● Transmission (gear) oils ● Coolant/anti-freeze ● Fork oils and suspension fluids ● Brake/clutch fluids ● Spray lubes, degreasers and solvents

Conversion Factors — REF•26

34 Nm × 0.738 = 25 lbf ft

- Formulae for conversion of the metric (SI) units used throughout the manual into Imperial measures

MOT Test Checks — REF•27
- A guide to the UK MOT test ● Which items are tested ● How to prepare your motorcycle for the test and perform a pre-test check

Storage — REF•32
- How to prepare your motorcycle for going into storage and protect essential systems ● How to get the motorcycle back on the road

Fault Finding — REF•35
- Common faults and their likely causes ● How to check engine cylinder compression ● How to make electrical tests and use test meters

Technical Terms Explained — REF•48
- Component names, technical terms and common abbreviations explained

Index — REF•52

REF•2 Tools and Workshop Tips

Buying tools

A toolkit is a fundamental requirement for servicing and repairing a motorcycle. Although there will be an initial expense in building up enough tools for servicing, this will soon be offset by the savings made by doing the job yourself. As experience and confidence grow, additional tools can be added to enable the repair and overhaul of the motorcycle. Many of the specialist tools are expensive and not often used so it may be preferable to hire them, or for a group of friends or motorcycle club to join in the purchase.

As a rule, it is better to buy more expensive, good quality tools. Cheaper tools are likely to wear out faster and need to be renewed more often, nullifying the original saving.

> **Warning: To avoid the risk of a poor quality tool breaking in use, causing injury or damage to the component being worked on, always aim to purchase tools which meet the relevant national safety standards.**

The following lists of tools do not represent the manufacturer's service tools, but serve as a guide to help the owner decide which tools are needed for this level of work. In addition, items such as an electric drill, hacksaw, files, soldering iron and a workbench equipped with a vice, may be needed. Although not classed as tools, a selection of bolts, screws, nuts, washers and pieces of tubing always come in useful.

For more information about tools, refer to the Haynes *Motorcycle Workshop Practice TechBook* (Bk. No. 3470).

Manufacturer's service tools

Inevitably certain tasks require the use of a service tool. Where possible an alternative tool or method of approach is recommended, but sometimes there is no option if personal injury or damage to the component is to be avoided. Where required, service tools are referred to in the relevant procedure.

Service tools can usually only be purchased from a motorcycle dealer and are identified by a part number. Some of the commonly-used tools, such as rotor pullers, are available in aftermarket form from mail-order motorcycle tool and accessory suppliers.

Maintenance and minor repair tools

1 Set of flat-bladed screwdrivers
2 Set of Phillips head screwdrivers
3 Combination open-end and ring spanners
4 Socket set (3/8 inch or 1/2 inch drive)
5 Set of Allen keys or bits
6 Set of Torx keys or bits
7 Pliers, cutters and self-locking grips (Mole grips)
8 Adjustable spanners
9 C-spanners
10 Tread depth gauge and tyre pressure gauge
11 Cable oiler clamp
12 Feeler gauges
13 Spark plug gap measuring tool
14 Spark plug spanner or deep plug sockets
15 Wire brush and emery paper
16 Calibrated syringe, measuring vessel and funnel
17 Oil filter adapters
18 Oil drainer can or tray
19 Pump type oil can
20 Grease gun
21 Straight-edge and steel rule
22 Continuity tester
23 Battery charger
24 Hydrometer (for battery specific gravity check)
25 Anti-freeze tester (for liquid-cooled engines)

Tools and Workshop Tips REF•3

Repair and overhaul tools

1 Torque wrench (small and mid-ranges)
2 Conventional, plastic or soft-faced hammers
3 Impact driver set
4 Vernier gauge
5 Circlip pliers (internal and external, or combination)
6 Set of cold chisels and punches
7 Selection of pullers
8 Breaker bars
9 Chain breaking/riveting tool set
10 Wire stripper and crimper tool
11 Multimeter (measures amps, volts and ohms)
12 Stroboscope (for dynamic timing checks)
13 Hose clamp (wingnut type shown)
14 Clutch holding tool
15 One-man brake/clutch bleeder kit

Specialist tools

1 Micrometers (external type)
2 Telescoping gauges
3 Dial gauge
4 Cylinder compression gauge
5 Vacuum gauges (left) or manometer (right)
6 Oil pressure gauge
7 Plastigauge kit
8 Valve spring compressor (4-stroke engines)
9 Piston pin drawbolt tool
10 Piston ring removal and installation tool
11 Piston ring clamp
12 Cylinder bore hone (stone type shown)
13 Stud extractor
14 Screw extractor set
15 Bearing driver set

REF•4 Tools and Workshop Tips

1 Workshop equipment and facilities

The workbench

- Work is made much easier by raising the bike up on a ramp - components are much more accessible if raised to waist level. The hydraulic or pneumatic types seen in the dealer's workshop are a sound investment if you undertake a lot of repairs or overhauls (see illustration 1.1).

1.1 Hydraulic motorcycle ramp

- If raised off ground level, the bike must be supported on the ramp to avoid it falling. Most ramps incorporate a front wheel locating clamp which can be adjusted to suit different diameter wheels. When tightening the clamp, take care not to mark the wheel rim or damage the tyre - use wood blocks on each side to prevent this.
- Secure the bike to the ramp using tie-downs (see illustration 1.2). If the bike has only a sidestand, and hence leans at a dangerous angle when raised, support the bike on an auxiliary stand.

1.2 Tie-downs are used around the passenger footrests to secure the bike

- Auxiliary (paddock) stands are widely available from mail order companies or motorcycle dealers and attach either to the wheel axle or swingarm pivot (see illustration 1.3). If the motorcycle has a centrestand, you can support it under the crankcase to prevent it toppling whilst either wheel is removed (see illustration 1.4).

1.3 This auxiliary stand attaches to the swingarm pivot

1.4 Always use a block of wood between the engine and jack head when supporting the engine in this way

Fumes and fire

- Refer to the Safety first! page at the beginning of the manual for full details. Make sure your workshop is equipped with a fire extinguisher suitable for fuel-related fires (Class B fire - flammable liquids) - it is not sufficient to have a water-filled extinguisher.
- Always ensure adequate ventilation is available. Unless an exhaust gas extraction system is available for use, ensure that the engine is run outside of the workshop.
- If working on the fuel system, make sure the workshop is ventilated to avoid a build-up of fumes. This applies equally to fume build-up when charging a battery. Do not smoke or allow anyone else to smoke in the workshop.

Fluids

- If you need to drain fuel from the tank, store it in an approved container marked as suitable for the storage of petrol (gasoline) (see illustration 1.5). Do not store fuel in glass jars or bottles.

1.5 Use an approved can only for storing petrol (gasoline)

- Use proprietary engine degreasers or solvents which have a high flash-point, such as paraffin (kerosene), for cleaning off oil, grease and dirt - never use petrol (gasoline) for cleaning. Wear rubber gloves when handling solvent and engine degreaser. The fumes from certain solvents can be dangerous - always work in a well-ventilated area.

Dust, eye and hand protection

- Protect your lungs from inhalation of dust particles by wearing a filtering mask over the nose and mouth. Many frictional materials still contain asbestos which is dangerous to your health. Protect your eyes from spouts of liquid and sprung components by wearing a pair of protective goggles (see illustration 1.6).

1.6 A fire extinguisher, goggles, mask and protective gloves should be at hand in the workshop

- Protect your hands from contact with solvents, fuel and oils by wearing rubber gloves. Alternatively apply a barrier cream to your hands before starting work. If handling hot components or fluids, wear suitable gloves to protect your hands from scalding and burns.

What to do with old fluids

- Old cleaning solvent, fuel, coolant and oils should not be poured down domestic drains or onto the ground. Package the fluid up in old oil containers, label it accordingly, and take it to a garage or disposal facility. Contact your local authority for location of such sites or ring the oil care hotline.

Note: It is antisocial and illegal to dump oil down the drain. To find the location of your local oil recycling bank, call this number free.

OIL CARE — FOLLOW THE CODE
OIL BANK LINE
0800 66 33 66
www.oilbankline.org.uk

In the USA, note that any oil supplier must accept used oil for recycling.

Tools and Workshop Tips REF•5

2 Fasteners - screws, bolts and nuts

Fastener types and applications

Bolts and screws

● Fastener head types are either of hexagonal, Torx or splined design, with internal and external versions of each type **(see illustrations 2.1 and 2.2)**; splined head fasteners are not in common use on motorcycles. The conventional slotted or Phillips head design is used for certain screws. Bolt or screw length is always measured from the underside of the head to the end of the item **(see illustration 2.11)**.

2.1 Internal hexagon/Allen (A), Torx (B) and splined (C) fasteners, with corresponding bits

2.2 External Torx (A), splined (B) and hexagon (C) fasteners, with corresponding sockets

● Certain fasteners on the motorcycle have a tensile marking on their heads, the higher the marking the stronger the fastener. High tensile fasteners generally carry a 10 or higher marking. Never replace a high tensile fastener with one of a lower tensile strength.

Washers (see illustration 2.3)

● Plain washers are used between a fastener head and a component to prevent damage to the component or to spread the load when torque is applied. Plain washers can also be used as spacers or shims in certain assemblies. Copper or aluminium plain washers are often used as sealing washers on drain plugs.

2.3 Plain washer (A), penny washer (B), spring washer (C) and serrated washer (D)

● The split-ring spring washer works by applying axial tension between the fastener head and component. If flattened, it is fatigued and must be renewed. If a plain (flat) washer is used on the fastener, position the spring washer between the fastener and the plain washer.

● Serrated star type washers dig into the fastener and component faces, preventing loosening. They are often used on electrical earth (ground) connections to the frame.

● Cone type washers (sometimes called Belleville) are conical and when tightened apply axial tension between the fastener head and component. They must be installed with the dished side against the component and often carry an OUTSIDE marking on their outer face. If flattened, they are fatigued and must be renewed.

● Tab washers are used to lock plain nuts or bolts on a shaft. A portion of the tab washer is bent up hard against one flat of the nut or bolt to prevent it loosening. Due to the tab washer being deformed in use, a new tab washer should be used every time it is disturbed.

● Wave washers are used to take up endfloat on a shaft. They provide light springing and prevent excessive side-to-side play of a component. Can be found on rocker arm shafts.

Nuts and split pins

● Conventional plain nuts are usually six-sided **(see illustration 2.4)**. They are sized by thread diameter and pitch. High tensile nuts carry a number on one end to denote their tensile strength.

2.4 Plain nut (A), shouldered locknut (B), nylon insert nut (C) and castellated nut (D)

● Self-locking nuts either have a nylon insert, or two spring metal tabs, or a shoulder which is staked into a groove in the shaft - their advantage over conventional plain nuts is a resistance to loosening due to vibration. The nylon insert type can be used a number of times, but must be renewed when the friction of the nylon insert is reduced, ie when the nut spins freely on the shaft. The spring tab type can be reused unless the tabs are damaged. The shouldered type must be renewed every time it is disturbed.

● Split pins (cotter pins) are used to lock a castellated nut to a shaft or to prevent slackening of a plain nut. Common applications are wheel axles and brake torque arms. Because the split pin arms are deformed to lock around the nut a new split pin must always be used on installation - always fit the correct size split pin which will fit snugly in the shaft hole. Make sure the split pin arms are correctly located around the nut **(see illustrations 2.5 and 2.6)**.

2.5 Bend split pin (cotter pin) arms as shown (arrows) to secure a castellated nut

2.6 Bend split pin (cotter pin) arms as shown to secure a plain nut

Caution: If the castellated nut slots do not align with the shaft hole after tightening to the torque setting, tighten the nut until the next slot aligns with the hole - never slacken the nut to align its slot.

● R-pins (shaped like the letter R), or slip pins as they are sometimes called, are sprung and can be reused if they are otherwise in good condition. Always install R-pins with their closed end facing forwards **(see illustration 2.7)**.

REF•6 Tools and Workshop Tips

2.7 Correct fitting of R-pin. Arrow indicates forward direction

Circlips (see illustration 2.8)

● Circlips (sometimes called snap-rings) are used to retain components on a shaft or in a housing and have corresponding external or internal ears to permit removal. Parallel-sided (machined) circlips can be installed either way round in their groove, whereas stamped circlips (which have a chamfered edge on one face) must be installed with the chamfer facing away from the direction of thrust load **(see illustration 2.9)**.

2.8 External stamped circlip (A), internal stamped circlip (B), machined circlip (C) and wire circlip (D)

● Always use circlip pliers to remove and install circlips; expand or compress them just enough to remove them. After installation, rotate the circlip in its groove to ensure it is securely seated. If installing a circlip on a splined shaft, always align its opening with a shaft channel to ensure the circlip ends are well supported and unlikely to catch **(see illustration 2.10)**.

2.9 Correct fitting of a stamped circlip

2.10 Align circlip opening with shaft channel

● Circlips can wear due to the thrust of components and become loose in their grooves, with the subsequent danger of becoming dislodged in operation. For this reason, renewal is advised every time a circlip is disturbed.

● Wire circlips are commonly used as piston pin retaining clips. If a removal tang is provided, long-nosed pliers can be used to dislodge them, otherwise careful use of a small flat-bladed screwdriver is necessary. Wire circlips should be renewed every time they are disturbed.

Thread diameter and pitch

● Diameter of a male thread (screw, bolt or stud) is the outside diameter of the threaded portion **(see illustration 2.11)**. Most motorcycle manufacturers use the ISO (International Standards Organisation) metric system expressed in millimetres, eg M6 refers to a 6 mm diameter thread. Sizing is the same for nuts, except that the thread diameter is measured across the valleys of the nut.

● Pitch is the distance between the peaks of the thread **(see illustration 2.11)**. It is expressed in millimetres, thus a common bolt size may be expressed as 6.0 x 1.0 mm (6 mm thread diameter and 1 mm pitch). Generally pitch increases in proportion to thread diameter, although there are always exceptions.

● Thread diameter and pitch are related for conventional fastener applications and the accompanying table can be used as a guide. Additionally, the AF (Across Flats), spanner or socket size dimension of the bolt or nut **(see illustration 2.11)** is linked to thread and pitch specification. Thread pitch can be measured with a thread gauge **(see illustration 2.12)**.

2.11 Fastener length (L), thread diameter (D), thread pitch (P) and head size (AF)

2.12 Using a thread gauge to measure pitch

AF size	Thread diameter x pitch (mm)
8 mm	M5 x 0.8
8 mm	M6 x 1.0
10 mm	M6 x 1.0
12 mm	M8 x 1.25
14 mm	M10 x 1.25
17 mm	M12 x 1.25

● The threads of most fasteners are of the right-hand type, ie they are turned clockwise to tighten and anti-clockwise to loosen. The reverse situation applies to left-hand thread fasteners, which are turned anti-clockwise to tighten and clockwise to loosen. Left-hand threads are used where rotation of a component might loosen a conventional right-hand thread fastener.

Seized fasteners

● Corrosion of external fasteners due to water or reaction between two dissimilar metals can occur over a period of time. It will build up sooner in wet conditions or in countries where salt is used on the roads during the winter. If a fastener is severely corroded it is likely that normal methods of removal will fail and result in its head being ruined. When you attempt removal, the fastener thread should be heard to crack free and unscrew easily - if it doesn't, stop there before damaging something.

● A smart tap on the head of the fastener will often succeed in breaking free corrosion which has occurred in the threads **(see illustration 2.13)**.

● An aerosol penetrating fluid (such as WD-40) applied the night beforehand may work its way down into the thread and ease removal. Depending on the location, you may be able to make up a Plasticine well around the fastener head and fill it with penetrating fluid.

2.13 A sharp tap on the head of a fastener will often break free a corroded thread

Tools and Workshop Tips REF•7

- If you are working on an engine internal component, corrosion will most likely not be a problem due to the well lubricated environment. However, components can be very tight and an impact driver is a useful tool in freeing them **(see illustration 2.14)**.

2.14 Using an impact driver to free a fastener

- Where corrosion has occurred between dissimilar metals (eg steel and aluminium alloy), the application of heat to the fastener head will create a disproportionate expansion rate between the two metals and break the seizure caused by the corrosion. Whether heat can be applied depends on the location of the fastener - any surrounding components likely to be damaged must first be removed **(see illustration 2.15)**. Heat can be applied using a paint stripper heat gun or clothes iron, or by immersing the component in boiling water - wear protective gloves to prevent scalding or burns to the hands.

2.15 Using heat to free a seized fastener

- As a last resort, it is possible to use a hammer and cold chisel to work the fastener head unscrewed **(see illustration 2.16)**. This will damage the fastener, but more importantly extreme care must be taken not to damage the surrounding component.

> **Caution:** Remember that the component being secured is generally of more value than the bolt, nut or screw - when the fastener is freed, do not unscrew it with force, instead work the fastener back and forth when resistance is felt to prevent thread damage.

2.16 Using a hammer and chisel to free a seized fastener

Broken fasteners and damaged heads

- If the shank of a broken bolt or screw is accessible you can grip it with self-locking grips. The knurled wheel type stud extractor tool or self-gripping stud puller tool is particularly useful for removing the long studs which screw into the cylinder mouth surface of the crankcase or bolts and screws from which the head has broken off **(see illustration 2.17)**. Studs can also be removed by locking two nuts together on the threaded end of the stud and using a spanner on the lower nut **(see illustration 2.18)**.

2.17 Using a stud extractor tool to remove a broken crankcase stud

2.18 Two nuts can be locked together to unscrew a stud from a component

- A bolt or screw which has broken off below or level with the casing must be extracted using a screw extractor set. Centre punch the fastener to centralise the drill bit, then drill a hole in the fastener **(see illustration 2.19)**. Select a drill bit which is approximately half to three-quarters the diameter of the fastener and drill to a depth which will accommodate the extractor. Use the largest size extractor possible, but avoid leaving too small a wall thickness otherwise the extractor will merely force the fastener walls outwards wedging it in the casing thread.

- If a spiral type extractor is used, thread it anti-clockwise into the fastener. As it is screwed in, it will grip the fastener and unscrew it from the casing **(see illustration 2.20)**.

2.19 When using a screw extractor, first drill a hole in the fastener . . .

2.20 . . . then thread the extractor anti-clockwise into the fastener

- If a taper type extractor is used, tap it into the fastener so that it is firmly wedged in place. Unscrew the extractor (anti-clockwise) to draw the fastener out.

> ⚠️ **Warning:** Stud extractors are very hard and may break off in the fastener if care is not taken - ask an engineer about spark erosion if this happens.

- Alternatively, the broken bolt/screw can be drilled out and the hole retapped for an oversize bolt/screw or a diamond-section thread insert. It is essential that the drilling is carried out squarely and to the correct depth, otherwise the casing may be ruined - if in doubt, entrust the work to an engineer.

- Bolts and nuts with rounded corners cause the correct size spanner or socket to slip when force is applied. Of the types of spanner/socket available always use a six-point type rather than an eight or twelve-point type - better grip

REF•8 Tools and Workshop Tips

2.21 Comparison of surface drive ring spanner (left) with 12-point type (right)

is obtained. Surface drive spanners grip the middle of the hex flats, rather than the corners, and are thus good in cases of damaged heads **(see illustration 2.21)**.

- Slotted-head or Phillips-head screws are often damaged by the use of the wrong size screwdriver. Allen-head and Torx-head screws are much less likely to sustain damage. If enough of the screw head is exposed you can use a hacksaw to cut a slot in its head and then use a conventional flat-bladed screwdriver to remove it. Alternatively use a hammer and cold chisel to tap the head of the fastener around to slacken it. Always replace damaged fasteners with new ones, preferably Torx or Allen-head type.

HAYNES HiNT

A dab of valve grinding compound between the screw head and screwdriver tip will often give a good grip.

Thread repair

- Threads (particularly those in aluminium alloy components) can be damaged by overtightening, being assembled with dirt in the threads, or from a component working loose and vibrating. Eventually the thread will fail completely, and it will be impossible to tighten the fastener.
- If a thread is damaged or clogged with old locking compound it can be renovated with a thread repair tool (thread chaser) **(see illustrations 2.22 and 2.23)**; special thread

2.22 A thread repair tool being used to correct an internal thread

2.23 A thread repair tool being used to correct an external thread

chasers are available for spark plug hole threads. The tool will not cut a new thread, but clean and true the original thread. Make sure that you use the correct diameter and pitch tool. Similarly, external threads can be cleaned up with a die or a thread restorer file **(see illustration 2.24)**.

2.24 Using a thread restorer file

- It is possible to drill out the old thread and retap the component to the next thread size. This will work where there is enough surrounding material and a new bolt or screw can be obtained. Sometimes, however, this is not possible - such as where the bolt/screw passes through another component which must also be suitably modified, also in cases where a spark plug or oil drain plug cannot be obtained in a larger diameter thread size.
- The diamond-section thread insert (often known by its popular trade name of Heli-Coil) is a simple and effective method of renewing the thread and retaining the original size. A kit can be purchased which contains the tap, insert and installing tool **(see illustration 2.25)**. Drill out the damaged thread with the size drill specified **(see illustration 2.26)**. Carefully retap the thread **(see illustration 2.27)**. Install the

2.25 Obtain a thread insert kit to suit the thread diameter and pitch required

2.26 To install a thread insert, first drill out the original thread . . .

2.27 . . . tap a new thread . . .

2.28 . . . fit insert on the installing tool . . .

2.29 . . . and thread into the component . . .

2.30 . . . break off the tang when complete

insert on the installing tool and thread it slowly into place using a light downward pressure **(see illustrations 2.28 and 2.29)**. When positioned between a 1/4 and 1/2 turn below the surface withdraw the installing tool and use the break-off tool to press down on the tang, breaking it off **(see illustration 2.30)**.

- There are epoxy thread repair kits on the market which can rebuild stripped internal threads, although this repair should not be used on high load-bearing components.

Tools and Workshop Tips REF•9

Thread locking and sealing compounds

● Locking compounds are used in locations where the fastener is prone to loosening due to vibration or on important safety-related items which might cause loss of control of the motorcycle if they fail. It is also used where important fasteners cannot be secured by other means such as lockwashers or split pins.

● Before applying locking compound, make sure that the threads (internal and external) are clean and dry with all old compound removed. Select a compound to suit the component being secured - a non-permanent general locking and sealing type is suitable for most applications, but a high strength type is needed for permanent fixing of studs in castings. Apply a drop or two of the compound to the first few threads of the fastener, then thread it into place and tighten to the specified torque. Do not apply excessive thread locking compound otherwise the thread may be damaged on subsequent removal.

● Certain fasteners are impregnated with a dry film type coating of locking compound on their threads. Always renew this type of fastener if disturbed.

● Anti-seize compounds, such as copper-based greases, can be applied to protect threads from seizure due to extreme heat and corrosion. A common instance is spark plug threads and exhaust system fasteners.

3 Measuring tools and gauges

Feeler gauges

● Feeler gauges (or blades) are used for measuring small gaps and clearances **(see illustration 3.1)**. They can also be used to measure endfloat (sideplay) of a component on a shaft where access is not possible with a dial gauge.

● Feeler gauge sets should be treated with care and not bent or damaged. They are etched with their size on one face. Keep them clean and very lightly oiled to prevent corrosion build-up.

3.1 Feeler gauges are used for measuring small gaps and clearances - thickness is marked on one face of gauge

● When measuring a clearance, select a gauge which is a light sliding fit between the two components. You may need to use two gauges together to measure the clearance accurately.

Micrometers

● A micrometer is a precision tool capable of measuring to 0.01 or 0.001 of a millimetre. It should always be stored in its case and not in the general toolbox. It must be kept clean and never dropped, otherwise its frame or measuring anvils could be distorted resulting in inaccurate readings.

● External micrometers are used for measuring outside diameters of components and have many more applications than internal micrometers. Micrometers are available in different size ranges, eg 0 to 25 mm, 25 to 50 mm, and upwards in 25 mm steps; some large micrometers have interchangeable anvils to allow a range of measurements to be taken. Generally the largest precision measurement you are likely to take on a motorcycle is the piston diameter.

● Internal micrometers (or bore micrometers) are used for measuring inside diameters, such as valve guides and cylinder bores. Telescoping gauges and small hole gauges are used in conjunction with an external micrometer, whereas the more expensive internal micrometers have their own measuring device.

External micrometer

Note: *The conventional analogue type instrument is described. Although much easier to read, digital micrometers are considerably more expensive.*

● Always check the calibration of the micrometer before use. With the anvils closed (0 to 25 mm type) or set over a test gauge (for

3.2 Check micrometer calibration before use

the larger types) the scale should read zero **(see illustration 3.2)**; make sure that the anvils (and test piece) are clean first. Any discrepancy can be adjusted by referring to the instructions supplied with the tool. Remember that the micrometer is a precision measuring tool - don't force the anvils closed, use the ratchet (4) on the end of the micrometer to close it. In this way, a measured force is always applied.

● To use, first make sure that the item being measured is clean. Place the anvil of the micrometer (1) against the item and use the thimble (2) to bring the spindle (3) lightly into contact with the other side of the item **(see illustration 3.3)**. Don't tighten the thimble down because this will damage the micrometer - instead use the ratchet (4) on the end of the micrometer. The ratchet mechanism applies a measured force preventing damage to the instrument.

● The micrometer is read by referring to the linear scale on the sleeve and the annular scale on the thimble. Read off the sleeve first to obtain the base measurement, then add the fine measurement from the thimble to obtain the overall reading. The linear scale on the sleeve represents the measuring range of the micrometer (eg 0 to 25 mm). The annular scale

3.3 Micrometer component parts

| 1 | Anvil | 3 | Spindle | 5 | Frame |
| 2 | Thimble | 4 | Ratchet | 6 | Locking lever |

REF•10 Tools and Workshop Tips

on the thimble will be in graduations of 0.01 mm (or as marked on the frame) - one full revolution of the thimble will move 0.5 mm on the linear scale. Take the reading where the datum line on the sleeve intersects the thimble's scale. Always position the eye directly above the scale otherwise an inaccurate reading will result.

In the example shown the item measures 2.95 mm **(see illustration 3.4)**:

Linear scale	2.00 mm
Linear scale	0.50 mm
Annular scale	0.45 mm
Total figure	**2.95 mm**

3.5 Micrometer reading of 46.99 mm on linear and annular scales . . .

3.7 Expand the telescoping gauge in the bore, lock its position . . .

3.4 Micrometer reading of 2.95 mm

3.6 . . . and 0.004 mm on vernier scale

3.8 . . . then measure the gauge with a micrometer

Most micrometers have a locking lever (6) on the frame to hold the setting in place, allowing the item to be removed from the micrometer.
● Some micrometers have a vernier scale on their sleeve, providing an even finer measurement to be taken, in 0.001 increments of a millimetre. Take the sleeve and thimble measurement as described above, then check which graduation on the vernier scale aligns with that of the annular scale on the thimble **Note:** *The eye must be perpendicular to the scale when taking the vernier reading - if necessary rotate the body of the micrometer to ensure this.* Multiply the vernier scale figure by 0.001 and add it to the base and fine measurement figures.

In the example shown the item measures 46.994 mm **(see illustrations 3.5 and 3.6)**:

Linear scale (base)	46.000 mm
Linear scale (base)	00.500 mm
Annular scale (fine)	00.490 mm
Vernier scale	00.004 mm
Total figure	**46.994 mm**

Internal micrometer

● Internal micrometers are available for measuring bore diameters, but are expensive and unlikely to be available for home use. It is suggested that a set of telescoping gauges and small hole gauges, both of which must be used with an external micrometer, will suffice for taking internal measurements on a motorcycle.
● Telescoping gauges can be used to measure internal diameters of components. Select a gauge with the correct size range, make sure its ends are clean and insert it into the bore. Expand the gauge, then lock its position and withdraw it from the bore **(see illustration 3.7)**. Measure across the gauge ends with a micrometer **(see illustration 3.8)**.
● Very small diameter bores (such as valve guides) are measured with a small hole gauge. Once adjusted to a slip-fit inside the component, its position is locked and the gauge withdrawn for measurement with a micrometer **(see illustrations 3.9 and 3.10)**.

Vernier caliper

Note: *The conventional linear and dial gauge type instruments are described. Digital types are easier to read, but are far more expensive.*
● The vernier caliper does not provide the precision of a micrometer, but is versatile in being able to measure internal and external diameters. Some types also incorporate a depth gauge. It is ideal for measuring clutch plate friction material and spring free lengths.
● To use the conventional linear scale vernier, slacken off the vernier clamp screws (1) and set its jaws over (2), or inside (3), the item to be measured **(see illustration 3.11)**. Slide the jaw into contact, using the thumbwheel (4) for fine movement of the sliding scale (5) then tighten the clamp screws (1). Read off the main scale (6) where the zero on the sliding scale (5) intersects it, taking the whole number to the left of the zero; this provides the base measurement. View along the sliding scale and select the division which

3.9 Expand the small hole gauge in the bore, lock its position . . .

3.10 . . . then measure the gauge with a micrometer

lines up exactly with any of the divisions on the main scale, noting that the divisions usually represents 0.02 of a millimetre. Add this fine measurement to the base measurement to obtain the total reading.

Tools and Workshop Tips REF•11

3.11 Vernier component parts (linear gauge)

1 Clamp screws
2 External jaws
3 Internal jaws
4 Thumbwheel
5 Sliding scale
6 Main scale
7 Depth gauge

In the example shown the item measures 55.92 mm **(see illustration 3.12)**:

Base measurement	55.00 mm
Fine measurement	00.92 mm
Total figure	**55.92 mm**

3.12 Vernier gauge reading of 55.92 mm

● Some vernier calipers are equipped with a dial gauge for fine measurement. Before use, check that the jaws are clean, then close them fully and check that the dial gauge reads zero. If necessary adjust the gauge ring accordingly. Slacken the vernier clamp screw (1) and set its jaws over (2), or inside (3), the item to be measured **(see illustration 3.13)**. Slide the jaws into contact, using the thumbwheel (4) for fine movement. Read off the main scale (5) where the edge of the sliding scale (6) intersects it, taking the whole number to the left of the zero; this provides the base measurement. Read off the needle position on the dial gauge (7) scale to provide the fine measurement; each division represents 0.05 of a millimetre. Add this fine measurement to the base measurement to obtain the total reading.

In the example shown the item measures 55.95 mm **(see illustration 3.14)**:

Base measurement	55.00 mm
Fine measurement	00.95 mm
Total figure	**55.95 mm**

3.13 Vernier component parts (dial gauge)

1 Clamp screw
2 External jaws
3 Internal jaws
4 Thumbwheel
5 Main scale
6 Sliding scale
7 Dial gauge

3.14 Vernier gauge reading of 55.95 mm

Plastigauge

● Plastigauge is a plastic material which can be compressed between two surfaces to measure the oil clearance between them. The width of the compressed Plastigauge is measured against a calibrated scale to determine the clearance.

● Common uses of Plastigauge are for measuring the clearance between crankshaft journal and main bearing inserts, between crankshaft journal and big-end bearing inserts, and between camshaft and bearing surfaces. The following example describes big-end oil clearance measurement.

● Handle the Plastigauge material carefully to prevent distortion. Using a sharp knife, cut a length which corresponds with the width of the bearing being measured and place it carefully across the journal so that it is parallel with the shaft **(see illustration 3.15)**. Carefully install both bearing shells and the connecting rod. Without rotating the rod on the journal tighten its bolts or nuts (as applicable) to the specified torque. The connecting rod and bearings are then disassembled and the crushed Plastigauge examined.

3.15 Plastigauge placed across shaft journal

● Using the scale provided in the Plastigauge kit, measure the width of the material to determine the oil clearance **(see illustration 3.16)**. Always remove all traces of Plastigauge after use using your fingernails.

Caution: Arriving at the correct clearance demands that the assembly is torqued correctly, according to the settings and sequence (where applicable) provided by the motorcycle manufacturer.

3.16 Measuring the width of the crushed Plastigauge

REF•12 Tools and Workshop Tips

Dial gauge or DTI (Dial Test Indicator)

● A dial gauge can be used to accurately measure small amounts of movement. Typical uses are measuring shaft runout or shaft endfloat (sideplay) and setting piston position for ignition timing on two-strokes. A dial gauge set usually comes with a range of different probes and adapters and mounting equipment.

● The gauge needle must point to zero when at rest. Rotate the ring around its periphery to zero the gauge.

● Check that the gauge is capable of reading the extent of movement in the work. Most gauges have a small dial set in the face which records whole millimetres of movement as well as the fine scale around the face periphery which is calibrated in 0.01 mm divisions. Read off the small dial first to obtain the base measurement, then add the measurement from the fine scale to obtain the total reading.

In the example shown the gauge reads 1.48 mm (see illustration 3.17):

Base measurement	1.00 mm
Fine measurement	0.48 mm
Total figure	**1.48 mm**

3.17 Dial gauge reading of 1.48 mm

● If measuring shaft runout, the shaft must be supported in vee-blocks and the gauge mounted on a stand perpendicular to the shaft. Rest the tip of the gauge against the centre of the shaft and rotate the shaft slowly whilst watching the gauge reading **(see illustration 3.18)**. Take several measurements along the length of the shaft and record the maximum gauge reading as the amount of runout in the shaft. **Note:** *The reading obtained will be total runout at that point - some manufacturers specify that the runout figure is halved to compare with their specified runout limit.*

● Endfloat (sideplay) measurement requires that the gauge is mounted securely to the surrounding component with its probe touching the end of the shaft. Using hand pressure, push and pull on the shaft noting the maximum endfloat recorded on the gauge **(see illustration 3.19)**.

3.19 Using a dial gauge to measure shaft endfloat

● A dial gauge with suitable adapters can be used to determine piston position BTDC on two-stroke engines for the purposes of ignition timing. The gauge, adapter and suitable length probe are installed in the place of the spark plug and the gauge zeroed at TDC. If the piston position is specified as 1.14 mm BTDC, rotate the engine back to 2.00 mm BTDC, then slowly forwards to 1.14 mm BTDC.

Cylinder compression gauges

● A compression gauge is used for measuring cylinder compression. Either the rubber-cone type or the threaded adapter type can be used. The latter is preferred to ensure a perfect seal against the cylinder head. A 0 to 300 psi (0 to 20 Bar) type gauge (for petrol/gasoline engines) will be suitable for motorcycles.

● The spark plug is removed and the gauge either held hard against the cylinder head (cone type) or the gauge adapter screwed into the cylinder head (threaded type) **(see illustration 3.20)**. Cylinder compression is measured with the engine turning over, but not running - carry out the compression test as described in *Fault Finding Equipment*. The gauge will hold the reading until manually released.

Oil pressure gauge

● An oil pressure gauge is used for measuring engine oil pressure. Most gauges come with a set of adapters to fit the thread of the take-off point **(see illustration 3.21)**. If the take-off point specified by the motorcycle manufacturer is an external oil pipe union, make sure that the specified replacement union is used to prevent oil starvation.

3.21 Oil pressure gauge and take-off point adapter (arrow)

● Oil pressure is measured with the engine running (at a specific rpm) and often the manufacturer will specify pressure limits for a cold and hot engine.

Straight-edge and surface plate

● If checking the gasket face of a component for warpage, place a steel rule or precision straight-edge across the gasket face and measure any gap between the straight-edge and component with feeler gauges **(see illustration 3.22)**. Check diagonally across the component and between mounting holes **(see illustration 3.23)**.

3.22 Use a straight-edge and feeler gauges to check for warpage

3.18 Using a dial gauge to measure shaft runout

3.20 Using a rubber-cone type cylinder compression gauge

3.23 Check for warpage in these directions

Tools and Workshop Tips　REF•13

- Checking individual components for warpage, such as clutch plain (metal) plates, requires a perfectly flat plate or piece or plate glass and feeler gauges.

4　Torque and leverage

What is torque?

- Torque describes the twisting force about a shaft. The amount of torque applied is determined by the distance from the centre of the shaft to the end of the lever and the amount of force being applied to the end of the lever; distance multiplied by force equals torque.
- The manufacturer applies a measured torque to a bolt or nut to ensure that it will not slacken in use and to hold two components securely together without movement in the joint. The actual torque setting depends on the thread size, bolt or nut material and the composition of the components being held.
- Too little torque may cause the fastener to loosen due to vibration, whereas too much torque will distort the joint faces of the component or cause the fastener to shear off. Always stick to the specified torque setting.

Using a torque wrench

- Check the calibration of the torque wrench and make sure it has a suitable range for the job. Torque wrenches are available in Nm (Newton-metres), kgf m (kilograms-force metre), lbf ft (pounds-feet), lbf in (inch-pounds). Do not confuse lbf ft with lbf in.
- Adjust the tool to the desired torque on the scale (see illustration 4.1). If your torque wrench is not calibrated in the units specified, carefully convert the figure (see *Conversion Factors*). A manufacturer sometimes gives a torque setting as a range (8 to 10 Nm) rather than a single figure - in this case set the tool midway between the two settings. The same torque may be expressed as 9 Nm ± 1 Nm. Some torque wrenches have a method of locking the setting so that it isn't inadvertently altered during use.

- Install the bolts/nuts in their correct location and secure them lightly. Their threads must be clean and free of any old locking compound. Unless specified the threads and flange should be dry - oiled threads are necessary in certain circumstances and the manufacturer will take this into account in the specified torque figure. Similarly, the manufacturer may also specify the application of thread-locking compound.
- Tighten the fasteners in the specified sequence until the torque wrench clicks, indicating that the torque setting has been reached. Apply the torque again to double-check the setting. Where different thread diameter fasteners secure the component, as a rule tighten the larger diameter ones first.
- When the torque wrench has been finished with, release the lock (where applicable) and fully back off its setting to zero - do not leave the torque wrench tensioned. Also, do not use a torque wrench for slackening a fastener.

Angle-tightening

- Manufacturers often specify a figure in degrees for final tightening of a fastener. This usually follows tightening to a specific torque setting.
- A degree disc can be set and attached to the socket (see illustration 4.2) or a protractor can be used to mark the angle of movement on the bolt/nut head and the surrounding casting (see illustration 4.3).

4.2 Angle tightening can be accomplished with a torque-angle gauge . . .

4.1 Set the torque wrench index mark to the setting required, in this case 12 Nm

4.3 . . . or by marking the angle on the surrounding component

Loosening sequences

- Where more than one bolt/nut secures a component, loosen each fastener evenly a little at a time. In this way, not all the stress of the joint is held by one fastener and the components are not likely to distort.
- If a tightening sequence is provided, work in the REVERSE of this, but if not, work from the outside in, in a criss-cross sequence (see illustration 4.4).

4.4 When slackening, work from the outside inwards

Tightening sequences

- If a component is held by more than one fastener it is important that the retaining bolts/nuts are tightened evenly to prevent uneven stress build-up and distortion of sealing faces. This is especially important on high-compression joints such as the cylinder head.
- A sequence is usually provided by the manufacturer, either in a diagram or actually marked in the casting. If not, always start in the centre and work outwards in a criss-cross pattern (see illustration 4.5). Start off by securing all bolts/nuts finger-tight, then set the torque wrench and tighten each fastener by a small amount in sequence until the final torque is reached. By following this practice,

4.5 When tightening, work from the inside outwards

REF•14 Tools and Workshop Tips

the joint will be held evenly and will not be distorted. Important joints, such as the cylinder head and big-end fasteners often have two- or three-stage torque settings.

Applying leverage

● Use tools at the correct angle. Position a socket wrench or spanner on the bolt/nut so that you pull it towards you when loosening. If this can't be done, push the spanner without curling your fingers around it **(see illustration 4.6)** - the spanner may slip or the fastener loosen suddenly, resulting in your fingers being crushed against a component.

4.6 If you can't pull on the spanner to loosen a fastener, push with your hand open

● Additional leverage is gained by extending the length of the lever. The best way to do this is to use a breaker bar instead of the regular length tool, or to slip a length of tubing over the end of the spanner or socket wrench.
● If additional leverage will not work, the fastener head is either damaged or firmly corroded in place (see *Fasteners*).

5 Bearings

Bearing removal and installation
Drivers and sockets

● Before removing a bearing, always inspect the casing to see which way it must be driven out - some casings will have retaining plates or a cast step. Also check for any identifying markings on the bearing and if installed to a certain depth, measure this at this stage. Some roller bearings are sealed on one side - take note of the original fitted position.
● Bearings can be driven out of a casing using a bearing driver tool (with the correct size head) or a socket of the correct diameter. Select the driver head or socket so that it contacts the outer race of the bearing, not the balls/rollers or inner race. Always support the casing around the bearing housing with wood blocks, otherwise there is a risk of fracture. The bearing is driven out with a few blows on the driver or socket from a heavy mallet. Unless access is severely restricted (as with wheel bearings), a pin-punch is not recommended unless it is moved around the bearing to keep it square in its housing.

● The same equipment can be used to install bearings. Make sure the bearing housing is supported on wood blocks and line up the bearing in its housing. Fit the bearing as noted on removal - generally they are installed with their marked side facing outwards. Tap the bearing squarely into its housing using a driver or socket which bears only on the bearing's outer race - contact with the bearing balls/rollers or inner race will destroy it **(see illustrations 5.1 and 5.2)**.
● Check that the bearing inner race and balls/rollers rotate freely.

5.1 Using a bearing driver against the bearing's outer race

5.2 Using a large socket against the bearing's outer race

Pullers and slide-hammers

● Where a bearing is pressed on a shaft a puller will be required to extract it **(see illustration 5.3)**. Make sure that the puller clamp or legs fit securely behind the bearing and are unlikely to slip out. If pulling a bearing

5.3 This bearing puller clamps behind the bearing and pressure is applied to the shaft end to draw the bearing off

off a gear shaft for example, you may have to locate the puller behind a gear pinion if there is no access to the race and draw the gear pinion off the shaft as well **(see illustration 5.4)**.

> **Caution: Ensure that the puller's centre bolt locates securely against the end of the shaft and will not slip when pressure is applied. Also ensure that puller does not damage the shaft end.**

5.4 Where no access is available to the rear of the bearing, it is sometimes possible to draw off the adjacent component

● Operate the puller so that its centre bolt exerts pressure on the shaft end and draws the bearing off the shaft.
● When installing the bearing on the shaft, tap only on the bearing's inner race - contact with the balls/rollers or outer race with destroy the bearing. Use a socket or length of tubing as a drift which fits over the shaft end **(see illustration 5.5)**.

5.5 When installing a bearing on a shaft use a piece of tubing which bears only on the bearing's inner race

● Where a bearing locates in a blind hole in a casing, it cannot be driven or pulled out as described above. A slide-hammer with knife-edged bearing puller attachment will be required. The puller attachment passes through the bearing and when tightened expands to fit firmly behind the bearing **(see illustration 5.6)**. By operating the slide-hammer part of the tool the bearing is jarred out of its housing **(see illustration 5.7)**.
● It is possible, if the bearing is of reasonable weight, for it to drop out of its housing if the casing is heated as described opposite. If this

Tools and Workshop Tips REF•15

5.6 Expand the bearing puller so that it locks behind the bearing . . .

5.7 . . . attach the slide hammer to the bearing puller

method is attempted, first prepare a work surface which will enable the casing to be tapped face down to help dislodge the bearing - a wood surface is ideal since it will not damage the casing's gasket surface. Wearing protective gloves, tap the heated casing several times against the work surface to dislodge the bearing under its own weight **(see illustration 5.8)**.

5.8 Tapping a casing face down on wood blocks can often dislodge a bearing

● Bearings can be installed in blind holes using the driver or socket method described above.

Drawbolts

● Where a bearing or bush is set in the eye of a component, such as a suspension linkage arm or connecting rod small-end, removal by drift may damage the component. Furthermore, a rubber bushing in a shock absorber eye cannot successfully be driven out of position. If access is available to a engineering press, the task is straightforward. If not, a drawbolt can be fabricated to extract the bearing or bush.

5.9 Drawbolt component parts assembled on a suspension arm

1 Bolt or length of threaded bar
2 Nuts
3 Washer (external diameter greater than tubing internal diameter)
4 Tubing (internal diameter sufficient to accommodate bearing)
5 Suspension arm with bearing
6 Tubing (external diameter slightly smaller than bearing)
7 Washer (external diameter slightly smaller than bearing)

5.10 Drawing the bearing out of the suspension arm

● To extract the bearing/bush you will need a long bolt with nut (or piece of threaded bar with two nuts), a piece of tubing which has an internal diameter larger than the bearing/bush, another piece of tubing which has an external diameter slightly smaller than the bearing/bush, and a selection of washers **(see illustrations 5.9 and 5.10)**. Note that the pieces of tubing must be of the same length, or longer, than the bearing/bush.

● The same kit (without the pieces of tubing) can be used to draw the new bearing/bush back into place **(see illustration 5.11)**.

5.11 Installing a new bearing (1) in the suspension arm

Temperature change

● If the bearing's outer race is a tight fit in the casing, the aluminium casing can be heated to release its grip on the bearing. Aluminium will expand at a greater rate than the steel bearing outer race. There are several ways to do this, but avoid any localised extreme heat (such as a blow torch) - aluminium alloy has a low melting point.

● Approved methods of heating a casing are using a domestic oven (heated to 100°C) or immersing the casing in boiling water **(see illustration 5.12)**. Low temperature range localised heat sources such as a paint stripper heat gun or clothes iron can also be used **(see illustration 5.13)**. Alternatively, soak a rag in boiling water, wring it out and wrap it around the bearing housing.

> ⚠ **Warning:** *All of these methods require care in use to prevent scalding and burns to the hands. Wear protective gloves when handling hot components.*

5.12 A casing can be immersed in a sink of boiling water to aid bearing removal

5.13 Using a localised heat source to aid bearing removal

● If heating the whole casing note that plastic components, such as the neutral switch, may suffer - remove them beforehand.

● After heating, remove the bearing as described above. You may find that the expansion is sufficient for the bearing to fall out of the casing under its own weight or with a light tap on the driver or socket.

● If necessary, the casing can be heated to aid bearing installation, and this is sometimes the recommended procedure if the motorcycle manufacturer has designed the housing and bearing fit with this intention.

Tools and Workshop Tips

● Installation of bearings can be eased by placing them in a freezer the night before installation. The steel bearing will contract slightly, allowing easy insertion in its housing. This is often useful when installing steering head outer races in the frame.

Bearing types and markings

● Plain shell bearings, ball bearings, needle roller bearings and tapered roller bearings will all be found on motorcycles **(see illustrations 5.14 and 5.15)**. The ball and roller types are usually caged between an inner and outer race, but uncaged variations may be found.

5.14 Shell bearings are either plain or grooved. They are usually identified by colour code (arrow)

5.15 Tapered roller bearing (A), needle roller bearing (B) and ball journal bearing (C)

● Shell bearings (often called inserts) are usually found at the crankshaft main and connecting rod big-end where they are good at coping with high loads. They are made of a phosphor-bronze material and are impregnated with self-lubricating properties.

● Ball bearings and needle roller bearings consist of a steel inner and outer race with the balls or rollers between the races. They require constant lubrication by oil or grease and are good at coping with axial loads. Taper roller bearings consist of rollers set in a tapered cage set on the inner race; the outer race is separate. They are good at coping with axial loads and prevent movement along the shaft - a typical application is in the steering head.

● Bearing manufacturers produce bearings to ISO size standards and stamp one face of the bearing to indicate its internal and external diameter, load capacity and type **(see illustration 5.16)**.

● Metal bushes are usually of phosphor-bronze material. Rubber bushes are used in suspension mounting eyes. Fibre bushes have also been used in suspension pivots.

5.16 Typical bearing marking

Bearing fault finding

● If a bearing outer race has spun in its housing, the housing material will be damaged. You can use a bearing locking compound to bond the outer race in place if damage is not too severe.

● Shell bearings will fail due to damage of their working surface, as a result of lack of lubrication, corrosion or abrasive particles in the oil **(see illustration 5.17)**. Small particles of dirt in the oil may embed in the bearing material whereas larger particles will score the bearing and shaft journal. If a number of short journeys are made, insufficient heat will be generated to drive off condensation which has built up on the bearings.

5.17 Typical bearing failures

● Ball and roller bearings will fail due to lack of lubrication or damage to the balls or rollers. Tapered-roller bearings can be damaged by overloading them. Unless the bearing is sealed on both sides, wash it in paraffin (kerosene) to remove all old grease then allow it to dry. Make a visual inspection looking to dented balls or rollers, damaged cages and worn or pitted races **(see illustration 5.18)**.

● A ball bearing can be checked for wear by listening to it when spun. Apply a film of light oil to the bearing and hold it close to the ear - hold the outer race with one hand and spin the inner race with the other hand **(see illustration 5.19)**. The bearing should be almost silent when spun; if it grates or rattles it is worn.

5.18 Example of ball journal bearing with damaged balls and cages

5.19 Hold outer race and listen to inner race when spun

6 Oil seals

Oil seal removal and installation

● Oil seals should be renewed every time a component is dismantled. This is because the seal lips will become set to the sealing surface and will not necessarily reseal.

● Oil seals can be prised out of position using a large flat-bladed screwdriver **(see illustration 6.1)**. In the case of crankcase seals, check first that the seal is not lipped on the inside, preventing its removal with the crankcases joined.

6.1 Prise out oil seals with a large flat-bladed screwdriver

● New seals are usually installed with their marked face (containing the seal reference code) outwards and the spring side towards the fluid being retained. In certain cases, such as a two-stroke engine crankshaft seal, a double lipped seal may be used due to there being fluid or gas on each side of the joint.

Tools and Workshop Tips REF•17

● Use a bearing driver or socket which bears only on the outer hard edge of the seal to install it in the casing - tapping on the inner edge will damage the sealing lip.

Oil seal types and markings

● Oil seals are usually of the single-lipped type. Double-lipped seals are found where a liquid or gas is on both sides of the joint.
● Oil seals can harden and lose their sealing ability if the motorcycle has been in storage for a long period - renewal is the only solution.
● Oil seal manufacturers also conform to the ISO markings for seal size - these are moulded into the outer face of the seal (see illustration 6.2).

6.2 These oil seal markings indicate inside diameter, outside diameter and seal thickness

7 Gaskets and sealants

Types of gasket and sealant

● Gaskets are used to seal the mating surfaces between components and keep lubricants, fluids, vacuum or pressure contained within the assembly. Aluminium gaskets are sometimes found at the cylinder joints, but most gaskets are paper-based. If the mating surfaces of the components being joined are undamaged the gasket can be installed dry, although a dab of sealant or grease will be useful to hold it in place during assembly.
● RTV (Room Temperature Vulcanising) silicone rubber sealants cure when exposed to moisture in the atmosphere. These sealants are good at filling pits or irregular gasket faces, but will tend to be forced out of the joint under very high torque. They can be used to replace a paper gasket, but first make sure that the width of the paper gasket is not essential to the shimming of internal components. RTV sealants should not be used on components containing petrol (gasoline).
● Non-hardening, semi-hardening and hard setting liquid gasket compounds can be used with a gasket or between a metal-to-metal joint. Select the sealant to suit the application: universal non-hardening sealant can be used on virtually all joints; semi-hardening on joint faces which are rough or damaged; hard setting sealant on joints which require a permanent bond and are subjected to high temperature and pressure. **Note:** *Check first if the paper gasket has a bead of sealant impregnated in its surface before applying additional sealant.*
● When choosing a sealant, make sure it is suitable for the application, particularly if being applied in a high-temperature area or in the vicinity of fuel. Certain manufacturers produce sealants in either clear, silver or black colours to match the finish of the engine. This has a particular application on motorcycles where much of the engine is exposed.
● Do not over-apply sealant. That which is squeezed out on the outside of the joint can be wiped off, whereas an excess of sealant on the inside can break off and clog oilways.

Breaking a sealed joint

● Age, heat, pressure and the use of hard setting sealant can cause two components to stick together so tightly that they are difficult to separate using finger pressure alone. Do not resort to using levers unless there is a pry point provided for this purpose (see illustration 7.1) or else the gasket surfaces will be damaged.
● Use a soft-faced hammer (see illustration 7.2) or a wood block and conventional hammer to strike the component near the mating surface. Avoid hammering against cast extremities since they may break off. If this method fails, try using a wood wedge between the two components.

Caution: If the joint will not separate, double-check that you have removed all the fasteners.

7.1 If a pry point is provided, apply gently pressure with a flat-bladed screwdriver

7.2 Tap around the joint with a soft-faced mallet if necessary - don't strike cooling fins

Removal of old gasket and sealant

● Paper gaskets will most likely come away complete, leaving only a few traces stuck on

> **HAYNES HINT**
>
> *Most components have one or two hollow locating dowels between the two gasket faces. If a dowel cannot be removed, do not resort to gripping it with pliers - it will almost certainly be distorted. Install a close-fitting socket or Phillips screwdriver into the dowel and then grip the outer edge of the dowel to free it.*

the sealing faces of the components. It is imperative that all traces are removed to ensure correct sealing of the new gasket.
● Very carefully scrape all traces of gasket away making sure that the sealing surfaces are not gouged or scored by the scraper (see illustrations 7.3, 7.4 and 7.5). Stubborn deposits can be removed by spraying with an aerosol gasket remover. Final preparation of

7.3 Paper gaskets can be scraped off with a gasket scraper tool . . .

7.4 . . . a knife blade . . .

7.5 . . . or a household scraper

REF•18 Tools and Workshop Tips

7.6 Fine abrasive paper is wrapped around a flat file to clean up the gasket face

7.7 A kitchen scourer can be used on stubborn deposits

8.1 Tighten the chain breaker to push the pin out of the link . . .

8.2 . . . withdraw the pin, remove the tool . . .

8.3 . . . and separate the chain link

8.4 Insert the new soft link, with O-rings, through the chain ends . . .

8.5 . . . install the O-rings over the pin ends . . .

8.6 . . . followed by the sideplate

8.7 Push the sideplate into position using a clamp

the gasket surface can be made with very fine abrasive paper or a plastic kitchen scourer **(see illustrations 7.6 and 7.7)**.

● Old sealant can be scraped or peeled off components, depending on the type originally used. Note that gasket removal compounds are available to avoid scraping the components clean; make sure the gasket remover suits the type of sealant used.

8 Chains

Breaking and joining final drive chains

● Drive chains for all but small bikes are continuous and do not have a clip-type connecting link. The chain must be broken using a chain breaker tool and the new chain securely riveted together using a new soft rivet-type link. Never use a clip-type connecting link instead of a rivet-type link, except in an emergency. Various chain breaking and riveting tools are available, either as separate tools or combined as illustrated in the accompanying photographs - read the instructions supplied with the tool carefully.

> ⚠ **Warning:** The need to rivet the new link pins correctly cannot be overstressed - loss of control of the motorcycle is very likely to result if the chain breaks in use.

● Rotate the chain and look for the soft link. The soft link pins look like they have been deeply centre-punched instead of peened over like all the other pins **(see illustration 8.9)** and its sideplate may be a different colour. Position the soft link midway between the sprockets and assemble the chain breaker tool over one of the soft link pins **(see illustration 8.1)**. Operate the tool to push the pin out through the chain **(see illustration 8.2)**. On an O-ring chain, remove the O-rings **(see illustration 8.3)**. Carry out the same procedure on the other soft link pin.

> **Caution:** Certain soft link pins (particularly on the larger chains) may require their ends to be filed or ground off before they can be pressed out using the tool.

● Check that you have the correct size and strength (standard or heavy duty) new soft link - do not reuse the old link. Look for the size marking on the chain sideplates **(see illustration 8.10)**.

● Position the chain ends so that they are engaged over the rear sprocket. On an O-ring chain, install a new O-ring over each pin of the link and insert the link through the two chain ends **(see illustration 8.4)**. Install a new O-ring over the end of each pin, followed by the sideplate (with the chain manufacturer's marking facing outwards) **(see illustrations 8.5 and 8.6)**. On an unsealed chain, insert the link through the two chain ends, then install the sideplate with the chain manufacturer's marking facing outwards.

● Note that it may not be possible to install the sideplate using finger pressure alone. If using a joining tool, assemble it so that the plates of the tool clamp the link and press the sideplate over the pins **(see illustration 8.7)**. Otherwise, use two small sockets placed over

Tools and Workshop Tips   REF•19

8.8 Assemble the chain riveting tool over one pin at a time and tighten it fully

8.9 Pin end correctly riveted (A), pin end unriveted (B)

the rivet ends and two pieces of the wood between a G-clamp. Operate the clamp to press the sideplate over the pins.

● Assemble the joining tool over one pin (following the maker's instructions) and tighten the tool down to spread the pin end securely **(see illustrations 8.8 and 8.9)**. Do the same on the other pin.

> ⚠ **Warning: Check that the pin ends are secure and that there is no danger of the sideplate coming loose. If the pin ends are cracked the soft link must be renewed.**

Final drive chain sizing

● Chains are sized using a three digit number, followed by a suffix to denote the chain type **(see illustration 8.10)**. Chain type is either standard or heavy duty (thicker sideplates), and also unsealed or O-ring/X-ring type.

● The first digit of the number relates to the pitch of the chain, ie the distance from the centre of one pin to the centre of the next pin **(see illustration 8.11)**. Pitch is expressed in eighths of an inch, as follows:

8.10 Typical chain size and type marking

8.11 Chain dimensions

Sizes commencing with a 4 (eg 428) have a pitch of 1/2 inch (12.7 mm)

Sizes commencing with a 5 (eg 520) have a pitch of 5/8 inch (15.9 mm)

Sizes commencing with a 6 (eg 630) have a pitch of 3/4 inch (19.1 mm)

● The second and third digits of the chain size relate to the width of the rollers, again in imperial units, eg the 525 shown has 5/16 inch (7.94 mm) rollers **(see illustration 8.11)**.

9 Hoses

Clamping to prevent flow

● Small-bore flexible hoses can be clamped to prevent fluid flow whilst a component is worked on. Whichever method is used, ensure that the hose material is not permanently distorted or damaged by the clamp.

a) A brake hose clamp available from auto accessory shops **(see illustration 9.1)**.
b) A wingnut type hose clamp **(see illustration 9.2)**.
c) Two sockets placed each side of the hose and held with straight-jawed self-locking grips **(see illustration 9.3)**.
d) Thick card each side of the hose held between straight-jawed self-locking grips **(see illustration 9.4)**.

9.1 Hoses can be clamped with an automotive brake hose clamp . . .

9.2 . . . a wingnut type hose clamp . . .

9.3 . . . two sockets and a pair of self-locking grips . . .

9.4 . . . or thick card and self-locking grips

Freeing and fitting hoses

● Always make sure the hose clamp is moved well clear of the hose end. Grip the hose with your hand and rotate it whilst pulling it off the union. If the hose has hardened due to age and will not move, slit it with a sharp knife and peel its ends off the union **(see illustration 9.5)**.

● Resist the temptation to use grease or soap on the unions to aid installation; although it helps the hose slip over the union it will equally aid the escape of fluid from the joint. It is preferable to soften the hose ends in hot water and wet the inside surface of the hose with water or a fluid which will evaporate.

9.5 Cutting a coolant hose free with a sharp knife

REF•20 Security

Introduction

In less time than it takes to read this introduction, a thief could steal your motorcycle. Returning only to find your bike has gone is one of the worst feelings in the world. Even if the motorcycle is insured against theft, once you've got over the initial shock, you will have the inconvenience of dealing with the police and your insurance company.

The motorcycle is an easy target for the professional thief and the joyrider alike and the official figures on motorcycle theft make for depressing reading; on average a motorcycle is stolen every 16 minutes in the UK!

Motorcycle thefts fall into two categories, those stolen 'to order' and those taken by opportunists. The thief stealing to order will be on the look out for a specific make and model and will go to extraordinary lengths to obtain that motorcycle. The opportunist thief on the other hand will look for easy targets which can be stolen with the minimum of effort and risk.

Whilst it is never going to be possible to make your machine 100% secure, it is estimated that around half of all stolen motorcycles are taken by opportunist thieves. Remember that the opportunist thief is always on the look out for the easy option: if there are two similar motorcycles parked side-by-side, they will target the one with the lowest level of security. By taking a few precautions, you can reduce the chances of your motorcycle being stolen.

Security equipment

There are many specialised motorcycle security devices available and the following text summarises their applications and their good and bad points.

Once you have decided on the type of security equipment which best suits your needs, we recommended that you read one of the many equipment tests regularly carried out by the motorcycle press. These tests compare the products from all the major manufacturers and give impartial ratings on their effectiveness, value-for-money and ease of use.

No one item of security equipment can provide complete protection. It is highly recommended that two or more of the items described below are combined to increase the security of your motorcycle (a lock and chain plus an alarm system is just about ideal). The more security measures fitted to the bike, the less likely it is to be stolen.

Lock and chain

Pros: *Very flexible to use; can be used to secure the motorcycle to almost any immovable object. On some locks and chains, the lock can be used on its own as a disc lock (see below).*

Cons: *Can be very heavy and awkward to carry on the motorcycle, although some types will be supplied with a carry bag which can be strapped to the pillion seat.*

● Heavy-duty chains and locks are an excellent security measure **(see illustration 1)**. Whenever the motorcycle is parked, use the lock and chain to secure the machine to a solid, immovable object such as a post or railings. This will prevent the machine from being ridden away or being lifted into the back of a van.

● When fitting the chain, always ensure the chain is routed around the motorcycle frame or swingarm **(see illustrations 2 and 3)**. Never merely pass the chain around one of the wheel rims; a thief may unbolt the wheel and lift the rest of the machine into a van, leaving you with just the wheel! Try to avoid having excess chain free, thus making it difficult to use cutting tools, and keep the chain and lock off the ground to prevent thieves attacking it with a cold chisel. Position the lock so that its lock barrel is facing downwards; this will make it harder for the thief to attack the lock mechanism.

Ensure the lock and chain you buy is of good quality and long enough to shackle your bike to a solid object

Pass the chain through the bike's frame, rather than just through a wheel . . .

. . . and loop it around a solid object

U-locks

Pros: Highly effective deterrent which can be used to secure the bike to a post or railings. Most U-locks come with a carrier which allows the lock to be easily carried on the bike.

Cons: Not as flexible to use as a lock and chain.

● These are solid locks which are similar in use to a lock and chain. U-locks are lighter than a lock and chain but not so flexible to use. The length and shape of the lock shackle limit the objects to which the bike can be secured **(see illustration 4)**.

Disc locks

Pros: Small, light and very easy to carry; most can be stored underneath the seat.

Cons: Does not prevent the motorcycle being lifted into a van. Can be very embarrassing if you forget to remove the lock before attempting to ride off!

● Disc locks are designed to be attached to the front brake disc. The lock passes through one of the holes in the disc and prevents the wheel rotating by jamming against the fork/brake caliper **(see illustration 5)**. Some are equipped with an alarm siren which sounds if the disc lock is moved; this not only acts as a theft deterrent but also as a handy reminder if you try to move the bike with the lock still fitted.

● Combining the disc lock with a length of cable which can be looped around a post or railings provides an additional measure of security **(see illustration 6)**.

Alarms and immobilisers

Pros: Once installed it is completely hassle-free to use. If the system is 'Thatcham' or 'Sold Secure-approved', insurance companies may give you a discount.

Cons: Can be expensive to buy and complex to install. No system will prevent the motorcycle from being lifted into a van and taken away.

● Electronic alarms and immobilisers are available to suit a variety of budgets. There are three different types of system available: pure alarms, pure immobilisers, and the more expensive systems which are combined alarm/immobilisers **(see illustration 7)**.

● An alarm system is designed to emit an audible warning if the motorcycle is being tampered with.

● An immobiliser prevents the motorcycle being started and ridden away by disabling its electrical systems.

● When purchasing an alarm/immobiliser system, check the cost of installing the system unless you are able to do it yourself. If the motorcycle is not used regularly, another consideration is the current drain of the system. All alarm/immobiliser systems are powered by the motorcycle's battery; purchasing a system with a very low current drain could prevent the battery losing its charge whilst the motorcycle is not being used.

U-locks can be used to secure the bike to a solid object – ensure you purchase one which is long enough

A typical disc lock attached through one of the holes in the disc

A disc lock combined with a security cable provides additional protection

A typical alarm/immobiliser system

REF•22 Security

Indelible markings can be applied to most areas of the bike – always apply the manufacturer's sticker to warn off thieves

Chemically-etched code numbers can be applied to main body panels . . .

. . . again, always ensure that the kit manufacturer's sticker is applied in a prominent position

Security marking kits

Pros: *Very cheap and effective deterrent. Many insurance companies will give you a discount on your insurance premium if a recognised security marking kit is used on your motorcycle.*

Cons: *Does not prevent the motorcycle being stolen by joyriders.*

● There are many different types of security marking kits available. The idea is to mark as many parts of the motorcycle as possible with a unique security number **(see illustrations 8, 9 and 10)**. A form will be included with the kit to register your personal details and those of the motorcycle with the kit manufacturer. This register is made available to the police to help them trace the rightful owner of any motorcycle or components which they recover should all other forms of identification have been removed. Always apply the warning stickers provided with the kit to deter thieves.

Ground anchors, wheel clamps and security posts

Pros: *An excellent form of security which will deter all but the most determined of thieves.*

Cons: *Awkward to install and can be expensive.*

● Whilst the motorcycle is at home, it is a good idea to attach it securely to the floor or a solid wall, even if it is kept in a securely locked garage. Various types of ground anchors, security posts and wheel clamps are available for this purpose **(see illustration 11)**. These security devices are either bolted to a solid concrete or brick structure or can be cemented into the ground.

Permanent ground anchors provide an excellent level of security when the bike is at home

Security at home

A high percentage of motorcycle thefts are from the owner's home. Here are some things to consider whenever your motorcycle is at home:

✔ Where possible, always keep the motorcycle in a securely locked garage. Never rely solely on the standard lock on the garage door, these are usual hopelessly inadequate. Fit an additional locking mechanism to the door and consider having the garage alarmed. A security light, activated by a movement sensor, is also a good investment.

✔ Always secure the motorcycle to the ground or a wall, even if it is inside a securely locked garage.

✔ Do not regularly leave the motorcycle outside your home, try to keep it out of sight wherever possible. If a garage is not available, fit a motorcycle cover over the bike to disguise its true identity.

✔ It is not uncommon for thieves to follow a motorcyclist home to find out where the bike is kept. They will then return at a later date. Be aware of this whenever you are returning home on your motorcycle. If you suspect you are being followed, do not return home, instead ride to a garage or shop and stop as a precaution.

✔ When selling a motorcycle, do not provide your home address or the location where the bike is normally kept. Arrange to meet the buyer at a location away from your home. Thieves have been known to pose as potential buyers to find out where motorcycles are kept and then return later to steal them.

Security away from the home

As well as fitting security equipment to your motorcycle here are a few general rules to follow whenever you park your motorcycle.
✔ Park in a busy, public place.
✔ Use car parks which incorporate security features, such as CCTV.

✔ At night, park in a well-lit area, preferably directly underneath a street light.
✔ Engage the steering lock.
✔ Secure the motorcycle to a solid, immovable object such as a post or railings with an additional lock. If this is not possible, secure the bike to a friend's motorcycle. Some public parking places provide security loops for motorcycles.
✔ Never leave your helmet or luggage attached to the motorcycle. Take them with you at all times.

Lubricants and fluids

A wide range of lubricants, fluids and cleaning agents is available for motor-cycles. This is a guide as to what is available, its applications and properties.

Four-stroke engine oil

● Engine oil is without doubt the most important component of any four-stroke engine. Modern motorcycle engines place a lot of demands on their oil and choosing the right type is essential. Using an unsuitable oil will lead to an increased rate of engine wear and could result in serious engine damage. Before purchasing oil, always check the recommended oil specification given by the manufacturer. The manufacturer will state a recommended 'type or classification' and also a specific 'viscosity' range for engine oil.

● The oil 'type or classification' is identified by its API (American Petroleum Institute) rating. The API rating will be in the form of two letters, e.g. SG. The S identifies the oil as being suitable for use in a petrol (gasoline) engine (S stands for spark ignition) and the second letter, ranging from A to J, identifies the oil's performance rating. The later this letter, the higher the specification of the oil; for example API SG oil exceeds the requirements of API SF oil. **Note:** *On some oils there may also be a second rating consisting of another two letters, the first letter being C, e.g. API SF/CD. This rating indicates the oil is also suitable for use in a diesel engines (the C stands for compression ignition) and is thus of no relevance for motorcycle use.*

● The 'viscosity' of the oil is identified by its SAE (Society of Automotive Engineers) rating. All modern engines require multigrade oils and the SAE rating will consist of two numbers, the first followed by a W, e.g. 10W/40. The first number indicates the viscosity rating of the oil at low temperatures (W stands for winter – tested at –20°C) and the second number represents the viscosity of the oil at high temperatures (tested at 100°C). The lower the number, the thinner the oil. For example an oil with an SAE 10W/40 rating will give better cold starting and running than an SAE 15W/40 oil.

● As well as ensuring the 'type' and 'viscosity' of the oil match the recommendations, another consideration to make when buying engine oil is whether to purchase a standard mineral-based oil, a semi-synthetic oil (also known as a synthetic blend or synthetic-based oil) or a fully-synthetic oil. Although all oils will have a similar rating and viscosity, their cost will vary considerably; mineral-based oils are the cheapest, the fully-synthetic oils the most expensive with the semi-synthetic oils falling somewhere in-between. This decision is very much up to the owner, but it should be noted that modern synthetic oils have far better lubricating and cleaning qualities than traditional mineral-based oils and tend to retain these properties for far longer. Bearing in mind the operating conditions inside a modern, high-revving motorcycle engine it is highly recommended that a fully synthetic oil is used. The extra expense at each service could save you money in the long term by preventing premature engine wear.

● As a final note always ensure that the oil is specifically designed for use in motorcycle engines. Engine oils designed primarily for use in car engines sometimes contain additives or friction modifiers which could cause clutch slip on a motorcycle fitted with a wet-clutch.

Two-stroke engine oil

● Modern two-stroke engines, with their high power outputs, place high demands on their oil. If engine seizure is to be avoided it is essential that a high-quality oil is used. Two-stroke oils differ hugely from four-stroke oils. The oil lubricates only the crankshaft and piston(s) (the transmission has its own lubricating oil) and is used on a total-loss basis where it is burnt completely during the combustion process.

● The Japanese have recently introduced a classification system for two-stroke oils, the JASO rating. This rating is in the form of two letters, either FA, FB or FC – FA is the lowest classification and FC the highest. Ensure the oil being used meets or exceeds the recommended rating specified by the manufacturer.

● As well as ensuring the oil rating matches the recommendation, another consideration to make when buying engine oil is whether to purchase a standard mineral-based oil, a semi-synthetic oil (also known as a synthetic blend or synthetic-based oil) or a fully-synthetic oil. The cost of each type of oil varies considerably; mineral-based oils are the cheapest, the fully-synthetic oils the most expensive with the semi-synthetic oils falling somewhere in-between. This decision is very much up to the owner, but it should be noted that modern synthetic oils have far better lubricating properties and burn cleaner than traditional mineral-based oils. It is therefore recommended that a fully synthetic oil is used. The extra expense could save you money in the long term by preventing premature engine wear, engine performance will be improved, carbon deposits and exhaust smoke will be reduced.

Lubricants and fluids

● Always ensure that the oil is specifically designed for use in an injector system. Many high quality two-stroke oils are designed for competition use and need to be pre-mixed with fuel. These oils are of a much higher viscosity and are not designed to flow through the injector pumps used on road-going two-stroke motorcycles.

Transmission (gear) oil

● On a two-stroke engine, the transmission and clutch are lubricated by their own separate oil bath which must be changed in accordance with the Maintenance Schedule.
● Although the engine and transmission units of most four-strokes use a common lubrication supply, there are some exceptions where the engine and gearbox have separate oil reservoirs and a dry clutch is used.
● Motorcycle manufacturers will either recommend a monograde transmission oil or a four-stroke multigrade engine oil to lubricate the transmission.
● Transmission oils, or gear oils as they are often called, are designed specifically for use in transmission systems. The viscosity of these oils is represented by an SAE number, but the scale of measurement applied is different to that used to grade engine oils. As a rough guide a SAE90 gear oil will be of the same viscosity as an SAE50 engine oil.

Shaft drive oil

● On models equipped with shaft final drive, the shaft drive gears are will have their own oil supply. The manufacturer will state a recommended 'type or classification' and also a specific 'viscosity' range in the same manner as for four-stroke engine oil.
● Gear oil classification is given by the number which follows the API GL (GL standing for gear lubricant) rating, the higher the number, the higher the specification of the oil, e.g. API GL5 oil is a higher specification than API GL4 oil. Ensure the oil meets or exceeds the classification specified and is of the correct viscosity. The viscosity of gear oils is also represented by an SAE number but the scale of measurement used is different to that used to grade engine oils. As a rough guide an SAE90 gear oil will be of the same viscosity as an SAE50 engine oil.
● If the use of an EP (Extreme Pressure) gear oil is specified, ensure the oil purchased is suitable.

Fork oil and suspension fluid

● Conventional telescopic front forks are hydraulic and require fork oil to work. To ensure the forks function correctly, the fork oil must be changed in accordance with the Maintenance Schedule.
● Fork oil is available in a variety of viscosities, identified by their SAE rating; fork oil ratings vary from light (SAE 5) to heavy (SAE 30). When purchasing fork oil, ensure the viscosity rating matches that specified by the manufacturer.
● Some lubricant manufacturers also produce a range of high-quality suspension fluids which are very similar to fork oil but are designed mainly for competition use. These fluids may have a different viscosity rating system which is not to be confused with the SAE rating of normal fork oil. Refer to the manufacturer's instructions if in any doubt.

Brake and clutch fluid

● All disc brake systems and some clutch systems are hydraulically operated. To ensure correct operation, the hydraulic fluid must be changed in accordance with the Maintenance Schedule.
● Brake and clutch fluid is classified by its DOT rating with most motorcycle manufacturers specifying DOT 3 or 4 fluid. Both fluid types are glycol-based and can be mixed together without adverse effect; DOT 4 fluid exceeds the requirements of DOT 3 fluid. Although it is safe to use DOT 4 fluid in a system designed for use with DOT 3 fluid, never use DOT 3 fluid in a system which specifies the use of DOT 4 as this will adversely affect the system's performance. The type required for the system will be marked on the fluid reservoir cap.
● Some manufacturers also produce a DOT 5 hydraulic fluid. DOT 5 hydraulic fluid is silicone-based and is not compatible with the glycol-based DOT 3 and 4 fluids. Never mix DOT 5 fluid with DOT 3 or 4 fluid as this will seriously affect the performance of the hydraulic system.

Coolant/antifreeze

● When purchasing coolant/antifreeze, always ensure it is suitable for use in an aluminium engine and contains corrosion inhibitors to prevent possible blockages of the internal coolant passages of the system. As a general rule, most coolants are designed to be used neat and should not be diluted whereas antifreeze can be mixed with distilled water to provide a coolant solution of the required strength. Refer to the manufacturer's instructions on the bottle.
● Ensure the coolant is changed in accordance with the Maintenance Schedule.

Chain lube

● Chain lube is an aerosol-type spray lubricant specifically designed for use on motorcycle final drive chains. Chain lube has two functions, to minimise friction between the final drive chain and sprockets and to prevent corrosion of the chain. Regular use of a good-quality chain lube will extend the life of the drive chain and sprockets and thus maximise the power being transmitted from the transmission to the rear wheel.
● When using chain lube, always allow some time for the solvents in the lube to evaporate before riding the motorcycle. This will minimise the amount of lube which will

Lubricants and fluids REF•25

'fling' off from the chain when the motorcycle is used. If the motorcycle is equipped with an 'O-ring' chain, ensure the chain lube is labelled as being suitable for use on 'O-ring' chains.

Degreasers and solvents

● There are many different types of solvents and degreasers available to remove the grime and grease which accumulate around the motorcycle during normal use. Degreasers and solvents are usually available as an aerosol-type spray or as a liquid which you apply with a brush. Always closely follow the manufacturer's instructions and wear eye protection during use. Be aware that many solvents are flammable and may give off noxious fumes; take adequate precautions when using them (see *Safety First!*).

● For general cleaning, use one of the many solvents or degreasers available from most motorcycle accessory shops. These solvents are usually applied then left for a certain time before being washed off with water.

Brake cleaner is a solvent specifically designed to remove all traces of oil, grease and dust from braking system components. Brake cleaner is designed to evaporate quickly and leaves behind no residue.

Carburettor cleaner is an aerosol-type solvent specifically designed to clear carburettor blockages and break down the hard deposits and gum often found inside carburettors during overhaul.

Contact cleaner is an aerosol-type solvent designed for cleaning electrical components. The cleaner will remove all traces of oil and dirt from components such as switch contacts or fouled spark plugs and then dry, leaving behind no residue.

Gasket remover is an aerosol-type solvent designed for removing stubborn gaskets from engine components during overhaul. Gasket remover will minimise the amount of scraping required to remove the gasket and therefore reduce the risk of damage to the mating surface.

Spray lubricants

● Aerosol-based spray lubricants are widely available and are excellent for lubricating lever pivots and exposed cables and switches. Try to use a lubricant which is of the dry-film type as the fluid evaporates, leaving behind a dry-film of lubricant. Lubricants which leave behind an oily residue will attract dust and dirt which will increase the rate of wear of the cable/lever.

● Most lubricants also act as a moisture dispersant and a penetrating fluid. This means they can also be used to 'dry out' electrical components such as wiring connectors or switches as well as helping to free seized fasteners.

Greases

● Grease is used to lubricate many of the pivot-points. A good-quality multi-purpose grease is suitable for most applications but some manufacturers will specify the use of specialist greases for use on components such as swingarm and suspension linkage bushes. These specialist greases can be purchased from most motorcycle (or car) accessory shops; commonly specified types include molybdenum disulphide grease, lithium-based grease, graphite-based grease, silicone-based grease and high-temperature copper-based grease.

Gasket sealing compounds

● Gasket sealing compounds can be used in conjunction with gaskets, to improve their sealing capabilities, or on their own to seal metal-to-metal joints. Depending on their type, sealing compounds either set hard or stay relatively soft and pliable.

● When purchasing a gasket sealing compound, ensure that it is designed specifically for use on an internal combustion engine. General multi-purpose sealants available from DIY stores may appear visibly similar but they are not designed to withstand the extreme heat or contact with fuel and oil encountered when used on an engine (see *Tools and Workshop Tips* for further information).

Thread locking compound

● Thread locking compounds are used to secure certain threaded fasteners in position to prevent them from loosening due to vibration. Thread locking compounds can be purchased from most motorcycle (and car) accessory shops. Ensure the threads of the both components are completely clean and dry before sparingly applying the locking compound (see *Tools and Workshop Tips* for further information).

Fuel additives

● Fuel additives which protect and clean the fuel system components are widely available. These additives are designed to remove all traces of deposits that build up on the carburettors/injectors and prevent wear, helping the fuel system to operate more efficiently. If a fuel additive is being used, check that it is suitable for use with your motorcycle, especially if your motorcycle is equipped with a catalytic converter.

● Octane boosters are also available. These additives are designed to improve the performance of highly-tuned engines being run on normal pump-fuel and are of no real use on standard motorcycles.

REF•26 Conversion Factors

Length (distance)
Inches (in)	x 25.4	= Millimetres (mm)	x 0.0394	=	Inches (in)
Feet (ft)	x 0.305	= Metres (m)	x 3.281	=	Feet (ft)
Miles	x 1.609	= Kilometres (km)	x 0.621	=	Miles

Volume (capacity)
Cubic inches (cu in; in^3)	x 16.387	= Cubic centimetres (cc; cm^3)	x 0.061	=	Cubic inches (cu in; in^3)
Imperial pints (Imp pt)	x 0.568	= Litres (l)	x 1.76	=	Imperial pints (Imp pt)
Imperial quarts (Imp qt)	x 1.137	= Litres (l)	x 0.88	=	Imperial quarts (Imp qt)
Imperial quarts (Imp qt)	x 1.201	= US quarts (US qt)	x 0.833	=	Imperial quarts (Imp qt)
US quarts (US qt)	x 0.946	= Litres (l)	x 1.057	=	US quarts (US qt)
Imperial gallons (Imp gal)	x 4.546	= Litres (l)	x 0.22	=	Imperial gallons (Imp gal)
Imperial gallons (Imp gal)	x 1.201	= US gallons (US gal)	x 0.833	=	Imperial gallons (Imp gal)
US gallons (US gal)	x 3.785	= Litres (l)	x 0.264	=	US gallons (US gal)

Mass (weight)
Ounces (oz)	x 28.35	= Grams (g)	x 0.035	=	Ounces (oz)
Pounds (lb)	x 0.454	= Kilograms (kg)	x 2.205	=	Pounds (lb)

Force
Ounces-force (ozf; oz)	x 0.278	= Newtons (N)	x 3.6	=	Ounces-force (ozf; oz)
Pounds-force (lbf; lb)	x 4.448	= Newtons (N)	x 0.225	=	Pounds-force (lbf; lb)
Newtons (N)	x 0.1	= Kilograms-force (kgf; kg)	x 9.81	=	Newtons (N)

Pressure
Pounds-force per square inch (psi; lbf/in^2; lb/in^2)	x 0.070	= Kilograms-force per square centimetre (kgf/cm^2; kg/cm^2)	x 14.223	=	Pounds-force per square inch (psi; lbf/in^2; lb/in^2)
Pounds-force per square inch (psi; lbf/in^2; lb/in^2)	x 0.068	= Atmospheres (atm)	x 14.696	=	Pounds-force per square inch (psi; lbf/in^2; lb/in^2)
Pounds-force per square inch (psi; lbf/in^2; lb/in^2)	x 0.069	= Bars	x 14.5	=	Pounds-force per square inch (psi; lbf/in^2; lb/in^2)
Pounds-force per square inch (psi; lbf/in^2; lb/in^2)	x 6.895	= Kilopascals (kPa)	x 0.145	=	Pounds-force per square inch (psi; lbf/in^2; lb/in^2)
Kilopascals (kPa)	x 0.01	= Kilograms-force per square centimetre (kgf/cm^2; kg/cm^2)	x 98.1	=	Kilopascals (kPa)
Millibar (mbar)	x 100	= Pascals (Pa)	x 0.01	=	Millibar (mbar)
Millibar (mbar)	x 0.0145	= Pounds-force per square inch (psi; lbf/in^2; lb/in^2)	x 68.947	=	Millibar (mbar)
Millibar (mbar)	x 0.75	= Millimetres of mercury (mmHg)	x 1.333	=	Millibar (mbar)
Millibar (mbar)	x 0.401	= Inches of water (inH$_2$O)	x 2.491	=	Millibar (mbar)
Millimetres of mercury (mmHg)	x 0.535	= Inches of water (inH$_2$O)	x 1.868	=	Millimetres of mercury (mmHg)
Inches of water (inH$_2$O)	x 0.036	= Pounds-force per square inch (psi; lbf/in^2; lb/in^2)	x 27.68	=	Inches of water (inH$_2$O)

Torque (moment of force)
Pounds-force inches (lbf in; lb in)	x 1.152	= Kilograms-force centimetre (kgf cm; kg cm)	x 0.868	=	Pounds-force inches (lbf in; lb in)
Pounds-force inches (lbf in; lb in)	x 0.113	= Newton metres (Nm)	x 8.85	=	Pounds-force inches (lbf in; lb in)
Pounds-force inches (lbf in; lb in)	x 0.083	= Pounds-force feet (lbf ft; lb ft)	x 12	=	Pounds-force inches (lbf in; lb in)
Pounds-force feet (lbf ft; lb ft)	x 0.138	= Kilograms-force metres (kgf m; kg m)	x 7.233	=	Pounds-force feet (lbf ft; lb ft)
Pounds-force feet (lbf ft; lb ft)	x 1.356	= Newton metres (Nm)	x 0.738	=	Pounds-force feet (lbf ft; lb ft)
Newton metres (Nm)	x 0.102	= Kilograms-force metres (kgf m; kg m)	x 9.804	=	Newton metres (Nm)

Power
Horsepower (hp)	x 745.7	= Watts (W)	x 0.0013	=	Horsepower (hp)

Velocity (speed)
Miles per hour (miles/hr; mph)	x 1.609	= Kilometres per hour (km/hr; kph)	x 0.621	=	Miles per hour (miles/hr; mph)

Fuel consumption*
Miles per gallon (mpg)	x 0.354	= Kilometres per litre (km/l)	x 2.825	=	Miles per gallon (mpg)

Temperature
Degrees Fahrenheit = (°C x 1.8) + 32   Degrees Celsius (Degrees Centigrade; °C) = (°F - 32) x 0.56

*It is common practice to convert from miles per gallon (mpg) to litres/100 kilometres (l/100km), where mpg x l/100 km = 282

MOT Test Checks REF•27

About the MOT Test

In the UK, all vehicles more than three years old are subject to an annual test to ensure that they meet minimum safety requirements. A current test certificate must be issued before a machine can be used on public roads, and is required before a road fund licence can be issued. Riding without a current test certificate will also invalidate your insurance.

For most owners, the MOT test is an annual cause for anxiety, and this is largely due to owners not being sure what needs to be checked prior to submitting the motorcycle for testing. The simple answer is that a fully roadworthy motorcycle will have no difficulty in passing the test.

This is a guide to getting your motorcycle through the MOT test. Obviously it will not be possible to examine the motorcycle to the same standard as the professional MOT tester, particularly in view of the equipment required for some of the checks. However, working through the following procedures will enable you to identify any problem areas before submitting the motorcycle for the test.

It has only been possible to summarise the test requirements here, based on the regulations in force at the time of printing. Test standards are becoming increasingly stringent, although there are some exemptions for older vehicles. More information about the MOT test can be obtained from the TSO publications, *How Safe is your Motorcycle* and *The MOT Inspection Manual for Motorcycle Testing*.

Many of the checks require that one of the wheels is raised off the ground. If the motorcycle doesn't have a centre stand, note that an auxiliary stand will be required. Additionally, the help of an assistant may prove useful.

Certain exceptions apply to machines under 50 cc, machines without a lighting system, and Classic bikes - if in doubt about any of the requirements listed below seek confirmation from an MOT tester prior to submitting the motorcycle for the test.

Check that the frame number is clearly visible.

> **HAYNES HINT**
> *If a component is in borderline condition, the tester has discretion in deciding whether to pass or fail it. If the motorcycle presented is clean and evidently well cared for, the tester may be more inclined to pass a borderline component than if the motorcycle is scruffy and apparently neglected.*

Electrical System

Lights, turn signals, horn and reflector

✔ With the ignition on, check the operation of the following electrical components. **Note:** *The electrical components on certain small-capacity machines are powered by the generator, requiring that the engine is run for this check.*

a) Headlight and tail light. Check that both illuminate in the low and high beam switch positions.
b) Position lights. Check that the front position (or sidelight) and tail light illuminate in this switch position.
c) Turn signals. Check that all flash at the correct rate, and that the warning light(s) function correctly. Check that the turn signal switch works correctly.
d) Hazard warning system (where fitted). Check that all four turn signals flash in this switch position.
e) Brake stop light. Check that the light comes on when the front and rear brakes are independently applied. Models first used on or after 1st April 1986 must have a brake light switch on each brake.
f) Horn. Check that the sound is continuous and of reasonable volume.

✔ Check that there is a red reflector on the rear of the machine, either mounted separately or as part of the tail light lens.
✔ Check the condition of the headlight, tail light and turn signal lenses.

Headlight beam height

✔ The MOT tester will perform a headlight beam height check using specialised beam setting equipment **(see illustration 1)**. This equipment will not be available to the home mechanic, but if you suspect that the headlight is incorrectly set or may have been maladjusted in the past, you can perform a rough test as follows.

✔ Position the bike in a straight line facing a brick wall. The bike must be off its stand, upright and with a rider seated. Measure the height from the ground to the centre of the headlight and mark a horizontal line on the wall at this height. Position the motorcycle 3.8 metres from the wall and draw a vertical line up the wall central to the centreline of the motorcycle. Switch to dipped beam and check that the beam pattern falls slightly lower than the horizontal line and to the left of the vertical line **(see illustration 2)**.

Headlight beam height checking equipment

Home workshop beam alignment check

REF•28 MOT Test Checks

Exhaust System and Final Drive

Exhaust

✔ Check that the exhaust mountings are secure and that the system does not foul any of the rear suspension components.
✔ Start the motorcycle. When the revs are increased, check that the exhaust is neither holed nor leaking from any of its joints. On a linked system, check that the collector box is not leaking due to corrosion.
✔ Note that the exhaust decibel level ("loudness" of the exhaust) is assessed at the discretion of the tester. If the motorcycle was first used on or after 1st January 1985 the silencer must carry the BSAU 193 stamp, or a marking relating to its make and model, or be of OE (original equipment) manufacture. If the silencer is marked NOT FOR ROAD USE, RACING USE ONLY or similar, it will fail the MOT.

Final drive

✔ On chain or belt drive machines, check that the chain/belt is in good condition and does not have excessive slack. Also check that the sprocket is securely mounted on the rear wheel hub. Check that the chain/belt guard is in place.
✔ On shaft drive bikes, check for oil leaking from the drive unit and fouling the rear tyre.

Steering and Suspension

Steering

✔ With the front wheel raised off the ground, rotate the steering from lock to lock. The handlebar or switches must not contact the fuel tank or be close enough to trap the rider's hand. Problems can be caused by damaged lock stops on the lower yoke and frame, or by the fitting of non-standard handlebars.
✔ When performing the lock to lock check, also ensure that the steering moves freely without drag or notchiness. Steering movement can be impaired by poorly routed cables, or by overtight head bearings or worn bearings. The tester will perform a check of the steering head bearing lower race by mounting the front wheel on a surface plate, then performing a lock to lock check with the weight of the machine on the lower bearing (see illustration 3).
✔ Grasp the fork sliders (lower legs) and attempt to push and pull on the forks (see illustration 4). Any play in the steering head bearings will be felt. Note that in extreme cases, wear of the front fork bushes can be misinterpreted for head bearing play.
✔ Check that the handlebars are securely mounted.
✔ Check that the handlebar grip rubbers are secure. They should by bonded to the bar left end and to the throttle cable pulley on the right end.

Front wheel mounted on a surface plate for steering head bearing lower race check

Front suspension

✔ With the motorcycle off the stand, hold the front brake on and pump the front forks up and down (see illustration 5). Check that they are adequately damped.

Checking the steering head bearings for freeplay

Hold the front brake on and pump the front forks up and down to check operation

MOT Test Checks REF•29

Inspect the area around the fork dust seal for oil leakage (arrow)

Bounce the rear of the motorcycle to check rear suspension operation

Checking for rear suspension linkage play

✔ Inspect the area above and around the front fork oil seals **(see illustration 6)**. There should be no sign of oil on the fork tube (stanchion) nor leaking down the slider (lower leg). On models so equipped, check that there is no oil leaking from the anti-dive units.
✔ On models with swingarm front suspension, check that there is no freeplay in the linkage when moved from side to side.

Rear suspension

✔ With the motorcycle off the stand and an assistant supporting the motorcycle by its handlebars, bounce the rear suspension **(see illustration 7)**. Check that the suspension components do not foul on any of the cycle parts and check that the shock absorber(s) provide adequate damping.
✔ Visually inspect the shock absorber(s) and check that there is no sign of oil leakage from its damper. This is somewhat restricted on certain single shock models due to the location of the shock absorber.
✔ With the rear wheel raised off the ground, grasp the wheel at the highest point and attempt to pull it up **(see illustration 8)**. Any play in the swingarm pivot or suspension linkage bearings will be felt as movement.
Note: *Do not confuse play with actual suspension movement.* Failure to lubricate suspension linkage bearings can lead to bearing failure **(see illustration 9)**.
✔ With the rear wheel raised off the ground, grasp the swingarm ends and attempt to move the swingarm from side to side and forwards and backwards - any play indicates wear of the swingarm pivot bearings **(see illustration 10)**.

Worn suspension linkage pivots (arrows) are usually the cause of play in the rear suspension

Grasp the swingarm at the ends to check for play in its pivot bearings

REF•30 MOT Test Checks

Brake pad wear can usually be viewed without removing the caliper. Most pads have wear indicator grooves (1) and some also have indicator tangs (2)

On drum brakes, check the angle of the operating lever with the brake fully applied. Most drum brakes have a wear indicator pointer and scale.

Brakes, Wheels and Tyres

Brakes

✔ With the wheel raised off the ground, apply the brake then free it off, and check that the wheel is about to revolve freely without brake drag.

✔ On disc brakes, examine the disc itself. Check that it is securely mounted and not cracked.

✔ On disc brakes, view the pad material through the caliper mouth and check that the pads are not worn down beyond the limit **(see illustration 11)**.

✔ On drum brakes, check that when the brake is applied the angle between the operating lever and cable or rod is not too great **(see illustration 12)**. Check also that the operating lever doesn't foul any other components.

✔ On disc brakes, examine the flexible hoses from top to bottom. Have an assistant hold the brake on so that the fluid in the hose is under pressure, and check that there is no sign of fluid leakage, bulges or cracking. If there are any metal brake pipes or unions, check that these are free from corrosion and damage. Where a brake-linked anti-dive system is fitted, check the hoses to the anti-dive in a similar manner.

✔ Check that the rear brake torque arm is secure and that its fasteners are secured by self-locking nuts or castellated nuts with split-pins or R-pins **(see illustration 13)**.

✔ On models with ABS, check that the self-check warning light in the instrument panel works.

✔ The MOT tester will perform a test of the motorcycle's braking efficiency based on a calculation of rider and motorcycle weight. Although this cannot be carried out at home, you can at least ensure that the braking systems are properly maintained. For hydraulic disc brakes, check the fluid level, lever/pedal feel (bleed of air if its spongy) and pad material. For drum brakes, check adjustment, cable or rod operation and shoe lining thickness.

Wheels and tyres

✔ Check the wheel condition. Cast wheels should be free from cracks and if of the built-up design, all fasteners should be secure. Spoked wheels should be checked for broken, corroded, loose or bent spokes.

✔ With the wheel raised off the ground, spin the wheel and visually check that the tyre and wheel run true. Check that the tyre does not foul the suspension or mudguards.

✔ With the wheel raised off the ground, grasp the wheel and attempt to move it about the axle (spindle) **(see illustration 14)**. Any play felt here indicates wheel bearing failure.

Brake torque arm must be properly secured at both ends

Check for wheel bearing play by trying to move the wheel about the axle (spindle)

MOT Test Checks REF•31

Checking the tyre tread depth

Tyre direction of rotation arrow can be found on tyre sidewall

Castellated type wheel axle (spindle) nut must be secured by a split pin or R-pin

Two straightedges are used to check wheel alignment

✔ Check the tyre tread depth, tread condition and sidewall condition **(see illustration 15)**.
✔ Check the tyre type. Front and rear tyre types must be compatible and be suitable for road use. Tyres marked NOT FOR ROAD USE, COMPETITION USE ONLY or similar, will fail the MOT.

✔ If the tyre sidewall carries a direction of rotation arrow, this must be pointing in the direction of normal wheel rotation **(see illustration 16)**.
✔ Check that the wheel axle (spindle) nuts (where applicable) are properly secured. A self-locking nut or castellated nut with a split-pin or R-pin can be used **(see illustration 17)**.
✔ Wheel alignment is checked with the motorcycle off the stand and a rider seated. With the front wheel pointing straight ahead, two perfectly straight lengths of metal or wood and placed against the sidewalls of both tyres **(see illustration 18)**. The gap each side of the front tyre must be equidistant on both sides. Incorrect wheel alignment may be due to a cocked rear wheel (often as the result of poor chain adjustment) or in extreme cases, a bent frame.

General checks and condition

✔ Check the security of all major fasteners, bodypanels, seat, fairings (where fitted) and mudguards.

✔ Check that the rider and pillion footrests, handlebar levers and brake pedal are securely mounted.

✔ Check for corrosion on the frame or any load-bearing components. If severe, this may affect the structure, particularly under stress.

Sidecars

A motorcycle fitted with a sidecar requires additional checks relating to the stability of the machine and security of attachment and swivel joints, plus specific wheel alignment (toe-in) requirements. Additionally, tyre and lighting requirements differ from conventional motorcycle use. Owners are advised to check MOT test requirements with an official test centre.

REF•32 Storage

Preparing for storage

Before you start

If repairs or an overhaul is needed, see that this is carried out now rather than left until you want to ride the bike again.

Give the bike a good wash and scrub all dirt from its underside. Make sure the bike dries completely before preparing for storage.

Engine

● Remove the spark plug(s) and lubricate the cylinder bores with approximately a teaspoon of motor oil using a spout-type oil can (see illustration 1). Reinstall the spark plug(s). Crank the engine over a couple of times to coat the piston rings and bores with oil. If the bike has a kickstart, use this to turn the engine over. If not, flick the kill switch to the OFF position and crank the engine over on the starter (see illustration 2). If the nature on the ignition system prevents the starter operating with the kill switch in the OFF position, remove the spark plugs and fit them back in their caps; ensure that the plugs are earthed (grounded) against the cylinder head when the starter is operated (see illustration 3).

⚠ **Warning: It is important that the plugs are earthed (grounded) away from the spark plug holes otherwise there is a risk of atomised fuel from the cylinders igniting.**

> **HAYNES HiNT** On a single cylinder four-stroke engine, you can seal the combustion chamber completely by positioning the piston at TDC on the compression stroke.

● Drain the carburettor(s) otherwise there is a risk of jets becoming blocked by gum deposits from the fuel (see illustration 4).

● If the bike is going into long-term storage, consider adding a fuel stabiliser to the fuel in the tank. If the tank is drained completely, corrosion of its internal surfaces may occur if left unprotected for a long period. The tank can be treated with a rust preventative especially for this purpose. Alternatively, remove the tank and pour half a litre of motor oil into it, install the filler cap and shake the tank to coat its internals with oil before draining off the excess. The same effect can also be achieved by spraying WD40 or a similar water-dispersant around the inside of the tank via its flexible nozzle.

● Make sure the cooling system contains the correct mix of antifreeze. Antifreeze also contains important corrosion inhibitors.

● The air intakes and exhaust can be sealed off by covering or plugging the openings. Ensure that you do not seal in any condensation; run the engine until it is hot,

Squirt a drop of motor oil into each cylinder

Flick the kill switch to OFF . . .

. . . and ensure that the metal bodies of the plugs (arrows) are earthed against the cylinder head

Connect a hose to the carburettor float chamber drain stub (arrow) and unscrew the drain screw

Storage REF•33

Exhausts can be sealed off with a plastic bag

Disconnect the negative lead (A) first, followed by the positive lead (B)

Use a suitable battery charger - this kit also assess battery condition

then switch off and allow to cool. Tape a piece of thick plastic over the silencer end(s) **(see illustration 5)**. Note that some advocate pouring a tablespoon of motor oil into the silencer(s) before sealing them off.

Battery

● Remove it from the bike - in extreme cases of cold the battery may freeze and crack its case **(see illustration 6)**.

● Check the electrolyte level and top up if necessary (conventional refillable batteries). Clean the terminals.
● Store the battery off the motorcycle and away from any sources of fire. Position a wooden block under the battery if it is to sit on the ground.
● Give the battery a trickle charge for a few hours every month **(see illustration 7)**.

Tyres

● Place the bike on its centrestand or an auxiliary stand which will support the motorcycle in an upright position. Position wood blocks under the tyres to keep them off the ground and to provide insulation from damp. If the bike is being put into long-term storage, ideally both tyres should be off the ground; not only will this protect the tyres, but will also ensure that no load is placed on the steering head or wheel bearings.
● Deflate each tyre by 5 to 10 psi, no more or the beads may unseat from the rim, making subsequent inflation difficult on tubeless tyres.

Pivots and controls

● Lubricate all lever, pedal, stand and footrest pivot points. If grease nipples are fitted to the rear suspension components, apply lubricant to the pivots.
● Lubricate all control cables.

Cycle components

● Apply a wax protectant to all painted and plastic components. Wipe off any excess, but don't polish to a shine. Where fitted, clean the screen with soap and water.
● Coat metal parts with Vaseline (petroleum jelly). When applying this to the fork tubes, do not compress the forks otherwise the seals will rot from contact with the Vaseline.
● Apply a vinyl cleaner to the seat.

Storage conditions

● Aim to store the bike in a shed or garage which does not leak and is free from damp.
● Drape an old blanket or bedspread over the bike to protect it from dust and direct contact with sunlight (which will fade paint). This also hides the bike from prying eyes. Beware of tight-fitting plastic covers which may allow condensation to form and settle on the bike.

Getting back on the road

Engine and transmission

● Change the oil and replace the oil filter. If this was done prior to storage, check that the oil hasn't emulsified - a thick whitish substance which occurs through condensation.
● Remove the spark plugs. Using a spout-type oil can, squirt a few drops of oil into the cylinder(s). This will provide initial lubrication as the piston rings and bores comes back into contact. Service the spark plugs, or fit new ones, and install them in the engine.

● Check that the clutch isn't stuck on. The plates can stick together if left standing for some time, preventing clutch operation. Engage a gear and try rocking the bike back and forth with the clutch lever held against the handlebar. If this doesn't work on cable-operated clutches, hold the clutch lever back against the handlebar with a strong elastic band or cable tie for a couple of hours **(see illustration 8)**.
● If the air intakes or silencer end(s) were blocked off, remove the bung or cover used.
● If the fuel tank was coated with a rust

Hold clutch lever back against the handlebar with elastic bands or a cable tie

Storage

preventative, oil or a stabiliser added to the fuel, drain and flush the tank and dispose of the fuel sensibly. If no action was taken with the fuel tank prior to storage, it is advised that the old fuel is disposed of since it will go off over a period of time. Refill the fuel tank with fresh fuel.

Frame and running gear

- Oil all pivot points and cables.
- Check the tyre pressures. They will definitely need inflating if pressures were reduced for storage.
- Lubricate the final drive chain (where applicable).
- Remove any protective coating applied to the fork tubes (stanchions) since this may well destroy the fork seals. If the fork tubes weren't protected and have picked up rust spots, remove them with very fine abrasive paper and refinish with metal polish.
- Check that both brakes operate correctly. Apply each brake hard and check that it's not possible to move the motorcycle forwards, then check that the brake frees off again once released. Brake caliper pistons can stick due to corrosion around the piston head, or on the sliding caliper types, due to corrosion of the slider pins. If the brake doesn't free after repeated operation, take the caliper off for examination. Similarly drum brakes can stick due to a seized operating cam, cable or rod linkage.
- If the motorcycle has been in long-term storage, renew the brake fluid and clutch fluid (where applicable).
- Depending on where the bike has been stored, the wiring, cables and hoses may have been nibbled by rodents. Make a visual check and investigate disturbed wiring loom tape.

Battery

- If the battery has been previously removal and given top up charges it can simply be reconnected. Remember to connect the positive cable first and the negative cable last.
- On conventional refillable batteries, if the battery has not received any attention, remove it from the motorcycle and check its electrolyte level. Top up if necessary then charge the battery. If the battery fails to hold a charge and a visual checks show heavy white sulphation of the plates, the battery is probably defective and must be renewed. This is particularly likely if the battery is old. Confirm battery condition with a specific gravity check.
- On sealed (MF) batteries, if the battery has not received any attention, remove it from the motorcycle and charge it according to the information on the battery case - if the battery fails to hold a charge it must be renewed.

Starting procedure

- If a kickstart is fitted, turn the engine over a couple of times with the ignition OFF to distribute oil around the engine. If no kickstart is fitted, flick the engine kill switch OFF and the ignition ON and crank the engine over a couple of times to work oil around the upper cylinder components. If the nature of the ignition system is such that the starter won't work with the kill switch OFF, remove the spark plugs, fit them back into their caps and earth (ground) their bodies on the cylinder head. Reinstall the spark plugs afterwards.
- Switch the kill switch to RUN, operate the choke and start the engine. If the engine won't start don't continue cranking the engine - not only will this flatten the battery, but the starter motor will overheat. Switch the ignition off and try again later. If the engine refuses to start, go through the fault finding procedures in this manual. **Note:** *If the bike has been in storage for a long time, old fuel or a carburettor blockage may be the problem. Gum deposits in carburettors can block jets - if a carburettor cleaner doesn't prove successful the carburettors must be dismantled for cleaning.*
- Once the engine has started, check that the lights, turn signals and horn work properly.
- Treat the bike gently for the first ride and check all fluid levels on completion. Settle the bike back into the maintenance schedule.

Fault Finding REF•35

This Section provides an easy reference-guide to the more common faults that are likely to afflict your machine. Obviously, the opportunities are almost limitless for faults to occur as a result of obscure failures, and to try and cover all eventualities would require a book. Indeed, a number have been written on the subject.

Successful troubleshooting is not a mysterious 'black art' but the application of a bit of knowledge combined with a systematic and logical approach to the problem. Approach any troubleshooting by first accurately identifying the symptom and then checking through the list of possible causes, starting with the simplest or most obvious and progressing in stages to the most complex.

Take nothing for granted, but above all apply liberal quantities of common sense.

The main symptom of a fault is given in the text as a major heading below which are listed the various systems or areas which may contain the fault. Details of each possible cause for a fault and the remedial action to be taken are given, in brief, in the paragraphs below each heading. Further information should be sought in the relevant Chapter.

1 Engine doesn't start or is difficult to start
- [ ] Starter motor doesn't rotate
- [ ] Starter motor rotates but engine does not turn over
- [ ] Starter works but engine won't turn over (seized)
- [ ] No fuel flow
- [ ] Engine flooded
- [ ] No spark or weak spark
- [ ] Compression low
- [ ] Stalls after starting
- [ ] Rough idle

2 Poor running at low speed
- [ ] Spark weak
- [ ] Fuel/air mixture incorrect
- [ ] Compression low
- [ ] Poor acceleration

3 Poor running or no power at high speed
- [ ] Firing incorrect
- [ ] Fuel/air mixture incorrect
- [ ] Compression low
- [ ] Knocking or pinking
- [ ] Miscellaneous causes

4 Overheating
- [ ] Engine overheats
- [ ] Firing incorrect
- [ ] Fuel/air mixture incorrect
- [ ] Compression too high
- [ ] Engine load excessive
- [ ] Lubrication inadequate
- [ ] Miscellaneous causes

5 Clutch problems
- [ ] Clutch slipping
- [ ] Clutch not disengaging completely

6 Gearchange problems
- [ ] Doesn't go into gear, or lever doesn't return
- [ ] Jumps out of gear
- [ ] Overshifts

7 Abnormal engine noise
- [ ] Knocking or pinking
- [ ] Piston slap or rattling
- [ ] Valve noise
- [ ] Other noise

8 Abnormal driveline noise
- [ ] Clutch noise
- [ ] Transmission noise
- [ ] Final drive noise

9 Abnormal frame and suspension noise
- [ ] Front end noise
- [ ] Rear suspension noise
- [ ] Brake noise

10 Oil pressure warning light comes on
- [ ] Engine lubrication system
- [ ] Electrical system

11 Excessive exhaust smoke
- [ ] White smoke
- [ ] Black smoke
- [ ] Brown smoke

12 Poor handling or stability
- [ ] Handlebar hard to turn
- [ ] Handlebar shakes or vibrates excessively
- [ ] Handlebar pulls to one side
- [ ] Poor shock absorbing qualities

13 Braking problems
- [ ] Brakes are spongy, don't hold
- [ ] Brake lever or pedal pulsates
- [ ] Brakes drag

14 Electrical problems
- [ ] Battery dead or weak
- [ ] Battery overcharged

1 Engine doesn't start or is difficult to start

Starter motor doesn't rotate
- [ ] Engine kill switch OFF.
- [ ] Fuse blown. Check main fuse and ignition/starter circuit fuse (Chapter 9).
- [ ] Battery voltage low. Check and recharge battery (Chapter 9).
- [ ] Starter motor defective. Make sure the wiring to the starter is secure. Make sure the starter relay clicks when the start button is pushed. If the relay clicks, then the fault is in the wiring or motor.
- [ ] Starter relay faulty. Check it according to the procedure in Chapter 9.
- [ ] Starter switch not contacting. The contacts could be wet, corroded or dirty. Disassemble and clean the switch (Chapter 9).
- [ ] Wiring open or shorted. Check all wiring connections and harnesses to make sure that they are dry, tight and not corroded. Also check for broken or frayed wires that can cause a short to ground (earth) (see wiring diagram, Chapter 9).
- [ ] Ignition (main) switch defective. Check the switch according to the procedure in Chapter 9. Replace the switch with a new one if it is defective.
- [ ] Engine kill switch defective. Check for wet, dirty or corroded contacts. Clean or replace the switch as necessary (Chapter 9).
- [ ] Faulty neutral, side stand or clutch switch. Check the wiring to each switch and the switch itself according to the procedures in Chapter 9.

Starter motor rotates but engine does not turn over
- [ ] Starter clutch defective. Inspect and repair or replace (Chapter 2).
- [ ] Damaged idle/reduction or starter gears. Inspect and renew the damaged parts (Chapter 2).

Starter works but engine won't turn over (seized)
- [ ] Seized engine caused by one or more internally damaged components. Failure due to wear, abuse or lack of lubrication. Damage can include seized valves, followers, camshafts, pistons, crankshaft, connecting rod bearings, or transmission gears or bearings. Refer to Chapter 2 for engine disassembly.

No fuel flow
- [ ] No fuel in tank.
- [ ] Fuel tank breather hose obstructed.
- [ ] Fuel tap filter or in-line filter (carburettor models) or fuel pump assembly filter (fuel injection models) clogged. Remove the tap or pump and clean or renew the filter (Chapter 1 and 4).
- [ ] Fuel line clogged. Pull the fuel line loose and carefully blow through it.
- [ ] Float needle valve clogged (carburettor models). For all of the valves to be clogged, either a very bad batch of fuel with an unusual additive has been used, or some other foreign material has entered the tank. Many times after a machine has been stored for many months without running, the fuel turns to a varnish-like liquid and forms deposits on the inlet needle valves and jets. The carburettors should be removed and overhauled if draining the float chambers doesn't solve the problem.
- [ ] Fuel pump or relay faulty. Check the fuel pump and relay (Chapter 4).

Engine flooded (carburettor models)
- [ ] Float height too high. Check as described in Chapter 4.
- [ ] Float needle valve worn or stuck open. A piece of dirt, rust or other debris can cause the valve to seat improperly, causing excess fuel to be admitted to the float chamber. In this case, the float chamber should be cleaned and the needle valve and seat inspected. If the needle and seat are worn, then the leaking will persist and the parts should be replaced with new ones (Chapter 4).
- [ ] Starting technique incorrect. Under normal circumstances (i.e., if all the carburettor functions are sound) the machine should start with little or no throttle. When the engine is cold, the choke should be operated and the engine started without opening the throttle. When the engine is at operating temperature, only a very slight amount of throttle should be necessary. If the engine is flooded, raise the fuel tank and turn the fuel tap OFF and hold the throttle open while cranking the engine. This will allow additional air to reach the cylinders. Remember to turn the fuel tap back ON after the engine starts.

Engine flooded (fuel injection models)
- [ ] Faulty pressure regulator – if it is stuck closed there could be excessive pressure in the fuel rail. Check as described in Chapter 4.
- [ ] Injector(s) stuck open, allowing a constant flow of fuel into the engine. Check as described in Chapter 4.
- [ ] Starting technique incorrect. The throttle should be fully closed when starting the engine – a fully open throttle will cause the fuel supply to be shut off by the ECM. If the engine is flooded, set the engine kill switch to RUN and turn the ignition ON. Open the throttle fully and operate the stater motor for 5 seconds. The engine can then be started normally.

Compression low
- [ ] Spark plugs loose. Remove the plugs and inspect their threads. Reinstall and tighten to the specified torque (Chapter 1).
- [ ] Cylinder head not sufficiently tightened down. If a cylinder head is suspected of being loose, then there's a chance that the gasket or head is damaged if the problem has persisted for any length of time. The head bolts should be tightened to the proper torque in the correct sequence (Chapter 2).
- [ ] Incorrect valve clearance. This means that the valve is not closing completely and compression pressure is leaking past the valve. Check and adjust the valve clearances (Chapter 1).
- [ ] Cylinder and/or piston worn. Excessive wear will cause compression pressure to leak past the rings. This is usually accompanied by worn rings as well. A top-end overhaul is necessary (Chapter 2).
- [ ] Piston rings worn, weak, broken, or sticking. Broken or sticking piston rings usually indicate a lubrication or carburation problem that causes excess carbon deposits or seizures to form on the pistons and rings. Top-end overhaul is necessary (Chapter 2).
- [ ] Piston ring-to-groove clearance excessive. This is caused by excessive wear of the piston ring lands. Piston replacement is necessary (Chapter 2).
- [ ] Cylinder head gasket damaged. If a head is allowed to become loose, or if excessive carbon build-up on the piston crown and combustion chamber causes extremely high compression, the head gasket may leak. Retorquing the head is not always sufficient to restore the seal, so gasket renewal is necessary (Chapter 2).
- [ ] Cylinder head warped. This is caused by overheating or improperly tightened head bolts. Machine shop resurfacing or head replacement is necessary (Chapter 2).
- [ ] Valve spring broken or weak. Caused by component failure or wear; the springs must be renewed (Chapter 2).
- [ ] Valve not seating properly. This is caused by a bent valve (from over-revving or improper valve adjustment), burned valve or seat (improper carburation) or an accumulation of carbon deposits on the seat (from carburation or lubrication problems). The valves must be cleaned and/or renewed and the seats serviced if possible (Chapter 2).

Fault Finding REF•37

1 Engine doesn't start or is difficult to start (continued)

No spark or weak spark

- ☐ Engine kill switch turned to the OFF position.
- ☐ Battery voltage low. Check and recharge the battery as necessary (Chapter 9).
- ☐ Spark plugs dirty, defective or worn out. Locate reason for fouled plugs using spark plug condition chart and follow the plug maintenance procedures (Chapter 1).
- ☐ Spark plug caps/ignition coils faulty or not making good contact over the spark plugs. Check condition. Replace if cracks or deterioration are evident (Chapter 5).
- ☐ Ignition control unit (carburettor models) or ECM (fuel injection models) defective. Check the unit, referring to Chapter 5 or 4 for details.
- ☐ Pulse generator defective. Check the unit, referring to Chapter 5 (carburettor models) or 4 (fuel injection models) for details.
- ☐ Ignition or kill switch shorted. This is usually caused by water, corrosion, damage or excessive wear. The switches can be disassembled and cleaned with electrical contact cleaner. If cleaning does not help, renew the switches (Chapter 9).
- ☐ Wiring shorted or broken between:
    a) Ignition (main) switch and engine kill switch (or blown fuse)
    b) Ignition control unit or ECM and engine kill switch
    c) Ignition control unit or ECM and ignition HT coils
    d) Ignition control unit or ECM and pulse generator
- ☐ Make sure that all wiring connections are clean, dry and tight. Look for chafed and broken wires (Chapters 5 and 9).

Stalls after starting

- ☐ Improper choke action (carburettor models). Make sure the choke linkage shaft is getting a full stroke and staying in the out position (Chapter 4).
- ☐ Ignition malfunction. See Chapter 5.
- ☐ Carburettor or fuel injection system malfunction. See Chapter 4.

- ☐ Fuel contaminated. The fuel can be contaminated with either dirt or water, or can change chemically if the machine is allowed to sit for several months or more. Drain the tank and float chambers (Chapter 4). Also check that the fuel flows freely and is not being restricted.
- ☐ Intake air leak. On carburettor models, check for loose carburettor or throttle body-to-intake manifold connections, loose or missing vacuum gauge adapter screws or hoses, or loose carburettor tops (Chapter 4).
- ☐ Engine idle speed incorrect. Turn idle adjusting screw until the engine idles at the specified rpm (Chapter 1). On fuel injection models, also check the fast idle system wax unit and starter valves (See Chapter 4).

Rough idle

- ☐ Ignition malfunction. See Chapter 5.
- ☐ Idle speed incorrect. See Chapter 1.
- ☐ Carburettors or throttle bodies (starter valves) not synchronised. Adjust with vacuum gauge or manometer set as described in Chapter 1 (carburettor models) or Chapter 4 (injection models).
- ☐ Carburettor or throttle body (starter valve) or fuel injection system malfunction. See Chapter 4.
- ☐ Fuel contaminated. The fuel can be contaminated with either dirt or water, or can change chemically if the machine is allowed to sit for several months or more. Drain the tank and float chambers (Chapter 4).
- ☐ Intake air leak. On carburettor models, check for loose carburettor or throttle body-to-intake manifold connections, loose or missing vacuum gauge adapter screws or hoses, or loose carburettor tops (Chapter 4).
- ☐ Air filter clogged. Clean or renew the air filter element (Chapter 1).

2 Poor running at low speeds

Spark weak

- ☐ Battery voltage low. Check and recharge battery (Chapter 9).
- ☐ Spark plugs fouled, defective or worn out. Refer to Chapter 1 for spark plug maintenance.
- ☐ Incorrect spark plugs. Wrong type, heat range or cap configuration. Check and install correct plugs listed in Chapter 1.
- ☐ Ignition control unit (carburettor models) or ECM (fuel injection models) defective. Check the unit, referring to Chapter 5 or 4 for details.
- ☐ Pulse generator defective. See Chapter 5.
- ☐ Ignition HT coils/spark plug caps defective or not making good contact with spark plugs. See Chapter 5.

Fuel/air mixture incorrect

Carburettor models

- ☐ Pilot screws out of adjustment (Chapter 4).
- ☐ Pilot jet or air passage clogged. Remove and overhaul the carburettors (Chapter 4).
- ☐ Air bleed holes clogged. Remove carburettor and blow out all passages (Chapter 4).
- ☐ Fuel level too high or too low. Check the float height (Chapter 4).
- ☐ Carburettor intake manifolds loose. Check for cracks, breaks, tears or loose clamps. Renew the rubber intake manifold joints if split or perished.

Fuel injection models

- ☐ Fuel injection system malfunction (see Chapter 4).
- ☐ Fuel injector clogged (see Chapter 4).

- ☐ Fuel pump or pressure regulator faulty (see Chapter 4).
- ☐ Throttle body intake manifolds loose. Check for cracks, breaks, tears or loose clamps. Renew the rubber intake manifold joints if split or perished.

All models

- ☐ Air filter clogged, poorly sealed or missing (Chapter 1).
- ☐ Air filter housing poorly sealed. Look for cracks, holes or loose clamps and renew or repair defective parts.
- ☐ Fuel tank breather hose obstructed.

Poor acceleration

- ☐ Carburettors or throttle bodies leaking or dirty. Overhaul them (Chapter 4).
- ☐ Fuel injection system malfunction, faulty fuel pump, or pressure regulator (fuel injection models) – see Chapter 4.
- ☐ Timing not advancing. The pulse generator or the ignition control unit or ECM may be defective. If so, they must be renewed, as they can't be repaired. Check them (see Chapter 4 or 5).
- ☐ Carburettors or throttle bodies (starter valves) not synchronised. Adjust them with a vacuum gauge set or manometer as described in Chapter 1 (carburettor models) or Chapter 4 (injection models).
- ☐ Engine oil viscosity too high. Using a heavier oil than that recommended in Chapter 1 can damage the oil pump or lubrication system and cause drag on the engine.
- ☐ Brakes dragging. Usually caused by debris which has entered the brake piston seals, or from a warped disc or bent axle. Repair as necessary (Chapter 7).

REF•38 Fault Finding

2 Poor running at low speeds (continued)

Compression low

- [ ] Spark plugs loose. Remove the plugs and inspect their threads. Reinstall and tighten to the specified torque (Chapter 1).
- [ ] Cylinder head not sufficiently tightened down. If a cylinder head is suspected of being loose, then there's a chance that the gasket and head are damaged if the problem has persisted for any length of time. The head bolts should be tightened to the proper torque in the correct sequence (Chapter 2).
- [ ] Incorrect valve clearance. This means that the valve is not closing completely and compression pressure is leaking past the valve. Check and adjust the valve clearances (Chapter 1).
- [ ] Cylinder and/or piston worn. Excessive wear will cause compression pressure to leak past the rings. This is usually accompanied by worn rings as well. A top-end overhaul is necessary (Chapter 2).
- [ ] Piston rings worn, weak, broken, or sticking. Broken or sticking piston rings usually indicate a lubrication or carburation problem that causes excess carbon deposits or seizures to form on the pistons and rings. Top-end overhaul is necessary (Chapter 2).
- [ ] Piston ring-to-groove clearance excessive. This is caused by excessive wear of the piston ring lands. Piston renewal is necessary (Chapter 2).
- [ ] Cylinder head gasket damaged. If a head is allowed to become loose, or if excessive carbon build-up on the piston crown and combustion chamber causes extremely high compression, the head gasket may leak. Retorquing the head is not always sufficient to restore the seal, so gasket renewal is necessary (Chapter 2).
- [ ] Cylinder head warped. This is caused by overheating or improperly tightened head bolts. Machine shop resurfacing or head renewal is necessary (Chapter 2).
- [ ] Valve spring broken or weak. Caused by component failure or wear; the springs must be renewed (Chapter 2).
- [ ] Valve not seating properly. This is caused by a bent valve (from over-revving or improper valve adjustment), burned valve or seat (improper carburation) or an accumulation of carbon deposits on the seat (from carburation, lubrication problems). The valves must be cleaned and/or renewed and the seats serviced if possible (Chapter 2).

3 Poor running or no power at high speed

Firing incorrect

- [ ] Air filter restricted. Clean or renew filter (Chapter 1).
- [ ] Spark plugs fouled, defective or worn out. See Chapter 1 for spark plug maintenance.
- [ ] Incorrect spark plugs. Wrong type, heat range or cap configuration. Check and install correct plugs listed in Chapter 1.
- [ ] Ignition control unit or ECM defective. See Chapter 5 or 4.
- [ ] Ignition HT coils/spark plug caps defective or not making good contact with spark plugs. See Chapter 5.

Fuel/air mixture incorrect

Carburettor models

- [ ] Main jet clogged. Dirt, water or other contaminants can clog the main jets. Clean the fuel tap filter, the in-line filter, the float chamber area, and the jets and carburettor orifices (Chapter 4).
- [ ] Main jet wrong size. The standard jetting is for sea level atmospheric pressure and oxygen content.
- [ ] Throttle shaft-to-carburettor body clearance excessive. Refer to Chapter 4 for inspection and part replacement procedures.
- [ ] Air bleed holes clogged. Remove carburettor and blow out all passages (Chapter 4).
- [ ] Fuel level too high or too low. Check the float height (Chapter 4).
- [ ] Carburettor intake manifolds loose. Check for cracks, breaks, tears or loose clamps. Renew the rubber intake manifold joints if split or perished.
- [ ] Fuel pump faulty (see Chapter 4).

Fuel injection models

- [ ] Fuel injection system malfunction (see Chapter 4).
- [ ] Fuel injector clogged (see Chapter 4).
- [ ] Fuel pump or pressure regulator faulty (see Chapter 4).
- [ ] Throttle body intake manifolds loose. Check for cracks, breaks, tears or loose clamps. Renew the rubber intake manifold joints if split or perished.

All models

- [ ] Air filter clogged, poorly sealed or missing (Chapter 1).
- [ ] Air filter housing poorly sealed. Look for cracks, holes or loose clamps and renew or repair defective parts.
- [ ] Fuel tank breather hose obstructed.

Compression low

- [ ] Spark plugs loose. Remove the plugs and inspect their threads. Reinstall and tighten to the specified torque (Chapter 1).
- [ ] Cylinder head not sufficiently tightened down. If a cylinder head is suspected of being loose, then there's a chance that the gasket and head are damaged if the problem has persisted for any length of time. The head bolts should be tightened to the proper torque in the correct sequence (Chapter 2).
- [ ] Incorrect valve clearance. This means that the valve is not closing completely and compression pressure is leaking past the valve. Check and adjust the valve clearances (Chapter 1).
- [ ] Cylinder and/or piston worn. Excessive wear will cause compression pressure to leak past the rings. This is usually accompanied by worn rings as well. A top-end overhaul is necessary (Chapter 2).
- [ ] Piston rings worn, weak, broken, or sticking. Broken or sticking piston rings usually indicate a lubrication problem that causes excess carbon deposits or seizures to form on the pistons and rings. A top-end overhaul is necessary (Chapter 2).
- [ ] Piston ring-to-groove clearance excessive. This is caused by excessive wear of the piston ring lands. Piston renewal is necessary (Chapter 2).
- [ ] Cylinder head gasket damaged. If a head is allowed to become loose, or if excessive carbon build-up on the piston crown and combustion chamber causes extremely high compression, the head gasket may leak. Retorquing the head is not always sufficient to restore the seal, so gasket renewal is necessary (Chapter 2).
- [ ] Cylinder head warped. This is caused by overheating or improperly tightened head bolts. Machine shop resurfacing or head renewal is necessary (Chapter 2).
- [ ] Valve spring broken or weak. Caused by component failure or wear; the springs must be renewed (Chapter 2).
- [ ] Valve not seating properly. This is caused by a bent valve (from over-revving or improper valve adjustment), burned valve or seat (improper carburation) or an accumulation of carbon deposits on the seat (from fuelling or lubrication problems). The valves must be cleaned and/or renewed and the seats serviced if possible (Chapter 2).

Fault Finding REF•39

3 Poor running or no power at high speed (continued)

Knocking or pinking

- [ ] Carbon build-up in combustion chamber. Use of a fuel additive that will dissolve the adhesive bonding the carbon particles to the crown and chamber is the easiest way to remove the build-up. Otherwise, the cylinder head will have to be removed and decarbonised (Chapter 2).
- [ ] Incorrect or poor quality fuel. Old or improper grades of fuel can cause detonation. This causes the piston to rattle, thus the knocking or pinking sound. Drain old fuel and always use the recommended fuel grade.
- [ ] Spark plug heat range incorrect. Uncontrolled detonation indicates the plug heat range is too hot. The plug in effect becomes a glow plug, raising cylinder temperatures. Install the proper heat range plug (Chapter 1).
- [ ] Improper air/fuel mixture. This will cause the cylinders to run hot, which leads to detonation. Clogged jets or an air leak can cause this imbalance. See Chapter 4.

Miscellaneous causes

- [ ] Throttle valve doesn't open fully. Adjust the throttle grip freeplay (Chapter 1).
- [ ] Clutch slipping. May be caused by loose or worn clutch components. Refer to Chapter 2 for clutch overhaul procedures.
- [ ] Timing not advancing – faulty ignition control unit or ECM.
- [ ] Engine oil viscosity too high. Using a heavier oil than the one recommended in Chapter 1 can damage the oil pump or lubrication system and cause drag on the engine.
- [ ] Brakes dragging. Usually caused by debris which has entered the brake piston seals, or from a warped disc or bent axle. Repair as necessary.

4 Overheating

Engine overheats

- [ ] Coolant level low. Check and add coolant (Chapter 1).
- [ ] Leak in cooling system. Check cooling system hoses and radiator for leaks and other damage. Repair or renew parts as necessary (Chapter 3).
- [ ] Thermostat sticking open or closed. Test as described in Chapter 3.
- [ ] Faulty radiator cap. Remove the cap and have it pressure tested by a dealer.
- [ ] Coolant passages clogged. Have the entire system drained and flushed, then refill with fresh coolant.
- [ ] Water pump defective. Remove the pump and check the components (Chapter 3).
- [ ] Clogged radiator fins. Clean them by blowing compressed air through the fins from the rear side of the radiator.
- [ ] Cooling fan or fan switch fault (Chapter 3).

Firing incorrect

- [ ] Spark plugs fouled, defective or worn out. See Chapter 1 for spark plug maintenance.
- [ ] Incorrect spark plugs.
- [ ] Ignition control unit or ECM defective (Chapter 4 or 5).
- [ ] Pulse generator faulty (Chapter 4 or 5).
- [ ] Faulty HT ignition coils/spark plug caps (Chapter 5).

Fuel/air mixture incorrect

Carburettor models

- [ ] Main jet clogged. Dirt, water or other contaminants can clog the main jets. Clean the fuel tap filter, the in-line filter, the float chamber area, and the jets and carburettor orifices (Chapter 4).
- [ ] Main jet wrong size. The standard jetting is for sea level atmospheric pressure and oxygen content.
- [ ] Throttle shaft-to-carburettor body clearance excessive. Refer to Chapter 4 for inspection.
- [ ] Air bleed holes clogged. Remove carburettor and blow out all passages (Chapter 4).
- [ ] Fuel level too high or too low. Check the float height (Chapter 4).
- [ ] Carburettor intake manifolds loose. Check for cracks, breaks, tears or loose clamps. Renew the rubber intake manifold joints if split or perished.
- [ ] Fuel pump faulty (see Chapter 4).

Fuel injection models

- [ ] Fuel injection system malfunction (see Chapter 4).
- [ ] Fuel injector clogged (see Chapter 4).
- [ ] Fuel pump or pressure regulator faulty (see Chapter 4).
- [ ] Throttle body intake manifolds loose. Check for cracks, breaks, tears or loose clamps. Renew the rubber intake manifold joints if split or perished.

All models

- [ ] Air filter clogged, poorly sealed or missing (Chapter 1).
- [ ] Air filter housing poorly sealed. Look for cracks, holes or loose clamps and renew or repair defective parts.
- [ ] Fuel tank breather hose obstructed.

Compression too high

- [ ] Carbon build-up in combustion chamber. Use of a fuel additive that will dissolve the adhesive bonding the carbon particles to the piston crown and chamber is the easiest way to remove the build-up. Otherwise, the cylinder head will have to be removed and decarbonised (Chapter 2).

Engine load excessive

- [ ] Clutch slipping. Can be caused by damaged, loose or worn clutch components. Refer to Chapter 2 for overhaul procedures.
- [ ] Engine oil level too high. The addition of too much oil will cause pressurisation of the crankcase and inefficient engine operation. Check Specifications and drain to proper level (Chapter 1 and *Daily (pre-ride) checks*).
- [ ] Engine oil viscosity too high. Using a heavier oil than the one recommended in Chapter 1 can damage the oil pump or lubrication system as well as cause drag on the engine.
- [ ] Brakes dragging. Usually caused by debris which has entered the brake piston seals, or from a warped disc or bent axle. Repair as necessary.

Lubrication inadequate

- [ ] Engine oil level too low. Friction caused by intermittent lack of lubrication or from oil that is overworked can cause overheating. The oil provides a definite cooling function in the engine. Check the oil level (Chapter 1).
- [ ] Poor quality engine oil or incorrect viscosity or type. Oil is rated not only according to viscosity but also according to type. Some oils are not rated high enough for use in this engine. Check the Specifications section and change to the correct oil (Chapter 1).

Miscellaneous causes

- [ ] Modification to exhaust system. Most aftermarket exhaust systems cause the engine to run leaner, which make them run hotter.

5 Clutch problems

Clutch slipping
- [ ] Clutch cable incorrectly adjusted. Check and adjust (see Chapter 1).
- [ ] Friction plates worn or warped. Overhaul the clutch assembly (Chapter 2).
- [ ] Plain plates warped (Chapter 2).
- [ ] Clutch springs broken or weak. Old or heat-damaged (from slipping clutch) springs should be replaced with new ones (Chapter 2).
- [ ] Clutch release mechanism defective. Replace any defective parts (Chapter 2).
- [ ] Clutch centre or housing unevenly worn. This causes improper engagement of the plates. Renew the damaged or worn parts (Chapter 2).

Clutch not disengaging completely
- [ ] Clutch cable incorrectly adjusted. Check and adjust (see Chapter 1).
- [ ] Clutch plates warped or damaged. This will cause clutch drag, which in turn will cause the machine to creep. Overhaul the clutch assembly (Chapter 2).
- [ ] Clutch spring tension uneven. Usually caused by a sagged or broken spring. Check and renew the springs as a set (Chapter 2).
- [ ] Engine oil deteriorated. Old, thin, worn out oil will not provide proper lubrication for the plates, causing the clutch to drag. Renew the oil and filter (Chapter 1).
- [ ] Engine oil viscosity too high. Using a heavier oil than recommended in Chapter 1 can cause the plates to stick together, putting a drag on the engine. Change to the correct weight oil (Chapter 1).
- [ ] Clutch housing guide seized on gearbox input shaft. Lack of lubrication, severe wear or damage can cause the guide to seize on the shaft. Overhaul of the clutch, and perhaps transmission, may be necessary to repair the damage (Chapter 2).
- [ ] Clutch release mechanism defective.
- [ ] Loose clutch centre nut. Causes housing and centre misalignment putting a drag on the engine. Engagement adjustment continually varies. Overhaul the clutch assembly (Chapter 2).

6 Gearchange problems

Doesn't go into gear or lever doesn't return
- [ ] Clutch not disengaging. See above.
- [ ] Selector fork(s) bent or seized. Often caused by dropping the machine or from lack of lubrication. Overhaul the transmission (Chapter 2).
- [ ] Gear(s) stuck on shaft. Most often caused by a lack of lubrication or excessive wear in transmission bearings and bushings. Overhaul the transmission (Chapter 2).
- [ ] Selector drum binding. Caused by lubrication failure or excessive wear. Renew the drum and bearing (Chapter 2).
- [ ] Gearchange lever return spring weak or broken (Chapter 2).
- [ ] Gearchange lever broken. Splines stripped out of lever or shaft, caused by allowing the lever to get loose or from accident damage. Renew necessary parts (Chapter 2).
- [ ] Gearchange mechanism stopper arm broken or worn. Full engagement and rotary movement of selector drum results. Renew the arm (Chapter 2).
- [ ] Stopper arm spring broken. Allows arm to float, causing sporadic shift operation. Renew spring (Chapter 2).

Jumps out of gear
- [ ] Selector fork(s) worn. Overhaul the transmission (Chapter 2).
- [ ] Gear groove(s) worn. Overhaul the transmission (Chapter 2).
- [ ] Gear dogs or dog slots worn or damaged. The gears should be inspected and renewed if necessary.

Overshifts
- [ ] Stopper arm spring weak or broken (Chapter 2).
- [ ] Gearchange shaft return spring post broken or distorted (Chapter 2).

Fault Finding REF•41

7 Abnormal engine noise

Knocking or pinking

- [ ] Carbon build-up in combustion chamber. Use of a fuel additive that will dissolve the adhesive bonding the carbon particles to the piston crown and chamber is the easiest way to remove the build-up. Otherwise, the cylinder head will have to be removed and decarbonised (Chapter 2).
- [ ] Incorrect or poor quality fuel. Old or improper fuel can cause detonation. This causes the pistons to rattle, thus the knocking or pinking sound. Drain the old fuel and always use the recommended grade fuel (Chapter 4).
- [ ] Spark plug heat range incorrect. Uncontrolled detonation indicates that the plug heat range is too hot. The plug in effect becomes a glow plug, raising cylinder temperatures. Install the proper heat range plug (Chapter 1).
- [ ] Improper fuel/air mixture (carburettor models). This will cause the cylinders to run hot and lead to detonation. Clogged jets or an air leak can cause this imbalance. See Chapter 4.

Piston slap or rattling

- [ ] Cylinder-to-piston clearance excessive. Caused by improper assembly. Inspect and overhaul top-end parts (Chapter 2).
- [ ] Connecting rod bent. Caused by over-revving, trying to start a badly flooded engine or from ingesting a foreign object into the combustion chamber. Renew the damaged parts (Chapter 2).
- [ ] Piston pin or piston pin bore worn or seized from wear or lack of lubrication. Renew damaged parts (Chapter 2).
- [ ] Piston ring(s) worn, broken or sticking. Overhaul the top-end (Chapter 2).
- [ ] Piston seizure damage. Usually from lack of lubrication or overheating. Renew the pistons and bore the cylinders, as necessary (Chapter 2).
- [ ] Connecting rod upper or lower end clearance excessive. Caused by excessive wear or lack of lubrication. Renew worn parts.

Valve noise

- [ ] Incorrect valve clearances. Adjust the clearances by referring to Chapter 1.
- [ ] Valve spring broken or weak. Check and renew weak valve springs (Chapter 2).
- [ ] Camshaft or cylinder head worn or damaged. Lack of lubrication at high rpm is usually the cause of damage. Insufficient oil or failure to change the oil at the recommended intervals are the chief causes. Since there are no replaceable bearings in the head, the head and camshaft holder will have to be renewed if there is excessive wear or damage (Chapter 2).

Other noise

- [ ] Cylinder head gasket leaking.
- [ ] Exhaust pipe leaking at cylinder head connection. Caused by improper fit of pipe(s) or loose exhaust flange. All exhaust fasteners should be tightened evenly and carefully. Failure to do this will lead to a leak.
- [ ] Crankshaft runout excessive. Caused by a bent crankshaft (from over-revving) or damage from an upper cylinder component failure. Can also be attributed to dropping the machine on either of the crankshaft ends.
- [ ] Engine mounting bolts loose. Tighten all engine mount bolts (Chapter 2).
- [ ] Crankshaft bearings worn (Chapter 2).
- [ ] Cam chain tensioner defective, cam chain or guide blades worn. Renew according to the procedure in Chapter 2.

8 Abnormal driveline noise

Clutch noise

- [ ] Clutch outer drum/friction plate clearance excessive (Chapter 2).
- [ ] Loose or damaged clutch pressure plate and/or bolts (Chapter 2).

Transmission noise

- [ ] Bearings worn. Also includes the possibility that the shafts are worn. Overhaul the transmission (Chapter 2).
- [ ] Gears worn or chipped (Chapter 2).
- [ ] Metal chips jammed in gear teeth. Probably pieces from a broken clutch, gear or selector mechanism that were picked up by the gears. This will cause early bearing failure (Chapter 2).
- [ ] Engine oil level too low. Causes a howl from transmission. Also affects engine power and clutch operation (Chapter 1).

Final drive noise

- [ ] Chain not adjusted properly (Chapter 1).
- [ ] Front or rear sprocket loose. Tighten fasteners (Chapter 6).
- [ ] Sprockets worn. Renew sprockets (Chapter 6).
- [ ] Rear sprocket warped. Renew sprockets (Chapter 6).
- [ ] Rubber dampers in rear wheel hub worn. Check and renew (Chapter 7).

REF•42 Fault Finding

9 Abnormal frame and suspension noise

Front end noise

- [ ] Low fluid level or improper viscosity oil in forks. This can sound like spurting and is usually accompanied by irregular fork action (Chapter 6).
- [ ] Spring weak or broken. Makes a clicking or scraping sound. Fork oil, when drained, will have a lot of metal particles in it (Chapter 6).
- [ ] Steering head bearings loose or damaged. Clicks when braking. Check and adjust or replace as necessary (Chapters 1 and 6).
- [ ] Fork yokes loose. Make sure all clamp pinch bolts are tightened to the specified torque (Chapter 6).
- [ ] Fork tube bent. Good possibility if machine has been dropped. Replace tube with a new one (Chapter 6).
- [ ] Front axle bolt or axle clamp bolts loose. Tighten them to the specified torque (Chapter 7).
- [ ] Loose or worn wheel bearings. Check and renew as necessary (Chapter 7).

Rear suspension noise

- [ ] Fluid level incorrect. Indicates a leak caused by defective seal. Shock will be covered with oil. Renew shock or seek advice on repair from a Honda dealer or suspension specialist (Chapter 6).
- [ ] Defective shock absorber with internal damage. This is in the body of the shock and can't be remedied. The shock must be replaced with a new one (Chapter 6).
- [ ] Bent or damaged shock body. Replace the shock with a new one (Chapter 6).
- [ ] Loose or worn suspension linkage or swingarm components. Check and renew as necessary (Chapter 6).

Brake noise

- [ ] Squeal caused by pad shim not installed or positioned correctly (where fitted) (Chapter 7).
- [ ] Squeal caused by dust on brake pads. Usually found in combination with glazed pads. Clean using brake cleaning solvent (Chapter 7).
- [ ] Contamination of brake pads. Oil, brake fluid or dirt causing brake to chatter or squeal. Replace pads (Chapter 7).
- [ ] Pads glazed. Renew the pads (Chaper 7).
- [ ] Disc warped. Can cause a chattering, clicking or intermittent squeal. Usually accompanied by a pulsating lever and uneven braking. Renew the disc (Chapter 7).
- [ ] Loose or worn wheel bearings. Check (Chapter 1) and renew (Chapter 7) as necessary.

10 Oil pressure warning light comes on

Engine lubrication system

- [ ] Engine oil pump defective, blocked oil strainer gauze or failed relief valve. Carry out an oil pressure check (Chapter 1).
- [ ] Engine oil level low. Inspect for leak or other problem causing low oil level and add recommended oil (Daily (pre-ride) checks).
- [ ] Engine oil viscosity too low. Very old, thin oil or an improper weight of oil used in the engine. Change to correct oil (Chapter 1).
- [ ] Camshaft or journals worn. Excessive wear causing drop in oil pressure. Measure oil clearance (Chapter 2). Abnormal wear could be caused by oil starvation at high rpm from low oil level or improper weight or type of oil (Chapter 1).
- [ ] Crankshaft and/or bearings worn. Same problems as above. Measure oil connecting rod and main bearing oil clearance (Chapter 2).

Electrical system

- [ ] Oil pressure switch defective. Check the switch according to the procedure in Chapter 9. Replace it if it is defective.
- [ ] Oil pressure warning light circuit defective. Check for pinched, shorted, disconnected or damaged wiring (Chapter 9).

11 Excessive exhaust smoke

White smoke

- [ ] Piston oil ring worn. The ring may be broken or damaged, causing oil from the crankcase to be pulled past the piston into the combustion chamber. Replace the rings with new ones (Chapter 2).
- [ ] Cylinders worn, cracked, or scored. Caused by overheating or oil starvation. The cylinders will have to be rebored and new pistons installed.
- [ ] Valve oil seal damaged or worn. Replace oil seals with new ones (Chapter 2).
- [ ] Valve guide worn. Perform a complete valve job (Chapter 2).
- [ ] Engine oil level too high, which causes the oil to be forced past the rings. Drain oil to the proper level (Chapter 1).
- [ ] Head gasket broken between oil return and cylinder. Causes oil to be pulled into the combustion chamber. Renew the head gasket and check the head for warpage (Chapter 2).
- [ ] Abnormal crankcase pressurisation, which forces oil past the rings. Clogged breather is usually the cause.

Black smoke

Carburettor models

- [ ] Main jet too large or loose. Compare the jet size to the Specifications (Chapter 4).
- [ ] Choke cable or linkage shaft stuck, causing fuel to be pulled through choke circuit (Chapter 4).
- [ ] Fuel level too high. Check and adjust the float height(s) as necessary (Chapter 4).
- [ ] Float needle valve held off needle seat. Clean the float chambers and fuel line and renew the needles and seats if necessary (Chapter 4).

Fuel injection models

- [ ] Fuel injection system malfunction (see Chapter 4).

All models

- [ ] Air filter clogged (Chapter 1).

Brown smoke

Carburettor models

- [ ] Main jet too small or clogged. Lean condition caused by wrong size main jet or by a restricted orifice. Clean float chambers and jets and compare jet size to Specifications (Chapter 4).
- [ ] Fuel flow insufficient. Float needle valve stuck closed due to chemical reaction with old fuel. Float height incorrect. Restricted fuel line. Clean line and float chamber and adjust floats if necessary.
- [ ] Carburettor intake manifold clamps loose (Chapter 4).
- [ ] Faulty fuel pump (see Chapter 4).

Fuel injection models

- [ ] Fuel injection system malfunction (see Chapter 4).
- [ ] Faulty fuel pump or pressure regulator (see Chapter 4).

All models

- [ ] Air filter poorly sealed or not installed (Chapter 1).

Fault Finding REF•43

12 Poor handling or stability

Handlebars hard to turn
- [ ] Steering head bearing adjuster nut too tight. Check adjustment as described in Chapter 1.
- [ ] Bearings damaged. Roughness can be felt as the bars are turned from side-to-side. Renew bearings and races (Chapter 6).
- [ ] Races dented or worn. Denting results from wear in only one position (e.g., straight ahead), from a collision or hitting a pothole or from dropping the machine. Renew bearings (Chapter 6)
- [ ] Steering stem lubrication inadequate. Causes are grease getting hard from age or being washed out by high pressure car washes. Disassemble steering head and repack bearings with fresh grease (Chapter 6).
- [ ] Steering stem bent. Caused by a collision, hitting a pothole or by dropping the machine. Renew damaged part. Don't try to straighten the steering stem (Chapter 6).
- [ ] Front tyre air pressure too low (Chapter 1).

Handlebar shakes or vibrates excessively
- [ ] Tyres worn or out of balance (Chapter 7).
- [ ] Swingarm bearings worn. Renew worn bearings (Chapter 6).
- [ ] Wheel rim(s) warped or damaged. Inspect wheels for runout (Chapter 7).
- [ ] Wheel bearings worn. Worn front or rear wheel bearings can cause poor tracking. Worn front bearings will cause wobble (Chapter 7).
- [ ] Handlebar clamp bolts loose (Chapter 6).
- [ ] Fork yoke bolts loose. Tighten them to the specified torque (Chapter 6).
- [ ] Engine mounting bolts loose. Will cause excessive vibration with increased engine rpm (Chapter 2).

Handlebar pulls to one side
- [ ] Frame bent. Definitely suspect this if the machine has been dropped. May or may not be accompanied by cracking near the bend. Renew the frame (Chapter 6).
- [ ] Wheels out of alignment. Caused by improper location of axle spacers or from bent steering stem or frame (Chapter 6).
- [ ] Swingarm bent or twisted from accident damage. Renew the swingarm (Chapter 6).
- [ ] Steering stem bent. Caused by impact damage or by dropping the motorcycle. Renew the steering stem (Chapter 6).
- [ ] Fork tube bent. Disassemble the forks and renew the damaged parts (Chapter 6).
- [ ] Fork oil level uneven. Check and add or drain as necessary (Chapter 6).

Poor shock absorbing qualities
- [ ] Too hard:
  - a) Fork oil level excessive (Chapter 6).
  - b) Fork oil viscosity too high. Use a lighter oil (see the Specifications in Chapter 6).
  - c) Fork tube bent. Causes a harsh, sticking feeling (Chapter 6).
  - d) Rear shock shaft or body bent or damaged (Chapter 6).
  - e) Fork internal damage (Chapter 6).
  - f) Shock internal damage.
  - g) Tyre pressure too high (Chapter 1).
  - h) Incorrect adjustment settings (Chapter 6).

Too soft:
  - a) Fork or shock oil insufficient and/or leaking (Chapter 6).
  - b) Fork oil level too low (Chapter 6).
  - c) Fork oil viscosity too light (Chapter 6).
  - d) Fork springs weak or broken (Chapter 6).
  - e) Shock internal damage or leakage (Chapter 6).
  - f) Incorrect adjustment settings (Chapter 6).

13 Braking problems

Brakes are spongy, or lack power
- [ ] Air in brake line. Caused by inattention to master cylinder fluid level or by leakage. Locate problem and bleed brakes (Chapter 7).
- [ ] Pad or disc worn (Chapters 1 and 7).
- [ ] Brake fluid leak. See paragraph 1.
- [ ] Contaminated pads. Caused by contamination with oil, grease, brake fluid, etc. Renew pads (Chapter 7). Clean disc thoroughly with brake cleaner (Chapter 7).
- [ ] Brake fluid deteriorated. Fluid is old or contaminated. Drain system, replenish with new fluid and bleed the system (Chapter 7).
- [ ] Master cylinder internal parts worn or damaged causing fluid to bypass (Chapter 7).
- [ ] Master cylinder bore scratched by foreign material or broken spring. Repair or renew master cylinder (Chapter 7).

Brake lever or pedal pulsates
- [ ] Disc warped. Renew disc (Chapter 7).
- [ ] Wheel axle bent. Renew axle (Chapter 7).
- [ ] Brake caliper bolts loose (Chapter 7).
- [ ] Brake caliper sliders damaged or sticking (rear caliper), causing caliper to bind. Lubricate the sliders or renew them if they are corroded or bent (Chapter 7).
- [ ] Wheel warped or otherwise damaged (Chapter 7).
- [ ] Wheel bearings damaged or worn (Chapters 1 and 7).

Brakes drag
- [ ] Master cylinder piston seized. Caused by wear or damage to piston or cylinder bore (Chapter 7).
- [ ] Lever balky or stuck. Check pivot and lubricate (Chapter 7).
- [ ] Brake caliper binds on bracket (rear caliper). Caused by inadequate lubrication or damage to caliper slider pins (Chapter 7).
- [ ] Brake caliper piston seized in bore. Caused by wear or ingestion of dirt past deteriorated seal (Chapter 7).
- [ ] Brake pad damaged. Renew pads (Chapter 7).
- [ ] Pads improperly installed (Chapter 7).

14 Electrical problems

Battery dead or weak
- [ ] Battery faulty. Caused by sulphated plates which are shorted through sedimentation. Also, broken battery terminal making only occasional contact (Chapter 9).
- [ ] Battery cables making poor contact (Chapter 9).
- [ ] Load excessive. Caused by addition of high wattage lights or other electrical accessories.
- [ ] Ignition (main) switch defective. Switch either grounds (earths) internally or fails to shut off system. Renew the switch (Chapter 9).
- [ ] Regulator/rectifier defective (Chapter 9).
- [ ] Alternator stator coil open or shorted (Chapter 9).
- [ ] Wiring faulty. Wiring grounded (earthed) or connections loose in ignition, charging or lighting circuits (Chapter 9).

Battery overcharged
- [ ] Regulator/rectifier defective. Overcharging is noticed when battery gets excessively warm (Chapter 9).
- [ ] Battery defective. Replace battery with a new one (Chapter 9).
- [ ] Battery amperage too low, wrong type or size. Install manufacturer's specified amp-hour battery to handle charging load (Chapter 9).

REF•44 Fault Finding Equipment

Checking engine compression

● Low compression will result in exhaust smoke, heavy oil consumption, poor starting and poor performance. A compression test will provide useful information about an engine's condition and if performed regularly, can give warning of trouble before any other symptoms become apparent.
● A compression gauge will be required, along with an adapter to suit the spark plug hole thread size. Note that the screw-in type gauge/adapter set up is preferable to the rubber cone type.
● Before carrying out the test, first check the valve clearances as described in Chapter 1.

1 Run the engine until it reaches normal operating temperature, then stop it and remove the spark plug(s), taking care not to scald your hands on the hot components.
2 Install the gauge adapter and compression gauge in No. 1 cylinder spark plug hole **(see illustration 1)**.

Screw the compression gauge adapter into the spark plug hole, then screw the gauge into the adapter

3 On kickstart-equipped motorcycles, make sure the ignition switch is OFF, then open the throttle fully and kick the engine over a couple of times until the gauge reading stabilises.
4 On motorcycles with electric start only, the procedure will differ depending on the nature of the ignition system. Flick the engine kill switch (engine stop switch) to OFF and turn the ignition switch ON; open the throttle fully and crank the engine over on the starter motor for a couple of revolutions until the gauge reading stabilises. If the starter will not operate with the kill switch OFF, turn the ignition switch OFF and refer to the next paragraph.
5 Install the plugs back in their caps and arrange the plug electrodes so that their metal bodies are earthed (grounded) against the cylinder head; this is essential to prevent damage to the ignition system **(see illustration 2)**. Position the plugs well away from the plug holes otherwise there is a risk of

All spark plugs must be earthed (grounded) against the cylinder head

atomised fuel escaping from the plug holes and igniting. As a safety precaution, cover the cylinder head with rag and disconnect the fuel pump wiring connector (see Chapter 4). Turn the ignition switch and kill switch ON, open the throttle fully and crank the engine over on the starter motor for a couple of revolutions until the gauge reading stabilises.
6 After one or two revolutions the pressure should build up to a maximum figure and then stabilise. Take a note of this reading and on multi-cylinder engines repeat the test on the remaining cylinders.
7 The correct pressures are given in Chapter 1. If the results fall within the specified range and on multi-cylinder engines all are relatively equal, the engine is in good condition. If there is a marked difference between the readings, or if the readings are lower than specified, inspection of the top-end components will be required.
8 Low compression pressure may be due to worn cylinder bores, pistons or rings, failure of the cylinder head gasket, worn valve seals, or poor valve seating.
9 To distinguish between cylinder/piston wear and valve leakage, pour a small quantity of oil into the bore to temporarily seal the piston rings, then repeat the compression tests **(see illustration 3)**. If the readings show

Bores can be temporarily sealed with a squirt of motor oil

a noticeable increase in pressure this confirms that the cylinder bore, piston, or rings are worn. If, however, no change is indicated, the cylinder head gasket or valves should be examined.
10 High compression pressure indicates excessive carbon build-up in the combustion chamber and on the piston crown. If this is the case the cylinder head should be removed and the deposits removed. Note that excessive carbon build-up is less likely with the used on modern fuels.

Checking battery open-circuit voltage

⚠ *Warning: The gases produced by the battery are explosive - never smoke or create any sparks in the vicinity of the battery. Never allow the electrolyte to contact your skin or clothing - if it does, wash it off and seek immediate medical attention.*

Fault Finding Equipment REF•45

Measuring open-circuit battery voltage

Float-type hydrometer for measuring battery specific gravity

- Before any electrical fault is investigated the battery should be checked.
- You'll need a dc voltmeter or multimeter to check battery voltage. Check that the leads are inserted in the correct terminals on the meter, red lead to positive (+ve), black lead to negative (-ve). Incorrect connections can damage the meter.
- A sound fully-charged 12 volt battery should produce between 12.3 and 12.6 volts across its terminals (12.8 volts for a maintenance-free battery). On machines with a 6 volt battery, voltage should be between 6.1 and 6.3 volts.

1 Set a multimeter to the 0 to 20 volts dc range and connect its probes across the battery terminals. Connect the meter's positive (+ve) probe, usually red, to the battery positive (+ve) terminal, followed by the meter's negative (-ve) probe, usually black, to the battery negative terminal (-ve) **(see illustration 4)**.

2 If battery voltage is low (below 10 volts on a 12 volt battery or below 4 volts on a six volt battery), charge the battery and test the voltage again. If the battery repeatedly goes flat, investigate the motorcycle's charging system.

Checking battery specific gravity (SG)

⚠ *Warning: The gases produced by the battery are explosive - never smoke or create any sparks in the vicinity of the battery. Never allow the electrolyte to contact your skin or clothing - if it does, wash it off and seek immediate medical attention.*

- The specific gravity check gives an indication of a battery's state of charge.
- A hydrometer is used for measuring specific gravity. Make sure you purchase one which has a small enough hose to insert in the aperture of a motorcycle battery.
- Specific gravity is simply a measure of the electrolyte's density compared with that of water. Water has an SG of 1.000 and fully-charged battery electrolyte is about 26% heavier, at 1.260.
- Specific gravity checks are not possible on maintenance-free batteries. Testing the open-circuit voltage is the only means of determining their state of charge.

1 To measure SG, remove the battery from the motorcycle and remove the first cell cap. Draw

Digital multimeter can be used for all electrical tests

Battery-powered continuity tester

some electrolyte into the hydrometer and note the reading **(see illustration 5)**. Return the electrolyte to the cell and install the cap.

2 The reading should be in the region of 1.260 to 1.280. If SG is below 1.200 the battery needs charging. Note that SG will vary with temperature; it should be measured at 20°C (68°F). Add 0.007 to the reading for every 10°C above 20°C, and subtract 0.007 from the reading for every 10°C below 20°C. Add 0.004 to the reading for every 10°F above 68°F, and subtract 0.004 from the reading for every 10°F below 68°F.

3 When the check is complete, rinse the hydrometer thoroughly with clean water.

Checking for continuity

- The term continuity describes the uninterrupted flow of electricity through an electrical circuit. A continuity check will determine whether an **open-circuit** situation exists.
- Continuity can be checked with an ohmmeter, multimeter, continuity tester or battery and bulb test circuit **(see illustrations 6, 7 and 8)**.

Battery and bulb test circuit

REF•46 Fault Finding Equipment

Continuity check of front brake light switch using a meter - note split pins used to access connector terminals

Continuity check of rear brake light switch using a continuity tester

- All of these instruments are self-powered by a battery, therefore the checks are made with the ignition OFF.
- As a safety precaution, always disconnect the battery negative (-ve) lead before making checks, particularly if ignition switch checks are being made.
- If using a meter, select the appropriate ohms scale and check that the meter reads infinity (∞). Touch the meter probes together and check that meter reads zero; where necessary adjust the meter so that it reads zero.
- After using a meter, always switch it OFF to conserve its battery.

Switch checks

1 If a switch is at fault, trace its wiring up to the wiring connectors. Separate the wire connectors and inspect them for security and condition. A build-up of dirt or corrosion here will most likely be the cause of the problem - clean up and apply a water dispersant such as WD40.

2 If using a test meter, set the meter to the ohms x 10 scale and connect its probes across the wires from the switch **(see illustration 9)**. Simple ON/OFF type switches, such as brake light switches, only have two wires whereas combination switches, like the ignition switch, have many internal links. Study the wiring diagram to ensure that you are connecting across the correct pair of wires. Continuity (low or no measurable resistance - 0 ohms) should be indicated with the switch ON and no continuity (high resistance) with it OFF.

3 Note that the polarity of the test probes doesn't matter for continuity checks, although care should be taken to follow specific test procedures if a diode or solid-state component is being checked.

4 A continuity tester or battery and bulb circuit can be used in the same way. Connect its probes as described above **(see illustration 10)**. The light should come on to indicate continuity in the ON switch position, but should extinguish in the OFF position.

Wiring checks

- Many electrical faults are caused by damaged wiring, often due to incorrect routing or chaffing on frame components.
- Loose, wet or corroded wire connectors can also be the cause of electrical problems, especially in exposed locations.

1 A continuity check can be made on a single length of wire by disconnecting it at each end and connecting a meter or continuity tester across both ends of the wire **(see illustration 11)**.

2 Continuity (low or no resistance - 0 ohms) should be indicated if the wire is good. If no continuity (high resistance) is shown, suspect a broken wire.

Checking for voltage

- A voltage check can determine whether current is reaching a component.
- Voltage can be checked with a dc voltmeter, multimeter set on the dc volts scale, test light or buzzer **(see illustrations 12 and 13)**. A meter has the advantage of being able to measure actual voltage.
- When using a meter, check that its leads are inserted in the correct terminals on the meter, red to positive (+ve), black to negative (-ve). Incorrect connections can damage the meter.
- A voltmeter (or multimeter set to the dc volts scale) should always be connected in parallel (across the load). Connecting it in series will destroy the meter.
- Voltage checks are made with the ignition ON.

Continuity check of front brake light switch sub-harness

A simple test light can be used for voltage checks

A buzzer is useful for voltage checks

Fault Finding Equipment REF•47

Checking for voltage at the rear brake light power supply wire using a meter ...

1 First identify the relevant wiring circuit by referring to the wiring diagram at the end of this manual. If other electrical components share the same power supply (ie are fed from the same fuse), take note whether they are working correctly - this is useful information in deciding where to start checking the circuit.

2 If using a meter, check first that the meter leads are plugged into the correct terminals on the meter (see above). Set the meter to the dc volts function, at a range suitable for the battery voltage. Connect the meter red probe (+ve) to the power supply wire and the black probe to a good metal earth (ground) on the motorcycle's frame or directly to the battery negative (-ve) terminal **(see illustration 14)**. Battery voltage should be shown on the meter

A selection of jumper wires for making earth (ground) checks

... or a test light - note the earth connection to the frame (arrow)

with the ignition switched ON.

3 If using a test light or buzzer, connect its positive (+ve) probe to the power supply terminal and its negative (-ve) probe to a good earth (ground) on the motorcycle's frame or directly to the battery negative (-ve) terminal **(see illustration 15)**. With the ignition ON, the test light should illuminate or the buzzer sound.

4 If no voltage is indicated, work back towards the fuse continuing to check for voltage. When you reach a point where there is voltage, you know the problem lies between that point and your last check point.

Checking the earth (ground)

● Earth connections are made either directly to the engine or frame (such as sensors, neutral switch etc. which only have a positive feed) or by a separate wire into the earth circuit of the wiring harness. Alternatively a short earth wire is sometimes run directly from the component to the motorcycle's frame.
● Corrosion is often the cause of a poor earth connection.
● If total failure is experienced, check the security of the main earth lead from the negative (-ve) terminal of the battery and also the main earth (ground) point on the wiring harness. If corroded, dismantle the connection and clean all surfaces back to bare metal.

1 To check the earth on a component, use an insulated jumper wire to temporarily bypass its earth connection **(see illustration 16)**. Connect one end of the jumper wire between the earth terminal or metal body of the component and the other end to the motorcycle's frame.

2 If the circuit works with the jumper wire installed, the original earth circuit is faulty. Check the wiring for open-circuits or poor connections. Clean up direct earth connections, removing all traces of corrosion and remake the joint. Apply petroleum jelly to the joint to prevent future corrosion.

Tracing a short-circuit

● A short-circuit occurs where current shorts to earth (ground) bypassing the circuit components. This usually results in a blown fuse.

● A short-circuit is most likely to occur where the insulation has worn through due to wiring chafing on a component, allowing a direct path to earth (ground) on the frame.

1 Remove any bodypanels necessary to access the circuit wiring.

2 Check that all electrical switches in the circuit are OFF, then remove the circuit fuse and connect a test light, buzzer or voltmeter (set to the dc scale) across the fuse terminals. No voltage should be shown.

3 Move the wiring from side to side whilst observing the test light or meter. When the test light comes on, buzzer sounds or meter shows voltage, you have found the cause of the short. It will usually shown up as damaged or burned insulation.

4 Note that the same test can be performed on each component in the circuit, even the switch.

Technical Terms Explained

A

ABS (Anti-lock braking system) A system, usually electronically controlled, that senses incipient wheel lockup during braking and relieves hydraulic pressure at wheel which is about to skid.
Aftermarket Components suitable for the motorcycle, but not produced by the motorcycle manufacturer.
Allen key A hexagonal wrench which fits into a recessed hexagonal hole.
Alternating current (ac) Current produced by an alternator. Requires converting to direct current by a rectifier for charging purposes.
Alternator Converts mechanical energy from the engine into electrical energy to charge the battery and power the electrical system.
Ampere (amp) A unit of measurement for the flow of electrical current. Current = Volts ÷ Ohms.
Ampere-hour (Ah) Measure of battery capacity.
Angle-tightening A torque expressed in degrees. Often follows a conventional tightening torque for cylinder head or main bearing fasteners **(see illustration)**.

Angle-tightening cylinder head bolts

Antifreeze A substance (usually ethylene glycol) mixed with water, and added to the cooling system, to prevent freezing of the coolant in winter. Antifreeze also contains chemicals to inhibit corrosion and the formation of rust and other deposits that would tend to clog the radiator and coolant passages and reduce cooling efficiency.
Anti-dive System attached to the fork lower leg (slider) to prevent fork dive when braking hard.
Anti-seize compound A coating that reduces the risk of seizing on fasteners that are subjected to high temperatures, such as exhaust clamp bolts and nuts.
API American Petroleum Institute. A quality standard for 4-stroke motor oils.
Asbestos A natural fibrous mineral with great heat resistance, commonly used in the composition of brake friction materials. Asbestos is a health hazard and the dust created by brake systems should never be inhaled or ingested.
ATF Automatic Transmission Fluid. Often used in front forks.
ATU Automatic Timing Unit. Mechanical device for advancing the ignition timing on early engines.
ATV All Terrain Vehicle. Often called a Quad.
Axial play Side-to-side movement.
Axle A shaft on which a wheel revolves. Also known as a spindle.

B

Backlash The amount of movement between meshed components when one component is held still. Usually applies to gear teeth.
Ball bearing A bearing consisting of a hardened inner and outer race with hardened steel balls between the two races.
Bearings Used between two working surfaces to prevent wear of the components and a build-up of heat. Four types of bearing are commonly used on motorcycles: plain shell bearings, ball bearings, tapered roller bearings and needle roller bearings.
Bevel gears Used to turn the drive through 90°. Typical applications are shaft final drive and camshaft drive **(see illustration)**.

Bevel gears are used to turn the drive through 90°

BHP Brake Horsepower. The British measurement for engine power output. Power output is now usually expressed in kilowatts (kW).
Bias-belted tyre Similar construction to radial tyre, but with outer belt running at an angle to the wheel rim.
Big-end bearing The bearing in the end of the connecting rod that's attached to the crankshaft.
Bleeding The process of removing air from an hydraulic system via a bleed nipple or bleed screw.
Bottom-end A description of an engine's crankcase components and all components contained there-in.
BTDC Before Top Dead Centre in terms of piston position. Ignition timing is often expressed in terms of degrees or millimetres BTDC.
Bush A cylindrical metal or rubber component used between two moving parts.
Burr Rough edge left on a component after machining or as a result of excessive wear.

C

Cam chain The chain which takes drive from the crankshaft to the camshaft(s).
Canister The main component in an evaporative emission control system (California market only); contains activated charcoal granules to trap vapours from the fuel system rather than allowing them to vent to the atmosphere.
Castellated Resembling the parapets along the top of a castle wall. For example, a castellated wheel axle or spindle nut.
Catalytic converter A device in the exhaust system of some machines which converts certain pollutants in the exhaust gases into less harmful substances.
Charging system Description of the components which charge the battery, ie the alternator, rectifer and regulator.
Circlip A ring-shaped clip used to prevent endwise movement of cylindrical parts and shafts. An internal circlip is installed in a groove in a housing; an external circlip fits into a groove on the outside of a cylindrical piece such as a shaft. Also known as a snap-ring.
Clearance The amount of space between two parts. For example, between a piston and a cylinder, between a bearing and a journal, etc.
Coil spring A spiral of elastic steel found in various sizes throughout a vehicle, for example as a springing medium in the suspension and in the valve train.
Compression Reduction in volume, and increase in pressure and temperature, of a gas, caused by squeezing it into a smaller space.
Compression damping Controls the speed the suspension compresses when hitting a bump.
Compression ratio The relationship between cylinder volume when the piston is at top dead centre and cylinder volume when the piston is at bottom dead centre.
Continuity The uninterrupted path in the flow of electricity. Little or no measurable resistance.
Continuity tester Self-powered bleeper or test light which indicates continuity.
Cp Candlepower. Bulb rating commonly found on US motorcycles.
Crossply tyre Tyre plies arranged in a criss-cross pattern. Usually four or six plies used, hence 4PR or 6PR in tyre size codes.
Cush drive Rubber damper segments fitted between the rear wheel and final drive sprocket to absorb transmission shocks **(see illustration)**.

Cush drive rubbers dampen out transmission shocks

D

Degree disc Calibrated disc for measuring piston position. Expressed in degrees.
Dial gauge Clock-type gauge with adapters for measuring runout and piston position. Expressed in mm or inches.
Diaphragm The rubber membrane in a master cylinder or carburettor which seals the upper chamber.
Diaphragm spring A single sprung plate often used in clutches.
Direct current (dc) Current produced by a dc generator.

Technical Terms Explained REF•49

Decarbonisation The process of removing carbon deposits - typically from the combustion chamber, valves and exhaust port/system.
Detonation Destructive and damaging explosion of fuel/air mixture in combustion chamber instead of controlled burning.
Diode An electrical valve which only allows current to flow in one direction. Commonly used in rectifiers and starter interlock systems.
Disc valve (or rotary valve) A induction system used on some two-stroke engines.
Double-overhead camshaft (DOHC) An engine that uses two overhead camshafts, one for the intake valves and one for the exhaust valves.
Drivebelt A toothed belt used to transmit drive to the rear wheel on some motorcycles. A drivebelt has also been used to drive the camshafts. Drivebelts are usually made of Kevlar.
Driveshaft Any shaft used to transmit motion. Commonly used when referring to the final driveshaft on shaft drive motorcycles.

E

Earth return The return path of an electrical circuit, utilising the motorcycle's frame.
ECU (Electronic Control Unit) A computer which controls (for instance) an ignition system, or an anti-lock braking system.
EGO Exhaust Gas Oxygen sensor. Sometimes called a Lambda sensor.
Electrolyte The fluid in a lead-acid battery.
EMS (Engine Management System) A computer controlled system which manages the fuel injection and the ignition systems in an integrated fashion.
Endfloat The amount of lengthways movement between two parts. As applied to a crankshaft, the distance that the crankshaft can move side-to-side in the crankcase.
Endless chain A chain having no joining link. Common use for cam chains and final drive chains.
EP (Extreme Pressure) Oil type used in locations where high loads are applied, such as between gear teeth.
Evaporative emission control system Describes a charcoal filled canister which stores fuel vapours from the tank rather than allowing them to vent to the atmosphere. Usually only fitted to California models and referred to as an EVAP system.
Expansion chamber Section of two-stroke engine exhaust system so designed to improve engine efficiency and boost power.

F

Feeler blade or gauge A thin strip or blade of hardened steel, ground to an exact thickness, used to check or measure clearances between parts.
Final drive Description of the drive from the transmission to the rear wheel. Usually by chain or shaft, but sometimes by belt.
Firing order The order in which the engine cylinders fire, or deliver their power strokes, beginning with the number one cylinder.
Flooding Term used to describe a high fuel level in the carburettor float chambers, leading to fuel overflow. Also refers to excess fuel in the combustion chamber due to incorrect starting technique.
Free length The no-load state of a component when measured. Clutch, valve and fork spring lengths are measured at rest, without any preload.
Freeplay The amount of travel before any action takes place. The looseness in a linkage, or an assembly of parts, between the initial application of force and actual movement. For example, the distance the rear brake pedal moves before the rear brake is actuated.
Fuel injection The fuel/air mixture is metered electronically and directed into the engine intake ports (indirect injection) or into the cylinders (direct injection). Sensors supply information on engine speed and conditions.
Fuel/air mixture The charge of fuel and air going into the engine. See **Stoichiometric ratio**.
Fuse An electrical device which protects a circuit against accidental overload. The typical fuse contains a soft piece of metal which is calibrated to melt at a predetermined current flow (expressed as amps) and break the circuit.

G

Gap The distance the spark must travel in jumping from the centre electrode to the side electrode in a spark plug. Also refers to the distance between the ignition rotor and the pickup coil in an electronic ignition system.
Gasket Any thin, soft material - usually cork, cardboard, asbestos or soft metal - installed between two metal surfaces to ensure a good seal. For instance, the cylinder head gasket seals the joint between the block and the cylinder head.
Gauge An instrument panel display used to monitor engine conditions. A gauge with a movable pointer on a dial or a fixed scale is an analogue gauge. A gauge with a numerical readout is called a digital gauge.
Gear ratios The drive ratio of a pair of gears in a gearbox, calculated on their number of teeth.
Glaze-busting see **Honing**
Grinding Process for renovating the valve face and valve seat contact area in the cylinder head.
Gudgeon pin The shaft which connects the connecting rod small-end with the piston. Often called a piston pin or wrist pin.

H

Helical gears Gear teeth are slightly curved and produce less gear noise that straight-cut gears. Often used for primary drives.

Installing a Helicoil thread insert in a cylinder head

Helicoil A thread insert repair system. Commonly used as a repair for stripped spark plug threads **(see illustration)**.
Honing A process used to break down the glaze on a cylinder bore (also called glaze-busting). Can also be carried out to roughen a rebored cylinder to aid ring bedding-in.
HT (High Tension) Description of the electrical circuit from the secondary winding of the ignition coil to the spark plug.
Hydraulic A liquid filled system used to transmit pressure from one component to another. Common uses on motorcycles are brakes and clutches.
Hydrometer An instrument for measuring the specific gravity of a lead-acid battery.
Hygroscopic Water absorbing. In motorcycle applications, braking efficiency will be reduced if DOT 3 or 4 hydraulic fluid absorbs water from the air - care must be taken to keep new brake fluid in tightly sealed containers.

I

lbf ft Pounds-force feet. An imperial unit of torque. Sometimes written as ft-lbs.
lbf in Pound-force inch. An imperial unit of torque, applied to components where a very low torque is required. Sometimes written as in-lbs.
IC Abbreviation for Integrated Circuit.
Ignition advance Means of increasing the timing of the spark at higher engine speeds. Done by mechanical means (ATU) on early engines or electronically by the ignition control unit on later engines.
Ignition timing The moment at which the spark plug fires, expressed in the number of crankshaft degrees before the piston reaches the top of its stroke, or in the number of millimetres before the piston reaches the top of its stroke.
Infinity (∞) Description of an open-circuit electrical state, where no continuity exists.
Inverted forks (upside down forks) The sliders or lower legs are held in the yokes and the fork tubes or stanchions are connected to the wheel axle (spindle). Less unsprung weight and stiffer construction than conventional forks.

J

JASO Quality standard for 2-stroke oils.
Joule The unit of electrical energy.
Journal The bearing surface of a shaft.

K

Kickstart Mechanical means of turning the engine over for starting purposes. Only usually fitted to mopeds, small capacity motorcycles and off-road motorcycles.
Kill switch Handebar-mounted switch for emergency ignition cut-out. Cuts the ignition circuit on all models, and additionally prevent starter motor operation on others.
km Symbol for kilometre.
kmh Abbreviation for kilometres per hour.

L

Lambda (λ) sensor A sensor fitted in the exhaust system to measure the exhaust gas oxygen content (excess air factor).

Technical Terms Explained

Lapping see **Grinding**.
LCD Abbreviation for Liquid Crystal Display.
LED Abbreviation for Light Emitting Diode.
Liner A steel cylinder liner inserted in a aluminium alloy cylinder block.
Locknut A nut used to lock an adjustment nut, or other threaded component, in place.
Lockstops The lugs on the lower triple clamp (yoke) which abut those on the frame, preventing handlebar-to-fuel tank contact.
Lockwasher A form of washer designed to prevent an attaching nut from working loose.
LT Low Tension Description of the electrical circuit from the power supply to the primary winding of the ignition coil.

M

Main bearings The bearings between the crankshaft and crankcase.
Maintenance-free (MF) battery A sealed battery which cannot be topped up.
Manometer Mercury-filled calibrated tubes used to measure intake tract vacuum. Used to synchronise carburettors on multi-cylinder engines.
Micrometer A precision measuring instrument that measures component outside diameters (see illustration).

Tappet shims are measured with a micrometer

MON (Motor Octane Number) A measure of a fuel's resistance to knock.
Monograde oil An oil with a single viscosity, eg SAE80W.
Monoshock A single suspension unit linking the swingarm or suspension linkage to the frame.
mph Abbreviation for miles per hour.
Multigrade oil Having a wide viscosity range (eg 10W40). The W stands for Winter, thus the viscosity ranges from SAE10 when cold to SAE40 when hot.
Multimeter An electrical test instrument with the capability to measure voltage, current and resistance. Some meters also incorporate a continuity tester and buzzer.

N

Needle roller bearing Inner race of caged needle rollers and hardened outer race. Examples of uncaged needle rollers can be found on some engines. Commonly used in rear suspension applications and in two-stroke engines.
Nm Newton metres.
NOx Oxides of Nitrogen. A common toxic pollutant emitted by petrol engines at higher temperatures.

O

Octane The measure of a fuel's resistance to knock.
OE (Original Equipment) Relates to components fitted to a motorcycle as standard or replacement parts supplied by the motorcycle manufacturer.
Ohm The unit of electrical resistance. Ohms = Volts ÷ Current.
Ohmmeter An instrument for measuring electrical resistance.
Oil cooler System for diverting engine oil outside of the engine to a radiator for cooling purposes.
Oil injection A system of two-stroke engine lubrication where oil is pump-fed to the engine in accordance with throttle position.
Open-circuit An electrical condition where there is a break in the flow of electricity - no continuity (high resistance).
O-ring A type of sealing ring made of a special rubber-like material; in use, the O-ring is compressed into a groove to provide the sealing action.
Oversize (OS) Term used for piston and ring size options fitted to a rebored cylinder.
Overhead cam (sohc) engine An engine with single camshaft located on top of the cylinder head.
Overhead valve (ohv) engine An engine with the valves located in the cylinder head, but with the camshaft located in the engine block or crankcase.
Oxygen sensor A device installed in the exhaust system which senses the oxygen content in the exhaust and converts this information into an electric current. Also called a Lambda sensor.

P

Plastigauge A thin strip of plastic thread, available in different sizes, used for measuring clearances. For example, a strip of Plastigauge is laid across a bearing journal. The parts are assembled and dismantled; the width of the crushed strip indicates the clearance between journal and bearing.
Polarity Either negative or positive earth (ground), determined by which battery lead is connected to the frame (earth return). Modern motorcycles are usually negative earth.
Pre-ignition A situation where the fuel/air mixture ignites before the spark plug fires. Often due to a hot spot in the combustion chamber caused by carbon build-up. Engine has a tendency to 'run-on'.
Pre-load (suspension) The amount a spring is compressed when in the unloaded state. Preload can be applied by gas, spacer or mechanical adjuster.
Premix The method of engine lubrication on older two-stroke engines. Engine oil is mixed with the petrol in the fuel tank in a specific ratio. The fuel/oil mix is sometimes referred to as "petroil".
Primary drive Description of the drive from the crankshaft to the clutch. Usually by gear or chain.
PS Pfedestärke - a German interpretation of BHP.
PSI Pounds-force per square inch. Imperial measurement of tyre pressure and cylinder pressure measurement.
PTFE Polytetrafluoroethylene. A low friction substance.

Pulse secondary air injection system A process of promoting the burning of excess fuel present in the exhaust gases by routing fresh air into the exhaust ports.

Q

Quartz halogen bulb Tungsten filament surrounded by a halogen gas. Typically used for the headlight (see illustration).

Quartz halogen headlight bulb construction

R

Rack-and-pinion A pinion gear on the end of a shaft that mates with a rack (think of a geared wheel opened up and laid flat). Sometimes used in clutch operating systems.
Radial play Up and down movement about a shaft.
Radial ply tyres Tyre plies run across the tyre (from bead to bead) and around the circumference of the tyre. Less resistant to tread distortion than other tyre types.
Radiator A liquid-to-air heat transfer device designed to reduce the temperature of the coolant in a liquid cooled engine.
Rake A feature of steering geometry - the angle of the steering head in relation to the vertical (see illustration).

Steering geometry

Technical Terms Explained

Rebore Providing a new working surface to the cylinder bore by boring out the old surface. Necessitates the use of oversize piston and rings.
Rebound damping A means of controlling the oscillation of a suspension unit spring after it has been compressed. Resists the spring's natural tendency to bounce back after being compressed.
Rectifier Device for converting the ac output of an alternator into dc for battery charging.
Reed valve An induction system commonly used on two-stroke engines.
Regulator Device for maintaining the charging voltage from the generator or alternator within a specified range.
Relay A electrical device used to switch heavy current on and off by using a low current auxiliary circuit.
Resistance Measured in ohms. An electrical component's ability to pass electrical current.
RON (Research Octane Number) A measure of a fuel's resistance to knock.
rpm revolutions per minute.
Runout The amount of wobble (in-and-out movement) of a wheel or shaft as it's rotated. The amount a shaft rotates 'out-of-true'. The out-of-round condition of a rotating part.

S

SAE (Society of Automotive Engineers) A standard for the viscosity of a fluid.
Sealant A liquid or paste used to prevent leakage at a joint. Sometimes used in conjunction with a gasket.
Service limit Term for the point where a component is no longer useable and must be renewed.
Shaft drive A method of transmitting drive from the transmission to the rear wheel.
Shell bearings Plain bearings consisting of two shell halves. Most often used as big-end and main bearings in a four-stroke engine. Often called bearing inserts.
Shim Thin spacer, commonly used to adjust the clearance or relative positions between two parts. For example, shims inserted into or under tappets or followers to control valve clearances. Clearance is adjusted by changing the thickness of the shim.
Short-circuit An electrical condition where current shorts to earth (ground) bypassing the circuit components.
Skimming Process to correct warpage or repair a damaged surface, eg on brake discs or drums.
Slide-hammer A special puller that screws into or hooks onto a component such as a shaft or bearing; a heavy sliding handle on the shaft bottoms against the end of the shaft to knock the component free.
Small-end bearing The bearing in the upper end of the connecting rod at its joint with the gudgeon pin.
Spalling Damage to camshaft lobes or bearing journals shown as pitting of the working surface.
Specific gravity (SG) The state of charge of the electrolyte in a lead-acid battery. A measure of the electrolyte's density compared with water.
Straight-cut gears Common type gear used on gearbox shafts and for oil pump and water pump drives.
Stanchion The inner sliding part of the front forks, held by the yokes. Often called a fork tube.

Stoichiometric ratio The optimum chemical air/fuel ratio for a petrol engine, said to be 14.7 parts of air to 1 part of fuel.
Sulphuric acid The liquid (electrolyte) used in a lead-acid battery. Poisonous and extremely corrosive.
Surface grinding (lapping) Process to correct a warped gasket face, commonly used on cylinder heads.

T

Tapered-roller bearing Tapered inner race of caged needle rollers and separate tapered outer race. Examples of taper roller bearings can be found on steering heads.
Tappet A cylindrical component which transmits motion from the cam to the valve stem, either directly or via a pushrod and rocker arm. Also called a cam follower.
TCS Traction Control System. An electronically-controlled system which senses wheel spin and reduces engine speed accordingly.
TDC Top Dead Centre denotes that the piston is at its highest point in the cylinder.
Thread-locking compound Solution applied to fastener threads to prevent slackening. Select type to suit application.
Thrust washer A washer positioned between two moving components on a shaft. For example, between gear pinions on gearshaft.
Timing chain See **Cam Chain**.
Timing light Stroboscopic lamp for carrying out ignition timing checks with the engine running.
Top-end A description of an engine's cylinder block, head and valve gear components.
Torque Turning or twisting force about a shaft.
Torque setting A prescribed tightness specified by the motorcycle manufacturer to ensure that the bolt or nut is secured correctly. Undertightening can result in the bolt or nut coming loose or a surface not being sealed. Overtightening can result in stripped threads, distortion or damage to the component being retained.
Torx key A six-point wrench.
Tracer A stripe of a second colour applied to a wire insulator to distinguish that wire from another one with the same colour insulator. For example, Br/W is often used to denote a brown insulator with a white tracer.
Trail A feature of steering geometry. Distance from the steering head axis to the tyre's central contact point.
Triple clamps The cast components which extend from the steering head and support the fork stanchions or tubes. Often called fork yokes.
Turbocharger A centrifugal device, driven by exhaust gases, that pressurises the intake air. Normally used to increase the power output from a given engine displacement.
TWI Abbreviation for Tyre Wear Indicator. Indicates the location of the tread depth indicator bars on tyres.

U

Universal joint or U-joint (UJ) A double-pivoted connection for transmitting power from a driving to a driven shaft through an angle. Typically found in shaft drive assemblies.
Unsprung weight Anything not supported by the bike's suspension (ie the wheel, tyres, brakes, final drive and bottom (moving) part of the suspension).

V

Vacuum gauges Clock-type gauges for measuring intake tract vacuum. Used for carburettor synchronisation on multi-cylinder engines.
Valve A device through which the flow of liquid, gas or vacuum may be stopped, started or regulated by a moveable part that opens, shuts or partially obstructs one or more ports or passageways. The intake and exhaust valves in the cylinder head are of the poppet type.
Valve clearance The clearance between the valve tip (the end of the valve stem) and the rocker arm or tappet/follower. The valve clearance is measured when the valve is closed. The correct clearance is important - if too small the valve won't close fully and will burn out, whereas if too large noisy operation will result.
Valve lift The amount a valve is lifted off its seat by the camshaft lobe.
Valve timing The exact setting for the opening and closing of the valves in relation to piston position.
Vernier caliper A precision measuring instrument that measures inside and outside dimensions. Not quite as accurate as a micrometer, but more convenient.
VIN Vehicle Identification Number. Term for the bike's engine and frame numbers.
Viscosity The thickness of a liquid or its resistance to flow.
Volt A unit for expressing electrical "pressure" in a circuit. Volts = current x ohms.

W

Water pump A mechanically-driven device for moving coolant around the engine.
Watt A unit for expressing electrical power. Watts = volts x current.
Wear limit see **Service limit**
Wet liner A liquid-cooled engine design where the pistons run in liners which are directly surrounded by coolant (see illustration).

Wet liner arrangement

Wheelbase Distance from the centre of the front wheel to the centre of the rear wheel.
Wiring harness or loom Describes the electrical wires running the length of the motorcycle and enclosed in tape or plastic sheathing. Wiring coming off the main harness is usually referred to as a sub harness.
Woodruff key A key of semi-circular or square section used to locate a gear to a shaft. Often used to locate the alternator rotor on the crankshaft.
Wrist pin Another name for gudgeon or piston pin.

Index

Note: *References throughout this index are in the form - "Chapter number" • "Page number"*

A

Air filter – 1•20
Air filter housing – 4•6
Air injection system (DAI) – 4•35
Air temperature sensor – 4•22
Alternator – 9•23

B

Bank angle sensor – 4•23
Battery
 charging – 9•4
 check – 1•13
 removal, inspection and installation – 9•3
 specifications – 9•1
Body panels – 8•3
Bores (cylinder) – 2•44
Brake light bulb – 9•8
Brake light switches – 1•15, 9•10
Brakes
 bleeding – 7•12
 calipers – 1•26, 7•6, 7•7
 check – 1•15
 discs – 7•5
 fluid change – 1•21, 7•13
 fluid levels – 0•14
 hoses – 1•26, 7•12
 master cylinders – 1•26, 7•9, 7•10
 pads – 1•8, 7•2
 specifications – 7•1
Bulbs
 brake/tail light – 9•8
 headlight – 9•6
 instrument – 9•13
 turn signals – 9•9
 wattages – 9•2

C

Cables
 clutch – 1•8, 2•33
 choke – 1•13, 4•33
 lubrication – 1•11
 throttle – 1•13, 4•32
Calipers (brake) – 7•6, 7•7
Cam chain, tensioner blade and guide blades – 2•20
Cam chain tensioner – 2•14
Cam pulse generator – 4•22
Camshafts and followers – 2•16
Carburettors
 dismantling – 4•9
 float height check – 4•13
 overhaul – 4•8
 reassembly – 4•13
 removal and installation – 4•8
 separation and joining – 4•12
 synchronisation – 1•14
 throttle position sensor – 5•5
Catalytic converter – 4•38
Centrestand – 6•4
Chain (cam) – 2•20
Charging system – 9•22
Choke cable
 check and adjustment – 1•13
 renewal – 4•33
Clutch
 removal, inspection and installation – 2•27
 specifications – 2•5
Clutch cable
 check and adjustment – 1•8
 renewal – 2•33
Clutch lever – 6•6
Clutch switch – 9•17
Cockpit trim panels – 8•3

Compression test – 1•25
Connecting rods – 2•44, 2•45
Conversion factors – REF•26
Coolant temperature sensor (fuel injected models) – 4•21
Cooling system
 check – 0•14
 coolant level check – 0•15
 coolant reservoir – 3•8
 draining, flushing and refilling – 1•23
 fan and fan switch – 3•2
 hoses and unions – 3•9
 pressure cap – 1•15, 3•2
 radiator – 3•5
 temperature gauge and sender – 3•3, 9•13
 thermostat – 3•4
 water pump – 3•6
Crankcases – 2•41, 2•43
Crankshaft and main bearings – 2•50
Cush drive – 6•24
Cylinder bores – 2•44
Cylinder head – 2•21, 2•23

D

Dimensions (model) – 0•11
Diode – 9•17
Direct air injection system (DAI) – 4•35
Discs (brake) – 7•5
Drive chain
 check, adjustment, cleaning and lubrication – 1•5
 daily check – 0•13
 removal, cleaning and installation – 6•23
 specifications – 6•2

Index

E

Electrical system
- alternator – 9•23
- battery – 1•13, 9•3, 9•4
- brake light switches – 1•15, 9•10
- brake/tail light – 9•8
- charging system – 9•22
- clutch switch – 9•17
- diode – 9•17
- fault finding – 9•3
- fuses – 9•4
- handlebar switches – 9•15
- headlight – 1•16, 9•6, 9•7
- horn – 9•17
- ignition (main) switch – 9•14
- instruments – 9•11, 9•13
- lighting system – 9•5
- neutral switch – 9•16
- oil pressure switch – 9•14
- regulator/rectifier – 9•25
- sidestand switch – 9•16
- specifications – 9•1
- starter motor – 9•18, 9•19
- turn signals – 9•9, 9•10
- wiring diagrams – 9•26 et seq

Engine
- cam chain, tensioner blade and guide blades – 2•20
- cam chain tensioner – 2•14
- camshafts and followers – 2•16
- compression test – 1•25
- connecting rods – 2•44, 2•45
- crankcases – 2•41, 2•43
- crankshaft – 2•50
- cylinder bores – 2•44
- cylinder head – 2•21, 2•23
- idle speed – 1•7
- main and connecting rod bearings – 2•44, 2•50
- oil and filter change – 1•11
- oil cooler – 2•12
- oil level check – 0•13
- oil pressure check – 1•25
- oil pressure switch – 9•14
- oil pump – 2•35
- oil sump, strainer and pressure relief valve – 2•34
- piston rings – 2•49
- pistons – 2•47
- removal and installation – 2•8
- running-in procedure – 2•61
- specifications – 2•2
- starter clutch – 2•27
- timing rotor – 2•40
- valve clearance check – 1•21
- valve cover – 2•13
- valves – 2•23

Engine control module (ECM) – 4•24
Engine number – 0•9
Engine stop relay – 4•23
Evaporative emission control system (EVAP) – 1•21, 4•37
Exhaust system – 4•33, 4•38

F

Fairing and body panels – 8•3 et seq
Fan (cooling) – 3•2
Fast idle system wax unit – 4•27
Fault finding – REF•35 et seq
Filter
- air – 1•20
- engine oil – 1•11
- fuel – 1•26

Final drive
- check, adjustment, cleaning and lubrication – 1•5
- daily check – 0•13
- removal, cleaning and installation – 6•23
- specifications – 6•2
- sprockets – 6•23

Footrests – 6•3
Frame – 6•3
Frame number – 0•9

Front brake
- calipers – 7•6
- discs – 7•5
- fluid level check – 0•14
- lever – 6•6
- master cylinder – 7•9
- pads – 1•8, 7•2
- specifications – 7•1

Front forks
- adjustment – 6•19
- check – 1•17
- oil change – 1•26, 6•8
- overhaul – 6•10
- removal and installation – 6•7

Front mudguard – 8•6

Front wheel
- bearings – 7•17
- removal and installation – 7•14

Fuel system (carburettor models)
- carburettors – 1•14, 4•8 et seq
- check – 1•12
- filters – 1•26
- hoses – 1•26
- idle fuel/air mixture adjustment – 4•7
- idle speed – 1•7
- level warning light and sensor – 4•31
- pump – 4•29
- specifications – 4•1
- tank and tap – 4•3, 4•6

Fuel system (fuel injected models) – 4•17 et seq
- bank angle sensor – 4•23
- cam pulse generator – 4•22
- catalytic converter – 4•38
- engine control module (ECM) – 4•24
- engine coolant temperature sensor (ECT) – 4•21
- engine stop relay – 4•23
- fast idle system wax unit – 4•27
- fault diagnosis and checks – 4•19
- fuel cut-off relay – 4•24
- fuel pressure regulator – 4•21
- fuel pump – 4•30
- fuel rail and injectors – 4•20
- fuel reserve display – 4•31
- fuel supply system – 4•28
- ignition pulse generator – 4•23
- intake air temperature sensor (IAT) – 4•22
- manifold absolute pressure sensor (MAP) – 4•22
- oxygen sensor – 4•24
- starter valves – 4•26
- tank – 4•4
- throttle bodies – 4•24
- throttle position sensor – 4•21

Fuel tank and tap – 4•3, 4•6
Fuel tank trim panels – 8•3
Fuses – 9•2, 9•4

G

Gearchange
- lever – 6•3
- mechanism – 2•37
- selector drum and forks – 2•39

Gearshafts – 2•53, 2•54

H

Handlebar switches – 9•15
Handlebars – 6•5
Headlight
- aim – 1•16
- assembly – 9•7
- bulb – 9•6

Horn – 9•17
HT coils – 5•2

I

Idle speed – 1•7
Ignition (main) switch – 9•14
Ignition pulse generator
- carburettor models – 5•3
- fuel injected models – 4•23

Ignition system
- check – 5•2
- control unit (carburettor models) – 5•4
- engine control module (fuel injected models) – 4•24
- HT coils – 5•3
- pulse generator – 4•23, 5•3
- timing – 5•4
- timing rotor – 2•40

Immobiliser system – 5•5
Injectors (fuel) – 4•20
Instruments – 9•11, 9•13
Intake air temperature sensor – 4•22

L

LCD instruments – 9•13
Legal checks – 0•16
Levers (handlebar) – 6•5
Lighting system – 9•5
Linkage (rear suspension) – 6•17
Lubricants
- general information – REF•23
- recommended – 1•2

Index

M

Main bearings – 2•44, 2•50
Maintenance schedule – 1•2
Manifold absolute pressure sensor – 4•22
Master cylinder (brake) – 7•9, 7•10
Mirrors – 8•2
Mixture adjustment (carburettor) – 4•7
MOT test checks – REF•27
Mudguard (front) – 8•6

N

Neutral switch – 9•16

O

Oil (engine/transmission)
  oil and filter change – 1•11
  level check – 0•13
Oil (front forks) – 1•26, 6•8
Oil cooler – 2•12
Oil pressure check – 1•25
Oil pressure relief valve – 2•34
Oil pressure switch – 9•14
Oil pump – 2•35
Oil sump and strainer – 2•34
Oxygen sensor – 4•24, 4•38

P

Pads (brake) – 7•2
Performance data – 0•11
Pilot screw adjustment (carburettor) – 4•7
Piston rings – 2•49
Pistons – 2•47
Pressure regulator (fuel) – 4•21
Pressure relief valve – 2•34
Pulse generator (ignition)
  carburettor models – 5•3
  fuel injected models – 4•23
Pulse secondary air injection system (PAIR) – 1•19, 4•36
Pump (fuel) – 4•29
Pump (oil) – 2•35
Pump (water) – 3•6

R

Radiator – 3•5
Rail (fuel) – 4•20
Rear brake
  caliper – 7•7
  disc – 7•5
  fluid level check – 0•14
  master cylinder – 7•10
  pads – 1•8, 7•4
  pedal – 1•16, 6•3
Rear suspension
  check – 1•17
  linkage – 6•17
  shock absorber – 6•17
  swingarm – 6•19
Rear view mirrors – 8•2
Rear wheel
  bearings – 7•17
  removal and installation – 7•15
  sprocket coupling/rubber dampers – 6•24
Regulator/rectifier – 9•25
Routine maintenance – 1•1 et seq

S

Safety – 0•12, 0•16
Schedule (maintenance) – 1•2
Seat – 8•2
Seat cowling – 8•5
Security – REF•20
Selector drum and forks – 2•39
Shock absorber (rear)
  adjustment – 6•19
  removal and installation – 6•17
Sidestand – 6•4
Sidestand switch – 9•16
Spark plugs – 1•9, 1•10
Specifications
  brakes – 7•1
  clutch – 2•5
  cooling system – 3•1
  electrical system – 9•1
  engine – 2•2
  final drive – 6•2
  front forks – 6•1
  fuel system – 4•1
  ignition system – 5•1
  routine maintenance – 1•1
  transmission – 2•5
  wheels and tyres – 7•2
Speedometer and speed sensor – 9•12
Sprocket coupling/rubber dampers
  bearing – 7•18
  removal and installation – 6•24
Sprockets
  check – 1•5
  check and renewal – 6•23
  sizes – 6•2
Stands – 1•11, 1•17, 6•4
Starter clutch – 2•27
Starter motor – 9•18, 9•19
Starter relay – 9•18
Starter valves – 4•26
Steering head bearings
  check and adjustment – 0•13, 1•17, 1•25
  inspection and renewal – 6•16
Steering stem – 6•14
Storage – REF•32
Suspension
  adjustment – 6•18
  bearings – 1•25
  checks – 0•13, 1•17
  front forks – 6•7 et seq
  rear shock – 6•16
  rear suspension linkage – 6•17
  swingarm – 6•19
Swingarm
  bearings – 1•25
  inspection, bearing check and renewal – 6•22
  removal and installation – 6•20
Synchronisation
  carburettors – 1•14
  throttle bodies – 4•27

T

Tachometer – 9•13
Tail light – 9•8
Tank and tap (fuel) – 4•3, 4•6
Temperature gauge and sender – 3•3, 9•13
Tensioner (cam chain) – 2•14
Timing (ignition) – 5•4
Timing (valve) – 2•18
Timing rotor – 2•40
Thermostat – 3•4
Throttle cables
  check and adjustment – 1•13
  renewal – 4•32
Throttle bodies – 4•24
Throttle position sensor
  carburettor models – 5•5
  fuel injected models – 4•21
Tools – REF•2 et seq
Torque settings – 1•2, 2•6, 3•1, 4•2, 5•1, 6•2, 7•2, 9•2
Transmission
  gearchange mechanism – 2•37
  shafts – 2•53, 2•54
  specifications – 2•5
Turn signals – 9•9, 9•10
Tyres
  checks and pressures – 0•16
  general information and fitting – 7•19
  sizes – 7•2

V

Valve clearances – 1•21
Valve cover – 2•13
Valves – 2•23

W

Water pump – 3•6
Weight (model) – 0•11
Wheel bearings
  check – 1•25
  renewal – 7•17
Wheels
  alignment – 7•13
  check – 1•19
  inspection and repair – 7•13
  removal and installation – 7•14, 7•15
  specifications – 7•2
Windshield – 8•3
Wiring diagrams – 9•26 et seq

Haynes Motorcycle Manuals – The Complete List

Title	Book No
APRILIA RS50 & RS125 (93 - 05)	4298
Aprilia RSV1000 Mille (98 - 03)	♦ 4255
BMW 2-valve Twins (70 - 96)	♦ 0249
BMW K100 & 75 2-valve Models (83 - 96)	♦ 1373
BMW R850, 1100 & 1150 4-valve Twins (93 - 04)	♦ 3466
BSA Bantam (48 - 71)	0117
BSA Unit Singles (58 - 72)	0127
BSA Pre-unit Singles (54 - 61)	0326
BSA A7 & A10 Twins (47 - 62)	0121
BSA A50 & A65 Twins (62 - 73)	0155
DUCATI MK III & Desmo Singles (69 - 76)	◊ 0445
Ducati 600, 620, 750 and 900 2-valve V-Twins (91 - 05)	♦ 3290
Ducati 748, 916 & 996 4-valve V-Twins (94 - 01)	♦ 3756
GILERA Runner, DNA, Ice & SKP/Stalker (97 - 04)	4163
HARLEY-DAVIDSON Sportsters (70 - 03)	♦ 2534
Harley-Davidson Shovelhead and Evolution Big Twins (70 - 99)	♦ 2536
Harley-Davidson Twin Cam 88 (99 - 03)	♦ 2478
HONDA NB, ND, NP & NS50 Melody (81 - 85)	◊ 0622
Honda NE/NB50 Vision & SA50 Vision Met-in (85 - 95)	◊ 1278
Honda MB, MBX, MT & MTX50 (80 - 93)	0731
Honda C50, C70 & C90 (67 - 03)	0324
Honda XR80/100R & CRF80/100F (85 - 04)	2218
Honda XL/XR 80, 100, 125, 185 & 200 2-valve Models (78 - 87)	0566
Honda H100 & H100S Singles (80 - 92)	◊ 0734
Honda CB/CD125T & CM125C Twins (77 - 88)	◊ 0571
Honda CG125 (76 - 05)	◊ 0433
Honda NS125 (86 - 93)	3056
Honda MBX/MTX125 & MTX200 (83 - 93)	1132
Honda CD/CM185 200T & CM250C 2-valve Twins (77 - 85)	0572
Honda XL/XR 250 & 500 (78 - 84)	0567
Honda XR250L, XR250R & XR400R (86 - 03)	2219
Honda CB250 & CB400N Super Dreams (78 - 84)	0540
Honda CR Motocross Bikes (86 - 01)	2222
Honda CBR400RR Fours (88 - 99)	◊ ♦ 3552
Honda VFR400 (NC30) & RVF400 (NC35) V-Fours (89 - 98)	◊ ♦ 3496
Honda CB500 (93 - 01)	◊ ♦ 3753
Honda CB400 & CB550 Fours (73 - 77)	0262
Honda CX/GL500 & 650 V-Twins (78 - 86)	0442
Honda CBX550 Four (82 - 86)	◊ 0940
Honda XL600R & XR600R (83 - 00)	2183
Honda XL600/650V Transalp & XRV750 Africa Twin (87 - 02)	♦ 3919
Honda CBR600F1 & 1000F Fours (87 - 96)	♦ 1730
Honda CBR600F2 & F3 Fours (91 - 98)	♦ 2070
Honda CBR600F4 (99 - 02)	♦ 3911
Honda CB600F Hornet (98 - 02)	◊ ♦ 3915
Honda CB650 sohc Fours (78 - 84)	0665
Honda NTV600 Revere, NTV650 & NT650V Deauville (88 - 01)	◊ ♦ 3243
Honda Shadow VT1100 (USA) (85 - 98)	2313
Honda CB750 sohc Four (69 - 79)	0131
Honda V45/65 Sabre & Magna (82 - 88)	0820
Honda VFR750 & 700 V-Fours (86 - 97)	♦ 2101
Honda VFR800 V-Fours (97 - 01)	♦ 3703
Honda VFR800 V-Tec V-Fours (02 - 05)	♦ 4196
Honda CB750 & CB900 dohc Fours (78 - 84)	0535
Honda VTR1000 (FireStorm, Super Hawk) & XL1000V (Varadero) (97 - 00)	♦ 3744
Honda CBR900RR FireBlade (92 - 99)	♦ 2161
Honda CBR900RR FireBlade (00 - 03)	♦ 4060
Honda CBR1100XX Super Blackbird (97 - 02)	♦ 3901
Honda ST1100 Pan European V-Fours (90 - 01)	♦ 3384
Honda Shadow VT600 & 750 (USA) (88 - 03)	2312
Honda GL1000 Gold Wing (75 - 79)	0309
Honda GL1100 Gold Wing (79 - 81)	0669

Title	Book No
Honda Gold Wing 1200 (USA) (84 - 87)	2199
Honda Gold Wing 1500 (USA) (88 - 00)	2225
KAWASAKI AE/AR 50 & 80 (81 - 95)	1007
Kawasaki KC, KE & KH100 (75 - 99)	1371
Kawasaki KMX125 & 200 (86 - 02)	◊ 3046
Kawasaki 250, 350 & 400 Triples (72 - 79)	0134
Kawasaki 400 & 440 Twins (74 - 81)	0281
Kawasaki 400, 500 & 550 Fours (79 - 91)	0910
Kawasaki EN450 & 500 Twins (Ltd/Vulcan) (85 - 04)	2053
Kawasaki EX500 (GPZ500S) & ER500 (ER-5) (87 - 05)	♦ 2052
Kawasaki ZX600 (Ninja ZX-6, ZZ-R600) Fours (90 - 00)	♦ 2146
Kawasaki ZX-6R Ninja Fours (95 - 02)	♦ 3541
Kawasaki ZX600 (GPZ600R, GPX600R, Ninja 600R & RX) & ZX750 (GPX750R, Ninja 750R)	♦ 1780
Kawasaki 650 Four (76 - 78)	0373
Kawasaki Vulcan 700/750 & 800 (85 - 04)	♦ 2457
Kawasaki 750 Air-cooled Fours (80 - 91)	0574
Kawasaki ZR550 & 750 Zephyr Fours (90 - 97)	♦ 3382
Kawasaki ZX750 (Ninja ZX-7 & ZXR750) Fours (89 - 96)	2054
Kawasaki Ninja ZX-7R & ZX-9R (94 - 04)	♦ 3721
Kawasaki 900 & 1000 Fours (73 - 77)	0222
Kawasaki ZX900, 1000 & 1100 Liquid-cooled Fours (83 - 97)	♦ 1681
MOTO GUZZI 750, 850 & 1000 V-Twins (74 - 78)	0339
MZ ETZ Models (81 - 95)	◊ 1680
NORTON 500, 600, 650 & 750 Twins (57 - 70)	0187
Norton Commando (68 - 77)	0125
PEUGEOT Speedfight, Trekker & Vivacity Scooters (96 - 05)	◊ 3920
PIAGGIO (Vespa) Scooters (91 - 06)	◊ 3492
SUZUKI GT, ZR & TS50 (77 - 90)	◊ 0799
Suzuki TS50X (84 - 00)	◊ 1599
Suzuki 100, 125, 185 & 250 Air-cooled Trail bikes (79 - 89)	0797
Suzuki GP100 & 125 Singles (78 - 93)	◊ 0576
Suzuki GS, GN, GZ & DR125 Singles (82 - 05)	◊ 0888
Suzuki 250 & 350 Twins (68 - 78)	0120
Suzuki GT250X7, GT200X5 & SB200 Twins (78 - 83)	◊ 0469
Suzuki GS/GSX250, 400 & 450 Twins (79 - 85)	0736
Suzuki GS500 Twin (89 - 02)	♦ 3238
Suzuki GS550 (77 - 82) & GS750 Fours (76 - 79)	0363
Suzuki GS/GSX550 4-valve Fours (83 - 88)	1133
Suzuki SV650 (99 - 05)	♦ 3912
Suzuki GSX-R750, GSX-R1100 (85 - 92), GSX600F, GSX750F, GSX1100F (Katana) Fours	♦ 2055
Suzuki GSX-R600 (97 - 00) & GSX-R750 (96 - 99)	♦ 3553
Suzuki GSX-R600 (01 - 02), GSX-R750 (00 - 02) & GSX-R1000 (01 - 02)	♦ 3986
Suzuki GSX-R600/750 (04-05) & GSX-R1000 (03-06)	♦ 4382
Suzuki GSX600/750F & GSX750 (98 - 02)	♦ 3987
Suzuki GSF600 & 1200 Bandit Fours (95 - 04)	♦ 3367
Suzuki GS850 Fours (78 - 88)	0536
Suzuki GS1000 Four (77 - 79)	0484
Suzuki GS/GSX1000, 1100 & 1150 4-valve Fours (79 - 88)	0737
Suzuki TL1000S/R & DL1000 V-Strom (97 - 04)	♦ 4083
Suzuki GSX1300R Hayabusa (99 - 04)	♦ 4184
TRIUMPH Bonneville, T100, Speedmaster, America & Thruxton (01 - 05)	♦ 4364
Triumph Tiger Cub & Terrier (52 - 68)	0414
Triumph 350 & 500 Unit Twins (58 - 73)	0137
Triumph Pre-Unit Twins (47 - 62)	0251
Triumph 650 & 750 2-valve Unit Twins (63 - 83)	0122
Triumph Trident & BSA Rocket 3 (69 - 75)	0136
Triumph Daytona, Speed Triple, Sprint, Tiger (97 - 05)	♦ 3755
Triumph Triples & Fours (carburettor engines) (91 - 99)	♦ 2162
VESPA P/PX125, 150 & 200 Scooters (78 - 03)	0707
Vespa Scooters (59 - 78)	0126
YAMAHA DT50 & 80 Trail Bikes (78 - 95)	◊ 0800
Yamaha T50 & 80 Townmate (83 - 95)	◊ 1247

Title	Book No
Yamaha YB100 Singles (73 - 91)	◊ 0474
Yamaha RS/RXS100 & 125 Singles (74 - 95)	0331
Yamaha RD & DT125LC (82 - 87)	◊ 0887
Yamaha TZR125 (87 - 93) & DT125R (88 - 02)	◊ 1655
Yamaha TY50, 80, 125 & 175 (74 - 84)	◊ 0464
Yamaha XT & SR125 (82 - 02)	◊ 1021
Yamaha Trail Bikes (81 - 00)	2350
Yamaha 250 & 350 Twins (70 - 79)	0040
Yamaha XS250, 360 & 400 sohc Twins (75 - 84)	0378
Yamaha RD250 & 350LC Twins (80 - 82)	0803
Yamaha RD350 YPVS Twins (83 - 95)	1158
Yamaha RD400 Twin (75 - 79)	0333
Yamaha XT, TT & SR500 Singles (75 - 83)	0342
Yamaha XZ550 Vision V-Twins (82 - 85)	0821
Yamaha FJ, FZ, XJ & YX600 Radian (84 - 92)	2100
Yamaha XJ600S (Diversion, Seca II) & XJ600N Fours (92 - 03)	♦ 2145
Yamaha YZF600R Thundercat & FZS600 Fazer (96 - 03)	♦ 3702
Yamaha YZF-R6 (98 - 02)	♦ 3900
Yamaha 650 Twins (70 - 83)	0341
Yamaha XJ650 & 750 Fours (80 - 84)	0738
Yamaha XS750 & 850 Triples (76 - 85)	0340
Yamaha TDM850, TRX850 & XTZ750 (89 - 99)	◊ ♦ 3540
Yamaha YZF750R & YZF1000R Thunderace (93 - 00)	♦ 3720
Yamaha FZR600, 750 & 1000 Fours (87 - 96)	♦ 2056
Yamaha XV (Virago) V-Twins (81 - 03)	♦ 0802
Yamaha XVS650 & 1100 Drag Star/V-Star (97 - 05)	♦ 4195
Yamaha XJ900F Fours (83 - 94)	♦ 3239
Yamaha XJ900S Diversion (94 - 01)	♦ 3739
Yamaha YZF-R1 (98 - 03)	♦ 3754
Yamaha FZS1000 Fazer (01 - 05)	♦ 4287
Yamaha FJ1100 & 1200 Fours (84 - 96)	♦ 2057
Yamaha XJR1200 & 1300 (95 - 03)	♦ 3981
Yamaha V-Max (85 - 03)	♦ 4072
ATVs	
HONDA ATC70, 90, 110, 185 & 200 (71 - 85)	0565
Honda Rancher, Recon & TRX250EX ATVs	2553
Honda TRX300 Shaft Drive ATVs (88 - 00)	2125
Honda TRX300EX & TRX400EX ATVs (93 - 04)	2318
Honda Foreman 400 and 450 ATVs (95 - 02)	2465
KAWASAKI Bayou 220/250/300 & Prairie 300 ATVs (86 - 03)	2351
POLARIS ATVs (85 - 97)	2302
Polaris ATVs (98 - 03)	2508
YAMAHA YFS200 Blaster ATV (88 - 02)	2317
Yamaha YFB250 Timberwolf ATVs (92 - 00)	2217
Yamaha YFM350 & YFM400 (ER and Big Bear) ATVs (87 - 03)	2126
Yamaha Banshee and Warrior ATVs (87 - 03)	2314
TECHBOOK SERIES	
ATV Basics	10450
Motorcycle Basics TechBook (2nd Edition)	3515
Motorcycle Electrical TechBook (3rd Edition)	3471
Motorcycle Fuel Systems TechBook	3514
Motorcycle Maintenance TechBook	4071
Motorcycle Workshop Practice TechBook (2nd Edition)	3470
GENERAL MANUALS	
Twist and Go (automatic transmission) Scooters Service and Repair Manual	4082
Motorcycle Modifying	4272

◊ = not available in the USA   ♦ = Superbike

The manuals on this page are available through good motorcycle dealers and accessory shops.
In case of difficulty, contact: Haynes Publishing
(UK) +44 1963 442030   (USA) +1 805 498 6703
(FR) +33 1 47 17 66 29   (SV) +46 18 124016
(Australia/New Zealand) +61 3 9763 8100

MCL20.2/06

Preserving Our Motoring Heritage

The Model J Duesenberg Derham Tourster. Only eight of these magnificent cars were ever built – this is the only example to be found outside the United States of America

Almost every car you've ever loved, loathed or desired is gathered under one roof at the Haynes Motor Museum. Over 300 immaculately presented cars and motorbikes represent every aspect of our motoring heritage, from elegant reminders of bygone days, such as the superb Model J Duesenberg to curiosities like the bug-eyed BMW Isetta. There are also many old friends and flames. Perhaps you remember the 1959 Ford Popular that you did your courting in? The magnificent 'Red Collection' is a spectacle of classic sports cars including AC, Alfa Romeo, Austin Healey, Ferrari, Lamborghini, Maserati, MG, Riley, Porsche and Triumph.

A Perfect Day Out

Each and every vehicle at the Haynes Motor Museum has played its part in the history and culture of Motoring. Today, they make a wonderful spectacle and a great day out for all the family. Bring the kids, bring Mum and Dad, but above all bring your camera to capture those golden memories for ever. You will also find an impressive array of motoring memorabilia, a comfortable 70 seat video cinema and one of the most extensive transport book shops in Britain. The Pit Stop Cafe serves everything from a cup of tea to wholesome, home-made meals or, if you prefer, you can enjoy the large picnic area nestled in the beautiful rural surroundings of Somerset.

John Haynes O.B.E., Founder and Chairman of the museum at the wheel of a Haynes Light 12.

The 1936 490cc sohc-engined International Norton – well known for its racing success

The Museum is situated on the A359 Yeovil to Frome road at Sparkford, just off the A303 in Somerset. It is about 40 miles south of Bristol, and 25 minutes drive from the M5 intersection at Taunton.
Open 9.30am - 5.30pm (10.00am - 4.00pm Winter) 7 days a week, *except Christmas Day, Boxing Day and New Years Day*
Special rates available for schools, coach parties and outings Charitable Trust No. 292048